ARISTOTLE ON MEANING AND ESSENCE

OXFORD ARISTOTLE STUDIES

General Editors

Julia Annas and Lindsay Judson

Aristotle on Meaning and Essence

DAVID CHARLES

CLARENDON PRESS · OXFORD

OXFORD

UNIVERSITY PRESS

Great Clarendon Street, Oxford OX2 6DP

Oxford University Press is a department of the University of Oxford.
It furthers the University's objective of excellence in research, scholarship,
and education by publishing worldwide in

Oxford New York

Auckland Bangkok Buenos Aires Cape Town Chennai
Dar es Salaam Delhi Hong Kong Istanbul Karachi Kolkata
Kuala Lumpur Madrid Melbourne Mexico City Mumbai Nairobi
São Paulo Shanghai Taipei Tokyo Toronto

Oxford is a registered trade mark of Oxford University Press
in the UK and in certain other countries

Published in the United States
by Oxford University Press Inc., New York

© David Charles 2000

The moral rights of the author have been asserted
Database right Oxford University Press (maker)

First published 2000

First published in paperback 2002

All rights reserved. No part of this publication may be reproduced,
stored in a retrieval system, or transmitted, in any form or by any means,
without the prior permission in writing of Oxford University Press,
or as expressly permitted by law, or under terms agreed with the appropriate
reprographics rights organization. Enquiries concerning reproduction
outside the scope of the above should be sent to the Rights Department,
Oxford University Press, at the address above

You must not circulate this book in any other binding or cover
and you must impose this same condition on any acquirer

British Library Cataloguing in Publication Data
Data available

Library of Congress Cataloging in Publication Data
Data available

ISBN 0-19-825070-3 (hbk.)
ISBN 0-19-925673-X (pbk.)

1 3 5 7 9 10 8 6 4 2

Typeset by SNP Best-set Typesetter Ltd., Hong Kong
Printed in Great Britain
on acid-free paper by
T.J. International Ltd.,
Padstow, Cornwall

To my family

Preface

The study of meaning, essence, and necessity is a central part of the philosophical tradition we have inherited from classical Greece. Aristotle initiated the discussion of many of the topics in this area, and advanced debate on others beyond the level achieved by his predecessors. My primary aim is to gain a philosophical understanding of his work on these subjects.

How are we to achieve this type of understanding? Its acquisition requires us to focus on the arguments and motivations which led Aristotle to his views, to state then as precisely as possible, to see them as forming (where appropriate) a coherent overall theory, and (finally) to examine how far they withstand reasonable criticism. In these ways, we can assess the truth and importance of the views themselves.

If one aims to understand earlier writers in this way, one will place their work in some wider philosophical context. One may define that context historically in terms of those who influenced or were influenced by the writer in question. Alternatively, one may characterize it in terms of a broader conceptual framework shared with others who have, at varying times, engaged with similar issues. In this book I have followed the latter path, seeking to compare and contrast Aristotle's views with those of subsequent philosophers, including such present-day writers as Saul Kripke and Hilary Putnam. In this way, I hope to show that the study of Aristotle's work can deepen contemporary understanding of these topics.

If one attempts the latter project, one must avoid anachronism: the mistaken assimilation of Aristotle's views and concerns to those of our own day. The most important safeguard against this error is the careful reading of the range of relevant texts, which aims to place his views on particular topics in the context of his own arguments and basic interests. In this, much can be gained from a study of the many commentaries, written from a variety of philosophical standpoints, which have been dedicated to Aristotle's work over the centuries. A second defence is the requirement constantly to search for the conceptual resources which will enable us to see where past and present writers converge and where they diverge. For there can be no general presumption that ancient writers employed either precisely the same concepts as we do or, for that matter, radically different ones.

In writing on these themes, I am following an Oriel College tradition. My three most recent predecessors, Jonathan Barnes, Richard Robinson, and David Ross, have all written on these issues, combining high-grade philological skills and philosophical acumen. Before them, there was a line of Aristotelian philosophical scholars, working on similar questions, beginning with Richard Kilvington in 1326, and including (amongst others) Richard Whately, Edward Poste, and John Cook Wilson. They represent one part of the outstanding Oxford tradition in the study of ancient philosophy, to which I am deeply indebted.

My own interest in these topics stems from a reading group I organized on *Posterior Analytics* B.8–10 in 1983–5. We read these chapters slowly, often spending two or three hours on one or two lines. Such discussions have great merits: detailed attention to the text, the requirement for high standards of precision (both philosophical and philological), the opportunity for a free exchange of views between faculty and graduate students, and the sheer fun of shared work and enthusiasm. I owe a particular debt to the 1983–5 *Analytics* group, which included (at various times) Kei Chiba, Paula Gottlieb, Tomomasa Imai, Vassilis Karasmanis, Gavin Lawrence, Penelope Mackie, Christopher Megone, Michael Morris, Dory Scaltsas, Pantazis Tselemanis, Jennifer Whiting, and Michael Woods. I am sure that they all influenced my thinking on these topics.

Since then, I have given seminars on the *Analytics* with Jonathan Barnes and with Robert Bolton (at Rutgers University), on the *Metaphysics* with Michael Frede and with Montgomery Furth (at UCLA), on Aristotle's biological works with Allan Gotthelf and James Lennox, on the *Physics* with Lindsay Judson, and on *De Anima* with Shigeru Kanzaki and Kei Chiba (at Tokyo Metropolitan University). I have gained greatly from all of these and also from a long-lived discussion group on *De Anima*, which began in 1988 and continues to this day. Indeed, it was only through the latter's work that I came to see points of connection between Aristotle's account of thought and of colour perception and his analysis of definition and explanation in the *Analytics*. In this, I am indebted to (amongst others) Stephen Everson and, particularly, Michael Frede.

I began to write this book as a Fellow at the idyllic Center for Hellenic Studies in Washington DC in 1985/6, under the kindly and supportive Directorship of Zeph Stewart. I benefited then, as in 1994 and in 1998, from sabbatical leave granted by the Provost and Fellows of Oriel. Earlier versions of the following Chapters have appeared elsewhere:

Chapter 4: 'Aristotle on names and their signification', in Stephen Everson (ed), *Companions to Ancient Thought 3: Language* (Cambridge, 1994).
Chapter 11: 'Matter and Form: Unity, Persistence, and Identity' in T. Scaltsas, D. Charles and M. L. Gill (eds), *Unity, Identity, and Explanation in Aristotle's Metaphysics* (Oxford 1994).
Chapter 12: 'Natural Kinds and Natural History', in D. Devereux and P. Pellegrin (eds), *Biologie, Logique et Metaphysique* (Paris, 1990).
'Aristotle and the Unity and Essence of Biological Kinds', in W. Kullmann and S. Follinger (eds), *Aristotelische Biologie* (Stuttgart, 1997).

These papers, together with ones representing the basis of Chapters 2, 3, 5, 8, and 9 and Appendix 2, have been presented at conferences or seminars in a variety of places in Europe, the USA, and Japan. I am grateful to many audiences for interesting criticisms and difficult questions. I have also gained from detailed comments on specific topics from Justin Broackes, Victor Caston, Alan Code, Andrea Falcon, Mary Louise Gill, Terry Irwin, Yoshihiko Kaneko, Vassilis Karasmanis, Atsushi Kawatanai, Frank Lewis, Geoffrey Lloyd, Christopher Megone, Mario Mignucci, Pierre Pellegrin, Gerhard Seel, Richard Sorabji, Michael Wedin, and Audrius Zakarauskas.

I have learned from the discussion of related issues in contemporary philosophy. In this I am particularly indebted to Bill Brewer, John Campbell, Bill Child, Dorothy Edgington, Lizzie Fricker, Jennifer Hornsby, Ian Rumfitt, Paul Snowdon, Helen Steward, Tom Stoneham, Rowland Stout, and Timothy Williamson. Our weekly discussions, on a wide variety of topics, have been a constant source of illumination and encouragement.

In completing the book, I have been greatly assisted by helpful and searching comments on the penultimate draft from John Campbell, Lindsay Judson, and Timothy Williamson. Adam Beresford, Kei Chiba, and Greville Healey provided constructive and stimulating philosophical and philological advice on several versions. Without their support, I would not even now have finished the book.

Contents

PART II: ARISTOTLE ON DEFINITION, ESSENCE, AND NATURAL KINDS

Abbreviations

Introduction

This book is an essay on two themes in Aristotle's philosophy and their interconnection. The first is his account of the meaning of terms such as 'man', 'fish', and 'eclipse', which pick out kinds of objects or processes. The second is his theory of the essences of these kinds, the features we refer to in defining them, the ones that make them what they are. The first is discussed in Part I, the second in the Part II.

These two themes can be connected in a variety of ways. In one contemporary account, ordinary thinkers who grasp the meaning of natural-kind terms (such as 'man') must make (or be sensitive to) deep theoretical assumptions about the internal structure of a kind they already know to exist. (I set out a version of this view in Chapter 1.) On this basis, some modern essentialists have sought to vindicate talk of the essential features of objects and kinds. Indeed, in their view, if our practices are in good order, there is no need for any further metaphysical theory of essence.

Aristotle's account is fundamentally different. According to him, grasp of the meaning of a natural-kind term involves knowledge neither of the existence nor of the essence of the kind signified. As a consequence, he needed to formulate an independent metaphysical theory to vindicate claims about the essence and nature of kinds. He could not rely on the (supposedly) profound theoretical intuitions of ordinary thinkers. Indeed, in his view, they need not (in general) have intuitions of this type. While the modern essentialist's account involves a deep theory of meaning and little or no metaphysics, for Aristotle the balance is reversed. Because his relevant account of signification is comparatively shallow, it is the task of metaphysics and not of the philosophy of language to vindicate essentialist claims.

In Part I, I set out an interpretation of Aristotle's account of the meaning of natural-kind terms and of our understanding of them. My starting point is his discussion of *accounts of what terms signify* in the *Posterior Analytics* B.7–10 (Chapters 2 and 3). Here, Aristotle sets out three stages of scientific enquiry. At the first stage, one may possess an account of what a term signifies, but yet not know of the existence of the kind signified. At the second and third stages, one will (if all goes well) discover the existence and subsequently the essence of the relevant kind. I argue for this interpretation against a number of alternatives.

In Chapter 4 I consider Aristotle's discussion of the signification of such terms. In his view, this is determined (firstly) by the thoughts with which they are correlated and (secondly) by the kinds with which those thoughts are (in a certain way) causally connected. Indeed, it is this distinctive type of efficient causal connection which determines the object (or content) of the relevant thoughts, and thereby the signification of the term in question. This, I argue, is an account of the meaning of such terms, although it differs in certain respects from accounts of meaning with which we are familiar. In Chapter 5 I set out Aristotle's account of the object (or content) of thought and perception, on which his account of the meaning of kind terms is based.

At this point, there is a problem. How can the signification of a kind term be determined by the kind itself, if the thinker (at the first stage of scientific enquiry) does not know, in understanding the term, that the kind in question exists? For, if she does not know this, how can she know the signification of the term? Is there a major inconsistency in his account of these issues?

Aristotle can, and does, overcome this problem (as I argue in Chapter 6), but only at the cost of separating signification and understanding in ways which sharply distinguish his account from Fregean (and other modern) analyses of these issues. His discussion of what is involved in understanding a natural-kind term is equally distinctive. He focuses (I suggest) on the type of understanding possessed by master craftsmen, unaffected by scientific theory, who are able skilfully to engage with the kinds they encounter. Their grasp of the signification of these terms does not involve knowledge of either the essence or the existence of the kind in question. In Chapter 6 I examine a number of objections to my inter-pretation of Aristotle's account of signification, as given in Part I. I also consider some philosophical objections to the view itself.

The aim in Part II is to understand the metaphysical basis of Aristotle's essentialism. The distinctive nature of his approach emerges first in the interdependency he detects between the practices of definition and of explanation (when correctly understood). In *Posterior Analytics* B, neither practice is complete without the assistance of the other (Chapters 7–9). This interdependency rests, at the metaphysical level, on the co-determination of essence and causation: all essences are *per se* causes of a given type, and all such *per se* causes are essences. These two theses are developed and examined in Chapter 10.

In Chapters 11 and 12 I argue that Aristotle's discussion of substances and of animal kinds in the *Metaphysics* and the biological writings is based (in large measure) on the two theses outlined in Chapter 10. However, once again, there is a problem. While Aristotle succeeds in sustaining his *Analytics*-based account in his metaphysical writings, he encounters major problems in his study of biology. Not only does he fail to locate the type of unitary essence his theory requires, but, worse still, he appears to have come to believe that no such unitary essences could be found. It seems that his favoured area for scientific research did not contain the types of essence required by his scientific and metaphysical picture. There is, it appears, a crisis in Aristotle's essentialism, which can (given his biological discoveries) only be overcome at the cost of modifying several of his central *Analytics*-style claims about essence and the unity of kinds.

In Chapter 13 I review the basic components of Aristotle's picture (as it has emerged) and consider its distinctive metaphysical and epistemological foundations. Aristotle's account of essentialism is, I argue, distinct from that offered by its major competitors (whether conventionalist or Platonist, as these are characterized in Chapter 1), and is immune to some of the criticisms developed by (for example) Descartes, Locke, and Quine. Aristotle is not, in my view, the type of Aristotelian essentialist they attack. Indeed, the form of essentialism he defends is preferable (in certain major respects) to the alternatives currently available.

The book is constructed like a house with three storeys. On the ground floor, you will find (in Chapters 2, 3, 7–9 and 10 Sections 1 and 6) an analysis of Aristotle's discussion of signification, definition, and explanation in the *Posterior Analytics*. On the next floor, you will see (in Chapters 4, 5, 6) Sections 1 and 2, 10 Sections 4 and 5, 11 and 12) an account of his attempts to develop the *Analytics* model. Thus, in Part I some foundational issues concerning signification, left unresolved in the *Analytics*, are addressed elsewhere, while in Part II the more abstract *Analytics* view of explanation and definition is supplemented and made more determinate in the *Metaphysics* and biological writings. On the third floor (in Chapters 6 Sections 3–6, 10 Sections 2 and 3, and 13), there is an attempt to locate and assess Aristotle's accounts of signification and of definition in a broader conceptual context. Here, what is sought is an Aristotelian vantage point from which to see familiar non-Aristotelian discussions in a distinctive way. These more speculative sections offer the view from the highest window of a house whose lower storeys have been constructed in a more cautious style.

The scholarly basis of this book lies in the careful exegesis of complex and difficult texts. While this work is fundamental to my project, I have asterisked sections which can be omitted by those less preoccupied with detail of this type. A reader interested in Aristotle's philosophical picture and wishing to see only some part of its exegetical underpinnings may wish to follow a route consisting of the following Chapters or Sections: Chapter 1, Chapter 4 Sections 5 and 6, Chapter 5 Section 9, Chapter 6, Chapter 10 Sections 1, 2, and 4, Chapter 11 Section 6, Chapter 12 Sections 4, 7, and 10, and Chapter 13.

I

Meaning, Essence, and Necessity

1.1 INTRODUCTION

The study of meaning, essence, and necessity is of ancient vintage. Its subject matter, in so far as it concerns natural kinds, can be defined by a set of questions:

(A) How is the meaning of linguistic terms such as 'man', 'thunder', 'water', 'fish', or 'soul' determined? What is the relation between the meaning of these terms and what the speaker understands by them? Is an account of the former also an account of the latter?

(B) Man, it is said, is essentially rational and necessarily capable of acquiring a culture. What, if anything, makes these claims true? Is their source to be found in us as thinkers or in the kinds themselves? Or are they, in some way, the joint product of ourselves and the world? What is the relation between essence and necessity?

(C) How can we know that kinds possess some features essentially and some necessarily? How is it possible for us, on the basis of our knowledge of the relevant term and of some truths about this world, to come to know that man is essentially rational?

Question (A) concerns linguistic terms and their meaning, (B) the metaphysics of necessity and essentiality, and (C) the epistemology of necessary and essential truths. Aristotle laid the foundations for subsequent work on each of these topics. My first aim is to understand his answers to these questions.[1]

---

[1] My concern in this book is primarily with the essences of kinds not of individuals. Thus, I shall focus on such claims as:

Man is essentially rational

or

Water is necessarily composed of hydrogen and oxygen

and not on:

Socrates is essentially a man

or

Aristotle's views on these issues are different from the ones widely accepted today. Discernment of these differences has scholarly value. But there will be further philosophical gains if his ideas constitute (as they sometimes do in this area) a live, and challenging, alternative to those currently in fashion. For, the study of his views may assist us in our continuing attempts to address these topics.

Philosophers who work on the history of their subject make such claims as these more often than they substantiate them. However, in this particular area such hopes are well-founded. In the early days of 'modern' philosophy, Locke and Hume doubted whether we could have knowledge of metaphysical necessities in nature. They argued that the source of all intelligible discourse about necessity must lie in our ideas and concepts. Their rejection of Aristotle's account was further developed by their successors, Kantian and positivist alike. For them, our understanding of necessity is grounded either in the preconditions of rational thought or in our freely chosen conventions and practices. Indeed, it is only in the past three decades, as a result of developments in the study of modal logic, that this longstanding, anti-Aristotelian orthodoxy has been challenged. Some recent writers have even claimed to defend 'good old-fashioned Aristotelian essentialism'.[2] So, it should not be surprising that we still have something to learn from Aristotle on these topics. For, he dedicated much of his life to their study.[3]

1.2 ONE FORM OF MODERN ESSENTIALISM

In recent years there has been a sustained attempt to devise a philosophical theory which engages with the three questions set out above. While certain aspects of this theory have not been fully worked out, Hilary Putnam and others have developed a programme which I shall call the

---

This is necessarily water.

With regard to the individual Socrates, my concern is with the issue of whether (e.g.) he, considered *as a man*, is essentially rational, rather than with that of whether he is essentially a man.

[2] For use of this (or related) terminology, see for instance R. B. Marcus, *Modalities* (Oxford 1993), 45–70, B. Brody, 'Why Settle for Anything Less Than Good Old-fashioned Aristotelian Essentialism?', *Nous* 7 (1973), 351–65. The term 'old-fashioned' comes from Quine.

[3] Aristotle's writings on particular topics in areas as diverse as biology, psychology, and physics are motivated by his search for a general theory which answers these three questions. In what follows I shall omit many of the details of his account of natural kinds in the hope of grasping its general outline.

programme of modern essentialism.[4] My first task is to set out the general outlines of this programme.[5] Since I shall seek to be explicit where its more cautious proponents remain uncommitted, I shall refer to the view presented here as that of 'my modern essentialist'.[6]

According to my modern essentialist, certain terms in natural language, such as 'water' or 'gold', are correlated with natural kinds with essences. This is because they were introduced in one of two ways. The first requires us to point to particular samples of water. Here, in learning the term 'water', we acquire the intention to count a liquid as water (roughly) as follows:

(1) For every possible world, w, and every individual, x, in w, x is water if and only if x in w is the same liquid as *this* (or *these*) samples.[7]

In (1) the demonstrative '*this*' refers to a particular sample of water, one situated within the speaker's visual field. We intend to count something as water in any possible world (situation) only if it is the same liquid as *this* sample before us. There is a second route to learn the term 'water', which may be characterized as the 'stereotypical' one. Here, we acquire the intention to count a liquid as water (roughly) as follows:

(1′) For every possible world w, and every individual, x, in w, x is water if and only if x in w is a sample of the colourless, tasteless liquid that fills *these* lakes and rivers (or most of them).[8]

There is no need for a sample of water to be before us when we learn the term, provided that we refer to the liquid in our lakes and rivers, and intend to count something as water only if it is the same liquid as the one we find there. Of these formulations, (1) is the more basic. For, our grasp on the relevant liquid is grounded in our ability to pick out instances of it when confronted by it. We need to be able to distinguish water from other similar

---

[4] In my presentation of *modern essentialism* I derive my main inspiration from the writings of Hilary Putnam. Saul Kripke's work on these issues is marked by great caution on some of the questions which are central to our discussion.

[5] My concern is with those aspects of modern essentialism that are sometimes labelled 'non-trivial essentialism'. These are to be distinguished from trivial essentialist claims, such as those concerning the necessity of true identity statements involving genuine names. The latter, it appears, follow from the theory of reference alone. For this distinction, see N. Salmon, *Reference and Essence* (Oxford, 1982), 5.

[6] On some issues modern essentialists disagree. On others they have changed their views. My 'modern essentialist' is one who has been prepared to adapt his earlier formulations in the light of subsequent work. His position is, thus, something of an amalgam, although (I believe) a currently fashionable one. One version of this position is characterized by Penelope Mackie in her review of A. Sidelle, *Necessity, Essence and Individuation: A Defense of Conventionalism* (Ithaca, 1989), in *Mind* 99 (1990), 635.

[7] Putnam, *Philosophical Papers* ii. 232, 'Meaning and Reference', 128, in S. P. Schwartz (ed.), *Naming, Necessity and Natural Kinds* (Ithaca, 1977).

[8] Putnam, *Philosophical Papers*, ii. 229–30.

liquids in our lakes (or elsewhere). Thus, in what follows, I shall focus mainly on (1).

(1) and (1′) depend on the notion of 'the same liquid'. For my modern essentialist, this is grounded in the intuition that a liquid can look and taste like water (resemble water in its superficial properties) without being water.[9] Thus, he envisages our agreeing not to count something as water if it has a different fundamental physical property from that of the water with which we are familiar in this world.[10] He notes: 'whether something is or is not the same liquid as this may take an indeterminate amount of scientific investigation to determine'.[11] Since we may discover by scientific investigation whether two samples are indeed of the same liquid, we intend our usage of 'water' to be sensitive to scientific discoveries about what *being the same liquid* consists in. The latter is a theoretical relation to be made more precise by an empirical investigation conducted by the relevant experts.

One example of this approach is offered by Hilary Putnam. He characterizes *being the same liquid* as follows: two samples of water are samples of the same liquid only if they possess the 'same important physical properties',[12] ones which constitute the underlying (non-superficial) 'composition of water'.[13] This account can (perhaps) be best summarized as follows: two samples of water are samples of water only if both have the same basic determining and underlying property, which is to be discovered by scientific means. Thus, we might characterize our grasp on the notion of being the *same liquid substance* as follows:

(2) A sample s_1 in some possible world w_1 is a sample of the same liquid substance as sample s_2 in possible world w_2 if and only if sample s_1 in w_1 has the same determining and basic scientific physical feature as s_2 in w_2.

As things turned out, difference and similarity in micro-character constitute the relevant scientifically important differences and similarities. This was an a posteriori discovery. It took much scientific investigation to discover the fundamental scientific properties.[14] Still more may be needed.

---

[9] As Putnam notes in Schwartz (ed.), *Naming, Necessity and Natural Kinds*, 130.

[10] As Putnum suggests in Schwartz (ed.), *Naming, Necessity and Natural Kinds*, 129 (final four lines) and 130 (top twelve lines).

[11] As Putnum remarks in Schwartz (ed.), *Naming, Necessity and Natural Kinds*, 122–3.

[12] Schwartz (ed.), *Naming, Necessity and Natural Kinds*, 129, l. 20. Putnam is not always clear as to the precise interpretation of *being the same liquid*. Sometimes he writes as if he is assuming that possession of the same fundamental chemical properties (or 'microstructure') is the important feature at issue. Nathan Salmon (*Reference and Essence*, 185–6) understands him in the latter way. I have preferred his more cautious formulation, which allows that it is (possibly) a discovery that micro-structural features are the basic scientific ones.

[13] Putnam, 'Realism and Reason', in *Philosophical Papers* (1983), iii. 63, ll. 1–5.

[14] We are interested both in fundamental properties and in how such properties are structured. See *Naming, Necessity and Natural Kinds*, 122 (final three lines).

Thus, while in (2) we grasp a priori what it is for s_1 and s_2 to be members of the same kind, empirical research is required to specify what the determining physical features are.

(1) represents my modern essentialist's account of the way in which we fix the reference of the term 'water'. We know a priori that something is a sample of water if and only if it is a sample of the same liquid substance as *these* samples (pointing to instances of water). (2) explicates the ordinary thinker's a priori grasp on the idea of being the same liquid substance. It too is grounded in our positive reflections, conjectures, and thought experiments about what it is to be the same liquid. (2) goes beyond (1) because it introduces the idea of a scientifically based, theoretical, sameness relation. However, both are grounded a priori in the understanding of the ordinary speaker of the language.

(1) and (2) together explain certain features of our practice in using natural-kind terms. It should be no surprise that, given (1) and (2), the ordinary thinker defers to the scientist about what things are (e.g.) water. For, the former accepts that water has some determining physical feature of a type which it is up to the latter to discover. The pre-scientific thinker's use of these terms will march in step with that of the scientist because the former has ceded to the latter authority in determining what water is. Indeed, the term 'water' was introduced with the aim of correlating it with a natural kind whose essence the scientist is best placed to discover.

My modern essentialist's account allows that different people may use the term 'water' in the same way even though they disagree about many of the properties of water (including its fundamental one). Provided that they are all in contact with the same liquid and believe (at least implicitly) that the liquid has an (as yet possibly unknown) scientifically basic, determining feature, they can use the term with the same sense even if they hold differing beliefs. The scientist who knows that water has certain scientific properties unknown to (or falsely diagnosed by) the pre-scientific thinker can use the word with the same sense as his pre-scientific colleague. People with importantly different beliefs about water can be using the term 'water' with the same meaning.[15]

(1) and (2) have, it is claimed, 'startling consequences for the theory of necessary truth'.[16] If one adds the further premiss:

(3) Water, in this world, has as its fundamental physical feature being composed of hydrogen and oxygen,

it appears to follow that water, in any possible world in which it exists, must

---

[15] This applies at least to all who agree that (e.g.) water has a fundamental physical constitution and one which it must possess in all possible situations in which it exists. Both these features cause difficulties which are discussed below.

[16] As Putnam notes in Schwartz (ed.), *Naming, Necessity and Natural Kinds*, 128–9.

have that fundamental physical feature. Thus, we may conclude from (1), (2), and (3) that:

(4) If water is composed of hydrogen and oxygen in this world, it is necessarily composed of hydrogen and oxygen.[17]

My modern essentialist locates the source of necessity in (4) in our semantically deep pre-scientific referential intentions (especially as in (2)). At the outset, we agreed to attach the term 'water' to the liquid with the same scientific determining feature as this liquid in the actual world. We would count nothing as water if it lacked that determining feature. Thus, we assumed that water possesses a scientifically discoverable, determining physical feature, and that possession of that feature determines whether something is water in any possible world in which that liquid exists. There is no possibility of something being water and lacking this property because (in our view, as reflected by the referential intentions noted above) nothing could be correctly referred to as 'water' if it differed in this way from the water we encounter. Thus, the source of the necessity of such claims as:

Water is composed of hydrogen and oxygen

is to be found in the practices we follow in introducing the term 'water'. For these convert empirical truths about the actual structure of water (3) into necessary truths about how water has to be.[18]

According to my modern essentialist, no distinctive modal facts in reality are required to make (4) true. The injection of a modal element comes from us and our conventions and not from reality itself. As Putnam himself notes, the modern essentialist's proposal should not seem 'so very metaphysical':

---

[17] I interpret this claim as the following one:

$\Box \forall x$ [x is water x$\to$ x is composed of hydrogen and oxygen].

and not the far stronger:

$\forall x$ [x is water x$\to \Box$ x is composed of hydrogen and oxygen].

The former concerns the essences of kinds, the latter the essences of individuals. One can only derive the latter claim from the former by adding as a further premiss:

$\forall x$ [x is water $\to \Box$ x is water].

This premiss requires further support from an account of the essence of individuals. My present concern is with the essences of kinds.

[18] While this claim locates the source of the necessity of such statements as:

Water is H_2O.

in our linguistic conventions, it does not follow that such statements are about our linguistic conventions. They are about the world which we understand as we do in virtue of our possessing the conventions we do.

Rather [such a theory] seems to me to be what Carnap would have called an explication, a convention which has some intuitive appeal and which enables us to systematize our pre-analytic use of modal notions.[19]

Sentences such as (4) will be true solely in virtue of non-modal facts about this world and our acceptance of certain linguistic conventions.

My modern essentialist holds (1) and (2) as a priori truths grasped by ordinary thinkers, and adopts an explicitly conventionalist approach to (2). He has a near relative who agrees that both (1) and (2) are grasped a priori by pre-scientific thinkers, but denies that (2) is to be understood in a purely conventionalist fashion. The latter will interpret (2) as expressing our grasp on (e.g.) certain principles of possibility, understood as essential ingredients in any understanding of the world. In such an account, the a priori status of (2) rests on the preconditions of any thought about an intelligible world.[20] It is not appropriate to ask whether the source of such world-defining conditions lies solely in us or in the world. Indeed, there will be no priority as between our contribution and that of the world. Both are governed by one set of principles, which simultaneously determine our thought and the world about which we think.

Despite the important differences between this approach and that of my modern essentialist, both share the assumption (definitive, in my view, of modern essentialism) that the basis for (4) lies in the pre-scientific, implicit, a priori knowledge of ordinary thinkers (such as is involved in their grasp of the kind terms). They differ in that the latter group (whom I shall call 'democratic Kantians')[21] do not accord the ordinary thinker's assumptions a purely conventional status.

These accounts are taken to explain how we come to have knowledge of necessary properties of water. At the outset, we know, in grasping the relevant term, that water has some (as yet unspecified) scientifically fun-

---

[19] Putnam, *Philosophical Papers*, iii. 65. In this context Putnam is speaking of Saul Kripke's account of individual essences. But the point applies equally to their account of the essences of natural kinds. Indeed, Putnam represents himself in contrast to Kripke as adopting this conventionalist account of the matter in his own later writings: 'If I am right, then, *given these referential intentions*, it was always impossible for a liquid other than H_2O to be water . . . But the "essence" of water in this sense is a product of our use of the word, the kinds of referential intentions we have: this sort of essence is not "built into this world"'. (*Philosophical Papers* iii. 221, top 10 lines.)

[20] This second type of account goes further towards legitimizing our modal discourse than the first, purely conventionalist, one. It would be compatible with the first that we are in error in making the semantically deep assumptions noted in Putnam's account of these issues. Locke and Hume both argued that while people believe that there are objective modal connections in reality, they are mistaken to do so. In this they suggested what John Mackie has called in another context 'an error theory' of necessary connections and real essences. (See his *Ethics: Inventing Right and Wrong* (New York, 1977), Ch. 1.)

[21] Democratic Kantians are to be distinguished from élitist Kantians, who take the grounding for (4) to lie in the a priori knowledge of the élite thinker, whether scientist or metaphysician. In the first part of this book my concern is with the question of whether Aristotle is a conventionalist or a democratic Kantian. It is only in Chapter 13 that I consider whether he is an élitist Kantian.

damental property. When we discover by ordinary scientific means that in the actual world this is the property of being H_2O, we know that this is the relevant necessary property of water. We upgrade the results of respectably empirical science into necessary truths because of the commitments we accepted in grasping the relevant terms. There is no need for any special form of metaphysical speculation to explain how we come to have knowledge of necessities in nature. We can be essentialists without countenancing natural kinds, as classically conceived, possessed of their own essential properties quite independently of how we describe them.[22] Nor do we need a special faculty of intuition, or any distinctive epistemological capacity, to grasp them.

1.3 PROBLEMS AND ALTERNATIVES

Both forms of modern essentialist represent ordinary thinkers as assuming that:

(1) Water has an (as yet unknown) fundamental feature, of a type grasped by scientists, which determines its other features,[23]

(2) Water has one and the same feature in all possible worlds in which it exists which fixes the identity of the kind,

and

(3) The (as yet unknown) fundamental scientific feature (specified in (1)) is the feature (mentioned in (2)) which fixes the identity of water in all possible worlds in which it exists.

According to my modern essentialist, these assumptions have the status of a convention. According to his Kantian cousin, they are required for any rational thought about kinds. Either way, they are something grasped by all pre-scientific thinkers who understand the meaning of 'water'.

Many will object that ordinary thinkers do not make these three deep assumptions in understanding the term 'water'. We can certainly tell stories in which we appear to understand this term (as a kind term) without making these assumptions.

Story 1: The Cautious. Some may assume that water has a physically fundamental scientific feature in this world (assumption (1)) and believe that there are some properties which water must have if it is to exist

[22] The point is made by Putnam in *Philosophical Papers*, iii. 220. In this passage, Putnam (tentatively) represents himself as preferring the 'conventionalist' approach, and contrasts his account with Kripke's (*Philosophical Papers*, iii. 221).

[23] Ordinary thinkers need not assume that the particular feature in question can be discovered by scientists. It is enough that they believe that there is a kind-unifying feature of a type some of whose instances can be discovered by scientists.

(assumption(2)). But they may still remain agnostic as to whether the identity of the kind in all possible worlds rests on its possession of that fundamental scientific feature (assumption(3)). Perhaps they have never given the matter a moment's thought and would not know whether to accept assumption (3), if asked. They might think even that other necessary features of the kind are as important for its identity, or prefer to remain agnostic on this controversial topic. But, nonetheless, they use the term 'water' to refer to the relevant natural kind.[24]

Story 2: The Unsophisticated. Others may have no view as to whether water has a fundamental scientific physical feature (as required by assumption (1)), even though they think that water does have some properties in all worlds in which it exists which determine its identity (as is required by assumption (2)). They may be confident that there are some properties which water must have to be water, but not believe that these are the scientifically fundamental ones. They may think of water as having the same important properties as these samples, but regard as important only those intrinsic properties which are relevant to their skills, not those which feature in a master physical science.[25] They may have no view as to whether the remaining properties of water flow from one fundamental scientific feature. Indeed, they may not have grasped the idea of a determining physical feature of the type a physical scientist might uncover. But, nonetheless, they may accept that water is a kind, and that as such it must possess certain properties whenever it exists. In this way, more primitive people may succeed in grasping genuine kinds, and using terms to refer to them. Such kinds may indeed have fundamental scientific features, but they are of no interest to the people who introduce the term.

Both stories attribute to ordinary thinkers, using natural-kind terms, assumptions semantically shallower than those required by my modern essentialist. Of course, confident and sophisticated thinkers may often make the latter assumptions in using natural-kind terms. But this cannot by itself show that all ordinary thinkers who master natural-kind terms always make assumptions of this type. Indeed, as the two stories suggest, we can (it appears) grasp these terms without them.[26]

Many, favouring modern essentialism, will wish to reject the conventionalist interpretation of (2). But what alternative basis can be provided

---

[24] For consideration of related issues, see Graeme Forbes's *The Metaphysics of Modality* (Oxford, 1985), 193 ff.

[25] For a view of this type, see David Wiggins's 'Putnam's Doctrine of Natural Kind Words' in P. Clark and B. Hale (eds.), *Reading Putnam* (Oxford, 1994), 203.

[26] Nor is the issue altered if one invokes the idea of a pre-scientific thinker's reliance (via some deference mechanism) on his experts. For, there is no reason to assume (1) that his experts are scientists rather than craftsmen, or (2) that he has ceded authority to them over matters in remote possible worlds. He need never have considered the latter question at all.

for this claim? Nathan Salmon once characterized (2) as 'irreducibly metaphysical', and 'if knowable at all, knowable a priori', 'the product of a *sui generis* branch of philosophy'.[27] But these formulations, despite their salutary caution, offer little insight into the metaphysical basis or knowability of (2). If (2) is to be understood in ways other than those proposed by my modern conventionalist, its basis and knowability need to be explained.

At this point, some have emphasized the primitive and irreducible nature of necessity.[28] But this move by itself is unsatisfactory, because it is itself compatible with a wide variety of distinct metaphysical theories. Thus, my modern essentialist could agree that necessity is irreducible. So too could Plato, opting for a rich metaphysical theory in which necessities and essences are real independent features of the natural world. The same is true for the Kantian, whether democratic or elitist.[29] Irreducible necessary truths could be based on the a priori convictions of the ordinary thinker (as in my modern essentialist's account), or on some yet to be specified metaphysical picture. As theorists, we need to know which of these options is to be preferred.[30]

Some modal realists seem to think that we (or some of us) have a special sort of intuition which allows us to detect what must be the case, a form of privileged access to the metaphysical grid which binds this world and all other possible worlds.[31] In their view, there are natural kinds with their own essential features existing independently of us, and we are aware of them by intuition or some other special epistemological faculty. However, this form of Platonism can only be successful if it can resist the objections brought by Locke and other empiricist writers. For, they challenged the very coherence of this position on epistemological grounds.

Some modern writers have been attracted to the view that (2) is knowable a posteriori, 'the product of scientific discovery, of scientific theories'.[32] Thus, Saul Kripke once wrote:

---

[27] Salmon, *Reference and Essence*, 263 f.

[28] As Kripke does in *Naming and Necessity*, 18–19, esp. n. 18.

[29] An élitist Kantian is one who, like his democratic cousin (introduced in the previous section), believes that the source of necessity does not lie either in us or in the world, but in a set of principles which simultaneously define both together. The élitist Kantian holds that this insight is the result of philosophical investigation, not one immediately accessible to all concept users.

[30] This issue is acute if one follows Salmon in separating trivial and non-trivial essentialism (*Reference and Essence*, 5). (See n. 5 above.) For, one needs to know the basis for non-trivial essentialist claims.

[31] This type of view is criticized by Saul Kripke in *Naming and Necessity*, 43–5. It is sometimes (perhaps implausibly) associated with the writings of David Lewis (e.g. 'Counterpart Theory and Quantified Modal Logic' *JP* 65 (1968), 113–26).

[32] Keith Donnellan, 'Rigid Designators, Natural Kinds, and Individuals' (unpublished, 1974). This paper, originally read at a UCLA Philosophy Colloquium, is cited by Salmon, *Reference and Essence*, 165.

Science attempts, by investigating basic structural traits, to find the nature and thus the essence (in the philosophical sense) of a kind.[33]

Indeed, he went so far as to comment that his views:

suggest that a good deal of what contemporary philosophy regards as mere physical necessity is actually necessity *tout court*.[34]

However, he did not endorse this proposal, cautiously concluding that he was uncertain as to 'how far this line can be pushed'. His caution was fully justified. For, to sustain his suggestion, he would need to show how scientific theory could give us knowledge of what is the case not merely in this world, but in all possible worlds. One would need to know how (if at all) physical necessity is converted into metaphysical necessity. These fundamental questions would need to be resolved before Kripke's suggestion could be vindicated.[35]

Contemporary debate on these issues has two poles. At one, the foundations for talk of necessity lie in our conventions, in the deep a priori assumptions chosen by ordinary thinkers. At the other, they are the product of a substantive metaphysical theory. The first option makes great, apparently implausible, demands on the ordinary thinker. The second presupposes an (as yet to be developed) metaphysical theory of how the world has to be, and an epistemological account of how we can grasp that this is so. But little has been done to make good these latter presuppositions.

1.4 ARISTOTLE'S ESSENTIALISM INTRODUCED

We seem to oscillate between three traditional options. All essentialists may agree that:

(*) F is an essential feature of kind K if and only if F is the feature selected when we define K.[36]

But this bi-conditional claim can be interpreted in several ways. For my modern essentialist, essential features are made such because we have a set of definitional procedures. These definitional procedures are conventional, and embedded in our grasp of natural-kind terms. Metaphysical priority is given to the right-hand side of (*). For the Platonist, by contrast, essential features are there to be seen, graspable by anyone capable of

[33] Kripke, *Naming and Necessity*, 138.
[34] Kripke, *Naming and Necessity*, 164.
[35] As Salmon notes, *Reference and Essence*, 264.
[36] For some parallel distinctions, see my 'Aristotle and Modern Moral Realism' in R. Heinaman (ed.), *Aristotle and Modern Realism* (London, 1995).

reason-based intuition. For him, priority is given to the left-hand side of
(*). The Kantian denies that priority should be given to either side of (*).
In his view, our definitional practices cannot be understood without reference to essential features of objects, but the latter cannot be understood
without reference to our definitional practices. It is already a mistake to
ask which side of (*) is prior.

Are these the only alternatives? Is there a form of metaphysical account,
distinct from those just sketched above, which is immune to traditional
empiricist criticisms?

Aristotle, I shall argue, sought to devise just such an account. His
writings, far from adopting (ahead of his time) any form of the modern
essentialist programme, constitute a well-defended attempt to vindicate
the claims of traditional metaphysics without attributing to the ordinary
thinker the deep a priori assumptions invoked by my modern essentialist.
Further, his metaphysical account differs in fundamental ways from the
Platonist and Kantian options introduced above.[37] Thus, his views cannot
be assimilated to any of the three options just outlined.[38]

Aristotle (as I shall argue in Part I) developed an account of the meaning
and understanding of natural-kind terms which does not require us, as
users, to have intentions with the degree of semantic depth presupposed
by my modern essentialist. According to his account, one can understand
the term 'water' as a natural-kind term without having any views as to
whether water possesses a fundamental scientific feature. Nor need one
intend to defer to scientific specialists who have such knowledge. For
Aristotle, it is the craftsman not the scientist who is the key to understanding terms for natural kinds. The craftsman can grasp terms for natural
kinds without making the semantically deep assumptions implicit in my
modern essentialist's account.

If this is correct, Aristotle cannot have sought to explain the source and
nature of necessity of claims such as (4) on the basis of our pre-scientific
linguistic intentions.[39] Their status has to be explained independently of

---

[37] Platonism, so characterized, does not necessarily involve either of the two following
theses:

(a) The world is composed fundamentally of universals, conceived as necessary entities.

(b) The fundamental components of reality can be known a priori.

Thesis (b) is labelled 'epistemological Platonism' in Chapter 10 Section 6. If Plato held some
version of (a) and (b), his views would represent one species within the broader genus of
Platonism (as I have defined it).

[38] Of the options previously considered, Aristotle's views approximate most closely
to Kripke's (cautious and unendorsed) suggestion that science uncovers metaphysical
necessities. But Aristotle's view of science, as it will emerge, is one permeated by essentialist thinking.

[39] It is not merely that appeal to pre-scientific intuitions is insufficient to account for the
source and nature of the necessity of claims such as (4). Aristotle, as I understand him, also
rejects the necessity of any appeal to such intuitions.

resources drawn from the philosophy of language or an account of pre-scientific thought. If so, Aristotle needed to develop the type of meta-physical and epistemological theory required by any who are drawn to essentialism but wish to reject my modern essentialist's programme. I shall argue (in Part II) that in doing so he proposed an account distinct from and preferable to the three traditional metaphysical options set out above.

1.5 EXISTENCE: FURTHER DIFFERENCES BETWEEN ARISTOTLE AND MY MODERN ESSENTIALIST

In my modern essentialist's account, (1) requires the ordinary thinker to use particular examples to fix the extension of the term 'water'. Instances of water are counted as such because they are related in an appropriate way to this sample of water. Further, if the term 'water' refers to a kind, its reference is fixed by the expression 'the kind of which these are instances'. This is how we grasp the reference of the phrase 'that kind'. The ordinary thinker is accredited with a mechanism for fixing the reference of the term 'water' which essentially involves the use of examples. His grasp of these is (partially) constitutive of his grasp of the term.

My modern essentialist is explicitly committed to the ordinary thinker's using examples in this way.[40] He makes the following assumption:

Existence Assumption: If one understands the term 'water', one must therein know that the kind has instances.

For, it is a constitutive condition of understanding 'water' (on this account) that one knows of certain instances that they are (in fact) instances of water (or is in contact with someone who does). In one version, one who understands the term must be able to discriminate instances of water from instances of other kinds (or is prepared to defer to someone who can). More cautiously, at the centre of the relevant practice, there must be someone who knows that the relevant kind is instantiated and which kind it is (viz. the one instantiated by (some of) those examples). In another version, to master the term one must stand in some less demanding form of epistemically reliable connection with actual instances of water (one which does not require anyone to be able to distinguish them from samples of certain other kinds).

[40] It should be noted, however, that Kripke's own writings suggest a marked degree of caution about the use of reference-fixing devices of this type. (See *Naming and Necessity*, 121 ff, 136.)

Both versions of modern essentialism require one who understands the term 'water' to have knowledge of certain instances of water (or be dependent on someone who does), although they disagree about the precise conditions required for such knowledge. Both would reject the view that one can understand 'water' without having any knowledge (either directly or derivatively via one's experts) of any of its instances.[41] Thus, my modern essentialist accepts (first) that one element of the meaning of a natural-kind term is determined by its referent and (second) that one understands its meaning by having knowledge (either directly or indirectly) of its instances as instances of that kind.[42] He must reject the possibility of our distinguishing (e.g.) in the earlier stages of scientific investigation between:

(i) knowing the meaning of a natural kind term;

and

(ii) knowing that there is a kind referred to by this term.

In his account, there can be no determinate grasp on the meaning of such a term without knowing (derivatively or directly) that the kind in question is instantiated (by certain cases). For, one cannot understand the term 'water' without knowing that water is in fact instantiated by certain specific examples.

While some find this aspect of modern essentialism problematic,[43] my modern essentialist aims to show that our grasp of kind terms essentially involves knowledge of the existence of relevant instances.[44] For

[41] One could perhaps use the term 'water' without being able even derivatively to identify its instances. But, for my modern essentialist, in such a case one would not understand the term, but merely 'parrot' it.

[42] See, e.g. Putnam's remarks in Clark and Hale (eds.), *Reading Putnam*, 282–3. Here, he insists that the mind is to be conceived in terms of 'a system of object-and-quality involving abilities', such that to possess the relevant concept of (e.g.) gold is to have 'the beginnings of an identificatory ability'. The required ability is one which cannot be fully explained without reference to the objects (or kinds) one is able to identify (perhaps with the aid of one's experts). Thus, to master the relevant term requires one to have an identificatory ability which essentially involves actual cases of the kind. While Putnam's views on these topics may have altered over the years, my modern essentialist is one for whom (as Evans and McDowell have insisted) mastery of a natural-kind term involves the ability (at least with assistance) to identify actual instances of that kind. Thus, my modern essentialist is not a proponent of the 'dual component account' in which one can master a term without the relevant ability. (In earlier days, Putnam was sometimes taken to be just such a dual-component theorist. See McDowell's 'Putnam on Mind and Meaning', *Philosophical Topics* 20 (1992), 35–48, and C. McGinn's 'The Structure of Content', in A. Woodfield (ed.), *Thought and Object* (Oxford, 1982).)

[43] See, e.g. Paul Boghossian's 'What the Externalist Can Know A Priori', *PAS.* 97 (1997), 161–75.

[44] See, e.g. Bill Brewer's *Perception and Reason* (Oxford, 1999), 262 ff.

Aristotle, by contrast, knowledge of the meaning of a kind-term need not involve anyone's having knowledge of the existence of instances of the kind. I shall argue that he separates these two stages of enquiry, and thus rejects my modern essentialist's Existence Assumption. The challenge he faces is that of showing that one can determinately grasp natural-kind terms without knowing (even derivatively) of some cases that they are instances of that kind.[45] My modern essentialist thinks that it cannot be done. In Part I I shall examine Aristotle's (complicated) attempt to show that it can.

1.6 NECESSITY, AND ESSENTIALITY

There is one further issue on which Aristotle and my modern essentialist differ. In Aristotle's account not all necessary properties of a kind are essential to it. Thus, he thought that:

'Man is a rational animal'

expresses an essential truth, while

'Man is a humorous animal'

or

'Man is capable of acquiring a culture'

are only necessary truths. For my modern essentialist, by contrast, 'essentialism' consists solely in the belief that objects or kinds have certain properties necessarily, or (as he would say) in all possible worlds.[46] This is quite different from Aristotle's view, since it fails to respect his central distinction between necessary and essential features,[47] both of which are possessed by a kind in all possible worlds in which it exists.

At this point Aristotle faces two challenges. He must show how the distinction between necessary and essential features can be maintained. It cannot be enough to point to the fact that we have intuitions about essences distinct from (and more demanding than) those concerning merely necessary properties.[48] He needs to establish that these intuitions

---

[45] If examples are involved in Aristotle's account of the acquisition of natural-kind terms, they must play a role different from that envisaged by my modern essentialist.

[46] This understanding is captured in both (1) and (2).

[47] This point was emphasized by Joan Kung in 'Aristotle on Essence and Explanation', *PS* 31 (1977), 361–83.

[48] These points have been made recently by Kit Fine in a series of important papers. See, e.g. 'Essence and Modality', *Philosophical Perspectives: Logic and Language* 8 (1994), 1–16. Fine appears to base his claims on shared intuition. He has not (so far) been concerned to support them on the basis of a more general metaphysical or epistemological theory.

are metaphysically well grounded. Further, he must indicate how we are to make sense of the logical grammar of claims involving necessary and essential features without referring to possible worlds.

1.7 OUTLINE OF WHAT FOLLOWS

In the first part of this book (Chapters 2–6) I shall argue that, for Aristotle, the meaning of natural-kind terms is semantically shallow and can be grasped even if no one has knowledge of the existence of the kind. Thus, Aristotle (or so I shall argue) rejects two of my modern essentialist's central assumptions, those which concern *semantic depth* and *existence*. His views (or so I shall claim) constitute an interesting and defensible alternative to these (and other) modern orthodoxies.

My investigation begins with an analysis of Aristotle's discussion of definition in *Posterior Analytics* B. Chapters 2 and 3 argue that (in his account) one begins scientific enquiry with a grasp of what the term signifies, which does not require one to have knowledge of the existence of the kind. At this stage one need not know anything of the existence or of the essence of the kind. In Chapters 4–6 I shall argue that (notwithstanding initial appearances to the contrary) his view of the significance of names and of the content of thought is consistent with this account. In Chapter 6 I shall attempt to assess the strengths and weaknesses of Aristotle's proposal.

Aristotle needs to vindicate claims concerning necessity and essence without relying on the assistance of the pre-scientific thinker. I shall examine his attempts to do this in Chapters 7–12. In the final chapter, I shall argue that his views constitute a distinctive and attractive theory of these issues, a high-grade alternative to those currently in fashion (Chapter 13).

I

Aristotle on Signification, Understanding, and Thought

2

Posterior Analytics *B.8–10: the Three-Stage View*

2.1 INTRODUCTION

Posterior Analytics B.10 contains some of Aristotle's most sophisticated thoughts on definition. A first approach to a translation might run as follows:[1]

[A] Since a definition is said to be an account given in reply to the 'What is —?' question, it is clear that one kind of definition will be an account given in reply to the question 'What is it that a name or other name-like expression signifies? An example of such a question is 'What does "triangle" signify?'[2] [B] When we grasp that what is signified exists, we seek the answer to the 'Why?' question. But it is difficult to understand in this way [viz. via an answer to the 'Why?' question] things which we do not know to exist. We have stated the source of this difficulty above: that we do not know whether or not the thing exists, except in an accidental way. [C] An account may be one in two ways: either by being stitched together, like the *Iliad*, or because it shows that one thing belongs to one thing non-accidentally.

[D] The above is one definition of definition, but another definition is an account which shows the answer to the 'Why?' question. In this way the first type of definition signifies [something] but does not prove anything, whereas the latter type will clearly be like a demonstration of what F is, differing from a demonstration in the arrangement of terms. [E] For, there is a difference between saying why there is thunder and what thunder is. For, one will say in the first case 'because fire is quenched in the clouds'. But what is thunder? It is the noise of fire being quenched in the clouds. Thus, the same account is given in more than one way, first as a continuous demonstration and second as a definition. [F] Another definition of thunder is 'noise in the clouds'. This is the conclusion of a demonstration of what it is. [G] The definition of immediates is an undemonstrable positing of what they are.

[H] One definition, therefore, is an undemonstrable account of what a thing is. One is a deduction of what it is, differing in aspect from the demonstration. A third is a conclusion of the demonstration of what it is. (93^b29–94^a14)

---

[1] This is offered as a revisable first attempt at a translation of this chapter. I have separated eight sections between 93^b29 and 94^a14, [A]–[H], solely for ease of reference.

[2] In this translation, I follow Ross, *Aristotle's Prior and Posterior Analytics* (Oxford, 1949), in deleting *ti esti* in 93^b31. (But see below.)

Aristotle ends with a summary of what has been achieved in the last three chapters (B 8–10). He writes:

So it is clear from what has been said [i] in what way there is a demonstration of the what it is and in what way not, [ii] of what things there is a demonstration of the what it is, and of what things not, [iii] in how many different ways 'definition' is predicated, [iv] in what way definition proves the what it is and in what way not, [v] of what things there is a definition and of what things not, [vi] what the relation is between definition and demonstration, and [vii] in what way it is possible for them to be of the same thing, and in what way not.

Of the issues mentioned, (ii) and (iii) are addressed primarily in B.8 and 9, while (iii), (iv), and (v) are the concern of B.10. The discussion of (vi) and (vii) spans B.8, B.9, and B.10.

In this Chapter and the next I shall focus on Aristotle's discussion of issues (iii), (iv), and (v). My main aim is to argue that B.10 sets out Aristotle's *three-stage view of scientific enquiry*, and to support my interpretation by considering the relevant sections of B.8. I shall also investigate his account of the form and role of accounts of what names signify. In Chapters 4, 5, and 6 I shall discuss Aristotle's account of names and their signification. In Part II (Chapters 7 and 8) the issues raised by (i), (ii), (vi), and (vii) concerning the relation between definition and demonstration will be discussed.

2.2 INITIAL EVIDENCE FOR THE THREE-STAGE VIEW: SECTIONS [A] AND [B] OF B.10

In sections [A] and [B] of B.10, Aristotle appears to separate three distinct stages of enquiry as follows:

Stage 1: This stage is achieved when one knows an account of what a name or another name-like expression signifies (section [A]: 93^b30–2).

Stage 2: This stage is achieved when one knows that what is signified by a name or name-like expression exists (section [B]: 93^b32).

Stage 3: This stage is achieved when one knows the essence of the object/kind signified by a name or name-like expression (section [B]: 93^b32–3).[3]

---

[3] For the answer to the 'Why?' question is (in this context) to be identified with the essence of the phenomenon (see *Post. An.* B.2, 90^a15, B.8, 93^a4). Some might refer to the essence (so understood) as the basic essence and allow other derived features also to be part of the essence. Aristotle sometimes refers to the latter type of feature as 'in the essence' (see B.6, 92^a7 ff.). Both types of feature need to be distinguished from any non-accidental features which are not (for any reason) part of the essence. (*Idia* may be of this type.)

Stage 1 is, apparently, distinguished from Stage 2, since it is the answer (in the case of a name) to the question:

What does 'triangle' signify?

and not to the question:

Does the triangle exist?

One can complete Stage 1 without completing Stage 2 in a variety of ways. In some cases, there may be no kind or object which is signified by the relevant linguistic expression (e.g. 'goatstag'). In others, the name may signify a kind although one does not (as yet) know that the kind exists. Here, one may proceed, at Stage 2, to establish the existence of (e.g.) the triangle (as Aristotle remarks in A.10, 76^a35–6). There is a further transition involved in the step from Stage 2 to Stage 3. Aristotle comments that it is difficult to achieve Stage 3 if one does not possess at Stage 2 non-accidental knowledge that what is signified by the name exists (section [B]: 93^b32–5).

If Aristotle does accept the three-stage view, two consequences immediately follow.

(i) It cannot be (in his view) an essential part of knowing an account of what a name or another name-like expression (e.g. for a kind) signifies that one knows that the kind is instantiated.[4]

(ii) It cannot be (in his view) an essential part of knowing an account of what a name or another name-like expression (e.g. for a kind) signifies that one knows that all members of the kind actually have an essence, still less what the essence is. For, one could only know this when one knows that the kind in question exists. But this knowledge can only be achieved at Stage 3 after one has passed Stage 2.

Indeed, it remains an open question whether knowing the account of what a name like 'man' signifies even involves knowing that the kind, man, if it exists, has an essence.

In this Chapter I shall argue that (in B.8–10) Aristotle holds the three-stage view of scientific enquiry and that he regards the first stage (grasp of an account of what the name signifies) as not essentially involving (in any case) knowledge either of the existence of the relevant kind or that the kind has an essence (yet to be discovered). If this is correct, he cannot have accepted in B.8–10 either of the assumptions implicit in the modern essentialist's programme, (1) and (2), which were introduced in the previous Chapter.[5]

---

[4] For a contrasting view, see Robert Bolton's 'Essentialism and Semantic Theory in Aristotle: *Posterior Analytics* II.7–10', *PR* 85 (1976), 523 ff.

[5] (1) encapsulates the enquirer's knowledge of the existence of the kind, (2) his knowledge that the kind has an essence yet to be discovered. (See Ch. 1 Sect. 1.2.)

2.3 THE FIRST SENTENCE OF B.10

The argument of the first sentence appears to run as follows.

(1) It is said that definition is an account of what something is. (Premiss)

From this premiss Aristotle derives (C):

(C) It is obvious that one type of definition is an account of what a name or another name-like expression signifies.[6]

But why is this obvious? The assumption linking premiss (1) and (C) appears to be:

(2) One type of account of what something is is an account of what a name or another name-like expression signifies.[7] (Premiss)

---

[6] In what follows I shall focus on the case of names and leave on one side the category of other name-like expressions. Ross identified these with terms such as 'straight line' or 'complex angle' which are name-like, but not (simple) names. An alternative is to regard as name-like expressions 'accounts which signify the same as names' (B.7, 92^{b}27–8). This latter suggestion might be strengthened by construing the subsequent line as follows:

(e.g.) that which is signified by the answer to the question 'What is "triangle"?'

In this interpretation, one would retain the *to* from the MSS and take it as a place-holder for the subject phrase *ti esti trigonon* (as W. Detel suggests, *Aristoteles: Analytica Posteriora* (Berlin, 1993), 675–6). '*Trigonon*' (or perhaps better '*trigonou*') might be taken to refer to the term 'triangle'. If so, the answer to the question 'What is "triangle"?' would be a phrase like 'figure with internal angle sum of two right angles'. So, the whole phrase would mean:

(e.g.) that which is signified by a phrase like 'figure with internal angle sum of two right angles'.

One might ask what this phrase signifies if one does not know what (e.g.) 'right angle' signifies. So understood, Aristotle is envisaging two questions:

What does 'triangle' signify?

and

What is signified by the phrase used to answer the question 'What does "triangle" signify?'

Both answers could be useful in teaching.

   While this interpretation is attractive, I shall not rely on it in what follows. The text is too short and too uncertain to allow one to place confidence in any of these readings.

[7] I take the logical form of these claims to be:

(1) ∀x [x is a definition ↔ x is an account of what something is]. (Premiss)

(2) ∀x [x is an account of what a name signifies → x is an account of what something is]. (Premiss)

(C) ∀x [x is an account of what a name signifies → x is a definition]. (From (1) and (2))

From (2), it follows that some accounts of what something is are accounts of what a name signifies. From (C), it follows that some definitions are accounts of what names signify. I take *horismos* as the subject of the conclusion because this seems to be the topic of the chapter and the next passage begins with the term '*horos*' which seems to refer back to '*horismos*' in 93^{b}29 and to contrast this type of definition with another.

Presumably, if the claim in (C) is obvious, this can only be because P(2) is also obvious.

How is the argument to be understood? In one traditional account (2) is interpreted as follows.[8] The question:

What is *triangle*?

is to be understood as:

What is 'triangle'?

and taken as equivalent to:

What does 'triangle' signify?

In *Posterior Analytics* A.1 Aristotle uses the phrases:

What is what is said [i.e. what is a given term, such as 'triangle']?

and

What does 'triangle' signify?

interchangeably ($71^a13–15$).[9] These questions can both be answered by a claim of the form:

'Triangle' signifies . . .

where the dots are filled by an account which says what the term signifies. Alternatively, they can be answered by saying

'Triangles' are . . .'

where the dots are filled by a phrase which tells us what the term 'triangle' signifies. This is one way in which one might explain the meaning of the term 'triangle' to someone who does not understand the English term. To him, one might say:

'Triangles' are three-sided figures.

Accounts of what names signify appear to be of the form:

This name signifies *this* (B.7, $92^b32–4$)

where *this* is replaced by an account which signifies the same as the name ($92^b5–7$). There can, as the immediate context makes clear, be accounts of this type whether or not there is an object or kind in the world signified by the name. For, there can be an account of what 'goatstag' signifies

---

[8] This was the line taken by the Greek commentators, Themistius (*Paraphrasis* p. 51, 14 ff.), Eustratius (*Commentarium* p. 128, 20–35) and Philoponus (*Commentarium* p. 372, 8–19).

[9] In this passage, '*to legomenon*' is in apposition to '*to trigonon*', which must itself be a term and not an object since it is the signifier and not the signified.

($92^{b}5$–7). Thus, if this interpretation of Aristotle's argument is accepted, there can also be a type of definition of what 'goatstag' signifies.

I shall argue that this traditional interpretation is correct. However, there is a problem. In B.7 Aristotle limits the term *definition* to accounts of things that exist ($92^{b}26$–8). This being so, how can he accept in B.10 that there is a type of definition (*horismos*) associated with the name 'goatstag', since there are no goatstags? Nor is his restricted use of the term 'definition' confined to one passage in B.7. In B.3 ($90^{b}16$–17) 'definitions' are said to be accounts which give knowledge of essence. But, since non-existents lack essences ($92^{b}28$), there can be no definitions of non-existents. Further, in B.3, at $90^{a}36$, Aristotle introduces the phrase 'what something is' in the context of proof and demonstration. But, since there can be no demonstrative proofs about goatstags, there should not be a 'what something is' (of this type) in their case. Indeed, throughout book B of the *Posterior Analytics* Aristotle restricts the use of the phrase 'what something is' to accounts of existing objects or kinds.

There are two ways to respond to this problem. One, implicit in the traditional account, is to suggest that in B.10, $93^{b}29$–32 Aristotle is expanding the range of definition to allow for a type of definition which gives an account of what names signify, and not restricting definitions to accounts of some object or kind. If so, there can be a type of definition which states what names for either existents or non-existents signify. On this understanding, Aristotle will accept in premiss (2) that an account of what 'F' signifies is an account that, in the way explained above, gives a reply to the 'What is F?' question (even if there is no kind or object signified by the name). I shall call this 'the liberal interpretation'.[10]

The alternative, restrictive, interpretation accepts that Aristotle's full constraints on definition are in force in the first sentence of B.10 and exclude the very possibility of there being a definitional account of what 'goatstag' signifies. On a restrictive reading, one would interpret premiss (2) above as:

(2*) Some accounts of what F is will be identical with some accounts of what names signify,

from which one can derive:

---

[10] Aristotle sometimes uses the phrase 'F *tis*' to indicate not a type of F but rather something like an F in the *alienans* use of '*tis*' in which self-control is described as a virtue of a sort (See *NE* $1128^{b}34$). Can '*tis*' in $93^{b}30$ be taken in this *alienans* way (with *horismos* understood)? While it is difficult to find an exact parallel for the *alienans* use with the relevant noun suppressed, such a use may not be impossible. However, the liberal interpretation does not require this reading. For, as argued above, Aristotle can relax his constraints on definition, in the case of accounts of what terms signify, without describing them as only 'definitions of a kind'. Indeed, the liberal interpreter may prefer to take such accounts as definitions (of what terms signify and not of things).

(C*) It is obvious that some definitions of F will be identical with some accounts of what 'F' signifies.[11]

The restrictive interpretation has two distinctive features. First, the claims in (2*) and (C*) concern a certain subset of accounts of what names signify (those which signify existents with essences). Second, these accounts of what 'F' signifies will be identical in content with some genuinely definitional accounts of what F is. As a consequence, only a subset of accounts of what names signify will be counted as definitions.[12]

There are two possible versions of the restrictive interpretation. In both, definitional accounts of what names signify are confined to cases of terms which signify existents and reveal something of their essence. As a consequence, in both, these accounts of what the terms signify will be the same in content as (some) genuine definitions of the kind. But in the first version it is not required that one knows, in grasping this type of account, that the kind in question exists. For, one may not know that the account of what the term signifies in fact defines the kind. This might be discovered later, when one comes to know that the kind in question exists and has a certain essence. One will not know what is definitional solely on the basis of one's grasp of the account of what the term signifies. Something further is required.

According to the second version, by contrast, grasping a definitional account of what a name signifies involves knowledge of the existence and essence of the kind signified. For, if the account of what the name signifies is indeed definitional of the kind, one will (according to this view) know that this is so in grasping it. So understood, Aristotle's view would be similar to that of my modern essentialist, as set out in Chapter 1. Indeed, one might justifiably regard Aristotle as the founding father of this version of modern essentialism.[13]

Of these two versions of the restrictive interpretation, the first is fully

---

[11] Thus understood, the logical form of these sentences would run as follows.

(1) ∀x [x is a definition of F ↔ x is an account of what F is]. (Premiss)

(2) ∀x [x is a member of a given subset of accounts of what a name signifies → x is an account of what F is]. (Premiss)

(C) ∀x [x is a member of a given subset of accounts of what a name signifies → x is a definition of F]. (From (1) and (2))

(2) and (C) could alternatively be understood as identity claims between some accounts of what a name signifies and some accounts/definitions of what F is.

[12] This view was taken by Ross, apparently following Averroes and Zabarella. In more recent discussions, it has become generally accepted. It is held in some version by Robert Bolton, Richard Sorabji in *Necessity, Cause and Blame: Perspectives on Aristotle's Theory* (London and Ithaca, 1980), 196 f., and by D. DeMoss and D. Devereux in 'Essence, Existence, and Nominal Definition in Aristotle's *Posterior Analytics* II.8–10', *Phronesis* 33 (1988), 133–54.

[13] As was suggested by Bolton in 'Essentialism', 515 ff.

consistent with the three-stage view, since knowledge of what a term signifies need not involve knowledge of the existence of the kind signified.
But the second is not, since it cannot allow there to be a distinction
between Stages 1 and 2 (in cases of successful enquiry). Further, the first
does not require that if we grasp a definitional account, we know that we
are doing so. In the second, by contrast, the definitional nature of such an
account will be transparent once we grasp it.

These three interpretations (i.e. the liberal and the two restrictive ones)
offer differing answers to four questions:

(A) Does Aristotle accept the three-stage view? Does he think that every
     case of scientific enquiry involves a first stage where one need not
     know of the existence of the kind, but must know an account of what
     the name signifies?

(B) Are any Stage 1 accounts identical in content (in Aristotle's view)
     with any definition of a kind?

(C) Does Aristotle think that if one grasps an account which is in fact
     definitional one knows that it is so? Is the definitional nature of that
     account transparent to the person who grasps it?

(D) Are all accounts of what names signify regarded by Aristotle as
     definitional in some way?

The differences can be represented as follows:

	(A)	(B)	(C)	(D)
Liberal:	Yes	No	Yes	Yes
Restrictive 1:	Yes	Yes	No	No
Restrictive 2:	No	Yes	Yes	No

I shall argue in favour of the liberal interpretation by defending
affirmative answers to questions (A) and (D), and a negative answer to
question (B). That is, I shall defend the three-stage interpretation of
scientific enquiry, in a form in which all correct Stage 1 accounts of what
names signify are definitional but different in content from any other
definition.

In the context of the book as a whole, an affirmative answer to (A) and
a negative answer to (B) are more important than an affirmative answer
to (D). However, since an affirmative answer to (C) appears plausible,[14]

---

[14] The argument runs as follows: definitions are accounts which reveal what something is
(B.3, 91^{a}1) and, thus, make its nature known to us (B.3, 90^{b}16). Thus, if we grasp an account
which makes known to us the nature of something, we grasp its definition. There is no more
to grasping a definition than grasping a knowledge-giving/revealing account of this type. If
so, there can be no case in which we grasp an account which makes a kind's nature known
to us but do not grasp its definition.
   This argument could be blocked in two ways:

the liberal interpreter needs to secure an affirmative answer to (D) to defend his affirmative answer to (A) and negative answer to (B). For, if (C) were answered in the affirmative and (D) in the negative, one would be forced to answer (A) in the negative and (B) in the affirmative (in line with the second restrictive interpretation).

The first section of B.10 offers *some* evidence in favour of affirmative answers (A) and (D), the two central aspects of the liberal view. Its support for the three-stage view has been indicated above (in Section 2). It also supports the claim that for Aristotle all accounts of what names signify are definitional. Or so I shall now argue.

(1) This section contains no explicit restriction to *some* accounts of what names signify. If a restriction to some accounts of what names signify had been intended, one would have expected a clear indication of this in the text.[15] However, there are no indications in the text that Aristotle is marking a restriction to a subset of definitions and to a subset of accounts of what names signify. Further, if the context at the beginning of B.10 is the one set by the earlier discussion of *all* accounts of what names signify (B.7, 92^{b}5–7, 26–33), Aristotle's remarks in this sentence should apply to all such accounts and not just to some.

But is this the context? Or has he shifted focus in the intervening chapters so that he is now concerned only with cases of successful enquiry into existing kinds? For, if that were so, the relevant accounts of what names signify might, in B.10, be restricted to those which signify kinds with essences.

The immediate context at the beginning of B.10 is, it appears, set by the aporetic discussion in B.7. That was the last time that the phrase 'accounts of what names signify' was used. It would be an extremely abrupt (not to say misleading) transition if Aristotle were now to use the very same phrase in a far more restricted fashion. For, since his goal in B.10 is to

(A) Perhaps we do not label such an account a 'definition'. But is mere labelling what is at stake (in Aristotle's account)? For, one could equally well say (if this is all that is at stake) that we have a definition, and merely do not label it as such.

(B) Perhaps (in Aristotle's view) we can know the nature of the thing but not know that we know it. Perhaps he also thinks that we cannot have a definition unless we do not merely know the nature of the thing but also know that we do. If so, we will be able (in his view) to know the nature of a thing but not have a definition of it.

(B) would (if successful) give Aristotle reason for thinking that one could have an account which makes a nature known to us without having a definition of it. But there is no evidence of any of these moves in Aristotle's discussion in *Posterior Analytics* B. Further, they are clearly controversial, and would need to be defended in some detail. Worse still, Aristotle defines definitions in terms of making things known to us (90^{b}16), and not in terms of making us know that we know things.

[15] The first '*tis*' must modify '*horismos*', and the phrase mean one type of definition. If '*tis*' had been intended to qualify '*logos*', it would have had to be placed after '*logos*' (cf. *de An.* A.4, 407^{b}32) or (possibly) '*estai*' (cf. *de An.* frag. 4, 68).

resolve the problems raised in B.7 and the preceding chapters, one would have expected him either to use the phrase with precisely the same sense as previously or to signal clearly his more restricted use.[16]

(2) On the liberal interpretation, it is indeed obvious that accounts of what names signify are a type of definition, since (as set out above) 'What does "F" signify?' can easily be taken as an example of the 'What is F?' question. By contrast, it is *not* immediately obvious that all (or indeed any) accounts of what terms signify will be definitional accounts of what the kind is. For, the latter will be of the form:

Fs are essentially . . .

where F specifies the kind and not its name, and the gap is filled by a description which refers to the essence of the kind. But it is not obvious that such accounts are needed to teach a child the signification of terms such as 'gold'? Why cannot that be done by telling her that gold is a metal which looks yellow in certain light (assuming that this is not part of its essence)? Answers to these questions cannot be assumed as obvious at the outset. Further, there is no preparation for such a step in the immediate context. Indeed, in B.7 Aristotle had made precisely the opposite assumption: that accounts of what names signify are distinct from accounts of what something is (92b26–8). Given this background, the transitions at the beginning of B.10 are easier to understand on the liberal, rather than the restrictive, style of interpretation.

(3) The first sentences of B.10 contain some indication that Aristotle is making the liberalizing moves required if he is to take answers to the 'What does "F" signify?' question as definitions and as proper answers to the 'What is . . . ?' question. To do so, he needs to introduce some relevant wider use of the term 'definition' and the what is . . . ? question. But this is precisely what is suggested in the first sentence of B.10, where Aristotle notes that definitions and answers to the 'What is . . . ?' question *are said to be* coterminous. For, in this context, the use of 'is said' may be taken to

[16] It may be objected that in B.7, 92b26 ff. Aristotle dismisses as absurd the possibility of taking as definitions accounts of what names signify, which do not 'take hold' of the 'what it is'. Thus, it might be said, he dismisses the possibility that there might be accounts of what names signify which do not take hold of the essence. If so, in B.10 his focus will be restricted to accounts of what names signify for the special case of names which signify existents with essences. However, this reply is unconvincing for several reasons. First, in 92b26 ff. Aristotle seeks to show only that accounts of what names signify which do not take hold of the 'what it is' are not *definitions*. He does not attempt to show that they are not *accounts* of what the relevant name signifies. Indeed, he in no way challenges their status as accounts in these sentences (92b30–1), only their status as definitions. Further, it would be a big step (requiring argument) to disqualify as *accounts* statements which say what (e.g.) 'goatstag' signifies. For, answers to question like 'What does "goatstag" signify?' would most naturally be taken as accounts (unless further argument is provided), since they tell us something: what the name signifies.

signal a relaxation of the standard constraints on definition. Indeed, it may invoke some popular view about what definition is.[17]

There is further evidence of Aristotle's making the necessary liberalizing move later in B.10. This would require him to contrast the wider use of definition introduced in the first sentence of B.10 with his own standard one. Thus, at $93^{b}38$ he distinguishes between the 'one definition of definition' just given and another one which is to follow. The complex phrase suggests that the first definition is not a definition on the same level as the ones that follow, but is rather an example of a definition of a different type. Since the next three are connected with proof, the first will be different if it is not similarly proof-connected. This will be so if the first type of definition is an account of 'What does "F" signify?'. Since such accounts are said not to be involved directly in proof ($92^{b}32$–3), they will be a definitions of a radically different type from the three that follow.

These three arguments should incline us to favour the liberal view that all accounts of what names signify are definitions (and so to answer question (D) in the affirmative). This view certainly has the advantage of allowing us to give a straightforward interpretation of the first sentence of B.10, while at the same time preserving intact Aristotle's general constraints on definition. For (on this reading), the latter apply to definitions of things and not to definitional accounts of what terms signify. Both versions of the restrictive interpretation, by contrast, have to give contorted accounts of the argument at the beginning of B.10 in order to represent Aristotle as imposing the same constraints on definitional accounts of what terms signify as on accounts of the kinds themselves.

The first section of B.10 seems, on balance, to favour both the three-stage view and the contention that all accounts of what names signify are definitional. However, to secure the liberal view, one must, in addition:

(1) show that this view coheres well with Aristotle's route to resolve the *aporiai* in B.7. (This issue is discussed in the next Chapter),

(2) establish that this view coheres well with the remainder of B.10, where Aristotle apparently introduces three further kinds of definition, and

(3) show that this view is consistent with Aristotle's discussion in the earlier chapters (B.8–9).

I shall attempt to establish (2) and (3) in the remainder of this Chapter. In discussing (2), I shall also examine the further liberal claim that no account of what a term signifies is to be identified with any definitional account of the kind signified.

---

[17] 'It is said' ('*legetai*') is used in these chapters of the *Analytics* to describe the views of others (see B.8, $93^{a}1$) rather than to state doctrine Aristotle himself accepts.

2.4 SECTION [B] OF B.10: THE THREE-STAGE VIEW DEVELOPED?

Aristotle continues his discussion in B.10 as follows:

When we grasp that what is signified exists, we seek an answer to the 'Why?' question. It is difficult to understand in this way [via an answer to the 'Why?' question] things which we do not know to exist.[18] We have stated the source of this difficulty above: viz. we do not know whether or not the thing exists, except in an accidental way. (93^{b}32–5)

The reference is to 93^{a}20 ff, where Aristotle writes:

It is impossible to know what a thing is, if we are ignorant that it is. Sometimes we grasp that it exists accidentally, sometimes by having something of the thing itself ... In the case where we know accidentally that the thing exists, we are in a hopeless position as regards finding out what it is; for, we do not even know that it is. And to seek for what something is when one does not know that it is, is to seek for nothing. But when one possesses something of the thing itself, it is easier to seek. Thus, how we stand as regards finding out what something is is determined by the way that we know that it exists. (93^{a}20–2, 24–9)

In both passages, Aristotle claims that if one fails to know non-accidentally that the thing exists, it is difficult to determine what the thing is (93^{b}33–4; 93^{a}26–7). Why is this so?

Failure to know non-accidentally that the kind exists arises because of a failure to grasp any of its non-accidental properties (93^{a}25–6). For, it is only if one grasps some non-accidental property that one can know non-accidentally that the kind exists (93^{a}26). Further, non-accidental knowledge that the kind exists is needed if one is to be able easily to conduct a worthwhile enquiry (93^{a}26–8). Without it, there is nothing to direct one's investigation in the correct direction. One is seeking for nothing (93^{a}27). If the search turns out to be successful, it will be a piece of good fortune. For, if one fails to know non-accidentally that the kind exists, one cannot, without great difficulty, search for what it is. In such a case, one will not have advanced at all towards knowledge of 'the what it is'.[19]

---

[18] I take 'in this way' to refer to progress to Stage 3 in investigation. It has been suggested that 'in this way' should be taken to refer rather to grasp on Stage 1 or Stages 1 and 2. However, both these alternatives are problematic. It is not at all clear (with regard to the first option) why it should be difficult to grasp an account of what a name signifies in cases where we do not know that the kind exists. Indeed, Aristotle envisages that this is just what we do when we do grasp an account of what the name signifies in the case of 'goatstag' or indeed 'triangle' (cf. A.10, 76^{a}33 ff.). Further, it is completely platitudinous to say that it is difficult to know a thing to exist if we do not know it to exist! Indeed, the problem mentioned in the next lines appears to refer back to the discussion in B.8 of the difficulty of the transition from Stage 2 to 3, and not of the difficulty of arriving at Stage 2.

[19] I construe 93^{a}25–6 as making the following point: If one knows only accidentally that the kind exists one can have no grasp at all of any non-accidental property of the kind. For, if one had some grasp on a non-accidental property of the kind, one would be able to know non-accidentally that it exists.

Accidental knowledge that the kind exists involves a grasp on merely accidental features of the kind. By contrast, if one grasps a non-accidental property of the kind, one can grasp non-accidentally that the kind exists. Both these cases are distinguished from one in which one is completely ignorant of the kind's existence (93^a20–2). For, failure to possess non-accidental knowledge is compatible with having some idea that the kind exists, and need not make one totally ignorant of whether it exists or not. There is at least one step in between failure to know and ignorance (see 93^a20–1).

Aristotle, in B.8, distinguishes three states:

(i) complete ignorance of whether the kind exists

(ii) accidental knowledge that the kind exists

(iii) non-accidental knowledge that the kind exists.

If one is in state (i), one cannot (on this basis) come to know what the kind is (93^a20). If one is in state (ii), one can come to know this but only with extreme difficulty because one has no clear idea of what one is seeking. Indeed, it is as if one were seeking nothing. However, even so, it may not be impossible to find the answer, since, beginning with its accidental properties, one may be able to work towards a grasp of its non-accidental ones. By contrast, if one is in category (iii), it is easier to arrive at a grasp of what the kind is.

Later, in B.10, 93^b32–4, Aristotle collapses the distinction between category (i) and (ii), and makes the strongest claim true of both (i) and (ii) together. The best one can hope for if one fails to attain category (iii) is extreme difficulty in grasping what the kind is. This will be so if one is in category (ii). To say that those in category (i) will find this search difficult is (of course) an understatement. But this should not cause confusion, since Aristotle, in B.10, is considering all who fall outside category (iii). Difficulty in search is characteristic of all except those fortunate enough to be in category (iii).

The pressing question, for our purposes, is this: how is non-accidental knowledge that the kind exists to be achieved? One model, suggested by the three-stage view, runs as follows. On the basis of a Stage 1 account, one knows that the kind, if it exists, possesses some specified property.[20] At Stage 2, one discovers that the kind does indeed possess this property non-accidentally. The initial grasp on an account of what 'F' signifies provides a *springboard* from which one can come to know non-accidentally that F

---

[20] In such an account, one will grasp some property which the kind (if it exists) has non-accidentally. This formulation does not entail that one grasps that the kind (if it exists) has that property non-accidentally. For, it does not require that one knows that one thinks of the property as a non-accidental property of the kind (if it exists). In this context, I follow Aristotle in using the phrase 'non-accidental'. This, as it stands, may include both essential and necessary features of the kind. (For further discussion of this issue, see below.)

exists, and, thus, for a successful investigation of what F is. According to the springboard reading, grasp of a Stage 1 account is a helpful first step towards coming to know of the existence and the essence of the relevant kind.

If the springboard reading is correct, the first two stages in the case of the triangle mentioned in the first section of B.10 might be of the following type:

Stage 1: 'Triangle' signifies plane figure with three angles.

Stage 2: There are plane figures with three angles. So triangles exist.

On the basis of the Stage 1 account, the most that one can claim to know is that triangles, if they exist, are plane figures with three angles. This can be known without having any knowledge of the existence of the triangle (B.7, 92^{b}16–18). At Stage 2 one would establish (perhaps by constructive proof) that there are figures of this precise type.[21] Armed with this information one may search more easily for an answer to the 'Why?' question (Stage 3). For, one might seek to detect that feature of the triangle from which its three-angledness follows.

---

[21] On the role of constructive proof, see I. Mueller, *Philosophy of Mathematics and Deductive Structure in Euclid's Elements* (Cambridge, Mass., 1981) and W. Knorr 'Construction as Existence Proof in Ancient Geometry', *Ancient Philosophy* 3 (1983), 125–47. It is one of several ways to establish existence of geometrical figures.

An example of a constructive method, beginning with two angles and one straight line, might run as follows:

Construct two opposing internal angles on the line, ensuring that their combined angle sum is less than two right angles. Continue the lines formed by the angles until they meet.

This method will allow one to construct any type of triangle (and not merely (e.g.) the isosceles), and nothing but triangles. Thus, it will give knowledge of the existence of the triangle, and not merely of some type of triangle. Aristotle is careful to separate knowledge concerning triangles from knowledge about types of triangle (cf. *Post. An.* A.24, 85^{b}9–13, also 73^{b}31–9).

Proclus, in his *Commentary on Euclid's Elements* 1 (384), comments on a route of this type, when he writes:

If we think of a straight line with perpendiculars standing at its extremities and then think of these perpendiculars coming together to produce a triangle, we see that . . . they reduce the size of the right angles which they make with the straight line (translation by Glenn R. Morrow (Princeton, 1970))

Here, Proclus links this method of construction with Aristotle's readiness to take the property of having angle sum equal to two right angles as one the triangle's non-accidental properties. For, he continues:

the amount taken away from the original right angles is gained at the vertical angle as they converge and so of necessity makes the three angles equal in sum to two right angles

Proclus takes this method to show, 'in line with common notions', that triangles have an internal angle sum of two right angles (*Post. An.* B.8, 93^{a}33 f.), even though (in his view) the proof of the latter theorem may be given in different terms. I am indebted at this point to discussion with Vassilis Karasmanis.

There is evidence in favour of the springboard reading in Aristotle's discussion in B.8. There, Aristotle is principally concerned to distinguish between Stages 2 and 3, grasping that a kind exists and grasping what it is (93ᵃ28–9). Thus, he writes:

> In those cases in which we grasp something of the what it is, we proceed thus: let eclipse be A, moon C, screening by the earth B. To ask whether the moon is eclipsed or not is to seek whether B is or is not. And that is no different from seeking whether there is an account of it. (If B exists, we say that the moon is eclipsed.) . . . When we discover it [viz. that B exists], we know at the same time that the moon is eclipsed and why it is eclipsed. (93ᵃ29–32, 35–6)

In this passage, Aristotle is considering someone who knows something of eclipses, and proceeds to come to know that they exist. The discovery of their existence depends on coming to know something of their causal ancestry: viz. they are caused by the earth being screened. This is how we discover (in this case) that the moon is eclipsed: by finding an account of why the eclipse occurs, a relevant middle term. Before we know this, we have some grasp of what type of phenomenon it is (e.g. a sort of light deprivation affecting the moon), but lack an account of why it occurs. In this case our original grasp of the type of phenomenon *cannot* include knowledge that it exists. For, that grasp is prior to and independent of the knowledge that the phenomenon exists. Thus, as predicted by the three-stage view, our initial grasp of what eclipses are (e.g. deprivations of light (93ᵃ23)) is separable from our discovery that eclipses exist. So, what does one's original grasp of eclipses consist in?

Some light is shed on this by the preceding lines. There Aristotle writes:

> Sometimes we grasp that something exists accidentally, sometimes we grasp that something exists by having something of the thing itself; e.g., in the case of thunder, that it is a certain type of noise in the clouds, or, of an eclipse, that it is a certain type of light deprivation, or, of man, that it is a certain type of animal, or, of the soul, that it moves itself . . . And in the cases where we possess something [of the thing], it is easier to search. Thus, how we stand with regard to finding out what something is is determined by the way we know that it exists. (93ᵃ21–4, 28–30)

In cases where we have non-accidental knowledge that eclipses exist, we do so because we already grasp something of what eclipses are.[22] The

---

[22] The structure of this passage is reasonably clear. Aristotle distinguishes cases where we grasp that the thing exists incidentally from those where we grasp that it exists by having something of the thing itself (93ᵃ21–2). He then describes the difficulty involved in proceeding to knowledge of the 'what it is' when we only know accidentally that the thing exists (93ᵃ24–7). Next he returns to the case in which we know that the thing exists by 'having something of it'(93ᵃ28). He concludes these remarks in the next line by saying that 'as we know that it is, so we stand to the what it is'(93ᵃ28–9). All is clear as long as one keeps separate three different uses of the verb '*echein*' in this passage.

phrase 'having something of the thing itself' refers to the same stage as is marked out by the phrases 'having something [of the thing]' in 93ª28, and 'having something of the "what it is"' in 93ª29.[23] Thus, since the latter must refer to a stage prior to knowing that the kind exists, so must the former. If so, our grasp of what eclipses are—a type of deprivation of light—is a necessary condition for grasping non-accidentally that there are eclipses. In these cases, we come to know non-accidentally that there are eclipses by discovering that there are deprivations of light of the appropriate type. This is possible because armed with some information about eclipses we can proceed to Stages 2 and 3. Since this information directs our investigation into whether there are eclipses, its grasp cannot essentially involve our knowing that the kind exists.[24]

(a) 93ª21, 27, 28 (second use): having that it is/whether it is—this use is equivalent to 'knowing that it is'(93ª25, 26);

(b) 93ª22, 28 (first instance), 29: having something of the thing/of what it is;

(c) 93ª28 (third use): standing in a given relation to . . .

[23] The phrase 'by having something of the thing' in 93ª22 could (in principle) refer to two distinct steps. It could refer to the information one brings, to one's encounter with the thing, on the basis of which one comes to recognize the thing. Here, the information will serve as the springboard for coming to know that the thing exists. Alternatively, it could refer to the *mode* in which one comes to know the thing: i.e. to the information one picks up in encountering the thing. The springboard interpretation is preferable for two reasons:

(a) It refers to the same stage as is marked out in 93ª29 ff. where it must mark out a stage preliminary to knowing of the existence of the thing. For, this knowledge is arrived at in the process described in 93ª30 ff.

(b) The focus of the discussion is on a *search* for something: either to know what something is (93ª27 f.) or to know that it exists (93ª30 ff.). But in the context of a search one needs something to guide one. Otherwise, one would not know whether or not one's search was successful.

[24] How is the phrase 'a certain type of . . .' to be understood? Bolton ('Essentialism') suggested that this phrase should be taken to refer to certain particular instances known to be members of the kind. But this view, which requires that in knowing the relevant account one knows that the kind exists, is inconsistent with the three-stage view. There are two other alternatives. 'A certain' could mean:

(ii*) 'a kind of . . .', as (e.g.) sharks are a kind of fish

or

(ii#) 'a certain type of fish', where 'a certain' is a place-holder for a definite description to be supplied, as (e.g.) sharks are the type of fish with distinctive properties A, B, and C.

In (ii*) the relevant claim is only that sharks form one determinate kind of fish, but there is no requirement that one can now uniquely describe that type of fish. In (ii#) the claim is that the speaker can uniquely describe the kind, using a definite description currently in his possession. (ii*) takes 'a certain' as part of the content grasped by the thinker, while (ii#) construes it as a proxy for a quite different content he actually has.
  (ii*) seems preferable for three reasons:

(a) The phrase 'having something of the thing: e.g. . . . .' (93ª22) suggests that what follows is itself part of the content grasped by the thinker, not a place-holder for a fuller specification of that content.

If this is correct, the enquirer's grasp on what eclipses of the moon are prior to his knowing of their existence will simply consist in his knowing that, if they exist, such eclipses are instances of a type of light deprivation. This is the information he would have prior to knowledge of the existence or essence of the phenomenon. But where does such knowledge come from? An answer is provided by Aristotle's discussion of the void in *Physics* Δ.7, where he envisages a person knowing (at the same early stage of investigation) that the void is a place, if there is one, which is deprived of body (214^{a}16–17). But here the source of the knowledge is clear. It is based on an account of what the name 'void' signifies:

'void' is a place in which there is nothing. (213^{b}31)

Thus, in both cases the account of what the name signifies will give us knowledge that the kind, if it exists, has a given property. Such accounts do not give us knowledge that the kind in question exists.

At Stage 1 one will have some idea of what it would be for there to be eclipses, but will not as yet have established that there are any. Aristotle gives a further example of a similar predicament:

Nor is it different from asking of which of a contradictory pair is there an account: of its [a triangle's] having or not having internal angles equal to two right angles. (93^{a}33–5)

Here, one does not know whether triangles (*as such*) have or lack a given property: having an internal angle sum of two right angles.[25] When one finds a proof one will know both that this feature belongs to all and only triangles (or closed figures with three angles) and why this is so. The proof might run as follows:

The total angles made by one line when it touches another line are equal to two right angles. The total angle sum of a closed figure with three internal angles is equal to that made by the line touching another. Therefore, the internal angles of such a closed figure equal two right angles.[26]

This proof establishes that triangles as such possess the relevant feature (cf. *Post. An.* A.9, 76^{a}5–7; *Soph. El.* 6, 168^{b}2). Thus, one would at the same

(b) In the fourth example Aristotle cites a phrase uniquely true of the soul: 'the thing that moves itself'. Since this is clearly part of the content of the relevant thought, it is best to interpret the other phrases as playing a similar role. Thus, sometimes the content is a definite description, but not always. At other times an indefinite phrase will do.

(c) One has succeeded in 'grasping something of the thing/of the what it is' if one thinks of man as a type of animal. Nothing more specific (or conclusion-like) than this is needed.

[25] For, this might be a feature only of some types of triangle: e.g. isosceles triangles, or the ones one has so far drawn. One could not know, merely on the basis of a few examples, that this is a feature of all triangles as such.

[26] This form of proof follows that outlined in Euclid *Elementa* 1.32, which rests in turn on Euclid *Elementa* 1.13. Aristotle discusses it (or some near variant of it) in *Meta.* Θ.9, 1051^{a}24–6.

time establish that triangles as such have an internal angle sum equal to two right angles, and why this is so.[27]

In this case, as in that of the triangle and the eclipse, one has, prior to proof, no knowledge of the existence of the phenomenon in question. In the latter cases, knowledge of the accounts of what the names 'triangle' and 'eclipse' signify will not involve knowledge of the existence of the kind in question. In this way, the springboard interpretation supports the three-stage view proposed by the liberal interpreter.

2.5 SECTION [C]: 93[b]35–7: VARIETIES OF STAGE 1

What is involved in grasping an account of what a name signifies?

In the case of 'thunder', the person who grasps the account of what 'thunder' signifies is able at Stage 2 to know non-accidentally that thunder exists. If the argument of the previous section is correct, one grasps at a stage prior to discovery of existence that:

with respect to thunder it is a type of noise in the clouds. (93[a]22–3)

If so, Aristotle envisages that at Stage 1 one knows only that thunder, if it exists, is a type of noise in the clouds. One knows this on the basis of an account of what the term signifies, without therein knowing of thunder's existence.

In B.8 Aristotle describes a case in which one comes to learn that thunder exists. He writes as follows:

Let cloud be C, thunder A, quenching of fire B. B belongs to C (for fire is quenched in the clouds), and A (i.e. noise) belongs to C also. And B is the account of A: the first term. (93[b]10–12)

Here, too, one discovers that thunder exists when one discovers that noise belongs to the clouds because fire is quenched. Prior to this discovery, one will not know that thunder exists. Rather, if armed with an account of what the term signifies, one will know only that 'thunder' signifies a type of noise in the clouds. This Stage 1 knowledge enables one to conduct a successful enquiry into what exists (so as to possess non-accidental knowledge), and, at the third stage, to discover more fully what thunder is.

In this example, the terms used in the account of what 'thunder'

---

[27] This proof rests on (a) an understanding of the nature of the straight line (see *Physics* B.9, 200[a]17–18), and (b) an account of the triangle as a closed figure with three internal angles, such as might be derived from an account of what 'triangle' signifies. This type of proof does not consist simply in giving a method to construct triangles with a given property. It aims rather to explain why triangles, so constructed, have the features they do. Constructive proofs may establish the 'that' without yet establishing the 'why'.

signifies ('a type of noise in the clouds') belong to one thing non-accidentally because thunder is a natural unity. This will be one of the cases specified in 93^{b}35–7:

> An account is one in two ways, one by being stitched together like the *Iliad*, the other by showing that one thing belongs to one thing non-accidentally.

The latter phrase will pick out accounts like the one of what 'thunder' signifies.[28] In this type of account, one thing belongs to another non-accidentally. For, the account focuses on those features of thunder which need to be explained by the presence of its more fundamental properties. This type of initial account (as emphasized above) is the one that leads to successful enquiry and discovery of existence.

The other type of account specified in the passage cited is one which, like the *Iliad*, depends not on the natural unity of a genuine kind but on a man-made unity which we create. One clear example would be that of 'goatstag'. Here, the account might run as follows:

> 'Goatstag' signifies animals which are part goat and part stag.

But in this case, unlike the previous one, the unity of the account flows from us and not from the world. Although there is no one thing of which this account is predicated, knowledge of it will allow us to say:

> Goatstags are animals which are part goat and part stag, if there are any such animals.

As in the case of thunder, we will not know, on the basis of these accounts, of the existence of the relevant kind. In both cases, Stage 1 accounts will provide the springboard for an investigation into the question of whether the kind exists. Indeed, at Stage 1 the enquirer need not know which of the two types of account he possesses. In both cases, the accounts hold up a target for an investigation into the existence of the kind signified.

Both types of account are *bona fide* accounts of what the names signify. They should, thus, be included among the accounts of this type discussed in the first sentence of this paragraph (at 93^{a}29–32). The sentence, so understood, indicates that the paragraph as a whole is concerned with all accounts of what names signify, and not merely with that subset of such accounts which are correlated with names for existents. If so, the paragraph as a whole provides a context in which its first sentence should be taken as claiming that all accounts of what terms signify are definitions (in line with the liberal interpretation).

Are there more than these two types of accounts of what names signify?

---

[28] There may be other types of account which are relevant to this passage which are also one in this way: (e.g.) the accounts reached at Stage 3. However, since the only account explicitly mentioned is at Stage 1, 93^{b}35–7 must refer (at least in part) to accounts at that stage.

In particular, would grasp of an accidental property of the phenomenon be a good case of understanding something tied together by us? It would certainly not have the role of guiding our investigation which is played by a non-accidental predication. Nor would it be an example of a statement which is tied together by us, since the latter are distinguished from statements which represent accidental properties of things (*Meta.* Z.4, 1030^{b}7–10, 12–13). If so, we may conclude that the only cases allowed in 93^{b}35–7 are ones which either predicate one thing of one thing non-accidentally or are examples of ones which are tied together by us like the *Iliad*: e.g. that of 'goatstag'. There appears to be no third case.

As should now be clear, the sentence bracketed in the Ross text (93^{b}35–7) is important for an understanding of the first two sentences of the chapter. Indeed, the natural flow of the passage appears to be this:

(1) It is said that all and only definitions are accounts of what F is. (Premiss)

(2) There is a certain type of account of what F is which is an account of what 'F' signifies. (Accounts of what 'F' signifies are examples of a type of account of what something is.) (Premiss)

(3) It is obvious that one type of definition of F will be an account of what 'F' signifies. (From (1) and (2))

(4) Once one grasps that what is signified exists, one seeks an answer to the 'Why?' question.

(5) Accounts of what names signify can be unities in two ways: either like the *Iliad* or by non-accidental predication.

The importance of (5) is clear. One type of account, like the one correlated with 'thunder', can lead to non-accidental knowledge that the kind exists. This type of account involves non-accidental predication (see (5)) and guides the enquiry in the way indicated by proposition (4). The other type, like the one associated with 'goatstag', cannot play this role but is, nonetheless, a type of account appropriate for being a definition of what the name signifies. The final sentence is important because it distinguishes these two types of account of what the name signifies.

If this is correct, the earlier lines 93^{b}33–5 might appear something of a parenthesis:

(4′) It is difficult to proceed to an answer to the 'Why?' question in cases where we do not know the thing exists . . . as has been said before.

But it would be a mistake to transfer the brackets from 93^{b}36–7 to ^{b}33–5. For, while the earlier lines do not add directly to the flow of the argument, they do indicate part of the role of accounts of what names signify: as Stage 1 of the three-stage enquiry. In effect, (4′) captures the role played by some accounts of what names signify in successful enquiry, while (2), (3), and (5) emphasize that all accounts of what names signify are definitions.

Section [C], so understood, provides additional evidence in favour of the three-stage view and of the claim that all accounts of what terms signify have the status of being definitions. It completes the liberal interpretation of the first paragraph. Can this interpretation be sustained in the remainder of the chapter?

2.6 SECTIONS [D]–[G]: 93^{b}38–94^{a}10: FURTHER DEFENCE OF THE LIBERAL READING OF B.10

The view of Stage 1 of enquiry sketched in the previous sections gives a natural reading of the next two sections of chapter 10, labelled as [D] to [F] in the translation offered at the beginning of the Chapter.

The account of what 'thunder' signifies, let us assume, runs as follows:

'Thunder' signifies a type of noise in the clouds.

From this, one may extract the information that thunder is a type of noise in the clouds, if it exists. But one will not have as yet established that thunder exists. By contrast, the second definition is one which is related to the proof that noise belongs to the clouds. For, it adverts to the further term (e.g. 'fire being quenched'), which allows us to demonstrate that noise belongs to the clouds. This type of definition:

Thunder is noise in the clouds caused by fire being quenched.

shows the answer to the 'Why?' question.

The second definition rests on a demonstration of the form:

Fire being quenched belongs to the clouds.

Noise belongs to fire being quenched.

Noise belongs to the clouds.

Thus, Aristotle writes:

The same account is given in more than one way, first as a continuous demonstration and second as a definition. (94^{a}6–7)

How is this type of definition related to accounts of what terms signify?

There are several differences. The second type of definition is connected with demonstration, while there can be no demonstration that a term signifies anything (B.7, 92^{b}33). Thus, the second type of definition cannot be about the signification of words but must be about the nature of things.

If so, the two types of definition cannot be identical because their aims and relations are different: the first concerns the significance of 'thunder', the second the nature of thunder.

This fundamental difference can be illustrated in a different way. The constraints which govern the second type of definition arise from the explanatory structure of the kind, while those that govern the first are based in the account of the signification of its name. As Aristotle remarks, the latter is connected with signification, the former with proof (93^b39 ff.). Even if the very same words were used in giving both accounts, they would be used to do different things in the two cases.

These definitions also differ in other respects. The conclusion of the syllogism given above establishes that thunder exists. If the second definition is merely a grammatical variant of this syllogism, it too must give us the knowledge that the kind exists. So, to understand that this definition is true is to know that the kind in question exists. It will be grasped at Stage 3 when one already knows of the existence of the kind. By contrast, one can understand that the account of what 'thunder' signifies is correct without knowing of the existence of thunder. For, the account of what the name signifies does not give us the knowledge that the phenomenon exists. It is grasped at Stage 1 before one has knowledge of the existence of the kind. Thus, the two definitions differ in the existential information possessed by one who grasps them. For, they are grasped at different stages in the enquiry.

There is a further difference. The second definition consists in a specific claim about a uniquely identified kind. Thunder is the kind of noise in the clouds with one determinate cause. That is the kind it is. By contrast, the original account of what the name signifies is general in form:

'Thunder' signifies a type of noise in the clouds.

The latter phrase ('a type of noise in the clouds') is not sufficient uniquely to identify the specific type of noise in question. It says that thunder is a type of noise, but does not state which type it is. If so, since these two claims differ in respect of their degree of specificity, they cannot be semantically identical. More generally, if Stage 1 accounts can be general but Stage 3 definitions must uniquely specify the kind, there can be no general requirement that the content of the two types of account be identical. Even if both involve the same terms 'noise in the clouds', the logical force of these terms is different. For, at Stage 1 one has the general thought of a (*tis*) type of noise in the clouds, while at Stage 3 one can identify that type of noise as the one caused by fire being quenched. Nor is this an accident. If there are to be proofs about thunder, the kind in question must be uniquely individuated. Thus, the appropriate definitions must contain enough information to identify the kind in question.

Aristotle continues by considering a third type of definition:

Again, a definition of thunder is noise in the clouds. This is the conclusion of a demonstration of what it is. (94ᵃ7–9)

How is this related to the account of what the name 'thunder' signifies? Are they the same? They certainly appear to use the same terms.

There are, however, differences between the third definition and the first, which mirror those already detected between the second and the first. The first type of definition is concerned with the significance of the term 'thunder', the third with the nature of the phenomenon itself. For, the third is closely connected with demonstration, while the first cannot be (B.7, 92ᵇ33). Thus, the third type of definition requires features which are inherent in the causal structure of kinds rather than in the signification of the relevant term. The two definitions are of different things: the former concerns the significance of 'thunder', the latter thunder itself.

There are further differences. If one knows an account of what a name signifies, one need not know that the kind in question exists. By contrast, if one knows something based on a conclusion of a demonstration, one must know that the kind in question exists. For, such conclusions establish that the kind in question exists. Thus, one who possesses the latter style of definition must know something not required for knowledge of what the term signifies. The two definitions have different roles, because they are related to different stages in enquiry.

There is a further, semantic, difference between the two types of account. The third definition, in registering the information encapsulated in the conclusion, refers to that very type of noise in the clouds (there mentioned) about which certain causal truths have been established by demonstration.[29] It must, therefore, be a specific claim about one uniquely specified phenomenon: thunder. By contrast, the first definition is, as noted above, general in form, and fails uniquely to identify the type of noise in question. While it says that thunder is a type of noise in the clouds, it does not state which it is. Thus, the *definiens* as well as the *definienda* will be different in the two cases. Even if some of the same terms are used ('noise in the clouds') at Stage 1 they are used to make an indefinite claim about a type of noise (*tis*), while in the second they uniquely identify the phenomenon in question.

---

[29] This type of definition could be stated as follows:

Thunder is that type of noise in the clouds, which is caused by fire being quenched.

As such, it will differ from the second type of definition, which appears to run as follows:

Thunder is the type of noise in the clouds which is caused by fire being quenched.

For, in the latter, but not the former, the causal antecedents are used to specify the relevant type of noise. In the former, it is assumed that one can specify what thunder is independently of its causal origins.

The first type of definition also differs from the fourth one introduced in 94^{a}9–10:

The definition of immediates is an undemonstrable positing of what they are.

An example of such an account appears to be:

To be a monad is to be an indivisible unit,[30]

which is different in form from:

'The monad' signifies an indivisible unit.

For, the former answers the question:

What is a monad?

while the latter answers the question:

What is a 'monad'?

This difference in form is important; for, it explains why claims concerning undemonstrables can appear among the starting points of demonstration (A.8, 75^{b}31 ff., B.9, 93^{b}22), while claims about what terms signify can never be used either as premises or conclusions in such demonstrations.[31] As before, the fourth type of definition concerns the phenomenon signified and not the term which signifies. The differing connections with proof indicate a major difference in the type of claim made in these two cases.[32]

If these arguments are correct, there is reason not to identify any of the three definitions discussed in 93^{b}38–94^{a}10 with accounts of what names signify.[33] If so, as required by the liberal interpretation, definitional accounts of what names signify will constitute a form of definition distinct from any of the others specified in B.10. One cannot know solely on the

---

[30] This is to take the example cited in B.9 as an instance of an 'immediate'(93^{b}24): something which is a starting point for a science, such as the unit. So understood, immediates will be distinct from immediate propositions (such as are referred to in B.8, 93^{a}36).

[31] This is not to say that definitional claims about the monad (or, for that matter, the point, the line . . .) are ever actually used in demonstrations. Indeed, as Vassilis Karasmanis points out, such definitions are not used in Euclid's proofs ('The Hypotheses of Mathematics in Plato's *Republic* and his Contribution to the Axiomatization of Geometry', in P. Nicolopoulos (ed.), *Greek Studies in the Philosophy and History of Science* (1990), 127.) However, the fact that such claims are of a form which can be used in demonstration separates them from claims about what terms signify. For, the former (unlike the latter) are claims about how the world is (rather than about the signification of terms). Thus, the former are part of science (understood as an organized body of claims about the world) while the latter are not.

[32] The issue of the existential commitments of *theses* is complicated, and will be discussed in the next Chapter.

[33] This was the line taken by Themistius in his *Paraphrasis* (p. 51, 3–26) and, with certain caveats, by Philoponus.

basis of an account of what a name signifies that there is a real kind which it signifies, still less what its essence is.[34]

2.7 SECTION [H]: 94ᵃ11–14: ARISTOTLE'S SUMMARY of B.10

Aristotle continues (in section (H), as translated above) with a reference back to the three types of definition. This passage is initially puzzling, since it refers to only three types of definition, while the chapter has referred to four. Worse still, this passage seems to state a conclusion drawn from what precedes. So, why are only three definitions mentioned?

Our discussion suggests a solution to this puzzle. There are indeed four distinct definitions in this chapter, but they are not all of the same thing. The first concerns an account of what terms signify, the last three definitions of things or kinds. In the concluding paragraph of B.10, the three definitions mentioned are definitions of things, relevant to the specification of 'what a thing is' and connected with proof (94ᵃ15, 16–17), not accounts of what terms signify (B.3, 90ᵃ36, B.10, 93ᵇ38–9). After the first paragraph of B.10, Aristotle's attention seems confined to these definitions because he considers only accounts that are linked with proof.

Some scholars have argued that there are no more than three definitions in the whole of B.10.[35] But this is a mistake. While it is correct that there are only three types of definition of *kinds* in B.10, there are more than three types of definition. Their mistake was to fail to see that the first type of definition (the one connected with signification) is of a fundamentally different type from those that follow. As a consequence, they assumed that all four definitions had to be of the same thing, and, thus, were forced to identify the first with one of the remaining three mentioned in the chapter. But, as we saw in the preceding section, this cannot be done.

In these respects, traditional four-definition interpreters were correct. However, some made a further move which we can now see to have been mistaken. For, they thought that if accounts of what names signify were not identical with accounts of kinds, they would have to be about quite different items: meanings, denizens of a neo-Platonic realm, completely distinct from the world of things. No further move of this type is required. For, as we have seen, accounts of what 'thunder' signifies will mention properties which are features of the phenomenon, although they do so in

---

[34] If one knows a real definition of the phenomenon thunder, and knows that the term 'thunder' signifies that phenomenon, one will be able to derive an account of what that term signifies. For, the latter must specify some non-accidental feature of thunder (albeit in the general way indicated above).

[35] Ross accepts the three definition view.

a non-specific way. Since such accounts refer (indefinitely) to (e.g.) a type of noise in the clouds, they specify in a general way features of reality. The difference between these accounts and real definitions of thunder lies in their differing degrees of specificity, and not in the type of entity invoked. For, in the case of thunder, the account of what the term signifies will refer (in indefinite mode) to some non-accidental property of the phenomenon.

At this point, one can see the attraction of the three-definition inter-pretation. Scholars wishing to resist the other-worldly, neo-Platonic, version of Stage I accounts proposed to *identify* the account of what 'tri-angle' signifies with some account of the essence of triangles. But, as we have seen, this radical move was mistaken. While three-definition exegetes were correct to insist that some definitional accounts of what names signify concern things in the world, they should not have identified such accounts with any other definition.[36] The liberal interpretation shows how accounts of what names signify can be (in some way) about things without being identical with any real definition of the kind.

2.8 INTERIM CONCLUSIONS AND SCEPTICAL CHALLENGES

I have argued, thus far, for the three exegetical claims characteristic of the liberal interpretation, as set out in Section 2.3:

(A) Aristotle develops in B.8–10 a three-stage view of scientific enquiry, in which grasp of the first stage does not require knowledge of the exis-tence or of the essence of the kind under investigation.

(D) All accounts of what names signify are definitional accounts, even though they are not definitions of the kinds investigated.

(B) Accounts of what names signify are not identical with any of the three types of definition of the kind signified.

If (A), (B), and (D) are correct, both versions of the restrictive interpre-tation must be rejected. All three are inconsistent with the second restric-tive interpretation, and (B) and (D) with the first. Further, if (A) is correct, Aristotle's account of what names signify cannot be assimilated to that outlined by my modern essentialist. For, in Aristotle's view, grasp of this account does not essentially involve knowledge of the existence of the kind.

[36] It should be noted that the positions occupied by the two traditional opposing views of B.10 do not exhaust the field. If one group erred in identifying definitional accounts of names and things, the other was mistaken in thinking that accounts of what terms signify were not concerned with real-world objects.

My interpretation of B.8 and B.10 rests on five premisses:

(1) To grasp an account of what the name signifies is to have sufficient knowledge to go on to establish whether or not the thing exists and what it is—a kind of 'springboard' for further investigation.

(2) All (genuine) accounts of what names signify are definitions.

(3) To grasp an account of what a name signifies is (in some cases) to grasp 'something of the thing' (93ᵃ22).

(4) Knowledge of an account of what the term signifies does not involve one knowing of the existence of the thing.

(5) One can grasp something of the thing in the general way manifest when one thinks of thunder as 'a type of noise in the clouds'.

I shall consider objections to each of these in turn.

(a) Premiss 1

Some will object that in the immediate context of 93ᵃ20–8, Aristotle is focusing on knowledge of existence and of what the thing is (Stages 2 and 3), and not on any preceding stage. For, he begins by noting that one cannot arrive at Stage 3 save via Stage 2 (ᵃ20). In 93ᵃ21, he discusses various ways in which one can know of the existence of the thing: sometimes by having something of the thing, sometimes accidentally. If so, the phrase 'having something of the thing' might be taken to describe what is involved in knowing of the existence of the thing. That is, the phrase might specify the way in which we have knowledge (in certain cases) of the existence of the phenomenon, and as such involve features drawn from both Stages 1 and 2. It need not be restricted to features drawn from Stage 1 (as in the springboard interpretation sketched above). Rather, it will describe a *mode* of having knowledge of the thing at Stage 2.[37]

I have argued above for the springboard reading of 93ᵃ20–36. However, even if my interpretation of 93ᵃ20–9 were rejected, it remains difficult to resist it in lines 93ᵃ30–6. For, there one has a grasp on eclipses which enables one to investigate their existence. So, one must have a grasp on eclipses which is not existence-involving. Similarly with the triangle example. Thus, even if one were to prefer the *mode* reading of the lines up to 93ᵃ30, the following lines would force one to distinguish two separate elements which had previously been taken together, stages which

---

[37] The sense of 'knowledge' appears to remain constant in B.8, and there is no place for a clear distinction between ordinary and scientific knowledge in this context. 'To have' ('*echein*' (93ᵃ20, 26, 29, 30)) is used, apparently interchangeably, with 'to know' ('*eidenai*' (93ᵃ20, 25, 26, 36, ᵇ2–3)). Nor is there a gap between the use of 'knowing' in 93ᵃ35–6 and in 93ᵃ20–1.

correspond respectively to Stage 1 and Stage 2. If so, at Stage 1, one will grasp a specification of what (e.g.) 'triangle' or 'eclipse' signifies without knowing of the existence of the kind in question.

(b) Premiss 2

Some will object that Aristotle could not have allowed that an account of what 'goatstag' signifies could be a definition because (in their view) in *Posterior Analytics* B.7 he rules out the possibility of definitions of non-existents. If so, it will be claimed, some version of the restrictive view must be correct. Or else, Aristotle's views in B.7 and B.8–10 are inconsistent.

I shall consider this objection in the next Chapter. It should be noted, however, that its starting point lies in the aporetic chapter B.7 rather than in the chapters where the *aporiai* are resolved. Further, it assumes that Aristotle accepts throughout B.8–10 that there can be no definition of any kind in the case of non-existents. But, since in these chapters Aristotle is making distinctions which aim to overcome these *aporiai*, it cannot be safe to assume that all B.7 claims remain intact. Some will have to be modified to overcome the problems raised. Thus, if (as the liberal interpreter suggests) in B.10 one type of definition is connected with accounts of what terms signify and another with accounts of things, Aristotle could easily insist that only the latter be confined to existents while allowing that the former need not be. For, in this way the requirement in B.7 that all definitions be of existents will be shown to apply to real definitions of existing kinds, but not to accounts of what names signify. In general, it seems (methodologically) better to see Aristotle in B.10 as modifying the views in B.7 that led to *aporia* rather than as treating those assumptions as fixed and secure. If so, the present objection is not powerful.

(c) Premiss 3

Some might accept the three-stage reading of B.8, but deny that this says anything about accounts of what terms signify. According to this view, accounts of what names signify will be introduced in B.10 without further preparation in the immediately preceding discussion in B.8. Indeed, their role in successful investigation will not be discussed prior to B.10 save in the aporetic sections of B.7.

If this objection is sustained, Aristotle's whole discussion of accounts of what names signify will be woefully incomplete. For, if we exclude back references to B.8, B.10 leaves us in the dark about the precise role and nature of these accounts. Thus, it seems preferable (on methodological grounds) to regard the relevant B.10 discussion (93^{b}29–37) as depending on the stage of enquiry marked out in B.8 (at 93ᵃ30–6) as prior to the discovery of existence of the phenomenon. In this way, B.10 builds on the argument of B.8 by showing that accounts of what names signify give us Stage 1 knowledge that (e.g.) thunder, if it exists, is a type of noise in the clouds.

This reply can be strengthened. The first sentences of B.10 explicitly look back to B.8 (93ᵃ32–5). Indeed, the example of the triangle makes clear the backwards connection. For, as we know from B.7, knowledge of what the term 'triangle' signifies is separate from knowledge of the existence of the phenomenon (92ᵇ15–16). While B.8 does not contain any discussion of the transition from one to the other, it introduces at the relevant spot (93ᵃ29 ff.) the similar case of establishing the existence of a feature of the triangle: its having angle sum equal to two right angles. This offers a parallel to what is involved in establishing the existence of the triangle. If so, even though accounts of what names signify make their first appearance in B.10, they are best seen as located at the space prepared (and, to some extent, indicated) for them in the argument of B.8.

(d) Premiss 4

It may be objected that in 93ᵃ30–6 Aristotle is exclusively concerned with 'scientific knowledge' of the existence of kinds. But this (it will be said) is quite consistent with someone knowing in some everyday sense of the existence of thunder before they have scientific knowledge of its existence. Indeed, it will be suggested, this is precisely what is envisaged in 93ᵃ20–30, where (it will be claimed) one has everyday knowledge of the existence of certain phenomena prior to scientific proof. If so, one cannot conclude that the first stage of enquiry involves no knowledge at all of existence. Perhaps it only falls short of scientific knowledge of existence.

It is, however, hard to sustain this objection in the immediate context of B.8. For, the very same term is used throughout for knowledge in 93ᵃ20–9 and ᵃ29–ᵇ2—*eidenai* (ᵃ20, 25, 26, 36, 93ᵇ3)—without any indication that he is referring to different types of knowledge in different places (as the objector would require). Rather, Aristotle's claims appear to concern the same type of knowledge (without further qualification) throughout the chapter. Thus, when at 93ᵇ15 he makes the general and unqualified claim that there can be no coming to know what something is without proof, he appears to commit himself to the strong thesis that all routes to knowledge in these cases are through proof. Unscientific knowledge appears absent from the present discussion. Nor is it difficult to see why. In these chapters, Aristotle is concerned with the existence and nature of kinds, what such kinds have or are *as such*. It will not do for his purposes to establish that *some* triangles have a given feature or that (e.g.) isosceles triangles exist. For, he is concerned to establish not merely that some specific type of triangle exists or has a given feature, but that there is a wider kind of which (e.g.) the isosceles is an example. For this reason, one could not know that triangles exist merely by pointing to examples of triangles. For such examples could not establish the existence of the wider kind, triangle, rather than of some narrower kind (e.g. scalene triangle).[38]

(e) Premiss 5

It was argued above that the initial account of what 'thunder' signifies will specify it as a type of noise in the clouds. But, if this is correct, how can the enquirer on this basis proceed to discover the existence or nature of thunder? For, since there are other kinds of noise in the clouds (sheep on misty mountains, cloud-covered volcanoes . . .), how can we discover the existence of *thunder* rather than of any of the other types of noise in the clouds? It appears that the enquirer does not have the resources to discover that the relevant specific kind exists. If so, it will be said, the original account must be more specific. Surely, there must be more content if it is to do what is required to be a springboard for Stage 2? Perhaps we need to think of thunder as being noise in the clouds caused in a given way (if there is any such noise), or as noise in the clouds accompanied by lightning (if there is any such thing)? Surely our thoughts at Stage 1 must have more specificity than has so far been allowed?

This objection rests on a major (and controversial) assumption: that all the information needed to determine the extension of the relevant name will be available to the enquirer at Stage 1. However, it could well be that there are features which determine the extension of the term, which are not available at Stage 1. Thus, if (for example) the signification of the term is determined (in part) by the enquirer being in causal contact of a given type with the world, the extension of the term will be fixed by features not (necessarily) accessible to the enquirer, and not grasped as part of his account of what the term signifies. For, if external features can play some role in determining the signification of the term, they need not be part of the Stage 1 account of what the name signifies but still could be (subsequently) used in establishing the existence of the relevant kind. Indeed, one might at this stage exploit the causal connection to latch on to that kind rather than another.

This objection cannot be met until we have a clearer grasp of how the signification of the name is determined (in Aristotle's account). So we will return to this issue in Chapter 4. There is a lacuna here that needs to be filled.[39]

---

[38] For further discussion of this issue see Ch. 3 Sect. 3.5.

[39] Some will see immediately that larger issues concerning the role of external factors in determining signification are central to this discussion. While they are correct, I ask them to be patient. These issues will come to the fore in Chapter 4.

2.9 SEMANTIC DEPTH

If the arguments above are correct, one cannot know at Stage 1 that the kind has an essence, yet to be discovered. One cannot know this until one knows of the existence of the kind. Thus, Stage 1 accounts will not involve the type of semantic depth discussed in the previous Chapter. However, a further question remains: need one know at Stage 1 that the kind, if it exists, has an essence (even though one does not know what it is)?

The evidence of *Posterior Analytics* B.8–10 is not conclusive on this issue. The examples cited in B.8 (93^{a}22 ff.) do not explicitly refer to any internal essence of the kinds in question. There is certainly no necessity to understand phrases such as 'a type of light deprivation' or 'a type of animal' as alluding to an essence (yet to be discovered) which holds the kind together. However, they could (no doubt) be understood in this way.

Aristotle proceeds to discuss the case of the eclipse in more detail (93^{a}30–^{b}7), and begins by separating two types of example. In the first, one grasps the existence of the thing by grasping a basic middle term (93^{a}30–6). In the second, one grasps its existence by grasping an intermediate term (93^{a}36–^{b}14). But is a grasp on these middle terms required at Stage 1 or is it achieved only at Stage 2? If one needs to grasp at the outset the middle term (e.g. the earth's interposition), one will need to know at Stage 1 that if there are eclipses they are caused by the earth's interposition.

It is clear that Aristotle does not assume that at Stage 1 one must know that if there are eclipses they are brought about by the earth's interposition. For, he continues by saying that this case is no different from one in which one searches for an account of eclipse (93^{a}32). In the latter case, there is no requirement that one already have a prime candidate in mind for the middle term. One is merely looking to see whether there is one. So, since these cases are said to be the same, it cannot be known in either that 'interposition by the earth' is the middle term (if there is one). Thus, the astronomer who looks for B is best described as looking for a cause which turns out to be B (93^{a}31).

But need the astronomer know at Stage 1 that if there are eclipses they must have an essence (even if he does not know what it would be)? The discussion suggests that the enquirer who has knowledge of the existence of eclipses will know that there is some cause which accounts for their occurrence (93^{a}30–2, see B.2, 90^{a}8). But this does not require that the speaker know (in initially understanding the term) that if eclipses exist they have a hidden determining factor. For, the account at Stage 1 might be shallower. The enquirer at Stage 1 might need to know only that if eclipses exist they have some sort of causal structure present (while remaining agnostic as to whether there is one determining factor which holds that nature together).[40]

Aristotle's second example (93ª36–ᵇ2) takes the issue further. He writes:

Let C be moon, A eclipse, B inability to cast shadows at full moon with nothing obvious in between. If B belongs to the moon, and A belongs to B, then it is clear that there is an eclipse, but not why, and we know that there is an eclipse, but not what an eclipse is.

According to this passage, we can know that there is an eclipse without knowing its fundamental cause. All we need know is that there is some causal structure (or nature) present. If so, there can be no requirement that on the basis of Stage 1 we know that eclipses, if they exist, have one fundamental cause. For, in grasping their existence, we do not rely on its having a fundamental causal structure. Thus, it is natural to think that we must be able (at Stage 1) to grasp what eclipses are without knowing that if they exist they have a fundamental (or determining) cause of this type.

In the case at issue, in establishing the existence of the eclipse, one needs to know something of the nature (or causal structure) of the phenomenon. To find that eclipses manifest a specific inability of the moon, the one manifested in its failure to cast a shadow at full moon when nothing is in between, is to find something of their causal structure.[41] This inability, of

[40] It is not obvious that any reference to causal material is required at Stage 1. Perhaps one refers to causation only at Stage 2, when one seeks to establish that the kind exists. Thus understood, causal notions would not be part of the account of what the term signifies, and would only be relevant in establishing the existence of the kinds in question. I return to the topic in Chapter 6.

[41] The phrase 'not being able to cast shadows . . . at a full moon' can be interpreted in more than one way. It might specify:

(a) the inability of the moon—if full and if nothing is in between—to cast shadows,

or

(b) the inability of the moon, when full and nothing is in between, to cast shadows.

In (a), the moon may have the same conditional inability (to cast-no-shadows-when-full) even when it is not full. In (b), by contrast, the moon will lack the relevant unconditional inability to cast shadows when it is not full. It has the relevant inability only under the conditions specified.

(A similar contrast is clearly marked by David Pears in 'Ifs and Cans', *Questions in the Philosophy of Mind* (London, 1975), 142 ff.)

Of these interpretations, I prefer (a) for two reasons:

(1) It specifies an inability which is present when and only when there is an eclipse. As such, it allows one to determine whether or not any given case is one of an eclipse—provided that one can establish that the inability responsible for the current light failure is the same one as is responsible for the failure to cast shadows when the moon is full. This makes the case closely parallel to that of the triangle discussed above.

course, will not be the basic causal factor, since its presence in turn needs to be explained. (See, for the suggestion of further explanation, $93^{b}12$–14.) But it is still an account (one *logos* among many ($93^{b}14$)) of some aspect of the nature of the eclipse. It is a factor which distinguishes eclipses from things that look like eclipses but are not.[42]

The most that could be extracted from this passage (concerning Stage 1) is the claim that if the kind exists it has some causal nature.[43] But this involves no commitment to the view that the kind has one determining feature (or essence). While the latter may emerge as the enquiry progresses, the enquirer (at Stage 1) need only have a comparatively shallow grasp of the nature in question. He will think of it merely as a kind with some internal causal structure, but that is all.

These passages provide some support for a shallower view of the understanding of the ordinary thinker than is suggested by my modern essentialist.[44] But they do not make it absolutely clear what is required, or why. Does one need to grasp a feature which is, in fact, part of the essence, or will it be enough to grasp a feature which is, in fact, necessary? Since these issues are left unresolved, there remain major gaps in Aristotle's account.

---

(2) In general, Aristotle appears to prefer (unconditionally) to attribute to subjects conditional powers—if conditions are such and such?—to act in certain ways (cf. *Meta.* Θ.5, $1048^{a}16$–21). That is, he seems reluctant to think of their capacities as coming and going depending on the circumstances in which they find themselves. For further discussion of this issue, see my *Aristotle's Philosophy of Action* (London, 1984), 24 ff.

In (a) there is reference to some aspect of the permanent structure of the eclipse, although not to the fundamental cause of the relevant inability (as specified in $93^{b}5$: quenching . . . interposition). In (b), by contrast, there would be reference only to what is a cause in certain cases of eclipses, and not in all. In neither need one know anything about the essence of the kind (if it exists).

[42] Ross, commenting on this passage, says (p. 631):

At this point Aristotle's account takes a curious turn. He represents the question of whether the moon suffers eclipse as being solved not, as we might expect, by direct observation or inference from a symptom, but by asking whether the interposition of the earth . . . occurs.

But this development need not seem strange. In investigating whether there are eclipses, one needs to be able to distinguish (in some cases) between eclipses and things that look like (but are not) eclipses. Situated as we are, this can only be done by investigation of the relevant cause (compare the possible case discussed at *Post. An.* B.2, $90^{a}25$ ff.). Indeed, one should be able to make this distinction in all cases. For, then one will know of the existence of eclipses, and not of some subset of eclipses (e.g. those at full moon).

[43] This can only be extracted if one makes an assumption stronger than those noted in n. 40 above.

[44] There is no commitment to the claim, essential to (2) in my modern essentialist's account, that the kind has a determining and underlying (necessary) physical feature (see Ch. 1, Sect. 1.2). This difference is independent of the modern essentialist's tendency to describe all non-accidental properties as essential.

2.10 FURTHER GAPS IN ARISTOTLE'S ACCOUNT

In the *Analytics* passages (as so far considered) Aristotle's accounts of what names signify appear to be distinct (in the ways noted) from definitions of kinds, and to have a specific role in scientific enquiry. However, Aristotle has said nothing (directly) about how the signification of such names is determined, or about the role (if any) in this of accounts of what names signify. Nor has he explained how it is that names and such accounts can signify the same (B.7, 92^b27f.). These questions will be examined in Chapters 4–6. But, before considering these, it is important to secure the interpretation offered of B.8–10 by examining the wider context of *Posterior Analytics* B as a whole. That is the task of the next Chapter.

Other major issues are raised by Aristotle's discussion in B.8–10. Why does he connect definitions of things so closely with demonstration? What is the nature of this connection? What is its theoretical basis? These issues will be examined in Part II (Chapters 7–13).

3

Preparation for the Three-Stage View

3.1 INTRODUCTION

My main aim in this chapter is to place the analysis I have offered of *Posterior Analytics* B.8–10 in the wider context of book B as a whole. The liberal interpretation rests on three claims:[1]

(A*) In B.8–10 Aristotle accepts a three-stage view of scientific enquiry, and at Stage 1 the enquirer lacks knowledge of the existence of the kind signified.

(D*) At Stage 1, the enquirer will possess a definitional account of what a name signifies.

(B*) Stage 1 accounts of what names signify are different in content from subsequent accounts of the kind itself.

In the present Chapter I shall support claims (A*) and (D*) by suggesting that, in the context of *Posterior Analytics* B:

(1) The three-stage view is Aristotle's answer to some of the problems he raises in the aporetic chapters B.3–7, and especially in B.7 (Sections 3.2–3.6).

(2) Aristotle resolves some of the *aporiai* of B.3–7 by liberalizing the constraints he initially imposed on acceptable definition, and (thus) by allowing accounts of what names signify to count as definitions (Section 3.6).

(3) The three-stage view carries forward the discussion of B.1–2 (Section 3.7).[2]

I shall also argue that crucial elements of the three-stage view are to be found elsewhere in the *Analytics* (Section 3.8). It forms an essential structural feature of the *Posterior Analytics* as a whole.

---

[1] See Ch. 2, Sect. 2.3. (A*), (D*), and (B*) are liberal answers to issues (A), (D) and (B) raised there.

[2] This Chapter does not aim to provide further evidence in favour of (B*). The precise content of such definitions is only discussed in B.8–10.

It must be ceded at the outset that not all the *aporiai* raised in *Posterior Analytics* B.3–7 are resolved by introducing the three-stage view. Others require a fuller account of the nature of definition at Stage 3. These latter difficulties will be discussed in Chapters 7 and 8.

3.2 B.7 92ᵇ4–25: INDEPENDENCE PROBLEM

Aristotle concludes B.7 with the following very striking aporetic remark:

From this, then, it is evident that definition and deduction are not the same, and that deduction and definition are not of the same thing; and, in addition, that definition neither demonstrates nor proves anything, and that you cannot become aware of what a thing is either by definition or demonstration. (92ᵇ35–8)

In Sections 3.2–3.4 I shall consider the arguments which led him to these conclusions in B.7, and in Sections 3.5–3.6 suggest that the three-stage view (as developed in B.8–10) constitutes part of his answer to the problems raised in B.3–7. For, that view enables him to challenge one of the key assumptions he had made in setting up the *aporiai*.

In B.7 there are several interconnected arguments in favour of a negative answer to the question:

Can a definer prove what a thing is? (92ᵃ34–5, 92ᵇ4)

One runs thus:[3]

How can you prove what a thing is? For, it is necessary for the person who knows what a man or anything else is, to know that it exists (for, in respect to that which does not exist, no one knows what it is; you may know what the account or name *signifies*, e.g. when I say 'goatstag', but it is impossible to know what a goatstag is). But, if you are to prove what it is *and* that it is, how can you do both by the same argument? For, a definition and a demonstration show *one* thing; but what a man is and that a man is are different. (92ᵇ4–11)

This argument suggests that one cannot know what a thing is if one does not know that it exists. But (it claims) one cannot show by the same argument both that the kind, man, exists and what a man is, since an argument makes one thing clear, and these two claims would require different conclusions. This argument aims to show that there can be no *one* proof which shows both that man exists and what man is. It cannot establish that there can be no proof of what a man is. The most it can demonstrate is that the proof of what a man is must be different from the proof that man exists.

---

[3] I omit the first (92ᵃ35–ᵇ3), which is directed to showing the impossibility of proving what something is in any of the possible styles of proof. This argument concerns Stage 3 not Stage 1.

Aristotle immediately moves to supplement the first argument. He writes as follows:

Next, we say that it is necessary for everything that a thing is to be proved by demonstration, unless it is its essence. But being is not the essence of anything; for, that it is is not a kind. Therefore, there will be a demonstration that the thing exists. And this is what sciences actually do. The geometer assumes what 'triangle' signifies and proves that it is. Now, when you define what it is, what will you prove except what a triangle is? If so, you will know by definition what a triangle is, but you will not know if it is. But that is impossible. ($92^b 12$–18)

This argument suggests that the definer (as distinct from the geometer who establishes the existence of the triangle) reveals what a triangle is. But if this is so, and what the definer reveals is distinct from and independent of the proof that the triangle exists (as argued in $92^b 4$–11), it will be possible to know the real definition of a triangle without knowing that triangles exist. However, this consequence is one which Aristotle takes to be an impossibility.[4]

These two arguments work closely together. The proof that the triangle exists must either be identical with or distinct from the proof of what it is essentially. However, the first argument shows that these two proofs cannot be identical, and the second establishes that they cannot be distinct. Therefore, Aristotle concludes, there can be no proof of what a triangle is.

These arguments turn on the following assumptions:

 (i) The claim that F exists is different in form from the claim that F is essentially G.

 (ii) If these claims are different, it must be possible to know one without knowing the other.

(ii) is a very strong *Independence Assumption*, which Aristotle employs elsewhere in the aporetic chapters. Thus, in B.3 he argues:

To know what is demonstrable is to have a demonstration. But, since there is a demonstration of some claims (like *all triangles are F*), clearly there will be no definition of this—for, that way someone would know them in virtue of the definition without having the demonstration; for, nothing prevents him from having one without the other. ($90^b 9$–13)

This argument turns on two premisses:

(1) If a proposition Q is demonstrable, one can know Q only if one has a demonstration of it.

(2) If Q is both demonstrable and definable, it would be possible to know Q by the definitional route but still lack a demonstration of it.

---

[4] See, e.g. B.8, $93^a 18$ ff.

From (2) it follows that:

(3) Even if Q is demonstrable, it is possible to know Q and lack a demonstration of it.

Aristotle infers from this that if one has a demonstration of Q, Q cannot be defined.[5] The second premiss encapsulates the Independence Assumption: if demonstration and definition are separate in any way, then it must be possible to grasp one without the other. If so, one will be able to define F without grasping any demonstration.

If one accepts the Independence Assumption, one is faced with a problem:

Independence Problem: If definition is different in any way from demonstration, it will be possible to know the definition without knowing the conclusion of a demonstration sufficient to establish the existence of the kind defined. But this is impossible.[6]

The Independence Problem could be solved if one could not establish what F is without thereby establishing that F exists. For, then, although establishing the definition would be distinct from establishing the existence of the kind, one could not do the former without doing the latter. The three-stage view sets out the required steps. In it, while Stages 2 and 3 are treated as distinct, it is not possible to arrive at Stage 3 (the discovery of essence) without reaching Stage 2 (establishing existence) (93ª18–20). But, before we consider the details of Aristotle's solution, we should analyse a further problem raised in B.7. Aristotle's solution should apply to all these difficulties simultaneously.

3.3 B.7: 92ª34–b3, 19–25: THE FORMAL PROBLEM INTRODUCED

In B.4 and B.6 Aristotle argued that whole definitions could not be demonstrated in the conclusions of the form of syllogism he favoured.[7] Conclusions of demonstrations could not be of the form:

---

[5] In fact, Aristotle could have drawn a stronger conclusion from these premisses:

No one proposition can be known by both a definitional and a demonstrative route.

It is initially surprising that Aristotle does not challenge premiss 1, but takes it as a basic datum. This argument is analysed by Barnes, *Aristotle's Posterior Analytics*, 2nd edn. (Oxford, 1994), 207.

[6] The converse problem: 'How can they be so related that one cannot know the demonstration without knowing the definition?' is not one which troubled Aristotle to the same extent. This is because the Independence Problem as formulated above violates Aristotle's claim that one knows 'the that' before one knows 'the why?' (89b29, 93b32, 93ª17 ff.).

[7] I shall examine these arguments in more depth in Chapter 7.

Thunder is noise in the clouds.

Rather, they would have to be of the form:

Noise is in the clouds. (See B.8, 93^{b}11 ff.)

But then, how are the latter related to definitions of thunder? For, there is nothing in this conclusion that links it with the *definiendum*. By contrast, the former conclusions, arrived at by the method of general deduction, make explicit reference to the phenomenon to be defined.

In B.7 Aristotle raises this problem in the following way:

If the definition is 'equidistant from the middle', why . . . is this what a circle is? One might say it is a definition of mountain-gold. (92^{b}20–22)

If what is demonstrated is not the whole definition, how does one show that it is the *definiendum* which has been defined? Indeed, what makes the type of statement that can be derived by a demonstration at all relevant to the project of definition?

The problem may be stated as follows:

Formal Problem: If the conclusion of the syllogism is different in form from the definition, how can demonstration be of use in establishing definitions?

To establish definitions on the basis of demonstrations alone, one would need to show that:

(i) the conclusion of a demonstration is of the appropriate form to be a definition,

and

(ii) the conclusion is the definition of what is to be defined.

If the methods of general deduction or division method had been adequate, Aristotle would have solved the Formal Problem. But, if his arguments of B.4–6 are correct, these methods are inadequate (See Chapter 7). If so, how can one solve the Formal Problem?[8]

---

[8] This problem is important for the first argument in B.7, 92^{a}35–^{b}3. This may be summarized as follows: One cannot prove what something is essentially in any of the ways in which proof is possible. This is not possible by demonstration or by inductive argument. Demonstration has, it appears, been ruled out by the arguments of B.3–6. Aristotle takes it to follow from this that one cannot make clear from something which has been agreed that something else follows (92^{a}35–7). But induction is also incapable of establishing that everything is F since nothing is different. For, by induction, you do not prove what a thing is, but that either it is or is not (92^{b}1). The conclusion of induction seems to be propositions of the form:

All gall-less are long-lived.

based on propositions about instances of gall-less animals which are long-lived. But this method does not yield claims of the form:

Aristotle's aporetic conclusion at the end of B.7 is that there is no way of solving the Formal Problem which also satisfies other basic constraints on definition.[9] There is a dilemma. If one resolves this problem (by the method of general deduction or division), one does so at the cost of failing to meet further general constraints on definition. But if one meets the latter constraints on definition (e.g. by some other method), one fails to resolve the Formal Problem. There is, it appears, no way of doing both.

One of Aristotle's basic goals in B.8–10 is to solve both the Formal and Independence Problems without relying on the methods he has shown to be inadequate in B.4–6. His difficulty will become even clearer when we consider his comments on a further, radically different, type of definition.

3.4 THE FINAL ARGUMENT OF B.7: 92^{b}26–34: ACCOUNTS OF WHAT NAMES SIGNIFY

Most of the arguments of B.7 are directed against the claim that definitions can establish what F is. In the final argument of B.7 Aristotle considers another proposal:

If it is the case that the definer proves either what a thing is or what its name signifies, then if a definition has nothing at all to do with what a thing is, it could just be an account signifying the same as a name. But that's absurd. For, in the first place, there could be definitions even of non-essences and things that do not exist—for, one can signify even things that are not. Second, all accounts could be

All gall-less are necessarily long-lived,

A fortiori, induction cannot prove that the essence of F is G. Aristotle explains this by saying that induction does not establish conclusions of the appropriate form for definitions. The conclusions of induction are of the form:

All gall-less are long-lived,

and not of the appropriate form:

Men are essentially biped animals.

Thus, induction is dismissed because it cannot solve the Formal Problem at 92^{a}38–^{b}1. For, if the form of the conclusion is different from that of the definition, how can such a conclusion be of use in establishing definitions?

[9] These are discussed in detail in Chapter 7. They concern the conditions under which one comes to know that a given property is essential or explanatorily basic. Roughly, they require that:

(1) one should be able to come to know a correct definition of F

and

(2) one should be able to grasp an explanatory basic property of F.

definitions; for, one could posit a name for any account whatsoever, so we would speak definitions and the *Iliad* would be a definition. Also, no demonstration could demonstrate that this name signifies this; nor then do definitions make this clear in addition. (92^b26–34)

The proposal under discussion is that 'a definition would signify the same thing as a name'. This view has several merits in the context of B.7. It seems to solve the Formal Problem. If definitions are of the form:

'Thunder' signifies the same as 'noise in the clouds'

one would immediately grasp that the *definiens* was related to the *definiendum*. Further, this proposal neatly sidesteps the Independence Problem. If definitions are of this form, one can grasp them without knowing the kind exists. Even if one could not grasp what F is without knowing that F exists, one could grasp an account of what 'F' means without knowing that F exists. So, this proposal avoids the problems Aristotle noted earlier in discussing the proposal that a definition of F is an account of what F is.

However, as was to be expected, Aristotle's discussion of this new proposal consists (in part) in his arguing that if one avoids the Formal and Independence Problems in this way, one has to surrender other basic conditions for definition:

(a) Some of the accounts derived in this way will not be proper unities, but will be like the *Iliad* (92^b28–32).

(b) Some of the accounts derived in this way will not be of essences, since they will not be of existents.

For, accounts of this type are not relevant to the essence of the object defined (92^b26–8). Further, they break the connection between definition and demonstration; for, no demonstration can prove that:

'Thunder' signifies a type of noise in the clouds.

The basic dilemma which confronts Aristotle at the end of B.7 is clear. If definition is taken to be of what F is, and this definition is distinct from the conclusion of a demonstration, one faces the Independence and Formal Problems. But if definition is taken to be of what a name signifies, one can avoid these problems, but only if one is prepared to violate some basic conditions on what it is to be a definition. There is no way of solving the Independence and Formal Problems which respects important conditions on what it is to be a definition. If so, it appears, we cannot have any knowledge at all of definitions (92^b35–8).

This *aporia* rests on a hidden assumption, which can be stated thus:

Basic Assumption: There is *one* form of definition which simultaneously resolves the Independence and Formal Problems and satisfies further basic conditions on being a definition.

The *aporiai* of B.7 show, in effect, that there can be no *one* such form of definition. No one type of definition can both link the phenomenon to the *definiens* (in the ways required to resolve the Independence and Formal Problems) and at the same time satisfy Aristotle's basic requirements on definition. Accounts of what names signify can discharge the first task but not the second. Accounts of the essence of the thing meet the second requirement but cannot resolve the Formal and Independence Problems. The *aporiai* of B.7 can only be broken if, in place of one definition, one devises a variety of different but interconnected types of definition, severally performing the distinct tasks set for definition in B.7.

3.5 INDEPENDENCE PROBLEM RESOLVED

The three-stage view, with its definitional Stage 1 accounts of what terms signify, is precisely what is required to meet this challenge. The Independence Problem can be resolved within the three-stage view. On this account, one must establish that F exists before establishing what F is (93^a16–29). This is because the syllogism which reveals what F is has F's existence as its conclusion, and F's fundamental cause as its middle term. For example, one knows what thunder is when one can construct this syllogism:

Noise belongs to fire-being-extinguished.

Fire is being extinguished in the clouds.

Noise belongs to the clouds.

It is the middle term, 'fire-being-extinguished', which reveals what thunder is, not the conclusion. The syllogism represents an answer to the question 'Why is there noise in the clouds?' (Stage 3 knowledge), and, therefore, requires that the existence of noise in the clouds is previously established (Stage 2 knowledge).

Stages 2 and 3 are distinct, since it is possible to know that thunder exists without knowing what thunder is. For example, one might grasp a middle term which linked 'noise' and 'the clouds' in an appropriate way, but which did not invoke the essence (93^a36–$^b2$). Thus, it is possible to arrive at Stage 2 (non-accidentally) without arriving at Stage 3.

This feature of the three-stage view has the added merit of resolving another traditional exegetical problem. In a variety of passages Aristotle makes 'knowledge that' precede inquiry into the 'Why?' question. Thus, he writes:

When we know the that, we seek the because (89ᵇ29), and
We seek the because when we grasp the that. (93ᵃ17)

However, elsewhere he holds that, in the case of what is capable of being demonstrated, to achieve knowledge is to be in possession of a demonstration. Thus, he writes in 90ᵇ9–10:

to know in the case of what is demonstrable is to possess a demonstration

and in 71ᵇ28 ff.:

to know in the case of what is demonstrable non-accidentally is to grasp a demonstration.

These passages seem to be in conflict in two ways.

(i) The first set of passages requires that knowing that (e.g.) 'A is C' precedes knowing its cause. But if 'A is C' is demonstrable, and that is known non-accidentally only when the demonstration is known, this truth cannot be known before one knows the cause.

(ii) The first set suggests that knowing that 'A is C' precedes knowing its cause. But in the cases with a middle term one can only know that 'A is C' when one knows its middle term or cause.

Let us take (ii) first. Aristotle may accept that for us to know that 'A is C' requires our knowing that there is a middle term which articulates the connection in the conclusion. But this is compatible with our subsequently proceeding to discover what the middle term is (e.g. in cases where the middle term initially discovered is not 'immediately' joined to A and/or C). In such cases, we will (as Aristotle says) grasp 'that the kind exists, but not the answer to the "Why?" question' (93ᵃ35–6). This is to be contrasted with other cases, in which the first middle term we grasp is the one used in demonstration. For, there we will grasp that 'A is C' at the same time as we grasp the relevant middle term. (See 93ᵃ17–20.)

In cases of the first type, we will know that:

A belongs to C

but not (as yet) know that:

It is demonstrable that A belongs to C,

since the middle term involved in the first claim need not be one from which one can demonstrate that:

A belongs to C.

In such cases, we can know that 'A belongs to C' is true, but not (as yet) possess a demonstration. We may even know that there is a demonstration that 'A belongs to C' is true, but not yet know what the demonstration is.

These cases are to be separated from ones in which we know that:

It is demonstrated that A belongs to C

because we possess a demonstration of it. For, here we will grasp a demonstration which involves a basic middle term (e.g. D) from which the conclusion can be demonstrated.

The existence of these different routes to know that 'A is C' does not require us to distinguish two senses of 'knowledge'. 'It is known' in:

(1) It is known that C belongs to A

can mean the same as in:

(2) It is known by demonstration that C belongs to A.

All that is required is that the ways to knowledge of:

A is C

are different in the two cases. The first yields a grasp of truth, the second of demonstrative truth. It can be the same proposition known and the same sense of knowledge in the two cases.[10]

It is instructive to note that there are at least two ways in which one can fall short of knowing by demonstration that 'A is C', where this is demonstrable.

(a) One grasps a further middle term D, from which one can demonstrate that 'A is C', but has not yet constructed a demonstration.

(b) One grasps some middle term B, and grasps that there is a demonstration that 'A is C', but has not as yet grasped the relevant middle term (viz. D) from which such a demonstration can be constructed.

In both cases one grasps only accidentally that 'C belongs to A is demonstrably true'. But in both one would know non-accidentally that 'A is C'. For, although one would know that 'A is C' is true, one would not know that it is demonstrable. To grasp the latter one would need to grasp that 'A is C' is the conclusion of a demonstrative syllogism. In this way, one can know that 'A is C' is true, but not yet know that 'A is C' is demonstrably

---

[10] It is not absolutely essential that the objects of knowledge be the same. In the first, the proposition might be:

A belongs to C.

In the second, it might be:

A belongs of necessity to C.

Aristotle does not always pay sufficient attention to the precise logical form of his claims in these passages to allow us to distinguish clearly between the two alternatives canvassed here. For an opposing view, see Myles Burnyeat's paper 'Aristotle on Understanding Knowledge', in E. Berti (ed.), *Aristotle on Science* (Padua, 1981), 97–139.

true. One comes to know the latter at the third stage, after one has found a demonstration of the required form.

In this way, the three-stage view, with its clear separation between knowing that 'A is C' (at Stage 2) and knowing that 'A is C' is demonstrably true (at Stage 3), provides an unproblematic and conservative resolution of a traditional exegetical puzzle. That it does so is further evidence in favour of attributing it to Aristotle.

3.6 THE FORMAL PROBLEMS RESOLVED

There were two aspects of the Formal Problem raised in B.7. In order to resolve the first, Aristotle needed to show how conclusions of successful demonstrative syllogisms can be directly connected with the phenomenon to be defined. Accounts of what terms signify (as Aristotle envisages them) provide part of the route to achieve this goal. Thus, for example, if one knows that:

'Thunder' signifies the same as 'a specific type of noise in the clouds',

and also establishes that:

Noise belongs in the clouds,

one is on the way to establishing that:

Thunder exists.[11]

One will also know that one has the basis for a full definition of thunder, given that 'thunder' and 'noise in the clouds' have the same significance. And when one grasps that thunder is the noise in the clouds caused by fire being quenched, the connection with the thing defined is made legitimate by (a) the efficient causal connection between noise and extinction, and (b) the fact that 'thunder' signifies noise in the clouds. Thus, the account of what the name signifies links the *definiendum* (thunder) with the conclusion of the relevant syllogism.[12]

In this account, one cannot prove that:

[11] But there is still a problem. For, since there might be other types of noise in the clouds apart from thunder, one has not yet established that thunder exists (rather than some other form of noise in the clouds). I shall return to this issue in Ch. 4 Sect 4.4.

[12] If this is the role of accounts of what terms signify, they need have no greater depth than is present in the conclusion of the demonstrative syllogism. Since the conclusion itself does not refer to the essence of the kind (as that reference is supplied by the middle term), there is no need for the account of what the term signifies to do this either. This remark provides some support for the view (sketched in the previous Chapter, Section 2.11) that accounts of what names signify need not refer to an essence (as yet to be discovered) of the kind in question.

Thunder exists

in the favoured apodeictic style without knowing the account of what 'thunder' signifies. There can be no knowledge of Stage 2 truths without already passing Stage 1. But it is clearly possible to arrive at Stage 1 without arriving at Stage 2, as is clear in B.7 in the cases of 'goatstag' and 'triangle'.[13] Indeed, this possibility is needed to make sense of the possibility of going on to establish that thunder exists. Thus, given Aristotle's earlier separation between Stages 2 and 3, he is committed by this strategy to the three-stage view (as set out in the previous Chapter).

The other aspect of the Formal Problem is easily solved. It challenged one to say how conclusions of the form:

Noise belongs to the clouds

could be of use in establishing the *definiens*:

—noise in the clouds

since they differ in form. Aristotle took the relevant connection to be so transparent that he could say that *the same account* is said in different ways in the two cases (94ᵃ6–7, 8–9) differing only in syntactic arrangements (94ᵃ12–13). It is not a problem which preoccupied him once he had established the general connections between the three-stage view and definition.

Aristotle begins to solve the Formal Problem by introducing the 'significance connection' between terms and accounts of what those terms signify. This is how he ties the conclusion of the syllogism to the phenomenon to be defined. He is seeking to use his account of definition to resolve the Formal Problem while (at the same time) satisfying his other basic definitional conditions. He can meet the first of these requirements by taking accounts of what names signify as definitions of *some* type, even though they cannot satisfy his other conditions for being a definition. The latter are met by taking Stage 3 definitions as genuine definitions of things, even though they cannot (by themselves) resolve the Formal Problem. Each type of account can be counted as a definition because each performs one of the theoretical tasks required of definitions in B.7. The former tie the conclusion of the syllogism to the *definiendum*, the latter home in on the essence of the kind. In this way, Aristotle spreads the theoretical load which in the *aporiai* of B.7 is placed on one type of definition.

Aristotle, in dividing definitional tasks in this way, can weaken the demands made of each type of definition. Not all types of definitional account need be of existents or essences. Indeed, the type of definition required to solve the Formal Problem will not be of this type. Rather, it

---

[13] This is clear in A.10, 76ᵃ35 where Aristotle separates knowing the significance of 'triangle' and knowing of its existence.

can meet conditions on definition less demanding than those which are relevant at subsequent stages of enquiry. While accounts of what terms signify
supply answers to the:

What is it?

question (in the case of names and their significance), they need not satisfy
the more stringent requirements demanded of definitions of kinds.[14] This
is precisely as the liberal interpretation would predict.

These considerations also tell against the more restrictive interpretations set out in the previous chapter.[15] The latter argue that in B.7
Aristotle rules out the possibility of accounts of what names signify being
definitions. It is not just that these interpretations take one element in
an aporetic discussion as Aristotle's settled view. Worse still, their view
appears to misread the overall structure of the *aporiai* in B.7. For, if I am
correct, these arise because no *one* type of definition can be both essence-
invoking and an account of what the relevant name signifies. If so, one
cannot take any part of B.7 to show that all definitions must meet Aristotle's own most stringent conditions on definition. Indeed, his solution to
these *aporiai* depends on his separating different types of definition, none
of which meet all the demands set out in B.7. Thus, closer analysis of this
chapter as a whole (so far from being incompatible with the liberal interpretation) shows precisely why Aristotle developed the three-stage
account and liberalized his conditions on definition. He needed to do both
to overcome the aporiai discussed in B.3–7.[16]

3.7 THE PROBLEMS OF B.1–2: THEIR RESOLUTION

The first chapters of *Posterior Analytics* B, also indicate Aristotle's adherence to the three-stage view. In them, he initially separates four questions.

A	**B**
(1) Search for the fact.	(1) Search for the if it is.
(2) Search for the why.	(2) Search for the what it is.

[14] It would, of course, have been possible to restrict Stage 1 *definitional* accounts to those
correlated with terms which signify kinds with a real essence, and, thus, to rule out definitional accounts of what 'goatstag' signifies. But this move seems unattractive in the context
of B.7, where 'goatstag' and 'triangle' are treated in similar fashion. Further, as I have argued,
it is unmotivated, since Aristotle attempts to devise Stage 1 definitions which do not themselves meet his own most stringent constraints on being a definition.

[15] See Ch. 2 Sect. 2.3.

[16] For the opposing view, see the discussions by Ross, *Aristotle's Analytics*, 635 f.; Bolton,
'Essentialism', 514 ff.; Sorabji, *Necessity, Cause and Blame*, 198; and DeMoss and Devereux,
'Essence', 133–56.

Examples of A(1) are: Search for whether the moon is eclipsed or not, or whether the earth moves or not (89^{b}26–30). When we discover that the moon is eclipsed, we seek the answer to the 'Why?' question. B(1) is initially exemplified by search as to whether or not there is a centaur or a god: When we know that god exists, we seek what it is (89^{b}34). Questions in B(1) focus on whether something is (without qualification), not on whether it has some particular feature. In the first chapter, the examples of B(1) are substances (god, man, centaur). In the second chapter, some are substances (sun, moon, earth), but some are attributes (night (90^{a}5)). The basic demarcation between A(1) and B(1) depends on the form of the question. In A(1) it is: Does S (a substance) possess P (a property)? For B(1) the form of the question is: Does S exist? (or, Does S exist as a substance?).

Let us focus initially on the questions A(1) and B(1). The general form of these questions appear to be to discover whether:

(i) there is or is not a centaur or a god, (89^{b}32–3)

(ii) the moon is or is not, (90^{a}5, 90^{a}12)

(iii) the triangle sun/moon/earth is or is not, (90^{a}12–13)

(iv) the moon is eclipsed, (90^{a}3)

(v) there is an eclipse or not. (90^{a}26)

Aristotle's argument strongly suggests that knowledge of existence is not required for an understanding of the terms involved. For, the cases are ones in which (as in B.8, 93^{a}30ff.[17]) one knows enough about what (e.g.) eclipses are to discover if they exist, but does not yet know that they exist. One does not know at the outset that god exists. Indeed, his ontological status might turn out to be no better than that of the centaur or goatstag!

The remaining two stages of the three-stage enquiry are also distinguished in B.2. At Stage 2, one knows that (e.g.) triangles exist or that the moon is eclipsed. In this, one knows that there is some appropriate middle term which explains the fact or the existence of the triangle. To search for this is to enquire whether there is a relevant middle term or not (90^{a}6f., 9–11).

Stage 3 involves the discovery of what the middle term is. For, this will answer A.2 and B.2. In both these stages (2 and 3), the search is directed to discovery related to the middle term. At Stage 2, the issue is whether there is one. At Stage 3, the issue is what it is. These stages are logically separable even if they happen simultaneously (90^{a}26ff.).

At the end of B.2 Aristotle needs to show how enquiries of the type

---

[17] See Ch. 2 Sect. 2.5.

envisaged fit into his proof theory, and how they are related to the search for definition (90^{a}35 ff.). The three-stage view, as set out in B.8–10, constitutes his attempt to meet these two goals. At Stage 1, one begins with a definitional account of what the term signifies. In the case of man (89^{b}35), one might start with 'man' signifies the same as 'a certain type of two-footed animal' (93^{a}24).

Thus, one knows that man is an animal, if there is such an animal, with two-feet . . . The search for a middle term is the search for something which explains why *being two-footed* belongs to *animal* in this case.[18] Once we know that there is some relevant middle term, we know that the phenomenon exists.[19] The role of accounts of what names signify is to hold up targets for existence proofs of this type.

But why require at Stage 2 that one knows that there is a middle term, even if the identity of the middle term can remain veiled? Perhaps, at Stage 2, in discovering that the kind exists one discovers that it has some internal structure even if one does not know what its basis is. Perhaps it is here that knowledge of existence and of some causal structure is introduced, and not at Stage 1, as is suggested in the picture advanced by my modern essentialist (outlined in Chapter 1). I shall leave the task of a more precise interpretation of what is involved at Stage 2 to Chapter 6.

If this account is correct, Aristotle can consistently hold that existence is predicated of a kind, and that existence is established by grasping that there is a middle term. For the way to establish that the kind exists is to grasp an articulated account of what the term signifies which allows one to ask the 'Why?' question, and to discover that there is an answer to it—even if one does not yet know what it is. Indeed, it is just this which makes it appropriate for Aristotle to introduce his proof theory to establish existence. But if he is to do this, he needs accounts of what names signify at Stage 1 which do not involve knowledge of existence, but which provide the basis for a suitably articulated question which existence proofs can answer. This is why Stage 1 definitional accounts of 'man' and 'triangle' are stated in ways which do not require one to know of the existence of the phenomenon. For, they are introduced in order to allow us to establish existence. But, if this is so, it is difficult to see why similar accounts of 'centaur', 'goatstag', or 'god' should not be treated as definitions. For, they are similar in form, play the same role in investigation, and encapsulate the same type of knowledge state.

---

[18] The detailed nature of this enquiry is examined in Chapter 11.

[19] For a contrasting view of B.2, see A. Gomez-Lobo, 'On the So-called Question of Existence in Aristotle, *An. Post.* 2.1–2' *RM* 34 (1980), 71–89. Gomez-Lobo rightly emphasizes the difficulty of finding a middle term linking a term (such as 'man') and 'exist', but concludes from this that the question is not the one articulated in B.8 (on which I have concentrated), but rather a different one such as: 'Is this a man?'(p. 87).

3.8 DEFINITIONS: THESES: STAGE 1 ACCOUNTS*

At the beginning of *Posterior Analytics* A, Aristotle writes:

There are two ways in which it is necessary to know (*gignoskein*) things in advance. In some cases, it is necessary to assume in advance (*prohypolambanein*) that they exist, of some it is necessary to understand (*sunienai*) in advance what the thing said is, and of others both: e.g. the fact that everything is affirmed or denied truly— one must assume that this is so; of the triangle, one must assume that it signifies this, and of the unit both what it signifies and that it is. For, each of these is not equally clear to us. (71ᵃ11–17)

In this passage Aristotle distinguishes two kinds of claim which can be assumed or understood prior to proof:

(i) what given terms signify

(ii) that certain things exist or are so

In some cases, such as that of the unit, one assumes in advance both what the relevant term signifies and that the unit exists. In others, one needs to assume just what the term signifies. The difference between these two cases is that, while the unit is a starting point for proof, the triangle can be established to exist by proof. In the latter case, knowledge of existence is not assumed when one grasps the significance of the name (see also A.10, 76ᵃ32–6, 76ᵇ6–9, 15 f.). And this is as the three-stage view understands Stage 1. One grasps the significance of the terms 'triangle', 'odd', or 'cube' independently of and prior to grasping a proof of the existence of the features they signify.[20]

---

[20] It was argued in Chapter 2, Section 2.8 that accounts of what names signify of the form:

'Thunder' signifies a type of noise in the clouds.

are never used in proof (see B.7, 92ᵇ33). This view appears confirmed by Aristotle's remark in *Post. An.* A.10, 76ᵇ35 ff.:

Definitions (*horoi*) are not hypotheses (for nothing is said to be or not to be), but hypotheses are used as premisses, while definitions one needs only to understand.

The closest reference for 'definitions' in this context appears to be the accounts of what terms signify discussed previously in A.10 at 76ᵃ34 f., 76ᵇ7–12, 15, 17–21. It should be noted that they are introduced with the crucial '*ti* . . .' question in 76ᵃ34 f., in a context which clearly marks this out as a question about terms and not things. (See, for a similar use of the '*ti* . . .' question, *Post. An.* A.1, 71ᵃ14, cited in Ch. 2 Sect. 2.3.)

It is sometimes suggested by those who hold that all definitions are of things and are, thus, all related to proof that Aristotle is discussing *terms* and not *definitions* in this passage, and that '*horoi*' should be translated accordingly. However, a remark about *terms* would be a surprising addition at this stage in the argument, without any preparation in A.10. It seems far preferable to construe this remark as referring (demonstratively) to the definitions used in B.10. For, these (if I am correct) do not assert existence and cannot be used as premisses.

But what of the unit? Here, Aristotle says that one needs to know in advance both what the term signifies and that it is. Are these separate stages? Or, in the case of first principles, does grasp of what the term signifies involve knowledge of the existence of the unit? Is this a counter example to the separation between Stages 1 and 2 in the three-stage view?[21]

There is no reason to understand accounts of what (e.g.) the 'unit' signifies in this way. If accounts of what a name signifies are as above, these will be of the form:

'The unit' signifies an indivisible quantity.

The very most that can be extracted from this, by way of existential information, is that:

The unit is a quantity, if there is one such, which is indivisible.

As such it would be distinct from the claim that:

The unit is/exists as an indivisible quantity,

which could also be assumed at the outset of the enquiry ($71^{a}15, 76^{a}32-4$). While one can easily move from an account of what 'unit' signifies to the claim that the unit exists, it is a move nonetheless.

If this is correct, hypotheses may be of the form:

The unit is/exists as an indivisible quantity.[22]

As such, they will be distinct from accounts of what terms signify. They would also be distinct from definitional theses (in A.2, $72^{a}14-24$), although both are said to be a species of proposition.[23] Aristotle treats the postulation of what the unit is as a *thesis* but not a *hypothesis*. *Hypotheses*, he writes, 'assume one or other part of a contradiction' ($72^{a}18-20$). Definitional theses, by contrast, do not involve this assumption. How is this to be understood? The passage runs as follows:

A *thesis* which asserts one or other of the parts of the contradiction—I mean, that something is or that something is not, is a *hypothesis*; a thesis which does not do this is a *definition*. For, a definition is a *thesis*: the mathematician posits the unit to

---

[21] For parallel passages, see also $76^{a}31-6$ and $93^{b}25$ f. In the latter, Aristotle distinguishes the mathematician's 'hypothesis' about what the monad is from the hypothesis that it exists.

[22] Differing views of the form of hypotheses are helpfully discussed by Goldin in *Explaining the Eclipse: Aristotle's Posterior Analytics 2.1–10* (Michigan, 1996). I assume that, for Aristotle, 'to exist' is always 'to exist as something'. The something may be specified in categorial terms (e.g. to exist as a substance, see *Meta.*Δ.7, $1017^{a}22-30$, Z.1, $1028^{a}10-13$) or in a more specific fashion (e.g. to exist as a member of a genus of substance, with some specific *differentiae*, see *Meta.*H.2, $1042^{b}15$ff.). At this point, I am indebted to discussion with Paolo Crivelli.

[23] For, both are starting points for demonstrations and as such propositions ($72^{a}14-15$). Further, if hypotheses are species of theses, the latter must all be propositions.

be what is quantitatively indivisible; but this is not a *hypothesis*, because what a unit is and that it is are not the same. $(72^a18–24)^{24}$

Why do definitional theses not 'assert one or other part of a contradiction' and why are they separable from the hypothesis that the unit is (or exists as) something? An example of such a definition is:

To be a unit is to be an indivisible quantity.

Why is this distinct from any hypothesis? Conversely, if existence claims say that indivisibility belongs to quantity, why is this claim different from a definitional thesis? How can the latter fail to assert that the unit exists as an indivisible quantity?

The difference may be one of form. A definitional thesis, unlike the hypothesis suggested, does not assert that the unit is/exists as what is quantitatively indivisible. It rather states that what it is to be/to exist as a unit is to be/to exist as an indivisible quantity. But this does not say that the unit (in fact) exists as an indivisible quantity. It merely says what it is for the unit to exist. The hypothesis, by contrast, *asserts* that there are units. At the level of hypotheses, one has two contradictory propositions:

(i) The unit exists as an indivisible quantity.

(ii) The unit does not exist as an indivisible quantity.

One can refrain from asserting either by saying:

(iii) To be/exist as a unit is to be/exist as an indivisible quantity.

For, this states that to exist as a unit is to exist as an indivisible quantity, but does not state that the unit exists as an indivisible quantity.[25]

---

[24] In this translation, I take the phrase '*einai ti*' to be equivalent to 'something exists' rather than 'exists as something'. However, my argument for the separation of hypotheses, theses, and accounts of what the term signifies does not rest on this. Indeed, for my purposes, this phrase could be interpreted to mean 'to be something' (where 'something' referred either to its being a substance or its being a substance of a given kind. (See n. 19.))

[25] This interpretation agrees with B. Landor ('Definitions and Hypotheses in *Posterior Analytics* 72^a19–25 and 76^b35–77^a24', *Phronesis* 26 (1981), 313) in separating hypotheses as containing assertions of existence from definitional theses, which do not. However, it is unclear how Landor secures the latter result. He writes:

To posit that a unit is what is indivisible in quantity is to affirm the definiens ('what is indivisible in quantity') of the definiendum (unit).

If the phrase cited as *definiens* is *used* in this context, it is unclear why the assertion that:

The unit is what is indivisible in quantity.

does not assert that the unit exists as what is indivisible. If he intends to say:

'The unit' is 'what is indivisible in quantity'.

he clearly avoids an assertion of existence, but does so only by taking this thesis to be quite different from any which could be used in demonstration.

In certain scientific contexts one requires hypotheses (such as (i)) which assert one or other side of the contradiction. One has to move from (iii) to (i) in contexts where one wishes to make scientific assertions about what is the case. Since neither Stage 1 accounts nor theses make assertions of this type, they can be contrasted with hypotheses. However, theses will differ from accounts of what the name signifies since the latter concern the signification of terms, while the former do not. These three types of expression play differing roles in Aristotle's account. Once they are distinguished, there is no pressure to see accounts of what names signify as encapsulating knowledge of the existence of the kind. There can be such accounts whether or not the kind in question exists.[26]

Landor argues cogently against equating the definitional theses (and hypotheses) of 72ᵃ17 ff. with the *horoi* (and hypotheses) specified in A.10, 76ᵇ35 ff. This distinction could be maintained even if one construed the *horoi* of 76ᵇ35 ff. as definitional accounts of what terms such as 'odd', 'even', 'irrational', etc. signify. For, these definitions are not among the premisses of demonstration, since they concern the signification of terms and not objects or kinds. Further, since these definitional accounts concern terms such as 'odd' they are neither universal ('all') nor particular ('some') claims about members of any kind (77ᵃ3–4).

[26] In this argument, I have translated '*lambanein*' as 'assume' or 'posit'. If, however, '*lambanein*' were taken rather to mean 'to assume as immediately known without proof being required', then a *hypothesis* would not merely assume the existence of (e.g.) gold, but would assume the existence of gold as immediately known without proof being required. If so, a *thesis* might itself assume the existence of gold, but would not treat its existence as immediately known without proof being required. And in this way—contrary to my suggestion— a *thesis* might also involve the assumption of existence, although it would not treat the existence of (e.g.) instances of gold as self-evident and not requiring proof. And, if so, these passages would not show that the existence of instances is not assumed by a definition of the type under discussion. They would show only that their existence was not treated as self-evident and in need of no further scientific justification. (For this view, see Robert Bolton's paper, 'Aristotle on the Signification of Names', *Language and Reality in Greek Philosophy: Proceedings of the Greek Philosophical Society 1984/5* (Athens, 1985), 153–62.)

This objection is ingenious, but it seems difficult to accept that '*lambanein*' does, in the context of these chapters, mean 'posit as self-evident without further need of proof', rather than (merely) 'posit the existence of' (as mentioned above). I offer two reasons:

(1) This verb is very prominent in *Post. An.* A.10, from which two of the relevant passages are drawn: 76ᵃ31–6 and 76ᵇ35–8. It is used at least eleven times: 76ᵃ33, 34, 76ᵇ1, 3, 6, 7, 15, 19, 20, 27, 31. In several of these cases (outside the key passages) it is hard to see how '*lambanein*' can mean 'posit as self-evident without further need of proof'. Thus, in 76ᵇ16 ff. Aristotle writes that demonstrative sciences posit/*lambanei* which each of the attributes (i.e. attributive terms) signifies. Thus, Aristotle writes:

Nothing, however, prevents some sciences from overlooking some of these: (e.g.) from not positing (hypotheses) that its kind exists, if it is obvious . . . and from not assuming (*lambanei*) what the attributes signify, if they are clear.

In this passage, it is taken as a reason for not assuming what an attribute signifies that it is self-evident that it does not exist. But if '*lambanein*' meant 'posit as self-evident without further need of proof', it would be (at very least) an extremely paradoxical reason for not assuming as self-evident what an attribute signifies, that its existence is indeed self-evident! The passage reads far more easily if '*lambanein*' is taken to mean 'assume the existence'. For, if the attribute obviously exists, to assume its existence is to understate one's cognitive stage with respect to attribute—and, thus, its self-evidence is indeed good reason for not

These considerations support the attribution to Aristotle of a clear and general distinction between Stages 1 and 2 in scientific enquiry. This distinction can be preserved even if in grasping the relevant definitional thesis one must know (e.g.) that the unit exists. For the latter is a definitional account of the phenomenon, and not of the significance of the term. Thus, even if here there is no separation between Stages 2 and 3 in enquiry, there is a further stage clearly separated from Stage 1.

3.9 CONCLUSION

In this Chapter, I have argued (in answer to question (A) in Section 2.3 of the previous Chapter) that the three-stage view (as developed in B.8–10) is Aristotle's answer to some of the problems raised in *Posterior Analytics* B.7, and that it builds on his proposals in *Posterior Analytics* B.1–2 and A.1–2 and 10. More generally, it constitutes one part of his strategy for showing that one can have knowledge of the signification of terms prior to an enquiry into the nature and existence of the kind in question. This is important in the *Analytics*, since it allows for the possibility of scientific investigation and discovery in both these areas. In this way, Aristotle can avoid Meno's paradox (A.1, 71ª29 ff.), which seems to show that genuine discovery is impossible. That paradox requires that it be a condition for knowing the signification of the relevant term that one knows of the existence or nature of the kind signified. And this is precisely the premiss which the three-stage view rejects.[27]

merely positing its existence! Thus, if '*lambanein*' is to have a single sense throughout the passage, it is that of 'assuming'/'positing' and not that of 'assuming'/'positing as self-evident without further need of proof'. And this supports my initial account of the thesis/hypothesis distinction with respect to definition as one between positing a definition, and asserting that what is defined exists.

(2) The evidence for the use of *lambanein* as 'posit as self-evident without further need of proof' is inconclusive. It is true that in 76ª32–4 starting points are posited, and these indeed are often self-evident and cannot be further proved. Equally it is true that one application of *hypothesis* in 72ª19–20 is to self-evident truths which are, no doubt, taken as self-evident, and without further need of proof. But none of this shows that '*lambanein*' should mean 'posit as self-evident and without further need of proof': it only shows that some things which are posited are indeed self-evident, and without further need of proof. Elsewhere (e.g. 76ᵇ32–4), the things that are posited (e.g. in the case of teacher) are neither self-evident nor free from the need for further proof.

[27] There are several forms of Meno's paradox. In one, one cannot discover the nature of a kind because grasp of that is already involved in understanding the relevant name. In another, one could not discover the existence of a kind, since knowledge of that is already involved in understanding the name. Both have the same form; one discovers either nothing or only what one already knew. Aristotle wishes to allow that one can come to know of the existence as well as the nature of the kind. It is difficult to see how the modern essentialist can account for one's coming to know of the kind's existence. For, that is already presupposed in his understanding the term.

This Chapter has given some further grounds in favour of taking all Stage 1 accounts as a type of definition (whether or not they are of names for existents (see Section 3.6)). For, they all play one of the roles required of definition: they link the term to be defined with an account which is the object of enquiry. Further, there is no evidence in B.7 which suggests that Aristotle separated definitional from other accounts of what names signify on the grounds that only the former signify existents (Sections 3.2–3.4). His strategy appears rather to be to liberalize and diversify his account of definition so as to allow (*inter alia*) that all accounts of what names signify can be a type of definition. These considerations amount to further evidence in favour of an affirmative answer to question (D), raised in Section 2.3 of the last Chapter.

In what follows, the three-stage view is central. For, commitment to this requires Aristotle to think of all Stage 1 accounts as capable of being understood without knowledge of the existence of the kind signified. And this claim (now apparently secure) exercises a major influence on his discussion of signification and understanding.[28]

---

[28] In the overall context of this study, it is more important to establish that Aristotle held the three-stage view than that he regarded all Stage 1 accounts as definitional.

4

The Signification of Names

4.1 INTRODUCTION

Aristotle's three-stage view of scientific enquiry, outlined in the last two Chapters, contains several claims relevant to his account of signification:

C(1) Accounts of what terms signify play a role in guiding enquiry at Stages 2 and 3 (B.8, 93ª29–36, B.10, 93ᵇ29–35). Such accounts can be understood without knowledge of the existence of the kind signified. There can be accounts of what terms signify whether or not there is an existing kind signified by the term.

According to C(1), there can be (definitional) accounts of what 'goatstag' signifies (B.7, 92ᵇ6f., cf. B.10, 93ᵇ35–7), which are 'stitched together' by us.[1] There will also be definitional accounts of what the terms 'thunder' or 'triangle' signify, distinct from definitional accounts of the kinds themselves.

C(2) What is signified by a term at Stage 1 is (in some cases) the very same thing that is discovered to exist at Stage 2 (see 93ᵇ32: 'when we discover that what is signified exists').

C(1), I have argued, is a central feature of Aristotle's strategy in the *Analytics*. C(2) is a claim to which he regularly returns both there and elsewhere.[2]

In addition to C(1) and C(2), there are two further relevant claims which need to be investigated.

C(3) (At least some) accounts of what names signify the same as names.

In B.7, 92ᵇ26–8 Aristotle writes that if definition were to establish what the name signifies and not to grasp the essence of the kind, 'it would be an

---

[1] See Ch. 3 Sect. 3.8.
[2] See, e.g. his use of 'signify' to capture the relation between (e.g.) names and substances, such as man and horse, in *Cat.* 1ᵇ25–7. In *Post. An.* A.22, 83ª24f. Aristotle speaks of terms which signify substances as signifying either that thing or the type of thing it is. In all these cases, 'signification' links linguistic terms and substances in the world.

account signifying the same as a name'. It remains unclear, however, whether all such accounts signify the same as the relevant names, or only some of them.

C(4) There can be several different accounts of what one name signifies. (Thus, 'pride' might be taken as equivalent to 'not tolerating insult' or to 'indifference to misfortune' ($97^{b}21$ ff.) if pride were just one condition).

For, accounts of this type pick out non-accidental features of a kind (B.8, $93^{a}20$–4), and there can be several distinct non-accidental features of one kind.

Our first, and most immediate, problem is that C(1)–C(4) appear (at least at first sight) to be inconsistent. For, according to C(1), a definitional account of what a name signifies can be understood without knowing of the existence of the kind or object signified. But, if C(2) is correct, names on occasion signify what exists. How is this possible? Surely, a correct account of what *these* names signify should involve reference to the existence of the object or kind they signify? But if the enquirer understands this account in grasping the name, he will (contrary to C(1)) know of the existence of the kind signified. Further, if C(3) is correct, names and the relevant accounts will signify the same thing. But, given C(2), this is only possible if the account signifies (in some cases) a kind in the world. Thus, if the thinker understands this account, he will surely know which kind is signified. But, if so, he will know (contrary to C(1)) that the kind in question exists.

C(3) gives rise to a second problem. If C(3) applies to this case, 'the account of what "pride" signifies' will signify the same as 'pride'. But, according to C(4), there can be several different accounts of what 'pride' signifies, each picking out a different non-accidental feature of the phenomenon. How can these claims be consistent? Must 'pride' be ambiguous? Or do some accounts of what names signify fail to signify the same as the name?

Aristotle does not resolve these issues in the *Analytics*. While he makes a number of claims about names, their signification, and accounts of what names signify, he does not develop a full or unified account of these issues.[3] Indeed, the precise status of some of C(1)–C(4) is left obscure in that work. Is Aristotle really committed to C(3) and C(4)? Or did he introduce them

---

[3] This view of *Post. An.* B.8–10 represents a mid-position between two opposed interpretations. Robert Bolton ('Essentialism') took these chapters to present Aristotle's explicit account of the signification of kind terms. By contrast, John Ackrill did not accept that any general account of signification was even assumed in these texts ('Aristotle's Theory of Definition: Some Questions on *Post. An.* 2.8–10.' in Berti (ed.), *Aristotle on Science*. The mid-position is to argue that an account of signification is presupposed but not made explicit in these chapters.

only for specific dialectical purposes? Are they meant to apply to all accounts or only to some?[4]

Did he do better elsewhere? Did Aristotle develop an account of signification which sustains (at least some of) C(1)–C(4)? Did he provide answers to any of the following questions, central for an account of signification:

(A) Under what conditions does a name signify a particular kind or object?

(B) Under what conditions do two names have the same significance?

(C) Under what conditions do a name and an account have the same significance?

I shall argue in the next three Chapters that he did provide answers to these three questions which validate C(1)–C(4). In the present Chapter, I shall trace the outline of his approach, which rests on his discussion of thought in *De Anima*. This account (I shall suggest in Sections 4.2–4.4) underwrites claims C(2) and C(4). It is also consistent with C(1) and a version of C(3) (see Section 4.5). In Section 4.6 I shall argue that his account of the signification of the relevant names and expressions is an account of their meaning. In the next Chapter, I shall seek to secure the interpretation of Aristotle's account of thought which is presupposed in the present Chapter. Finally, in Chapter 6, I shall complete and assess the theory that has emerged.

4.2 THE BASIS OF AN ACCOUNT: SIMPLE NAMES AND THEIR SIGNIFICATION

Aristotle's remarks near the beginning of *De Interpretatione* contain one element of his account of signification. There he writes:

Spoken sounds are symbols of affections in the soul, and written marks are symbols of spoken sounds. And just as written marks are not the same for all, neither are spoken sounds. But what these are in the first place signs of— affections in the soul—are the same for all; and what these affections are like- nesses of—things in the world—are clearly the same for all. These matters have

---

[4] More precisely, C(3) is introduced in the context of a *reductio* (92^{b}26–7), although it seems that it is not the premiss that Aristotle rejects. The examples mentioned in C(4) are not explicitly said to be accounts of what the term signifies. Nothing (in what follows) hangs on taking the examples mentioned in B.13, 97^{b}15 ff. as cases of accounts of what names signify.

been discussed in the work *De Anima*, and do not belong to the present subject. (16ᵃ3–9)

Written marks and spoken sounds are signs—in the first instance—of 'affections of the soul', which appear to be thoughts, in this context (16ᵃ10, 14).[5] Names are signs for thoughts which are not yet combined with other thoughts that are signs for verbs so as to make affirmations, capable of truth and falsity.

Let us begin with names, successfully applied to objects or kinds: 'Cicero' or 'man'.[6] The written mark 'A' is a sign—in the first instance—of a given thought, the thought of Cicero or of man. The significance of 'A' is fixed by *the thought with which it is conventionally correlated*. The identity of a thought is determined by the answer to the question: 'What is this thought about?'(or, in Aristotle's terms, by the form received in that thought (see below)). Thus, the significance of 'A' is fixed by the answer to the question: 'What is the relevant thought about?'

What, in Aristotle's view, determines what the thought is about? In this passage, Aristotle says only that thoughts (all or some) are likenesses of things in the world *(homoiōmata)*, a topic which he notes he has discussed elsewhere (in fact, in *De Anima*). He is content to point his reader to the place to look for a more detailed account of *likeness* (16ᵃ8–9).

In Aristotle's discussion of perception and thought in *De Anima* the notion of likeness plays a major role. In cases of successful thinking and perceiving, entities in the world liken the relevant faculty to themselves. Likening is a causal process in which the starting point is

---

[5] On this account, written and spoken expressions are conventional signs of states of the soul: 16ᵃ10, 19. They are conventional signs of such states because they are both signs *(sēmeia)* and symbols *(sumbola)*. There may be signs which are not symbols and hence non-conventional (e.g. natural signs), and symbols which are not signs because not semantically significant. Aristotle's mixture of conventional (symbolic) and non-conventional (likening) relations is his attempt to disentangle two separate strands confused by Plato in the *Cratylus* (e.g. 430ᵈ5 ff., cf. 386ᶜ ff.). For a contrasting view, see N. Kretzmann's 'Aristotle on Spoken Sounds and Significance by Convention' in J. Corcoran (ed.), *Ancient Logic and Modern Interpretations* (Dordrecht, 1974). Parts of Kretzmann's view are convincingly criticized by Pantazis Tselemanis in 'Theory of Meaning and Signification in Aristotle' in *Language and Reality in Greek Philosophy* (Athens, 1985), 194–9. I shall consider the remainder of his view in discussing the notion of likeness below. Aristotle says practically nothing in *De Int.* about the conventional aspect of significance, and I shall follow his example.

[6] Aristotle's category of names includes common nouns and proper names (e.g. 'man', 'horse', 'Socrates'). Simple names have no relevant internal semantic structure (*De Int.* 16ᵃ20–6 (see Sect. 4.3)). It is very important to note that Aristotle does not say that all affections of the soul are likenesses of things in the world. He confines himself to saying that 'what affections are likenesses of are things in the world' (16ᵃ7 f.), which leaves open the possibility that some affections (e.g. those concerning goatstags) are not likenesses of anything (see Sect. 4.3). In particular, he does not say that all names are related to affections which are likenesses of things in the world.

(e.g.) a particular external object.[7] This process (in successful cases) results in the patient being made like the agent in certain relevant respects.[8] The efficient cause explains the relevant general features of the thought or perception: what it is about, its object. When this occurs, the form is transferred from the agent to the patient. Likening of this type occurs in successful cases, when the faculties involved are functioning as they should. In such cases, the objects liken the relevant faculties to themselves in the form-transferring way. This type of process is what makes the perception or thought the one it is.[9] When this occurs, the relevant faculty receives the form of the external object.[10] Likening, therefore, is an asymmetric causal process in which the relevant object or kind (with its form) is (1) the efficient cause of the relevant perception or thought, and (2) explains the general features of the perception or thought (what it is about). Further, (3) likening of the appropriate kind occurs when the relevant faculties are functioning as they should. ((1)–(3) constitute the basic account of likening.[11])

This account provides one central feature of Aristotle's account of names and their signification. According to *De Interpretatione* 16ᵃ3 ff., the significance of a simple linguistic expression 'A' is fixed *in the first instance* by what the thought with which it is conventionally correlated is about. Let us call this thought θ_1. If we apply the *De Anima* model in those cases where the thoughts are likenesses to things in the world (in this way), θ_1 is about the object which causes that thought in the likening (form-transferring) mode. In such cases the significance of 'a' will be fixed, *in the*

---

[7] For perception, see (e.g.) *De An.* B.5, 418ᵇ3–6. For thought (*De An.* 417ᵇ16–19, Γ.4, 429ᵃ13–18, 430ᵃ3–4), Aristotle applies his 'likening model' in both cases. This is a specific causal relation in which the cause 'likens the effect unto itself' (cf. *GC* A.7 324ᵃ9–11) so that the effect is 'made like' the cause. In this way, the wax which receives the imprint of the ring is likened to the ring which produces it. This means more than that it resembles the ring. For, that would be true also of marks which happened to look like the ring, but were not produced by it in this way. I shall develop this interpretation in more detail in the next Chapter.

[8] Aristotle's efficient or 'making' causes (e.g. the art of house-building) make the effect be a certain way (e.g. be organized in given ways), and do not merely bring the effect into existence. They make objects have given properties ('A causes B to be G'), where the latter are capable of having those properties (cf. *Meta.* Θ.7, 1049ᵃ5–8).

[9] I am further assuming that for Aristotle the efficient cause is constitutive of the processes it causes (cf. *Meta.* Z.17, 1041ᵃ29–32). The result could not be thunder/a thinking of thunder unless it was caused by fire being quenched/thunder (cf. *Post. An.* B.10, 94ᵃ5–6, B.8 93ᵇ10–19). (For further discussion, see Ch. 8.)

[10] This formulation rests on the assumption that there are objects with their own forms. It is not intended as a (reductive) analysis of what it is for the form to be transferred.

[11] This account of 'likening' presupposes that objects and kinds are as they are, with their own forms, independently of our thinking about them as we do. There is, thus, a substantial commitment to a form of realism at the basis of Aristotle's account. We are seen as living in a world in which divisions between objects and between kinds are not the result of our choosing to classify undifferentiated matter one way rather than another. Such divisions flow from distinctions, whose existence does not rest on our preferred mode of classification. The basis for this type of realism is discussed in Part II.

second instance, by the objects or kinds in the world which cause θ_1 in the form-transferring way. The latter step is fundamental to determining the significance of 'a', since it fixes what θ_1 is about, and this in turn determines the significance of 'a'.

On this interpretation, names of this type for objects or kinds (e.g.) K_1 will signify as follows:

'a' signifies the kind K_1 if and only if K_1 produces the thought θ_1 (with which 'a' is conventionally correlated) by the likening route.

When this occurs the thinking faculty will be likened to K_1 in the form-transferring way. On this account, there are two semantically relevant relations:

'a' signifies IMMEDIATELY θ_1 if and only if θ_1 is the thought with which 'a' is conventionally correlated.

What is signified by 'a' is what is cited in answer to the question: 'What is θ_1 about?' This relation will be common to all cases and is the prime object of signification. In certain cases where the content of the thought is produced by the form-transferring route by a kind in the world:

'a' signifies MEDIATELY K_1 if and only if K_1 produces θ_1 by the form-transferring route.

In these cases, what is signified mediately fixes what is signified immediately by 'a'.

In this interpretation, the significance of a simple name is fixed *in the second instance* by objects or kinds in the world. However, since there is no explicit reference in the text to the latter relation, some may doubt whether Aristotle accepts here the existence of a second signifying relation.[12] But the basis of the interpretation offered can be preserved even if it is shown that Aristotle rejected the idea of a second signification relation *in this passage*. For, even if a name signified the thought alone, provided that the latter's content was fixed in the way described, the significance of the name would still be determined by the relation between the thinking faculty and the object in the world (even though the latter would not now be labelled as a semantic relation). But this reply is too concessive, since elsewhere (e.g. *Post. An.* B.10, 93^{b}32) Aristotle takes what is signified by a term to be the very thing that is discovered to exist. This and other passages require there to be a

---

[12] Perhaps, '*prōton*' might mean (i) 'in the canonical way' (as understood with '*kuriōs*': e.g. *NE* Θ.4, 1157^{a}30; *De An.* A.10, 403^{b}29), and be contrasted with some less canonical ways, perhaps not even including any relation to things in the world; or it might mean (ii) 'with nothing in between' (e.g. *Post. An.* 81^{b}31–5), and not be contrasted with any other case involving words and things. Both these possible uses of '*prōton*' are indicated in Bonitz, *Index Aristotelicus* ad loc.

signification relation which reaches from our words beyond our thoughts to the world.[13]

This account provides a limited answer to question (A):

Under what conditions does a name (of the type discussed in *De Interpretatione* 1) signify a kind?

In these cases, what is signified by the name is what is discovered to exist at Stage 2 in the enquiry. This is because what is signified$_{MED}$ by the term is a kind in the world, and this fixes the signification$_{IMM}$ of the term. In such cases, it is not possible to specify what is signified by a term without mentioning the kind in the world to which it is related in the relevant efficient causal way.[14]

This model vindicates C(2) in the previous section. What is signified by the term 'man' is a kind in the world. But the model does not (as yet) make clear the answer to either question (B) or (C) above (even in the case of the names so far discussed). One might, of course, conjecture (on the basis of the discussion so far) that two names (of this type) will have the same significance if and only if they are both correlated with thoughts brought about by the same objects. But, while this conjecture is possible, it is certainly not guaranteed by anything said so far.

Aristotle's discussion elsewhere, however, appears to support this conjecture. Thus, he writes:

Things are called synonyms when they share a name and the account of what the thing is which corresponds to the name is the same, like animal in man and cow. Each of these is called by the same name 'animal', and the account of what the object is is the same. (*Cat.* 1ª6–10)

Objects and properties may be 'synonyms' on this account, but so can two

---

[13] See also *Post. An.* A.1, 71ª15. Some might object that these passages might be translated without taking the 'semantic' relation to involve objects. Thus, the passages might mean only that what is signified by the term (e.g. a concept in the mind) is found to be (e.g.) exemplified in the world, in which case, there need be no word-world semantic connection. However, there is good evidence that Aristotle did conceive of the relevant semantic relations as reaching to the world. For, this explains (i) the problems he has with names for non-existents, which on occasion seem to signify nothing (*De Int.* 18ª25); (ii) why he thought of particles and propositions as 'non-significant' (*Poetics* 1456ᵇ38 ff.); (iii) why 'is', 'every', and 'and' have no significance by themselves (*De Int.* 16ᵇ24, 20ª13); (iv) his claim that a name signifies one thing (*Meta.* Γ.4, 1006ᵇ12 f.), and that the name 'sun' signifies a substance (*Meta.* Z. 15, 1040ª32); (v) his claim that names are 'symbols' for things in the world (*Soph. El.* 1, 165ª6 ff.).

[14] Such cases are described in some modern writings as 'world-involving' or 'non-individualist'. See, for examples, Tyler Burge's papers 'Individualism and the Mental' *Midwest Studies* 4 (1979), 73–121, and 'Cartesian Error and Perception' in P. Pettit and J. McDowell (eds.), *Subject, Thought and Context* (Oxford, 1986), 117–36. See also Gareth Evans's *Varieties of Reference* (Oxford, 1982), chs. 6–8 and John McDowell's 'Singular Thought and the Extent of Inner Space' *in Subject, Thought and Context*, 137–68.

token names when (and only when) they have the same morphology and the accounts which correspond to the relevant names are the same.[15] Names are synonyms only if they have the same significance (otherwise they are homonyms). If so, in this case, the two token names will have the same significance because they are both correlated with one kind. In that case, the accounts corresponding to them will be the same. For, it is this feature which explains their having the same significance, not their having the same morphology (since homonyms also have that feature).

Aristotle makes the further move of claiming that two distinct names, like 'cloak' and 'garment' (with distinct morphology), will have the same significance provided that they are correlated with the same kind (*Soph. El.* 6, 168ᵃ27–32).[16] Here, too, the account which corresponds to the two names is the same. Thus, it appears that two names such as 'A' and 'B' will have the same significance provided that they signify the same object, and this will be so only if the answer to the question 'What is a?' is the same as the answer to the question 'What is b?'[17]

---

[15] 'Homonymy' and 'synonymy' are often taken to apply in this passage only to objects and not to names, on the grounds that only objects can have names in common while names cannot (at least without regress!). But names can also be homonyms or synonyms in the following way: they are homonyms if they share only the name (i.e. the same morphological unit), but differ with regard to the account of the thing which corresponds to the name; they are synonyms if they share both the same morphological unit and account. A term can also be a paronym if its morphology is derived from another with a distinct morphological ending. On this interpretation, both objects and names can be homonyms and synonyms, depending on whether they share, with regard to their name, only a morphological unit or something more. Thus, Aristotle will talk in *Cat.* 1 indifferently of names and objects and only distinguish between them in *Cat.* 2 ('of things said' . . . 'of things that are' 1ᵃ20). Elsewhere, Aristotle appears to speak of objects and of names as synonyms and homonyms (objects: e.g. *Top.* Δ.3, 123ᵃ28, *Meta.* Z.10, 1035ᵇ1 ff.; names: e.g. *Topics* A.15, 106ᵃ21, ᵇ4, Θ.13, 162ᵇ38, *Soph. El.* 5, 167ᵃ24, *NE* E.1, 1129ᵃ30). Bonitz notes both uses of these terms (*Index Aristotelicus* ad loc.). This can be explained (without use/mention confusion) if the interpretation proposed of *Cat.* 1 is accepted; in it, both objects and names can be synonyms and homonyms. However, even if only objects can be called 'synonyms', it is easy to derive an account of a synonym's name. Objects are synonyms if they share the same morphologically structured name and account. Names are synonyms if they share the same morphological structure and are correlated with the same accounts.

[16] Indeed, on occasion Aristotle appears to refer to such cases as '*sunonuma*' (see *Top.* Θ.13, 162ᵇ37, *Soph. El.* 5, 167ᵃ24, *Rhet.* Γ.2, 1405ᵃ1, *Meta.* Γ.4, 1006ᵇ15–18).

[17] This account suggests that the following expressions will have the same significance:

'Cicero': 'Tully'

'gold': 'the substance whose essence is atomic number 79'

'man': 'biped animal'

This suggestion seems confirmed by Aristotle's discussions of the paradoxes of knowledge: Section 4. Names and definitions may, in this view, signify the same, without names having to signify the essences which are the subject matter of those definitions. (On this issue, see App. 1.)

This line of thought suggests a way in which names and certain phrases can signify the same (C(3) above). 'Man' and 'biped animal' will signify the same if the answer to e.g. 'What is man?' is the same as the answer to 'What is biped animal?' They will signify the same because the thoughts with which they are correlated are the same in the relevant respect: both being brought about in the form-transferring way by the same kind in the world. Had the kinds been distinct, the expressions could not have had the same significance, even if they had both been true of objects or kinds which invariably co-occurred. Thus, 'possessor of weight' and 'occupier of three-dimensional space' will differ in significance, if the essence of the two kinds is distinct. Conversely:

a type of noise in the clouds

and

a type of noise accompanied by lightning

will both have the same significance as 'thunder' provided that all three expressions are correlated (in the relevant way) with the same kind. In this way C(4), set out in the previous section, can be vindicated.

On this account, 'thunder' will not signify the same as 'the quenching of fire in the clouds', which specifies thunder's efficient cause. For, the efficient cause and its effect are distinct objects. In the case of substances, 'man' will signify the same as 'biped animal' or 'biped animal with a given essence'. However, the name will not signify its essence, soul of a given kind, provided that the enmattered kind and its essence are different, and 'man' in its basic use signifies the composite species (matter and form/shape) and not its form/shape or essence alone (See *Meta.* H.3, 1043^b2–4, $^a30$–6). So, while names of this type do signify kinds (or species) with essences, it is not correct to say that they signify that essence. For, that requires a distinct name with a distinct significance.[18]

Phrases may have the same significance as names provided that they both signify the same objects non-accidentally. This can only occur if the account specifies a non-accidental feature of the kind. Had it not done so, the answer to the relevant 'Why?' question would not point to the essence of the phenomenon. Thus, genuine accounts of what a name signifies must specify some non-accidental property of the kind. If they fail to meet this condition, they cannot constitute proper accounts of what the name signifies. This condition confirms the restriction on accounts noted in Chapter 2: accounts of what names signify must select some non-accidental feature

---

[18] See, e.g. *Post. An.* B.8, 93^a24–6. It is difficult to advance at all in scientific investigation when one possesses a grasp of only the accidental properties of thunder (93^b31–5). One can, of course, say things about thunder, and be in contact with thunder, but one still lacks thoughts about thunder if one only possesses an accidental account of thunder.

of the kind. Both names and intersubstitutable accounts signify the same kinds non-accidentally.[19]

This model suggests a way to complete Aristotle's view of the signification of some names and of accounts of what such names signify. There can be accounts of 'thunder' as 'a type of noise in the clouds' or 'a type of noise accompanied by lightning'. 'Thunder' will signify the same as both, provided that they are all correlated non-accidentally with the same kind. This will be so if all three expressions are non-accidentally true of one object. It is the latter fact, that they all signify mediately (in the way specified) the same kind, that grounds their sameness of significance.

This model generates its own distinctive set of problems:

(i) How do names (like 'goatstag') for non-existents have significance?

(ii) How are statements about existence to be understood?

(iii) How are statements involving propositional attitudes to be understood?

Further, something more has to be said to account for the apparent difference in significance between distinct accounts of the same phenomenon. For 'noise accompanied by lightning' and 'noise in the clouds' must (it seems) in some way signify something different.

I shall argue in Sections 4.3 and 4.4 that Aristotle seeks to answer these three questions (i)–(iii) in a way which is consistent with, and motivated by, the general pattern of the account so far developed.

4.3 GOATSTAGS, NON-SIMPLE NAMES, AND EXISTENCE

In the *Analytics* there are accounts of what empty terms such as 'goatstag' and 'void' signify. Examples might be:

'void' signifies a place deprived of body (*Phys.* Δ.6, 214^{a}16 f.)

and

'goatstag' signifies a kind of animal, which is the offspring of goat and stag.

But how can Aristotle accept accounts of this type, if he is committed to the view of signification given in the last Section? Clearly, the signification of these terms cannot be determined by the process of 'likening' of

---

[19] At this point (as in Chapter 2) non-accidental features may include essential and necessary features (including *idia*). If accounts of kinds were to be confined to their essential features, this would mark a further restriction on the type of non-accidental features involved. See the discussion in Chapters 5 and 6 of the idea of the form being transferred.

thoughts to kinds in the world. So, how do such terms signify anything at all?

Aristotle begins *De Interpretatione* 2 by remarking that names themselves have no parts which signify 'in separation' or 'in their own right' (16ᵃ20 f.). Thus, in 'Kallippos' the parts, such as '—horse', do not signify in the way they would in the phrase 'the fine horse' (16ᵃ21 f.). He then adds:

> It is not, however, the same for compound names as for simple ones. In the latter there are no parts which signify anything. In the former, the parts tend to signify (*bouletai*), but they signify nothing when separated, as for example 'boat' in 'pirate boat' (16ᵃ23–6)

Elsewhere he notes that in 'double words' parts do signify (*semainei*) but not 'in their own right' (16ᵇ32 f.). Thus, Aristotle's basic distinction is between simple names (16ᵃ23) which have no parts which signify anything (at least in the context of such names), and compound names (like 'pirate boat' or 'goatstag') whose parts do (in some way) signify, but nonetheless do not (in this context) signify anything 'in their own right'. The account in the previous Section has been of simple names. How are compound names to be represented?

Aristotle's discussion is very condensed. Indeed, it is not even clear whether 'Kallippos' is used as an example of a simple name or a compound one.[20] However, his brief remarks suggest that in compound names the parts contribute to the significance of the compound whole, which is to be determined by the significance of the parts plus their mode of combination. The 'goat—' plays some role in determining the significance of the compound, but does not function as a separate signifying expression. Its role is not to signify the kind, goat, but to play a role in forming a new semantically significant term: (e.g.) offspring of goat and stag.

In the basic case, the significance of simple names is fixed by the answer to the question: What is the thought about with which they are conventionally correlated? This question is answered by pointing to the object or kind in the world to which the thought is likened. In the case of compound names, the relevant thought is about the compound object (goatstag) formed by parts connected (by the thinker). The content of his thought is not determined by a likening relation between it (viz. the whole) and things in the world. For, that relation is blind to the internal complexity of the relevant thought.[21] Thus, the immediate significance of a compound term is a complex thought, which is about the complex entity formed by the thinker in his mind. Such compound terms may, of course, have mediate

---

[20] Ammonius took it to be a simple name, Ackrill a compound one.

[21] It is a consequence of this account that 'pirate boat' is not given its significance in the same way as 'pirate' or 'boat. Strictly speaking, 'pirate boat' is not given its significance by the likening relation to things in the world any more than 'goat stag' is. For, the fact of the existence of pirate boats is not what determines the significance of the term.

significance in terms of the kinds in the world (if any) of which they are true. But they can have immediate significance without having mediate significance. Thus, the term 'goatstag' has immediate significance on the basis of the semantic contribution its parts make to the relevant complex thought, although there is no kind in the world to which that complex thought corresponds.

Aristotle does not spell out his proposal for compound names, since his focus remains mainly on simple names (which lack constituents which are, in any way, semantically significant). One version of his proposal would run as follows:

$$\text{'g'—signifies(IMM)} \to \theta \left\{ \begin{array}{l} \nearrow \theta_1 \nearrow K_1 \text{ goat: } \text{kind of animal with feature F} \\ \searrow \theta_2 \searrow K_2 \text{ stag: } \text{kind of animal with feature G} \end{array} \right.$$

The immediate significance of 'goatstag' would be determined by the content of the compound thought (θ), with which it is conventionally correlated. The content of this thought will in turn be fixed by the thought contents of simple thoughts θ_1 and θ_2 which are placed (by the thinker) in relation R (e.g. offspring of). The role of θ_1 and θ_2 is not (in this context) to signify things in the world, but rather to serve as an input (with the content they have) to an operation which yields a new significant thought. While θ_1 and θ_2 have the content they do because they are brought about in the likening way by things in the world, their role in compound thoughts is not to signify those kinds. Rather, the significance they acquire through being used to signify kinds is used by the thinker to form a new complex thought, with which the compound term is conventionally correlated. Thus, the linguistic expression 'goatstag' signifies immediately the complex thought θ, whose content is: offspring of goat and stag. The latter provides the answer to the question: 'What is the thought θ about?'

At this point, a major difference between simple and compound (or complex) names becomes evident. The significance of the simple and compound names is fixed in radically different ways. As a consequence, while simple thoughts must signify one object or kind in the world, compound names need not.[22] For, the significance of the latter is fixed in a way which

---

[22] I assume that (e.g.) man and goat are unitary kinds of this type, even though they might decompose under further metaphysical analysis into (e.g.) rational animal. They are proper unities *qua* genuine species of animal, with their own 'principle of movement and rest'. By contrast, goatstag is not a unitary kind (since there are no goatstags), nor is goatman (even if all goats and men were classified as such). For, these are not genuine kinds, but are constructs of our thoughts. At this point, Aristotle's claims about simple names rest on metaphysically based ideas of what is to count as a genuine unitary kind.

does not depend on their being one kind in reality which brings them about in the likening way. Of course, complex names may signify objects or kinds (mediately), but it is not a condition of their having significance that they do so.[23]

If this is correct, 'goatstag' can be significant, even if there is no kind which is mediately signified. The term has as its immediate signification the thought whose content is: offspring of goat and stag. There is nothing more to the significance of this name than is given in the account of what the name signifies. But in other cases (such as that of 'pirate boat') there will also be objects which are signified mediately. Similarly for complex expressions such as 'noise accompanied by lightning' and 'noise in the clouds'. While these signify *mediately* the same kinds in the world, they differ in their *immediate* significance because the thoughts with which they are correlated are different in their semantically relevant components.

This account will apply straightforwardly to those empty names which, like 'goatstag', contain semantically active constituents. However, it cannot work for those empty names which are not semantically compound, such as, e.g. 'void', 'Socrates' (if Socrates does not exist (*Cat.* 13^{b}31)) or chimera (cf. Alexander of Aphrodisias, *Ad Meta.* 990^{b}14). Does Aristotle also have a strategy for these cases?

He considers an apparently simple name of the relevant type in *De. Interpretatione* 8. There he writes:

If one name is given to two things which do not make up one thing, there is not a single affirmation. Suppose, for example, that one gave the name 'cloak' to man and horse. Then:

Cloak is white

would not be a single affirmation. For, to say this is not different from saying:

Horse and man is white

and this is not different from saying:

Horse is white and man is white.

So, if this signifies many things and is more than one affirmation, clearly the first either signifies many things or nothing. For, there is nothing which is a man and a horse. (18^{a}18–26)

In this passage, Aristotle does no more than indicate that the thought

Cloak is white

can be semantically complex even though the name itself lacks semantic parts. Presumably, the immediate signification of the name 'cloak' is given by means of a combination of semantically active names (even though

---

[23] In the case of 'pirate boat' or 'author of the *Ethics*' the primary significance will be given by the complex thought with which the terms are correlated, the secondary significance by the object in the world with which the complex thought is correlated: e.g. Aristotle. Thus, complex names and expressions have separable primary and secondary significations.

'cloak' does not include these as parts). Here, the immediate signification of the name is determined by our combining two distinct semantically significant names. However, Aristotle only commits himself to the cautious claim that *if* this name is significant, its significance depends on its being correlated with many objects (in a given relation).[24] Thus, the most we can conclude is that while some non-compound names are given to one thing, others (like 'cloak') are not. The significance of the latter group (if they have one) depends on the significance of complex expressions such as 'man and horse' with which they are conventionally correlated. This group will include any (semantically) simple significant empty names, since their immediate significance must be dependent on some combination of simple names (joined together by us: e.g. 'unicorn' might be understood as 'horse with horn', etc.).

According to this model, there cannot be single affirmations when the grammatical subject, even if non-compound, fails to signify one existing object or kind. For, in single affirmations there must be one object with which the relevant term is correlated. Thus, the signification of empty names is fixed in a way which precludes their being used in single affirmations, since in these cases there is no one object (of the appropriate type) with which they are correlated and which produces the relevant affection of the soul.[25] All significant empty names must be either

---

[24] If the expression was not correlated with many objects, but was a simple empty name, it would signify nothing. This is not to say that Aristotle suggest here that no empty name is significant (as Ackrill suspected, *Aristotle's Categories and De Interpretatione* (Oxford, 1963), 132). It is rather to note that unless the empty name is complex in one of the ways indicated, it will lack significance because there is no entity in the world with which it is appropriately related. On this interpretation, the alternatives canvassed in 18ᵃ23–6 are as follows: either the name 'cloak' is treated as significant and complex, and there are several affirmations, or it is not significant (because it is not treated as complex). In the first alternative, the first affirmation (viz. 'Cloak is white' (18ᵃ25)) is equivalent both to 'Man-and-horse is white' and 'Man is white and horse is white' without distinction (as Aristotle says (18ᵃ21–3)), because 'Man-and-horse' is interpreted in the way indicated in the final sentence. In the second alternative, 'cloak' is not treated as equivalent to either, and is, therefore, a simple name with no reference—and hence not significant. Ackrill's interpretation, by contrast, takes Aristotle to distinguish between 'Man-and-horse is white' and 'Man is white and horse is white' (despite Aristotle's apparent insistence to the contrary (18ᵃ21–3)). Further, it requires Aristotle to treat the complex name 'Man-and-horse' as insignificant because empty. This is an unfortunate consequence, since Aristotle elsewhere clearly regards some empty names (such as 'goatstag') as significant (as Ackrill himself notes). Nor is the suggestion (to mitigate this consequence) that 'man-and-horse' is an impossible object (since no man could possibly be a horse) finally convincing. For, there is no indication that Aristotle is speaking here of impossible objects, nor any sign that he saw a relevant difference between 'man-horse' and 'goat-stag'.

[25] This will be so also if there is no proper unity referred to by a given term. Thus, 'Pride is F' would not say one thing of one thing, if there was more than one thing which was pride (97ᵇ13–24). Some compound names for unitary entities can also signify one thing in the required way (cf. *De Int.* 20ᵇ15–18), and, thus, form constituents of single affirmations. But the compound name is a special case of a constituent in a single affirmation, and the basic case of the latter involves simple names.

semantic compounds (like 'goatstag') or compounds at the level of thought (like 'cloak'). Both will only appear in complex affirmations, and both are partially dependent for their significance on the simple names which comprise the relevant complex names or expressions.

Aristotle can allow that the sentences:

Goatstags do not exist (21^a32 f.)

and

Pegasus does not exist

are meaningful if the immediate significance of 'goatstag' and 'Pegasus' is fixed in the way suggested. The first sentence will be equivalent to:

It is not the case that there are animals which are the offspring of a goat and a stag

and will be true. In a similar way:

Goatstags are found in Bosnia

will be false, as this would be equivalent to the sentence:

Animals which are the offspring of a goat and a stag are found in Bosnia.[26]

Aristotle's discussion of existential issues in *De Interpretatione* and *Categories* appears to be influenced by this account of simple names and single affirmations.[27] In single affirmations, one thing is predicated of one actual thing (non-accidentally). Thus, in singular cases, it will follow from:

a is F

---

[26] This is not intended as a full account of the logical form of categorical statements involving names such as 'goatstag'. In particular, I do not investigate here whether complex statements of this type can be accommodated within the framework of Aristotle's syllogistic (involving A, I, O, and E claims). Perhaps other machinery (e.g. drawn from predicate calculus) is required at this point. Aristotle does not consider these issues in detail because he focuses almost exclusively on categorical statements for simple terms. I am indebted at this point to discussions with Alex Orenstein.

[27] In simple, single affirmations, 'one thing is said of one thing non-accidentally' (*De Int.* 18^a13 f.); by contrast, there can be non-simple, single affirmations which are one by conjunction of such claims. The simplest, and most basic, case of a simple, single affirmation involves one simple name plus a predicational tie; for, all other cases of simple, single affirmations will involve names compounded out of a simple name. At the basis of Aristotle's doctrine of simple, single affirmations is his account of simple names. He attempts to specify their signification independently of their role in such affirmations in virtue of his favoured likening-relation. While the *De Int.* is in large measure neutral on the issue of whether, in Aristotle's view, an account of names is prior to an account of affirmations (or vice versa), his approach in general appears to favour taking the signification of names as basic.

that

a exists as (e.g.) a substance.

Similarly, from the plural affirmations of this type such as:

All A's (men) are F

it will follow that:

Some A's (men) are F

since here also one thing (being F) is predicated of one thing (e.g. the kind, man, or perhaps the class of men).[28] In both cases the subject term must refer to one actual thing (individual, kind, or class). Had there been no such kind or class, there could not have been a single affirmation. In that case, 'man' would have been dependent for its significance on a complex thought in the way in which 'void' is.[29]

These existential consequences can only be avoided if sentences such as:

a is F

and

All A's are F

are, despite appearances, not single affirmations. In that case, the 'a' term will be like 'cloak' or 'goatstag'.[30] By contrast, a genuinely single affirmation such as:

Thunder is loud

will entail:

Thunder exists as a process/quality.

[28] It remains a moot point whether any class would count as a genuine unity of the appropriate type.

[29] This account of one basic ingredient in Aristotle's logical square of opposition does not require that the language as a whole contain no empty terms, only that single affirmations do not. (To complete it one requires a detailed specification of what is signified by 'All A's'. But that lies outside the scope of this Chapter.) It should be contrasted with Timothy Smiley's approach to these issues in 'Syllogism and Quantification', *Journal of Symbolic Logic* 27 (1962), 58–72. Smiley preserves the logical square by employing a 'many-sorted' logical system in which every subject term refers to an existing object. But this, at a stroke, banishes such empty names as 'goatstag', 'void', or 'Socrates' from the language, contrary to Aristotle's explicit examples in *De Int.*, *Cat.*, and *Phys.*

[30] The variety of cases of names which Aristotle discusses in *De Int.* alone ('Kallippos', 'Homer', 'goatstag', 'cloak') makes it unprofitable to ask whether *all* Aristotelian names are existence-presupposing. (See, for example, Michael Wedin's and William Jacobs's discussions of the claim that all singular, affirmative sentences imply the existence of a bearer of the grammatical subject of the sentence ('Aristotle on the Existential Import of Singular Sentences', *Phronesis* 23 (1978), 179–96, and 'Aristotle and Nonreferring Subjects', *Phronesis* 24 (1979), 282–300, respectively). There is a rich variety of cases, which can be classified initially as follows:

For, if 'thunder' is a simple name, thunder must exist.[31]

In this section, I have considered Aristotle's main discussion of empty names and existential statements involving names in *De Interpretatione* (and the *Categories*). The likening account, as introduced in Section 4.2, explains several features of Aristotle's views. In particular, it shows why he had to give a different account of the signification of compound and simple names. Further, it makes it clear why (in his account) names

Names which can occur in a single affirmation (which says one thing of one thing)		Names which can occur only in complex affirmations	
Simple Names	Compound Names	Simple Names	Compound Names
Kallippos	pirate ship	cloak	Homer the poet
man	rational biped	Pegasus	goatstag
	(name-like expressions)	void	

Simple names in single affirmations presuppose the existence of their bearer. Any name which can occur meaningfully in a single proposition entails the existence of its bearer. But there are simple and compound names ('Pegasus', 'goatstag', etc.) which do not entail or presuppose the existence of their bearer, even if they occur in (non-single) affirmative sentences of the form 'a is F.'. Earlier discussions of these topics appear to overlook these complexities in Aristotle's account.

[31] Aristotle may employ a similar strategy in considering a further type of complexity in the subject-place (cf. *De Int.* 20^{b}15–17). One example of this type of case is:

Homer is F (e.g. a poet). (*De Int.* 21^{a}24–5)

Aristotle claims that in this case it does not follow that

Homer exists

because 'is F' is not predicated non-accidentally of Homer 'in his own right' in the original sentence (*De Int.* 21^{a}25–7). In that sentence 'is F' may be predicated non-accidentally of Homer-the-poet but not of Homer himself (as 'good' is predicated of A-the-shoemaker and not of A himself in the sentence 'A is a good shoemaker' *De Int.* 21^{a}14–16). If so, the sentence is about a complex object Homer-the-poet and not about one object (Homer), and it will not follow from it that:

Homer exists.

However, Aristotle does not attempt to state under what conditions sentences are about one thing rather than a complex, and so does not make it clear (in general terms) when the relevant existential consequences can be avoided. In this case, 'Homer' is presumably to be correlated with a complex thought whose content is fixed not solely by Homer himself. But Aristotle gives no indication of why this is so. At this point, Aristotle's account runs out. His interest is, as always, focused on the central case of simple names for one proper, natural unity. This unity need not be a metaphysical simple, but can be a kind, like man. The key notion appears to be that of a natural unity (with its own internal structure), and not that of a metaphysical simple which resists further analysis.

occurring meaningfully in single affirmations must entail the existence of their bearer. For, their significance is fixed by the object with which they are correlated in the likening way.

But the first of these points gives rise to a problem: if the ways in which simple and complex names signify differ to this extent, why did Aristotle insist that knowledge of both was independent of knowledge of existence? How did he hold on to C(1), the claim required by the three-stage view in the *Analytics*? Before addressing this pressing problem, I shall consider one further relevant aspect of Aristotle's discussion: his remarks on certain paradoxes involving knowledge and belief.

4.4 KNOWLEDGE, BELIEF, AND SUBSTITUTION*

To recapitulate: on Aristotle's account, two simple names ('a', 'b') have the same significance (mediately and immediately) if and only if they signify the same object. In this case, the object designated by 'a' will be essentially the same as that designated by 'b'. Further, a name will signify the same (mediately) as an account provided that they are both non-accidentally correlated with the same object. In this way, co-signification is fixed by how the world is.

This account has implications for the analysis of belief and knowledge contexts. If 'Tully' has the same significance as 'Cicero', then, if John believes that Tully is a Roman, surely he must also believe that Cicero is a Roman (even if John is unaware that Cicero is Tully)? For, if two terms co-signify, they should be intersubstitutable in these contexts. Was Aristotle aware of this consequence? Did he accept it? Or did he have some way of avoiding it?

Aristotle's relevant remarks on these topics are brief and elliptical. In *De Sophisticis Elenchis* 179^a35–8 he writes that if two objects or kinds are the same in essence, then whatever is true of one is true of the other. Indeed, he formulates the following general principle:

It is only to things which are indistinguishable in essence and one that all the same attributes belong.

Cicero is the same in essence as Tully, as is water as H_2O. These cases are distinguished from another group of which Aristotle writes:

it is not necessary in all cases that what belongs to the subject only accidentally is true of the thing itself

In this group will be placed attributes which do not belong to the subject in virtue of its own nature, such as:

The man is *musical*. (cf. *Meta.* Δ.7, 1017^{a}8–10)[32]

Koriskos is *the man approaching*.

This statue is *mine*

For, to be Koriskos is not the same as to be the man approaching because it is not part of the essence of Koriskos to be the man approaching.[33] Here, according to Aristotle, the following inference pattern does not hold:

a is F

a = the G

The G is F.

Thus, if

Koriskos is known to me, and

Koriskos = the man approaching

it will not follow that

The man approaching is known to me.[34]

---

[32] It will also include:

The musician is *a man*. (*Meta.* Δ.7, 1017^{a}8–10)

where it is not of the musician *as such* that being a man is predicated, but of (e.g.) Polykleitos. (Similarly with 'The musician builds.') When the subject is a substance or kind, properties that belong to it *as such* will be its essential properties. But when the subject is not a substance by itself but (e.g.) a substance *qua* musician, the properties that belong to it *as such* need not be essential properties of the substance itself; rather, they will be properties which belong to it *qua* musician; and these need not be essential properties of that substance (e.g. man), if other types of substance can be musicians (on this, see L. Spellman's 'Referential Opacity in Aristotle', *HPQ* 7 (1990), 21 ff.). This formulation does not essentially involve regarding Polykleitos the musician as a 'kooky object' distinct from Polykleitos (as is suggested by F. Lewis, 'Accidental Sameness in Aristotle', *PS* 42 (1982), 2, 4–5, 7, 24, and G. Matthews, 'Accidental Unities' in M. Schofield and M. Nussbaum (eds.) *Language and Logos* (Cambridge, 1982), 227–8, 230–5. Rather, Polykleitos is contingently identical with Polykleitos the musician, since Polykleitos may have existed without being Polykleitos the musician.

[33] Aristotle appears in this passage to think that Koriskos *qua* man approaching has an essence *(ousia)* distinct from that of Koriskos. And this supports the view that Koriskos the man approaching is a separate object from Koriskos, one with its own essence. However, in the present context, 'indistinguishable in *ousia*' may mean only 'indistinguishable in some canonical account *(logos)* of what they are', and need not involve attributing a separate essence to Koriskos *qua* man approaching. For, in this context, 'being good' and 'being good and about to be asked' have separate *ousiai*, although (presumably) both lack Aristotelian essences (properly speaking).

[34] Aristotle applies the same strategy to the following inference pattern (179^{b}4–6):

This (statue) is mine.

This (statue) is an artwork.

This artwork is mine.

This latter pattern of inference will only be valid if the identity statement is a necessary one, and the relevant terms ('a', 'the G') denote objects or their essential properties.[35] By contrast, since Koriskos is not necessarily identical with the man who approaches, it does not follow that since I know Koriskos but do not know the man approaching, I both know and do not know Koriskos.[36] More generally, if the identity in question is contingent, there will be no valid substitution in contexts of this type.

Aristotle appears to accept the following principle as valid:

(1) S knows who a is

    <u>a is the same in essence as B</u>

    S knows who b is.

Since this principle is a general one, he should also accept:

(2) S knows that Fa

    <u>a is the same in essence as b</u>

    S knows that Fb.

For, if a and b are the same in essence, they will share all the same properties. Thus, if 'a' and 'b' signify the same objects non-accidentally, one may substitute 'a' for 'b' in 'knows that . . .' contexts. Nor should this result surprise us, given Aristotle's account of co-signification. If 'a' and 'b' co-signify in the appropriate way, they should be validly intersubstitutable.[37]

Aristotle's admittedly telegrammatic discussion of an alternative solution (which he rejects) reveals a similar pattern of thought. He writes:

The conclusion does not follow, if it means that I made the statue, since I may only possess it. The example is less striking, however, since it is tempting to spot ambiguity in 'mine' (made by me, 'belonging to me'). Aristotle, however, argues that, since this statue is not essentially mine, the conclusion does not follow.

[35] The crucial requirement is that the terms pick out things which are essentially identical. This relation is stronger than that of necessary identity, since certain features may pass the latter test (e.g. having gills) but not be part of the essence of the phenomenon.

[36] I prefer 'know who—is' for *eidenai* in this context to the alternative 'be acquainted with—', since it seems (as Sandra Peterson points out, *The Master Paradox* (Princeton Ph.D. thesis, 1969), 20) that if one is acquainted with a, and a = b, then one is acquainted with b (even if one does not know one is). An alternative would be to translate the verb as 'to one's knowledge acquainted with—', in which case (also) one would be to one's knowledge acquainted with Koriskos, but not to one's knowledge acquainted with the man approaching. Peterson's own final suggestion that the immediate context itself be construed as a case of *oratio obliqua* ('knows that—') (p. 32) seems to go beyond the text. I am indebted in this section to her excellent discussion of the relevant issues. See also her paper 'Substitution in Aristotelian Technical Contexts', *PS* 47 (1985), 249–57.

[37] Sandra Peterson did not discuss the relation between the substitution principle which Aristotle accepts and the account of signification. But this connection appears a central one in discussing *oratio obliqua* contexts.

Some people say that it is possible to know and not to know the same thing, but not in the same respect. When they do not know the man approaching, but do know Koriskos, they say they know and do not know the same thing but not in the same respect. (*Soph. El.* 179^{b}7–11)

Aristotle's own proposal, presumably, allows that one may know with regard to the man approaching that he is approaching, but not know that he is Koriskos. (In 179^{b}30–3, Aristotle is extending his original account to cover 'intensional' contexts.) The alternative proposal, by contrast, will not work in some cases (179^{b}27); presumably, those which cannot be analysed in terms of the person knowing and not knowing the same thing in a different aspect. Thus, he comments:

the person knows concerning Koriskos that he is Koriskos, and concerning the man approaching that he is approaching. (179^{b}27f., 31–3)

In this proposal (but not in Aristotle's) one can substitute 'Koriskos' for 'the man approaching' in the context:

S does not know with regard to the man approaching that he is Koriskos

to yield:

S does not know with regard to Koriskos that he is Koriskos.

Thus, here, free substitution of all co-referring expressions is permitted (whether or not they are non-accidentally true of the same object). However, as Aristotle objects, since S does know with regard to Koriskos that he is Koriskos, it follows that he both knows and does not know the same thing ('that he is Koriskos') with regard to the same thing (Koriskos). Thus, Aristotle concludes, the alternative proposal fails because it cannot provide a general solution for the whole range of relevant paradoxes.[38]

Aristotle's own account depends on his accepting the more rigorous substitution principle set out above, a principle congruent with his account of co-signification. However, his position may appear unacceptable. For,

---

[38] The opponent might (of course) accept that S knows and does not know with regard to Koriskos that he is Koriskos. However, in this case he is not (as Aristotle points out) employing his favoured strategy of finding a different aspect as the relevant object of belief. However, Aristotle's criticism is not by itself conclusive. His opponent might insist that one can hold—about Koriskos—distinct attitudes to the claim 'he is Koriskos'. For, in locutions of the form:

Of a, S knows that he is F.

the first place (filled by 'a') appears to be extensional and outside the context of S's knowledge. If so, the opponent would not think that he had much to 'explain away' in this case. What Aristotle really needed (for his purposes) was a case in which S knows that a is F and does not know that a is F (although not perhaps in the same mode).

surely one can know that Cicero is a Roman, grasp the significance of 'Tully', and still not know that Tully is a Roman? Can his substitution principle avoid refutation by the very examples which led Frege to articulate his own distinctive theory? Does Aristotle have anything further to say in his defence?[39]

It would be foolish to claim that Aristotle focused sharply on these issues in the passages cited or elsewhere. However, his remarks suggest one move which mitigates the appearance of paradox. In discussing intentional action (*NE/EE* 1135ª23–30), Aristotle separates accidental and non-accidental knowledge. Thus, he writes:

I call 'intentional' an action within one's power where one acts knowingly and not in ignorance of who is being affected, with what, and for what good—and one knows each of these non-accidentally . . . for, it is possible that the person struck should be one's father, and one know that the person is a man or one of the bystanders, but be ignorant that it is one's father.

In this case one knows non-accidentally that one is striking a bystander or a man, but only knows accidentally that it is one's father. This type of ignorance (accidental knowledge) is to be distinguished from cases where one has no idea that one is striking anybody at all. If one applies this distinction to the case of simple names, one arrives at the following position. While it is true that if one knows that Cicero is a Roman, and knows the signification of 'Tully', one will know that Tully is a Roman, the premiss and conclusion will involve different types of knowledge. For, one will know non-accidentally that Cicero is a Roman but only know accidentally that Tully is a Roman. It will not follow from the fact that one knows non-accidentally that Cicero is a Roman that one knows non-accidentally that Tully is a Roman. Thus, in an example of the type cited, the assailant might know non-accidentally that he is striking Cicero, but only know accidentally that he is striking Tully. For, it is only the claim that Cicero is a Roman that plays a role in the explanation of his intentional action.

If this is correct, the accidental knower will know (in line with the *Sophisticis Elenchis* substitution principle) that Tully is a Roman (Fb), even though he does not know this in the way which would be required if he were to be able (e.g.) to act intentionally on it. Slightly more fully, he may know Fb accidentally even though he is not able to use this knowledge in his practical reasoning. In a similar case, on which Aristotle comments, one may know in some way (e.g.) that this mule is sterile (perhaps on the basis of past perception or reasoning), while still thinking actively that this mule is in foal (*Pr. An.* 67ᵇ5–10). Here, too, one will know that this mule is sterile (Fb) but not in the way required if one is to use that knowledge in one's

---

[39] Compare Nathan Salmon's strategy in *Frege's Puzzle* (Boston, 1982), ch. 8.

reasoning. In these cases, the subject may have knowledge that Fb even though he has not grasped this claim in the way required for him to be able to use it in his reasoning.

Aristotle does not specify (in any further detail) the distinct ways of knowing he has introduced. However, his remarks suggest that (in his view) one may substitute 'a' and 'b', when these terms have the same significance, in knowledge contexts, without intolerable paradox. For, while (in the case envisaged) the thinker will know that Tully is a Roman, he will not know it non-accidentally. He does not grasp this piece of knowledge in the way in which he knows that Cicero is a Roman.[40] His non-accidental knowledge of the latter is manifested by his ability to use it in some further way in his thinking.[41]

While these remarks must remain speculative, they suggest that Aristotle had at his disposal some resources with which to defend his approach to substitution and co-signification. In his account, the distinctions required to analyse belief and knowledge contexts will stem from features distinctive of these particular states, not from his account of signification. The latter will legitimize the general principle of co-substitution sketched above, and will be appropriate in a wide variety of contexts, including modal ones. The further additions required to analyse non-accidental knowledge will not themselves be part of his general account of signification. Thus, he can distinguish what is needed to legitimize substitution in contexts involving (non-accidental) knowledge from what is required for his account of co-signification. But, in making this distinction, his account is fundamentally non-Fregean.

---

[40] Accidental knowledge need not require different objects of knowledge, as accidental causation need not require distinct processes separate from essential causes. (On this, see my *Aristotle's Philosophy of Action*, 50–1.) There are certain analogies between Aristotle's strategy (so understood) and recent responses to Frege's puzzle—e.g. Nathan Salmon's in *Frege's Puzzle*. Aristotle's ways of knowing correspond in some measure to Salmon's guises. Both, at least, are non-identical with Fregean senses (see Sect. 4.6). But there are also important differences, since Aristotle appears to allow free substitution within certain propositional contexts (e.g. 'know'), and not within others (e.g. 'know non-accidentally'). Hence, his motivation for permitting certain substitutions is specific to certain propositional attitudes, and cannot be the result simply of the sameness of significance of certain singular terms and a compositional semantics for attitude ascriptions (as in Salmon's proposal). There is (for Aristotle) non-accidental knowledge of a proposition only when it is known in a given way.

[41] In this way, what is known by nature can be the same as what is known by us, even if we do not grasp what is known in the same way or order as the active intellect itself does (cf. *Post. An.* A.2, 71^{b}33 ff.). For, what is known can be precisely the same thing, even though it is thought about in different ways. Here, Aristotle may be following a traditional pattern of Greek thought in which we and the gods can know the same thing, even though we do not think of it in the same way. On this general topic, see F. Letoublon's interesting essay, 'Les dieux et les hommes: le langage et sa reference dans l'antiquité grecque archaique' *Language and Reality in Greek Philosophy: Proceedings of the Greek Philosophical Society* (Athens, 1985), 92–9.

4.5 ARISTOTLE'S PROBLEM

So far, the following picture has emerged:

(A) Simple names signify (mediately) substances and kinds (on pain of being meaningless), while compound names need not do so. In the case of simple names, the content of the thought with which the name is correlated is determined by the kind (or object) in the world which imprints itself on us (through the likening process).

However, the arguments of Chapters 2 and 3 led us to the following conclusion:

(B) In Aristotle's view, one can grasp an account of what a simple name signifies without knowing of the existence (or of the essence) of the object or kind in question. For, at the first stage of the three stages of scientific enquiry, one can grasp the significance of 'triangle' without knowledge of the existence or essence of the phenomenon.

How are (A) and (B) consistent? One can generate the appearance of inconsistency as follows:

(1) Our thoughts about a kind are individuated (in part) by the kinds which cause them. (Premiss)

(2) When we have a thought, we know which thought we have. (Premiss)

(3) When we know which thought we have, we know what individuates it. (From (1) and (2))

(4) When we have a thought about a kind, we know which kind it is which causes it. (From (3))

(5) Accounts of what the name 'K' signifies are thoughts about that kind (when 'K' is a simple name). (Premiss)

(6) In grasping an account of what 'K' signifies, we know which kind it is which causes the thought. (From (4) and (5))

If (6) is correct, in grasping an account of what 'K' signifies we will know which kind is signified, and therein know that the kind in question exists. But this is plainly inconsistent with the three-stage view, as set out in Chapters 2 and 3. For, a crucial feature of that view is that one can grasp accounts of what names of kinds signify without knowing of the existence of the relevant kind. Are Aristotle's semantic intuitions, after all, inconsistent?

There are (at least) two ways to respond to this challenge. One is to show that (despite what has been said so far) Aristotle did not accept (A) or (B). An alternative is to suggest that he found a way of holding these

claims without inconsistency. Of the two claims that generate the inconsistency, (A) is (at present) the more weakly supported. For, the major
argument in its defence has rested on the (so far unconfirmed) report of
a connection between names, thought, and the objects and kinds that make
up the world.[42] However, (A) is in fact secure (or so I shall argue in the
next Chapter). If so, Aristotle can only avoid this problem by showing that
(A) and (B) are, appearances notwithstanding, consistent.

In the argument just given, (1) will be supported by the argument of the
next Chapter. (2) seems hard to reject. For, surely if we have a thought we
must (in some way) know which thought it is. (5) is an obvious truth. So,
if the argument is to be broken, Aristotle must challenge the inference
from (2) to (3)? Can this be done? Did he do it?

In Aristotle's terms, one might possess an account of what 'K' signifies
without knowing that the kind exists, if one does not know that the
signification of the name is in fact determined by that kind. In such a case
one will not know that there exists one unified phenomenon that brought
about these thoughts, still less be able to distinguish that phenomenon
from all others. While the content of the relevant thought will be determined by the kind that is signified, the thinker need not know which kind
that is (in the way required to distinguish that kind from all others, either
real or imaginary). Rather, in having a thought about eclipses, she may
think of them as possessing certain features which would locate them, if
they exist, in an ordered world: e.g. being a certain unified property of the
moon. But, in knowing this, she need not know *everything* about what
makes the thought the thought it is. In particular, she need not know that
the thought in question is (constitutively) brought about by an existing
kind in the world. Indeed, she may not know whether or not this case is
like that of 'goatstag'. In brief, she need not know that the kind in question exists.

There are three reasons, implicit in our previous discussion, for thinking
that Aristotle followed this route.

First, this proposal makes good sense of Aristotle's discussions of existence claims (as set out in Section 4.3) and of existence proofs (as deployed
in *Analytics* B). Stage 1 accounts allow us to articulate questions in an
appropriate form for us to attain knowledge of the existence of the kind.
Thus, to establish that thunder exists is to establish that noise belongs to
the clouds, by finding an appropriate middle term. In this way, one will
establish that thunder is a genuine unity.[43] In doing so, one goes beyond
what is required for an understanding of the name.

Second, this account fits well with Aristotle's own use of accounts of

---

[42] For further support for (A), see App. 1.

[43] See also Sect. 4.6 below. On the view sketched here, existence can be a property of
objects or kinds (in Aristotle's account), and need not in general be a property of properties. For a contrasting view, see G. E. L. Owen's paper: 'Aristotle on the Snares of Ontology',
in R. Bambrough (ed.), *New Essays on Plato and Aristotle* (London, 1965).

what names signify (as set out in Chapter 2, Section 2.5). If the (immediate) signification of a simple term is determined by the thinking faculty being likened to an object, the information embedded in the account of what it signifies may be in the form of an indefinite reference ('a specific type of . . .'), or of a definite description which purports, but fails, to be unique. For, it is not this information that determines the signification of that term. If so, a thinker may grasp an account of what the term signifies without possessing uniquely identifying knowledge of the kind signified. His account is an account of thunder (and not of any noise in the clouds) because it is that very phenomenon which brings about the thought, the thinker's grasp of which the account expresses. For, it is a causal connection to the relevant phenomenon which fixes the signification of the term. But the thinker who grasps that term need not grasp everything about the relevant thought. In particular, the individuating information about its origin may escape him.[44]

Third, we have been prepared (to some extent) for a move of this type by Aristotle's discussion of the paradoxes of knowledge. For there, two terms 'a' and 'b' can have the same significance, and the thinker know the significance of each, without his knowing that they have the same significance. His preparedness to doubt that a = b in no way undermines the claim that 'a' and 'b' have the same significance. There can be features of the signification of these terms (their co-signification) which are not transparent to the thinker. (In a similar fashion, since the thinker may not know whether pride has one essence, she may not know whether or not 'pride' is a 'univocal' term (*Post. An.* B.13, 97^{b}15–25).)

These three points highlight the role played by accounts of what terms signify. The first suggests their use in searching for knowledge of existence and essence of a kind. One example of this role is provided by Aristotle's discussion of the enquiry into the existence of ice. If 'ice' signifies the same as 'solid water', to establish that ice exists is to establish that solidity belongs to water.[45] The question about ice's existence is now, according to Aristotle, posed in a form in which it can be answered and knowledge gained.[46] If this is correct, there is no difficulty in understanding how existence proofs can establish that ice exists (e.g. as a substance) by establishing that solidity

---

[44] This suggestion fills a gap in the earlier discussion of Ch. 2; see closing paragraphs of 2.8.

[45] The precise form of the question is important. To establish that ice exists/does not exist (e.g. as a substance) is not (in Aristotle's account) to establish that solidity belongs/does not belong to solid water (or ice). And this is fortunate since the latter claims are either tautologous or inconsistent.

[46] Owen (in 'Aristotle on the Snares of Ontology') criticized Aristotle's view on the grounds that the substitution of 'ice' (or 'solid water') for 'water' in the sentence which states that 'being solid belongs to water' made the sentence tautologous. For, it now says that 'being solid belongs to solid water'. However, Owen's criticism rests on a mistaken view of Aristotle's substitution rules for stage 1 accounts. (It is only if one succumbs to this mistake that one is tempted to interpret 'exists' in Aristotle as equivalent to the existential quantifier, and treat 'ice exists' as saying that the property of icehood is instantiated: Owen,

belongs to water. For, such accounts provide the information required for a successful enquiry (of Aristotle's form) into the nature and existence of the kind (viz. 'ice' signifies solid water). But it is fully consistent with this account that 'exists as a substance' be treated as a predicate of 'ice'. For, it is by means of an existence proof (involving 'solid water') that the simple existential claim is established. Further, even if 'ice' is a simple term which signifies a substance, one can understand what 'ice' signifies (on the basis of an account of what it signifies) without knowing that it exists. Thus, it is not a referential tautology to assert that ice exists.

In the account offered, the central role of accounts of what names signify is to express the thinker's understanding of the immediate signification of a term, such as 'man'. In the best case, his initial understanding of the term will give him a preliminary and partial account of the kind which will be of use in his subsequent enquiry into the nature and existence of the kind. Such accounts provide, in effect, the base camp from which we can begin our ascent to knowledge of the kind. With the information they provide, and our methods of investigation, we will (in the end) come to have knowledge of the existence, extension, and nature of the kind.[47] But such knowledge lies in the future, and is not part of what it is to grasp an account of what the name signifies. Further, the role of Stage 1 accounts cannot be to fix either the reference or the extension of the term.[48] For, answers to these questions will emerge in the context of enquiry, and need not be known at Stage 1. At the beginning of enquiry, we may have thoughts about kinds (provided by the likening model) without knowing enough about them to determine the reference (or extension) of the relevant terms.

4.6 ARISTOTLE'S THEORY? ITS COMMITMENTS

If the proposal made in the previous section is confirmed, Aristotle's account of names will have (in addition to (A) and (B)) two further elements.

(C) (A) and (B) are consistent because (in the case of simple names) the

'Aristotle on the Snares of Ontology' 82 ff.). Even in *Post. An.* B.8 (93^{b}9–12), where Aristotle comes closest to Owen's suggestion, he substitutes part of the *definiens* (noise . . .) for the *definiendum* (thunder), and not all of it. However, in the conclusion he switches back to 'noise' and omits 'thunder', and, thus, avoids any suspicion of the difficulty Owen considers. (Further, even if he had maintained 'thunder' in the conclusion, this would not generate Owen's problem. The proof of existence would then conclude with the non-tautologous claim that 'Thunder belongs in the clouds.')

[47] As Aristotle emphasizes in *Post. An.* B.8, 93^{a}21–30, the methods are restricted to finding that there is a middle term, and what it is. The information required is just what is needed for this: two terms which can be connected in this way.

[48] For a contrasting view about the function of such accounts, see Robert Bolton's remarks on their 'essential reference fixing role' ('Essentialism', 537).

(immediate) signification of the name is determined by features beyond those of which the thinker need have knowledge in understanding the term (such as are expressed in his account of what the term signifies).

(D) (C) is possible because the signification of the name is determined by the content of the thought with which the name is conventionally correlated, and the content of that thought is (in turn) determined by the substance or kind in the world which produces it. The account of what the name signifies expresses the speaker's understanding of that name by showing his grasp on the thought with which the name is correlated. But the thinker need not know (at the outset) how the content of the thought with which the name is correlated is determined. For all he knows, its content might be determined in the way in which thoughts concerning goatstags are determined.

Can this proposal be secured exegetically? It certainly has merits. It shows how Aristotle can consistently hold the three-stage view (sketched in Chapters 2 and 3) together with the account of signification and thought given in the earlier sections of this Chapter (and the next). More generally, (A)–(D) allow Aristotle to underwrite the four claims, C(1)–C(4), set out in Section 4.1 above, without inconsistency.

It is, however, one thing to show that Aristotle would have been well advised to follow a given route, another to establish that he actually did so. In the absence of any explicit endorsement by Aristotle of (A)–(D), only indirect evidence can be available. In addition to that already provided, further support can only come from evidence that Aristotle was aware of the distinctive shape and commitments of the theory sketched in this Chapter. Is such evidence available?

The theory (as it emerged) is complex and has two major distinctive features, which I shall label (D1) and (D2). Once we grasp these, we can test how far Aristotle saw and attempted to make good the distinctive philosophical commitments that this theory involves.

(D1) In the basic case, the immediate signification of a name is given by the content of the thought with which it is conventionally correlated. However, the content of this thought does not determine the reference of the term in the way in which Frege and many others have proposed. It is not the case that the reference is given by the object which 'fits' the thoughts which express the thinker's understanding of the name. For, his understanding of the name (in terms of general descriptions) need not be sufficient to enable him to distinguish the bearer of the name from all other objects (real and imaginary). Rather, the content of the thought is itself fixed by the object to which the thinking faculty is likened. In this way, the 'likening' relation puts us (as thinkers) in contact with a genuine kind which we proceed to investigate.

In Aristotle's theory, although the signification of a simple name is determined (fundamentally) by an object or kind in the world, the thinker's understanding of that name need not be accounted for in terms of his grasp of the object signified. For, in the context of enquiry, one may understand a name and then go on to discover that the object signified exists. Nor need one (on the basis of resources available to one at the beginning of the enquiry) 'know which' object is signified in the way required if one is to be able to distinguish the bearer of the name from all other objects. As far as one's understanding goes, there need be nothing to distinguish this case from one in which there is no real object signified.

The signification of names is fixed (in Aristotle's account) by resources which outrun the thinker's understanding of that term. Further, the conditions for co-signification depend on how the world is and not on our understanding of the terms themselves. In these two respects, Aristotle's account of signification is distinct from any version of the widely accepted Fregean account of meaning.[49] For, Aristotle does not accept that either the signification of a term or the conditions for its co-signification are determined by the thinker's knowledge or understanding of the term.[50]

The gulf that separates Aristotle's theory from Fregean ones may explain why some have doubted whether he was interested in meaning at all.[51] His account of signification is certainly not an account of meaning, if

[49] I take orthodox Fregean sense theories to be committed to the following claims:

(a) To grasp the sense of a term is to grasp something which determines its reference.

(b) Senses are transparent; if two senses are the same, and one grasps both, one is able to grasp that they are identical without further reflection.

(c) Senses are not object-dependent (with the exceptions of the senses of 'I', 'now', 'this'); one can grasp the sense of a name and there not be an object to which the name refers.

See, for instance, M. Dummett, *Frege* (London, 1973). Revisionary interpreters of Frege—especially the 'new Oxford Fregeans' (e.g. G. Evans: *Varieties of Reference*, J. McDowell, 'On the Sense and Reference of Proper Names', *Mind* 86 (1977) 159–85)—deny that Frege held (c), and debate the nature of his understanding of (a). I take all Fregean theories to be committed to (b).

[50] Aristotle rejects both theses (a) and (b) mentioned above. He rejects both the classical version of Frege's thesis (a) in which the understander must have a definite description of the object before his mind, and the 'new version' in which the sense grasped by the thinker determines the reference of the name simply because the sense cannot be specified without mentioning the referent. For, in Aristotle's view, one can have an account of what the term signifies (even in the case of an existent) without knowing of the existence of the object.

[51] See T. H. Irwin's 'Aristotle's Concept of Signification', in Schofield and Nussbaum (eds.), *Language and Logos*, 240–66. Others have held that Aristotle lacks a theory of meaning because he uses the term 'signify' in a wide variety of ways. Thus, in some contexts it points to a word-world relation, in others to a world-world one. But why should this feature be worrying? There is, after all, the same variety of usage in English between what Grice calls 'natural' and 'non-natural' meaning. ('Meaning', *P.R.* 66 (1957), 121–126.) A similar argument would show that there can be no account of the meaning of names in English! All that is needed is that Aristotle employ the term 'signify' univocally in cases where it relates (e.g.) names and objects.

all such accounts have to consist in dictionary definitions or to provide one who understands them with a way to determine the extension of the term. But there is a more generic conception of meaning. In it, to give the meaning of a name 'α' is to state something which determines those conditions under which indicative sentences containing 'α' are true or false (in so far as they contain 'α'). Frege's theory of sense is one attempt to do this, explicit definitional accounts of meaning another. But so too is Aristotle's theory. Take the case of simple names. In Aristotle's view, 'α' means A (an object or kind) if and only if A is the cause (in suitable conditions) of the thought with which 'α' is conventionally correlated. Thus, the indicative sentence 'α is F' will be true when A is F, and false when A is not F. Further, an object will be incorrectly named 'α' (e.g. in non-ideal conditions) if it is other than A. Aristotle (as we saw in Section 4.3) offers a somewhat different account of the signification of complex names. But here too he seeks to explain how linguistic expressions can be correctly and incorrectly applied.[52] Thus, 'goatstag' will be incorrectly applied to goats, if the signification of that term is fixed (as Aristotle suggests) by some combination of thoughts of goats and stags. In these ways, Aristotle's account of signification meets the conditions given above for accounts of the meaning of names (although it is a non-Fregean theory).[53]

(D2) Aristotle's theory is a complex one. For, while the meaning of simple names is determined by the substances and kinds to which they refer, the meaning of compound names is not determined in this way. For this reason, it is a mistake to describe Aristotle's theory as one in which 'meaning amounts to reference'. There is no need for each significant name to have a referent (e.g. 'goat-stag', 'hippo-centaur'); only simple names in single affirmations need do so.[54] While both simple and complex names signify the object of the thought with which they are correlated, they differ precisely because those objects are themselves determined in radically different ways.[55]

[52] For a contrasting view which appears to confine a theory of meaning to (e.g.) dictionary definitions, see Irwin's, 'Aristotle's Concept', 241–3. Irwin is best seen as asking how Aristotle can be offering an account of meaning (if he is not aiming to give dictionary equivalents). I have been helped at this point by discussions with Michael Morris.

[53] My claims are, of course, confined to the meaning of names and name-like expressions. They do not amount to the claim that Aristotle devised an account of meaning for all expressions of the language. For a somewhat similar approach to the meaning of names, see Nathan Salmon's characterization of a variety of 'naive' theories in *Frege's Puzzle*, ch. 2. It would be a major, but worthwhile, task to compare Aristotle's account of other expressions (such as predicates and relations) with that proposed by Salmon.

[54] It should be noted that Aristotle rejects Plato's theory of ideas in part on this ground (cf. Alexander of Aphrodisias, *Commentary in Metaphysica* 82.1).

[55] Hamlyn's view that for Aristotle meaning is reference can be criticized on different grounds also. For Aristotle, two terms (a, b) can have the same reference, but differ in significance if the correct answer to the question 'What is a?' is different from that to 'What is b?' (e.g. weight, volume). In general, the view that Aristotle is offering a 'denotational theory' of meaning ignores the role he attributes to thought in the determination of meaning. (See Sect. 4.2 above.)

If Aristotle holds (D1) and (D2), he incurs a number of substantial-philosophical commitments. Here are three:

(PC1) He needs to provide an account of the content of thought which can stand as the basis for this type of account of signification. For, without a theory of content and of 'likening', his account of signification is (at best) incomplete.[56]

(PC2) He needs to explain how we come to have thoughts of this type at all. How come we are so lucky as to have our thinking faculties likened to kinds and substances in the world?

(PC3) He needs to explain how the signification of our terms can outrun our understanding of them. How is it possible for us to grasp a term which (in fact) signifies a kind, without being able to discriminate that kind from all others? Can we really understand terms without having the required knowledge of what they signify?

(PC3) has several aspects. First, Aristotle needs to show how we can have thoughts which are individuated in a given way without knowing this fact about them. He must show how the nature of these thoughts can be (on occasion) veiled from us. Second, he needs to show how we came to possess thoughts (with determinate content) which are about objects, without knowing which object or kind they are about.[57] Third, he should show how we can have thoughts about kinds without knowing that, if they exist, they have an essence. How can this be, if it is a requirement that in having thoughts about kinds something of their form is transferred? Surely this must put us in contact with their essences?

Did Aristotle accept these commitments? Did he attempt to develop a way of meeting these demands? If we find Aristotle at work on these

---

[56] Compare Gareth Evans's attack on the claim that all who use names understand them, or have thoughts about their referents, in the way suggested by the 'Photographic Model' (*Varieties of Reference*, 82–100 f.). Evans, a neo-Fregean, rejects the 'Photographic Model' in favour of the claim that all thinkers who use a name must have the ability to identify the referent (p. 403) and be able to 'distinguish the object of their judgement from all other things' (p. 89), either by having a description which uniquely identifies (e.g.) thunder or a propensity to recognize thunder demonstratively when confronted by it (p. 93). Since Aristotle did not accept these Fregean requirements, he needs to show how without them we can latch on to the signification of a name.

[57] Some may not find (PC3) puzzling. They believe that our grasp on the signification of a term rests merely on our standing in some causal relation with the object. But the difficulty with their view is clear. What makes it the case that this type of causal connection gives the thinker an understanding of the term. Causal impact seems not to be enough for understanding. But if one adds to the bare causal requirement the suggestion that the thinker must be able knowledgeably to discriminate the relevant object or kind, one has already embraced some form of the Fregean option (which Aristotle, it appears, rejects). It may appear that Aristotle is attempting to find a space for his theory where none really exists!

projects, we will have further evidence that he held the position defined by (A)–(D). In the next Chapter, I shall argue that he accepted (PC1) (and the first part of (PC3)), and in Chapter 6 turn to his discussion of (PC2) and the other aspects of (PC3). If I am correct, Aristotle attempted (with no little success) to develop precisely the type of account of thought and meaning which is required to meet (PC1)–(PC3).

5

Signification and Thought

5.1 INTRODUCTION

Several claims in the last Chapter rest on a hypothesis about Aristotle's view of the relation between a thought and the kind or object which that thought is about. In outline, the hypothesis runs as follows: in the central case (corresponding to a simple name in a single affirmation), what makes a thought one about an object or kind is that the thinking faculty is *likened* to that object or kind in the form-transferring way. The relevant type of *likening* occurs (it is claimed) when:

  (i) the object or kind is the efficient cause of the thought,

 (ii) the efficient cause explains the relevant general features of the thought (viz. what it is about, its content), and

(iii) the thinker's thinking faculty is functioning correctly.

In this Chapter, I shall seek to confirm this hypothesis by providing exegetical arguments in favour of these claims. If successful, these arguments underwrite the account of signification offered in the last Chapter. My arguments will rest on an interpretation of Aristotle's analogy between perception and thought, as this is developed in *De Anima*. While this analogy is rich in detail, I shall focus only on those aspects which concern the object of thought and perception.

It should be noted that if these arguments succeed, success comes with a heavy price. The result is that we cannot avoid the threat of inconsistency uncovered in the previous Chapter (Section 4.5) simply by denying that Aristotle held the account of signification developed in that Chapter. The tension between it and the three-stage view (as developed in Chapters 2 and 3) has to be resolved in some other way.

5.2 THE ANALOGY INTRODUCED

At the beginning of *De Anima* Γ.4 Aristotle writes:

If thinking is like perceiving, it should consist in being acted upon by what is thought about or in something else of this kind.[1] So, it [viz. the noetic part] must be impassive, and receptive of the form, and potentially of the same type [sc. as the object of thought: *to noeton*] but not identical with it, and be related to the objects of thought as the faculty of sense is to sensible objects. (429[a]13–18)

Here, Aristotle sets out several key elements of his analogy between thought and perception:

(a) both involve a part of the soul being acted on by their respective objects;

(b) in both, the relevant part of the soul receives the form (without the matter);

(c) in both, the part of the soul is potentially of the same type as the external object which acts upon it, but is not identical with it.[2]

Aristotle clarifies (c) elsewhere by adding a further claim:

(d) both faculties are potentially identical with the form received (Γ.8, 431[b]28 ff.)

Thus, he writes:

These faculties must be identical with either the objects themselves or their forms. But they are not identical with their objects: for, the stone does not exist in the soul, but only the form of the stone.

Aristotle has already developed (a) and (b) in discussing perception, when he wrote:

Perception consists in being moved and acted upon . . . for, it seems to be a sort of quality change (B.5, 416[b]33–5, cf. also 418[a]3–6)

and

---

[1] The qualification 'or in something else of this kind' could be taken in two ways: (a) If the comparison between thinking and perceiving is precise, and perceiving is not a straightforward case of 'being acted upon' (*De An.* B.5, 417[b]2 f., [b]15, 418[a]1–3), neither is thinking. (b) If the comparison is less precise, thinking (unlike perceiving) might not exactly involve being acted upon by its object. In the present context, (a) is preferable, since it makes Aristotle's inference to the characteristics which perception and thinking share immediately intelligible. By contrast, (b) would make this problematic, since it would not be clear that perception and thinking are sufficiently alike for the inference to be valid. For, (b), unlike (a), renders it unclear why the objects of thought and perception should be similarly related to their respective faculties.

[2] See *De An.* B.5, 418[a]3–6: 'the sentient subject is potentially such as the object of sense is actually. During the process of being acted upon [viz. by the object of sense] it is unlike it, but by the end of the process it has become like it'. The object of sense in this context is the external object which causes the relevant result. By analogy, in the case of thought, the object of thought must be (e.g.) the stone which is thought about, and not the form of the stone which is present in the mind. This is why the thinking faculty is held to be identical with the form of the stone (when it thinks of it), and not with the external stone (to which it is likened) (cf. Γ.8, 431[b]28 ff.).

Each sense organ is receptive of the perceived object without the matter (Γ.2, 425^{b}23 f.).

(a)–(d) point to a sustained analogy between perception and thought. Although Aristotle develops this analogy cautiously and is aware of several major disanalogies,[3] it offers (I shall argue) the basis for his account of the relation between the thinker and the object of her thoughts. In particular, his discussion of perception lays the foundation for the four claims laid out in the previous Section. Claims (i) and (ii) are supported in Section 5.3, and claim (iii) in Section 5.4.

5.3 THE ANALOGY DEVELOPED: PERCEPTION AND LIKENING: CLAIMS (i) AND (ii)

While Aristotle makes extensive use of the analogy between perception and thought, he makes comparatively few remarks about its basis. In *De Anima* Γ.9 he notes that the power of discrimination (*krisis*) is common to both intellect (*dianoia*) and perception (432^{a}15–17), and in Γ.3 says that in perceiving and thinking the soul discriminates (*krinei*) and cognitively grasps (*gnōrizei*) (427^{a}19–21). Since discrimination of this type involves our being correct (or incorrect (428^{a}3–5)), both perception and thought must involve cognitive discrimination of their relevant objects.[4] My aim is to

---

[3] In *De An.* Γ.4 alone several disanalogies emerge:

(1) The impassivity of the thinking and perceptual faculties is distinguished (429^{a}29–^{b}6). The latter can be destroyed by 'excessive sensible objects', while the former is not adversely affected by 'highly intelligible objects'.

(2) The sensible faculty involves a physical organ, and is inseparable from the body (429^{a}26, ^{b}4–5), while neither is true of the thinking faculty.

(3) In the case of theoretical knowledge of things without matter, that which thinks and that which is thought about are identical (430^{a}2–6). In the case of perception or knowledge of particular external objects or enmattered kinds this is not so (cf. 417^{b}25–8, 430^{a}6–8, 432^{a}1–3). This is because, in the distinctive case of abstract thought, the relevant object does not exist independently of the thinking faculty. (See below.)

Of these, (3) alone is directly relevant to the issue of the object of thought, and is discussed below. (3) goes beyond Aristotle's identification of thinking with the relevant form (which is common to all cases of perceiving and thinking).

[4] In *De An.*, Aristotle takes discrimination as a basic notion together with the capacity to move in space (Γ.9, 432^{a}15–19). He is not attempting to give an account of what makes it the case that a creature discriminates, but only of what it discriminates (in varying cognitive states). (For a defence of this translation of *krisis*, see T. Ebert in 'Aristotle on What is Done in Perceiving', *Zeitschrift für Philosophische Forschung* 37 (1983), 181 ff.) Aristotle holds that if one discriminates A, this essentially involves one's being able to discriminate its contrary or opposite (e.g. *De An.* A.5, 411^{a}4 f., Γ.3, 427^{b}5). In this, discrimination is governed by the same constraints as knowledge (cf. e.g. *NE/EE* E.1, 1129^{a}13 ff., *Meta.* B.2,

examine the nature of the discrimination involved in both cases by considering the four claims (a)–(d) set out in the last Section.

Aristotle's fourth claim (d) is not as perplexing as it may initially seem. It amounts only to this: a given case of (e.g.) seeing is the one it is because it is a case in which (e.g.) blue is seen. More generally, what makes a perception one perception is that it is of one object at one time (*De Sensu* 447^{b}16–18). This is how (according to Aristotle) we individuate perceptions: by their objects and their times. Thus, 'perceiving' can be identified with the form perceived; for, the latter makes a given perceiving the one it is.

Aristotle develops this point in considerable detail in the case of thought in *De Anima* Γ.6. There he writes:

if one thinks of each of the halves (of a line) separately, then one divides the time also; and then it is as if they were lengths themselves. But if one thinks of the whole as made up of halves, then one does so in a time made up of both halves. (430^{b}11–14)

His point is this: my thought of the line is a single (undivided) thought provided that it is of a single (undivided) object. If I think of each of the halves of the line separately, I have two thoughts (one for each side of the division). If I make up a line from these two halves, I have a third thought (of a divided but conjoined line) separate from any of the other thoughts so far mentioned. The general principle is that what makes each thought the thought it is its object. Thus, what makes my present thought the one it is that it is one of Kyoto, and not (e.g.) of the southern section of that ancient city.

The perceiving faculty is potentially of the same type as what is perceived in that it can be made like it in some relevant respect. Aristotle concludes *De Anima* B.5 as follows:

996^{a}20 ff.). If one can discriminate what is white this essentially involves being able to discriminate it from what is not white (one can 'tell them apart'). Similarly, to be able to discriminate this object essentially involves being able to discriminate it from what is not this object (e.g. other objects, nothing), at least in some cases. Discrimination essentially involves being able to distinguish cognitively between different cases in some way (e.g. 'This is A rather than not A', 'This is a and that is not a'). For Aristotle, discriminating A goes beyond merely differential behavioural response to A; for, one could respond differentially to A and to not-A, but not do so in virtue of the same discriminating capacity. That said, certain further questions remain:

(a) If I can discriminate white from non-white in this way, does this require me to be able to discriminate what is white as white? (Could I achieve this while discriminating what is white (e.g.) in terms rather of a theoretical pattern of light rays.)

(b) If I can discriminate this object from other objects, does this require me to be able to discriminate it as an object? (Does the latter require some further conceptual machinery?)

These questions are taken up in what follows.

The sentient subject is potentially such as the object of sense is actually. Thus, during the process of being acted upon it is unlike, but at the end of the process it has been made like (*homoiotai*) the object and is like it. (418ª3–6)

But what does the phrase 'a is made like b' mean? Throughout *De Anima* B.5, Aristotle refers to his general account of affecting and being affected as developed in *De Generatione Corruptione* A.7. Thus, he raises one specific difficulty for the *De Generatione Corruptione* account as follows:

> Now, some say that the like is affected only by the like. But in the sense in which this is possible or impossible we have already stated in our general account of acting and being acted on. (416ᵇ35–417ª2)

and later cites the solution he reached there:

> Therefore, as we have said, a thing is acted upon in a way by the like, and in a way by the unlike; for, while it is being acted upon it is unlike, but when it has suffered it is like, the object. (417ª18–20)[5]

In *De Generatione Corruptione* Aristotle claims that if one thing affects another, they must be distinct in species but the same in genus (distinct in form, but with the same type of matter (324ª5–7)). Agent and patient (e.g. the hot and the cold) are initially both like and unlike. They are unlike in that one is hot and the other cold, but like in that they have enough in common for the hot to heat the cold (cf. *GC* 323ᵇ29–324ª5). The agent brings into play the patient's potentiality for being thus affected. A potentially hot object is made actually hot by the agency of the actually hot object, which assimilates the cold object to itself, and makes it like it itself (viz. hot):

> This is why it is indeed plausible to say that fire heats and the cold cools, and that, to speak generally, what is active (the agent) makes the patient like itself. (324ª9–11)

When this occurs, the patient is likened to the agent by being made like it in some relevant respect (*De An.* B.5, 418ª5–6).[6] The resultant state of the patient is a *liken-ness* of the agent's active power. Thus, the cold is (in the state of having been) made hot by the hot, and this is why it is actually hot.

---

[5] It matters little, for present purposes, if the explicit reference in this passage is to *GC* or to Aristotle's earlier discussion of food and digestion (*De An.* B.4, 416ᵇ5–9). For, in the latter discussion Aristotle also employs his *GC* thesis to explain the truth and error in two conflicting views: 'like is fed by like' and 'like is fed by unlike' (416ª29–32). Food is initially unlike the digestive faculty, but is made like it by digestion. Indeed, part of the point of Aristotle's introducing the case of digestion may be familiarize his audience and readers with his *GC* structures.

[6] The Greek terms reveal the importance of efficient causality: the agent makes the patient like itself (*homoioun* (*GC* A.7, 324ª10f.)). The patient is made like the agent (*homoiotai* (*De An.* B.5, 418ª6)). When this occurs, something is produced (a state of the patient) which is a liken-ness (*homoiōmata*) of the agent (*De Int.* 1, 16ª7 f.).

The role of the efficient cause is central here. Aristotle's claim is not merely that the effect is like or resembles the cause in terms of its relevant quality. The type of likeness in question has to be understood as the result of a given type of causal process in which the patient is likened to the agent. Objects which were always hot to the same degree without causal contact would be like one another, but would not be liken-nesses of one another. Here, as elsewhere, the efficient cause is an important element in the essence of the coming into being of states or things.[7] Since Aristotle identifies the result of being acted on with the activity of being acted on,[8] the resultant likeness (the result of being acted on) is essentially the result of this type of causal process.

This model commits Aristotle, in the case of proper perception, to the following view: what is seen (let us say a red object) induces in the perceiver a result which is a likeness of the red in the object. This result could not be the one it is unless it was produced by the red of an object in this way. Had the patient always been in a state which resembled the redness of objects, she would not be in *that* type of resultant state—even if (*per impossibile*) she had a visual experience whose content exactly resembled the shade of red of the red object before her. Without the efficient causal connection she would not be in a state which was (in the relevant respects) a likeness of that red.

The causal model is central to Aristotle's account of perceiving and thinking. Thus, he writes of proper perception:

the sense is what is receptive of the forms of sensible objects without the matter, just as the wax receives the design of the signet ring without the iron or gold, and receives the gold or bronze design, but not as gold or bronze (B.12, 424[a]17–21)

In this case, it is not just that the wax resembles the signet ring by bearing the same design. The crucial point is that the wax is causally affected by the ring, and is, thus, made like the ring in certain relevant respects. This, no doubt, is why Aristotle focuses here (and elsewhere)[9] on the analogy with wax imprinted by a ring: for, an imprint is what it is because it is imprinted by a ring. Further, an imprint is an imprint of the type it is because it is printed in by a ring of this type. This is the way in which the patient is likened in relevant respects to the agent.

Both these points are general. The agent not only brings it about that

---

[7] See, e.g. *Meta.* Z.17, 1041[a]29–32. The examples of thunder and eclipse in *Post. An.* B.8 fall within this general pattern: they are essentially the product of a given type of cause.

[8] See *Meta.* Θ.8, 1050[a]21–3. For further discussion of this point, see my 'Aristotle: Ontology and Moral Reasoning' (*OSAP* 4 (1986), 135 ff.).

[9] See *De Mem.* 1, 450[a]31 ff. where, talking of memory, Aristotle writes: 'the stimulus produced [viz. perception] engraves a sort of impression of the percept, just like men who make an impression with a seal'.

the patient is in a certain state, but also (if all goes well) determines the quality of that state. Thus, the teacher does not just cause the learner to learn something. If successful, she determines what it is that the learner learns: i.e. what it is that is 'printed' on to the learner's mind. Both flow, if all goes well, from her potentiality to teach.

Aristotle proceeds to apply this model to the case of perception of proper sensibles. He writes:

Similarly, the sense, in each case, is acted upon by what has colour, flavour, or sound, not in the way in which each such thing is called what it is, but in so far as it has a given quality and in accordance with the relevant ratio/account (*logos*). (B.12, 424ᵃ21–5)

In perceiving red, the perceptual faculty is determined in relevant respects by the red in the object before it. It is not, with regard to proper perception, determined by other aspects of the object, such as its being a pillar box or this pillar box, etc. When perception occurs, the perceptual faculty is made like the relevant cause in that its state is made to be a certain way by the relevant quality of the agent.

What exactly is the nature of the internal state that is brought about? Aristotle does not spell out what the relevant account or ratio is in this passage (424ᵃ25). Elsewhere, he speaks of movements in the patient as being proportionate to the agent (*De Mem.* 2, 452ᵇ12), when there are in the patient shapes and movements similar (*homoia*) in some way to things outside. He also claims that in the case of perception there is something in the patient proportionate to the form of the sensible object (452ᵇ16 f.), but does not develop an account of what the type of proportionality is, or of whether the *relata* are psychological or physiological phenomena. The most that can safely be extracted from these passages is the claim that the quality of the relevant perceptual faculty is determined by the external object in the manner, whatever it is, which is appropriate for that faculty.[10] This measure of qualitative similarity between agent and patient does not commit Aristotle to any particular account of its nature (e.g. in exclusively representational or physiological terms).

Thus far, we have considered only the successful interactions in which (e.g.) the teacher actually teaches the student. This approach corresponds to Aristotle's general practice of defining capacities in terms of how they are actualized in optimal conditions: what a thing can do is defined by what it achieves when it is operating at its most successful. For example, one's

---

[10] There can, of course, be similarity relations between internal states produced in this way. Thus, for example, someone may remember a name somewhat like (*paromoia*) the one they seek (*De Mem.* 2, 452ᵇ5–7), or when asleep one's images may resemble people when they are only like them (*De Insom.* 3, 461ᵇ19 f., 23–6). In these cases, there is similarity between two objects without the causal interaction between them which generates 'liken-ness'.

capacity to lift weights is defined by the maximum one can lift and one's capacity to see is defined by the smallest object one can see (as in eye testing) (cf. *De Caelo* A.11, 281ª15–26). There can be other cases of lifting or seeing, which are incomplete or unsuccessful in certain ways.[11]

So far, I have discussed those aspects of Aristotle's account of perception which fall under claims (a), (c), and (d) in the previous Section. These three components, taken together, yield the following picture:

(i) What makes a perception the one it is is the *form* which is cognitively discriminated.

and

(ii) What makes that discrimination the one it is is what causally produces it (in optimal conditions) in the favoured way.

It is important to take both these elements together in this manner. If one focuses exclusively on (i), one is left with no resources to account for what makes the discrimination the one it is. If one focuses only on (ii), one might overlook the fact that it is the presence of these causal processes that *constitutively* determines what is discriminated.

One aspect of this account resembles Brentano's famous claim that Aristotle's notion of 'taking on the Form without the matter' essentially involves the perceiver perceptually discriminating (and, thus, being aware of) an object. However, my conclusion is based on considerations derived from the role of discrimination as defined by (a), (c), and (d), which are fundamentally distinct from Brentano's. In particular, they do not rest on construing 'taking on the Form without the matter' as being confined to awareness of an object.[12] For all that has been said, it may also essentially involve, in the case of perception, a change in the eye jelly as well as awareness of an object. The presence of a physiological process is in no way excluded merely by reference to discrimination of an object. Indeed, in my view, careful consideration of the analogy suggests that some physiological process is essentially involved in perceiving, although this is not so in the analogous case of thinking.[13] (Nor should this difference surprise us, since the two cases are related by analogy and need not be the same in all relevant respects.) Although detailed consideration of these issues would take us far away from our present concerns, it is important to note that

---

[11] In discussing processes in *Phys.* Γ.1–3, Aristotle introduces goal-directedness with capacities for change, and not with individual changes (cf. 202ª21–6, 201ª10 ff.). This allows that individual processes may be incomplete or inadvertent in failing to reach a goal of the type at which the capacity is directed. On this, see my *Aristotle's Philosophy of Action*, 24–5.

[12] As Brentano claimed when he interpreted (e.g.) 'taking on the Form without the matter' in terms of 'psychical indwelling' or 'mental inexistence' (*Psychology from an Empirical Standpoint* trans. C. Rancurello, D. B. Terrel, and L. McAlister (London, 1973), 125 n. See also his *Psychology of Aristotle*, trans. R. George (Berkeley, 1977).)

[13] On this issue, see Sect. 5.5 below.

acceptance of one aspect of Brentano's claim does not commit one to any radical anti-materialist conclusions.

5.4 PERCEPTION AND ERROR: CLAIM (iii)*

My interpretation of Aristotle's treatment of perception further differs from Brentano's in several ways. Most importantly, I have argued that Aristotle offered the basis of a solution to Brentano's famous problem: What makes this perceiving a perceiving of A? Aristotle's answer (in my view) rests on the role he gives to the causal conditions which in optimal conditions produce the perceiving and determine the identity of the intentional state. Brentano thought that Aristotle had failed to answer this question. This was because he took elements (b) and (d), rather than (a), as the central ingredients in Aristotle's account. Thus, by my lights, he failed to see the significance for his problem of the causal resources which Aristotle deployed.[14]

Brentano was drawn to his interpretation because he thought that Aristotle's account of 'taking on the Form without the matter' should apply (in precisely the same way) to veridical and non-veridical cases of perception. If one can be visually affected by 'what is not' (as in cases of illusion or hallucination), there can be no type of efficient causal interaction which is essential for either illusory or veridical perception.[15] From this Brentano concluded that likening could not be an essential constituent in his account of perception (or thought).

But did Aristotle consider that in a case of perceptual illusion of A the perceiver receives the form of A without its matter? Is there any element of likening to determine the relevant content in the case of illusion? Generally, can Aristotle account for cases of perceptual error within the general framework so far developed?

I shall begin with the latter, more general, question. Aristotle remarks cautiously in *De Anima* that 'perception [*aisthēsis*] of proper objects is true, or only capable of error to the least possible degree' (Γ.3, 428^{b}18f.). In *De Insomniis* he gives examples of error regarding the proper sensibles when he writes:

If we look for a long time at one colour—e.g. white or green—any object to which we shift our gaze appears to be of that colour. (*De Insom.* 2, 459^{b}11–13)

[14] For a clear statement of Brentano's problem, see H. Field 'Mental Representation', *Erkenntnis* 13 (1978) 9–61.

[15] This is a consequence of Brentano's fundamental move in understanding Aristotle: to interpret 'taking on the Form without the matter' in terms of the scholastic notion of 'objective', the immanent object of perception or thought (*Psychology from an Empirical Standpoint*, 210 n. 6, 229 n. 23).

In this chapter, Aristotle also gives examples of perceptual illusion involving common sensibles (e.g. movement, being one). Thus, he writes:

The same persistence of vision occurs when we turn from moving objects—e.g. fast flowing rivers; for then objects really at rest appear to be moving. (459^b18–20)

Elsewhere, he gives a further example:

So, when the fingers are meshed one object looks (or appears) to be two. (460^b20 f.)

Aristotle's discussion of these cases is rich and intricate. He envisages cases where 'not only will one thing look or appear to be two, but the perceiver will also *think* that it is two' (460^b22–3). He contrasts these cases with examples in which one object will look to be two, but the person will not think that this is so. So there are two types of (e.g.) visually based error:

Stage 1: One object *looks* to be two.

The sun/moon *looks* to be a foot across.

Stage 2: One object *seems* to be two.

The sun/moon is *taken to be* a foot across.

Let us focus on Stage 1. At the end of *de Insomniis* 2, Aristotle concludes:

The cause of the deception (Stage 1) is that things look to us as they do not only when the object of sense moves the sense organ, but also when the sense is moved by itself, provided that it is stimulated in the same way as by the object of sense (460^b23–5).

The idea seems to be this: for men in fever, marks on the wall look to be (e.g.) *animals* because the marks stimulate their sense organs in the same way as they would be stimulated by animals of that kind. The marks on the wall may only bear a slight resemblance to these animals. But the fever does the rest by bringing it about that the sense is stimulated by them in just the way it would be if there were animals there (and everything was functioning properly).

But why then do the marks on the wall look to us (in fever) to be animals? On one view, this would be impossible. If the content of the appearance-state was determined in every instance by its actual cause, what would appear to the men in fever would be the actual cause (i.e. the marks on the wall). For, these are the actual cause of their 'looking-state'. But if these lines look to be animals, what determines the content of the illusion cannot be its actual cause.

In the cases described of veridical perception and illusion, the movements in the sense organ are of the same general type. The lines look to the men in fever to be animals, because their sense organs are stimulated in the way in which they would be stimulated if they were functioning well and they were seeing an animal. Aristotle does not say whether the relevant movements in the sense organ are to be understood as occurring at the phenomenal or the physiological level (see, for the latter, *De Insom.* 3, 461ᵃ4 ff.). As interpreters we can remain neutral on these issues since in this context they are not Aristotle's central concern. It is enough for his purposes if (a) the relevant movements are typed by what occurs when all is functioning well, and (b) there are movements of this type when illusion occurs. He need go no further than this in the present context.[16] (In particular, he does not need to claim that there is a common 'narrow-content' representational state present in cases of perception and illusion.[17])

Aristotle adds a second point in discussing these cases:

perceptions persist even after the external perceptible object has gone (*De Insom.* 2, 460ᵇ2–4),

and

stimuli arise from perceptions ... in cases which have their origin in the body. (460ᵇ30)

This suggests a further condition which applies at least in some cases: The lines look to be animals/Kleon provided that (i) the sense organ is stimulated in the way it would be if an animal/Kleon was actually there and all was functioning well, and (ii) it is so stimulated in part because it has been stimulated by an animal/Kleon in the past (when all functioned well). It is not sufficient for the lines to look to be Kleon that one is in the state one would be in if one saw Kleon when the perceptual faculty was functioning as it should be. One might equally be in a state of that type when one saw Kleon's twin brother. One must also be in that state (in part) because of one's past (successful) seeings of Kleon.[18] Indeed, this is what makes the illusion an illusion of Kleon and not of his twin brother.

[16] This structure can apply both to misperceiving what is white as green, and to errors in further states which are not directly perceptual but are the result of movements set up by perception. Thus, Aristotle distinguishes (in *De An.* Γ.3, 428ᵇ18–20 and 25–8) between false perception and false imagination produced by perception. Aristotle in this context appears to separate cases of seeing and mis-seeing A, which involve immediate processes in the perceptual faculty, and imagining A when the object is not present to the perceiver in the same direct way. The latter correspond to his official account of *phantasia*; but he uses *phainetai* in describing both cases.

[17] I leave it open (at this stage) whether Aristotle insisted on there being one common representational state of the relevant kind. Victor Caston has argued that he was committed to this view, in 'Why Aristotle Needs Imagination' (*Phronesis* 41/1 (1996) 20 ff.) and 'Aristotle and the Problem of Intentionality' (*Philosophy and Phenomenological Research*, 58/2 (1998), 249 ff.). The issues are complex and require detailed analysis.

[18] The second condition is important in cases of twins or lookalikes. What makes it the case that I imagine (or see) Cicero coming towards me, and not his twin brother (whom I have not met), is that it is my seeing Cicero, and not his twin, in the past that is causally responsible for my present state. This would remain the case even if I had met both of them, provided that it was my seeing Cicero, and not his twin, that was causally responsible for my present perceptual state. This condition is relevant to the issues Caston discusses in 'Aristotle and the Problem of Intentionality', 287 ff.

When is the organ functioning as it should? Is it failing to do so when the sun looks to be a foot across? Is not this just how the sun should look from this distance? Aristotle seems to reason as follows in this case: The sense organs can only be functioning properly when objects look to be the size they actually are.[19] Thus, when the sun looks to be a foot across, the sense organ cannot be functioning as it should because the object in question is not the size it appears to be. Conversely, it is functioning well with regard to nearby objects which are a foot across (e.g. feet); for, it presents them as being the size they actually are.[20]

However, the notion of accurate information is not, by itself, sufficient to capture Aristotle's account of the proper functioning of sense organs. If this was all that was involved, a perceiver could equally well see (when their sense organs function properly) red or a given mixture of white and black light (as in Aristotle's account of derived colours in *De Sensu* 3, 439^{b}19ff.). But proper perception is of red or of green, and not of some appropriate mix of basic colours. Why is this so? Aristotle adds a further feature to his account of proper functioning which accommodates this difficulty. In (e.g.) visual perception, the nature of the sense organ involves transparent water in the eye jelly (*De An.* Γ.1, 425^{a}4 ff.), since it is this which the relevant colour affects (*De An.* B.7, 418^{a}29-^{b}1). The proper objects of perception are constrained in part by the physiological substratum involved in the relevant capacity; for, this limits the content of the relevant discrimination (in some way) to one which concerns red rather than a theory-based mix of basic colours, since the latter cannot arise from this physical change in the transparent alone. Aristotle is concerned to

---

[19] This teleological account explains primarily why animal sense organs function as they do in general, and only derivatively (if at all) why on occasion we humans make the specific and distinctive discriminations that we do (e.g. between blue and green). At the level of perception an animal (e.g. a frog) would see yellow moving objects (as such) rather than (e.g.) flies or sources of carbohydrate, even though it needs to eat flies or sources of carbohydrate to survive. Survival needs determine that we have the type of sense organs we do (in Aristotle's account), but do not make it the case that specific animals perceptively discriminate those objects which they need for survival as such (e.g. as potatoes, rather than as small, brown, round objects). Indeed, if the frog can survive in its actual situation by discriminating black, buzzing objects, why attribute to it discrimination of flies? This is one of the points at which Aristotle's account differs from the version of teleological theory proposed by Ruth Millikan (*Language, Thought and Other Biological Categories* (Cambridge, Mass., 1984)). In her view, because the frog needs to eat flies to survive, the frog's visual system discriminates flies (as such), rather than (e.g.) black buzzing dots. In this respect, Aristotle's view of the physiology involved constrains the content of perception more rigorously than Millikan's does but at the same time allows for cross-species perceptions of the same objects.

[20] This account accommodates several of Aristotle's examples in these chapters. Thus, one finger may appear to be two as the sense organ is stimulated in the way in which it would be stimulated (when the sense organ is functioning properly) by two objects. Further, in such a case, the past experience of correct functioning may be alive, and causally active, in the present awareness. A similar account will apply to Aristotle's examples of objects at rest appearing to move (459^{b}19–21), and of mistakes in colour perception.

emphasize the constraining role of the basic physical elements in his account of the proper objects of perception (*De An.* Γ.1, 425ᵃ8 ff.):

So we are left to suppose that there is no sense organ apart from water and air.

The key notion to successful functioning (in Aristotle's account) is the registering of accurate information by senses designed to be responsive to the medium in which animals move.[21,22]

For the reasons given above, Aristotle's account of perception is not a simple, efficient, causal one. Since it essentially involves some teleological elements, it allows him to classify perceptual experiences in terms of their causes *when* (in the ways explained) *all is functioning well*. In this way, one can misperceive red objects as green, when one receives the form of green without its matter in cases of perceptual illusion. Thus, the causal element can (*pace* Brentano) remain constitutive of perceptual content, even in cases of misperception or illusion. On this view, Aristotle can (as Brentano insisted) allow that in cases of illusion the perceiver receives the form without the matter, but still take the likening element to be constitutive of the relevant content. For, the states are individuated by what produces the relevant effect if all is functioning well.

It will be objected that Aristotle on occasion appears to rule out the possibility of error concerning the special sensibles. Thus, Aristotle claims:

(1) with proper objects, error is impossible (*De An.* B.6, 418ᵃ12–14),

and that:

(2) sight cannot be deceived be as to the fact of colour, but (e.g.) as to what the coloured object is and where it is.

---

[21] Aristotle speaks of perception as common to all animals (*De An.* Γ.3, 427ᵇ8), and treats it across species (e.g. in *De An.* Γ.13, 435ᵇ18–21) for all animals that share the same medium. Hence, what perception discriminates (e.g. moving, black dots) will be the same (in this account) for frogs (who want to eat them), flies (who want to mate with them), and humans (who, e.g., want to drive them out of the kitchen). In this respect, different 'consumer' needs in different animals do not distinguish different objects of perception. At this point also Aristotle's account differs sharply from Ruth Millikan's with regard to the content of perception.

[22] Aristotle adds to his basic account a teleological explanation of why we have sense organs of the type we do. We have vision as animals which need to move to survive, since it allows us to see objects at a distance (Γ.12, 434ᵇ26–8). But this requires us to see objects through a medium, which is transparent, since we live in air or water (Γ.12, 434ᵇ28–30, Γ.13, 435ᵇ21–4). This teleological role explains why we have sense organs which register effects in the transparent and nothing more; for, our basic sense organs are designed to register these changes (and nothing else). This is why our sense organs are functioning correctly when we visually discriminate red rather than a given spectral mix of colours: for, they were not built to be responsive to the latter type of theoretical ratio. In this case we discriminate red as red. When we make accurate discriminations with our sense organs, we are naturally well placed to survive and flourish.

Elsewhere he goes further.[23] Thus, in *De An.* Γ.7 he writes:

(3) seeing with respect of a proper object is true, but whether the pale object is a man or not is not always true. (430ᵇ29–30)

For, this seems to require (a) that the proper object be a specific colour and (b) that *seeing* with regard to it always be true.[24] Nor is 430ᵇ30 ff. a solitary example. Even in *De Anima* Γ.3 Aristotle writes:

(4) perception of proper sensibles is always true. (427ᵇ13 f.)

The objection runs as follows: If Aristotle rules out error with regard to special perception, he cannot have adhered to the theory outlined above. For, that allows for the possibility of error in the case of special perception.

This objection can be resisted. First, even if Aristotle had accepted that special perception was unerring, this could be because he held (as a further thesis) that conditions for special perception were always optimal (or, at least, good enough to avoid error). However, it is fairly clear that the four bits of evidence cited do not establish that Aristotle held this view.

Passage (4) is introductory, and is qualified by the more cautious formulation offered later in the same chapter (428ᵇ18 f.). There, Aristotle notes that error is not possible when 'the sensation is present' (428ᵇ27–9), but does not specify in detail what that involves, although it must include the sensed object being present (428ᵇ29 f.). If so, we can plausibly extrapolate the following view:

(P) If the sensed object is present, and this controls the nature of the sensation, no error is possible with regard to a special sensible.

---

[23] It should be noted that (1) and (2) claim only that vision is always correct with regard to colour (as Aristotle notes in 418ᵃ14 (see also *De Sensu* 4, 442ᵇ8)). This need mean no more than that there can be no mistake about the fact that the visual faculty grasps some colour. If so, Aristotle's claim of inerrancy need come to no more than this:

The visual system cannot be mistaken as to whether there is some colour which it discriminates (since it can only operate if some colour affects it).

This claim does not require that the visual system is infallible about which colour it discriminates, as it allows that it may be mistaken about which colour is before it, and thus take a pale object as green (see Γ.3, 428ᵇ21).

[24] (b) is required to mark the contrast with the case of complex seeing which can on occasion be false. (a) might be challenged as follows: 'Why not take "a proper object" to mean (e.g.) colour, and not some specific colour (in line with the interpretation offered of 418ᵃ12–14 above)?' The reply is twofold: first, if this was what was intended, the reference to 'pale' would be misleading in 430ᵇ30, since there could (it might appear) be error about the pale even in a non-complex judgement. (If Aristotle does not compare seeing the pale with seeing that the pale is a man, he is not comparing like with like.) Second, in this context, the analogy drawn is that between seeing and thinking of a specific definition or the essence of a particular object (430ᵇ26–8, ᵇ15–17). If so, the former must also be seeing a specific object.

If (P) is Aristotle's claim, he can assert (without inconsistency) in the same passage (428^b18–28) that error is possible with regard to special sensibles, and that a special sense, in the presence of its object, etc., is always correct.

In these ways Aristotle can allow for a limited form of inerrancy in special perception within the framework of a general account of perception which is built on efficient and teleological elements. When the special senses are functioning well, we receive accurate information registered by senses of a type designed to work well in the medium in which we live. There may indeed be perceptual errors whose content is determined by the likening materials outlined above. Thus, *pace* Brentano, the likening account can be constitutive of the content of perceptual states, where perceptual form is received without matter.

5.5 PERCEPTION OF COMMON SENSIBLES: THE CAUSAL MODEL EXTENDED

Aristotle treats both proper and common sensibles in *De Anima* B.5 as cases of *per se* causes of perception, and distinguishes these from accidental perception where 'the percipient is not acted on as such by the thing perceived' (418^a23 f.). Although proper perception of individual sensibles is the basic case of perception,[25] common perception also involves *per se* objects of perception (418^a24 f.). How can this be? I shall argue that it is Aristotle's adherence to the causal assimilation model (as set out in Section 5.3) that explains this aspect of his treatment of the common sensibles. His use of this model (I shall suggest) shows his interest in issues of content determination.

The model of causal likening can be extended from proper perception (e.g. of colours) to perception of common sensibles (number, rest, movement, shape, size (Γ.1, 425^a15–17)). Indeed, this model explains how a perceiver can arrive at cross-modal discriminations of the form:

one red and heavy object,

---

[25] Why is proper perception the basic case? Aristotle writes that this is so because 'those *per se* perceptibles which are special to each sense are most strictly perceptible in that it is to these that the special nature of the several senses is directed' (418^a25–6). His thought appears to be that the distinctive nature of each sense is directed towards its special sensibles, while, since there is no distinctive sense targetted at common sensibles, the senses, with their own distinctive essences, have to work together (cf. *De An.* Γ.1, 425^a31–2). Thus understood, common sensibles are only perceived by an individual sense when it works together with other senses. This perception is secondary (according to Aristotle) because one needs to understand the individual senses with their distinctive essences before one can understand how such senses cooperate in recognizing where special sensibles co-occur (425^a22–4).

where *one object* is immediately grasped as such in perception. For, in such a case the relevant perceptual discrimination will be of one object provided that it is brought about, in favourable conditions, by one object. Similarly, perception would be of this one yellow, bitter object (425ᵇ1–3) provided that it was brought about, in appropriate conditions, by this one object. Causal assimilation to one cross-modal moving object explains why perception is of one such object rather than of (e.g.) one visual object and one tactile object (in which case further inference would be required to reach the discrimination of one cross-modal object). What is common to special and common perception is that both involve the *per se* efficient causal impact of objective features on the discriminator, as captured by the causal likening model. Accidental perception, by contrast, does not involve this type of causal likening.

Aristotle's discussion of common sensibles in *De Anima* Γ.1 suggests that he is thinking of them in the way suggested by the causal model. He argues that there can be no special sense for common sensibles from the following premises (425ª16–24):

P(1) We perceive all the common sensibles (movement, rest, shape, size, number, oneness) 'by movement' (425ª17–18),

P(2) We can perceive these (or at least number) by the special senses (425ª19f.); for, each sense perceives one object.[26]

From these premises Aristotle concludes that there can be no special sense for, common sensibles; for, if there were we would perceive them as we now perceive what is sweet by sight. The latter occurs when we perceive both (e.g. the pale, the sweet) separately and—as a further step—cognize that they co-occur (425ª22–7).[27] We have no access via sight to the sweetness of the object, but rather conjoin two perceptual experiences and infer that, since the pale is sweet, we see the sweet. By contrast, in the case of common sensibles no further inferential step of this type is required. We

---

[26] Each of the five senses senses a unity: one colour, one sound, etc. An instantaneous single act of perception implies one object (*De Sensu* 7, 447ᵇ21 ff.), the type of oneness mentioned in 425ª17.

[27] Error is more common with regard to common sensibles than special sensibles because, in the former case, there are additional sources of error over and above what is involved in discriminating (e.g.) white. In particular, the judgement about *which* object is white allows for misidentification of two qualitatively similar particulars. Thus, there is a type of error present in the second case that is absent from the first. Aristotle further separates this type of misidentification from errors concerning other common sensibles, such as size and movement, which belong to (but do not constitute the identity of) the substances to which the proper sensibles belong (Γ.3, 428ᵇ27 ff.). In the latter cases Aristotle says that error is even more frequent, presumably because there is a still greater variety of possible sources of mistake (over and above misidentification of the individual involved).

can have direct access to one white object P(2), since its oneness impacts on the special senses.[28]

If this is correct, the common sensibles will causally impact on the senses in a manner somewhat similar to that achieved by the special sensibles. But common sensibles themselves differ from special sensibles in that their causal impact is not unique to one sense, but can be shared by several. This is why Aristotle includes among common sensibles one object, and not one (e.g.) visually perceived object.[29] Thus, the senses can operate together in immediately perceiving one bitter and yellow object (Γ.1, 425ᵃ31 ff.), without any inferential step (beyond what is given in perception) identifying the visual with the tasted object.[30] In the case of any individual sense organ, common and special sensibles are *per se* causes of its processes or quality changes. Since the former category includes

---

[28] This account (with its emphasis on causal impact) gives a role to 'by movement' which separates the case of the common sensibles perceived from those where 'we perceive what is sweet by sight' (425ᵃ22–3), and, thus, provides an answer to those who thought (like R. D. Hicks, *Aristotle: de Anima* (Cambridge, 1907), 428) that it had no role (thus understood). Hicks's alternative suggestion is to construe 'by movement' to mean 'our perception of all other common sensibles depends on our perception of movement'. But this is wholly perplexing: magnitudes and shapes may be perceived equally whether or not they are moving; number and unity are recognized by (e.g.) break in continuity, and Aristotle makes no attempt to show how our perception of continuity rests on our perception of movement. In *Phys.* Δ.11, 219ᵃ12 ff., magnitude, time, and movement are all instances of the continuous. Had this been the basis of Aristotle's thought, he should have claimed that we perceive movement and magnitude by the continuous, and not continuity by movement.

[29] That the object seen is cross-modal (open to several sensory modalities) is highly significant in Aristotle's account. Had the effect of one or three moving red objects on the visual system (in his theory) been that (e.g.) the eye jelly was reddened in a distinctive way for one or three moving objects, he would have had to show (a) that what was seen was one moving object rather than one visually appearing (modality-specific) quasi-object, (b) that this effect on vision paralleled in some undisclosed physiological way a comparable effect on the senses of touch and hearing, and (c) that the perceiver could grasp 'straight off' (without inference or reflection) that these effects were effects of the same object. That Aristotle makes no attempt to discharge these obligations suggests that he is not understanding perception of common sensibles on precisely the same model as perception of white, etc. Rather, in both, taking on the form involves discrimination of one, white, object.

[30] This formulation is intended to be neutral as regards the question of whether there could be (satisfactory) perception of common sensibles if we had only one sense (e.g. vision). In fact, Aristotle suggests that in such a case we would be less aware of the common sensibles (such as size) and all sensibles would seem to be of the same type (i.e. visibles), since we would never encounter a case of an object which had size but no colour (Γ.1, 425ᵇ6–9). This is presumably because in such a case we would lack our perception of size and merely perceive coloured-sizes. Similarly, we would not perceive one object but one coloured-object, and, thus, lack the perceptions we currently enjoy of one object (which we may or may not experience as coloured). As it is, we perceive each of the common sensibles (one, moving, three-dimensional object) as distinct from coloured-one, coloured-size, coloured-shape, etc. Thus, it appears that (in Aristotle's view) for us to have satisfactory perception of common sensibles it is essential that we have several distinct senses which operate together. When individual senses perceive one object, they do so only as a part of a unified sense faculty.

shape and size, the objects grasped by the senses in this direct way at the outset are three-dimensional objects with their own weight and volume. In Aristotle's account, perceivers do not begin with (e.g.) purely visual, two and a half-dimensional objects without full spatial size or weight, and then construct three-dimensional spatial objects out of these more elementary beginnings. Rather, they are immediately given cross-modal, three-dimensional objects typically grasped by the senses working in co-operation.[31]

It will be objected that the cases of common and special perception are more radically distinct than has so far been allowed. Perception of common sensibles appears not to involve any physiological process (e.g. the eye jelly reddening) of the type found in the case of special sensibles. Indeed, it might appear that there could be no one physiological process of this distinctive type since the impact of common sensibles is shared by distinct sense faculties. If so, some will conclude that the causal assimilation cannot apply to the case of common perception.

This objection is correct in one important respect. Aristotle does not spell out the type of quality change which results from common sensibles, or the route by which it is brought about. However, he makes it clear that he thinks that in this case what occurs must essentially involve receiving the relevant form (without the matter) of the one moving object perceived. For, when he talks of perceptually receiving the form of a stone (Γ.8, 431^{b}19), he must be referring to a quality change but not one of the type involved in 'being-reddened' or 'being-hardened' by external objects. So, he has to extend the notion of perceptually receiving the form, itself a quality change, beyond the range of the special sensibles. Indeed, this is required if he is to apply his favoured formula of taking on 'the Form without the matter' to the perception of particulars (as he wishes to do (see B.5, 417^{b}22 ff.)).

Consideration of the case of common sensibles shows the range of the causal-likening model. It need not be confined to the type of physiologically based account offered for special perception.[32] Indeed, it can be applied even in cases where no physiological account of this type is offered. In the case of perception of common sensibles, several sense organs can

[31] This point is of major importance in understanding the distinctive nature of Aristotle's epistemological starting point. Unlike (e.g.) Kant, for whom the starting point is 'inner sense' with its not fully spatial (two and a half-dimensional) objects, Aristotle begins with fully spatial (three-dimensional) objects at the outset. Hence, his project is not to 'construct' fully spatial objects from those in inner sense, or to argue that inner sense presupposes three-dimensional external objects. His starting point is a radically non-Cartesian awareness of three-dimensional fully spatial objects.

[32] For a contrasting view, see Stephen Everson's discussion of these issues in *Aristotle on Perception* (Oxford, 1997), 148–57. It is difficult to see how Everson can explain the fact that Aristotle's visual perceiver sees a square object (which is red) rather than a square-red object.

together receive the relevant form of one moving object, when they discriminate one such object (in favoured cases) under the causal influence
of one continuous moving object.[33] The goal of the senses operating in
unison is knowledge of the movement, size, and number of the fully spatial
objects we encounter (Γ.1, 425^b4 f.). When all is functioning well, we will
discriminate one moving object *as* one moving object.[34]

What is common to the account of special and common perception is
the use of the idea of causal likening to explain our discrimination of their
respective objects. In this way, we can perceptually discriminate one
moving object in a way which parallels that in which we perceptually discriminate white or red. But this point of similarity allows for considerable
differences between the ways in which the likening occurs. While both may
involve physiological changes in the subject, the point of similarity does
not consist in there being physiological changes of the same type. The type
of changes may vary considerably, provided that, in both, the subject discriminates the relevant objects in an appropriate way. It appears to be this
latter feature that makes both cases ones where one 'takes on the Form
without the matter'. If so, the discussion of common sensibles supports the

[33] Aristotle, in his discussion of common sensibles, regards them as *per se* causes of
perception along with special sensibles, in contrast with accidental sensibles. Hence, he
must have believed that they, unlike accidental sensibles, make a distinctive (efficient)
causal impact on the perceptual faculty. If so, the perceptual faculty has to be such as to be
responsive both to colour and sound (each via an individual faculty) and to one, shaped,
moving, object (as an integrated sense faculty). (See n. 30.) Thus, there must be a distinctive
impact of one such object on the integrated sense faculty, which cannot be fully understood
in terms of its impact via any one medium (e.g. light) on any one sense (e.g. vision). The
impact rather is one which can only be understood in terms of the interconnected activities
of the distinct faculties working in unison. Aristotle does not attempt to articulate in what
this integrated perceptual process (*kinesis* (Γ.1, 425^a17)) consists. His claim is only that the
perceptual faculty as a whole is responsive to the impact of the oneness, size, or motion of
an object, but not to accidental sensibles (e.g. being the son of Kleon), presumably because
it is not designed to be causally affected directly (as a perceptual system) by facts about
parentage.

[34] In this case, we will discriminate the object of our perception *as* an external object
because we take what appears to us *as* of something else. Aristotle compares this with seeing
a picture as a portrait of someone (*De Mem.* 1, 450^b30 f.), and distinguishes it from seeing a
picture in its own right (and not as a portrait of someone). In both cases, the picture would
be a picture of Koriskos, provided that it is caused in the right way. But what would make
it true that we saw it *as* a portrait of Koriskos is that we viewed it successfully with the goal
of finding out about real, three-dimensional objects in the external world (and, thus, were
interested in (e.g.) the causal history of the picture, etc.). If it is not seen as a portrait, what
fixes what is seen is the causal history of the picture (who it is of). When it is seen *as* a portrait, we need to add our interest in finding out about the external world (via the painting)
to the basic causal story. Since, for Aristotle, both these cases are examples of imagination,
it cannot be correct to view imagination as a general faculty of seeing as (as Martha Nussbaum suggested in her essay on 'The Role of *Phantasia* in Aristotle's Explanations of
Action', in *Aristotle's de Motu Animalium* (Princeton, 1978), 221–69). For, only the second
case involves seeing the picture as a portrait, while the first does not. Further, recognition
of proper and common sensibles involves 'seeing as' but no imagination.

line of interpretation of 'taking on the Form without the matter' given above (Section 5.3 *ad fin.*).

5.6 THE ANALOGY APPLIED: THOUGHT

According to the interpretation developed above, a perceiver (in Aristotle's account) correctly visually discriminates A as A provided her perceptual faculty is (efficiently) causally affected by A via the appropriate medium (light), and her faculty is functioning as it should to receive accurate information from that medium. If his account of thought (Γ.4, 429^a13-17) is analogous, a thinker will (in his account) correctly *noetically* discriminate A as A provided that her noetic faculty is (efficiently) causally affected by A via the appropriate medium, and her noetic faculty is functioning as it should to receive accurate information from that medium. What makes my thought a thought of Kleon, or of water, or of the essence of water (if these are all objects of thought) is that I am in the state I would be in when these objects causally affect (via the appropriate medium) my thinking faculty and it is functioning as it should. My thought would be a thought of Kleon (and not his twin brother) or water (and not a water lookalike), provided that it is Kleon and water (and not their close relatives) which causally affect my thinking faculty in the appropriate way.

In *De Anima* Γ.4–6 and 8, Aristotle (I shall argue) attempts to implement this strategy and to make it more determinate and defensible. His discussion raises several major issues:

(a) In Γ.5 Aristotle speaks of intellect (*nous*), and not of the objects of thought, as the efficient cause of thoughts in the passive intellect. Intellect is described as like skill (430^a12) and as the maker of everything (430^a15). But in Γ.4, the efficient cause is the object of thought. How are these claims consistent?

(b) In the case of perception, the perceptual faculty receives information from its medium (e.g. light) and its nature is designed to fulfil this role. In the case of thought, the role of light is played by the active mind (430^a15). But what does this mean? In what ways, if any, are our thoughts constrained by the nature of the active intellect? Aristotle addresses these topics in some detail in Γ.5 (430^a14-17) and Γ.4 (429^a18-^b6).

(c) In perception, the perceptual faculty functions well when it accurately registers information transferred by its medium. What counts as success for the thinking faculty? And how can it err, if it does err? Aristotle addresses these issues also in Γ.3 and Γ.5.

(d) In perception, Aristotle took proper and common sensibles to be *per se* causes of perception. What range of objects is thinkable, and can they all be accommodated within one uniform account of thinking? In Γ.4 and Γ.5 Aristotle focuses on thoughts of universals (water, flesh, straight line, straightness), and does not discuss thoughts of particulars. I shall follow his example.[35] In Γ.6 he distinguishes between simple thoughts and complex ones in ways which parallel his discussion of proper sensibles.

To consider these issues in this way is to follow the route suggested by Aristotle's analogy between perception and thought. His discussion raises many issues, pertaining to topics as diverse as theology and materialism, which lie outside our immediate area of concern. I shall attempt to focus (as far as is possible) solely on the issue of the content of thought: what makes a thought the thought it is.

5.7 THE ROLE OF THE ACTIVE INTELLECT

The active intellect, as introduced in Γ.5, has two separable roles.

(1) It is the efficient cause of passive thoughts, which (like skill) makes passive thoughts what they are. Here, the active intellect takes over the role of the objects of thought as efficient causes of thought.

(2) It is regarded as an analogue of light, the medium in the case of perception. Thus, Aristotle writes:

There is one kind of intellect, which is such as to become all things. And there is intellect of another kind, such as to make all things. This is a type of positive state like light; for, in a way light makes potential colours actual. (430ᵃ14–17)

What are these roles? Are they consistent? It appears that in (1) the intellect is compared with the objects perceived, but in (2) it is compared not with the objects but with the medium (between those objects and the perceiver). How can one thing be compared with both? For, the objects perceived and the light in which they are active are distinct.

Let us take each claim separately. (1) encourages the following line of thought: the reason why Aristotle can substitute the active intellect and

---

[35] Elsewhere Aristotle allows for thought of individuals, such as Kleon (*De An.* Γ.6 430ᵇ5–6), and knowledge of particulars (B.5, 417ᵇ26–8). These cases seem relatively unproblematic given the analogy with perception: what makes my thought a thought of Kleon is that Kleon causally affects my thinking faculty in the appropriate way. And this will be so if it gives me relevant knowledge of individuals in (e.g.) knowledge of who that person is. (Aristotle, however, does not specify the goal of the thinking faculty with regard to individuals in these passages, and so offers no suggestions as to what 'knowing who' involves.)

objects of thought in this way is that they are strictly identical.[36] Indeed, Aristotle says as much:

> The knowing activity (sc. of the active intellect) is identical with its object. (Γ.5, 430ᵃ19 f.)

The active intellect just is identical with the set of its objects, the organized and intelligible world. From this perspective, Aristotle's introduction of the active intellect as the efficient cause (like skill) of the operation of the passive mind becomes readily comprehensible (430ᵃ11–15).[37] For, since it is (when fully active) identical with its objects, both it and its objects can equally be described as the cause of the passive mind's operation. So, while one might have expected Aristotle to speak of the objects of thought as the efficient cause of passive thought (on the basis of the analogy with perception) he can substitute active intellect for objects of thought in this role without inconsistency.

How is the identity of the active intellect and the objects of thought to be interpreted? What is the significance of the analogy between the active intellect and light in its role in colour perception? This analogy, central to Aristotle's discussion of *De Anima*, must be considered in some detail.

For Aristotle, light is the activity of the transparent as such (418ᵇ10, 419ᵃ10). It is an aspect of the essence of colour (in *De Anima*) to produce change in the actually transparent (419ᵃ10–12), a change of a given kind in the quality of the light. While the eye itself contains transparent elements, colour is not defined in *De Anima* B.7 by reference to the perceiver, but rather in terms of an ability to produce change in the transparent. Light makes potential colours such as green actual by itself (as the positive state of the transparent) being active in a given way (a way distinct from that in which it is active when black or red, etc.). When light is active in this way and impacts on S's perceptual faculty, which is functioning as it should, S perceives green.[38]

In *De Anima* B.7, the picture looks like this:

ability of the object to change the transparent	change in the transparent when active ('the activity of colour')	perception

---

[36] I am indebted to Michael Frede for many discussions of issues concerning the active intellect. Through these I came to see that the (strong) identity of active intellect and the object of thought (which Frede advocates in 'La theorie aristotelicienne de l'intellect agent', in Dherbey (ed.), *Corps et Ame*, 377–90) is 'of a piece' both with Aristotle's colour analogy and with his *Analytics*-based co-determination thesis (as I understood them). For detailed discussion of the latter, see 10.5 below.

[37] Skill is taken as a paradigm case of an efficient cause in *Phys.* B.3, 195ᵇ23–5.

[38] Light itself is not a quality change (*alloiōsis*), but a state (*hexis*). Yet it is a state which can be affected in given ways by given objects, as (e.g.) virtue is a state which is well disposed to proper objects (H.3, 246ᵃ10–12, 246ᵇ18–20).

Aristotle says little about the nature of the activity of colour in *De Anima*, and nothing further about the nature of the relevant ability.[39] The discussion in *De Anima* is (at least) consistent with the view that an object is able to move the transparent because of a mixture of basic colours at its periphery. Elsewhere he notes that the activity of colour fills the medium between the object and the eye, and does so instantaneously (*De Sensu* 447^{a}9–11). It is this changed state of the transparent which affects the eye in a distinctive way. But while Aristotle insists that the activity of colour is not an effluence of bodies (particles), he offers little, if any, positive characterization of its qualities. We have to look elsewhere for clues as to how he thought of light.

Aristotle treats sound and colour as analogous, and claims that the activity of sound occurs in the medium (B.8, 419^{b}6–10) between the object and the hearing. Hence, this sound needs to be distinguished from the 'sounding' (Γ.2, 426^{a}7–8) which occurs in the sentient subject, when the air inside the ear is affected by the sound which enters it (B.8, 420^{a}10–14). For, the latter continues in existence only for as long as the hearing occurs (Γ.2, 426^{a}15–18), while the original sound will have a different duration.[40] Similarly, colour (i.e. the colour-relevant activity of light) occurs in the medium, but 'colouring' (i.e. what goes on in the eye when perception takes place) occurs in the sentient subject and lasts only as long as she sees the colour (426^{a}15–16).

This distinction between sound (or colour) in the medium and sounding (or colouring) in the sentient subject allows Aristotle to conclude that the early physiologists were mistaken in thinking that (e.g.) colours could not exist without perceivers (426^{a}21 f.), but correct to assert that the operation of the sensible (as such) could not exist without a perceiver. For this latter activity (viz. the colouring of the type which endures as long as seeing does) requires a perceiver (426^{a}21–6). Indeed, this is why Aristotle can distinguish between what it is to be a colour and what it is to be seen (*Meta.* K.9, 1065^{b}31–3); for, the latter involves colour affecting the percipient, while the former is its activity *qua* colour (in the medium, without essentially affecting anything else).[41]

What occurs in the medium? Sounds are (in Aristotle's view) produced

---

[39] In *De Sensu* 3, there are attempts at a more positive characterization of particular colours (e.g. white, black (439^{b}15–18)). The situation is made more complicated by Aristotle's further claim that the eye itself involves the transparent. (See below.)

[40] Hearing can either be hearing sounds or hearing both noise and silence (*De An.* B.9, 421^{b}4–6, cf. 422^{a}22–4). So, in one mode hearing is the active exercise of one's auditory capacities, even if no sound is heard (i.e. listening out for), while in another it is hearing a sound which lasts as long as the sounding does. Both of these are activities of the relevant capacities, and as such must be distinct from the mere capacity to hear which is possessed by objects which can hear, but are not hearing at present (Γ.2, 425^{b}28–30).

[41] On this issue, I agree with Justin Broackes's discussion of colour in 'Aristotle, Objectivity and Perception', *OSAP* 17 (1999), 61, and with his able (and to my mind decisive) criticisms of certain aspects of Sarah Broadie's earlier article 'Aristotle's Perceptual Realism' (*Ancient Minds: Southern Journal of Philosophy* 31, suppl. (1993), 137–59.)

by something striking against something else, and occur in their own medium (analogous to light (419^{b}29–30)). Thus, it is not stricken air which approaches the ear, but rather air which in some way carries sound because of its distinctive sound-conducting capacity (what earlier commentators described as '*to dieches*'). In the parallel case, water carries sound without air travelling through it, and without making actual waves. Further, Aristotle cannot have thought that echoes literally involve bouncing masses of air (as both Alexander and Philoponus rightly insisted in commenting on 419^{b}25–7).[42] Rather, in this case successive bits of air between the source and the wall are shaped into a unified mass until the air adjoining the wall transfers the sound to the wall, which in turn starts the process up again in a changed direction. Thus, sound is a distinctive activity of the air which realizes its sound-conducting capacity, and it is this activity which is reflected when sound affects smooth or concave surfaces (419^{b}28). If the analogy is sustained, colour should be an activity of the same general kind in air or water which realizes their capacity *qua* transparent. What occurs in the case of colour is a continuous instantaneous activity which pervades the whole medium between source and observer. It is because of this activity in the medium that colours are known by us. Further, this activity (like that of sound) is not a wave of a bodily type.[43]

Many of the details of this account are obscure. However, Aristotle has done enough to present an outline of his intended analogy between perception and thought. The active intellect is presented as the analogue of light, which, when active in given ways, is the efficient cause of the perceiver's perception of red. If so, the analogy will run as follows:

ability of the object to 'modify' the active intellect	activity of the universal in the active intellect	thoughts of object or universal (in the passive intellect)

In the case of objects containing matter (Γ.4, 430^{a}5–8),[44] the relevant universals will exist actually only when there is an appropriate activity in the active intellect. It is in virtue of this activity that the universals are known by us. Both colours and universals exist independently of us in media of distinctive types, which causally impact on us and assimilate our relevant

[42] Philoponus, commenting on *De An.* in *Analytica Posteriora*, ed. M. Wallies (Berlin, 1909), p. 340, 32 f.; p. 360, 19 ff. (where he cites Alexander with approval). Philoponus appears to think of echoes as involving the activity of sound itself being reflected. Thus, it is not only that sound involves a continuous propagation of a state which pervades the whole medium between source and observer, but also that its activity can be redirected when it hits a wall. This Aristotelian doctrine is implicit in his own discussion of echoes (*De An.* B, 419^{b}25 ff.), and his analogy with light's reflection. As Sambursky notes in 'Philoponus' Interpretation of Aristotle's Theory of Light', *Osiris* 13 (1958), 121–3, this doctrine still falls short of the Stoic innovation of *sound waves* of corporeal entities.

[43] For a contrasting view, see Myles Burnyeat's paper 'Aristote voit du rouge et entend un "do": combien se passe-t-il de choses? Remarques sur *De Anima*, 2, 7–8', in G. R. Dherbey (ed.), *Corps et Ame* (Paris, 1996), 149–67.

[44] Cases not involving matter (430^{a}3–5) are discussed in the penultimate section.

faculties to themselves.[45] In both cases, the faculties have as their goal receiving their appropriate objects in this way, and function correctly when they do so.

Light makes all colours actual by being affected in certain ways appropriate to its nature (Γ.5, *hexis* (430ᵃ15)). How does the light of the active intellect make all universals actual by itself being appropriately affected? Aristotle's use of light resembles (as has been frequently noted) the Platonic analogy of the sun in the *Republic*, which represents the role of the form of the good. This makes each relevant object what it is (*Rep.* H, 508aff.) in virtue of the latter's being located in its own niche in an organized and intelligible world. If the analogy is sustained, what it is for a universal to be active will be for it to occupy a given niche in an organized and intelligible order. The active intellect, so understood, will be the organized structure in which each of the relevant universals is active. As an intellect, it is the appropriate locus, the 'place for such forms' (Γ.4, 429ᵃ27 f.).[46] However, unlike Plato's sun, the active intellect is not itself a distinct object. By analogy with light, its role is as the abiding and structured space in which distinct universals themselves are active.[47]

If this is correct, our minds (passive intellects) will function properly when they receive objects intelligibly organized in a coherent structure of this type.[48] What the passive mind receives will be forms of kinds located

---

[45] For a somewhat contrasting view of this aspect of the analogy, see Michael Frede's 'La theorie aristotelicienne de l'intellect agent', 382–3.

[46] This account takes the reference to light as to what is affected in given ways, and not to what can be affected in given ways. If it were the latter, the identification between nous and *noeta* would come under strain. For, *noeta* cannot be identified with the medium in which they are active.

[47] Aristotle immediately notes a disanalogy between light and the active intellect. The active intellect is essentially in activity, and as such has no potentiality (Γ.5, 430ᵃ17–18). If it had possessed a potentiality, its actualization would require explanation. Since it lacks a potentiality, it is always in activity and is unmixed and separate. Thus, it differs from light, which is itself the actualization of a capacity. As Aristotle remarks, the activity of the intellect has no intermittence (430ᵃ22), and in itself is immortal and eternal (430ᵃ23).

[48] Aristotle tackles related issues in the central books of the *Metaphysics*. It is sometimes held that there universals have only potential existence outside the mind, and only exist actually in the mind (e.g. G. Hughes, 'Universals as Potential Substances' in M. Burnyeat (ed.), *Notes on Book Zeta of Aristotle's Metaphysics* (Oxford, 1979), 107–26 and J. Lear, *Aristotle: The Desire to Understand* (Cambridge, 1988), 292). The colour analogy is consistent with these claims provided that one understands 'universals' existing actually in the mind' to mean that they exist only in God's mind/the active intellect. Thus understood, the universal doghood may exist only potentially in actual dogs. For it to exist actually the relevant universal needs not only to be instantiated in such dogs but also to fall within an intelligible order of other universals which are related in law-like ways. If, *per impossibile*, there were dogs but no such organized world order, doghood would only exist potentially. (This would be the analogue of potential colours without any light.) Particular animals may, of course, come to instantiate doghood as they develop into maturity from the foetus stage. But this means that they come to have the potential to affect the divine mind in the way which exemplifies doghood. (This would be the analogue of things coming to have the potential to affect the light in a way which exemplifies redness—e.g. by being painted!)

in an organized and intelligible world. If so, it will achieve its goal when we think of such objects and kinds as occupying their appropriate place in an objective world order. Further, such objects and kinds will only be known to us because they occupy a place in that order. As in the case of perception, the content of our passive thought will be determined by the causal elements which produce the relevant thoughts (when the thinking faculty is functioning as it should).[49]

While these aspects of the analogy seem relatively clear, others remain obscure. While it is part of the nature of the red colour to move the light in a given way, there may be more to its nature than this. It is true that when one sees an object as red, one sees it as such in virtue of its disposition (now realized) to affect the medium in a given way. But this truth in no way rules out the possibility that the object has some further property (e.g.) of being red (as Aristotle suggests in *De Sensu* in his theory of colour mixture and degrees of transparency (439^b8–10, 439^b20–440^b23)). Equally, while it may be part of the nature of a universal to move the active intellect in a given way; it does not follow that its nature consists solely in this ability. When one thinks of an object as F, one thinks of it as such in virtue of its ability (now realized) to fit into an organized and intelligible world order in a given way. Its playing the latter role may also depend on the object's having a given form which does (in fact) affect the medium in the way specified. But it need not. Perhaps to be F is just to fit in a given way into an organized and intelligible world. These ontological issues are left unresolved in *De Anima*, where Aristotle aims to uncover just enough structure to account for the relation between thought and its objects. We shall return to these ontological questions in Part II.

5.8 THOUGHT AND ERROR*

If Aristotle's analogy with colour perception provides the basis for his account of veridical thought, what (if anything) can he say about mistaken thought (see Γ.3, 427^b8–11)?[50]

Aristotle's discussion of error in thought is complicated by his

---

[49] Since this is the role of the passive intellect, it must itself be capable of organizing objects in the appropriate way, and in this (at least) correspond to the active intellect itself. This is why our intellect` is said to be like the independent active intellect (*NE* K.7, 1177^a15–17) or even identical with it.

[50] Aristotle sometimes speaks of intellect as, like knowledge, always correct (*Post. An.* B.19, 100^b6–8), and in *De Anima* notes that 'thinking of indivisibles' is never false (*De An.* Γ.6, 430^a26–7). The first usage must refer only to successful cases of thought, and not to all cases of thinking. The latter is more problematic, but must refer to a special doctrine of Aristotle's concerning indivisible concepts and not to his view of thinking in general.

distinction between thoughts of simples and of complexes (involving predication). Of the former, Aristotle writes:

> Thought is not always something true or false. When thought is of what something is with respect to its essence and there is no predication it is true. (Γ.6, 430^{b}26–8)

This parallels Aristotle's discussion of the objects of the proper senses (Γ.6, 430^{b}28 ff.) which seems to require at least:

(P) If one is in *proper* visual contact with a special sensible, no error is possible.

Proper visual contact requires the presence of the visible object as the immediate and controlling cause of the perception. Since our special visual systems are set up so as to be directly sensitive to their proper objects, error will not occur if all is functioning well. If the analogy holds, Aristotle should accept in the case of thought:

(P*) If one is in *proper* epistemic contact with (or genuinely thinks of) an indivisible object, no error is possible.

Here, since our noetic faculty is set up so as to be directly sensitive to its proper objects, error will not occur if all is functioning well. Just as our special senses are such as to (e.g.) see the nature of colour, so our noetic faculty is such as to grasp the natures of its proper objects.[51] Further, since their objects are simple, the only alternative to proper contact is ignorance, not error.[52]

It does not, however, follow from (P*) that if one believes one is thinking of an indivisible object (O), one actually is. For, it is possible that one could be affected by a different simple object (Q) or by a complex object (R) in the way one would be affected by O if the thinking faculty were

---

[51] Neither (P) nor (P*) depends on the respective proper objects being defined as those which make this impact on us when all is functioning well. Rather, they are substantial claims to the effect that our faculties have the capacity to be affected by their respective objects in this way.

[52] Aristotle makes this clear in his discussion of grasp of incomposites in *Meta.* Θ.10, which are presumably to be identified with the simples mentioned in Z.17, 1041^{b}9–11. There, he writes that in these cases 'falsity does not exist, nor error, only ignorance'(1052^{a}1–2). This is because here there is either being in touch with the incomposite or failing to be in touch; the former is correct, the latter is ignorance (1052^{b}24–5). There is no room for error in the case of incomposites (including incomposite substances, which are identical with their essences, and the essences of composite substances, but excluding composite substances) (see 1051^{b}26–7). (Aristotle throws in his favoured rider 'except accidentally' (1051^{b}26); but it is difficult to see what this adds, since Aristotle's focus is on (*inter alia*) absolute simples. Perhaps, by 'except accidentally' he intends the following qualification: if error is possible concerning these matters it occurs in ways not linked to our grasping them as simples, but (e.g.) through our misdescribing them in complex propositions or mislocating them in a genus tree (i.e. in some way which involves complexity imported by us).

functioning properly.[53] Equally, it seems possible that one could be affected by a simple object in the way one would be affected by a complex object if the thinking faculty were functioning properly. If the analogy with perception is maintained, the thought in these cases would be of the object which would have set up an affection of this type had all been functioning properly. However, while this would permit the possibility of error concerning simples in the thinking faculty, Aristotle does not investigate this possibility in *De Anima*.[54] In particular, he does not address in detail the question of what makes two affections be of the same type. There is a further consequence of this account. If it is correct, it does not follow that if one is (in fact) thinking of a simple object, one knows that one is. For, one need not know that one's thinking faculty is indeed controlled in the appropriate way by an external object. How the thought is brought about need not be transparent to the thinker. The way the thought is presented to the thinker may mask the identity of the thought.

This point serves to illuminate one aspect of Aristotle's remarks about thought. He sometimes insists that 'images' or 'phantasms' are the means by which thoughts are presented to subjects. Thus, he writes:

Whenever one contemplates, one must at that moment contemplate with an image. (*De An.* Γ.8, 432^{a}8–10)[55]

---

[53] If the faculty is functioning correctly, thinking will be correct (*Post. An.* B.19, 100^{b}6–8). Compare Aristotle's remarks on seeing (*horan* (*De Insomniis* 1, 459^{a}1–4)) as always being true. In *Meta.* Θ.10, 1051^{b}31 f., Aristotle writes that for incomposites either one thinks them or one does not (error is not possible); but this does not mean that whenever one believes one thinks of a simple one does do so. There is a limited disanalogy with the case of perceiving: thinking (of this type) conceptually requires success, but perceiving (*aisthesis*) does not. This is why the analogue of thinking is proper perceptual contact, not merely perceiving. For, 'perceiving' (for Aristotle) is akin to 'being affected in one's sense organs', and this (unlike seeing or thinking) does not require success.

[54] Aristotle writes:

with regard to what is identical in species the mind thinks of it in an indivisible unit of time and by an indivisible mental act. It grasps these things accidentally in this way, and not in so far as the latter (viz. what thinks and when) are divisible, but in so far as they are indivisible. For, there is present in the objects something indivisible, although probably not separable, which makes the relevant time and the duration one. For, this applies for anything continuous. (Γ.6, 430^{b}14–20)

Aristotle holds that in any case where we grasp a divisible unity of this type as one, our grasp of it is accidental (and not a full grasp of the kind in question, which, presumably, would require us to grasp it as a complex). However, this accidental grasp of unity is possible because the relevant objects or kinds contain something properly indivisible (e.g. an essence) which makes the object itself a unity (of a kind), even though it is a composite.

[55] I am indebted to Michael Wedin's discussion of this passage in *Mind and Imagination in Aristotle* (New Haven, 1988), 113–16. He emphasizes that the role of *phantasia* in this passage is to capture how the thought is presented to the thinker. However, he does not develop this point in the way I suggest, and he may not agree with a development of the type proposed.

If one contemplates with an 'image' of this kind, one need not know the type of route by which the thought was produced (*De Mem.* 450^{b}25–9). Indeed, for all one knows, it might have been produced by an external object or by a combination of one's own thoughts. When the thought is presented to a subject in an image, the subject need not know what produced it. The presence of the 'image' is precisely what is required to express the fact that the way in which the thought is presented to the subject masks its identity conditions. Thus, when Aristotle writes that the thinking faculty 'thinks its forms in images' which occur simultaneously with the thought, he appears to be emphasizing the fact that when one thinks, the precise identity of the thoughts one has need not be transparent to one. One need not know, in thinking, that the thoughts one has are caused in an appropriate way by an appropriate object.[56]

Indivisibles are the analogues of the simples grasped by the special senses (430^{b}30–2). Thinking of them is contrasted with the kind of thinking which involves predication and may allow for further kinds of error (430^{b}28–30). In the latter cases, we may combine simples to form non-existent complexes (such as centaurs or goatstags). Error is possible here because the combinations we make are not controlled by the objects in the way that they are in the case of special perception or thought of indivisibles. As in the case of common sensibles, when there is combination by us in addition to the objects of the special senses, there is a further possible source of error.[57]

5.9 THE ANALOGY RECONSIDERED

In this Chapter, I have argued that Aristotle's use of an analogy between perception and thought supports several claims concerning thought and its object.

(A) In the basic case, S's thought is a thought about a kind or object (when all is functioning well) provided that S's thinking faculty is likened to the relevant kind or object. When this occurs the thinker is able to locate that kind in an independent, intelligible, world order.

---

[56] This is not to say that there is one state which correctly describes in the same way how all thoughts strike the subject. There may be two types of 'image' depending on whether or not the thought which strikes the subject is appropriately caused by an external object.

[57] If the thinking faculty malfunctions and the thinker mislocates or misdescribes A, it would be affected by complex object A in the way it would have been by complex object B or simple object C had the faculty been functioning properly (if the analogy with perception holds). And this would be because of the operation of past thinking of B or C. But Aristotle does not develop in *De An.* Γ.6 a positive account of the content of erroneous thought (since he is focusing throughout on successful cases of thinking).

In this account, the nature and content of these thoughts are (constitutively) dependent on external objects. There is internal light (thoughts with content) because of the way in which the external objects impact on us. In this way, the cases of thought and perception are analogous.

The analogy generates two additional theses concerning thought:

(B) In the case of simple objects our thinking can be successful because our noetic faculty is such as to be able to grasp the nature of its proper objects.

(C) If error is possible in the case of simple objects, this is because our noetic faculty can be stimulated by an object O in the same way as it would be by another simple (P), if all was functioning well.

There is a further consequence:

(D) The thinker need not know if they are having a simple thought when they are having one.

For, as before, the thinker need not know what makes the thought the one it is. Thus, they will grasp the relevant thought even though they do not know that the thought is one of a simple object.

(D) is important, since it shows how a thinker can have a thought which is about a given object or kind without knowing which object or kind it is. This is precisely what is required if Aristotle is to countenance the possibility (central to our concerns)[58] that a thinker can have a thought whose content is determined by a given kind without knowing which kind that is (in the way required to distinguish it from all other kinds, real or imaginary). Thus, it seems that (D) offers one part of Aristotle's way out of escaping the apparent inconsistency which threatened his account in the previous Chapter (Section 4.5).[59]

While (B), (C), and (D) are interesting and important claims, they are not fully developed in *De Anima*. The main burden of the analogy is carried by (A), which I have interpreted as a claim about the content of thought.

My account of the analogy faces an immediate difficulty. In the case of perception, 'receiving the relevant form' from an object clearly involves acquiring a form at that time. (When this occurs, the perceiver actualizes her potential to perceive.) However, in the case of thinking, the transition (on which Aristotle focuses) is that from potentially thinking that p (in the mode of the scholar who has acquired relevant knowledge in the past) to actually thinking that p. But this transition does not involve the subject's *acquiring* a new form at all. Rather, the form itself will typically have been

---

[58] As set out in the final Section of the last Chapter.

[59] More specifically, it offers a way of addressing the first part of (PC3), set out in Section 4.6 of the previous Chapter.

acquired at a previous stage when the person originally became knowledgeable in the relevant area (cf. Γ.4, 429^{b}7–9). That she has originally acquired it in this way explains why she can now exercise her knowledge by herself (without the impact of external objects which themselves produce the activity (B.5, 417^{b}19–21)).[60]

The difficulty takes the form of a dilemma. If Aristotle's discussion of thinking does not focus on the original acquisition of a form, he is not comparing like with like. For, he is comparing the acquisition of a perceptual form with the exercise of an already acquired thought. But, since these cases are unlike, there can (it seems) be no strict analogy between them. However, if the strict analogy is maintained, Aristotle is focusing either on the acquisition of forms in the two cases or on the specific efficient causes which lead to particular episodes of perceiving or thinking.[61] But in neither case can the analogy focus on what makes a thought (or perception) have the content it does. Thus, to conclude: either the analogy is broken-backed or it does not concern the determination of content.

Aristotle does not focus throughout on the acquisition of forms. For he takes as analogous the perceiver who sees a particular object whose form he has not previously acquired, and the thinker who has already acquired the relevant form and is exercising his ability to think of that form (see B.5, 417^{b}18–19). Thus, he writes that the thinker 'has already become' all of the relevant objects of thought (Γ.4, 429^{b}8–9). They exist in his soul in some way before their actual use (B.5, 417^{b}23). In actively thinking, he exercises a capacity he has already acquired. If so, Aristotle's focus cannot be on the original acquisition of the form in question.

In fact, the situation is more complicated. For, elsewhere Aristotle compares some thinkers to a wax tablet which bears no actual writing before it is written on (Γ.4, 430^{a}1–2). But this suggests that the relevant objects are not present in any way prior to actual thinking. These thinkers may have the general ability to think grammatically, but need not possess already the specific grammatical form.

How can Aristotle cover both these cases within one common framework? His main point cannot be confined to one which concerns either the

---

[60] In perception and knowledge of particulars, the productive cause is particular and external. In the case of thinking, by contrast, the universals are present 'in some way' in the soul, and hence thinkers can think of them when they please (B.5, 417^{b}22 ff.). The universals are present 'in some way' presumably because the thinker has the ability to think of them. But this is compatible with his actually thinking of them involving the universals actually impacting on him. The difference with perceiving is not that there is no comparable receiving of the form in the two cases, but that only in the case of thinking can we put ourselves in a position to receive the form (since thinking is within our power by ourselves).

[61] This interpretation has been proposed by Michael Wedin in *Mind and Imagination in Aristotle*.

initial acquisition of a form or the use of a form already acquired. Further, since the causal routes involved in these two cases are very different, his point cannot depend on there being one type of causal route involved in the production of both types of specific thought.

How can the analogy survive the presence of these major differences? What is common to the two cases of thought under consideration? It seems that, in both, the thinking faculty is affected by the relevant universal (whether or not previously acquired), and that its relevant states are then causally dependent on the universal in some appropriate way (if all is functioning well). There can be thinking of this type whether or not the specific capacity has already been acquired.[62] Since the relevant states are thoughts with contents, in both cases the contents of the relevant thoughts are determined by the universal on which they are causally dependent. In both, therefore, what makes it the case that the subject has the thoughts she does is that she is causally affected in some way by the external world.

This account of thought allows Aristotle to preserve his analogy with perception. In both, the content of the relevant state is determined by the subject's being affected in some (causal) way by relevant objects in the external world. The faculty in the two cases is likened (in differing ways) to some object. But there is an obvious disanalogy. In the case of perception, the content is acquired at the same time as it is determined. But this need not be so in the case of thought. However, the presence of this disanalogy does not (in any way) call into question the point of analogy. For, the analogy is pitched at such a general level that it cannot be affected by a more specific disanalogy of this type.

It should be noted that in *De Anima* Γ Aristotle says very little on the more specific issue of how we come to acquire particular thoughts. His only remarks are in Γ.8, where he says that no one can think if they have not previously perceived (432^{a}7f.), and that the objects of thought are somehow present in the objects of imagination (432^{a}8f.). But these remarks are not developed into an account of how we acquire specific universals.[63] (It is only elsewhere that he attempts to provide such an account. For further discussion, see the next Chapter.) His lack of detailed comment on this topic can be easily understood if his chief focus is (as I have suggested) on the issue of the determination of content. For, while his account

---

[62] This preserves the parallel with perception. The capacity to see mauve or this mauve does not depend on the antecedent acquisition of either of the specific capacities involved. It is rather a consequence of the general capacity to see a whole range of colours and coloured objects, which matches the grammarian's ability to think new thoughts about grammatical categories and the grammaticality of particular sentences.

[63] It is to the passages in *Post. An.* B.19 and *Meta.* A.1 which are discussed in the next Chapter that one needs to look for such an account. In this Chapter, the focus has been on the content of perception and thought, and no attempt has been made to extend this to the content of imagination. (That awaits a further study.)

of the latter may require that some story be told about how we acquire the relevant thoughts, that story is not itself part of the theory of content determination. It is rather a background necessary condition for the account of content determination.

What then survives of the analogy? There are three features in the account of thought which parallel the case of perception.

(a) It is *because* the universal is as it is that the thought is as it is (and not vice versa); so the universal is the controller of the thought.

(b) The thinking faculty is affected by the universal, as the perceptual faculty is by its proper object. In both cases, the relevant form will be received, if all is functioning well.

(c) Given (a) and (b), one can detect activity and passivity in both cases.

These conditions give content to the idea of an efficient causal process linking universal and thinking faculty.[64] It will be enough if (i) the operation of the mind is itself controlled by the nature of the external object, and (ii) there is a causal process beginning with the object and involving the subject's activity which results in the thought. When the thinker's thought of a universal is dependent in these two ways on a universal, the thinking faculty is causally affected by that universal. The analogy is preserved if there is an asymmetric causal relation of the type captured by (a)–(c).

This analogy is consistent with there being major differences between the two cases. In addition to the one already mentioned, the types of causal pattern involved in the two cases may be radically different. Thus, thought need not involve the impact of spatial forms characteristic of perception. There need be no quasi-perceptual forms travelling through a spatial medium from objects of thought to make a quasi-physical impact on the thinker. Nor need perception involve only the apprehension of the type of forms characteristic of thought. Perception (unlike thought) may involve

---

[64] Aristotle's discussions of efficient and teleological causation are both in need of further investigation. For the former, see M. Frede's essay on 'The Original Conception of Cause', in his *Essays in Ancient Philosophy* (Minnesota, 1987), and for the latter see my 'Teleological Causation in the *Physics*' in L. Judson (ed.), *Aristotle's Physics* (Oxford, 1991). Aristotle's active efficient causes are objects whose capacities are exercised in the relevant interactions. They are, thus, essentially structured phenomena, with their own distinctive form, and are fundamentally different from unstructured events which are used as causes in some influential twentieth-century theories, such as those of Donald Davidson. (On this, see my *Aristotle's Philosophy of Action*, 30–6, 44 ff.) Putnam objects to all theories of content which involve efficient causation on the basis that they essentially involve unstructured (Davidsonian) events, which cannot explain 'how the constituents of events connect with subsentential parts of speech' ('Aristotle after Wittgenstein', in R. W. Sharples (ed.), *Modern Thinkers and Ancient Thinkers* (London, 1993), 124). His objections do not engage with Aristotle's use of efficient causation, since Aristotle is opposed *au fond* to the Davidsonian account of events and causation.

a detailed story about a medium and the physical organ involved in the acquisition of the perceptual form. Indeed, the main lines of the analogy could be preserved even if perceptual forms were essentially spatial, and noetic forms essentially non-spatial.[65]

5.10 THE ANALOGY AND ITS GAPS

The general form of theory which has emerged is distinctive. In the cases of both thought and perception the content of the relevant state is determined by the object to which the faculty is likened (when all is going well). For, it is then that the relevant form is transferred from object to subject. There is a secondary point of analogy. In neither case need one be aware that the thought (or perception) is produced by an object in the favoured way. Thus, one need not know, in having a thought or perception of A, that there is (e.g.) an existing object or kind that produces that thought or perception.

This general framework has two major gaps. Aristotle needs to show how we can acquire thoughts of the relevant type. This topic is discussed in Chapter 6. Further, Aristotle needs to clarify and defend the ontological claim (sketched in 5.7) that the world is (in some way) an organized and intelligible structure of the type he envisages, containing forms which are transferred to the subject. His attempt to vindicate this assumption is one of my main concerns in Part II of this book (see especially 10.5 and 13.2).

The analysis suggested above is inconsistent with an alternative (initially attractive) account of Aristotle's viewpoint. Aristotle, as we have seen, identifies certain objects of thought with the active intellect. Further, he holds that we, while thinking, engage in an activity of the type which the active intellect always enjoys. Perhaps these claims should be taken to suggest that the principles that govern our thought are the same as those which govern the world. More specifically, Aristotle might be taken to suggest that it makes no sense to ask how we come to have thoughts of this type or how the world has kinds of the type we think about. For, both our thoughts and the world are governed by the very same constitutive principles. No further vindication can be given of our entitlement to such

---

[65] It is, in any event, a mistake, from an Aristotelian viewpoint, to expect all the relevant causal processes to involve physical elements of the kind present in the case of special perception. Indeed, there is no indication of the presence of this precise type of physiological change in the case of the common sensibles. It is enough that the activity of the senses is causally controlled in some (unspecified) way by the external object. Neither in this case nor in that of thought need there be a physical impact of precisely the type found in the case of special perception.

thoughts. For, our thoughts and reality are both instances of the same activity of the same intellect.

However, this (no priority) interpretation[66] cannot be reconciled with the causal account of the determination of content which (I have argued) Aristotle favours. For, the content of thought, and not merely acts of thinking, is causally determined by the world. Thus, when Aristotle talks of the world imprinting itself on us and our psychological states, he is embracing a form of realism inconsistent with the no-priority interpretation.

If this is correct, we cannot avoid filling the two gaps mentioned above.[67] However, before turning to Aristotle's attempts to do this, there is one further objection to my account which should be considered.

5.11 THOUGHTS OF OBJECTS WITHOUT MATTER*

It will be objected that the interpretation offered cannot apply to examples such as the essence of flesh or water or the straight (429^b16–17). Of this Aristotle writes:

in the case of things without matter the very same thing is the knower and the known (Γ.4, 430^a3 f.)

In these cases (unlike those which involve matter) the thing known appears not to be even potentially present in any material object. If so, how can the causal model be appropriate? What is the cause?

It would, clearly, be a major undertaking to spell out Aristotle's account of thought of entities of this kind. My aim is a modest one: to sketch how the analogy with perception can be preserved in such cases.

According to Aristotle, the relevant universals exist in the active intellect alone, and are not even potentially present in material objects (430^a3–8). Thus, they may be seen as analogues of those general features of the light which are characteristics of the medium and not of the objects which give rise to its activity. Such features might include relations between actual colours (comparative brightness, colour matching, colour composition, spectral position), which are features of the colours themselves rather than of the coloured objects (e.g. pillar boxes) which are disposed to produce them. While there could not be such colours unless there were objects with such capacities, the properties of colours themselves could be conceived as activities of the light independently of the objects which gen-

---

[66] For talk of no-priority theories, see Ch. 1 Sect. 1.3.

[67] Further, if the no-priority view is to be rejected, one needs to explain why Aristotle invoked the active intellect at all at this stage in his enquiry. I return to this question in Chapter 10.5.

erate them. Thus, colour science can focus on colours and their properties and not on the objects which give rise to them.[68]

The analogy, so understood, would run as follows. When we think theoretically, our thoughts are (e.g.) of the essence of flesh or water because of the features these universals possess solely in virtue of their presence in the active intellect. But what does this mean? Perhaps, no more than this: The essence of water is what it is because it occupies a given position in the intelligible order (e.g. because it occupies a given slot in that order, related to the slots occupied by (e.g.) hydrogen and oxygen). These thoughts would, of course, be matter-dependent because we could not have them unless the enmattered kind existed. But in thinking of water's essence, we may focus only on its structural relations (whether taxonomic or explanatory) with other features in the intelligible world, and not on the enmattered kind itself. Theoretical science (like colour science) focuses on features which are in this limited way separable from material objects.

Is this story consistent with Aristotle's remarks in *De Anima*? Some of his remarks suggest this type of model. Thus, in Γ.7, 431^{b}12–15, he writes:

Abstracted objects, as they are called, the mind thinks of as if it was thinking of the snub-nosed—*qua* snub-nosed, it could not be thought of apart from flesh, but *qua* hollow, if it were actually so conceived, it would be thought of as apart from the flesh in which hollowness resides.

When one thinks of the snub-nosed as such (as when one thinks of man) one cannot think of this apart from the body/matter, or without the assistance of the perceptual faculty (Γ.4, 429^{b}13–17). But when one thinks of it solely as hollow one ignores its physical properties, and focuses solely on something with a geometric shape in abstract space. In this way, the hollow is an object with its own place in an intelligible world. Although it is not in reality separable from material objects, it is something whose nature depends on its standing in its own niche in abstract space (the distinctive light of the active intellect).

If the analogy with light is understood in this way, objects which are (in this way) separable from matter can assimilate the passive thinking faculty to themselves.[69] In this way, Aristotle's discussion of mathematical entities

[68] In *De Sensu* 3, Aristotle discusses colours in this type of way when he talks (e.g.) of 'the multiplicity of colours being due to the fact that the components may be combined in various ratios' (440^{b}18 ff.), and rejects other views of their composition (e.g. 439^{b}25–440^{a}6). This appears to be an essay in colour science.

[69] When so grasped they are grasped as separable from matter, unlike our thoughts of water which are of what is inseparable from matter. Because they are separable features, they cannot be analysed (at least without qualification) as the realizations of capacities of physical objects. For, when considered as unmixed with matter they could not be seen as essentially the realizations of material capacities. And this is why Aristotle does not regard them as existing potentially in the matter, but as essentially features of the active intellect itself.

and essences in *De Anima* can exemplify a pattern of efficient causal and teleological factors similar to that he detects in cases where the relevant universal is essentially enmattered. His treatment of these issues, although somewhat sketchy, need not be inconsistent with his basic analogy between perception and thought.[70]

---

[70] His remarks on these issues in *De Anima* are incomplete. Thus, in Γ.4, 429^{b}19–22, he asserts that we do have such thoughts of essences and purely mathematical objects, but does not say at all clearly how this is achieved. I have merely sketched a model which preserves some analogy with the case of perception. It would take us far from our present study to examine these issues in detail. For further discussion of related issues, see Edward Hussey's essay in his (commentary on) *Aristotle's Physics III–IV* (Oxford, 1983), 182–4, I. Mueller's 'Aristotle on Geometrical Objects', *Archiv für Geschichte der Philosophie* 52 (1970), 156–67, and J. Lear's 'Aristotle's Philosophy of Mathematics', *PR* 91 (1982), 161–93.

6

Understanding, Thought, and Meaning

6.1 INTRODUCTION

In Chapter 4, we detected an apparent inconsistency in Aristotle's account of signification. The problem arose because he held the following two claims:

(A) Simple names must signify (mediately) substances and kinds (on pain of lacking all significance), while compound names need not. In the former case, the content of the thought (with which the name is correlated) is determined by the kinds in the world which imprint themselves on our psychological states.

(B) One can grasp an account of what a simple name signifies without knowing of the existence (or of the essence) of the object or kind in question. For, at Stage 1 of the three stages of scientific enquiry, one can grasp the significance of (e.g.) 'eclipse' without knowledge of the existence or essence of the phenomenon (as was argued in Chapters 2 and 3).

It seems hard to deny that Aristotle held both (A) and (B). Indeed, the grounds for attributing (A) to him have been strengthened by the argument of the last Chapter. Did he find a way to hold both consistently?

In Chapters 4 and 5, we found some evidence of the route he attempted. To recapitulate: his account of signification (for a simple name) rests on the content of the thought with which that name is conventionally correlated. In these cases, content is (constitutively) determined by the form of the object or kind on which the thinker (in having this thought) is causally dependent.

However, the thinker who has this thought need not know which object or kind it is which makes that thought the thought it is. He need not see through to the fundamental determining conditions of the thought in question. Its basic nature can be (to some degree) obscure to him.[1]

This account raises several urgent questions. One stems from the discussion of Chapter 5.

---

[1] See Ch. 4 Sect. 4.6; Ch. 5 Sect. 5.7.

(A) How can an enquirer come to have thoughts of this type at all?

This question is pressing because it might seem mysterious that the enquirer could come to have any thoughts of the relevant type, or that her thinking faculty could be 'likened' in this way to kinds in the world.[2] Dissolution of this mystery does not require an *analysis* of the 'likening' relation. It will be enough if we can show how a process of this type can come about.[3]

A second question presses hard on the first:

(B) How can a thinker come to have a thought which is about a determinate kind without knowing which kind it is?[4]

The appearance of paradox is not dispelled by Aristotle's claim (noted above) that the *content* of the relevant thought need not be completely transparent to the thinker. For this does not explain how she could come (in the first place) to have a thought about an object (in the world) without knowing which object it is about. That still seems mysterious.

Two other questions remain to be considered. One, which concerns semantic depth, was raised in Chapter 2:[5]

(C) How can an Aristotelian thinker grasp a thought about a kind without (at least) thinking that, if the kind exists, it has an essence?

In the terms of the previous discussion: how much of the relevant form does the thinker need to grasp in order to have a thought about a kind? Indeed, it might seem that this question has become more pressing as a result of the last Chapter. For, the thinker must receive *something* of the form in question if she is to think about the relevant kind. It is not enough for her to stand in any (undemanding) type of causal relation with it. How can she grasp the form without knowing something of the essence or underlying structure of the kind?

A further question concerns knowledge of existence, and arises from the discussion of Chapters 4 and 5:

(D) How can an (Aristotelian) thinker grasp a thought about a kind without knowing of the existence of the kind?

---

[2] This is (PC1) of the final Section of Chapter 4. For similar misgivings see Putnam's *Reason, Truth and History* (Cambridge, 1981), 50–1.

[3] This distinction grounds the difference between reductive and (e.g.) supervenience theories in the philosophy of mind. See, for this distinction, the Introduction to D. Charles and K. Lennon (eds.), *Reduction, Explanation and Realism* (Oxford, 1992). In the present context, we are seeking to make it non-mysterious how a concept can be acquired. But this does not demand an analysis of concept acquisition in terms which do not refer to concepts. Nor is there an attempt to reduce the notion of form to more basic notions. The relevant notion of form is further elucidated in the account of definition given in Chapter 10 Sections 10.1–2.

[4] This is (PC3) of the final Section of Chapter 4 come back to haunt us!

[5] See also App. 1.

While we have taken this possibility as a datum in previous Chapters, we still need to explain in detail how this can occur.

In Section 6.2 I shall seek to answer these questions 'at one go' through an analysis of Aristotle's account of the route to the possession of thoughts of kinds (on the basis of perception). If successful, this Section will support the attribution to Aristotle of the theory outlined in Chapter 4. In Section 6.3 I shall assess what is distinctive about his theory (as it has emerged in Chapters 2–5) and in Section 6.4 examine the distance that separates it from that of my modern essentialist. It will become clear that (unlike the latter) the basis for Aristotle's essentialist claims lies in his metaphysics and not in his account of language or of the thought of the ordinary thinker.[6]

6.2 THE ROUTE TO THOUGHT

In *Post. An.* B.19 Aristotle writes of the origin of thoughts (tied as they are to grasp of universals) as follows. I shall begin with a non-committal translation:

Many memories form a single experience. And from experience or from the completed universal that has come to rest in the soul (the one apart from the many, whatever is one and the same in all these things) arises the starting point of skill and knowledge—of skill if it deals with how things come into being, of knowledge if it deals with what is the case. (100ᵃ5–9)

The outline is clear: memory yields experience and the latter gives rise in turn to thought of universals, the starting point of knowledge (100ᵇ12–15). But the details are obscure. For, we need to know what is involved in *experience*, and how it differs from *memory*, from *thought*, and from *knowledge*. What is involved in 'a universal coming to rest in the soul'? Further, and central to an answer to question (A), we need to understand the nature of the transition from experience to thought.

The text itself is problematic. I have translated the second sentence neutrally:

from experience or from the complete universal that has come to rest in the soul (100ᵃ6–7)

But this phrase can be understood in several ways. It might mean:

(a) from experience—that is, from the complete universal that has come to rest in the soul—

[6] See Ch. 1 Sect. 1.6.

in which experience involves grasp of the complete universal, (and the 'or' is epexegetic[7]), or alternatively:

(b) from experience, or from the complete universal . . .

In (b), 'or' could be a corrective 'or rather', and the whole phrase mean:

(b1) from experience, or rather from the complete universal that has come to rest in the soul[8]

Alternatively, the 'or' might serve to indicate two separate ways in which the starting point of skill and knowledge might arise:[9]

(b2) from experience or from the complete universal that has come to rest in the soul arises the starting point of skill and knowledge . . .

It is not clear that the *Analytics* phrase by itself supports either an (a)- or a (b)-style reading. Experience, for all that is said there, could either be of universals or of particulars. Perhaps it will be argued (in support of a (b)-style reading) that experience cannot involve a grasp of whole universals, since if it did there would be no further step beyond experience required to attain the starting point of knowledge and skill. However, this consideration is not decisive. For perhaps something more than a universal 'standing in the soul' is required as a starting point for *knowledge*. Maybe this requires universals to be connected with each other in some further way (as perhaps is indicated in 100^{b}1–3). If so, experience may enable one to grasp solitary or disconnected universals, but one will still lack the starting points of knowledge.

There is, however, a closely parallel passage in *Metaphysics*. A.1 which strongly favours a (b)-style reading. There, Aristotle writes:

Skill comes to be when from many notions (*ennoēmata*) of experience one universal judgement about similar objects is formed. To have a judgement that when Kallias was ill of this disease this helped, and similarly for Socrates, and many others, is the task of experience. But to judge that something is beneficial for *all* people of *a certain type*, marked off into one class, when they are ill of this disease—e.g. to phlegmatic or bilious people when burning with fever—is the task of skill. (981^{a}5–12)

Aristotle notes that experience is as good a guide to action as skill, and that men with experience can be more successful than those who lack it

---

[7] See, e.g. Barnes, *Aristotle's Posterior Analytics* (Oxford, 1975), 253: 'the connective "or" is presumably epexegetic—i.e.' Also, Ross, *Aristotle's Analytics*, 674: 'from experience—i.e. when the whole universal has come to rest in the soul'.

[8] See, e.g. J. H. Lesher 'The Meaning of *Nous* in the Posterior Analytics,' *Phronesis* 18 (1973), 59: ' "from experience, or rather from the universal . . ." is perhaps preferable'.

[9] And this could be taken to mean that both are alternative routes to both skill and knowledge, or that one is a route to skill, and the other to knowledge.

but possess only general accounts of the same phenomena (981ᵃ12–15). His reason is revealing:

This is because experience concerns particulars, while skill concerns universals, and actions and productions are concerned with individuals. (981ᵃ15–17)

In the first of these passages Aristotle distinguishes the things noticed in experience ('notions') from the genuine universals (981ᵃ16, 21) involved in a universal judgement about similar cases (981ᵃ7 f.). If the distinction holds, the *whole universal* which rests in the soul cannot be grasped by experience, but must be the object of a distinct faculty. And this clearly favours a (b)-style reading.[10]

What then are the 'notions of experience', and why are they not universals? Aristotle's example concerns judgements of the form:

This worked for Kallias and Socrates . . . when they suffered this disease

and is contrasted with judgements about what works for all people of a certain type (eg. phlegmatic) with a certain kind of disease (e.g. fever). The many *notions* of experience appear to essentially involve claims of the form:

This worked for this man with this illness.

However, reference to past cases may be misleading, since Aristotle also employs experience in his discussion of artisans who make objects (981ᵃ30 ff.) and doctors who treat particular patients (981ᵃ18–20). It appears that 'notions of experience' must also be capable of being expressed in judgements of the form:

This works/will work for this man with this illness.[11]

In all cases the judgements are (what I shall call) essentially particular-orientated. The person with experience can pick out particular people as the ones to be treated by this medicine, but will still lack the resources to say (or understand) what groups them together as a unit. Thus, she may be able to say correctly 'This case is like that one', but not yet grasp in general

---

[10] Is it (b1) or (b2) which is to be preferred? While Aristotle speaks of experience making skill (*Meta.* 981ᵃ4), the role of experience is not confined to the acquisition of skill. Thus, the acquisition of grasp of starting points in (e.g.) astrology stems from experience of astrology (*Pr. An.* A.30, 46ᵃ18–21). Perhaps experience and the universal's lodging in the soul by a different route (e.g. by teaching) are both routes to knowledge and skill. But the 'or' may be better understood in this context as the corrective 'or rather', as Aristotle appears to emphasize that the canonical route to thought lies through memory and experience.

[11] Indeed, this is one reason why experience differs from memory (100ᵃ3 f.). The latter in this context concerns only the retention of past instances (*monē* (99ᵇ36, 100ᵃ3)), while the former has a dynamic quality which goes beyond past cases. Indeed, this is why we should listen to the unproved sayings of the experienced who see clearly what to do in a given situation (*NE/EE* 1143ᵇ11–14).

terms what the relevant likeness consists in. Her ability comes to no more than her being able to say: 'This individual (Socrates) is like that one (Kallias) in (e.g.) that respect' (pointing to some demonstrated feature of Socrates).[12]

Similar remarks may apply to her grasp of this illness or this medicine. In each case, the relevant person with experience has no more grasp on *illness* or *medicine* than is given by her ability to discriminate particular instances on the basis of their being like other particular cases.[13] She will lack the conceptual sophistication required to understand the illness as (e.g.) *fever of a general type*, in terms which do not essentially involve reference to other particular cases. Thus, she will not grasp universals, if the latter are to be understood as wholly general and completely abstracted from particular cases. But precisely this understanding of universals seems to be what is suggested both by the examples given in *Metaphysics* A.1 and by the phrase 'the universal . . . the one *over and above* the many' (as used in *Post. An.* 100ᵃ6f.). For, the latter clearly expresses the idea of a universal as something to be understood without any essential reference to particular cases.[14]

The person with *knowledge* (981ᵃ29f.) possesses a fully conceptual grasp on the type of illness involved, while the one with *experience* lacks this and can only spot similarities between particular cases (without being able to say in purely descriptive terms what the similarity consists in).[15] Some might describe both as having the *concept* of the relevant illness,

---

[12] The person with experience has the ability to identify objects (and other phenomena) without having thoughts about the kind of object in question. Thus, they can identify objects without using 'sortal concepts', if the latter require general thoughts about the kinds of objects involved. Of course, one cannot have Aristotelian thoughts about objects without invoking the sortal notions. Indeed, this is how the thoughts of the master craftsman differ from the judgements of those guided only by experience. (See also n. 26 below.)

[13] The person with experience does not grasp a confused universal. Indeed, she is in no way confused, but possesses the ability to pick out particular cases of (e.g.) an illness perfectly (or highly reliably). She does not make mistakes comparable to that of those who call all men 'father' (*Phys.* A.1, 184ᵇ3ff.) or possess a similarly 'confused whole'. This is one reason why one should not attribute to people of experience the 'confused universals' discussed in *Phys.* A.1. Aristotle's position is far more radical: people with experience lack universals altogether. If so, he does not succumb to the following line of thought: People with experience can grasp cases together and so must possess some kind of universal; but, since they do not possess high-grade genuine universals, they must possess confused low-grade ones. For a contrasting view, see R. Bolton's 'Aristotle's Method in Natural Science' in L. Judson (ed.), *Aristotle's Physics*, (Oxford, 1991) 6ff.

[14] This marks an important difference from Putnam's account, with its essential use of indexicals. (See Chapter 1.)

[15] Elsewhere, Aristotle characterizes the former as a case of *thinking*, and distinguishes it from particular-directed perceiving and imagining. (See *De An.* Γ.8, 432ᵃ12f., B.5, 417ᵇ23–5). In this Section, I take *knowledge* (of the relevant type) to involve *thought* as its starting point, and understand both to be distinct from lower-level, particular-directed states (such as *experience*).

since both can discriminate instances when confronted by them, but this labelling is misleading. Aristotle's point is this: the content of a knowledgeable person's thoughts is fully general, involving universals which contain no essential reference to particular cases, but the person with experience alone enjoys a distinctive type of content, essentially constituted by reference to particular cases.[16] He emphasizes the relevant difference as follows:

we think that master craftsmen in each craft are more worthy of honour and know in a truer sense and are wiser than manual workers, because they know the causes of what is done, while the latter, like lifeless things, do what they do, as fire burns— but while lifeless things perform each of these by nature, manual workers perform them through habit (*Meta.* A.1, 981^{a}30–^{b}5)

The manual workers have experience and react on its basis without grasp on the relevant universals. From the perspective of the thinker, they are like a natural force because they lack a proper understanding of what they are doing.

Aristotle's discussion of thought and experience shows how we can come to have thoughts about kinds in a non-mysterious way. We do not (in his view) merely find ourselves with rich thoughts about man, thunder, and eclipse. We acquire such thoughts when we step beyond experience and grasp the relevant universals. Thus, the doctor might move from realizing that this medicine works for this illness to a view about the type of illness in question and the type of medicine it is (*Meta.* A.1 981^{a}11–12). Such transitions arise from the successful operation of experience in 'low-level' skill, and give rise to the thought that there is a unified kind before one.

What does the doctor need to understand if she is to grasp the relevant universal? Can she know that she is in touch with a genuine nature in the world, while lacking theoretical ideas about what the basis for such a nature is? Can she believe that the term 'dropsy' latches on to a distinct nature in reality, while having no view as to whether there is one underlying feature (its essence) which holds the kind together?

There is good evidence for a positive reply to this question. Aristotle insists that the craftsman needs a grasp 'sufficient for his task'(*NE* A.7, 1098^{a}30f.), and distinguishes this from that of the geometer (or scientist). In the case of the doctor, her aim is to use her skill to restore the patient to health (see *Meta.* Z.7, 1032^{b}18f.). For this, she must have some idea of what health is, but she does not need to understand it in terms of basic science (e.g. as a mixture or imbalance of heat and cold) as a Pythagorean

---

[16] For this distinction, see Evans, *Varieties of Reference*, 124, 158, and A. Cussins, 'The Connectionist Construction of Concepts', in M. Boden (ed.), *The Philosophy of Artificial Intelligence* (Oxford, 1990), 23.

doctor would.[17] Her conception of her goal may be a functional one, defined in terms of the patient's ability to perform certain tasks in a satisfactory way. She need not even consider the possibility of a deep scientific account of health. It is not needed for the purposes of producing the result at which she aims (*NE/EE* Z.4, 1140ª10–13).

Similar remarks any apply to her grasp on the type of illness in question. She may understand that if the patient has a given condition he will have (or develop) certain other features as well. In this way, his temperature or lethargy may serve as a 'litmus test' for the presence of other features of the same condition. If she can isolate the feature in question she will know that other features are also present. In this respect, her state is like that of the person described in *Posterior Analytics* B.8 as knowing that there are eclipses because he knows that there exists, as a phenomenon, a specific inability of the moon: to cast a shadow under certain specified conditions. He has a test which will enable him to tell whether an eclipse is occurring, and whether other features of eclipses will follow, but need not know that there is any fundamental scientific cause of such occurrences. The latter idea is not needed for his purposes.

The skilled doctor may also understand that if she treats one feature of the patient's condition in one way, other features will react in a given way. At the level of the universal, she will see the condition, dropsy, as containing a set of interlocking capacities. On this basis she will know that if she does one thing to it, a certain result will follow. Indeed, it is just this type of knowledge which enables her to realize that she is dealing with an objective kind with its own 'internal principle of change and rest' (*Phys.* B.1, 193ᵇ3–6). For, it is a kind of illness with its own distinctive set of interlocking causal capacities, whose presence is not explained by her activity.[18] Indeed, as she will see, these features of the illness limit what she can do for the patient.

The skilled doctor, of the type envisaged, will be able to teach (*Meta.* A.1, 981ᵇ7f.). For, she will know, on the basis of her understanding of the illness, *why* it is best to treat a given type of condition in one way rather than another. She will also have similarly based ideas about what can and cannot be usefully done for patients with this condition. She will be interested to find out when her inability to cure patients arises not from her

---

[17] In the Hippocratic writings, doctors who take as their starting points (or basic postulates) the hot, the cold, the wet, and the dry are frequently attacked. It has been suggested that Philolaus is one of those attacked in this way (see G. E. R. Lloyd's 'Who is attacked in *On Ancient Medicine?*', Phronesis 8 (1963), 108–26, and C. A. Huffman, *Philolaus of Croton* (Cambridge, 1993). Those attacked required the doctor to understand diseases in terms of a small number of starting points, drawn from basic physical theory. In their view, skills had to be based on theoretically supported postulates of this type.

[18] This distinguishes natural kinds from artefacts.

lack of skill (for perhaps that could be remedied), but from the nature of their condition.

What has been said about the doctor will apply to any master craftsman. A skilled carpenter will come to think of certain kinds of wood as (by nature) having certain interlocking features, which can be used in given ways in his work. He will think of elm as one type of wood amongst many, with differing natures, useful for different purposes. Part of his skill will consist in knowing which type of wood is best suited for what type of purpose. But neither the doctor nor the carpenter need have any views about what, if anything, holds together the varying features of the illness, health, or the wood (e.g. that these possess one underlying feature, molecular or evolutionary, which *explains* their possession of a number of interlocking causal capacities). However, while they may never have raised this issue, they, nonetheless, have the idea of a determinate natural kind, with its own distinctive features, existing independently of themselves.

These resources provide an answer to question (C). The skilled craftsman may grasp the kind without thinking of it as possessing an underlying essence of a scientific kind. His grasp on the kind is not of a proto-scientific type, as would be exemplified by one who described the kind as one with an underlying essence yet to be discovered. There is no need for his thoughts to have that degree of depth. For, while he aspires to know everything about the kind that he needs for his skill, he need not know any biological or molecular theory about the wood's structure or historical evolution (nor even that there could be any such theory).[19]

There are several heroes (and heroines) elsewhere in Aristotle's thought whose role corresponds to that of the master craftsman. The virtuous know how to act and can explain why they act in that way, but need not know the fundamental principles concerning human well-being which make their mode of action correct. Indeed, they may have no view as to whether there are any underlying principles of this type. Thus, they will lack the kind of explanation of why what they do is correct which the ethical philosopher might provide.[20] Similarly, the orator (discussed in the *Rhetoric*) may know how to argue without knowing the basis of his practice in a theory of logical validity. Equally, he may know what the emotions are and how to engage with them without having the beginnings of a scientific account of their nature or essence.[21] All of these can have thoughts about kinds or

[19] This is not to say that the skilled artisan cannot be interested in the deeper understanding of the kind which the scientist can provide. Indeed, he may be prepared to defer to the scientist's greater knowledge in some cases. However, that said, he can grasp the significance of the kind term without even imagining that there is a deeper form of understanding to be had of the kinds with which he interacts. (See also Chapter 13.)

[20] On this, see (for instance) my *Aristotle's Philosophy of Action*, 185 n. 21.

[21] On this, see J. M. Cooper's 'Aristotle on Emotion' in D. J. Furley and A. Nehamas (eds.), *Aristotle's Rhetoric* (Princeton, 1994), 205–9.

phenomena without thinking that they must possess basic, unifying, determining features. The master craftsman does not stand alone.

So, how is the transition made from experience to thought? Aristotle says that we grasp the first universals by induction (100^b4), and notes that in this way perception instils the universal (100^b5). He also says that 'we perceive the universal' (100^a17), but does not spell out any of these remarks in detail. Induction, in this context, presumably refers to a cognitive process which leads from particular cases to universal;[22] but this tells us nothing until we know the nature of the process itself. Barnes remarks that: 'Aristotle nowhere gives [an account] of how such concepts as *man* are derived from data of perception'.[23]

It is certainly true that Aristotle nowhere gives a detailed account of how such a derivation will go. However, he does provide some indications. The first stage will involve *experience* (as discussed above), focusing on specific discriminations of particular cases. The relevant transition is from this to a grasp on a universal, which involves no essential reference to particulars. The end product will not simply be an abstraction from experience, since the universals must cohere among themselves in an organized way (100^a11-$^b2$). Consequently, one cannot justify the resulting universals solely by reference back to experience. For, there are additional, explanatory, constraints present at the level of thought which are not present in experience.

This account does not make the transition mysterious. Reflection on what is common in the particular cases of illness one has confronted and treated, and how they differ from other somewhat similar cases, gives an initial impetus towards grasping the relevant universal and seeing its connections with, and distinctions from, other related universals. Initially, one may introduce a term (e.g. 'dropsy') as a way of labelling the instances one thinks of as examples of one type of illness. One may grasp some of the symptoms which one has found in general terms (nausea and lethargy followed by fever), and also note which medicines work for which patients. For, one is concerned to see which types of treatment work for which patients and which do not, and to find some way of rep-

---

[22] As Barnes remarks: 'perception instils the universal by induction simply because our first grasp of universal A depends on our having perceived a quantity of individual A's. Thus construed 100^b3-5 says no more than that concept acquisition proceeds from the less to the more general' *(Aristotle's Posterior Analytics*, 256). This appears to be the case in the acquisition of universals also (*NE/EE* Z.3, 1139^b28-30; Z.11, 1143^b1-5).

[23] Barnes, *Aristotle's Posterior Analytics*, 255. He rests this conclusion on the correct claim that 'it is hard to see how . . . man could be either a proper or a common sensible'. But we can only draw his conclusion if we ignore the role of experience in Aristotle's account. Barnes is drawn to do this because he believes that experience itself involves universals and universal judgements (*Aristotle's Posterior Analytics*, 255), 'perceiving things as A's'. But this seems over-hasty in the light of the clear distinction in *Meta.* A.1 between universals and the notions grasped by a person with experience.

resenting this knowledge at a general level (e.g. so as to communicate it to others).

If one follows a route of this type, one has some reason to think that one is in touch with a genuine kind. This thought is underwritten by the similarities one sees in the cases with which one interacts.[24] While it is a step beyond experience to grasp in general terms the illness with which one is dealing, it is one which arises naturally *from* experience. It is true that Aristotle does not fully specify the nature of the process involved (the mechanisms or the rules of derivation), but he says enough to constrain its operation and render it intelligible. It is not clear that a philosophical account of concept acquisition need do more. Aristotle has, at least, indicated how it is that we can grasp universals by a process which begins with experience and culminates in thought (in successful cases).[25]

When the master craftsman has been through a process of this type, he has acquired (in favourable circumstances) a thought about an existing kind. When this occurs, his thinking faculty has been likened to the kind (in a way which meets the requirements specified in Chapter 5). His thoughts are causally dependent (in the appropriate way) on the kind in question.[26]

Is it possible, within this general framework, to see how one might pass Stage 1 without as yet passing Stage 2? The following story suggests that it is.[27] Imagine a doctor treating a series of severely ill patients with a set

[24] The process is not merely a causal one. It provides the thinker with some justification for having the thought contents he does. (See, for further discussion, Ch. 13 Sects. 13.5 and 13.7.)

[25] More would be required if one were attempting to analyse 'likening' in terms of the conditions under which one came to acquire the relevant concepts. But there is no need to see Aristotle as engaging in that task. His goal need only be to make it intelligible how we can come to have such concepts.

[26] In this way, the master craftsman will come to grasp a variety of specific kinds. One account of this process runs as follows: Given his general understanding of (e.g.) 'animal', and his skilled interaction with particular animals, specific kinds will become visible to him. If so, it is not merely that he groups certain animals together for his own purposes (e.g. guarding the house, ploughing the field, etc.). Rather, he will distinguish separate kinds, with distinctive natures, when in the course of his activity he finds that some (e.g.) eat, move, breathe in one way, others in another. His kind concepts will not be merely the pragmatic ones (recommended by conceptualist writers), designed simply to serve his needs and purposes. But neither will they be formed (as some professedly 'realist' writers urge they should be) solely by looking at distinct patterns of causal connections, without reliance on any grasp of the relevant genus: (e.g.) animal. For, some grasp of the latter is required, in this account, to uncover specific animal kinds. (This is why, in *Post. An.* B.19, 100ᵃ11 ff., Aristotle emphasizes the need for the thinker to gain several universals *together* in the relevant genus.) So understood, Aristotle's account conforms neither to standard realist nor conceptualist options.

[27] At this point, my task is to show how these claims are (1) mutually consistent and (2) consistent with Aristotle's general account of concept acquisition. It cannot be proved (by more direct evidence) that Aristotle proceeded in this way. The account may be taken as one which offers the best explanation of Aristotle's claims in this area.

of symptoms, which she does not recognize as those of a known disease. She finds that some treatments work in some cases, and begins to note some similarities between the cases that can be treated in this way. She may speculate as to whether what had initially appeared to be a set of unconnected and disparate symptoms is (in fact) the manifestation of one unified condition, with a variety of interconnected features. This is merely a hypothesis on her part (perhaps one of many), since she lacks the evidence required (by her lights) to sustain the claim that these symptoms are thus connected. For example, she does not (as yet) know how the varying aspects of the condition affect one another, whether there is a common course the illness follows, or how far its various aspects can be treated in the same way. So, she cannot as yet determine whether the cases before her are instances of the same condition (with complications) or of a number of different conditions.[28] Nonetheless, on the basis of her limited experience of the disease, she has a hunch that there is one such condition, with its own causal structure, common to all the cases before her, which she calls 'dropsy'. She could say:

'Dropsy' signifies a unified medical condition with the following symptoms . . .

or (transferring to the level of use):

Dropsy is the unified medical condition, if there is one, with the following symptoms . . .

Something further would be required to establish the existence of one condition: e.g. repeated successful manipulation of symptoms ('if I do this, that will happen . . .'), some understanding of how different aspects of the illness are interconnected, or a prognosis of how the illness develops in standard cases. Without this, the doctor will be able to formulate an account of what 'dropsy' signifies (which she uses in her hypothesis[29]) without knowing of the existence of dropsy.

In this case, let us imagine, the doctor's hypothesis is correct and there is indeed a unitary disease of the type indicated. She was, in fact, interacting with one disease, without knowing that she was doing so. Her interactions with the kind, although not sufficient (by her lights) to generate knowledge of its existence, are sufficient to give her thoughts about it. So, at the end of a successful enquiry she will be entitled to say that she was right all along about dropsy. She has a thought of one unified kind throughout, even though (at the outset) she does not know that this is so. At the

---

[28] Since there could be other illnesses in her immediate vicinity which she could not tell apart from dropsy, her methods may not be reliable even in her situation. She could be very lucky in her hypothesis.

[29] For this use of hypothesis see *Post. An.* B.9, 93^{b}24 f. These issues are discussed in Ch. 3, Sect. 3.8. See also the discussion of Stage 1 accounts in Ch. 2 Sect. 2.9.

outset her thinking faculty is 'likened' to the kind, even though she does not know that this is the case.[30] As is required to answer question (D), raised in Section 6.1, she has a thought about dropsy without knowing that there is, in fact, such a kind.

But what does she possess when she first has a thought about dropsy? She does not have (at this stage) the practical ability to tell (by her own lights) that the cases before her exemplify one separate condition, rather than (for example) several different conditions with overlapping and somewhat similar symptoms. Thus, she need not have the resources to distinguish this illness from all others, real and imaginary. Indeed, she may even think it equally probable (for all she knows) that the cases before her exemplify several conditions rather than one.[31] Of course, she knows that if there is a common condition, all or many of these are cases of it. But since she does not (as yet) know that there is a common condition, she is not able knowledgeably to discriminate those cases which do have the illness in question. All she can say is that if there are any cases of dropsy, these (or some of them) are they. But she does not as yet know that these are cases of dropsy.

Her hypothesis is that there is one type of illness which all (or many) of these cases share. Further, she has latched on (through her interactions with the kind) to some of its genuine, non-accidental, features. In this way, something of the nature of the illness has impressed itself upon her.[32] It is the fact that this is so that makes her thought one about dropsy. Because of the impression the kind has made on her, she has latched on to enough of its features to go on to search (in the mode discussed in Chapters 2 and 3) for answers to questions about its existence and essence. She has, in effect, a point of access to an epistemic trail which culminates (if all goes well) in knowledge of the existence and nature of the kind with which she is interacting.[33] But she does not have this latter knowledge at the

---

[30] One should distinguish between the conditions required for likening and those required for likening plus knowledge of the existence of the kind.

[31] She also lacks the resources to distinguish the type of situation in which her hypothesis is correct from those (which could easily arise) in which it is not, even though she may be lucky enough to be in a situation where her hunches are correct. For this reason, although she can, as it happens (in her actual situation), reliably pick out cases of dropsy, she seems to lack knowledge. For, there are (as she may be aware) many 'proximate' situations (indistinguishable by her from this one) in which her hunch would be mistaken.

[32] We can understand in this way the significance of Aristotle's cautious phrases in *Post. An.* B.8, 93[a]22 and [a]29.

[33] One might propose that such accounts determine the reference of the term in the following way:

'T' signifies a kind K for thinker S if and only if S, when using 'T', has in his possession an account A, which provides him with information on whose basis alone he can (given his methods) come to have knowledge of the existence and nature of K.

That is, 'T' might signify the kind about which the thinker would come to have knowledge on the basis solely of the account he then possesses (plus his epistemic methods). The

beginning of her enquiry. Her case shows that it is possible to arrive (as Aristotle requires) at Stage 1 without yet achieving Stage 2. In this way, his account can be acquitted of the charge of inconsistency.

The master craftsman will, of course, often be able to make the transition to Stage 2 of enquiry. He may come to have good reason to believe that he has grasped a genuine universal. This will happen if (for example) he can interact successfully with the kind, predict what will happen if he acts in one way rather than another, piece together what types of effect one type of treatment has, detect the course of a given condition, and differentiate it from other close cases. In this way, he will see its position as one among several universals which form the basis for an interconnected map of illnesses and treatments.[34]

Naturally, he can make mistakes. In some cases, he may think that a series of instances have one common set of interlocking capacities when they do not. Thus, he may mistakenly 'lump together' elm and beech wood. But in both cases the idea of there being an objective kind with its own distinctive nature plays a central role in his thinking. Further, when he is right, there seems to be no reason to deny him knowledge of the existence of the kind.

Aristotle emphasizes the possibility of mistakes arising in the acquisition of thoughts. Thus, in *Physics* A.1 he writes:

What are at first clear to us and obvious are things which are rather confused. Later the elements and principles of these become known to us by analysis. This is why we advance from these [sc. confused] universals to specific ones. For, the whole [sc. which embraces all the specific cases] is more known in the light of perception, and the universal is a whole of a type; for, the universal embraces many things as parts. (184^a21–6)

---

epistemic methods in question would be those involved in arriving at Stages 2 and 3 of successful enquiry.
This proposal is committed to the claim that:

'T' signifies a kind K (for S at t) if and only if S would come to have knowledge of K in a given way on the basis of information S possesses at t.

But, even if this proposal were extensionally correct, it would not tell us what makes it true that 'T' signifies K at a stage before S comes to have knowledge of it. For, the fact that he would come to have knowledge of K in the future cannot be what makes it true that he then signifies K. If so, this proposal appears to be a consequence of the correct theory of signification-determination, and not its basis. Nor is it clear that the proposal is even extensionally correct. For, presumably, 'T' could signify K, even if S was not able (given his methods) to come to have knowledge of its existence or essence (e.g. if the kind was too complex for S to analyse).

[34] In this Section, I have not addressed the question of how one comes, in Aristotle's account, to grasp the first universals as such (100^b3–5). While my concern has been with the mastery of such concepts as man or animal, I have not sought to account for one's grasp on animal as a first principle. On the latter issue, see Ch. 10 Sect. 10.6.

These universals, which have parts, must be contrasted with the indivisible infimae species (such as man) discussed in *Posterior Analytics* 100ª15 ff. Aristotle gives no examples of the compound universals he introduces in *Physics* A.1, but compares this case with that of the name '*kuklos*', which signifies a whole in a confused way (since it is a homonym signifying both a circular object, such as Stonehenge, and a geometric circle) which definition divides into more specific elements. *Cycle*, by analogy, would be a confused universal initially grasped if the person who grasped it did not distinguish between the two. Elsewhere, as we have seen, Aristotle offers the example of pride. One might begin by thinking of pride as one thing, even though it subsequently turned out that there was no one phenomenon involved: e.g. if there was no common account of why some proud people were indifferent to misfortune and others could not tolerate insults (*Post. An.* B.13, 97ᵇ23–5). In both cases, one has arrived at a compound universal and entertains a confused thought because there is no unitary set of capacities of the required type in the cases before one.

However, although such mistakes are possible, the master craftsman will frequently get it right. In these cases, he will grasp a genuine thought of a kind and know that the kind exists. In the terminology of the earlier account, he will successfully achieve both Stages 1 and 2.

6.3 THE DISTINCTIVE NATURE OF ARISTOTLE'S ACCOUNT OF SIGNIFICATION

In Chapter 4, I noted that Aristotle's theory of signification is not a version of the Fregean theory. For, according to Aristotle, one can understand a name without having discriminating knowledge of the object named.[35] The argument of the previous Section supports this view. At Stage 1 of her enquiries into dropsy, the doctor need not know which illness she is investigating, since she will lack the ability knowledgeably to distinguish this condition from all other conditions (whether real or imaginary). She forms a hypothesis about (what is in fact) an existing kind (with which she

---

[35] Traditional Fregeans hold that the sense of a name is what is grasped by the thinker, and that this semantically determines the reference (e.g. by giving a definite description which uniquely fits the object). Revisionary Fregeans take the sense to be what the thinker grasps and to be what is (metaphysically) determined by the reference (since the sense, in their view, just is a mode of presentation of the referent). Thus, in their view, the thinker who knows the sense of a term knows which object it refers to. Aristotle, in effect, separates what the thinker grasps (as expressed by the account of what the name signifies) and the thought itself (which is determined by the object or kind in the world). In this way, he can allow a thinker to grasp a name without possessing distinguishing knowledge of its object.

interacts), without knowing of its existence. It is only at Stage 2 that she (by her own lights) achieves this knowledge and, thus, comes to know (in the Fregean mode) which object it is that she is thinking of. In this way, she makes the transition (as she sees it) from not knowing to knowing of the existence of the kind. (It would make nonsense of how she sees the transition to insist that she knew all along of the existence of the kind without knowing that she knew.[36])

Aristotle is able to characterize the thinker's progress in this way because he does not accept that grasping an object in thought involves 'knowing which' object it is that is grasped (in the way required to distinguish it from all others).[37] This is because, as is clear in the case of the craftsman, the account of content determination is not identical with an account of what the competent thinker knows. Semantics is one thing, epistemology another. The thinker can be 'likened' to the kind when she engages with instances of it, spots some similarities between cases, and gains some information about what the illness is like. But this does not require her to be able knowledgeably to discriminate the kind which is the causal source of her information. Nor does it require her to be able to tell who has the illness, or that certain cases are cases of the illness. The most she need know is that these (or some of them) are cases of the illness, if there are any cases of it. While the content of her hypothesis is 'informed' by the illness in question, she is not (as yet) in a position to know either that the illness exists or that certain people are suffering from it.

It is sometimes said that there are only two types of account of thought and signification. *Either* one attributes to the thinker thoughts about an object or kind solely in virtue of his standing in a causal relation with it *or* one requires that he possess discriminating knowledge of the object or kind in question,[38] such as might enable him (fallibly) to discriminate the object or kind from all others.[39]

Aristotle's strategy appears to differ from both of these accounts. For, while he does not accept the latter (Fregean) option, he does not accept the first one either. Thus, he does not think that to grasp the signification

---

[36] Aristotle gives no indication at all of this type of formulation. His view seems to be that at Stage 1 one lacks knowledge of the existence of the kind, not merely knowledge that one knows. Nor is this surprising. Aristotle's view of knowledge appears to require some grasp by the thinker on something which makes the relevant claim true (*Post. An.* A.2, 71^{b}10–12). Thus, his account of knowledge involves some component other than merely following a route, which (in fact) reliably leads to knowledge.

[37] For a contrasting claim, see John McDowell's formulations in 'Singular Thought and the Extent of Inner Space,' 140.

[38] Gareth Evans presents these alternatives in *Varieties of Reference*, 83.

[39] See Evans' comments on Russell's Principle in *Varieties of Reference*, 106 ff. McDowell emphasizes the fallibility of the relevant knowledge in 'Singular Thought and the Extent of Inner Space', 141.

of a kind term is simply to stand in some bare causal connection with the kind (which may, as a result, mean nothing to the thinker). The relevant type of connection has to be one in which something of the nature of the kind is made manifest to the thinker. They will engage with the kind in such a way that they gain some information about it, even if their information is not enough to enable them to tell that kind apart from all others (even ones in their immediate vicinity). They are in a position to form a hypothesis about the kind, even though they lack the type of knowledge on which the Fregean insists.[40]

Aristotle, further, has no reason to accept the characterization of the information gained by the thinker which is offered by a proponent of the bare causal thesis.[41] For, the information the Aristotelian thinker gains is constitutively tied to the kind which causes it. It is the imprint which that kind with its nature makes on him.[42] There need be no way of specifying how things are with the subject ('internally') in these cases which does not advert to the external world, as it is presented to the subject. The qualifications (of the 'if it is' form) do not require a separate form of internal content such as may be needed to allow an internalist account of knowledge.[43] Rather, they express a measure of epistemic reservation about whether the world is as it appears to be. Thus, there need be no 'distinct and separate' form of content which captures their role.

In Aristotle's account, the signification of terms is determined by features separate from those which determine our knowledge of the objects in question. Given this separation, he has no need of any of the following strategies:

(i)   to define a separate form of internal content as the focus for internalist constraints on knowledge (as in the dual-component theory)

(ii)   to insist that the thinker knows which object he is signifying (in either the orthodox or the neo-Fregean style)

(iii) to hunt for some version of a reliabilist account of knowledge to accommodate externalist elements in the account of meaning

[40] For objections to the pure causal theory of reference, see Gareth Evans's paper 'The Causal Theory of Names' (*PASS* 47 (1973), 187 ff.). In it, he cites the example of 'Madagascar', first attached (in some variant) to part of the mainland of Africa, and then (as a consequence) mistakenly transferred by the Portuguese to the offshore island that now bears the name.

[41] See, for example, Colin McGinn's 'The Structure of Content' in A. Woodfield (ed.), *Thought and Object* (Oxford, 1982), 230. He separates two components of meaning, one dependent on a causal connection with the object, a second 'conceptually disparate and . . . independent' (p. 230). Each component aims 'to specify the whole of a part of meaning' (p. 231).

[42] For the basis of these formulations, see Ch. 5 Sect. 5.2.

[43] It will become even clearer in Chapters 7–10 that the information gathered by the understander cannot be characterized without reference to the external world.

(iv) to allow that one grasps the significance of a term by standing in some bare causal relation with the object or kind

In his view (as this has emerged in the past Chapters) one can understand a name without knowing which object it denotes (in the Fregean manner), but one cannot understand it solely in virtue of standing in any type of causal connection with the object. One understands a name for a kind when one receives sufficient information about its nature (from engagement with its instances) to be able to form a hypothesis about it which (in favourable conditions) one can substantiate. The nature of the kind is (in some measure) given to one in one's experience of individual cases, even though one is not in a position then to know that this is so.[44] For, it is only at a later stage that one can come to know of the existence and nature of the kind.

Aristotle's approach stems from his interest in our understanding of the names we use in *enquiry*. Here, our understanding of our terms (what we know about their bearers) is determined by factors different from those which fix their signification. For this reason, Aristotle's account of the signification (or meaning) of names is not to be identified with an account of our understanding of their signification (or meaning).

6.4 ARISTOTLE AND MODERN ESSENTIALISM

We are now in a position finally to contrast Aristotle's account of our understanding of natural-kind terms with that proposed by the modern essentialist.[45] There are three points of difference:

(1) The skilled doctor (mentioned above) who has thoughts about dropsy is in a position akin (epistemically speaking) to one who knows that:

The void is a place, if there is such a place, which is deprived of body.

Her formulations will begin with Stage 1 accounts of what terms signify such as:

'Dropsy' signifies a certain kind of medical condition.

Accounts of what names signify express the grasp the thinker has on her thought. They show her grasp on the form which she has acquired by the

---

[44] At least in the case of kinds grasped through perception. It would take a further study to see whether and in what way this style of account applies to terms for triangles and other mathematical entities. Since there is no obvious analogue for perception in this case, it may be that one requires a fuller description of the phenomenon than in the perceptual case. Perhaps one needs the type of description of triangle as 'closed three-sided figure' mentioned in Chapter 2.   [45] See Ch. 1.

process set out above. When she has grasped such a form, she has been 'likened' to the kind in question. However, the thinker, in grasping such a thought, need not know whether there is (in reality) a kind which brings this thought about, or that the cases before her are actually cases of one condition. This by itself is sufficient to distance Aristotle's account from that of the modern essentialist (as set out in Chapter 1). For, his doctor can understand the term 'dropsy' without knowing of the existence of the kind. It is not a requirement on his mastery of the term that he 'knows which' kind it signifies.[46]

(2) The doctor's knowledge can be distinguished in a second way from that required of the understander by my modern essentialist (as introduced in Chapter 1). She need not possess the idea of a proto-scientific kind, of a kind (that is) with one core feature which explains the rest. For, this goes considerably beyond what is required for her to grasp the concept of dropsy, or of man. Indeed, she can know of the existence of the illness without thinking of it in that way. At these stages, she can have thoughts of a natural kind without any of the semantic depth required for thought of kinds as endowed with explanatorily basic properties. There is no need for her to think of man or dropsy as proto-concepts in a master science (like physics) in order to master the relevant thought or know of the existence of the kind.

Both (1) and (2) stem from a common source. Aristotle (as I have emphasized) develops his account of what names signify in the context of a thinker's *enquiry* into the nature and existence of a kind. At the initial stage of such an enquiry, one can understand a term for a natural kind without knowing of its existence or its hidden essence, or even that if it exists it has such an essence. No doubt, at a later stage in enquiry we will know of the existence and nature of the kind. But this further knowledge is not essential to our initial mastery of the terms. Most modern discussion focuses on what is involved in understanding a term once an enquiry is well advanced (or completed). But Aristotle concentrates on the absolute minimum required for the understanding of a term, as exemplified by what the thinker knows at the beginning of the enquiry.

(3) In order to grasp the significance of a kind term, one must have a general thought about the kind which is the causal source of one's information. Such general thoughts mark the imprint of the kind on us (when we are 'likened' to it). We do not grasp the significance of the term when we refer to the kind simply as 'the kind of which these are instances'. For,

---

[46] The argument for this is given in Section 6.2. My modern essentialist has a Fregean understanding of the 'knowing which' requirement. However, as mentioned in Chapter 1 Section 1.3, others might think to interpret the knowledge requirement differently (in a reliabilist fashion). I have presented some considerations against this view in Section 6.2 above. The doctor appears to signify dropsy even in cases where she only has a hunch that it is one genuine condition.

this phrase could also be used by a person with experience who lacks a thought, and merely has the ability to pick out its instances. If his thought is to be of a kind, it has to involve more than this. In particular, for Aristotle, it has to involve the understanding of the kind as a distinctive type of phenomenon, occupying its own slot among many other such kinds. In Aristotle's formulation, one needs to think of man as a certain distinctive kind of animal. It is not enough to think of man as the kind of which these are examples.[47] For, that would not distinguish a thought about man from a thought about animal.

This third difference stems from the care Aristotle takes in separating thought and experience. From his perspective, the ordinary person's dealings with examples may give him good grounds for thinking that there is indeed a kind of this type with which he is interacting. But his grasp on the kind must be general and cannot be constituted simply by his grasp on the phrase 'that of which these are examples'. He needs some general way to characterize the causal source of his information, although this need not involve any claims about its hidden determining basic features.[48]

To summarize (1)–(3): We may, in Aristotle's view, at the beginning of an enquiry be agnostic or mistaken about the basic internal features of the kind with which we interact. Indeed, we may not know that the kind has a basic internal feature at all. So, it is no objection to Aristotle's account that we, as thinkers, 'very often have the structure of the things we refer to dead wrong'.[49] For, all that is required is that we have received enough information from our interactions with the kind to be in a position from which we can come to have knowledge (in time) of its existence and basic structure. There is no requirement that we already have that knowledge at the initial stage in our enquiry.

While this account is attractive, it comes with a high cost. If one accepts it, one cannot develop from a study of our ordinary linguistic knowledge

---

[47] Thoughts at Stage 1 of enquiry cannot (in Aristotle's account) contain indexicals referring to particular instances of the kind. For the level of conceptualization he requires of us as thinkers precludes reference to individual cases. In Aristotle's view, to refer to a kind as 'that kind, the one these instances instantiate' would not (even in successful cases) distinguish between the kinds man, animal, and mammal. In his account, more is needed to latch on to one kind, such as grasp on some features which are (i) necessary properties and (ii) locate the kind as (e.g.) an illness or a metal, with its own slot in a relevant genus. Nor is the situation improved if we add that 'instances are of the same kind if they are governed by the same laws as these'. For, this mode does not differentiate man, mammal, and animal, since these are all (presumably) governed by laws (albeit different ones). (Further, the master craftsman need have no notion that there are laws at all, even though he grasps the existence of the relevant kind.)

[48] Since thought (and knowledge) is concerned with universals, the role of examples (in Aristotle's account) can only be to give evidence for the existence of a kind designated by the term. They cannot play a constitutive role in our understanding of the kind term kind itself. (Contrast the view of the modern essentialist, as set out in Ch. 1 Sect. 1.4.)

[49] Putnam, 'Aristotle after Wittgenstein', 129.

(or pre-scientific thought) the resources necessary to render coherent metaphysical essentialist claims (as my modern essentialist does in Chapter 1). The basis for the coherence of such claims has to be found elsewhere.

We are now at the turning point in our investigation. Aristotle's discussion of natural-kind terms does not involve (I have argued) attributing to the ordinary thinker thoughts with the degree of semantic depth required by my modern essentialist. He cannot render essentialist claims coherent on the basis of the linguistic knowledge or a priori thoughts of the ordinary thinker. His justification has to be found elsewhere, in an independent metaphysical account of essence and necessity. In the next part of the book, I shall examine how far he succeeded in this project.

6.5 SOME OBJECTIONS*

For Aristotle (according to my interpretation) it is a condition of a simple name signifying an object (or kind) that the thought (with which the name is conventionally correlated) be causally dependent in the form-transferring way on that object (or kind). So, the thought has to capture something of the form of the object (or kind). But the thinker who grasps that thought need not know that he is capturing something of the form of a real kind. For him, any such claim may have the status of a hypothesis. Thus, knowledge of the account of what the name signifies need not involve knowledge of the existence of the kind. In this way, he has shown how to hold consistently the three-stage view (as set out in Chapters 2 and 3) and the realist account of thought and signification (deployed in Chapters 4 and 5).

At this point, it may be helpful to consider some objections to the line of interpretation have offered. The first challenges the account of signification given above, the second and third call into question the distinctness of the three stages, while the fourth disputes the authority given to Stage 3 over the preceding stages. While some of these objections are narrowly exegetical, others challenge the consistency and philososphical value of Aristotle's position.

Objection 1: Signification, Stage 1, and Error

It has been suggested that this account misrepresents Aristotle's position by demanding too much of each thinker who uses (e.g.) the term 'man' or 'soul'. Surely, it will be said, they can use these terms without any grasp of the type suggested on the nature of the kind itself? Did not many of Aristotle's predecessors have thoughts about (e.g.) the soul while fundamentally misconceiving its nature? Some thought of it as a ratio of elements, or a certain type of harmony, and lacked the resources to think of it as an actuality of a certain type of body (in the correct Aristotelian fashion). Perhaps they belonged to a community, all of whose members lacked the resources to have Aristotelian thoughts about the soul because they all misconceived its nature. However, notwithstanding their errors about the nature of the soul, they used the term 'soul' to signify the soul. Had they failed to do so, Aristotle could not have argued that they had false beliefs about the soul. (Or so the objection runs.[50])

It is important to note that Aristotle (as I interpret him) is not vulnerable to the full force of this objection. First, he allows that some thinkers can grasp only accidental features of a kind, while still using the relevant term meaningfully.[51] However, this is only because the significance of the name is fixed by its being correlated with thoughts caused in the form-transferring way by the relevant kind. Many people can use a natural-kind term without the proper style of account, provided that the significance of that term is determined in the way indicated in Chapter 4. Second, to possess an account of (e.g.) soul requires only that one has a grasp on *some* of its nature. It does not require that one be correct about the precise theoretical specification of that kind: e.g. as an actuality. It is enough that one thinks of the soul as a starting point, or substance, 'which moves itself'[52] or 'by which one perceives and moves'.[53] For, these formulations pick out some part of the distinctive nature of the soul.[54]

If there is to be a counter example to my interpretation, it will be given by describing a situation in which all of a society (according to Aristotle)

---

[50] Travis Butler, 'On David Charles' Account of Aristotle's Semantics for Simple Names', *Phronesis* 42 (1997), 21–34. The final move in Butler's argument could easily be questioned. Perhaps Aristotle is intent on making the best sense he can of his predecessor's failed attempts at thoughts about the soul. For him to make sense of their views does not require that those views (as expressed by them) make sense.

[51] See *Post. An.* B.8, 93ª25–7.   [52] See *Post. An.* B.8, 93ª24.

[53] See *De An.* A.2, 403ᵇ26 f.

[54] I take Aristotle's basic understanding of 'soul' in *De Anima* to be 'a starting point (*arche*), that which makes things alive'(see A.1, 402ª6, A.2, 405ᵇ11 f., B.2, 414ª4, 12, B.4, 415ᵇ8). This is further expanded in terms of 'what makes things grow, perceive, think, move'. It is because the soul is understood in this way that all can discuss it, no matter what their metaphysical views may be. So understood, there is no real question as to the existence of the soul (provided there are living creatures). Aristotle further argues, dialectically (A.1, 403ª29 ff.), that if one thinks of the soul in these ways, one cannot regard it as (e.g.) a harmony. For, to do so is to give up on the soul's role as a self mover or starting point (A.4, 407ᵇ34 f., 408ª15 ff.). The formulations given in B.1, in terms of 'first actuality of living body', are Aristotle's first attempts at a general, theoretically defensible, statement (*logos*) of what the soul is (412ª5 f., 413ª9 f.: they are revised and made more precise in B.2–3). While they do not constitute an account of what the term 'soul' signifies, they do capture in Aristotle's terminology (via the idea of substance) the (generally shared) idea of the soul as a starting point. Although earlier thinkers did not use this terminology, Aristotle takes them to have (tacitly) accepted this idea (no matter what else they said) if they allowed (in line with majority opinion) that the soul is a starting point.

use a term to signify (e.g.) the soul, but none of them grasps anything of its proper nature. Thus, no one would locate the kind in its correct genus (as a substance)[55] or grasp any of its non-accidental, distinctives features. Aristotle's discussions of earlier views of the soul do not provide such a counter example. For, as he emphasizes, he takes over from his predecessors the characteristics that distinguish the soul (see *De An.* A.1, 403[b]26 f.). Further, even if some of his predecessors, on occasion, rejected the view that the soul is a substance, Aristotle gives no indication that this was ever the majority view. Indeed, he is at pains to point out that when they thought of the soul as a ratio or harmony, they were at odds with popular views about its nature.[56]

But could there be a counter example of the required type? Could Aristotle accept that a term might signify (e.g.) the soul when no one (at that time) had a thought of the appropriate type about it? If everyone's thoughts picked out only accidental properties, what would make their thoughts ones of the soul, rather than of (e.g.) some other, unrelated, and possibly non-existent entity (e.g. being an animal south of the Danube . . .)? Their understanding of the term would not be linked with the right kind. They would not have sufficient access to the relevant form to count as having a thought about the soul. Indeed, for this reason, their term would lack determinate significance. They would lack the information required to carry out an investigation into the existence or nature of the relevant kind.[57]

This point can be generalised. To have an (Aristotelian) account of what a name for a kind signifies requires that one thinks of it as located in an appropriate genus and possessed of some of its non-accidental properties. Thus, it is not enough that one thinks of gold as something yellow and malleable, if one lacks the idea of the distinctive, interconnected nature of gold as a kind of metal.[58] For, in that case, one's term 'gold' would signify not gold, but whatever is yellow-looking and malleable by us.[59] Aristotle's

---

[55] They would (in Aristotle's view) have succeeded in placing the soul in the right genus if they saw it as a starting point, even if they did not employ precise Aristotelian terminology of '*ousia*' and '*entelecheia*'.

[56] See *De An.* A.4, 407[b]32–408[a]34, esp. 407[b]34 ff.

[57] This is not to say that Aristotle could not take such a group to be intending to talk about something of which he had a thought. But this would not require him to think that they did in fact have a name which determinately signified that object or kind. It would rather be that he interpreted them thus to give them a determinate thought, even when they lacked one.

[58] Locke, *Essay on Human Understanding*, III. ix. 17. Locke lists a number of particular properties of 'colour, weight, fusibility, and fixedness which . . . gives it the right to the name (gold), which is therefore its nominal essence'. According to his account (*Essay* III. x. 18–19), we observe simply 'a complex . . . of properties' and have no genuine grasp of the nature to which they belong (although we aim to fill this gap by invoking the idea of 'the real essence', 'whereof we have no Idea at all').

[59] Similar points could be made about a society made up entirely of people who judged by experience not by thought. For, what would make their judgements be about gold rather than anything that looked to them a given way?

master craftsman grasps that there is one nature (with which he interacts) in which these differing features are interlocked. His understanding is manifested in an indefinite number of claims he can make about how the metal will react in different situations, and what he can and cannot do to it. His grasp on the metal allows him to track gold through a variety of actual and possible situations. This understanding grounds his ability to think of gold as a genuine kind of metal, with its own non-accidental properties, and to signify that kind by the term 'gold'.

In these respects, Aristotle demands more of one who masters a natural-kind term than does Locke. There is no way, in Aristotle's account, of picking out a kind without the type of understanding enjoyed by the master craftsman: of a kind, with a distinctive nature occupying a distinctive slot in its genus. But Aristotle does not require that at this stage one must have the idea of a fundamental (physico-chemical) determining feature or hidden scientific structure (as suggested by my modern essentialist). His position is importantly distinct from that occupied by my modern essentialist and from that which Locke made his own.[60] Both fail to appreciate the importance of the type of grasp on the nature of kinds which Aristotle's master craftsman enjoys. For, he has an understanding of kinds which is more than merely a grasp on a number of properties but does not involve the postulation of a (possibly) unknown basic scientific essence.

Objection 2: The Relation of Stages 1 and 2

It will be objected that the account offered excessively restricts what is involved in accounts of what the name signifies. Surely, it will be said, a thinker can, on occasion, grasp more than indicated above. Perhaps, after investigation, his account of what the term signifies could be deepened so as to include information about the existence of the kind. Equally, his account might come to include information about the basic explanatory (or essential) features of the kind. Surely, with regard to our natural-kind terms, we know that the relevant kind exists and that it has an essence. Is not our understanding of these terms permeated with these scientific beliefs?

There are two ways in which one might answer this objection. On one view, a Stage 1-style account is essential for any enquirer's account of what

---

[60] Thus, one cannot go directly from finding difficulties with one of these views to acceptance of the other. For, to do so is to pass over Aristotle's attractive mid-position. However, Locke made precisely this mistake in his attack on the abuse of words by Scholastic philosophers in *Essay* III. x. 19. So, too, does my modern essentialist in moving directly to his own account from his rejection of the Lockean account of natural-kind terms as 'a bundle of descriptions'.

the term signifies. If more is added, the additional features are not part of the account of what the name signifies. That will remain the same throughout all stages of scientific enquiry, and will be non-committal with regard to the existence and underlying structure of the kind.

There is an alternative version of the three-stage view. In this version, each name is originally introduced with a non-existence-committing account of the type mentioned above. Later, as knowledge increases, the account of what the name signifies will evolve to include additional information about the existence and even the essence of the kind. Such information may be a feature of the later accounts, but not of the earliest one. On this view, the non-existence-committing account will be an element in the most minimal type of account of what a name signifies, but not in subsequent more developed ones. The essential nature of such accounts will change over time.

Does Aristotle opt for the first or second of these replies? It is not clear whether in *Posterior Analytics* B.10 he is claiming that each person's account of what a name signifies always retains a non-existence-committing core or only that the original account of what a name signifies (when that account is first developed) always does.

The latter is the more cautious (and convincing) claim. To challenge it, one would need to find a case where knowledge of the existence of the kind was presupposed in the type of account given when a name is introduced. This would not be like the case described above in which the doctor points to examples and says: 'These are instances of dropsy, a condition with features A, B, C . . . if anything is'. For, there she could not justifiably simultaneously introduce a name for a kind and presuppose the latter's existence.

But could there be cases where the account of what a name for a kind signifies is introduced in a way which presupposes knowledge of the existence of the kind? Surely a master craftsman could discover the existence of a separate kind of wood and only subsequently devise an account for the name he gives it. Here the name, and its account, would be introduced for a kind already known to exist. (Perhaps our ancestors already knew of the existence of some separate kinds, which they then dubbed as 'horse', 'man' . . .) In such cases, there would not be the same type of first stage of enquiry as is present in the doctor's investigation into dropsy.

Are there then two groups of natural-kind terms? One group functions like 'dropsy', the other like 'man' or 'horse'? While both may be grasped at the craftsman level without any idea of a scientific essence, only the former are non-committal with regard to knowledge of existence? Is Aristotle focusing exclusively on the first type and (mistakenly) ignoring the second?

This objection is powerful. It must be ceded that some *names* could be introduced as names of kinds already known by the name-introducers to exist. In such cases, there is no ground for insisting that the account of what the name signifies is neutral with regard to knowledge of existence. However, in such cases the existence of the kind would be originally grasped by the master craftsman with an expression like 'the kind with the following features G, H, K . . .'. At a stage prior to his introducing the name 'teak' he would need to have established that these features cohered in the way required if there is to be a kind. Thus, prior to his introduction of the name, he would need to establish that there is in fact a genuine unified kind with this feature. There would, thus, be a hypothetical stage prior to his establishing the existence of the kind. This case could be described as one in which the craftsman began with '*a name-like expression*' (e.g. 'the kind with features A, B, and C) and then moved on to Stage 2.[61] It so happens in this case that a name-like expression rather than a name is introduced at Stage 1.

A similar story can be told in the case of 'man' and 'horse'. It was surely a discovery that there was a kind which contained individuals of different sizes, ages, colours, and sexes. This could not be established just by looking at instances. Further, this would be a discovery whether or not one introduced the kind with the name 'man' or with a name-like expression 'kind with features G, H, K . . .'. There will be a gap between Stage 1 and Stage 2 wherever one is not justified in asserting solely on the basis of examples that there is a genuine kind before one. Given the constraints on Stage 2, this will be so in every case.

Objection 3: The Stages and Knowledge

A further objection runs as follows: let us agree that if at Stage 3 one has infallible knowledge of the nature of the kind, this stage is clearly distinct from Stage 2, if there one has only fallible knowledge of the existence of the kind. However, if Stages 2 and 3 are distinguished in these ways, what is the basis for separating Stages 1 and 2? Surely in both cases one has fallible knowledge of the existence of the kind. This will be so, even if at Stage 1 the person is cautious about claiming to have knowledge. Conversely, the objector will say, if Stages 1 and 2 are separated on the grounds that at Stage 2 one has infallible knowledge of the existence of the kind, one will have collapsed the distinction between Stages 2 and 3. For, infallible knowledge of the existence of a kind requires knowledge of its distinctive essence. Either way, the objector will conclude, one has only two stages of inquiry and not three.

If this objection is to be met, Aristotle must point to real epistemic differences between the three stages he has separated. Can this be done?

---

[61] See *Post. An.* B.10 and 14.

According to Aristotle, at Stage 2 the enquirer has knowledge of the existence of the kind. The latter includes knowledge (in general terms) of what treatments work and what their effects are, what will happen if a person with the disease eats certain foods, the likely course of the condition if there is no intervention, etc. When the enquirer has this information, she is entitled to claim to know that the kind exists. For, she has the type of sustained interaction with the kind (conceived as a kind) required for this claim.

This stage can be separated from earlier and later ones in the same way. At Stage 1, one will have had considerably more limited interaction with the kind. One may have been in contact with instances of the kind, but is not yet entitled to claim to know that they form a natural grouping. For, one will not have the type of grasp on the interdependence of symptoms required for this claim. More specifically, one will have no appropriate ground for the claim that the cases before one form a unified kind of disease, rather than several. One will merely see a number of apparently similar symptoms in a variety of cases. On this basis, one may conjecture that all are cases of dropsy, but need not know that this condition actually exists.

At Stage 2, the doctor will have appropriate grounds for the claim that there is a unified condition before her, although her grounds will not be as strong as the ones available at Stage 3. For, at the final stage, she will have an explanation (of the appropriate type) of why the features of the condition hang together as they do, of why the condition arises, and of why its course is as it is. When one has information of this type about the kind, one's knowledge claims about it will be indefeasible. This knowledge will arise from the deeper type of interaction one has with the kind at Stage 3. For these reasons, Stage 3 considerations appear to have authority over those available at Stage 2.[62]

Objection 4: The Authority of Stage 3 over Stages 1 and 2

Hilary Putnam objects to Aristotle's account on the basis that 'more than one thing can be called knowing the nature of dogs' depending on our different interests (e.g. as evolutionary biologist, molecular biologist), and 'these different viewpoints can lead to different decisions in certain cases' about (e.g.) whether artificially synthesized dogs (with the same molecular structure as existing dogs) are real dogs or not.[63]

Putnam's point can be stated like this: in the account given, it is assumed

---

[62] At least in cases where there is a unified essence. For further complications, see Ch. 12, final Sects.

[63] Putnam, 'Aristotle after Wittgenstein', 132, 134.

that when one grasps the term 'dog', one form is transferred from the kind to the thinker. But this need not be so. In some cases, there is not one form which is transferred but several, even though the thinker does not distinguish them. (Indeed, in some cases, the differences may only emerge at Stage 3.)

It is not clear, however, that this is an objection to Aristotle's account (as presented here). In the case Putnam describes, 'dog' could be like 'pride', a homonym between 'evolutionary-dog' and 'molecular-dog' (with their differing accounts). Two forms might be transferred in different cases, even though speakers did not initially distinguish between them. There are two forms transferred because there are two separate kinds in reality, each of which impacts at different times on thinkers.

Putnam's examples would constitute an objection to Aristotle's actual account only if it were clear that the term 'dog' (as originally acquired) is (i) determinate in all respects and (ii) applicable both to evolutionary and molecular dogs. For, this would mean that one and only one determinate form was transferred at the outset. Indeed, some will say that only one form is transferred since thinkers (*ex hypothesi*) did not distinguish between these two types of dog. However, Aristotle need not accept either that one determinate form is transferred or that the original thinkers are the final arbiters on this issue. Indeed, he denies these claims.[64] There could be two homonyms as there would be in the case of pride (if there were no one explanation of both the types of pride mentioned in *Posterior Analytics* B.13, 97^{b}15 ff.). The fact that thinkers confuse two types of pride in no way shows that they master one determinate form. What determines that they grasp two names rather than one rests with reality and not with their pre-scientific intuitions.

Putnam's objection may arise from a deeper source. If there were no fact of the matter about which essences natural kinds possess, their forms could not be individuated using Aristotle's resources. For, these depend on there being one underlying essence which does the required work of demarcating kinds and individuating their forms. In the absence of any such metaphysical constraint, it will rest with us to divide kinds as we decide. However, if this is Putnam's point, it is an objection to Aristotle's metaphysical picture rather than to the theory of significance he built on these foundations.[65] (I shall return to the metaphysical issue in Chapter 13.)

---

[64] This point also highlights the gap which divides Aristotle's picture and Locke's. For, the locus of authority for questions of significance lies (in his picture) with the world and not with the reflective judgements of the ordinary speaker.

[65] Putnam may well think that since we can only individuate the relevant forms using our conceptual resources, such forms cannot provide the basis for an account of our thoughts or concepts. I attempt to unpick this style of argument in Chapter 13 Section 13.4.

6.6 CONCLUSION

According to my modern essentialist, the theory of meaning (or the theory of thought) enables us to render intelligible essentialist claims. Nothing is required from a further metaphysical account of essence. In Aristotle's theory, the situation is reversed. Far fewer demands are made of the theory of meaning. The ordinary thinker need have no notion of the kind as possessing a hidden essence (or basic determining feature) yet to be discovered. Aristotle has to make essentialist claims intelligible in a fundamentally different way. In his view, problems in metaphysics cannot be resolved by attributing profound metaphysical intuitions to the ordinary thinker.[66] They need to be addressed in their own terms.

---

[66] In the terminology of Chapter 1, Aristotle is not a modern essentialist of either a conventionalist or a democratic Kantian type. He could, of course, be an élitist Kantian, for whom it is the thoughts of the idealized thinker (and not the pre-scientific one) which constitute truth in a given area. (See Chs. 10 and 13.)

II

*Aristotle on Definition, Essence, and
Natural Kinds*

7

Definition and Demonstration: the Difficulties Raised in Posterior Analytics *B.3–7*

7.1 INTRODUCTION

At the beginning of B.8 Aristotle writes:

> We must consider again which of these points is correct and which is not, and what a definition is and whether there is in some way demonstration and definition of what a thing is, or in no way at all. (93ª1–3)

A new start is required because he had reached an impasse at the end of the previous chapter:

> From these considerations, it is evident that definition and deduction are not the same thing, and that deduction and definition are not of the same thing; and as well as that, that definition neither demonstrates nor proves anything, and that you cannot become aware of what a thing is either by definition or by demonstration. (92ᵇ35–8)

Aristotle proposes to avoid some of these difficulties by replacing the method of general deduction (and of division) with a method based on demonstration.[1] Thus, he writes:

> One way of doing this is the way just examined—proving what a thing is via something else (i.e. another definition). For, in the case of deducing what a thing is, the middle term must state what the thing is, and in the case of what is proper, the middle term must be proper. This means that you will be proving one account of what it is to be the given thing, but failing to prove another. Now, that this could not be a demonstration was said earlier: rather, it is a general deduction concerning what it is. But let us say in what way a demonstration is possible, speaking again from the beginning. (93ª9–17)[2]

---

[1] Some of these difficulties (as argued in Chapters 2 and 3) can be overcome by drawing the distinctions required by the three-stage view. However, others can only be met by developing a more detailed account (i) of how demonstration, definition, and deduction are connected, and (ii) of how we acquire knowledge of the relevant essential definitions.

[2] The argument runs as follows (where S stands for 'the cause is to be represented as a middle term', V for 'the method of general deduction is used', and W for 'the method of demonstration is used'):

There are several questions raised by this passage:

(1) What is the difference between the account given in B.4 and 6 (the so-called method of general deduction), and the one offered in B.8?
(2) What advantages does Aristotle see for his own proposal over the methods discussed earlier? What does this show about his view of the connection between definition and demonstration?

In this Chapter, I shall begin to answer (1) by examining Aristotle's criticisms of these earlier proposals. In the next, I shall address (2) by considering Aristotle's positive account, as it is developed in B.8 and 16–18. My general goal in these two Chapters is to understand the interconnections which Aristotle discerns between definition and demonstration.[3]

7.2 THE FIRST CRITICISMS OF THE METHOD OF GENERAL DEDUCTION: B.4

Aristotle gives several criticisms of the method of general deduction in B.4. The first runs as follows:

If both premisses contain what a thing is, the account of what it is to be that thing contained in the middle term will be prior. (91ª25–6)

Aristotle cites as an example a syllogism whose conclusion is:

A Φ def all C.

where 'C' is a term designating man, and 'A' designates what it is to be a man (e.g. two-footed animal).[4] Of this case, he notes:

If this is to be established by a syllogism, then 'A' must be predicated of all 'B'. (91ª28 f.)

$[S \rightarrow [VvW]]$

But the method of general deduction is inadequate as a means of demonstrating the cause. Therefore:

$[S \rightarrow W]$

So, if 'P' stands for 'to know what something is is the same as to know the cause of its being', and RR for 'the cause is something else and demonstrable', the whole structure of the argument is this:

$[P \rightarrow [R \rightarrow S]]$ & $[S \rightarrow W]$.

Further, since P is well supported, one can infer not only that:

$[P \rightarrow [R \rightarrow W]]$

but also that W is true when R is true: the method of demonstration is required to represent the cause in cases where this is different.

---

[3] Aristotle divides a number of cases relevant for his enquiry in 93ª5–7.
[4] By 'φ def' I intend 'belongs definitionally to', and by 'φ nec' 'belongs necessarily to'.

This is because the relevant syllogism must be of the form:

A Φ def all B.

<u>B Φ def all C.</u>

A Φ def all C.

Aristotle notes:

There will be another account [viz. of what C is] as the middle term[5] [viz. an account in the form B φ def C, intermediate between A Φ def B, and A Φ def C], which will also state what man is. So, you are assuming what one has to prove. For, B will be what man is as well. (91ᵃ30–2)

Aristotle's point here is a general one. If one's conclusion is:

Being a two-footed animal (A) belongs def all men (C).[6]

there will be a further term (the B-term: e.g. being rational) introduced in the minor premiss, which also specifies the essence of man. This latter specification has not been *proved* but *assumed*.[7]

---

[5] Reading *toutou* rather than *touto* with the MSS and Barnes, and taking this to refer to A. Ross reads *touto* and takes this to refer to B, translating 'This—viz. B—will state the essence of man'.

[6] It is important to note that in B.4 Aristotle is concerned with conclusions which give definitions such as:

Being a two-footed animal Φ def all men.

He is not focusing on the target he had previously taken in B.3 in which the relevant conclusion was:

A Φ necessarily to all C.

where A was being two-footed, and C was being an animal (90ᵇ34–6). These conclusions are not of the right form to be definitions, because they lack the appropriate predicational tie found in true definitions ('in a definition, it is not the case that one thing is predicated of one thing' (90ᵇ34 f.)). In B.4, by contrast, he is envisaging syllogisms whose conclusions are definitions of the form:

A Φ def all C,

where C is the term to be defined, and the predicational tie:

A Φ def all B,

is appropriate for definition.

[7] This mode of argument is apparent elsewhere in this chapter. In 91ᵃ33 ff., Aristotle writes:

We must enquire in the case of two propositions and in what is primitive and immediate. For, then what is being said becomes clear. Those who prove through conversion what soul is (or what man is) . . . postulate what was set out at the beginning; for example, if someone were to require that soul is what is explanatory of its being alive, and that this is a number that moves itself; for, it is necessary to postulate that soul just is a number that moves itself, in the sense of it being just the same thing. (91ᵃ33–8)

The syllogism at issue here appears to be this:

In assessing this argument, it is important to note that in seeking for a definition of C's. Aristotle is looking for something which (i) is possessed by all and only C's, and (ii) is included in the essence of C (91^a15–17). (Let us call this factor 'A'). These are stringent demands. (i) requires 'A' and 'C' to convert (be true of all and only the same objects), and so excludes the possibility that 'A' might extend further than 'C', as 'animal' extends further than 'man'. (ii) requires that 'A' should belong in the specification of C's essence (see 91^b1, 7), and not merely pick out a necessary feature of C. Thus, 'A' could not be 'being capable of laughter' even though all and only men have this capacity.

One possible reply to Aristotle's first argument in B.4 would run as follows:

Why exclude the possibility that the conclusion is of the form:

A Φ def all C

and the middle term is *not* a definition of C? For, a syllogism of this form would prove a definition of C without presupposing one in the minor premiss.

A Φ def all B.

B Φ def all C.

A Φ def all C.

In this case, the A-term is 'being self-moved number', the B-term 'being explanatory of life', and the C-term 'being soul'. Aristotle insists that if:

A Φ def all C

is proved, one must assume that:

B Φ def all C

instantiates the right type of unity (91^b1). But this will only be so if it is true that:

B Φ def all C.

If this were not so:

A Φ def all C

would not follow, even if one assumed:

A Φ def all B.

As he notes, unless it is also true that:

B Φ def all C

one cannot be assured of the right type of unity in the minor premiss. He then cites the example of *being an animal* and *being a man* given above. For, here, while it is the case that:

Being an animal Φ all men

this does not instantiate the required unity of definition. The terms do not convert, and the statement is not one of identity.

Aristotle deploys several arguments against this type of reply. The first runs as follows:

> If you do not assume in this way by doubling up [viz. by taking both premisses as definitions], it will not be necessary that A is predicated of C in the account of what it [viz. C] is, if, although A is predicated of B in what it [viz. B] is, B is not always predicated in the what it is of the various things it is predicated of. But both premisses do contain the what it [viz. C] is: therefore B will have to hold of C in what it [viz. C] is. (91ª21–3)

Aristotle's argument here appears to be the following: The schema:

A Φ def all B.

B Φ nec all C.

A Φ def all C.

will not be universally valid. Indeed, he offers a counter example in the penultimate section of this chapter, in which:

Being an animal belongs nec all men.

is the relevant minor premiss(cf. 91ᵇ4–7). For, in this case, while it is true that:

Being F Φ def all animals

and

Being an animal Φ nec all men

it will not be the case that:

Being F Φ def all men.

Take the case where 'being F' is 'being alive' or 'being capable of perception'. Here, the term might give the essence of the genus but not of the species, since it does not specify a feature possessed by all and only men (91ª15). This term cannot specify the essence of man.

It is sufficient for Aristotle's purposes to show that this mode of argument is not universally valid. For, if this is so, one cannot establish by these methods alone that:

A Φ def all C.[8]

---

[8] Barnes, in his commentary (p. 199), discerns a stronger argument at work in 91ª22–3:

[A Φ def all B] and [not[B Φ def all C]] ⊢ [not[A Φ def all C]].

However, it is not obvious that this is needed for Aristotle's argument at this point. It is not required to block the claim that one can demonstrate:

A Φ def all C.

Thus, Aristotle concludes:

> If you do not assume in this way [viz. an essential middle term], you will not have deduced that A is what it is to be C [viz. that C Φ def to A] ... But if you do assume in this way, you will already have assumed what it is to be C: viz. B. Hence, it has not been demonstrated: for, you have assumed what was set at the beginning. (91^{b}7–11)

What conclusion can be drawn from this argument? There are at least two options:

(a) (more cautiously) *Some* definitions of this form can be demonstrated in this way, but *some* cannot.

by arguments of this form. Nor is it needed to allow Aristotle to conclude—as he does later in B.4:

if you do not assume this, you will not deduce that A is what it is to be C

For, this relies only on the claim that one cannot demonstrate:

A Φ def all C

unless one has:

B Φ def all C

among one's premises.

So, where does Barnes detect the stronger thesis at work in this chapter? He offers two texts in support of his claim:

[a] What a thing is is proper to it and predicated in the what it is. These [viz. what a thing is] necessarily convert. For, if A is proper to C, it is clear that it (viz. A) is also proper to B, and B to C. So, they are all proper to one another. [91^{a}15–18]

But this in no way supports the claim that:

A Φ def all B ⊢ B Φ def all A. (A: being rational, B: being a man).

All that it supports is:

A Φ all B ⊢ B Φ all A.

Since the next sentence (91^{a}18–21) raises a different point concerning the transitivity of 'belonging in the what it is', there is no support for the stronger thesis in these sentences.

[b] Both will contain the what it is. Therefore B will hold of C in the what it is [91^{a}24–5].

But it seems to be pressing the text too hard to see the following argument at work here:

Suppose A φ def B, A φ def C, and not (B φ def C). By conversion, A φ def C yields C φ def A. Since φ def is transitive, C φ def B follows from C φ def A and A φ def B. By conversion, B φ def C—which contradicts the original supposition.

Further, this interpretation cuts 91^{a}24 f. off from the preceding sentence which gives its ground:

It is not necessary that A Φ def all C, if A Φ def all B, and it is not the case that B Φ def all C.

For, this appears to be an argument merely for the weaker thesis, and not for the stronger one which Barnes detects.

(b) (more radically) *No* definition of this form can be demonstrated in this way because the conclusion is of the wrong form to be the conclusion of a demonstrative syllogism.[9]

It seems clear from the examples given in B.8 that Aristotle preferred the latter option.[10] So, what grounds did he have for rejecting (a)? Perhaps Xenocrates actually held that some (but not all) definitions can be demonstrated by the method of general deduction. Indeed, one can imagine him arguing for this view as follows:

In my favoured syllogism:

A Φ def all B.

B Φ def all C.

A Φ def all C.

the A-term is 'being a self-moved number', B is 'being explanatory of life', C is 'soul'. I agree, of course, that:

B Φ def all C

is assumed, and not proved. But this just shows that not *all* definitions of C can be demonstrated in this way. Some are prior, and these cannot be proved. However, one has good reason to believe them to be true, since from them true conclusions of the form:

A Φ def all C

actually follow. Thus, there could be demonstrative conclusions of the form:

Noise in the clouds Φ def all thunder

as well as definitions of the form:

Fire being extinguished Φ def all thunder

which are unproved. So, why should we restrict ourselves, as Aristotle does in B.8, to demonstrations whose conclusions (e.g. Noise/Thunder Φ nec the clouds.) do not state definitions at all?

---

[9] This option would be compatible with allowing that some definitions are *deduced*. Deduction differs from demonstration in not capturing the relative priority of premises and conclusions.

[10] For the relevant conclusions (93^a30 f., 93^b2 ff., 93^b10 ff.) contain claims of the form:

Eclipses happen to the moon

or

Noise occurs in the clouds

which are not definitions of either eclipses or thunder.

Xenocrates' point could be put like this. In B.4 Aristotle showed that one could not both:

(1) have demonstrations whose conclusions state definitional connections:

e.g. Thunder is def noise in the clouds

and

(2) have in these demonstrations definitional minor premisses which are themselves (at the same time) proved:

e.g. Fire being extinguished Φ def all thunder.

In B.8 Aristotle's favoured demonstrations lack definitions in both premisses and conclusions. But why drop both (1) and (2) together? Why not give up (2), accept that there are some assumed definitions, but insist that one can demonstrate some other definitions from them?

Some of Aristotle's arguments in B.6 provide an answer to this form of objection. Indeed, they appear to be directed against the type of position envisaged by Xenocrates in this (imagined) reply.

7.3 FURTHER CRITICISMS OF GENERAL DEDUCTION: B.6

Since the first argument of B.6 (92^a8–10) simply reiterates the arguments of B.4, we must look for possible replies to the Xenocratean objection in the remaining arguments of the chapter.[11] The second runs as follows:

---

[11] Aristotle begins B.6 as follows:

Can one actually demonstrate what a thing is essentially on a supposition as follows:

[1] What it is to be F is composed from the elements which are in the essence of F and are peculiar to F.
[2] Being G, H, I are the only things in the essence of F and are collectively peculiar to F.

So

[3] Being G, H, I is the definition of being F. (92^a6–9)

Now, in this case, the assumption is a special one—one concerning the nature of definition (1). But not all of Aristotle's examples in this chapter are of this form. Thus, his second example runs as follows:

One might prove [sc. a definition] from a supposition as follows: if being bad is being divisible, and for things which have a contrary being their contrary is contrary to them, and the good is contrary to the bad, and the divisible to the indivisible, one might prove that the good is indivisible. (92^a20–4)

In this case there is no assumption about the nature of definition itself explicit in the argument. And so, whatever arguments Aristotle employs against the latter case should be arguments against the general proposal of arriving at a conclusion of the form:

As in a deduction you do not assume [as a premiss] an account of what it is for
something to be deduced (for the proposition on which the deduction depends is
always part or whole), similarly it is not necessary for an account of what it is to
be F to be in the deduction; this should be kept separate from what is assumed in
the premisses; and, just as in answer to someone who asks whether something has
been deduced we say, 'This is what deduction is,' similarly in answer to someone
who says that what it is to be F has not been deduced we say: 'That is right, since
this is what we assumed it is to be F'. Hence, deductions must be made without
assuming accounts of what deduction is or accounts of what it is to be particular
things. (92^a11–19)[12]

This line of thought has received a bad press:

(a) Some have thought that it attempts to establish at 92^a11 that one
    should not use as a premiss in a deduction an account of what a defi-
    nition is because in a deduction one does not use as a premiss an
    account of what deduction is. Barnes describes this as 'dismal'.[13]

(b) Others have thought that it rules out the definition of deduction as a
    possible premiss on formal grounds (i.e. such a premiss would not be
    either a whole or a part of the conclusion). But this is (as Barnes
    notes[14]) false: one can use propositions of this type among the propo-
    sitions from which we reason.

A Φ def all C.

from a premiss which contains a definitional term of the form:

B* Φ def all C*.

where B* and C* are systematically connected (in a definitional way) with B and C.

[12] I understand 92^a13–4 to say that no *particular definition* (e.g. a definition of F) need be
included among the (relevant) premisses (as they are in the method of general deduction).
Rather, this sentence claims, such definitions should be established separately from such premisses and be used to confirm claims of the form: the definition of F has been deduced. If
this definition is to be established by a syllogism, the latter should not contain it among its
premisses.
    I interpret the passage as referring to particular definitions and not the definition of
definition for three reasons:
    (1) In the immediate context (92^a7, $^a9$, $^a24$) the phrase 'what it is to be something' refers
to particular definitions, such as may appear in the syllogisms of general deduction. It would
be a major shift of levels to begin to talk now of the definition of definition.
    (2) Such a shift of levels would be unmotivated in the present context. For, there is no
indication that the method of general deduction either was or should be concerned with the
definition of definition. For all that Aristotle says, it aimed only to establish particular definitions.
    (3) A shift of levels is not required to sustain the analogy with deduction. For, that
can be preserved even if Aristotle is comparing particular definitions with the whole practice of deduction. There would still be a common element: in neither is it legitimate to
assume in advance what is to be established by the syllogisms at issue. In this way the analogy
can be maintained without using the whole practice of definition as an element in the
comparison.
[13] Barnes, *Aristotle's Posterior Analytics*, 212.   [14] *Aristotle's Posterior Analytics*, 213.

(c) Still others have thought that Aristotle is insisting that if anyone wanted to demonstrate a definition they should hold back the definition of definition in order to produce it later if challenged.[15]

There is, however, an alternative, more charitable, reading of this passage, and of the analogy which it suggests between deduction and definition. Aristotle need not be taken to argue that one can never have premisses of the form:

F is defined as . . .

among one's antecedents. He is arguing rather that if one does so, one is resting on a prior and independent understanding of what F is, which is not based on, and cannot be justified by, our understanding of this syllogism (92^a13–18). Further, if our understanding of the definition of F depends on our grasp of any type of syllogism, the latter cannot be one which includes among its premisses definitions of F. Syllogisms more basic than these will be required to underwrite our grasp of that definition (92^a18–19).

On this interpretation, Aristotle is not arguing that we must always exclude propositions which define deduction from the class of those from which we reason. Rather, he is saying that not all deductions can involve premisses of this type, because our understanding of what deduction is is itself grounded in an understanding of syllogisms which do not contain any such premisses (92^a18f.). By analogy, he will claim that our grasp of the definition of F cannot itself be grounded in an understanding of syllogisms which include a definition of F among their premisses. For, the latter will presuppose an account of what F is and cannot ground it. Further, if our understanding of what F is is based on any syllogism, it cannot be one which includes this definitional connection among its premisses.

Aristotle (on this interpetation) will not simply be saying that we must always 'hold back' the relevant definition in order to produce it later if challenged. Rather, he is claiming that our way to establish what F is (if the case is analogous to that of deduction) cannot be based on a syllogism in which that definition is assumed. For, that definition has to be secured on independent grounds. Indeed, Aristotle appears to push the analogy further (in 92^a18–19). In the case of deduction, one cannot establish what it is to be a deduction on the basis of premisses which include a definition of deduction. Rather, we understand what this is by pointing to particular deductions (which do not include any definition of deduction) and saying, 'This is what deduction is'. In this way we grasp what deduction is on the

---

[15] These criticisms assume that (*pace* n. 12) Aristotle is concerned with the definition of definition in this passage. However, one might devise variants of these criticisms even if Aristotle is concerned only with particular definitions in this passage.

basis of deductions which do not themselves contain definitions of deduction. By analogy, we should grasp what the definition of F is on the basis of a deduction which does not contain among its premisses any particular definition of what F is. That is, our grasp of what F is (like our grasp of what deduction is) should rest on our understanding of a deduction which does not contain the relevant definition among its premisses. If so, we must be able to grasp the definition of F on the basis of some deductions whose premisses do not contain a definition of F. In both cases, the relevant definition (whether of deduction or of F) will be understood on the basis of deduction which does not contain it.[16]

If Aristotle accepts both these points, he is embracing a Definitional Constraint of the following form:

the appropriate method for coming to know a definition should give us grounds for the claim that this definition is correct, and do so in a way which essentially involves the use of deduction (of some kind).

But why should Xenocrates accept these constraints? Perhaps he thought that we can just 'see' that certain definitions are correct without any further support. Or perhaps he believed that these claims could be justified from resources independent of deduction or demonstration. Why should Xenocrates accept Aristotle's analogy with deduction?

Aristotle's best reply would be to show that the preferred route to establishing particular definitions must involve deduction of some kind. His third and fourth arguments in B.6 engage in some measure with these issues. The third aims to show that definitions are not *demonstrated* within the method of general deduction. He argues for this conclusion as follows:

This is the case, even if you prove from a hypothesis in the following way: '(1) That which is bad is, definitionally, that which is divisible, and (2) For things which have a contrary being their contrary is being contrary to what they are, and (3) The good is contrary to the bad, and the indivisible to the divisible, so it follows that being good is being indivisible'. For, here, too, you are assuming what has to be proved. Someone will say that what is assumed is a different term [viz. 'bad' and not 'good'], and also that in demonstrations one assumes that this is true of this. But I shall reply that you do not assume in a demonstration the same thing as the conclusion or something that has the same account as the conclusion and converts with it. (92ª20–7)

---

[16] On this understanding, 'the something' syllogized in 92ª19 refers *either* to any deduction (as in 92ª16) *or* to the type of deduction from which one can read off the definition of F. Aristotle leaves the limits of the analogy unclear. Did he, for example, require that the premisses involved in establishing the definition of F should lack all definitions (or only the definition of F)? The stronger requirement would parallel his injunction against including any premiss concerning the nature of deduction in a deduction which shows the nature of deduction. The answer to this question is to be found (if at all) in his positive account in B.8 and the following chapters.

What is the point of this argument?[17] Why does it tell against Xenocrates? Consider the type of syllogism which he favours:

A Φ def all B.   A: self-moved number

B Φ def all C.   B: being explanatory of life

A Φ def all C.   C: soul

Here, the relevant minor premiss states that:

Being explanatory of life Φ def all souls

and one infers that:

Being a self-moved number φ def all souls.

Aristotle, in effect, objects as follows in 92ᵃ25–7:

in a genuine demonstration, the B-term is not the same as the A-term, nor is it a term with the same definition as the A-term which converts with it. But in the first premiss of the case proposed:

A Φ def all B.

the A-term (being a self-moved number) has the same account as the B-term (being explanatory of life); for, the account of the A-term is given by the account of the B-term. If so, this syllogism is not a demonstration (as I understand them), since it violates certain structural constraints required of demonstrations.

But how deep does this argument go? Why should Xenocrates accept that definitional syllogisms have to be *demonstrations* of a type which Aristotle accepts? Aristotle's point can perhaps be put as follows. Although Xenocrates assumes that:

the soul's being explanatory of life

is prior to and explanatory of:

the soul's being a self-moved number

he gives no grounds for doing so. That is, he provides no basis for taking the B-term as giving the account *(logos)* of the A-term rather than vice versa. In effect, he has no grounds for taking the minor premiss:

B Φ def all C (i.e. B belongs definitionally to all C).

as being what gives the basic definition of C. For all he has said, the conclusion:

---

[17] For a discussion of hypothetical syllogisms in the *Topics*, see P. Slomkowski's, *Aristotle's Topics* (Leiden, 1977).

A Φ def all C

could be equally basic. So, there appears to be no priority involved.

If this is correct, Aristotle is assuming that a definition should reveal what is prior in the relevant account and capture what is (in some sense) basic about the kind in question. He is further assuming that the relevant type of priority will only be captured in a demonstration. That is, one must be able to establish, in grasping a proper definition, what the relevant basic or prior features are by showing how the relevant conclusion:

A Φ def all C

is underwritten by a more basic connection formulated in the premisses. In arguing thus, Aristotle is proposing a Priority Condition as part of his general Definitional Constraint:

The appropriate method for arriving at a definition of C should legitimize the claim that some feature is prior to all other features of C.

Xenocrates has two options at this point. Either he can reject the requirement that definition should capture what is prior or he can show how to meet this requirement without dependence on demonstration. Aristotle does not consider the first option. He must have assumed that definitions should capture what is prior in the approved way, and perhaps that Xenocrates himself would have accepted this.[18] But what of the second? Did Xenocrates have good reasons, independent of demonstration, for taking the B-term as the more basic? Could he have found some? Certainly none are provided. Nor is it easy to see how intuition could play this role. For, Aristotle is seeking *a method* which should give us good reason to believe that certain features are basic. Merely stating truly that they are will not give us the required knowledge. As we will see in the next Chapter, demonstration, with its connections with explanation, offers a route to establishing what is prior to what.[19]

Before that, there is one further consideration relevant to definition introduced in B.6.

7.4 UNITY, DIVISION AND DEMONSTRATION

The fourth argument which Aristotle employs in B.6 shares certain features with the third. It runs as follows:

---

[18] For further discussion, see Ch. 10 Sect. 10.3.

[19] In B.8, Aristotle refers back to this passage where he notes:

For, in the case of what a thing is, it is necessary for the middle term to give what a thing is ... Hence, you will prove the one but not the other instance of what it is to be the same object. Now, that this way will not be a demonstration was said earlier. (93[a]11–14)

And in both these cases—if you prove by a division or by this kind of deduction in this way—there is the same puzzle: Why will man be a two-footed terrestrial animal and not animal and terrestrial and two-footed? For, from the assumptions there is no necessity that what is predicated turn out to be a unity. It could be like the case of someone being musical and literate. (92ª27–33)

Aristotle is noting that in a syllogism of the style favoured by Xenocrates:

A Φ def all B.

B Φ def all C.

A Φ def all C.

one is merely assuming that the B-term marks out a unity, and has no proof that this is so. Thus, he is introducing a further condition, which might be called the Unity Condition as part of his Definitional Constraint:

The appropriate method for arriving at definitions should legitimize the claim that the *definiens* is a unity.

In Xenocrates' example, what is it that establishes that the soul is a self-moved number, and not self-moved and number? As before, the element crucial for definition is assumed and not established by Xenocrates' method.

   Aristotle employs similar arguments in B.5. in considering the method of division. These allow us further insight into the Unity Condition, and, more generally, into his Definitional Constraint. He had discussed the method of division in *Prior Analytics* A.31, where he provided a clear example:

Being animal Φ all men.

Being mortal or immortal Φ all animals

Being mortal or immortal Φ all men. (46ᵇ9–11)

One of the criticisms he employed there (*Pr. An.* A.31, 46ᵇ2–11) is repeated in *Posterior Analytics* B.5, 91ᵇ24–7. In division, Aristotle notes, one cannot prove that:

All men are mortal.

Here, too, he comments that in a syllogism of the form:

A Φ def all B.

B Φ def all C.

A Φ def all C.

one will prove the conclusion and not the minor premiss, even though both give an account of what it is to be C. His comment in B.6 deepens our understanding of this latter point. A and B in this syllogism have the same account (*logos*) and are convertible. But the presence of this feature prevents this deduction from being a genuine demonstration.

The most that division can establish is the disjunctive conclusion:

All men are either mortal or immortal.

A fortiori, it cannot establish:

It is necessary that man is mortal,

the claim needed for definition. This too is assumed by the divider (91^b17-21). Further, the disjunctive conclusion is not of the right form to be a definition (92^a1-4).[20] So, since division cannot give us the resources to know that a given statement is a definition of man, it fails to satisfy Aristotle's Definitional Constraint.

Aristotle develops his criticism of division further in B.5. First, he notes that even if the divider could (*per impossibile*) establish by his method that:

All men are mortal

he would have no ground for taking this as part of the essence of man (91^b24-6). Nor would he have grounds for taking this property as the complete essence of man. Why not add it, or subtract it, from the definition (91^b26-7)? The method of division does not determine what should be, and what should not be, included in the definition of man.

Aristotle makes another related point: Even if (*per impossibile*) the method of division generated claims of the form:

(1) All men are animals

and

(2) All animals are footed

it could not establish that:

(3) All men are necessarily footed animals.

(1) and (2) cannot establish the relevant necessity in (3) (91^b15-21). That would have to be assumed. Thus, the method cannot give us a route

---

[20] In *Pr. An.* 46^b20-2, 46^a37-^b2, Aristotle argued that division is contrary to the general form of the syllogism. In a syllogism of the form required for division:

All men are animals.

All animals are either mortal or immortal.

All men are either mortal or immortal.

the middle term (animal) is greater in extension than the first term (man). By contrast, in the standard syllogism the middle term is less in extension than the first term. Further, the conclusion of the division syllogism is not sufficient to show that all men are mortal. This is merely assumed (46^b2-11). But what is the significance of violating these conditions on the general form of the syllogism? Perhaps it appears important because, in these syllogisms, it is presupposed that man belongs to the genus animal (46^b5-8), and this is not established by the method.

to grasp the necessity of true definition (91^{b}24–6). Therefore, it fails to explain what is essential for the kind, and so what is relevant for its definition.

Aristotle makes a further point, directly relevant to the Unity Condition. If one defines man as follows:

Man is two-footed, wingless, mortal (92^{a}1)

one has no reason for taking the *definiens* to be a genuine unity. What reason is given by this method for thinking that this *definiens* is a genuine unity while musical literate thing is not (cf. 92^{a}30–3)?

A defender of the method of division might attempt to reply to this criticism as follows: If one could establish (possibly *per impossibile*) by this method that:

Man is necesssarily terrestrial

and

Man is necessarily two-footed

one would have good grounds for the conclusion:

Man is necessarily terrestrial and two-footed.

It might be agreed that the method of division cannot by itself establish that both these *differentiae* belong to man. However, it would be enough if it could establish that individual *differentiae* belong to man. For, then it could use an agglomerative principle to establish that:

Man is necessarily F and G.

Further, if the method of division were able to establish:

Man is necessarily terrestrial

and

Man is necessarily two-footed

one could establish that:

Man is necessarily terrestrial and two-footed

in a way which showed that being terrestrial and two-footed was not an accidental unity (unlike musical and literate). It would indeed be necessary that man is terrestrial and two-footed, and this would follow from the individual necessities and the principle of agglomeration.

This reply, however, would prove inadequate by Aristotle's lights. The agglomerative principle will give us no reason to accept that:

Man is necessarily terrestrial and two-footed.

For, it does not establish that the individual modal claims:

Man is necessarily two-footed

and

Man is necessarily terrestrial

are both true of one and the same thing. This point will apply to any *differentiae* terms, no matter how basic, which the divider uses:

Man is animal, two-footed, featherless, terrestrial, mortal. (92^a1)

For, we need to show that one and the same kind (man) is both necessarily two-footed and necessarily terrestrial. Perhaps the term 'man' is ambiguous, and picks out one kind as two-footed and another as terrestrial.

This latter criticism gives further insight into Aristotle's conditions in this passage. In grasping a definition one needs a method which shows why a given set of properties are all necessarily true of the same thing. That is, one needs to show why man is both two-footed and terrestrial at the same time. It is not enough that one of these terms is a unity. It must also provide the basis for establishing that the kind possesses all the features of the kind which are mentioned in the definition. Explanations of this type will underwrite the unity of definition.

The method of division fails to satisfy this constraint in part because it cannot meet either the Unity or Priority Conditions. Indeed, the latter can better be seen as one Simple Condition:

The appropriate method for arriving at definitions should give us good grounds for the claim that:

(a) There is one feature which is a prior feature of the relevant kind

and

(b) That feature should explain why the kind possesses all the other necessary features specified in the definition.

7.5 SUMMARY

By the end of B.7, Aristotle has in place the Simple Condition and the Definitional Constraint. Further, he has argued that neither the method of division nor that of general deduction have the resources to meet the requirements set by the Simple Condition. If they were the only methods available whereby we can arrive at definitions, we would not be able to 'become aware of what a thing is either by definition or demonstration'(92^b35–8). What is needed is a method which meets the Simple Condition and simultaneously satisfies the other aspects of the Definitional Constraint. This, as I shall argue in the next Chapter, is precisely what Aristotle was attempting to dicover in much of the remainder of the *Analytics*.

Although the method of general deduction fails, it has one major advantage. It offers a simple way of establishing definitions, because its conclusions *are* definitions. If this method fails, it might appear that one cannot use deduction or demonstration in establishing definitions. For, if their conclusions do not contain definitions, they will not be relevant to the definitional task. At the end of B.7 Aristotle has arrived at an impasse. Either one uses a method (like that of general deduction) which has definitions in the conclusion but which violates the Definitional Constraint and the Simple Condition. Or, alternatively, one may satisfy these requirements but fail to generate the type of conclusions needed for definitions.[21] This is the dilemma that needs to be broken in B.8 and the following chapters. We shall follow Aristotle's attempts to do so in the next Chapter.

The Definitional Constraint and the Simple Condition have been introduced as conditions on how we come to know a definition of a particular kind. However, it is natural to enquire whether these epistemic conditions rest on a metaphysical conception of what features are relevant for a good definition. This question too will be addressed in the next Chapter.

---

[21] See Chapters 2 and 3 for further consideration of the Independence and Formal Conditions. These focus on the problems encountered if the syllogism's conclusion is not a definition.

8

Demonstration and Definition: Aristotle's Positive Views in Posterior Analytics B.8–10 and B.16–18

8.1 INTRODUCTION

Aristotle needed to find a method to establish which features of a kind define it. The definitional features, thus secured, should be (in some way) prior and sufficient to underwrite the unity of the kind. His method should essentially involve the use of demonstration. In this way, he could satisfy the Simple Condition and Definitional Constraint, which he employed in his criticisms of the methods of general deduction and division.

In the context set by B.3–7, Aristotle's aim was even more precisely defined. He had to achieve these goals in a way which was not vulnerable to the Formal and Independence Problems (as set out in Chapter 3). Thus, he had to show how demonstration could be of use in the definitional task, even though the relevant demonstrations did not have as their conclusions definitions of the kind.[1]

Part of Aristotle's solution has already been considered.[2] The conclusions of the relevant syllogisms need not contain both *definiens* and *definiendum*, provided that they are systematically connected to the term to be defined. The relevant link is provided by the Stage 1 account of what the term signifies. Thus, if 'thunder' signifies the same as 'a certain type of noise in the clouds', the demonstrative conclusion:

Noise belongs to the clouds

is connected in an obvious way to the term to be defined. For, as suggested above, Aristotle's accounts of what the term signifies provide the

---

[1] The phrase 'definitional task' is intended to be neutral at this point as between two options: the task of searching for definitions, and the task of laying out definitions once discovered. Demonstrations cannot contain both the term defined and its definition in the conclusion.

[2] See Chs. 2 and 3 above.

springboard for an investigation into the existence and nature of the kind.[3]

The stage is now set for Aristotle's attempt to satisfy his own Simple Condition and Definitional Constraint. I shall first consider his discussion in B.8, 93^a16-^b14. Investigation of the demonstrations used there (Section 8.2) and in B.16–17 (Section 8.3) will enable us to understand part of his strategy for connecting definition and explanation in *Posterior Analytics* B. But the resulting picture is more complicated than it might at first seem (Sections 8.4 and 8.5).

8.2 DEMONSTRATION, GENERAL DEDUCTION, AND EFFICIENT CAUSATION: THE BASIC CASE

Aristotle offers two examples of syllogisms in B.8 to illustrate the connection between the practice of definition and of demonstration. They run as follows:

[EXAMPLE 1] Being eclipsed belongs to all things being screened by the earth.
Being screened belongs to the moon (or perhaps to all moons of kind K).

Being eclipsed belongs to the moon (all moons of kind K).[4]
(93^a30-1)

[EXAMPLE 2] Thunder/Noise belongs to all fire-quenchings.
Fire-quenching belongs to the clouds (all clouds of kind K).

Noise belongs to the clouds (all clouds of kind K). (93^b9-12)

---

[3] More precisely, they fulfil two roles:

(a) They give the basis for an appropriately articulated two-term statement which is the starting point for a search for the relevant middle term (which explains why the two terms are so connected).

and

(b) They indicate an as yet not fully specified type of (e.g.) noise, which can be specified further at the second and third stage of enquiry.

[4] The precise logical form of these syllogisms has been the subject of much discussion. I assume (for present purposes) that they are in the Barbara form, and contain no singular terms. Thus, I prefer to construe reference to the moon as to (e.g.) the moon in certain stages of its career.

In these examples, although an effect is demonstrated, the conclusions do not contain definitions.[5] Even when the term being defined (e.g. 'eclipse') appears in the conclusion, the latter is not a definition of eclipse (or even of eclipse of the moon).

Why is this method preferable to that involving general deductions? In these demonstrations, the middle term (e.g. 'fire-quenching') specifies the efficient cause of:

(1) an eclipse of the moon

and

(3) noise occurring in the clouds

We can answer the 'Why?' question by giving the efficient cause of the phenomenon specified in the conclusion.

The causal order displayed in these demonstrations is relevant to the issue of priority encapsulated in the Simple Condition. In the case of thunder, the quenching of fire is causally more basic than the occurrence of noise in the clouds, because the former is the efficient cause of the latter.[6] This asymmetry is captured in syllogism (2), but not in the syllogisms of the method of general deduction. For, in the syllogism:

Noise in the clouds belongs def to all fire-quenchings.

Fire-quenching belongs def to all thunder.

Noise in the clouds belongs def to all thunder.

the middle term is not the efficient cause of noise in the clouds belonging to thunder. Indeed, this syllogism gives no ground for treating the second

---

[5] In this syllogism, I take the conclusion reached at 93^{b}10 f. *not* to be of the form:

Thunder is noise in the clouds.

It should be noted, however, that in B.10, 94^{a}7–9, Aristotle might appear to take this to be the conclusion 'of the demonstration of the what it is'. Is Aristotle's view inconsistent? Perhaps Aristotle is not over-concerned with the precise nature of the syllogism involved. (On these issues, see J. L. Ackrill, 'Aristotle's Theory of Definition' in Berti (ed.), *Aristotle on Science*, 359–63.)

However, in B.10, 94^{a}8 'this' can refer either to the phrase 'noise in the clouds' or to 'thunder is noise in the clouds'. The former seems preferable because it keeps the terms of the syllogism the same as those specified in 94^{a}4–7: 'noise', 'fire being quenched', 'the clouds'. To suppose otherwise is to deprive 'the clouds' of the status as a separate term which it clearly has in 94^{a}4 ff. and 93^{b}9 ff.

There remains a problem concerning the substitution of 'noise' and 'thunder' in 93^{b}9 ff. But this is a different issue, related to the permissible substitution of names and (parts of) accounts of what names signify.

[6] In this Chapter, I use interchangeably as translations for '*aition*', 'cause', 'causal explanation', and 'explanation'. This issue is discussed in more detail in Chapter 10.

premiss as prior to the conclusion. By contrast, through the practice of demonstration we grasp that a feature is definitionally prior because it is prior in the order of efficient causation. The quenching of fire is the start of a causal process which culminates in noise occurring in the clouds.

Why, for Aristotle, should our definitional practices depend on our way of explaining phenomena? It is not merely that we *know* that certain features are definitionally prior because they are causally prior (B.8, 93ª3–5). Rather, as he remarks in *Posterior Analytics* A.2, 71ᵇ31:

things are prior (i.e. by nature) since they are causes.

The order of definitional priority is determined by the order of causation. Fire being quenched is definitionally prior to noise in the clouds because it is causally prior. It is the efficient cause. What it is to be something (as captured in the definition) and the basic relevant cause are one and the same (B.2, 90ª14–15).[7] The dependence of our practice of definition on that of explanation reflects a metaphysical interconnection between essence and causation.[8]

We were prepared for a connection between defining and explaining by Aristotle's remarks in *Posterior Analytics* B.6. There, he suggested that there can be no account of particular definitions in terms independent of demonstration. Since demonstration captures the order of causation, there can be no account of particular definitions which is independent of the causal order.[9] In giving demonstrations we track, in the case of a kind, the metaphysical order of causation back to one cause of all its relevant necessary features. Had the order of causation not been connected in this way to the theory of definition, it would be (at least, epistemically) possible for there to be an alternative route to find what is definitionally prior. For, if definitional priority were not determined by causal priority, it would be (in principle) possible for us to come to know the former by a route independent of the latter. Aristotle, as we noted above, does not seriously consider the possibility of an alternative epistemic route of this type. So, his preference for the method of demonstration is, it appears, based on his assumption that the order of definition is metaphysically dependent on the order of causation. This is why we need to engage in demonstration to establish correct definitions.[10]

---

[7] Equally, since 'thunder' is taken to be equivalent in meaning to 'noise in the clouds', the quenching of fire is also definitionally prior to thunder.

[8] I use the terms 'practice of defining' and 'practice of explaining' to separate what we do in giving definitions/explanations from the subject matter of such definitions and explanations: essences and *explananda/explanantia* (or causes/effects).

[9] See Ch. 7.

[10] It may be objected that Aristotle's discussion of *nous* in the final chapter of the *Analytics* shows a route to grasp definitions which is independent of the theory of demonstration. I shall argue in Chapter 10 that this is not so. However, the present focus is restricted to the preceding chapters of *Post. An.* B.

Aristotle's remarks elsewhere suggest the same view. In B.16 ($98^{b}19$–21) he contrasts the syllogism which demonstrates the cause:

Things that are near do not twinkle.

The planets are near.

The planets do not twinkle.

with one which demonstrates the fact:

Things that do not twinkle are near.

The planets do not twinkle.

The planets are near.

Planets fail to twinkle (according to Aristotle) because they are near. They are not near because they fail to twinkle (A.13, $78^{a}37$ f.). The order of causation is fixed independently of the order of definition. However, he remarks in B.16 that:

It is clear that being screened by the earth (B) is the cause of the eclipse (A) and not vice versa: for, B is specified in the account of A, so that it is obvious that the latter is known via the former and not vice versa. ($98^{b}21$–4)

The order of efficient causation is *clear* because it is captured in the order of definition. But this, as we can now see, is because the order of definition is determined by the order of causation. The stars' position is definitionally prior to their failure to twinkle because the former is the efficient cause of the latter.[11] Here, too, the interdependence of our practices of definition and explanation reflects a metaphysical connection between essence and *explanans*/cause.

Other features of Aristotle's method rest on the same view. His 'immediate propositions' are a case in point (see B.8, $93^{a}36$). We reach, in giving explanations, an immediate proposition when there is no further cause which connects (e.g.):

(1) deprivation of light and the earth screening ($93^{a}30$–6)

---

[11] In B.16, $98^{b}22$ ff. Aristotle writes:

That the eclipse is not the cause of its being in between but the latter of the eclipse is clear; for, being in between is in the definition of eclipse, so that the latter is known by means of the former and not vice versa.

This might appear to take the order of definition to explain the order of causality (in opposition to the thesis developed above). However, Aristotle notes in this passage *not* that A causes B because A is used to define B, but rather that it is *obvious* that A causes B because A is used to define B. Obviousness is an epistemic notion, which reflects the order of our knowledge. But this is fully consistent with the line of interpretation developed to understand B.8–10, which concerns the metaphysical order of definition.

or

(2) noise and fire being quenched.

If there were a further cause, our investigation would be incomplete until we discovered it (93^b12-14). Immediate propositions are bedrock from a causal point of view. They describe a direct, unmediated, causal connection. No further cause can be invoked to account for the connection they express.[12] In B.8 two features are central to the examples of demonstration:

(1) In discovering the answer to the 'Why?' question, we trace the pattern and order of efficient causation.

(2) In discovering the answer to the 'Why?' question, we find at the end of our enquiry an immediate proposition. At this point, there is no further causal relation to be discovered relevant to the effect in question.

In both examples, the relevant causal pattern is one of efficient causation. By following this, we come to know the essence of the phenomenon in question. Here, what is definitionally prior (viz. the essence) is determined by what is causally prior.

A further example of this order of determination is suggested by Aristotle's identification of *the* essence with *the* cause (B.2 90^a14-15, see also the epistemic version in B.8 93^a3-4). If one traces back the relevant causal line from the effect, one will find *one* feature (*the* cause) which explains why (in the case of thunder) noise occurs in the clouds. This feature will also explain why thunder possesses its other necessary properties: why it is accompanied by lightning (for example), or why it is noisy. For, the presence of these properties will be explained because the fire, when quenched, produces noise and lightning. In this way, there is *one* efficient cause which brings about all the other necessary properties of thunder. This efficient cause would be discovered whichever of the relevant necessary properties

---

[12] In these examples of immediate propositions, we find two distinct phenomena which are immediately related. The cause in these cases is other than the phenomenon caused (93^b19, cf. 93^a7), as *fire being quenched* is other than *noise*. As such, immediate propositions of this type are different in kind from the cases discussed in B.9, where Aristotle is concerned (93^b21-5) with primary objects which are identical with their causes, or essences. It is crucial to separate immediate or primary *objects* (which are identical with their essences (93^b21-5)) from immediate *propositions* which state unmediated (causal) connections between distinct phenomena. (There may be a class of immediate propositions which are concerned with the relation between primary objects and their essences. If so, they will be a subclass of immediate propositions, whose other species will involve cases where the kinds or objects are distinct from their causes, but are non-mediately connected with them.) These two sets of cases are distinct, and confusion results if they are conflated. For a contrasting view, see R. Bolton's paper 'Definition and Scientific Method in Aristotle's *Posterior Analytics* and the *Generation of Animals*', in A. Gotthelf and J. Lennox (eds.), *Philosophical Issues in Aristotle's Biology* (Cambridge, 1987), 138–42.

had been the starting point of one's enquiry. For, it is the common cause of all the relevant features. Thus, the essence is the one cause of all the kind's derived necessary properties.

Aristotle, armed with the method of demonstration, can satisfy the requirements of his own Simple Condition. Thunder is a unity because there is *one* common efficient cause which explains the presence of its necessary properties. It is because fire is quenched that there is noise in the clouds, noise accompanied by lightning, etc. The presence of this prior feature underwrites the unity of the kind. Similarly in the case of man. Aristotle had asked: why do all the following properties belong to man:

footed, two-footed animal (92^a30)

and

featherless, footed, two-footed, mortal animal (92^a1)?

He now has an answer: because there is one common cause which explains man's possession of all of these properties. This one cause underwrites the unity of the kind. The relevant cause will be captured by the middle term of a syllogism in which each proposition says one thing of one thing non-accidentally (93^b36f.; cf. 72^a9). By contrast, there is no one cause which explains why something is both musical and literate. This is an accidental unity because the feature which explains one property fails to explain the other.

Aristotle's model of enquiry encapsulates a metaphysical picture. Enquiries of this type are successful when there is one common cause which is prior in the way specified to the other features of the kind. In the simple cases Aristotle discusses, the definitionally prior feature is the efficient cause. More generally, the prior feature will be the common cause in whatever causal mode is appropriate for the kind in question. The presence of this one feature will provide the basis for the unity of the kind.

Aristotle's model allows him to satisfy the requirements of the Definitional Constraint. Certain features will be relevant to definition if they possess the type of priority and unity required of good definition. They will possess the latter because they are causally prior and the one common cause of all the other relevant features of the kind. Such features will be mentioned in our definitions because they are causally prior unities of this type. Other features may be included in our definitions if they are immediate consequences of the one common cause. (For further discussion, see Chapter 9.)

These suggestions allow Aristotle to make substantial progress in the *Analytics*. His model satisfies the unity and priority requirements which he used to criticize rival proposals in B.5–6. Had he failed to meet them, his criticisms of those methods would have lost much of their force. The reasonable conclusion might have been that Aristotle's own requirements could not be met. Perhaps he should have jettisoned them and retained either the method of general deduction or division.

The grounds for Aristotle's preference for the method of demonstration have now become clear. He can use it to establish particular definitions because it will show which features are the causally basic, unifying features of the kind. Features cannot be known to be prior in this way unless they are seen as the basis for demonstrative explanation of the appropriate type. Without this, there would be no way to know which features are definitional. As Aristotle comments in his concluding remarks in B.8:

In cases where the cause is different from the effect, it is not possible to know what it is without demonstration, but there is no demonstration *of it.* (93^b18 f.)

Through giving demonstrations, we can use the notions of causal priority and of one unified cause to capture what is definitionally prior and to underwrite the unity of the *definiendum.* Further, the success of this method is non-accidental, since its epistemic virtues reflect the metaphysical dependence of definition on causation. In these respects, it is clearly preferable to the method of general deduction.

Aristotle's basic model has many gaps. In the cases so far considered, he has focused on examples involving efficient causation. Can this model be extended to cases involving other types of cause (see Sect. 8.5)? Nor have we understood other central aspects of the model. Why are certain features taken as the *explananda?* What constrains the appropriate causal connections? However, despite these gaps, we can reach an interim conclusion: In Aristotle's account causal priority (of some form) determines (in some measure) what is definitionally prior. In this way, our practice of definition rests on, and is partially determined by, our practice of explanation.

In the next Section, I shall investigate further the type of causal explanation which Aristotle employs in these contexts. It will soon become apparent that the connection between defining and explaining is more complicated than has so far been suggested. For, it turns out that it is appropriate to use certain forms of causal explanation because they are the right ones to yield definitions.

8.3 EXPLANATION AND ESSENCE: B.16–18: THE BASIC MODEL EXTENDED AND REFINED

In *Posterior Analytics* B.16–18 Aristotle discusses further the type of causal explanation to be used in arriving at definitions (see B.17, 99^a21 ff.). Examination of these passages may shed more light on the procedure he employed to satisfy the Definitional Constraint. For, several aspects were left obscure in B.8–10.[13]

In B.16–18 Aristotle considers two questions about causal explanation:

(A) If the *explanandum* is present, is the *explanans* always present?

(B) If the *explanans* is present, is the *explanandum* always present?

In Aristotle's own terminology, the relevant question is as follows:

(A*) If there is an eclipse, is there always a screening by the earth?

(B*) If there is a screening by the earth, is there always an eclipse?

As he puts it, do the relevant terms ('eclipse', 'interposition of the moon') convert? We might say: is the occurrence of the *explanans* (considered as a type) both necessary and sufficient for the occurrence of the *explanandum* (as a type)? (cf. 98ᵃ35–ᵇ4)

Aristotle's answers are cautious but revealing. One of his examples is biological. He asks:

Why do trees shed their leaves? If this is because of solidification of the sap, then if a tree sheds its leaves, solidification must belong to it. And if solidification occurs, in a tree, *not just in anything you like*, it must shed its leaves. (98ᵇ36–8)

Aristotle's requirement that the terms involved be equal in extension and convert cannot apply to all the cases of causal explanation he considers.[14] For, when the Athenians come to be at war with the Persians because they are the first to attack (B.11, 94ᵇ1 f.), the two terms cited ('being at war' and 'being the first to attack') do not convert. Since a war of this type needs at least two opponents, the aggressors and those who repond to aggression, not all who are at war can be the aggressors.[15] More generally, there are many different ways to come to be at war. So, the question is acute: Why is conversion *required* in the particular examples cited in B.16?

It is not immediately clear that the terms cited in the example above ('sap solidification', 'leaf loss') do convert. Do trees (or even broad-leaved trees) lose their leaves *only* when their sap solidifies? Aristotle is raising exactly this question when he asks:

[13] Thus, it is not clear whether all or any of the terms convert.
[14] Barnes argues powerfully that conversion is not the rule in all demonstrations (*Aristotle's Posterior Analytics*, 258–9). The substantial issue is whether there is any non-trivial group of demonstrations which require conversion.
[15] Another example of a causal explanation which does not meet this stringent requirement is given in *Post. An.* B.17, 99ᵇ4–5 in his discussion of the causes of longevity in different species.

is it true that if the *explanandum* (e.g. plants shedding their leaves) holds, the *explanans* also holds (e.g. their sap solidifying)? (98^a36–8; see 98^b30–2)

Surely there can be different explanations of why such trees lose their leaves. Perhaps, as Aristotle comments:

It is necessary that something explanatory is present, but not that everything which might be a cause is present. (98^b30–1)

In some cases, sap solidification might lead to leaf loss, in others the use of pesticide or the presence of disease (as there might be various explanations of why people are at war).[16]

There is a related question about the sufficiency of the proposed explanations. Why is it that if trees' sap solidifies, they must shed their leaves? Surely we can explain why some trees shed their leaves by saying:

it is because their sap solidifies,

without thinking that in every case when a tree's sap solidifies it will lose its leaves?

Aristotle has offered an answer to these questions given (in part) in the words already cited:

if solidification occurs, in a tree, *not just in anything you like*, it must shed its leaves. (98^b36–8)

His concern is to explain why (e.g. broad-leaved) trees *as such* and *universally* (98^b34) lose their leaves. He aims to find an explanation of why this happens to all such trees solely in virtue of their being such trees. Hence, if their sap could solidify without their leaves falling, one would not have explained *universally* why trees of this kind *as such* lose their leaves. One might, of course, have explained why these trees in certain conditions (e.g. when grown near a chemical plant) lose their leaves, but one could not explain why *all* broad-leaved trees *as such* do so.[17]

This strategy can be used to defend Aristotle's view that this type of explanation should provide necessary conditions for the occurrence of the effect. He is aiming at giving an explanation of the following form:

In *all* members of one kind K, a feature F which belongs to them *as such* always has one and only one cause C.

---

[16] Equally, there could be a case where trees shed their leaves from differing causes on differing occasions: e.g. in some cases because of chemical pollution, in others because of sap solidification. One cannot avoid this problem solely by limiting the cases in question to those involving trees (as Barnes suggests, *Aristotle's Posterior Analytics,* 253).

[17] Contrast the case of the Athenians coming to be at war with the Persians. There might well be no explanation of why the Athenians came to be at war, solely in virtue of their being Athenians. One would typically need to refer to something they had done (e.g. supported the Milesians), and not just to their nature.

In all broad-leaved trees, leaf loss (if it belongs to them all in virtue of their being broad-leaved trees) will always and only occur because of sap solidification. Explanations of this form will fail if some such trees' sap can solidify without their shedding their leaves. For, then, sap solidification alone will not account for their leaf loss. Equally, they will fail if some of their leaves can fall without their sap solidifying. Explanations of the desired form will apply to all actual and possible cases of broad-leaved trees losing their leaves. Otherwise, they cannot apply to *all* these trees *solely in virtue of their being such trees*, but only to such trees in certain conditions.

Aristotle clarifies his favoured explanatory structure further in B.17, 99ᵃ23–9. He notes that 'shedding leaves' applies to all vines, but that it extends further to figs and other types of tree. Thus, he writes:

> Shedding leaves [viz. B term] holds universally of all figs [D term]—for, I call *universal* that with which they do not convert, and *primitive universal* that with which severally they do not convert, but with which, taken together, they do convert and have the same extension. (99ᵃ32–5)

In this case, shedding leaves will be the *primitive* universal which applies to all and only trees of a given type (e.g. broad-leaved trees) which comprise the class of figs, vines, etc. What needs to be explained is why:

> Shedding leaves belongs to all and only broad-leaved trees.

The latter is the *primitive* universal to which leaf-shedding belongs. As before, all and only broad-leaved trees will shed their leaves, and leaf-shedding will belong to such trees *as such* (*Post. An.* A.4, 73ᵇ26 ff.). In this case, it appears to be in the nature of leaf-shedding to belong to broad-leafed trees and no others. That is, the type of leaf-shedding at issue is (partially) defined as something that happens to trees of that kind.[18] What governs the selection of the relevant primitive universals is that they satisfy the conversion requirements in this distinctive way. That is, the *explananda* are convertible and *per se* connected. (What is to be explained is why the type of leaf shedding found in these trees belongs to these trees as such.) There need be no such relation between being the Athenians and being at war.

If leaf-shedding belongs to all broad-leaved trees *per se*, the explanatory feature should also belong to such trees in this way. For, if this were not so, one would not have explained why leaf loss (of the relevant type) belongs to these and only these trees (solely in virtue of their being these trees). Thus, it must be in the nature of sap solidification (of the relevant type) to belong to trees of this type, and only to such trees. In explanations

---

[18] This will be a case of a *per se* 2 predication: i.e. one where it is in the nature of A to belong to B. By contrast, *per se* 1 predications are those where it is in the nature of B's that A's belong to them.

where the feature to be explained is one which belongs to the kind *per se*, the *explanans* must also belong to that kind in the same way. So, the *explanans* and *explanandum* must convert, because both are to be understood as belonging *per se* to the same kind. In this way, the explanations at issue are able to meet the convertibility requirements.

This form of explanation of why leaf-shedding of this type occurs in broad-leaved trees will invoke the fundamental essence of this type of leaf-shedding.[19] The explanatory syllogism will be the basis of an account of what this type of shedding leaves is. As Aristotle says:

What is shedding leaves? The solidifying of sap at the connection of the seed. (99ᵃ28 f.)

The explanatory syllogism in question would run as follows:

Shedding leaves Φ all and only solidifiers of sap.

(E) <u>Solidifying of sap Φ all and only broad-leaved trees.</u>

Shedding leaves Φ all and only broad-leaved trees.

Explanations of this form, which contain *primitive* universals in both the conclusion and the premises, will provide the basis for a full definition of the relevant phenomenon as the type of occurrence in broad-leaved trees which is brought on by their sap solidifying. They are structure-revealing explanations precisely because their conclusion contains a *per se* connection of this type. I shall call explanations with this feature *structural explanations*.

It is no accident that when we find structural explanations of this type we discover commensurate universals required for definition. Provided that the *explanandum* is a unitary property whose definition adverts to one kind to which it belongs primitively, an appropriate *explanans* will provide us with a basic definition of that property.[20] Aristotle's favoured mode of explanation is designed to allow us to come to know which features define the property in question. For, his explanations take as *explananda* features

---

[19] It might also be in the nature of broad-leafed trees to shed their leaves. In that case, there would be a *per se* 1 predication as well. However, this is not required in this context. One *per se* connection is enough for Aristotle's purposes.

[20] This claim is only that if a predicate belongs to its subject *primitively*, it is coextensive with it. This does not entail the far stronger claim (favoured by Zabarella in *Opera Logica* (Frankfurt, 1608)) that if a predicate belongs to two subjects non-primitively, it must belong to a common kind which embraces these two subjects primitively. Some predicates may *not* belong primitively to one proper subject at all. At best, like longevity, they may belong only to a conjunction of such subjects. Zabarella's proposal is effectively criticized by Barnes (in *Aristotle's Posterior Analytics*, 258), who concludes that *primitiveness* plays no role in generating commensurate universals. If my weaker construal of primitiveness is correct, primitive univerals will be commensurate, and *explananda* of this sort will lead to definitions.

and kinds (such as primitive universals) which are specified in such a way as to ensure their convertibility.

Nor need this method be confined to the definition of properties. If the feature to be explained is one which is used to differentiate the kind, the explanation will advert to the basic essence of the kind. Explanations of this type may result in definitions either of the feature or the kind. This is because the *explananda* are either the *differentiae* of a kind or a property which is itself defined as belonging to that kind. In the former case one will arrive at the essence of the kind, in the latter at the definition of the feature which belongs to the kind.

If we find structural explanations we will uncover definitions because their *explananda* are *per se* connected (in the ways indicated). It appears that, at this point, the practice of explanation depends on that of definition. For the *per se* connections the former invokes rest on definitional connections between feature and kind. Indeed, this is what distinguishes this form of explanation from the type involved in explaining why the Athenians come to be at war with the Persians.

This appearance is, I shall argue, confirmed by Aristotle's more detailed discussion of this form of explanation in the remainder of B.16 and B.17.

8.4 THE BASIC MODEL AMPLIFIED*

The importance of the principle that:

In one kind, one feature F of the appropriate type has one and only one cause C

emerges in Aristotle's discussion of a variety of cases which appear to threaten it. In the first group, leaf-shedding turns out not to be a unified phenomenon because there are two different explanations of why it can occur in what is one kind. Here, we should distinguish between natural and diseased leaf-shedding. If we find 'two accounts or more [of the phenomenon], it is clear that what we are seeking is not a single thing but several'. For example, if intolerance of insult and indifference to fortune have a different account, there will be two types (*eide*) of pride (97^b13-25). The absence of one feature jointly necessary and sufficient to explain all cases of pride would show that there are in fact two types of pride. Here, Aristotle accepts a principle of the following form:

P(1) If objects $k_i \ldots k_n$ are the same in species and there is a different explanation of why they possess a given property, there is more than one property to be explained.

Aristotle maintains the principle of conversion of cause and effect by separating various types of effect.

In a second group of cases, leaf-shedding might turn out not to belong *per se* to just one kind, such as figs. It belongs instead *per se* to a wider kind which involves figs and other trees as well. Aristotle gives a mathematical as well as a biological example.[21] Here, his strategy is to find a wider kind to which the relevant feature primitively belongs *per se*. In this way, he maintains his basic thesis that for one kind there is one explanation of the relevant phenomenon by introducing a wider kind to which the feature belongs *per se*.

The second type of case has the following structure:

A ϕ all and only B.

<u>B ϕ all D.</u>

A ϕ all D.

Here A and B (leaf-shedders and broad-leafed trees) are coextensive, but D (fig trees) is not coextensive with either. Aristotle's strategy is to find a group D* (sap solidifiers) to which D and other species belong, which is coextensive with A and B. This background group (D*) is the one which appears in the explanations not of why D's are A, but of why D and (e.g.) F's are A. (See B.18, 99^{b}7–8.)[22]

In both the first and second groups discussed, Aristotle shows how structural explanations generate definitions of the relevant properties. There is, however, a third group of cases which has a different structure. It runs as follows:

A ϕ all B.

<u>B ϕ all and only D.</u>

A ϕ all D.

[21] It runs as follows:

(1) Having external angles equal to four right angles applies to all triangles.

Here, the feature to be explained applies more widely than to the class of triangles. Aristotle's response is to argue that having external angles equal to four right angles applies to a larger group consisting of triangles, quadrangles, and perhaps others. Thus, we should say (according to Aristotle):

(2) Having external angles equal to four right angles applies to group G consisting of triangles, quadrangles . . .

Group G, which consists of triangles, quadrangles, etc., is co-extensive with the things that have external angles equal to four right-angles. Thus, the middle term which explains why (B) is true will also be co-extensive with this larger group. For, the latter is the group to which the property of having an angle sum equal to four right angles applies *as such*.

[22] This pattern is also to be found in the biological cases of leaf-shedding mentioned above.

Here, B is the cause of A's being D, but not of everything which is D. Aristotle introduces the case as follows:

But [23] indeed ⟨ in some cases ⟩ B is the cause of D's being A [with emphasis on the D]. In such cases A must extend further than B. If it did not, what reason is there for B to be the cause of this [viz. of A's belonging to all D]? (99^{a}35–7)

His line of thought appears to fall into several distinct stages:

(1) Take a case in which B (a middle term) is the cause of D's being A (99^{a}35 f.).

(2) This case is problematic, let us suppose, because A extends further than B. (If this were not so, B would not be the cause of D's being A but of some wider group (e.g. D's and E's) being A.[24] (99^{a}37).

Aristotle seeks to analyse this problematic case as follows:

(3) If A extends beyond D [e.g. to all E's and F's], and its presence beyond D is not explained by E's being B, then E's must be a group distinct from D [viz. apart from the group unified by feature B]. (99^{a}37–9).

If (3) were not so, and Es were not a group distinct from Ds, we would not be able to say:

A Φ all E.

while denying that:

E Φ all A. (99^{a}39–^{b}1)

For, if E's formed the same group as D's (viz the E* group) and:

A Φ all E*s.

were true, there would be commensurate universals of the form:

A Φ all E*'s (where E and D form this one unified group).

---

[23] I read in 99^{a}35 ff., 'τοις δὲ δὴ D' (or 'τοις δὲ') rather than 'τοις δὴ' as in the MSS, and take this to introduce a second case (distinct from that discussed in 99^{a}30–5, where all the terms convert when the appropriate group is specified). The second case introduced in 99^{a}36 cannot have this feature since the A and B terms do not convert. There must, therefore, be a break between these two passages. Since in the MSS 'δε' and 'δη' are both written in the same way, there is no better evidence for the present text than for my emendation. On the standard reading nothing is added by saying that B is the cause of D's being A, since this is already implicit in 99^{a}30–3.

[24] I translate '*ti mállon aition estai touto ekeinou*' as 'why is this [viz. B] rather the cause of that [viz. D's being A]?', and understand the implied contrast to be 'rather than B's being the cause of something other than D's being A'. The contrast should not be with 'rather than D's being A being the cause of B'. As Ross (*Aristotle's Prior and Posterior Analytics*, 673) and Barnes (*Aristotle's Posterior Analytics*, 258 ff.) note, Aristotle has several good reasons to rule out the latter possibility.

and there would be one explanation of why A belongs to all D and all E (99ᵇ1 f.). But if E is (as we shall assume) a unified group distinct from D (with its own separate explanation), there will not be commensurate universals of the form:

A Φ all and only E*

because D and E do not form a unified group. Here, there is no primitive universal E* to be introduced, as D and E do not form a genuine kind.

Aristotle is careful to add one important rider:

But will E be some one thing? We must enquire into this. Let it be C. (99ᵇ3 f.)

This caveat prevents one from concluding that E must be a unified group simply because it plays the specified role in explanation. E might turn out not to be a unified kind, but one which requires further division. Alternatively E might fall below the level of unified kinds. Aristotle's preferred form of explanation (of *per se* features via necessary and sufficient conditions) is itself constrained by the demand that the feature to be explained belong to a genuine unity.[25]

In this type of case, there is one property to be explained (e.g. longevity), but the explanation is different for different animals (e.g. quadrupeds and birds). The absence of one feature necessary and sufficient to explain the presence of this property in all cases forces us to distinguish between the kinds in question. There can indeed be, as Aristotle says:

several explanations of the same thing, but not *for things of the same sort.* (99ᵇ4–6)

There will be differences between the kinds of object under investigation in all cases where the same property is present but its presence is differently explained.

In this case, Aristotle commits himself to a further principle:

P(2) If the same property belongs to objects $k_i \ldots k_n$ but its presence is differently explained, objects $k_i \ldots k_n$ must differ in species (or in genus).

This thesis is also a reflection of his fundamental principle that for one kind K there is one and only one explanation of one genuine feature F. Here, this principle is used to differentiate kinds and not features. If the explanation is different for:

[25] There is no need to interpret these lines as indicating 'Aristotle's awareness of the weakness of the preceding lines' (as Barnes suggests in his note on 99ᵃ38, *Aristotle's Posterior Analytics*, 257.) They show rather the complexity of the conditions he required of the appropriate explanation.

A Φ all E.

and

A Φ all D.

the kinds involved must be distinct ($99^{b}2-4$).

In the third group of cases, one would not arrive at a definition of longevity, because it does not belong *per se* to one kind. Cause and effect fail to convert. There is no one element which explains longevity in kinds D and E. Explanations of this type cannot reveal the structure or definition of longevity. Nor need they generate definitions of the varying kinds (D and E), unless the relevant feature happens to be among the *differentiae* of these kinds. Although acceptance of P(2) forces one to separate and eventually define kinds when there are two explanations of the presence of one property, it need not lead us directly to a definition of either kind or feature. We do not automatically have in the third case a structural explanation of either the property or the kind.

This leads us to focus on a crucial point. The *explananda* in structural explanations are ones which belong to all the relevant kinds *per se*. Either the property is defined in terms of its belonging to a given kind, or the kind is defined in terms of its possessing certain properties. This type of explanation is distinguished (in part) by the fact that its *explananda* are definitionally connected. The *explananda* have to be of this type if they are to fit the convertibility schemata required if we are to discover essences by this route. When this is not so (as in the third case), we will no longer arrive at definitions of either property or kind. We need to think of (e.g.) leaf-shedding as leaf-shedding-in-these-trees for it to be the type of primitive universal required as an *explanandum*. In this way, Aristotle's favoured type of structural explanation appears to rest on *explananda* provided by our practices of definition (via their concern with the notion of primitive universals).

8.5 THE INTERDEPENDENCY OF DEFINING AND EXPLAINING

The interconnections between defining and explaining in Aristotle's account are close and intricate. In 8.2, we saw him using explanatory concerns to make determinate the intuitions concerning priority and unity which are involved in giving definitions. However, the story in 8.3 and 8.4 is subtly different. Here, his relevant form of structural explanation appears to rest on resources drawn from the practice of definition. For, the latter plays a role in providing the relevant *explananda* and in underwriting the convertibility of the terms required in structural explanations.

However, the arguments of 8.3 and 8.4 are incomplete. Aristotle needs to make clear *how* the practice of definition selects various features as the appropriate *explananda*. For, without that addition, some might interpret Aristotle as follows: In relying on definitional connections in arriving at the relevant *explananda* we are merely using results which are, at basis, dependent on our practice of explanation. No doubt, we can rely (epistemically) on definitional connections in looking for the *explananda*. But what makes these connections definitional is their (e.g.) being the immediate consequence of one underlying common cause. Similarly, it may be said, convertibility should be seen as the consequence of the presence of this type of causal structure. It need not be motivated by independent non-explanatory definitional resources. Perhaps our practice of definition rests throughout on that of explanation (without reciprocal support).

In the next Chapter, I shall seek to make good this lacuna. The relevant *explananda* are (in at least some cases) determined by aspects of the theory of definition, independent of the requirements of explanation. But to see this one needs a fuller grasp on the role of definition in B.13–15.

There are, nonetheless, further reasons (prior to B.13 ff.) to think that, for Aristotle, constraints implicit in our practice of definition are at work in determining the relevant pattern of explanation. Such constraints are not confined to the *explananda,* but also underlie some of the requirements placed on the *explanans*. Consider cases where there are several causal stories which explain the same phenomenon: efficient, teleological, grounding, etc. (B.11, 94^{b}27 f.). Here, Aristotle suggests that there can be efficient and teleological explanations of the occurrence of thunder (94^{b}31–4), and notes that this problem arises for a variety of natural phenomena (94^{b}34–6). What makes one of these causal stories the right one to yield the definition of the kind or feature in question?

Since Aristotle identifies the answer to the 'What is it?' and the 'Why?' questions (B.2, 90^{a}15), it is natural to think that only one of these causal stories gives us knowledge of the appropriate type of what the kind is. Definitions aim to give us knowledge of what the kind or substance is (see B.3, 90^{b}16, *Topics* Z.4, 141^{a}27 ff.). In the case of thunder, the efficient cause (fire being quenched in the clouds) makes it fully intelligible to us why thunder has the other genuine (or *per se*) features it has: being a noise, being accompanied by lightning, occurring under certain atmospheric conditions. The first two are consequences of fire being quenched, the third points to the surrounding circumstances required for fire to be quenched. By contrast, the teleological cause cited (to threaten those in Hades (94^{b}33–4)) would not make it clear why thunder occurs in the clouds or in certain atmospheric conditions, even if it explained why thunder was noisy. Only one of these explanations makes the nature of the kind fully intelligible to us in the way required to answer the 'What is F?' question.

This thesis can be generalized. In Aristotle's view, the efficient cause gives the basic essence of some phenomena, the teleological cause of others (*Meta.* Z.17, 1041ᵃ28–30). This can be true even if there is always one type of efficient and one type of teleological cause for the same phenomenon. Thus, anger may always be brought about by (e.g.) an insult, and aim at revenge (*De An.* A.1, 403ᵃ31 ff.). The latter constitutes the essence of anger, since it is this which makes the phenomenon fully intelligible to us. Once we understand that anger aims at revenge, we see that it has to be brought about by something which the angry person wishes to repay (e.g. an insult). This is because revenge has to involve reacting adversely to some wrong done. By contrast, if one knew only that a person was in a state brought about by an insult one would not thereby know that the person was looking for revenge. In order to know that, one would also need to know some further facts about their psychology. Only the teleological cause is sufficient by itself to make the phenomenon of anger fully intelligible to us.

A similar story can be told about the nature of (e.g.) houses, where there is one efficient cause (the art of house-building) and one teleological cause (safety for goods, etc.), each of which by itself can explain (in some way) all the relevant features of a house. However, only the teleological cause tells us 'what a house is'. Why? Not solely because it is a a common cause of all the relevant features of the house.[26] For, so too (*ex hypothesi*) is the efficient cause. There must be further constraints at work beyond those generated by the practice of explanation alone.

In the case of the house, the further element could be introduced as follows. If one had only the efficient causal story, something would remain unclear: why the art of building is the kind of art it is. One would merely take for granted (as an unexplained datum) why this art functions as it does. The teleological account is preferable because it shows why the efficient cause is as it is. Only one of these causal stories makes the nature of the phenomenon fully intelligible to us in the way required to answer the 'What is F?' question. Here, background assumptions about the requirements of good definition select which causal story is the relevant one for definitional purposes.[27]

Elsewhere, Aristotle appears to represent our practice of explanation as dependent on that of definition. Consider his contention that there cannot be explanatory chains of infinite length (A.19, 82ᵃ7 f).[28] He argues for this as follows: If there were such chains, one could not arrive at knowledge of what the kinds are or of their definitions (A.22, 82ᵇ37–83ᵃ1). Rather, definitions must be of finite length if we are to grasp them (see also 83ᵇ4–8). This argument is, at first glance, weak. Why would it follow from the fact

---

[26] See, e.g. *Meta.* H.2, 1043ᵃ15 ff.
[27] For further discussion of this point, see Ch. 10.
[28] I am indebted at this point to discussion with Henry Mendell.

that definitions cannot be of infinite length that demonstrations cannot be? What prevents there being explanations of infinite length which do not begin with definitions? Why should definition play this central role in the practice of demonstration?

The argument of the previous paragraph suggests an answer to these questions. Demonstrations, as Aristotle conceives them, must begin with statements which concern the essences of the kinds in question. For, this is a constraint on what demonstrating is. To demonstrate is to give an argument which begins with a statement about a causally basic (non-demonstrable) feature which can answer the 'What is F?' question. Thus, the demonstratively basic statement must be finite in length; for, otherwise it could not make the phenomenon fully intelligible to us. If demonstrations are to meet this requirement, they must begin with definitions which reveal the relevant essences.

This argument is revealing. Aristotle does not attempt to show that every science must contain a set of basic propositions which are underivable from the remainder, and then argue that these propositions must be definitions which can satisfactorily answer the 'What is F?' question. That is, he does not impose a structural constraint on demonstration, and argue that only a subclass of knowable propositions can meet it.[29] Rather, he begins with the substantial claim that demonstrations must begin with statements concerning essences, which (if they are to answer satisfactorily the 'What is F?' question) must be knowable by us. If so, the practice of demonstration is once again constrained by considerations drawn from our practice as definers.

These requirements serve to make the relevant type of structural explanation more determinate. The cause and effect convert, and both should belong *per se* to the kind. The cause cited must provide the basis for an answer to the relevant 'What is F?' question. That is, there must be one non-complex feature which is the common cause of (e.g.) the kind's other *per se* properties. Further, the nature of the common cause should not

[29] For a contrasting view, see Robin Smith's paper 'Immediate Propositions and Aristotle's Proof Theory', *Ancient Philosophy* 6 (1986), 47–55. Smith argues convincingly that Aristotle's arguments in *Post. An.* A.19–22 cannot depend on the claim that every regress of propositions must end in a basic set of premisses which are self-evident or epistemically immediate. For, Aristotle claims only that the starting points are definitions which reveal essences, and makes no reference to the epistemic notion of self-evidence in this passage. However, Smith concludes from this that the relevant starting points must merely be ones not deducible from any other true proposition, and then notes that there is no obvious step from this claim to any which concern (non-demonstrative) knowledge of definitions. On my view, the starting points are *non-demonstrable* because they are not the causal consequences of any further claim. Also, if they are to be *starting points of demonstration*, they must (a) be non-demonstrable and (b) state the relevant basic essence. If the relevant essences are the objects of non-demonstrative knowledge (as emerges in *Post. An.* B.8–10), the starting points of demonstration will themselves be capable of being known non-demonstratively.

stand in need of any further explanation. Rather, it should serve to make the whole phenomenon fully intelligible to us. These latter requirements follow from the demand that the relevant basic cause be used as the basis of the definition of the phenomenon.

Essences, in this account, are the starting points of demonstration and answer the 'What is F?' question. This conception of essence (and of definition) explains other features of Aristotle's explanatory practices. Thus, he insists that demonstrations must begin with *one* common cause and not a conjunction or disjunction of separate causes. These claims are natural if what is sought is the essence of the kind, a single cause which can provide the basis for the 'What is F?' question. Without this assumption, there would be nothing amiss with finding several separate causes for each of a kind's *per se* features. If we aim at definition, we will not be content with uncovering a conjunctive cause. For, that would fail to make all aspects of the kind transparent. In particular, it would not explain why all its features are interconnected in the way they are.

If this is correct, Aristotle's overall strategy can be formulated in terms of a mutual dependence between our practices of definition and of demonstration. While some of his claims about defining follow from his views about explaining, the constraints he imposes on structural explanation are (in some measure) grounded in the practice of definition. Each of these practices is incomplete without resources drawn from the other.

If this general picture is correct, Aristotle's account of the interdependency of the practices of definition and of demonstration involves a further thesis: the co-determination of essence and causation. Essences play a central role in a certain style of causal explanation, but the relevant type of causal story itself involves essences. This metaphysical thesis grounds Aristotle's epistemological claim that in knowing the answer to the 'Why?' question we know what the kind in question is. We achieve knowledge of essences by tracing back a certain pattern of explanation to its roots in a particular type of cause. But the relevant type of explanatory structure is one in which essences must be the basic *explanantia*. Essences and structural causation stand or fall together.

8.6 DEFINITION AND EXPLANATION: INTERDEPENDENCY AND ITS PROBLEMS

The interdependency of defining and explaining, introduced in the last Section, offers a way to understand Aristotle's claim in B.2 that the answer to the 'Why?' and to the 'What is it?' questions are one and the same. Why does he hold (at least) the following:

☐ [F is the essence/basic definer of A ↔ F is the fundamental explanatory feature in a given type of explanation]?

Aristotle (I have argued) requires that the type of explanation be a structural one, concerned with (e.g.) features which belong to the kind *per se*. We are now in a position to be able to understand his strategy more fully.

The initial claim in B.2 could be understood in a number of ways. On one view, the left-hand side of the bi-conditional, and in particular the notion of essence, is taken as basic. Here, the key metaphysical concept is that of one unified essence which constitutes the nature of a kind. This essence will indeed be the basis of a given pattern of explanation, but it can be understood as the essence in terms independent of its role in explanation. Successful explanations may invoke essences, but this is because such essences are the ontological building blocks on which good explanations rest.

There is a radical alternative to the first viewpoint. Here, one seeks to construct an account of what essence is from features which play a certain role in explanation. On this view, essences are to be defined in terms of their pivotal role in a form of explanation, which can be understood independently of the notion of essence. In this account, the right- and not the left-hand side of their bi-conditional is taken as basic. To be an essence is to play a given role in explanation.

We have seen reason to doubt that Aristotle held either of these alternatives. In his view, each side of the bi-conditional depends on the other. In his unified picture of defining and explaining, there are (at least) three key features (in cases where the cause is different from the effect).

(1) The Immediacy Condition

In searching for the definition of a phenomenon one reaches an immediate proposition, where no further cause can be invoked to explain the connection between the phenomenon and the feature invoked. This is causal bedrock. The causal feature invoked in the immediate proposition is causally prior to the features to be explained.

(2) The Unity Condition

The feature invoked in (1) must itself be one common cause of the other necessary features of the phenomenon which are explained.

(3) The Explanatory Condition

The feature invoked in (1) and (2) must be necessary and sufficient to explain why the phenomenon *as such* has the other properties it possesses *as such*.

These constraints arise from the practice of offering structural explanations. But, at crucial points, such explanations involve features drawn from our practices of definition. Thus, the relevant explanatorily basic feature is selected because it satisfies additional definitional constraints. The appropriate explanatory picture cannot be completed without the assistance of features drawn from the theory of definition.[30]

There is a further feature of Aristotle's account. In it, some kinds possess certain of their features in virtue of their belonging to wider-ranging kinds. The sub-kinds will be made what they are by their possessing distinctive unifying explanatory features which account for their possession of their distinctive necessary properties. Equally, the kinds to which they belong will be made what they are in the same way. Thus, both genera and species will be essentially defined by reference to that feature which is central in the relevant type of explanation of their possession of their other necessary properties. Thus, in addition to theses (1)–(3) above, Aristotle is committed to a further claim:

(4) The Hierarchical Conception

Kinds may possess features in virtue of their belonging to wider-ranging kinds of which they are sub-kinds. The definitions of the higher-order kinds will themselves be fixed in ways which meet (1)–(3).

These four features form the basis of Aristotle's picture of defining, explaining, and classifying as set out in these chapters of the *Analytics*. However, the account is still incomplete in several important aspects:

(A) We have not yet seen how the relevant *explananda* are to be determined. Are these fixed by resources independent of our practices of explanation? Does Aristotle use non-explanatory resources to fix (e.g.) the relevant primitive universals?

(B) We have not yet discovered the range of cases to which this model applies. How wide-ranging is the set of cases where the cause is separate from its effect? Can the model apply to kinds and substances?

Both (A) and (B) highlight areas where Aristotle's attempts to satisfy his own Definitional Constraint remain unclear. (A) is particularly pressing since (in addition to the reasons given above) it points to an incompleteness in his discussion of his central set of examples.

The Hierarchical Conception generates further questions:

(C) How are the species related to the higher-order kinds? Can one species fall within a variety of genera? If not, why not? Does

---

[30] For further discussion of B.2, 90ᵃ14 ff., see Ch. 10 Sect. 1.

Aristotle require that the properties which species possess are unique to that species?

(D) More generally, how is Aristotle's method of definition by genus and *differentia* connected to definition by causal essence of the type discussed in this Chapter. Are these different types of definition? If so, how can the notion of definition be dependent (in the ways suggested) on the account of explanation?

I shall examine questions (A), (C), and (D) in the next Chapter in considering Aristotle's further views of definition in *Posterior Analytics* B.13–15. Question (B) will be discussed in Chapters 10 and 11.

9

Towards A Unified Theory of Definition: Posterior Analytics B.13–15

9.1 INTRODUCTION

In Aristotle's account, definition and explanation are mutually dependent. His route to satisfy the Simple Condition and the Definitional Constraint (set out in Chapter 7) essentially involves the use of features drawn from the practice of explaining. But, as was argued in the last Chapter, the type of explanation at issue is itself constrained by the need to define the relevant phenomenon. Neither definition nor explanation can be completed without resources drawn from the other.

This form of interdependence between the practices of explanation and definition underlies the epistemological route which (in Aristotle's view) leads the enquirer to discover the essences of the kinds under investigation. In his three-stage view of scientific enquiry, Stage 3 involves explanation. Here, the enquirer discovers the essence by finding the feature which explains why the kind is as it is. It should be no surprise that this is so, since the type of explanation involved is itself constrained by features drawn from the practice of definition.

Does this interpretation cohere with Aristotle's discussion of definition in the intervening chapters of *Posterior Analytics* B.13–15? This question is pressing, because these chapters have sometimes been taken to contain elements inconsistent with the explanation-involving account I have proposed of B.8–10. In particular, it has been suggested that:

(1) In *Posterior Analytics* B.13–15, Aristotle developed a separate epistemic route to answer questions concerning existence, definition, and essence which does not involve the explanatory concerns prominent in B.8–10 and B.16–18.

(2) In *Posterior Analytics* B.13–15 Aristotle's metaphysical conception of the essence and definition of genera and species is independent of the explanatory concerns introduced in B.8–10 and B.16–18.

Discussion of the issues raised by these claims will enable us to consider questions (A), (C), and (D), raised at the end of the previous Chapter. For, we shall investigate how the relevant genera and species themselves are determined and by what route their essences are discovered. Further, we shall examine the issue (raised but not resolved in the last Chapter) of what determines the relevant *explananda* in structural explanation.

9.2 B.13, 96^a20–^b14

The first section of B.13 opens with the following claim:

How the *what it is* is placed in definitions (*horoi*)[1] has been given above, as has an account of the way in which there is or is not a demonstration or definition of the same thing. Let us now say how we should hunt out[2] the things that are predicated in the what it is. (96^a20–3)

These sentences reveal the aim of B.13: to hunt out the things that are predicated in *the what it is*. This goal, however, is capable of being understood in several ways, as can be shown by considering possible answers to the following questions:

(1) Is Aristotle in B.13 concerned with the same definitions (or accounts of what something is) as have been discussed in B.8–10? Or is he concerned with different accounts of what something is, independent of, and perhaps prior to, the explanation-involving definitions proposed in B.8–10?[3]

---

[1] '*Horos*' may mean either 'term' (as Barnes and Ross interpret it here) or 'definition' (for the latter use, see B.8, 93^b38 and B.13, 97^b25). In the context of the present sentence (96^a20–2), the latter seems preferable for three reasons:

(a) This sentence, so understood, precisely summarizes some of the results achieved in B.8–10 (as is to be expected given Aristotle's explicit back reference to 'what has been said before'). Aristotle, in those chapters, had initially asked in what way there is a definition of what something is (93^a1–2), and concluded by noting several ways in which there are definitions of what something is (94^a11–14).

(b) So understood, it represents Aristotle as recapitulating several of his major concerns from B.10, where he considered both how *what a thing is* can be set out in definitions, and how definitions are related to demonstrations. (For the latter, see B.10, 94^a14–16, 17–19, where the terminology is strikingly similar to that employed in the first lines of B.13.)

(c) By contrast, in the conclusion of B.10, Aristotle was not concerned with the narrower issue of how to express definitions by means of the *terms* used in demonstration. Indeed, some of the definitions considered in B.10 are not set out in demonstrative terms at all (94^a9–10, 16–17). Even when Aristotle does consider in this chapter the relation between definition and demonstration, he does not focus on the question of the relation between parts of the definition and specific demonstrative terms (see 94^a1 ff.).

[2] For similar uses of '*thereuein*' meaning 'look for', see *Post. An.* A.31, 88^a3 ff., *Pr. An.* A.30, 46^a10–12.

[3] Barnes and Ross favour the first alternative, Bolton the second (in 'Division, définition et essence dans la science aristotelicienne', Revue Philosophique 2(1993), 197–222). Bolton is led to his view by noting two difficulties in the first: (a) There is a mismatch between the

(2) If B.13 does discuss the same definitions as B.8–10, is its role merely to offer an (epistemological) path to discover the elements which have already been marked out as definitional by the considerations advanced in B.8–10? Or does it add additional (metaphysical) constraints to the account of *what something is* beyond those already clearly specified in B.8–10? If the latter, how are these additional features related to the earlier account of what something is?[4]

In this Chapter, I shall argue that while B.13 discusses the same definitions as B.8–10, it spells out some (metaphysical) constraints on definition which have been assumed, but not made explicit, in the earlier chapters. These latter constraints, rightly understood, are not only fully consistent with the explanation-involving view of definition developed in the previous Chapter, but actually amplify and deepen it. Taken together, they constitute a unified theory of definition and explanation. If this is correct, B.13 is not concerned with some distinct type of definition independent of (or prior to) the explanation-invoking account developed in B.8–10. Rather, it is permeated by the very same explanatory concerns as underlie the earlier discussion of definition. This, at least, is what I shall attempt to establish.

The first two sentences of B.13 set up a presumption that Aristotle remains concerned with the definitions he discussed in B.8–10. For, he appears to refer back to an earlier discussion of how essential features are to be placed in definitions, and to represent B.13 as intended to show how we should 'hunt out' the elements involved in those definitions. His target now appears to be to work out how to discover the elements involved in (at least some of) the definitions discussed in B.8–10. He may, of course, give prominence to features of these definitions which have not been emphasized earlier. But, nonetheless, the initial presupposition must be

demonstration-based definitions of B.8–10 and those of B.13, in that demonstration can be used to establish the presence of features beyond the essential ones specified in B.13 definitions (e.g. necessary ones). (b) It is not possible to line up all the definitions offered in B.13 with any one type of B.8–10 definition. I shall argue with regard to (a) that there are resources already implicit in B.8–10-style definitions which restrict their range to essential features, and that these draw on features only made fully explicit in B.13. (For an indication of Aristotle's awareness of the relevant difference, see B.8, 93^{a}11–13, although it is not fully developed there.) With regard to (b), I shall argue that while sections of B.13 may be concerned with several of the types of definition specified in B.8–10, these passages are not inconsistent with the earlier discussion.

[4] Barnes agrees that the task of B.13 is to arrive at B.8–10-style definitions (*Aristotle's Posterior Analytics*, 230), but argues that the chapter fails to do this because it does not succeed in marking out only essential features (as opposed to necessary ones), and rather merely rests on assumptions about which features are essential (e.g. p. 231). I shall argue that while B.13 does depend on certain assumptions about definitions which are present in B.8–10, it specifies the ingredients of definition in terms not fully explicit in the earlier chapters.

that in B.13 Aristotle is still concerned with the definitions discussed in B.8–10.

It is, however, far from obvious that B.13 implements this project. Indeed, the main exegetical problem becomes clear immediately,[5] when Aristotle's introduces his method of finding out what is predicated in the *what it is to be something* (96ᵃ22–3) in a way which reveals the *ousia*, or nature, of the phenomenon (96ᵃ34 f.).[6] It appears to be the following:

Collect a group of general terms $A_i \ldots A_n$, each one of which extends further than what is being defined, but which as a group apply to all of and only what is being defined.

Thus, Aristotle writes:

such things must be taken up to the first point at which just so many are taken that each will belong more widely but all of them together will not belong more widely; for, necessarily this will be the *nature* of the object (96ᵃ32–5)

He gives as an example the triple (three), to which (in his view) the following properties belong:

being a number, being odd, being prime in both ways (not being measured by number, and not being compounded from numbers) (96ᵃ35)[7]

Each of these properties belongs to other numbers, as (for example) being prime in this way belongs to the pair as well as the triple. But taken together all belong to nothing but the triple (96ᵇ1).

Aristotle claims that this account will show what it is to be the triple (96ᵇ4) and what its nature consists in (96ᵇ6), and do so by giving the relevant *differentiae* of the genus (as specified in 83ᵃ24 ff.). He argues for the latter claim as follows:

---

[5] B.13 is divided as follows in my discussion:

(a) 96ᵃ20–ᵇ14: Section 2.

(b) 96ᵇ15–25: Section 3.

(c) 96ᵇ25–97ᵃ2, 97ᵃ23–ᵇ5: Section 4.

(d) 97ᵇ5–26, together with B.14 and 15: Section 5.

[6] '*Ousia*' may be specified in this context as the genus or as a *differentia* of the genus (*Post. An.* A.2, 83ᵃ39 ff.; cf. 83ᵃ24–5). See also the discussion of B.9, 93ᵇ26–8 in the next Chapter, where (it is argued) *ousia* should also be separated from the cause of the *differentiae* being as they are.

[7] These definitions of prime and prime* depend on the claim, which Aristotle regards as plausible, that one is not itself a number but a measure of number (cf. *Meta.* N.1, 1088ᵃ6–8). We do not need to assess his grounds for this claim, since the issues raised here, such as concern *differentiae*, are at a far higher level of generality. I take 'prime' and 'prime*' as jointly one final *differentia*: being prime+ (96ᵃ38, ᵇ1). Thus, in 96ᵃ36 ff., I take the phrase to mean 'we take the property of both prime and prime*'. I am indebted here to discussion with Vasilis Karasmanis.

If $A_i \ldots A_n$ were not what it is to be the triple, it would extend further and be a genus (either named or unnamed); in which case it will belong to other things than the triple. But $A_i \ldots A_n$ does not extend further than the triple. So, it must be the nature (*ousia*) in question. ($96^b 6$–14)

This passage might suggest that Aristotle is recommending the following procedure to determine what something essentially is:

Take a group of terms which individually extend more widely than the kind under definition, and then extract that set of terms which, when taken together, are uniquely true of the kind in question.

This route might appear to offer a way to discover that a kind exists and to reveal its *ousia* (the nature of the kind) by listing a set of properties whose conjunction is co-extensive with the kind. Species and genera, thus introduced, need not be individuated in ways which involve their explanatorily basic features. If this is so, the methods advocated in B.13–15 would be distinct from, and independent of, the explanation-invoking account of definition and scientific enquiry we considered in the last Chapter. However, if there are two independent methods for arriving at definitions, it will be an unexplained coincidence if the definitions they generate are (ever) the same. There is no reason to expect the two methods to lead to the same answer to the question 'What is F?'

I shall argue that the appearance of an independent route is illusory. First, I shall seek to show that there is no inconsistency between Aristotle's discussions of definition, in B.8–10 and B.13–15. Second, I shall argue that this hypothesis is confirmed by other aspects of B.13, 14, and 15 (sections 2–5). Together B.8–15 give a unified account of definition.

There are two points of detail to be noted about the passage already cited ($96^b 6$–14). First, in introducing the discussion, Aristotle says that the terms $A_i \ldots A_n$:

extend beyond the kind in question, but do not extend beyond the genus ($96^a 24$ f.)

However, he does not say what counts as a genus or explain the significance of the restriction he introduces. There is a gap in the story: How are the relevant genera themselves determined?

Second, Aristotle does not say which set of properties (whose conjunction is co-extensive with the kind) form part of its being. There will regularly be a wider set of co-extensive properties, including non-essential but necessary ones (e.g. in the case of two, being prime+, less than three, and half of four, etc.), whose conjunction is co-extensive with the kind. So, how are the properties confined to those which fall within the nature (*ousia*) of the kind in question?

Aristotle gives some clue as to the answer to the latter question when he writes:

Such things would be taken up to *the point* at which first just so many are taken
that . . . ($96^{a}33$)

and

the nature is the *last* predication to hold of the atoms ($96^{b}12$ f.)

For, these lines suggest that there is an ordering of terms which, if followed, will enable one to arrive at a point from which one can *first* capture
(e.g.) what it is to be two. Beyond that, while there may be other terms
whose overlap applies to all and only dyads, these will not be part of
the relevant essence. But what fixes the relevant ordering? And what
determines what appears on the list? Can either or both of these questions be answered without invoking the explanation-based concerns of
B.8–10?

These questions can be raised in a more precise form by focusing on
Aristotle's favoured mathematical example: What determines that the
order in the case of the triple runs as follows:

number
odd
prime+: a combination of prime (not being measured by other numbers)
    and prime* (not being the sum of two numbers).

For example, why is odd prior to prime+? It is important to note that not
all prime+ numbers are odd (since two is an exception). Since odd does
not *subsume* prime or prime* (since that requires that all members of the
lower group belong to the higher group, i.e. that all primes are odd), the
priority relation cannot be that of subsumption.[8]

Two features seem to be at work here. The first, and most obvious, is that
there are fewer members of the group prime+ than of odd. But it is doubtful whether this by itself can separate those terms which are part of the
being of the thing from those which are not. For, on this basis, one could
replace being prime+ with being prime+ *and* less than fifteen, etc., or being
prime* with being prior to four in the number series.

The second feature is more important. Odd precedes prime in Euclid's
definitions of features of number. Nor was this order unmotivated,
since given a list of odd numbers one can extract a list of those which are
prime (on the basis of a method known in antiquity as 'Eratosthenes'

---

[8] Barnes suggests that Aristotle is employing the relation of subsumption here and
elsewhere in the chapter (*Aristotle's Posterior Analytics*, 231, 234), although he notes that
Aristotle's examples are not all cases of subsumption. This latter fact should (I think) be
taken to show that Aristotle is not in fact employing subsumption here (in which *all*
members of a lower group (e.g. prime+) belong to the group higher on the tree (e.g. odd)),
but is relying on some different ordering principle. I suggest an alternative principle in this
Chapter.

sieve').[9] If one also knows that two is the only even prime, one can find all prime numbers by this route. Further, if one knows that two and three are the only primes*, one can detect all primes+ in this way. There is, therefore, a method for detecting primes+ if one has already separated odd and even numbers, but there is no similar method for detecting odd and even numbers on the basis of a list of prime+ and non-prime+ numbers. For, there is no similar way to recover odd or even numbers from a list of primes+ or non-primes+. The latter distinction plays no part in the method for finding which numbers are even or odd. Thus, there is a significant asymmetry between odd and prime+: Knowing which numbers are odd is a step in a mathematical procedure towards discovering which are prime+, while knowing which are prime+ is not a step in a procedure towards discovering which are odd. This order of derivation justifies placing odd higher than prime+ in the list of *differentiae*.

Prime+ is better suited to playing the role of an intermediate *differentia* than the more complex *prime and less than fifteen*, because the method for selecting prime+ odd numbers pays no attention to what is above or below fifteen. Eratosthenes' sieve works indifferently above and below this number. The notions involved (prime, odd, prime*) are ones which should apply (in principle) to an unbounded set of numbers. Indeed, their status as *differentiae* is underwritten by their role in marking out genuine groups in this way across the whole number series. The species of prime+ odd numbers is marked out by a *differentia* (being prime+), whose status (and relative position) as a *differentia* is legitimized by its role in a general arithmetical practice.

The problem raised by the argument of B.13 can now be stated in a clearer form. Since definitions in the style of B.8–10 and those generated by the *differentia* model just considered relate to the *nature* of the objects involved, the results of the two methods should be systematically related. Indeed, if this were not so, there would be a crucial equivocation in Aristotle's account of the *nature* of (e.g.) the triple. However, the difficulty is that we have not yet seen how the trick is to be turned.

The hypothesis I wish to investigate runs as follows. The relevant differentiating features are the ones explained by the fundamental essence uncovered by the methods of B.8–10. Thus, the essence of the triple (if

---

[9] This method of finding odd prime numbers was called the 'sieve' by Eratosthenes (Iamblichus, *In Nicomachi Arithmeticam Introductionem*, ed. H. Pistelli (Leipzig, 1894), 1.13, 2–4). The 'sieve' works on odd numbers as follows: Set out a list of odd numbers:

3, 5, 7, 9, 11, 13, 15, 17, 19, 21, 23, 25 . . .

The sieve then subtracts all numbers divisible by three (and also presumably five and seven) to give a list of prime odd numbers:

3, 5, 7, 11, 13, 17, 19, 23 . . .

there is one) will explain why prime+ (understood as a combination of prime and prime*) belongs to odd number. The full definition of the triple would be as follows:

prime+ odd number with basic feature k, which explains in the appropriate way why prime+ belongs to odd number

If this is correct, the relevant *differentiae* will have two roles:

(a) They will fit into a pattern of mathematical procedures of the type sketched (a general derivational pattern which applies to all numbers).

and

(b) They will be explained in the appropriate way by the underlying essence.

Differentiae, so understood, will be ways of being members of a higher group which simultaneously meet conditions (a) and (b). They will mark out genuine kinds at varying levels of generality in a general, non-ad hoc, way which satisfies condition (b). As such, differentiating features of this type fall within the nature of the triple (96^b11). Indeed, there will be just as many *differentiae* in its nature as are required in the descending order to mark out the triple (in the approved way).

This hypothesis has considerable advantages in the context of B.13. Not merely does it render consistent Aristotle's two explicitly related discussions of definition in B.8–10 and B.13; it also shows how one can come to grasp all the relevant terms in the definition of the triple on the basis of one's grasp of the relevant genus/*differentia* structure. For, the latter will offer a way of 'hunting out' some of the features which are part of *what it is to be that kind.* Armed with this information one can proceed (in B.8–10 style) to grasp the remaining features which are definitional of the kind, by answering the 'Why?' question in the appropriate way.

This hypothesis fills a gap left in the last Chapter. While B.8–10 were concerned with the *explanandum* and *explanans* in demonstrations, they did not (as was noted) spell out in detail why certain features are selected as the relevant *explananda*. The genus/*differentia* structure, as demarcated in the present hypothesis, fills this gap: The appropriate *explananda* are (i) necessary properties of the kind and (ii) features specified in a pattern of derivation of the type exemplified by the mathematical case. This account will clarify which of the terms explained by the essence in this case are part of the definition: those which also fit into a pattern of differentiation of the type indicated by condition (a). As was suggested above,[10] the *explananda* are partially chosen on the basis of considerations which flow

[10] See Ch. 8 Sect. 3, 4, and 5.

from the practice of definition (as features which differentiate the genera in the required way).[11]

In B.8 Aristotle began his search for an answer to the 'Why?' question with an initial grasp of the thing itself. In the case of man, this was given by representing him as an animal of a certain type (93^a24). But it was not made explicit in that chapter why this was chosen as the starting point, or what made this the correct initial account (among non-accidental properties of the kind). The present hypothesis offers us a way of answering this question. 'Animal of a certain type (e.g. tame biped)' will be taken as the initial stage of enquiry because it is this description which locates man in its proper position in a genus/species tree. In the case of the triple, the initial account would specify it as odd prime prime* number, and, thus, locate it in its own niche in a genus/species tree. Full definitions will contain features of this type which are subsequently explained by the relevant essence.

This account, if correct, has further significant consequences for our understanding of Aristotle's schema of genera and *differentiae*, as introduced in B.13–15. His method will presuppose that there are features of the kind which are ways of being a higher-order kind (according to an appropriate pattern of derivation) but which are themselves explained by the underlying essence of the lower-level kind itself. Thus, the differentiating features will be those definitional features of the kind which are explained by the essence in the appropriate way. Not any sort of *differentia* will do this. Indeed, the result will only be achieved if the differentiation scheme in question is one which latches on to features which are part of the being of the kind (as Aristotle remarks in B.13, 97^a11–14). Thus, the appropriate differentiation scheme in the *Analytics* must meet two constraints:

(D.a)   It must be part of a general scheme of classification in which lower-order kinds are introduced by general, non-*ad hoc*, operations on higher-order ones.

and

(D.b)   It must point at each level to features which are appropriately explained by the essence in question.

This account of *differentiae* is explanation-involving in one crucial respect. In being *differentiae in accordance with being* (i.e. essence 97^a12 f.) the relevant predicates must not only locate the kind in its own niche in a natural order but do so in a way which points to genuine features of the kind

---

[11] Other terms explained by the essence (e.g. unique specific ones) would not be included in the definition (even though they are necessary properties of the kind) because they do not fit into the *differentiae* structure.

(appropriately explained by the essence). Thus, what counts as a *differentia* is delimited (but not wholly determined) by what is explained by the essence in the appropriate way. It is, of course, a substantial claim that there are features which can play both these roles, and a substantial recommendation that the relevant differentiation structure should be constrained by both these requirements.[12] For, the differentiating scheme not only points to a system of derivation of lower- from higher-order kinds, but also does so in a way which refers to non-accidental features of the relevant kinds which are explained by their essences.

In the arithmetical case it should come as no surprise that the differentiation scheme picks out non-accidental features of (e.g.) the triple. For, the pattern of derivation (odd, prime+) is one which rests on general properties of numbers (unlike being prime and less than fifteen, etc.). Given a system of this type, it is no accident that the features of the triple marked out are the non-accidental ones explained in the appropriate way by its essence. The system of differentiation appears designed to select non-accidental features of the numbers.

The hypothesis developed in the last few paragraphs is attractive. It renders the claims of B.13 consistent with those of B.8–10 (as promised at the beginning of B.13), and explains why the differentiation scheme in B.13 is in line with being (or essence (97^a13)). It also has interesting general implications for Aristotle's theory of definition and classification. However, it can only be secured (from an exegetical viewpoint) if we can see why he took definition and differentiation to be connected in the way suggested. There would have been a major gap in his theory if he had given no explanation of this connection. Fortunately, the next section of *Posterior Analytics* B.13 appears to provide the type of explanation required (or so I shall argue).

9.3 GENUS AS AN EXPLANATORY NOTION: 96^b15–25

This passage is a notoriously difficult one.[13] It runs as follows:

When you are dealing with a given subject [of enquiry], you should divide the genus into what are the first atoms in species—e.g. number into triplet and pair, then attempt to give definitions of these (e.g. of straight line, circle, and right angle);

---

[12] One might ask why it should be a derivative feature (and not the answer to the 'why?' question itself) which is the one which marks out the species in the descending tree? Aristotle, of course, focuses on cases where predicates extend beyond the kind (96^a24), and so will not be the unique essence (*to ti en einai*), and locates the *differentiae* amongst these in the case in point. It does not follow from this alone that the *differentiae* will always extend beyond the kind, or that it will always be a derivative feature which fills the role of the *differentia*.

[13] As Barnes comments: 'if it has a coherent interpretation, it remains to be found' (*Aristotle's Posterior Analytics*, 213).

and, after that, having grasped what the kind (genus) is (e.g. whether it is a quantity or quality), consider its proper affections through the first common elements.[14] For, properties of things that are compounded from the atoms will be clear from the definitions, because definitions and what is simple are the principles of everything, and properties belong non-derivatively to the simples alone, and to the other things derivatively. (96^{b}15–25)

This passage contains many difficulties. I shall begin by offering an interpretation which represents it as a natural extension of 96^{b}4–14. It runs as follows:

In examining a given subject matter such as numbers (*holon ti*), one should divide it into its first atomic species (e.g. two, three), and then try to formulate a definition of these. At this point one will avail oneself of terms like prime, odd, and prime*. A suggestion for a full definition of two might be:

even, prime, prime* with a given essence (what it is to be two)

After considering these definitions one does two things:

(a) seeks to determine the genus: number,

and

(b) discovers its distinguishing features by considering the properties of its first common elements.

The distinguishing features of number will presumably be *differentiae* such as being odd or even, prime or non-prime, prime* or non-prime*; the very features uncovered in seeking to define two and three. In this way, relevant *differentiae* emerge from consideration of the explanation-involving definitions of the first two elements in the domain. So, it is no accident that the *differentiae* selected pick out essential features of the numbers in question. For, they were chosen as *differentiae* precisely because they are elements in the definition of the basic cases. If these are definitional features for two and three, it is natural to assume that they are also definitional features of all numbers, since all others can be constructed from two and three (by addition).

However, there remains an obvious gap in Aristotle's account. The only differentiating properties so far attributed to derived numbers such as five or seven are those of being prime, non-prime*, and odd.[15] But these do not

---

[14] The proper affections could (grammatically) be either those of the genus or of the whole area under discussion. However, this issue need not detain us since one genus is taken here to cover one whole area of the appropriate type.

[15] In *De Caelo* 286^{a}6 ff., Aristotle notes a further feature of three: It has a beginning a middle and an end. Theon (46.14–8, 100.13–101.10) makes the same claims about three, and also notes that it is called 'perfect;' but for other reasons. The *differentiae* 'perfect' might be added to odd/even . . . as *differentiae* of numbers (see Iamblichus, *In Nicom. Arithm.*, 31–3).

specify what is distinctive of five as opposed to seven. Thus, the account of *differentiae* does not yet adequately distinguish between many of the infimae species of number.

While the existence of this problem (discussed acutely by Pacius) does not challenge the general thesis of the interdependence of differentiation and definition in B.13, it would, nonetheless, be less than satisfactory if it could not be resolved using the resources which that thesis allows us. One attempted solution would be to use the different modes of composition (*sunthesis*) involved in five and seven to determine (in some measure) the relevant infimae species (e.g. five will be composed from one concatenation of common numbers, seven from two). On this account, Aristotle will not hold that all the properties of five or seven are themselves the properties of the primary ones, provided that they are *either* properties of two or three *or* features of the way two and three are combined in their case. If so, the relevant features would belong to the derived species in accordance with (*kata*) the nature of the simples (96^{b}24 f.),[16] even though they are not all properties of simples.

Let us focus on the case of five. If its relevant properties were (e.g.) being odd, prime, and non-prime* and the product of only one concatenation of the basic elements, five would be marked out by features which individually extend beyond it, but which collectively do not (in line with Aristotle's injunction in 96^{a}32 ff.). These features are ones which either belong to two and three, or result from how they are combined to form five. Thus, they need not be (as Pacius apparently thought) confined to ones which belong to two and three, provided that their presence can be explained on the basis of the properties of two and three (including their powers of combination). This method can be generalized to cover all other numbers.[17]

[16] Barnes discusses this proposal first made by Pacius, critically (*Aristotle's Posterior Analytics*, 233), and rejects it. Pacius is taken to commit himself to the view that (e.g.) the quintuple's properties are confined to those of the triple and pair (e.g. odd/even, prime/non-prime), without considering their modes of combination. If this were his view, he would have been unable satisfactorily to distinguish between five and seven. But there seems no reason to interpret '*kata*' in 96^{b}24 to mean that all properties of the quintuple are ones which belong to the pair or triple. Perhaps rather they are consequences of the properties of the pair and triple plus their mode of combination. (Pacius' own formulations are actually fairly cautious. He commits himself only to the view that those properties that belong to both primary and derived species belong to the latter derivatively 'in so far as (*quatenus*) they are composed from the primary'. This does not require him to make the mistake of thinking that *all* features of derived species are shared by primary ones. However, since he offers no view on any features of the derived species which are not shared by the primary ones, his account is at best incomplete (Barnes, *Aristotle's Posterior Analytics*, 338)).

[17] Examples of the *differentiae* might be:

Four: even, non-prime, non-prime*, the result of one concatenation of basic elements.

Five: odd, prime, non-prime*, the result of one concatenation of basic elements.

If this line of interpretation is correct, Aristotle's discussion of numbers has achieved two goals:

(1) He has shown how one can arrive at a view of the relevant genus and its specific features by examining the definitional properties of two of its central cases.

(2) He has also shown how the other members of the genus can be marked out using these specific features (odd, even) together with the mode of combination of the common elements.

In the case of numbers, we can see why the initial differentiating features of individual numbers selected by these methods will be the ones explained by their distinctive essences. In the case of two and three, being odd, even, prime+, etc. were selected precisely because they played this role. In derived cases, there is a similar pattern. For example, if being the product of two and three is the essence of five, this will explain why it is odd (as it is not the product of two even numbers) and prime (given that is odd, and not divisible by three). Since the additional features used to differentiate five (e.g. its being non-prime*, the result of one concatenation of basic elements) depend on its being the product of two and three, these too will be explicable by its distinctive essence.

Within this conception, the genus of number is held together by a common thread: the features used in the definition of derived species can be seen to be the result of applying a series of operations to a small number of basic elements (e.g. two, three). Derived species (e.g. five, six . . .) fall within one genus provided that their differentiating properties depend on the definitional features (odd, prime . . .) and modes of combination of the basic elements.[18] Further, in their case, the essence itself may be based on

Six: even, non-prime, non-prime*, the result of two concatenations of basic elements.

Seven: odd, prime, non-prime*, the result of two concatenations of basic elements.

Eight: even, non-prime, non-prime*, the result of two concatenations of basic elements . . .

These *differentiae* would (in line with Aristotle's own injunction in 96ª32 ff.) individually extend beyond the relevant number, but collectively extend no further than it. (I include this list merely to show how such a system might work, not to claim that Aristotle actually had such a proposal 'in mind', when writing this passage.)

The relevant essences would be the essence of four, five . . . These could, but need not, be understood as (e.g.) the result of concatenating two and two, two and three . . .

[18] These cases show that it is a mistake to attempt to line up all of B.13 with any one of the B.8–10 definitions, or to criticize Aristotle if this cannot be done. The fact that his discussion is not limited to one of the B.10 definitions does not show that he is talking about some other form of pre-demonstrative definition. In B.13 Aristotle is pursuing the more general goal of showing how ideas about genus and *differentiae* can play a role *throughout* successful enquiry into essence and definition. Thus, at some points he focuses on definitions which correspond to conclusions of demonstrations, at others on full definitions which correspond to complete demonstrations. (The discussion of simples is reserved for B.19.)

some specific combination of two and three. Thus, there are three features involved in the arithmetical case:

(1) The general differentiating properties are shared by all numbers (e.g. odd/even, prime/non-prime, etc.).

(2) The additional differentiating features come from the mode of combination of the basic elements.

(3) The essence itself may be determined by facts about the combination of the basic elements.

Between them, these features generate the distinctive type of order to be found in the genus of number. Members of that genus are bound together by their shared possession of these three features. But this is a special kind of ordering, with its own distinctive properties. Aristotle needs to show that this idea of genera and *differentiae* can extend beyond the case of number to areas where the derived species are not composed from basic elements. In such a case, one would expect to find (1) but not (2) or (3) at work. Thus, he needs to devise a way of showing how certain species are differentiated which does not rest on the principle of composition.

9.4 EXTENSION BEYOND THE MATHEMATICAL CASE: BIOLOGY INTRODUCED*

Aristotle begins the task, just outlined, in the next section of the chapter by introducing the method of division, and sums up his general claims for this method later, in 97ᵃ23–ᵇ6.

Aristotle had written critically of division in *Posterior Analytics* B.5, but now reintroduces it in an apparently favourable manner as 'useful' for the type of procedure recently specified (96ᵇ25). Division in accordance with *differentiae* is to play something of the role taken by numerical order in the previous case:

Divisions in accordance with *differentiae* are useful in this procedure ... they are useful in deducing what something is (96ᵇ25–7)

Why does Aristotle reintroduce the method of division in the context of B.13? What has changed from B.5? Why is division useful in a way comparable to the distinctions marked out in the case of numbers?

If the mathematical case provides a partial parallel for the biological one, one would expect to find in the latter an analogue of condition (1). Thus, one should be able to organize a given subject matter by focusing on some special cases of individual species (e.g. man, horse . . .) and attempting to define these in the explanatory style of B.8–10. For example, one might define man as an animal capable of walking on two feet, with its own distinctive soul. On this basis, one would attempt to derive a view of the distinctive features of the genus, animal, as (e.g.) what is capable of movement, breathing, reproduction . . . In this way, one would hope to devise a system of *differentiae* which met two conditions:

(a*) They fit into a general and non-*ad hoc* procedure for deriving genuine kinds from other genuine kinds.

(b*) They are themselves explained in the relevant syllogism which incorporates the essence.

If the relevant *differentiae* point to ways of being members of the higher group which meet condition (b*), they will be (as Aristotle says) useful in 'deducing what something is'. For, they will point to the features to be explained by the essence. Indeed, it is because *differentiae* are of the type indicated by (b*) that they can play this role. That Aristotle emphasizes this use of *differentiae* strongly suggests that he sees their role as the one required by (b*).

Aristotle does not, however, say much that is relevant to condition (a*) in the biological case. As a result, we are given little indication of what is to replace composition from basic elements among specific *differentiae* in this case. He does, however, make an important point, when he writes:

It makes a difference which of the predicates is predicated first: e.g. to say animal tame two-footed or two-footed animal tame. For, if everything is made up out of something, and tame animal is a unity and man is made up out of this and the *differentia* (two-footed), it is necessary to postulate by dividing. (96^{b}30–5)

Aristotle emphasizes that it makes a difference what the relevant order is. This is because if [A + B] is a unity, and man is made up of [A + B] + C (with C as its *differentia*), it is necessary to postulate by dividing. This claim involves two aspects:

(i) The *differentia* C takes one from a unity to a unity (e.g. man).

and

(ii) To explain what man is is to explain why C belongs to [A + B]: Why does biped belong to tame animal?

Reference to the distinctive essence of man will answer the latter question by pointing to a feature which explains why bipedality belongs to the class of tame animals. The latter formulation gets the problem in the right form to be answered.

But why is this so? Would not the essence of man also explain why tameness belongs to the class of biped animal? What determines that this is the order of the *differentiae*?

Aristotle suggests that if *tame* is the first *differentia*, this is because it divides the whole genus of animal while *biped* does not. Being a biped is a way of being footed, as being split-winged is a way of being winged (96^b31 f., $^b38$ff.), and so is only a *differentia* among footed animals. But this remark does not take us very far. While this pattern of thought may explain why biped comes after tame, it says nothing about the relative positions of (e.g.) *tame* and *footed* as *differentiae*. Since all animals can be placed in the categories tame/wild, footed/footless, why begin with one rather than another?

The best clue is provided by clause (i). At each level, in Aristotle's view, one must have a properly unified kind, and not an *ad hoc* or unnatural collection of different kinds. Thus, tame animal is allowed as a species only if it is a unity.[19] Footed animal would be excluded if it did not form a genuine unified kind, but allowed of too much variation within its members. For similar reasons, aquatic, terrestrial, and aerial would be excluded, if they contain species too far apart to form a unified kind.

It is clear that there are background ontological assumptions about genuine unified kinds at work here. Indeed, the procedure of division is constrained by these assumptions. Its role is not to determine the unity of a kind (as it was in the account criticized in B.6), but rather to organize in some systematic way unities established by other means. Nor can division alone secure the appropriate ordering. Rather, it is itself constrained by two factors:

(a) It must begin with a unity (e.g. tame animal).

and

(b) It must add a further term (as a *differentia*) which generates a unified lower kind. Further, the presence of the relevant *differentia* will in turn be explained by the essence of the kind in the appropriate way.

Thus, the relevant *differentiae* will take us from unity to unity in a way which marks out the features to be explained at the lower level.

These conditions, taken together, mirror some of the constraints on *differentiae* in the mathematical case. Genuine biological *differentiae* will be features with two roles:

(a*) They will fit into a pattern of biological practice for deriving species of the kind indicated.

---

[19] I take it that these cases are only included *exempli causa*, and are not intended to correspond to Aristotle's own favoured views. On *wild* and *tame* as *differentiae*, see *PA* A.2.

and

(b*) They will themselves be explained in an appropriate way by the underlying essence.

(a*) refers to the required procedure for moving from unities to unities by means of *differentiae* which are themselves explained at the lower level. What is missing here is an account of the type of *differentiae* which will allow for this procedure. We are given no indication of what is to replace those features which depend on the combination of the basic elements (two and three) to distinguish species which are wild, four-legged, etc. In effect, we lack any clear idea of what the relevant type of *differentiae* will be, or of the nature of the order they define. So, no analogue is provided of conditions (2) and (3) in the arithmetical case. We are, however, told that division by *differentiae* is to mark out by divisional methods a descending sequence of genuine unities, and to do so in line with (a*) and (b*). If this goal is satisfactorily achieved, no unity will be excluded. Division, if successful, will allow us to see all relevant unities as part of a hierarchical structure of kinds with (at least) some basic shared *differentiae*.[20]

[20] Later (97ª35-ᵇ6), Aristotle envisages the following structure of kinds:

- (A) animal
- (B) bird   fish
- (C) split-winged   whole-winged

where level-B kinds are genuine unities because they are arrived at from a genuine unity (A) plus a *differentia* (e.g. being winged). One can then establish (if the schema of *differentiae* is adequate) that these are all the unities there are, provided that at the final stage—C—there is no further genuine *differentia* (i.e. there is no further genuine sub-kind to be marked out)—since what falls below this level is the same in kind as the level, and differs in a way not relevant to classification of kinds (because not explained by relevant reasons). In a complete *differentiae* system, no level will be missed out. For, if it was, one would not be able to grasp all the kinds by the favoured route:

unity A/animal [genus] + *differentia* 1 → proper unity B

If one skipped level B, and proceeded as follows

unity A/animal [genus] + *differentia* 2 → proper unity C

one would have the following division groupings at level C:

split-winged animals: whole-winged animals and wingless
             animals

and would overlook the unified kind of winged animals (birds). So, this procedure would ignore one kind with just the required type of unifying feature. A *differentia* term is correctly used in a sequence only if it is introduced at a point where no genuine kind is previously overlooked (winged animal). But this depends on prior assumptions about what are genuine kinds and an appropriate order of derivation, which this account does not generate or guarantee.

This sketch (albeit incomplete) of the role of genus and *differentiae* offers some insight into Aristotle's idea of using the genus to establish what belongs in the definition of sub-kinds. In an optimal case, one would be able to establish the distinguishing features (*ta sumbebēkota*) of the sub-species by seeing them as elements in a genus/*differentiae* tree of the appropriate kind. This is because the *differentiae* are themselves selected (in part) because they pick out what is to be explained by the essence in question (in the way required for definition). This will be so whether the *differentiae* are general ones, such as tame/wild or footed/non-footed, or specific ones which mark out differences between (e.g.) tame and footed animals.

The pattern at work in this account further exemplifies the thesis of the interdependence of definition and explanation introduced in the previous Chapter. The *explananda* accounted for by the essence are (in part) demarcated by definitional concerns which arise from our practice of defining by genus and *differentia*. But the pattern of differentiation itself is (in some measure) based on a view of what is to be explained on the basis of the essence in question. The same type of interdependence of explanation and definition is present here as in B.8–10 and B.16–18.

If this is correct, we can establish which features are the ones which follow from the essence and are part of the definition, in two ways. They will emerge either as the *explananda* to be derived from the essence of a sub-kind in the favoured way, or as the products of an appropriate genus/*differentia* tree. These two routes arrive at the same destination. In the favoured model of explanation (the one required for definition), the *explananda* are those features which not only follow from the essence but also fit into an appropriate structure of genus and *differentiae*. But, in turn, an appropriate structure of differentiation into genus and species will itself essentially involve the presence of features to be explained by the essence. Thus, if one possesses an appropriate differentiating procedure one will arrive in the case of man at (e.g.) biped tame animal. But equally if one begins with the essence of man (e.g. possessing a given kind of soul) and proceeds via an appropriate scheme of explanation one will arrive at these same features as the *explananda*. Nor is this an accident. The two discussions of definition, in B.8–10 and B.13, fit together because they both exemplify a common perspective in which the practices of definition and explanation are mutually interdependent. They were made for one another.

Aristotle's concepts of genus and *differentiae*, so understood, are partially based on his conception of explanation. Taken together, they provide a picture of a given area of investigation as an organized whole in which:

(a) Genera are kinds, all of whose sub-kinds can be ordered in an intelligible fashion using *differentiae*.

(b) *Differentiae* take one from kind to sub-kind in an intelligible way which picks out those features of the sub-kind which differentiate the sub-kind from its kind and are explained by its essence.

In this conception, *differentiae* mark out genuine unities by specifying some of their defining features in a way which shows them to be intelligibly related to higher-order kinds. Further, these features are the ones to be explained by the appropriate answer to the 'Why?' question. Genera are groups of objects which can be differentiated in this way.

9.5 THE CONSEQUENCES OF THE GENERAL PICTURE: EXPLANATION AND CLASSIFICATION IN B.14–15*

It is natural to expect Aristotle to employ this explanation-involving conception of genus, species, and *differentiae* in the remainder of B.13 and in the subsequent chapters (B.14–15). We have already seen how it is of use in understanding the discussion of pride in B.13, where concern with explanation was used to differentiate different types of pride (see Ch. 8 Sect. 4). It is also at work in B.14 and 15. Or so I shall argue.

In B.14, Aristotle discusses how problems are to be set out. One would naturally expect him to employ the model of differentiation he developed in B.13 to draw up a list of genera and species in line with these principles. In the immediate context of B.14 the only differentiating procedures available are those marked out in B.13. There is no other basis in the context for Aristotle's insistence that the appropriate divisions be made in a certain way ($98^a1–3$, see 96^b25). Further, kinds of the type introduced in B.13 are precisely what are required to raise problems in the right form. For, genuine features of such kinds (whether *differentiae* or not) will be explained by the essences of such kinds at the appropriate degree of generality. This is because these kinds are differentiated by features which are themselves explained by the underlying essence (in line with clause (b*) above). Thus, there is good reason for Aristotle to require problems to be set up using just the materials he has developed in B.13. For, these will set one on the road to discovering the answer to the appropriate 'Why?' question.

The model developed in B.14 appears to cohere well with the one we have discerned in B.13. The first example runs as follows:

animal

bird

species of bird (e.g. split-winged bird)

At each stage, Aristotle asks what properties belong to the relevant kinds and why:

(e.g.) Why are all animals F?

   Why are all birds G?

   Why are all split-winged birds H?

Here, it appears that the enquirer already possesses a structure of differentiation into genus and species which enables him to pose problems concerning the features of the genera and species at the right degree of generality (98^a4-8). In the light of the discussion of genus and *differentiae* in B.13, it is natural to expect the successful enquirer to possess a pattern of genera and species which allows him to select features to be explained at each level.

   If one withdraws the support provided by the model developed in B.13, there is no basis for the genus/*differentia* structure introduced in B.14. For, while it is true that these divisions are demarcated by names in common usage (98^a13 f.), Aristotle assumes both that common usage is correct in these cases and that his method can be extended to ones where there is no established name (98^a14 ff.). Nor is there any evidence that counter-predication is used in this passage (98^a1-12) to set up either the predicates or the kinds mentioned in the problems.[21] Further, if we had relied solely on established usage or counter-predication, there would be no guarantee that we had arrived at the right kinds for asking explanatory questions. For, kinds established independently of explanation-based *differentiae* might be irrelevant for explanatory purposes.

   Aristotle appears to rely on kinds differentiated as in B.13 in the second part of B.14, when he focuses on kinds and sub-kinds not marked out by names in common use (98^a14 ff.). He writes:

we must extract a common property and ask what things this follows, and what qualities follow it: e.g. in the case having a manyplies and lacking incisors, it follows animals with horns. And we should also enquire what animals having horns follows. For, it will be clear why (e.g.) having a manyplies belongs to them: because they have horns.

Aristotle asks himself two questions:

 (i) What objects/kinds have a manyplies? *Answer*: animals with horns.

 (ii) What objects have horns? *Answer* (not given): oxen, goats . . .

Question (ii) must be different from (i), as is signalled by 'Again . . .' in the text. Thus, while (ii) and (i) are both concerned with types of animal, the

---

[21] For a view of this sort, see J. G. Lennox's 'Between Data and Demonstration: The *Analytics* and the *Historia Animalium*, in A. C. Bowen (ed.), *Science and Philosophy in Classical Greece* (Pittsburgh, 1989), Ch. 12, and 'Divide and Explain: The *Posterior Analytics* in Practice' in Gotthelf and Lennox (eds.) *Philosophical Issues in Aristotle's Biology*, 90–116.

answers are different. In (i), Aristotle is assuming that there is a kind, such as horned animal, which lacks a common name (unlike 'bird' (98^{a}7)). These species might be described by a phrase (such as 'wingless quadruped' or 'horned animal') or by several names joined together.

In this passage, Aristotle relies on a structure of genus and *differentiae* which is already in place, and which marks out (e.g.) horned animals and goats as species in a descending tree.[22] In this case, unlike that discussed in the first part of B.14, 'horned animal' is not itself a name. But, nonetheless, there is a genus and *differentia* structure which yields questions at the right level such as:

Why do all horned animals have a manyplies?

and enables one to give derived answers to lower-level questions such as:

Why do oxen have manyplies?

In such a case, the answer depends on seeing oxen as falling below horned animal in a structure which has already been marked out on independent grounds. As before, the only available basis for this structure is the one provided in B.13. Further, the B.13 structure (96^{b}25) is useful because it introduces kinds with essences which can provide the answers to the problems raised in B.14. For, there what is sought is something which explains why the kind in question has its own genuine properties. Without the resources provided by the B.13 differentiation scheme it is unclear why the model set out in B.14 should be of use in setting out problems. For, if the connection between differentiation and explanation is dropped, there will be no reason to believe that the kinds distinguished in B.14 can assist us in setting out problems of the type required. For, they might lack essences of the type to be invoked for explanation.

The role of explanation-involving *differentiae* in individuating kinds is

---

[22] Aristotle is envisaging three stages:

(a) Establish $\forall x [Fx \rightarrow Hx]$, where 'Hx' means x has manyplies.

(b) Establish $\forall x [Gx \rightarrow Fx]$, where 'Fx' means x is horned.

and finally:

(c) What animals have F?

An answer to (c) might be: type A (goats), one of the kinds which are F (e.g. 99^{a}32–5). If so, there is no essential use of commensurate universals or counter-predication in this passage. These features enter at a further stage (cf. 99^{a}32–6) where one reaches the end of the explanatory project. Similarly, in B.17, 99^{b}5 ff., while all birds may have a given property, possession of this property need not be confined to birds (e.g. possession of a gut of a given kind), provided that not all animals possess a gut of this kind (cf. *HA* B.17; cf. 508^{b}14–17). It is not required that the universals at this stage belong exclusively to birds (cf. 99^{a}32–5), but some could apply to (e.g.) fish as well. Thus: 'Why do all birds have a gut of a given kind?' might be an acceptable problem, even if fish also had such a gut.

also clear in B.15. Aristotle notes that for a problem to be *one* problem, there must be one shared explanatory feature (whether numerically or in genus).[23] Thus, as in B.16 and 17, if the middle terms picking out the explanatory feature are different, either the relevant property to be explained is different or the objects differ in kind.[24] But this can only be because it is a condition on the kind being one that there is one essence which explains why it possesses its relevant properties. (Otherwise the property will turn out to be one 'by analogy' as in the cases discussed in B.14.[25]) This constraint is underwritten by the explanation-invoking account of differentiation developed in B.13. If kinds are differentiated by features which are explained in an appropriate way by the kind's essence (in line with requirement (b*) above), there will be one kind only if there is one essence of the appropriate type.

These claims clearly reflect the explanatory concerns manifested in Aristotle's method of differentiating genera and species. Kinds, sub-kinds, and *differentiae* are all selected (in part) on the basis of their role in explanation. This pattern is to be found throughout B.16–18, where difference in relevant middle term (cause) spells difference either in the property to be explained or the kind under explanation. But, as I have argued, it is also present in the earlier chapters, B.13–15, where kinds are individuated and *differentiae* selected (at least, in part) in line with the demands of explanation. Given this picture, it is no surprise in B.15 that if the rele-

---

[23] This chapter is interestingly discussed by J. G. Lennox in 'Aristotelian Problems' (1994). He argues (*contra* Ross and Barnes) that these two cases exhaust the ones in which the problem is the same. In Lennox's view, cases where the answers to problems are related because they 'fall under' one another are not ones where the problem is one (98ᵃ29–34). Whichever way this issue is resolved makes no difference to the issue presently under discussion.

[24] See Ch. 8 Sect. 8.5.

[25] At the end of B.14 Aristotle draws the following picture:

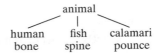

where there is an analogy between the cases because they belong to different genera. Aristotle remarks that some things will belong to:

human *qua* boned

and to:

fish *qua* spined, etc.

'as if these were one common nature', although they are not. By contrast, within one genus or species, there will be just such a common nature. So, if the idea of a common nature is an explanatorily based one, Aristotle will here too be relying on explanation-based concerns in his conception of the appropriate genus/species trees. For further discussion of the notion of 'common nature', see Chapter 12. In the immediate context of the *Analytics*, it seems clear in the light of the rest of B.14 and 15 that this is an explanatory notion.

vant explanatory middle term differs (and the property remains constant), the kinds (and the problems involved) must also be different. For, differentiation and explanation are tied closely together throughout this account.

9.6 TOWARDS A UNIFIED THEORY OF DEFINITON

I have argued that Aristotle's discussion of definition in B.13–15 is fully consistent with the explanation-involving practice of defining set out in B.8–10 and developed in B.16–18. Throughout, Aristotle is concerned with the same definitions. I have further argued that B.13–15 add to his earlier account by making explicit an account of genus, species, and *differentia* which deepens our grasp of the definitions considered in *Posterior Analytics* B.8–10. Throughout, Aristotle maintains the interdependence of defining and explanation. The features to be explained in the case of kinds are the ones which are used to differentiate the genus (in the way required for definition *per genus et differentiam*). But the differentiation scheme is itself further constrained by the need to use features which can be explained in the appropriate way by the essence of the relevant kinds.

In this Chapter, I have suggested that Aristotle's account in *Posterior Analytics* B of the definitions achieved by scientific enquiry forms a unified whole. His aim of finding the underlying causal basis of the kind (as emphasized in the previous chapter) fits closely together with his interest in locating kinds in appropriate genus/species trees. There is no need to see these two goals as generating two different types of definition. Rather, both aim to capture the same thing (the nature (*ousia*) of the kind in question). Further, they are closely connected because Aristotle's use of the notions of genus and *differentiae* is permeated by the explanatory concerns which motivate the search for the causal basis of the kind. Both goals flow from his constant focus on the subtle interdependences between explanation and definition, which emerge throughout his discussion.

In subsequent Chapters I shall investigate the application of this account of definition to issues in metaphysics and biology. There are many respects in which Aristotle's discussion of definition and classification in the *Analytics* is incomplete.[26] However, before considering these, I shall

---

[26] For instance, Aristotle does not consider the following questions:

(1) How far do the concepts of genus and *differentia* apply. If thunder is to be understood as *noise in the clouds*, is *noise* the genus, and *in the clouds* the differentiating term (specifying the place where; cf. *Meta*. H.2, 1042^{b}21)? Does something similar apply to the account of eclipse as *deprivation of light* (where deprivation is understood as like a genus).

examine further the precise nature and basis of Aristotle's thesis of the interdependence of definition and explanation, and consider a major exegetical challenge based on an interpretation of the final chapter of the *Analytics*. For, many see Aristotle as advancing in B.19 a fundamentally different, indeed opposite, view on these issues.

(2) How far does this account of definition cohere with definitions outside the *Analytics* of substance which use the concepts of matter and form?

(3) Can the explanation-involving system of classification suggested in B.13–15 be applied to any case other than mathematics? Does it work in the biological domain?

IO

Explanation and Definition: the Basic Model Reconsidered and Refined

10.1 INTRODUCTION

The last two Chapters have uncovered a common structure. In Aristotle's view, the practice of definition (as characterized in the *Analytics*) cannot be fully specified without the use of resources drawn from the practice of explanation. But the latter, in turn, is incomplete without the support of material taken from the former. The two practices are mutually dependent. Neither can stand alone.

To recapitulate: the priority and unity of the *definiens* cannot be captured without recourse to our causal explanatory practices, as these are revealed in demonstration.[1] But equally the relevant types of *explananda* and *explanantia* cannot be determined without assistance from the practice of definition. Thus, the *explanantia* are (a) features specific to the kind in question, (b) unities which it could not lack, and (c) ones which make the nature of the kind fully intelligible to us. In a similar way, the *explananda* (in the case of substances) are features which differentiate the kind in an appropriate genus/*differentia* tree.[2] The *per se* connections which are to be explained are delimited (in part) by our practices of definition. But here too definition does not stand alone. For, a feature can only be a *differentia* if it is explained in the appropriate way by the essence of the relevant phenomenon. Both definition and explanation have a role to play in the determination of *differentiae*. Neither is complete by itself.

These remarks show the importance of Aristotle's introductory remarks in B.2. He writes:

In all these cases it is clear that what it is and why it is are one and the same. What is an eclipse? Privation of light from the moon caused by the earth's screening. Why is there an eclipse? Or 'Why is the moon eclipsed?' Because the light fails when the earth screens it. What is a harmony? An arithmetical ratio of high and

---

[1] See Ch. 8 Sect. 8.2.

[2] See Ch. 9 Sects. 9.2–4. These features will be important elements of the form transferred from the kind to the thinker. (See Ch. 6 Sects. 6.1, 4–5.)

low pitch. Why does the high pitch harmonize with the low? Because an arithmetical ratio holds between them. (90ª14–21)

Aristotle's first question in this passage is:

(1) What is an eclipse?

which is answered as follows:

(2) Privation of light from the moon brought on by the earth's screening.

In this case, the 'Why?' question is posed as follows:

(3) Why does eclipse belong to the moon?

and answered by saying:

(4) Because light failure belongs to the moon brought on by the earth's screening.

The definition contains three elements: the efficient cause (the earth coming in between), what the efficient cause brings about (e.g. light failure), and what is affected by the efficient cause (the moon: *to proton paschon*). The definition is complex:

A (eclipse) = B (light failure) in C (the moon) brought on by D (earth screening).

The B and C places are filled by terms which are explained by the operation of the efficient cause (the B-term specifies the effect, the C-term the thing affected). The cause, D, is specified in such a way as to bring out its relevance to the effect:

It is because the earth is screened that light fails on the moon.

In this way, the structure and elements of the definition are determined by the relevant pattern of efficient causation. As Aristotle's argument develops it becomes clear that the relevant pattern of efficient causation is itself constrained by the theory of definition. For, the explanation is required to begin with the essence of the phenomenon (a simple, causally basic feature) and to explain (in favoured cases) the presence of a *differentia* (e.g. the eclipse's occurring *to the moon*). What is sought is an *unqualified* demonstration, the type of demonstration designed to reveal the essence of the kind.

Aristotle's introductory remarks in B.2 point to an identity between the defining features and those centrally involved in the appropriate form of explanation. Much of his subsequent discussion in *Posterior Analytics* B is directed to showing how this claim is to be understood.[3] The identity is a reflection of the interdependence of our practices of definition and of explanation.

---

[3] For rejected alternative understandings, see Ch. 8 Sect. 8.5.

Causally structured definitions of this type will be appropriate where 'the cause is different'. In some cases, the relevant cause might be a tele-ological one (e.g. preservation, in the case of a house). In others, it might be the grounding cause introduced in the mathematical cases in B.11 (94ᵃ24–34). The second case introduced in B.2 appears to be of this type, since the arithmetical ratio explains why there is a harmony of high and low notes of a certain kind.[4] In these cases the definition gives a structural description of the phenomenon, which picks out its causally salient fea-tures: the relevant cause, its effect, and the object affected. But, as becomes clear later, the relevant type of causation is constrained by demands which flow from the theory of definition.

The *Analytics*, so interpreted, articulates a unified account of these defi-nitions. Its completed definitions may refer to differentiation through genus and *differentia*, and to the unique, causally basic essence of the kind. These will have two dimensions:

(a) they will reveal the explanatorily basic feature of the kind,

and

(b) they will locate the kind in a wider context of other species within the same genus, at its appropriate point in a genus/species tree.

So understood, there is no contrast or tension between definition by genus and *differentia* and definition by causally basic feature. Both can be elements in one unified definition because both play a mutually sup-portive role in an appropriate constitutive causal story. Nor is their integration an accident. The *differentiae* are demarcated (in part) by their role as the *explananda* in the relevant causal story. But equally the *explananda* are themselves (in part) selected because they are *differentiae* which locate the particular kind in a wider system of classification. Some have argued that Aristotle offers several distinct theories of definition, which fail to form a unified whole: definition by genus and *differentia*, def-inition by basic causal feature, and definition by matter and form.[5] However, in the *Analytics*, the first two are integrated parts of one account of definition.

Interdependence between the practices of explanation and definition is

---

[4] In B.11, Aristotle notes cases where the teleological cause gives the basis for the rele-vant definitional account (94ᵃ22–23), and others in which 'given so an so, it is necessary that this is so'(94ᵃ21–2). Since Aristotle does not (in this passage) separate out the material cause, it is unclear whether the latter kind of cause is simply the material cause in disguise or whether it extends more widely. (Similarly with the mathematical example in 94ᵃ27 ff.) However, in all the cases mentioned the cause (specified by the middle term) is prior to the effect (as specified in the conclusion) in one of the three causal patterns specified. Further, there is no case in B.11 where the essence is said to be prior without the support of an effi-cient, grounding, or teleological causal story.

[5] See J. M. LeBlond's paper 'Definition in Aristotle', repr. in J. Barnes, M. Shofield, and R. Sorabji (eds.) *Articles on Aristotle 3: Metaphysics* (London, 1979), 63–79.

matched by a further metaphysical claim: that essences and the *explanantia* and *explananda* cited in structural explanation are co-determined. That is, if truths about the latter are determined, so are truths about the former (and vice versa). Indeed, a feature can only be essential if it is the *per se* structural cause, and can only be the latter if it is essential. The thesis of the co-determination of essences and *explanantia* concerns the structure of reality rather than our practices of definition or explanation.

Several questions naturally arise about these claims:

(1) What is the importance of Aristotle's claim that our practices of definition and explanation are interdependent?

(2) What is the basis of the constraints on definition, which are later made determinate by the theory of explanation?

(3) Does the interdependency of our practices of definition and explanation rest on the co-determination of essence and *explanantia*? Or vice versa? Or is neither more basic?

(4) Can the unified account of definition be extended to include the case of definition via matter and form?

I shall consider questions (1), (2), and (3) in the next three Sections, and (4) in the next Chapter. The parallel theses of interdependency and co-determination have epistemological consequences. For, we can come to know that certain features are essential by seeing their role as unified and immediate causes in a given form of explanation. There is no need for a special faculty of intuition to give us insight into the modal nature of reality. For, essences can be discovered by carrying through the distinctive type of explanatory project set out above. There is, however, a major objection to this line of interpretation. Many think that Aristotle, in the final chapter of the *Analytics*, develops an account of *nous* as a source of information about first principles, or about modal reality more generally, which can be acquired without any interest in explanation. I shall address this exegetical objection in Section 10.6.

10.2 THE IMPORTANCE OF THE INTERDEPENDENCY OF DEFINITION AND EXPLANATION

Aristotle ties together his answers to two questions. One is the definitional 'What is F?' question, the other an explanatory one ('What is required for F to exist as the kind of thing it is?'). More precisely, he argues that one cannot answer either of these questions without relying on material drawn from answering the other. Since the requirements for definition and explanation are mutually interdependent in this way, what defines a kind must be the same thing as what is required for it to exist. There is no possibility (in Aristotle's account) of these two coming apart. The definitional constraints are incomplete without the addition of material drawn from our practice of explanation.

The significance of Aristotle's claim becomes clearer if we consider the consequence of separating the theories of definition and of explanation. Once this happens, two questions become pressing. Why should the answer to the 'What is F?' question be the same as that to the question of what is required for F's existence? Indeed, why assume that the answer to the latter question has any relevance to the definition of the kind?

Once these questions are raised, one immediate response will be to say that we should *stipulate* that the explanatorily basic feature constitutes the definitional essence of the kind. This stipulation may reflect our preferences as definers, but need not register any further metaphysical truth.[6] We choose to make the explanatorily basic features into essential ones. Our choice, of course, is not an arbitrary one, since we may reasonably wish to have definitions which pick up explanatorily basic features and trace the explanatory connections in reality. But, nonetheless, it is we who convert explanatorily basic features into definitional ones.

This response rests on two assumptions. First, it presupposes that we, as definers, possess a determinate model of definition, quite independently of how the world is. In this model, our crucial definitional notions (such as may involve priority and unity) are complete without any assistance from the world. We merely note which features in the world satisfy our definitional model and conclude that they are (for that reason) definitional of the kind in question. We have a perfect definitional net (complete no matter what area it is used in) which allows us to make the explanatorily basic features we find in reality essential ones.[7] Second, this response requires us to be able to specify which features are explanatorily basic without any reliance on our practices of definition. There is just one pattern of explanation, marked out in ways independent of definition, which leads us to the definitions we seek.

---

[6] See the arguments deployed by Richard Sorabji (in *Necessity, Cause and Blame*, 213–16) to secure a connection between definitional essence and explanatorily basic feature, once one has introduced an account of definition and explanation which are conceptually independent of one another. Both his major arguments for the identification of definitional essence and explanatorily basic feature turn on the unsupported claim that what is explanatorily basic should be definitional. Richard McKirahan also engages with this issue when he seeks to explain the necessity of definition in *Principles and Proofs* (Princeton, 1992), 107 ff. But I am unable to see how he establishes the necessity of true definition from the resources he deploys.

[7] See, for the use of this analogy, David Wiggins's *Sameness and Substance* (Oxford, 1981), 141.

As we have seen, Aristotle rejects both assumptions. In his view there is no possibility of making determinate our definitional practices without invoking our explanatory ones. For this reason his account of definition is not a conventionalist one. Further, for similar reasons, his account of explanation is not one in which we grasp what is explanatorily basic in the required way without dependence on the constraints drawn from our practices of definition. There is no gap between definition and explanation which needs to be filled by stipulation. Aristotle's approach to these issues is not that of the conventionalist.

There is an alternative response to the questions raised above. If one recoils from conventionalism, but continues to separate our practices of definition and explanation, one will be drawn to say that certain features are essential, independently of their role in explanation. If so, it will seem natural to assume that definitional features (which are such independently of their explanatory role) can (in principle) be grasped as such in ways independent of our explanatory practices. There must be a route to knowledge of what has to be the case, the metaphysical structure of reality, which is not (essentially) dependent on our practices of explanation. It will be a discovery that features which figure in definition are the explanatorily basic ones. For, their having the latter role is not (in any way) what makes them essential.

Aristotle, if I am correct, must reject this response, one most often associated with Plato. For, it too rests on the assumption that it is possible to determine what is definitional independently of our practices of explanation. Both Platonist and conventionalist assume that our definitional practices are complete (or completable) without materials drawn from our understanding of the world's causal order. But it is precisely this assumption that Aristotle rejects. In his view, since our definitions cannot be completed without the use of materials drawn from our explanatory practices, there is no gap of the relevant kind between definition and explanation. The conventionalist and Platonist both attempt to fill a non-existent space.

For the Platonist, intellectual intuition by itself reveals to us the modal structure of reality. Once explanation and definition are separated, there is need for a non-explanation-based route (of this type) to grasp what is definitional. But no such intuition will be required in Aristotle's account. By contrast, we will (in his view) come to understand what features are essential by understanding the world through the lens of our interconnected practices of definition and explanation.[8] Thus, knowledge of essences will not depend on any special (and somewhat mysterious) form of metaphysical intuition. For, Aristotle does not see the need to divorce

---

[8] See Ch. 10 Sect. 10.1.

our practices of definition and explanation in the way which generates the need for intuitive knowledge of essences.[9]

Aristotle's insistence on the interdependency of our practices of definition and explanation is attractive. Once these practices are separated, we seem trapped (as in Chapter 1 Section 1.3) between an unacceptable form of Platonism and an unmotivated form of conventionalism. Aristotle avoids both extremes. Indeed, from his viewpoint, they share a common false assumption: that a full and determinate account of definition can be completed without dependence on our explanatory practices. Once this assumption is made explicit and undermined (in the way Aristotle does in the *Analytics*), one can resist the temptation to succumb to either of these implausible positions.

Aristotle's idea may be attractive, but is it defensible? We have yet to grasp its basis, examine its consequences, or assess its strengths and weaknesses. Thus far, we have merely noted the differences between his view and that of the standard Platonist and conventionalist alternatives. We require a deeper understanding of his own viewpoint and its strengths and weaknesses. We also need to 'unpick', in a more sustained manner, the two alternatives he rejects. In the remainder of this Chapter, I shall consider some of the origins, motivations, and consequences of Aristotle's view. In the final Chapter, I shall attempt to assess its merits, and compare them with those of the conventionalist and Platonist alternatives (see Ch. 13 Sect. 13.2).

10.3 THE ORIGINS OF ARISTOTLE'S DEFINITIONAL CONSTRAINTS

In the *Topics*, Aristotle articulates some general ideas about definitions. They, should, for example, capture the essence of what they define (A.5, 101^{b}38f.), and not merely state the latter's unique properties (E.5, 135^{a}10–12). He also attempts to make these claims more precise.

---

[9] The Platonist picture encounters a further difficulty at the metaphysical level. If one's starting point is a theory of definition (complete independently of truths about the causal structure of the world), it remains unexplained why the defining features (so understood) should provide the basis for the relevant form of causation. Why should the defining features be the very ones which are the basic explanatory building blocks? Could they not be definitional and fail to have any causal role at all? Something further is required, once definition and causation are separated, to explain why essences are (in reality) *per se* or fundamental causes. Perhaps the world was set up by some kindly providence (or demiurge) to ensure that this was the case. Without a metaphysical justification of this sort, there is no guarantee that essences of the type specified have any role in our understanding of the world.

The purpose of definition is 'to make something known' (Z.4, 142ª32–3). For this reason, the best type of definition should be through terms which are 'prior and more intelligible' (Z.4, 141ª29–33, 142ª7 ff.), because what is sought is one permanent definition of the thing in question. The relevant type of priority is exemplified by that of the point over the line, and of both over the cube (141ᵇ5–8). For, the point is (like the other examples Aristotle cites) the *principle* of what follows it (141ᵇ8 ff.). This, no doubt, is why it is to be used at the beginning of the demonstrations characteristic of teaching and learning (141ª29–31). The point is prior absolutely (141ᵇ27 ff.), and because it is the starting point of our investigation. In definition, we are engaged in a practice which aims to capture certain features in their proper order. There is, in Aristotle's account in the *Topics*, an order of priority which the best form of definition should capture.[10]

But what is the basis for such an order? Aristotle claims that there should be a single definition of each thing because each thing has one essence (Z.4, 141ª35 f.), and that this is why definition should be by means of what is prior and better known. The basic starting point (in these cases) is the one thing which is what it is to be each thing. Once we grasp this the whole phenomenon becomes known to us. Hence, the order of knowability is grounded in there being one feature which makes the thing what it is. Aristotle, in introducing a version of the unity condition we have seen at work in the *Analytics*, shows that his definitional constraints are grounded in views about the unity of the object.

But what is the essence in question? What makes it a unity? How are essences to be known? Indeed, more generally, what is the basis for talk of absolute priority, if understood as capturing the order of nature? In the *Topics*, Aristotle makes little progress in spelling out answers to these questions. He does suggest that genus is prior to *differentia* and that both are prior to the species defined (Z.6, 144ᵇ8–11), and that good definitions should locate species within a genus/*differentia* structure (A.5, 102ª31 ff., Z.6, 143ª29 ff.). Thus, he follows the tradition of using the method of genus and *differentiae* in definition (A.18, 108ᵇ5, 29; see also Δ.1, 120ᵇ11–12, 121ª7,

[10] There is also a different order of knowability dependent on where we begin (Z.4, 141ᵇ17–22, ᵇ35 ff.). Aristotle raises objections to attempts to give definitions on the basis of this latter order of knowability (such as the Meno-style definition of 'plane' as 'limit of solid' (141ᵇ22)). Indeed, he rejects such an attempt because it fails to meet the requirements he imposes on good definitions (being essence-revealing (141ᵇ23–5), capturing what is the appropriate unity (141ª35 f.), tracing the desired form of priority (141ª32–4)). (The considerations he adduces parallel those used in *Post. An.* B.7 (92ᵇ26 ff.) against treating accounts of what names signify as definitional.) However, the existence of a definitional practice of the type Aristotle criticizes shows that some were prepared to accept answers to the 'What is it?' question which did not meet his own stringent conditions. Such people might be amongst those who 'say' that all answers to the 'What is it?' question are definitional (*Post. An.* B.10, 93ᵇ29).

Δ.2, 122^{b}1–2). But he does not say what makes something a genus or a *differentia*, or how these are to be known. These notions, together with those of absolute priority and of requisite unity, are left indeterminate. Questions such as: 'Is being a wingless mortal animal a unity?' are left unaddressed. As a consequence, the nature of the essences captured in good definition remains underdetermined.

In *Posterior Analytics* (prior to B.8) *Topics*-style claims are used in what Aristotle describes as 'general' or 'logical' discussions (A.21, 82^{b}35 f., A.22, 84^{a}7 f., A.32, 88^{a}18 ff.). Definitions at this level satisfy the requirements set in the *Topics*: they are of essences (83^{a}24 f.), concern genus and *differentia* (83^{b}1 ff.), and make the thing defined known to us (83^{b}5–7). As becomes clear in *Posterior Analytics* B, such definitions must involve prior factors and be of unities. But, as we saw above, Aristotle argues in B.3–10 that these constraints cannot be met (or even be made fully determinate) without the addition of material drawn from our practice of explanation.[11] His crucial move is from the 'logical syllogism' to the method of causal demonstration (in B.8), from a 'logical' to a distinctively 'analytical' discussion. Without the further material thus introduced, Aristotle would have had no way of satisfying the logical conditions he had set himself. Indeed, the relevant ideas of priority and unity would have remained indeterminate.[12]

There are several layers in Aristotle's thought about definition. The *Topics* is concerned with the most general ('logical') notions, as set out above. In the *Analytics*, these are made more determinate by the addition of material drawn from his account of causal explanation. At the next level, the causal-definitional scheme of the *Analytics* is made even more determinate by the use of notions designed to interpret the physical world, such as matter, form, process, and goal. Definitions of substances at this level can only be secured if *matter* and *form* are added to the conceptual stock of the *Analytics*. But these will be more determinate versions of the types of definition introduced in the *Topics* and refined in the *Analytics*.[13]

---

[11] On this, see Chs. 7 and 8. Aristotle distinguishes 'logical' from 'analytical' in *Post. An.* A.22, 84^{a}7–8, where the latter invokes material drawn from the theory of demonstration (84^{a}10 ff.). The 'analytical' can be distinguished from the 'logical' and the 'physical' since (unlike the former) it is concerned with explanation but (unlike the latter) is not concerned with explanations specific to the details of a particular subject area. Thus, Z.17 might move from the logical to the analytical at 1041^{a}28 ff., without as yet reaching the level of the physical.

[12] This reflects the claims of Chapters 8 ff.

[13] At the most specific level, one would expect to find particular physical theories about particular types of phenomena employing the general framework arrived at through these stages of determination to analyse particular kinds or types of phenomena (such as biological kinds, eclipses . . .). These too should be placed within the general framework set by the levels above them in the relevant hierarchy.

254 Definition, Essence, and Natural Kinds

What is the epistemic status of Aristotle's claims about definition in the *Topics*? He is concerned with issues which are not peculiar to individual sciences, but which are the principles of everything (101^a37 ff.). His definitions are ones which will be accepted by all who are 'intellectually in good condition' (Z.4, 142^a9–11), and are not dependent on any particular experiential route or scientific discipline. Thus, his definitions reflect a generally held theory, available to anyone who thinks properly about these issues. All competent thinkers will have a theory of the world as containing kinds, standing in natural genera, with essences, which are prior and unities (in the ways suggested). They will also think of definition as what captures the essences in question.[14] Indeed, they are competent thinkers because they think of the world and definition in this way.[15]

The 'logical' level of thought, derived from the *Topics*, exercises an important influence on Aristotle's argument in the *Analytics*. Recall, for example, his criticisms of Xenocrates (as developed in Chapter 7). Aristotle objects that Xenocrates cannot satisfy the requirement that good definitions should be of prior features which underwrite the unity of the kind. But why should Xenocrates accept this assumption? Perhaps he should reject it, and cling to his original account of definition nonetheless.

Aristotle offered no explicit defence of the relevant assumption in *Posterior Analytics* B. As in the *Topics*, good definition is understood to be that which captures what is prior in the order of nature. This is taken as a background assumption which all competent participants in this discussion are bound to accept. It is not the type of claim which anyone (who knows what definition is) can reject. Xenocrates cannot maintain his position merely by denying that definition has to be of prior unities. For, if he had done this, he would no longer have been engaged in a (competent) discussion about definition.[16] Here, the background 'logical' theory is at work

---

[14] The epistemic status of these claims will depend on their expressing generally held intuitions, elements in a simple (non-scientific) theory to which all (in good epistemic condition) will subscribe. They will be a priori (not dependent on any particular type of experience) and may be taken as constitutive of what it is to be a definition. This formulation does not require these claims to be 'analytical' components of the meaning of the term 'definition' or to be known on the basis of the meaning of this term ('analytically certain', as Owen suggested in 'Tithenai ta phainomena'). More needs to be said on this issue, but its proper consideration lies outside the present study.

[15] It is not the case that the world is thus and so (solely) because this is what competent thinkers think. However, this leaves open the possibility that while thinkers are in good intellectual condition because they see the world in a given way, the world is the way it is because this is how thinkers in good condition see it. This latter possibility is a version of the no-priority view, discussed above.

[16] It is the kind of remark no one would make unless defending a thesis! (See *NE* 1.5, 1096^a1–2.)

setting the standards against which both Xenocrates and Aristotle's own proposals are to be judged.[17]

It may be objected that certain definitions do not (on Aristotle's own admission) encapsulate the relevant type of priority. Some may lack the requisite priority (e.g. the definitions of half and double (*Topics* Z.4, 142^{a}27 ff.)), since neither can be defined without the other. Others might be of objects such as white man which lack an appropriately unified cause (*Meta.* Z.4, 1030^{b}12 f.). If so, perhaps Aristotle's use of explanatory materials is restricted merely to one subset of definitions, such as might be given of substances or natural kinds. Perhaps he has a general theory of definition which is quite independent of these concerns.

However, Aristotle regards definitions which do not involve priority or unity as special cases (*Topics* 142^{a}32 f.), derivative and peripheral examples which do not share the salient features present in the case of substances (*Meta.* Z.4, 1030^{b}6 f.). If the argument given above is correct, one can see why this is so. Definitions of relations or improper unities will fail to manifest the type of priority and unity required by the 'logical' theory of definition. Definitions of substances are (justifiably) taken as the central case of definition (in part) because they reveal and make determinate the very features required by the general theory of definition.[18] It is not that Aristotle invokes explanatory concerns merely to accommodate one subset of cases (involving substances or natural kinds) where explanation is particularly appropriate. Nor is it that he merely stipulates that such cases are to be taken as the central instances of definition. It is rather that they are central because they meet the basic requirements of the general theory of definition.

10.4 DEFINITION AND ESSENCE: QUESTIONS OF PRIORITY

Definition in the *Topics* is concerned with essences and features in the world. It appears that there can be no stating what good definition is

---

[17] Similar remarks may be appropriate in considering Aristotle's use of 'logical' material in the earlier sections of *Meta.* Z. Many of his claims there (such as concern definition and priority) might be taken as ones on which all participants to the discussion should agree. Frank Lewis has called such assumptions 'big-tent' ones: open to all, no matter what their particular theories may be ('*Metaphysics* Zeta: A Budget Tour' (unpublished MS)). These issues require further detailed investigation.

[18] It is consistent with this claim that definitions of substances may be preferred to other definitions (such as those of eclipse or thunder) which also exemplify the relevant unity and priority conditions on other grounds (such as ontological basicness).

without reference to such phenomena. In the *Analytics*, the terms invoked in structural explanation (as discussed in Chapter 8) specify substances and features (such as essences) which belong *per se* to substances.[19] So, there can be no stating what structural explanation is without invoking essences in the world. Such explanations cannot be regarded simply as projections from us on to a neutral reality. For, if essences are features of the world, and serve as *per se* causes (in the favoured case corresponding to unqualified demonstration), such causes (*explanantia*) also must be things in the world. So understood, essences and causes cannot be merely projections from our practices of definition and explanation on to the world. For, those practices themselves cannot be understood without reference to real-world phenomena such as essences and kinds.

Does it follow from these considerations alone that the metaphysical co-determination of essence and causation is prior to and more basic than the interdependency of our definitional and explanatory practices? Not immediately. Perhaps neither thesis is prior to the other. Maybe we cannot specify our definitional practices without reference to essences or characterize what essences are independently of our definitional practices. Perhaps, equally, we cannot say what explanation is without mentioning real-world *explanantia*, or specify the latter without reference to explanation. Perhaps Aristotle thought that there was no way to say whether the interdependency of our practices was more or less basic than the interconnection of essence and *per se* structural cause?[20] Did he give reasons for taking one thesis as prior to the other?

Aristotle, I shall argue, held that the relevant metaphysical thesis is not dependent on the interdependency of our practices of definition and explanation. Indeed, he intended to use the former to justify the latter. Here are three reasons for this view:

(1) In the *Analytics*, Aristotle argues for the interdependency thesis by showing that our definitional practices are not sufficient (without the assistance of explanatory material) to provide adequate definitions. The interdependency thesis is not something that he can simply take for granted on the basis of existing definitional and explanatory practices. Indeed, his proposal seems to be a response to problems which he saw in the accounts of definition offered by earlier thinkers.[21]

---

[19] For the use of this structure in analysing the example of eclipse, see Barnes's discussion of 73ª34 in '*Aristotle's Posterior Analytics*', 2nd edn. (Oxford, 1994), 113.

[20] This form of no-priority view is discussed earlier in considering the role of the active intellect, in Chapter 5. (See also Ch. 1.)

[21] In Chapter 7, we discussed his criticisms of Xenocrates, and more generally of the methods of division and general deduction. It is tempting to see the interdependency thesis as Aristotle's way of addressing certain problems which he detected in the approach to definition taken by Socrates (as illustrated in the Meno) and by Plato elsewhere. Their methods, when they stayed at the 'logical' level, did not contain resources sufficient to establish def-

But what is the basis for his position? In B.2, 90ª14–15 Aristotle relies on the claim that there is an obvious connection between what a thing is and why that thing is as it is. Thus, he takes it as evident that there is a direct connection between something's being the thing it is and a certain type of causal story: one which explains its internal structure. In effect, he assumes at the outset that there is a fundamental connection between the basic essence of the thing and the causally basic starting point in the relevant form of causal explanation. Indeed, what it is to be the basic essence of the thing is (*inter alia*) to be a *per se* cause of a given type. If so, *Posterior Analytics* B begins with what appears to be a metaphysical thesis linking being and causality. His aim, therefore, is to give an account of definition and explanation which reflects this metaphysical interconnection.

(2) What are Aristotle's grounds for the metaphysical co-determination thesis, which is taken as basic in the *Analytics*? Does he argue for it on metaphysical grounds. Or does he elsewhere depend on the assumed inter-connection of our practices? A metaphysical defence of this thesis would require him to show that:

(1) If there were no natures, there would be no causes of a given type.

(2) If there were no causes of a given type, there would be no natures.

Aristotle, I shall suggest, defends (1) and (2) by direct metaphysical argument. While the full investigation of these topics would require an extended treatment, I shall merely sketch an outline of Aristotle's approach.[22]

(1) Per se *Causation and Chance: No Natures, No* per se *Causes*

If one accepts the co-determination thesis, basic causes (at least those cited in unqualified demonstrations) will be essential features of kinds. Such causes will be the central and clearest examples of *per se* causes (whether efficient or teleological).[23] If there were no natures of this type, there could be no *per se* causes.

---

initions. Further, because their methods did not essentially involve causal/explanatory con-siderations, they could not sustain claims about the priority and unity of definition. If this is correct, Aristotle's remarks on definition in the *Analytics* constitute his attempt to resolve the problems about definition which had troubled his predecessors. These issues require further study elsewhere.

[22] I have defended parts of this sketch in 'Teleological Causation in the *Physics*', 111 ff. However, other parts require a fuller discussion of Aristotle's views on chance and efficient causation. My sketch of the latter topic has been considerably influenced by discussions with Lindsay Judson.

[23] Such causes will not merely necessitate their effects but also show such effects to be consequences of the nature of the causes. It cannot be enough for A to cause B that the

Aristotle argues for a connection of this type in his discussion of cases of chance and accident or coincidence (*sumptoma*) in the *Physics*. He considers examples where two distinct 'streams' of causal processes happen to intersect at a given place and time. For example, one individual chooses to go to market for his own purposes, while a second individual (or set of individuals) go there for their own separate goals. The two streams intersect 'by chance' when the two individuals meet.[24] Here, as Aristotle insists, there is no *per se* cause of the intersection of the two processes. For, in such cases there is neither a mind nor a nature (B.6, 198ᵃ1–13) aiming at (e.g.) the repayment of the debt, which brings about these effects simultaneously. In the case of natural (non-intentional) processes, the absence of a nature of the appropriate type entails the absence of a *per se* cause.[25] Indeed, more generally, intersections of this type can have only incidental causes (see *Meta.* E.2, 1027ᵃ7 f.).[26] But this is because in the basic case there are natures acting as *per se* causes of the relevant effects. At this point, Aristotle is assuming that there is a metaphysical connection between causation and nature, not dependent on our explanatory or definitional practices. Indeed, his basic picture is of a world comprising simple natures (grounded in essences) as *per se* causes, standing in regular causal connections with one another. This viewpoint, and the corresponding account of chance, is a metaphysically driven one.

---

former necessitates the latter. The causal connection needs to be one which is intelligible to us in the light of the natures of the causes. For a contrasting view, see Richard Sorabji's suggestion that Aristotle analyses 'cause' in terms of necessitation alone (*Necessity, Cause and Blame*, Ch. 1).

[24] Similarly, it may happen that one causal process results in the development of sharp teeth, another in the development of flat teeth (*Phys.* B.8, 199ᵃ23 ff.). What is a chance or automatic result is that (in the theory under discussion) both processes happen at the same time and in the same place (199ᵃ27, 30). For further discussion of this passage, see my 'Teleological Causation in the *Physics*', 111 ff.

[25] It is fully consistent with this that the intersection is itself necessitated by antecedent conditions, such as the combined 'event' of A's being at P at t and B's being at P at t. However, such a combined event would not be a *per se* cause because it is not itself a nature or (in the case under discussion) the result of anyone's plan. Even if the world is fully necessitated, there will be examples of occurrences which lack *per se* causes. For a contrasting view, see Richard Sorabji's analysis of these passages in *Necessity, Cause and Blame*, Ch. 1. It is to be noted that occurrences of the type envisaged could remain coincidences even if (possibly *per impossibile*) they happened frequently. If so, infrequency may be a sign of 'chance' but cannot constitute it. (These issues are illuminatingly discussed by Lindsay Judson in 'Chance and "Always or for the Most Part"', in Judson (ed.), *Aristotle's Physics*, 78 ff.)

[26] A detailed analysis of *Meta.* E.2–3 lies outside the scope of the present work. Naturally, I am drawn to the view that 'those principles and causes which do not come to be' (1027ᵃ29–32) are ones which come to be without a *per se* cause of the appropriate type (viz. a nature or planning mind). This view, along with several alternatives, is discussed by Lindsay Judson in 'What Can Happen When You Eat Pungent Food', (in N. Avgelis and F. Peonidis (eds.), *Aristotle on Logic, Language and Science* (Thessaloniki, 1998)). I am indebted to Lindsay Judson for several helpful discussions of these issues.

(2) Nature and Teleology: No per se *Causes, No Natures*

A similar viewpoint permeates Aristotle's discussion of teleological causation. His basic defence of the role of teleology is this: If there were no
per se teleological causes, there would be no natures. Thus, he rejects
Empedocles' contention that 'the seeds' (essential to generation) come
about by chance, as follows:

> Anyone who asserts this does away with 'by nature' and 'nature' itself. For, what-
> ever arrives at some goal by a continuous movement from an internal starting
> point happens 'by nature'. The result is not the same for each, but yet it is not a
> matter of chance; but what occurs always tends towards the same goal, if nothing
> intervenes. (*Phys.* B.8, 199^{b}14–18)

His basic point is this: If one removes talk of goals, one undermines talk
of natures and natural processes. For, the latter are essentially defined in
terms of goals. Thus, both can be understood as essentially composed of
parts which are for the sake of a goal, which will be achieved if nothing
intervenes. This is what natures and natural processes are. Both are to be
defined in terms of the goals of their respective stages or parts. His defence
of teleological causation stops at this point. If it were not a genuine form
of causation, the world would contain no natures and no natural processes.
As required by the co-determination thesis, what it is to be a given thing
and what it is to be a given type of cause stand or fall together.[27]

Both these claims are made and supported on metaphysical grounds.
In the next Chapter, I shall argue that the second claim is central to
Aristotle's discussion of substance in *Metaphysics* Z, H, and Θ. There too
the interconnection of our practices of definition and explanation is given
a metaphysical basis in the relation between being and causation.

(3) Nor should Aristotle's preference for giving priority to metaphysical theses surprise us. For, in speaking of knowledge and perception, he
says that they are:

> the measure of things because we get to know something by them. Thus, they are
> measured by reality rather than themselves being the measurers of reality. (*Meta.*
> I.2, 1053^{a}31 ff.)

We have knowledge precisely because our states match up to reality. The
relevant test lies with nature not with us or with our practices. For the latter
are tested by nature itself.[28]

This perspective is evident in the case of the type of enquiry envisaged
in the *Analytics*. For, here we may go on investigating until we come finally

---

[27] For further discussion of this, and related issues, see my 'Teleological Causation in the
Physics'.
[28] I examine no-priority interpretations of Aristotle's ethical writings in my 'Aristotle and
Modern Realism', 135 ff.

to uncover the basic cause (B.8, 93ᵃ12–14). Here, it is nature which determines the end of our enquiry. What really is the case is not limited to what
we think (or even can think) now. We may perhaps be led to discover new
causes beyond those we now grasp (or even can grasp). Equally, we may
come to see that our present views are in some ways mistaken or inadequate (see, for example, B.13, 97ᵇ14 ff.). In these ways, what we come to
think will be determined (if all goes well) by how the world is.[29] Indeed,
in some cases our enquiries will be incomplete simply because we cannot
find in reality the features we seek.[30] Here, our practices answer to the
world. Authority lies there and not with our practices of definition and
explanation.

10.5 CO-DETERMINATION, INTERDEPENDENCY, AND THEIR INTERCONNECTIONS

In Section 10.2 we noted that, for Aristotle, our practices of definition and
of explanation are interdependent. In Section 10.3 we found that, in his
view, it is not possible to characterize definition without reference to
essences existing in the world. Indeed, in Section 10.4 we saw that, for
Aristotle, the interdependency of these practices rested on a metaphysical
thesis: the co-determination of essence and *per se* causation.

This combination of theses can be represented diagrammatically as
follows:

If our definitional practices are incomplete without material drawn from
our explanatory ones, and the latter rest on our ability to track *per se* causes
in the world, it follows that our definitional practices are incomplete

---

[29] I take it to be a constitutive feature of no-priority interpretations that they take what
the world is to be identical with what is thinkable. For this allows for the very same principles to govern our thought and the world we think about. But is 'what is thinkable' limited
to what is thinkable by us now or can it also include what is thinkable by us in ideal conditions. The latter is required to allow for enquiry. But, if so, what limits what is thinkable in
ideal conditions? Surely these limits come from the world and not from us. (Similar concerns will arise if one introduces the ideal thinker in ideal conditions. What constrains what
he/she thinks, apart from how the world really is?)   [30] See Ch. 12 Sect. 12.6 ff.

without the use of material drawn from our grasp on the world's *per se* causal structure. Conversely, if our explanatory practices are incomplete without material drawn from our definitional ones, and these in turn rest on our grasping essences in the world, our explanations rest on our ability to grasp essences in the world. Thus, we should add to the diagram above, two diagonal arrows:

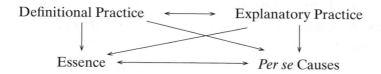

to capture the dependence of our definitional practices on the causal structure of the world, and that of our explanatory practices on our grasp of essences.

This interpretation allows us to understand more securely some of Aristotle's problematic remarks about thought and its objects. Indeed, his discussion in *De Anima* seems to illustrate (in a vivid way) three points which are central to our present concerns.

(1) One of his claims in *De Anima* (noted in our earlier discussion)[31] runs as follows:

(A) Our (passive) intellects function properly when and only when objects of a given type impact on us.

(B) Our (passive) intellects function properly when and only when we think of objects as organized in an intelligible and general structure.

(C) The active intellect is identical with a properly organized, general, and intelligible structure of thinkable objects (such as kinds).

(A) requires that we are causally influenced in our thinking by objects and kinds in the world. In the order of explanation (with regard to the content of our thought), as in the model developed in the last Section, priority is given to the world. Further, as required by (B), a thinker must be able to locate the kind in its appropriate niche in an organized and intelligible structure. (For, this is how thought differs from experience.[32]) Indeed, in successful and completed thought the thinker will be able to give definitions of the kind which are dependent in the ways specified on his practices of explanation.

But (B) does not by itself establish that it is an essential feature of a kind that it occupies a given slot in the structure of the world. Nor does it

---

[31] See Ch. 5 Sect. 5.4.   [32] See Ch. 6 Sect. 6.2.

underwrite the idea that the structure of the world is an intelligible and organized one. The most that (A) and (B) can guarantee is that we cannot think of a kind save as occupying a given place in the cosmos.

How does Aristotle sustain (C)? In *De Anima* he introduces at this point the active intellect, which he identifies with the objects of thought (including kinds and their essences). If this identity could be sustained, he could argue that kinds are essentially individuated by their position in an intelligible structure in the following way:

(D) It is a condition of our thoughts being the ones they are that they are thoughts of kinds located in an organized cosmos.

(E) A similar condition obtains for the thoughts of the active intellect.

(F) The thoughts of the active intellect are identical with the kinds of which it thinks.

So (G) Those kinds must be essentially individuated by their position in an organized and intelligible cosmos.

But what is the basis for (F)? Why should anyone identify the organized cosmos with the activity of the active intellect? Why regard the world and a certain form of mind as identical or as constructed on identical principles? One answer would be given by the no-priority interpretation, just considered. But we have seen reason both here and in Chapter 5 to reject this reading of Aristotle.[33]

If Aristotle accepts the co-determination thesis, he has an alternative way to support his conclusion ((G) above). For, if the essences of kinds are *per se* causes of a given type, kinds will be individuated by features which play a basic role in the world's causal order. Further, that order will be an intelligible one because the starting point for the relevant causal connections will lie in those essential features which make the kinds the ones they are. These causal connections will be completely perspicuous to us because they follow from the kinds' essences. (This claim rests on the presence of the downwards diagonal arrow from explanatory practice to essence.) In this way, the kinds will be wholly intelligible to us. For, their derived features will be seen to be causally dependent on their essences and to be made what they are by being so caused. (A similar story can be told for the genera to which species kinds belong.[34])

If this is correct, the world's causal order will be intrinsically intelligible,

---

[33] According to the no priority theorist, the world (as we grasp it) is governed by the same principles as our minds because no sense can be made of a world in categories other than those that govern our minds. Indeed, what we understand and the world so understood are identical. It makes no sense to ask whether these principles come from us or from the world. No sense can be made of giving priority to either side of the equation.

[34] See Ch. 9 Sects. 9.2 and 9.3.

exemplifying the type of knowability we seek.[35] While Aristotle's talk of the active intellect may encapsulate (in a vivid way) his view that the world is intelligible, its role will not be to explain that intelligibility. On the contrary, it is because the world's order is an intelligible one (in the ways underwritten by the co-determination thesis) that it can be understood in terms of the active intellect. While talk of the latter may introduce a high-level or theological description of an ordered and intelligible world, it is one available only after the hard work of metaphysics has been done. It is not an alternative way of doing that work.

While, according to the co-determination thesis, essences are (by metaphysical law) *per se* causes of a given type, they could not play this causal role unless they were unities with their own distinctive natures. It would be (at best) misleading to suggest that (for Aristotle) essences could be defined simply in terms of what plays a given causal role. For, in his account, the relevant causal role can only be played by essences, features which make the relevant kinds what they are. For similar reasons, it would be (at best) misleading to represent Aristotle as defining essences solely in terms of what is able to fit into an organized and intelligible world (see 5.7). For, in his view, it is only essences, with their own distinctive features, which can fit in this way into such a world. In this respect, the co-determination thesis serves to clarify some of the metaphysical issues left unresolved in his discussion of colour and the active intellect.

(2) There is a second way in which *De Anima* provides a model for Aristotle's metaphysical (co-determination) thesis and for his contention that our practices of defining and explaining are interdependent. In *De Anima*, Aristotle treats colours and the objects of thought as parallel. Colours (in his account) are real features of the world which impact on us, but ones which only impact on us because we are creatures with a certain form of sensibility. In a similar way, essences are features of the world which impact on us only because we engage in a certain form of thought. We can now see why this is so: we can only grasp essences of this type because we have definitional and explanatory practices of the type indicated. In neither case need the limited accessibility of the respective objects impugn their reality.[36] Both colours and the world's intelligible causal order are objective features, even though they are accessible only to those with specific definitional and explanatory practices or visual capacities. (This claim follows from the downwards vertical arrows linking the top and bottom levels of the diagram).

(3) There is one further point of comparison between Aristotle's discussions of thought and colour. In his view, our capacity to see can only be

---

[35] See Ch. 13 Sect. 13.3 for further discussion of the type of knowability involved here.

[36] See Ch. 5 Sect. 5.2. This issue is illuminatingly discussed by Justin Broackes in 'Aristotle, Objectivity and Perception', 61 ff.

understood in terms of our responsiveness to colours in the medium. Similarly, our capacity to think of essences will be (for him) grounded in our responsiveness to the causal order around us. For, the type of under-standing we seek (as encapsulated in the general theory of definition) cannot be made fully determinate without reference to how the world actually works. Our practices of definition depend on our being sensitive to causal patterns in the world. Just as we cannot make sense of visual per-ception without reference to colours existing in the medium, so we cannot make sense of the type of intelligibility we seek in definition without ref-erence to the structure of the world. (This claim follows from the down-wards diagonal arrow linking definitional practice and the *per se* causal structure of the world).

We can now see why, in Aristotle's account, our minds and the world must work on the same principles. For, our practices of definition and explanation are dependent (in the ways indicated) on the intelligible order of the world. That said, we would not have been able to grasp that intelli-gible order (or certain features as definitional) had our practices of defini-tion and explanation not been as they are. For, we can only discover, for example, what is the basic essence of a kind because we see it as the start-ing point in an appropriate form of explanatory account. If we had lacked definitional and explanatory practices of this type, the intelligible structure of reality would have escaped us.

In these three ways, Aristotle's discussion of thought, colour, and the active intellect sketches vividly, if incompletely, the metaphysical and epis-temological picture which he draws more fully elsewhere in terms of the interdependency and co-determination theses. Taken together, these two discussions present a distinctive and ingenious philosophical position, which will be investigated in detail in the final Chapter. There is, however, an immediate exegetical concern which must be addressed. Some will object that, whatever the philosophical plausibility of the position that has emerged, it cannot be Aristotle's own. For, they will say, in *Posterior Analytics* B.19 he developed an account of our grasp of first principles which appears to be completely independent of our practices of

---

[37] There has been considerable debate about whether in this chapter Aristotle is con-cerned with grasp of immediate (or simple) entities or with grasp of the immediate propo-sitions of science. Barnes concludes 'I feel obliged to concede that Aristotle did not realize that he was vacillating between two stories' (*Aristotle's Posterior Analytics*, 260). Ross, in effect, took the same view, finding evidence for Aristotle's concern both with the acquisi-tion of concepts (*Aristotle's Analytics*, 675) and with knowledge of the premisses of demon-stration (p. 675), and not fitting these two together in a unified way. Modrak (*Aristotle: The Power of Perception* (Chicago, 1987), 162) claims that Aristotle did not distinguish between primitive concepts and indemonstrable propositions, while, earlier, Kahn suggested ('The Role of nous in the Cognition of First Principles in *Posterior Analytics* 2.19', in Berti, (ed.) *Aristotle on Science*, 391, 395) that he was correct not to distinguish because 'there is no gap between a propositional and conceptual view of principles'. The difficulty arises because

explanation.[37] If this is correct, they will have challenged (in a most effective way) one of the central interpretative claims of the last three chapters. It is time to consider their objection in detail.

10.6 *NOUS* AND FIRST PRINCIPLES IN *POSTERIOR ANALYTICS* B.19

On one influential interpretation, we are able, according to Aristotle in B.19, to grasp first principles through the operation of *nous*, which captures the relevant definitions in a way fundamentally independent of explanatory concerns. Thus, even if the principles discovered in this way do indeed play an explanatory role, this is not constitutive of what it is to be a first principle. Rather, the practice of definition is seen as, at its basis, independent of the explanatory concerns sketched above. In B.19, Aristotle finally embraces a form of insight-based epistemology of exactly the type rendered redundant (or even obsolete) by the account developed in the preceding chapters of the *Analytics*.[38] In the end, he emerges as an epistemological Platonist.[39]

There are three exegetical claims which support this line of interpretation:

(1) In B.19 (100^b1–5) Aristotle shows how we can grasp first principles *as such* in a way independent of the practice of explanation.

Thus, for Aristotle, *nous* grasps the starting points of demonstration (100^b12) and is itself the starting point of discursive knowledge(100^b15). In these cases:

(2) Aristotle shows how we can grasp basic definitions in a way independent of the practice of explanation.

Aristotle begins by talking about immediate propositions (99^b17, 21), but later speaks of grasp of universals and of universals standing in the soul (100^a6, 15, 17, $^b2$, 3). However, it is not clear that this debate is a real one. The mathematician who grasps the simple unit understands that it is indivisible in quantity, and, thus, understands an immediate proposition of the relevant science. In grasping a basic external universal of this kind, a basic proposition of science becomes known to one. Indeed, Aristotle claims just this when he argues that nous grasps the immediate propositions of science (100^b9–14), and also (as the starting point of knowledge (100^b15)) grasps certain universals (100^b5–8). It is not merely a pun to the effect that nous grasps both types of starting point. Aristotle has indicated that he has reason to think that in grasping the basic universal, one grasps an immediate and basic proposition of science.

[38] For a recent statement of this view, see Michael Ferejohn's *The Origins of Aristotelian Science,* (New Haven, 1991), 4–5.

[39] For the epistemological Platonist, intuition is best seen as a separate faculty, distinct from our ability to think discursively. It is not to be understood merely as a distinctive exercise of our thinking faculty. For my characterization of Platonism, see Ch. 1 n. 37.

So, for example, we can come to have an intuitive grasp on the definition of animal, free from all concern with explanation. Since the activity of *nous* is described as 'more accurate' and 'truer' than knowledge (100^{b}8, 11), *nous* emerges as a high-grade form of perception, which enables us to see the starting points of demonstration without any assistance from our explanatory practices. If we add:

(3) The activity of *nous* not only does not involve (in its nature) discursive thought, but also does not depend on the latter for its epistemological credentials,

we must conclude that *nous* by itself provides the foundation of our knowledge of definitions and of essence. Indeed, what makes something essential will be independent of its role in explanation. If so, Aristotle will reject in B.19 both the interdependency and the co-determination theses. Either he changed his mind or he did not hold these theses in the first place.[40]

I shall challenge the attribution to Aristotle of the combination of claims (1), (2) and (3) which is required by the Platonist reading of B.19. The relevant sections of this chapter are best understood as rejecting (at least) claim (3), and as exemplifying certain central aspects of the interdependency thesis sketched above. Thus, I shall argue that Aristotle does not commit himself to the view that an intuitive grasp of the nature of primaries is the basis of our knowledge of definitional truths.

One might initially challenge the contention that Aristotle commits himself in B.19 to (1) on the basis of the reading of 100^{a}3 ff. offered in Chapter 6. There are two questions which Aristotle might be addressing in B.19. One is:

(A) How do those things which are starting points become known?

Another is:

(B) How do those things which are starting points become known *as starting points*?

Question (A) can be answered by giving an account of how (e.g.) the biologist comes to know what the animal is, which does not provide him with the resources to know that this is the *starting point* of biology. If B.19 is

---

[40] In Ch. 6 Sect. 6.2 I interpreted the earlier sections of B.19 (especially 100^{a}3–^{b}1) as being concerned with the acquisition of concepts (at the level of thought). However, as was noted there, this account did not engage with the issue of how we come (in Aristotle's view) to grasp something as first principles (or first universals). It is the latter issue which we must now address.

concerned exclusively with question (A), it will not offer a way to grasp (e.g.) animal as a starting point of the relevant science. The latter could be done by invoking the practice of demonstration, and by finding out what is first in the relevant series of demonstration. If so, since *nous* would not grasp first principles *as such*, there would be no intuition-based answer to question (B). Thus, there would be no evidence in B.19 in favour of claim (1).[41]

It is plausible, as was noted in Chapter 6, to see Aristotle as concerned in large measure in B.19 with question (A). Several considerations favour this view:

(1) He focuses initially on the general issue of how we grasp universals such as man and animal (100^b1–3). While some of the latter are immediates (i.e. the most general universals), others are not (e.g. man (100^b1)). The issue under discussion here appears to be: 'How are any universals grasped?', not 'How are some grasped as starting points?' In answering the first question one will consider (*inter alia*) those universals which are starting points, but one will not need to consider them as starting points.

(2) In B.19, 100^a10–$^b4$, Aristotle sketches an account of how we arrive at a grasp of universals via perception, memory, and experience.[42] It seems that:

(1) We grasp universals for species such as man (*infimae species*)[43] by a method which is essentially dependent on perception, memory, and experience. In grasping this, we grasp man as an animal of a given kind. We have a secure grasp on these universals when and only when we grasp several of them together in this way (100^a12–14).[44] We could not properly grasp the universal *man*, conceived of as an animal of a given kind, unless we also grasp *animal*, and perhaps other members of the same genus also.

[41] This line of reply would be attractive to an interpreter who thought that the whole of B.19 was concerned exclusively with the acquisition of concepts. This interpreter would seek to account for the problematic lines 100^b1 ff in the way used in Ch. 6 Sect. 6.2 to analyse 100^a3–$^b1$.

[42] See Ch. 6 Sect. 6.2.

[43] Man is given as an example of an 'indivisible' (*adiaphora*) in 100^a16–$^b2$. Man is an *infima species*. 'Adiaphora' is used elsewhere for *infimae species* (97^b31; 97^a37).

[44] Barnes emends the text to read 'until a position of strength is secured' reading '*alke*' for '*arche*', as he claims the latter 'makes no sense' if understood to mean 'principle' (*Aristotle's Posterior Analytics*, 254). But his emendation is not required. The text as it stands may be understood to mean 'until the initial point of rout is regained' (with Pacius and Ross), or 'until the original arrangement is regained' (as Michael Frede once suggested). On these readings, Aristotle's crucial point is to emphasize the regaining of a secure position/formation on the relevant part of the battlefield.

(2) We grasp first, or basic, universals, e.g. animal,[45] in a fundamentally similar way, through perception and induction.[46]

Thus, we might conclude that Aristotle in B.19 is offering a sketch of how we grasp universals, not a specific account of how we grasp first principles *as first principles*. Perhaps in B.16–18 he addresses these latter issues. For, there, explanation requires us to accept the existence of progressively higher-order species until we arrive at genera which are not themselves species of higher genera. On this basis, we can see that *animal* is a primary term, and determine what in a completed science is to count as a primitive universal. *Nous*, by contrast, may enable us to grasp those things that are the starting points of explanation, but we will not grasp them as starting points. We do the latter as the result of our study of the relevant pattern of demonstration.

(3) In the light of (1) and (2) one might read the first sentence of B.19 as asking the question: 'How do we come to have knowledge of those things that are first principles?' and not 'How do we come to know them as first principles?' For, the structure of science will show which are the first principles. The task of B.19 (on this account) is to show how we come to grasp those things which are (in fact) first principles. But we will know on independent, explanation-involving, grounds both what it is to be a first principle and what legitimizes the claim that certain features are first principles.

However, these three points are not sufficient, by themselves, to rule out the Platonist reading of B.19. For, Aristotle ignores (after the first sentence of B.19) considerations of demonstration, and focuses on an ordering of universals, apparently established without reference to demonstrative concerns. There must be, it seems, a non-demonstrative route to grasp what is first and what is subsequent in a series of universals (100^{a}13, ^{b}1–5). If so,

---

[45] In this context, '*ta prota*' (100^{b}4) must refer to most general universals such as the example given: animal (100^{b}3), and not scientific principles. '*Ta prota*' is used in this way elsewhere (76^{a}32). This interpretation preserves the parallelism with grasp of *infimae species*, such as man (100^{b}1). General universals (unlike *infimae species*) are described as 'without parts', since they are not parts of a more general whole (cf. *Meta.* Δ.3 1014^{b}6 ff).

[46] 'For, it is clear that it is necessary to grasp the most general universals by induction. For, indeed it is in this way that perception instils the universal' (100^{b}2–5). Induction is frequently used to describe the way we grasp universals from knowing particulars, and, thus, can refer to the same type of process (involving memory, experience, and grasp of universals described in 100^{a}4–15). There may be no further step involved in grasping the most general universals beyond those involved in grasping the more specific. Aristotle emphasizes that the two processes are similar: both involve a stand being made in the same way (100^{b}2–3), both involve perception (100^{b}4–5, 100^{a}15 f.). On this reading, '*kai gar*' is translated 'for, indeed', and not 'for, perception also . . .' If '*kai*' were translated in the latter way, this would mean 'since induction is involved in the relevant process beginning with particulars, this is the way in which perception also makes its contribution—namely by (i) perceiving . . . and (ii) in doing this, giving perceptual information about universals as an input to induction' (see below).

there will be a route to grasp what is primary which is independent of the practice of demonstration. So Aristotle, in B.19, must be engaging with question (B) as well as question (A). Since he appears to do this without invoking our explanatory practices, it is reasonable to conclude that he is invoking Platonist intuition to do so.

The situation is, in reality, even more complex. If Aristotle is answering both questions (A) and (B) in this way, he must accept that we can grasp some basic definitions, the ones from which science will begin, independently of our explanatory practices. Indeed, he seems to countenance (in the main sections of B.19) the possibility of our grasping all definitions (whether basic or derived) without assistance from our explanatory practices. We grasp not merely Stage 1 accounts of what terms signify in this way, but also correct definitions of (e.g.) the kind itself.[47] Surely, for this, we need Platonist intuition into the nature of things?

There is another way to resist the Platonist reading of B.19. Its most controversial claim can seem its most innocuous one: (3). I shall argue that our discussion of B.13–15 has given us good reason not to attribute (3) to Aristotle. He approaches the issues raised in B.19 forearmed with a characterization of the appropriate type of genus/*differentia* tree, which requires him to base the operation of *nous* on antecedent (discursive) explanatory practices. If so, there is not merely no reason to see Aristotle as invoking Platonist intuition in B.19; there is reason not to do so.

Aristotle's discussion of *differentiae* in B.13 shows what is involved in grasp on primary genus terms, such as animal. In that account, one sees man as a member of the genus, animal, from which it is differentiated by features explained by its essence. The *differentiae* in question distinguish members of the relevant genus in a way dependent on their explanatory essences. *Animal* is the first term in its genus because the other species can be derived from it in a system of differentiation (of this type).[48]

If this style of account is presupposed in B.19, the inductive process (specified in 100^b4) will track the pattern of differentiation, which constitutes the relevant genus/species structure. In the case at hand, one will see animal as the prime term because all others members of the relevant domain can be defined as animals of a given type. They are defined in terms of the distinctive ways in which they discharge their animal nature: move/breathe/eat/reproduce, etc. The features which differentiate animals will be the ones explained by their own distinctive essences (*qua* animals of type A). Prime terms, such as animal, are important precisely because they define the relevant subject matter in a way

---

[47] So understood, Aristotle begins B.19 with an account of the acquisition of concepts on the basis of experience (See Ch. 6), but ends with a description of our definitional grasp of primary items (in the world). The chapter represents an overview of several stages, elsewhere separated.   [48] See Ch. 9.

which marks out what is explanatorily important. They can be grasped as primary when the other members of their domain are seen as dependent on them in this way.

We are now in a position to sustain a thoroughly non-Platonist interpretation of the relation between the inductive process and the operation of nous in B.19; one fully consistent with Aristotle's discussion in B.13–15. *Nous* may grasp that (e.g.) animal occupies a certain niche in an organized system of definition and explanation. But it does so as a result of seeing animal as playing a central role in that system. *Nous* will recognize the results of (or the next step in) an inductive process which is grounded in a discursive understanding of this system of definition and explanation.[49] When we have become immersed in grasping this system, we may know how 'to go on' to see the primary terms. But the latter will be grasped as primary precisely because we see them as providing the basis for this definitional and explanatory structure.[50]

On the view just outlined, there is a striking analogy between the role of primary universals and that of the essences of substances. Both define their respective subject matters (the genus, the kind) and also explain why those subject matters have the features they do (i.e. why members of the genus (or kind) have certain differentiating features). They are both simultaneously explainers and definers of their respective objects. (Indeed, this is just as was to be expected given the interdependency of our practices of explanation and definition.[51])

---

[49] In a similar way one could grasp that the unit exists because of the way one comes to have knowledge of it. Thus, one could come to know of its existence when one sees that its existence is required if the pair and triple are to exist. Alternatively, one might know of its existence via perception of particulars and induction: if there are objects which are single entities, the unit exists. We are aware of many such particular entities, and hence can infer that the unit exists. This process is facilitated in the case of the unit because there is no further, distinct, essence of the unit to be grasped—as the cause and the unit are the same (*Post. An.* B.9). So, there is no chance of the unit turning out to be two distinct phenomena under investigation (unlike (e.g.) pride (97^b13–25)). In both cases, we can grasp with confidence that the unit exists independently of seeing it as the first element in a science.

L. A. Kosman argued that *nous* does not involve grasp of the existence of the starting points ('Understanding, Explanation and Insight in the *Posterior Analytics*', in E. N. Lee, A. P. D. Mourelatos, and R. M. Rorty (eds.), *Exegesis and Argument: Phronesis*, Suppl. 1 (1973), 384) on the basis of a reading of *Post. An.* I.13. But the inference is faulty, since nous may grasp that primitive universals exist on the basis of a previous inductive procedure.

[50] So understood, intuition need not be construed as a separate faculty, but may be taken simply as a distinctive exercise of a general faculty of reason. What is crucial for present purposes is that the activity of nous is supported by discursive thought in the ways suggested.

[51] In a similar way, the common axioms which concern equality and inequality (A.10, 76^a41, A.11, 77^a32) define the subject matter of (general) relations, and explain why other derived relations are as they are. Similar remarks will apply to common axioms about ratios and proportions, which are relevant not only in mathematics but also in other sciences as well (see Nicomachus, *Arithmetike Eisagoge*, 18; Iamblichus, *De Communi Mathematica Scientia* ed. N. Festo (Leipzig, 1891), 18–20). It is interesting to note that Proclus regards

A non-Platonist reading of B.19 may be possible. But why should we accept it? There are several reasons for doing so. First, it is natural to take the genus/species structure (invoked in 100^b2–4) as the one uncovered by the methods discussed in B.13 and employed in B.14. Otherwise, Aristotle would have provided no account of the type of definitional structure introduced in B.19. However, if this is correct, B.19's genus/species structure will rest on a system of *differentiae* permeated by explanatory considerations (as required by the argument of Chapter 9).

Second, in this account, nous can operate in a non-discursive manner without undermining induction's claim to be a process essentially involving discursive thought and inference. Nous can see certain objects in a given way provided that its operation arises out of and its results are constrained by a preceding inductive process. It sees what it sees because it is grounded in the preceding inductive stages. Thus, although it is itself non-discursive, its success is grounded in discursive reflection and inference.

Third, in this account, induction and demonstration remain distinct, but closely connected. The inductive procedure picks out the explanatorily relevant features of kinds in a hierarchical structure. But, as was noted in Chapter 9, it is precisely this structure which is relevant for explanation. In this way, we mark out derived species by means of features which are themselves related to their explanatory essences. It is, thus, no accident that the first terms in a genus of this type are the ones relevant for the starting points of demonstration. For, they are chosen because of their distinctive position in a differentiating system which itself rests on explanatory considerations. Although induction does not itself directly involve demonstration, it is permeated by our explanatory concerns. This is why induction can give us a route to grasp the structures relevant for explanation, even though induction itself does not involve the formulation of demonstrations.

If this non-Platonist reading is accepted, *nous* can only grasp certain features as the first elements in a science on the basis of an explanation-involving procedure of induction. Its epistemic authority will be derived from the process of induction on which it rests. Thus, *nous* will grasp as first principles items whose status is vindicated by their role in an

---

such axioms as common principles, studied by 'the science of being qua being' from which 'several sciences get their common propositions' (*Commentary on the First Book of Euclid's Elements*, ed. G. Morrow (Princeton, 1970), 9.19).

It might seem that the principle of non-contradiction does not fall easily into this pattern. For, as it is used as the basis for proof, it might be thought to define no distinctive subject matter. However, one might reply that 'logical' principles of this type define the nature of coherent speech and thought (*Meta.* Γ.4, 1006^a22, $^b5$–11). While a proper consideration of this topic would take us far away from our present task, one can see how the combined definitional/explanatory approach could be extended to this area also.

272

explanation-based system of differentiation of the type set out in B.13–15. Neither those chapters nor B.19 is committed to any version of epistemological foundationalism about first principles.

This non-Platonist reading of B.19 rests on a metaphysical basis. What makes primary universals *primary* is their central role in an interdependent system of definition and explanation. They mark out a subject matter in a way which makes clear its metaphysical and causal structure. If so, Aristotle's discussion in B.19, so far from undermining his earlier picture, in fact confirms it.

It will be objected that Aristotle's insistence on the epistemic superiority of *nous* (100^b8 ff.) commits him (notwithstanding our previous remarks) to a Platonist account of the role of intuition. This objection can be met. Let us grant that from the perspective of the completed science, one in which everything is set out in its proper order matching the hierarchic structure of reality, the primitives (such as the dyad or animal) will be known before anything else. Even so, this truth reflects the order of nature, not the order of our coming to know what is the case ($71^b31–72^a5$). Similarly the observation that primaries are better known than their consequences ($72^b26–32$) need exhibit nothing more than their role (in a completed science) in supporting a wide variety of consequences. Finally, Aristotle's remark that nous is more 'accurate than knowledge' (when it grasps immediate starting points of science) need only mean that what it grasps is closer to the relevant basic principles of science (100^b8; cf. $86^a13–21$). In a completed science one will rely most on first principles since these support a wide variety of consequences. They will sustain more weight than any particular conclusion drawn from them.

None of these claims shows that we must come to know primary terms before we know the others or that they are immediately believable (or self-evident). For, in the ways indicated, we can come to know that claims about primaries are (a) about first terms (b) about existent objects, and (c) particularly significant, without having started our enquiry with claims which concern first principles. There is no need to attribute any special epistemological authority to *nous* (in our enquiries) to allow for its special status in B.19. For, that may flow from its distinctive role and objects in a completed science, and not from its intrinsic epistemological powers.

To conclude: Aristotle's account of our grasp of first principles in B.19 is dependent, in the ways indicated, on our engagement with the explanation-based system of genus/species differentiation outlined in B.13–15. Thus, first principles have their special status because they play a central and distinctive role in Aristotle's interdependent stories of differentiation and explanation. We see certain items as primary when we understand that they play a central role in this story.

10.7. ISSUES AND CONSEQUENCES

If Aristotle accepts the general view outlined in Sections 10.3 and 10.4 above, several projects become pressing. One is to show how (if at all) substances can be analysed within his general metaphysical account of essence and explanation. Another is to establish how the interconnected practices of classification and definition devised in B.8–10 and 13–15 can be applied to a real scientific enterprise.[52] I shall examine in the next two Chapters whether (and how successfully) his discussions in the *Metaphysics* and the biological works carry through these projects.

There is a further philosophical issue to be assessed: How far is Aristotle justified in adopting the viewpoint sketched above? Does his picture withstand criticism? Is it properly motivated? I shall consider these issues in the final Chapter.

---

[52] I shall examine below the extent to which Aristotle carried over this *specific* aspect of his *Analytics* account into his biological writings. An affirmative answer does not commit one to the further claim that Aristotle sought to implement the whole *Analytics* picture of a fully axiomatized, complete, science in his biological writings.

II

Substance, Definition, and Essence

II.I INTRODUCTION

To what extent did Aristotle employ in the central books of the *Metaphysics* (Z, H, Θ) the strategy he develops in the *Analytics* to tackle issues concerning definition, essence, and explanation? This question can be subdivided and made more precise. Did he answer the question 'What is substance?' in a manner which meets the requirements for adequate definition set in the *Analytics* (noted in Chapter 7)? Are the practices of definition and explanation interconnected in the *Metaphysics* as they are in the *Analytics*?

I shall argue for an affirmative answer to both these questions. Aristotle's answers to questions such as 'What is man?' satisfy his own Definitional Constraint and Simple Condition.[1] Further, his discussion throughout reflects the interdependency of definition and explanation which is argued for in the *Analytics*. In both works, the account of definition is made determinate by the addition of causal material. Indeed, in general, we gain further insight into Aristotle's strategy in *Metaphysics* Z, H, and Θ if we see it in the light of his *Analytics* account of definition and explanation. Or so I shall suggest.

Aristotle notes in *Posterior Analytics* B.9 that his method of demonstration and definition applies not only to the cases of substance/attribute pairs discussed in B.8, but also to a wider category. Thus, he distinguishes two relevant kinds of example:

(1) In some, the thing and its cause are the same. Here, there will not be a separate middle term (or cause). (93^b21-5)[2]

---

[1] See Ch. 7 Sects 7.3–7.4. Aristotle typically focuses on examples (such as man) in considering the 'What is substance?' question. He supposes (I shall assume) that if he can provide a satisfactory answer to a range of specific 'What is . . . ?' questions for particular substances he will have the resources (e.g. matter, form . . .) to give a general answer to the 'What is substance?' question. His answers to such specific questions will be metaphysical (and not scientific) provided that they maintain the degree of generality (and independence of empirical detail) required in metaphysical enquiry.

[2] In 93^b21-5 Aristotle refers back to cases where the cause is not different. He now specifies such cases as those where the *what it is* is not different, and the objects are immediate or starting points with respect to the *what it is*. In these examples, the thing and its essence

(2) In others, the thing and its cause are distinct. Here, there will be a middle term which is the cause of the thing being as it is. ($93^{b}25$–8)[3]

However, Aristotle does not develop this suggestion or show how it can be applied to cases such as that of man (mentioned in B.1, $89^{b}34$). Is he attempting to implement this suggestion in the *Metaphysics*? If so, his discussion should exhibit (at least) three structural features.

SF(1) There should be a division between substances which are identical with their causes, and those which are not (to match his claims in *Posterior Analytics* B.9).

SF(2) There should be an *Analytics*-style interdependence between the explanatory story uncovered in SF(1) and the answer to the definitional 'What is F?' question. Each should depend on the other.

SF(3) There should be, in the case of composite substances, a basic unifying causal feature which explains the substance's possession of its other genuine properties in the way in which, for example, quenching of fire explains why noise belongs to the clouds.

SF(1) introduces the idea of a hierarchy of substances, SF(2) connects the practices of definition and explanation, while SF(3) provides a metaphysical basis for that connection.[4] Within this model, the definition of a composite substance could not be completed without reference to a

will be identical, as the unit and the essence of the unit are identical. The grammatical subject, however, is the thing (viz. the unit) and not its essence; for, its existence is hypothesized and it is it which 'has' an essence ($93^{b}23$, 24–5). Further, it is objects not essences which are referred to in the two adjacent sentences ($93^{b}21$, $93^{b}25$–8). So, in $93^{b}21$–5 Aristotle is referring (in subject place) to things which have essences, and distinguishing cases where the thing and its essence are not separated or distinct.

[3] In $93^{b}25$–8, Aristotle is concerned with objects or kinds where there is a middle term— where, that is, there is a cause separate from the object/kind which makes it the object/kind it is. In this sentence, '*ousia*' refers to substances or kinds, and not to the essences of such substances and kinds. For, it is the latter which are the cause of the substance (or kind) being the substance (or kind) it is. '*Ousia*' is used in this way in *Post. An.* B.2. Therefore, the middle term is sought for the existence of *ousiai* such as man, earth, sun, or triangle ($90^{a}8$–10). And what is sought is the answer to the 'Why?' question which gives the essence ($90^{a}14$–15). *Ousiai*, elsewhere, are exemplified by man ($83^{b}2$–6) and other particular species ($73^{b}7$). If so, in B.2 substance and essence are also to be regarded as separable, and the latter can be placed in a middle term with respect to the former. Thus, if, for example, man and the essence of man were to be different (*Meta.* H.3, $1043^{b}2$–3), man would be placed within the class of entities where the cause is different from the composite (which is caused to be as it is). By contrast, if soul and the essence of soul are identical, they would be placed in the category marked out by the preceding sentence ($93^{b}21$–5).

[4] I have discussed a version of the explanatory approach and some alternatives, in 'Matter and Form: Unity, Persistence and Identity' in T. Scaltsas, D. Charles, and M. L. Gill (eds.), *Unity, Identity and Explanation in Aristotle's Metaphysics* (Oxford, 1994), 75–105. The present Chapter marks an attempt to develop the explanatory approach further, and to connect it with the interdependency thesis developed in the previous Chapters.

feature which explains (in the favoured structural way)[5] why the composite substance is as it is. At the metaphysical level, this feature should be explanatorily (and ontologically) more basic than the composite and not an abstraction from it.

In this Chapter, I shall argue that each of these structural features plays a prominent role in the argument of the *Metaphysics*. Section 11.2 focuses on the role there of SF(1), and Sections 11.3–11.5 on that of SF(2) and SF(3). In Section 11.6 I shall consider some more general consequences of the resulting picture for the metaphysical account of substance that Aristotle presents in *Metaphysics* Z, H, and Θ.

11.2 HIERARCHY AND DEFINITION: *METAPHYSICS* Z.1–12

Aristotle refers to his discussion of definition in the *Analytics* in *Metaphysics* Z.12 when he says that he is taking up the topic 'in so far as it has been left open in the *Analytics*' (1037^{b}8–9). Further, in Z.4 he uses several points also deployed in the *Analytics*. For example, he emphasizes the importance of separating definitions of the essence of a thing from accounts which signify the same as a name (1030^{a}6–10). He argues, as in the *Analytics*, that if one were to identify the two, any account would be a definition, and even the *Iliad* itself would be a definition (cf. *Post. An.* B.7, 92^{b}30–2). By contrast, definitions should be accounts of unified substances (in the first instance (1030^{b}5 f., 1031^{a}1)), which say what it is to be that substance (1030^{a}16–17).

However, the points of similarity between *Metaphysics* and *Analytics* run considerably deeper than this. In Z.6, 1032^{a}4 ff., Aristotle writes:

It is clear that in respect of the things that are said in themselves and primary, each thing is identical with its essence.

This sentence recalls the 'starting points' mentioned in *Posterior Analytics* B.9 whose essences are immediate. But in Z.6 Aristotle is as reticent as in B.9 as to what objects fall within this category. While he notes that it is now easy to see how one can decide whether Socrates is identical with his essence, he does not give us an answer (1032^{a}6–8). But it emerges in Z.11 that the soul is the primary substance (1037^{a}5), and this is distinct from

---

[5] See the account of structural explanation in Chapter 8. This form of explanation places constraints on both the *explananda* and the *explanans*. The latter should answer the 'What is F?' question, the former be *per se* connected, and in the favoured case of substances include a *differentia* term.

man or animal, which is a composite of soul and matter (1037ᵃ6–8).⁶ Soul is the primary substance in the case of living animals since it is identified with form and essence (1035ᵇ14–16). Indeed, Aristotle claims that form is, in general, to be identified with essence (cf. Z.7, 1032ᵇ1–2, 14). Since essence is also to be identified with primary substance (1035ᵇ15), form is established in this way as primary substance.

Aristotle explicitly draws the conclusion that, in the case of living animals, soul is the primary substance and is identical with its essence. Thus, he writes in H.3 1043ᵇ2–4:

Soul and the essence of soul are identical, man and the essence of man are not, unless man is soul.

According to this passage, soul is a primary substance, and man *qua* composite of matter and soul is not. It is only in the former case that the substance is identical with the essence. The structure set out in *Posterior Analytics* B.9 is enriched in these chapters by the introduction of form (and in the case of man, soul) as the leading candidate for the role of primary substance.

If Aristotle is implementing the proposal contained in *Analytics* B.9, there should be different types of definition for composite and for primary substances. The former should resemble the complex definition of thunder given in B.10 (94ᵃ5):

noise in the clouds caused in a given way.

This definition includes other essential features of thunder as well as the answer to the 'Why?' question (sometimes identified with what it is to be thunder). The definition of man should include, by analogy, both the answer to the 'Why?' question (e.g. the soul) and other essential features of man which are explained by that answer. Further, if he follows the *Analytics* pattern, Aristotle should sometimes be tempted to speak of the soul alone as what man is, and sometimes to include other essential features also. For, in the *Analytics* both the cause of thunder and the cause plus other features are on occasion referred to as what thunder is.⁷

Composites are defined in precisely this way in *Metaphysics* Z.10–12.

---

⁶ Here too Aristotle preserves some detachment on the question of Socrates, noting that 'Socrates' may refer either to the soul or to the composite. In the former case, Socrates is identical with his essence, in the latter, not.

⁷ Thus, in *Post. An.* B.2, 90ᵃ31–3, Aristotle says that to know the answer to the 'Why?' question is to know what a thing is. Later, knowledge of what a thing is includes both the answer to the 'Why?' question and other features of thunder (cf. *Post. An.* B.10, 94ᵃ5–6). Correspondingly, sometimes the answer to the 'What is it?' question seems aligned with the discovery of the answer to the 'Why?' question (*Post. An.* B.2, 90ᵃ15, B.10, 94ᵃ9–10). But elsewhere it is construed more broadly to involve other features also (*Post. An.* B.10, 94ᵃ5).

Aristotle insists that it is a mistake to attempt to define them without reference to matter:

for, some things surely are this form in this matter or these things being so. (Z.11, 1036^{b}23 f.)

Thus, man (or animal) cannot be defined without reference to movement, or to the parts of man being in a certain condition (1036^{b}28–30). The definition of man should include reference to his form (or soul) and his matter (body, arranged in a given way). The former might be identified with what it is to be a man (strictly speaking), but the full definition will include form *plus* matter. In a similar way, what it is to be an eclipse might be given by referring to the earth standing between sun and moon, even though a full definition will also include deprivation of light (*Post. An.* B.8, 93^{a}23–32). On occasion Aristotle, in these chapters (e.g. Z.10, 1035^{b}14–16), speaks of the soul alone as 'the essence of the composite'. This is in line with our prediction. For, in the *Analytics* model full definitions can be represented as including both the essence (construed narrowly as the basic answer to the 'Why?' question[8]) and other (derived) essential features of the substance. The relevant full definition will include both prior and posterior elements (as do the full *Analytics* definitions of thunder and eclipse). Thus, there is no difficulty in accepting that form is prior to matter and (at the same time) that a full definition of the composite should include both.

These chapters, therefore, reveal the first structural feature-(SF1)-required if Aristotle is to follow the *Analytics* model. As suggested by *Posterior Analytics* B.9, some substances are identical with their essences, while others are not. Those in the first category are primary, those in the second derivative. Aristotle advances this discussion in two ways. He identifies, in the case of substances, form with essence, and suggests that while certain substances (e.g. soul) are identical with their essences, composites of matter and form (e.g. man) are not. These two additions, which introduce basic elements from his own physical theory (viz. matter and form), allow Aristotle to apply his *Analytics* style of definition to the case of substance. With their assistance, he can develop the hierarchy of substances required to justify his schematic claims in *Posterior Analytics* B.9. Souls are primary

---

[8] Attention to the variety of types of definition available in the *Analytics* makes it no surprise that Aristotle can sometimes restrict definition to the form of composite substances, while elsewhere including their matter. On this problem, see the papers of Michael Frede ('The Definition of Sensible Substances in *Metaphysics* Z', in D. T. Devereux and P. Pellegrin (eds.), *Biologie, logique et métaphysique chez Aristote* (Paris, 1990, 113–29) and Michael Ferejohn ('The Definition of Generated Composites in Aristotle's *Metaphysics*', in Scaltsas, Charles, and Gill (eds.), *Unity, Identity and Explanation*, 291–318). The *Analytics* structures show how form of a composite substance can be logically prior to matter, even though a full definition of the composite turns out to contain both.

substances, identical with their essences, while man is a non-primary substance compounded from soul and matter.[9]

These chapters reflect other *Analytics*-based concerns. In Z.10 Aristotle states that while there is a defining account of universals, there cannot be a definition of particular composite substances (1035^b34ff., esp. 1036^a4–6). He returns to this theme later, in Z.15, 1039^b27ff:

> There is no definition or proof of perceptible substances, because they have matter whose nature is such that it is capable of being and not being.

One of his arguments is that once such things are no longer immediately before one, definition and proof are impossible (1040^a1–4). This is, presumably, because one cannot know that they exist when they are unperceived, since they might have perished in the meantime. His discussion recalls the strictures on definition from the *Analytics*, where definitions are said to be always of universals (B.13, 97^b25). One can only have definitions of things one knows to exist (B.8, 93^a19–20). If one does not know whether things exist, one cannot know what they are (93^a26–7). In the required order of search, one cannot seek what things essentially are before one discovers that they exist (93^b32).[10] If one makes the additional (and no doubt controversial) assumption that since particular composites are perishable one cannot know that they exist unperceived, it follows that one cannot define particular perceptible substances (presumably because definitions should remain valid whether or not the substance is before one's gaze). Thus, the *Analytics*' constraints on definition, which connect it firmly with scientific proof, together with these further assumptions about perishable substances, compel Aristotle to reject the possibility of defining particular perceptible substances, such as Socrates or Kallias. If composite perceptible substances can be defined, it appears that these must be construed as examples of universals (such as man or horse), which can be the subject matter of Aristotle's science (cf. *Post. An.* B.17, 99^a21–4, 30–7), and not as particulars (Z.10, 1035^b27–31).[11]

Do the *Analytics*' strictures on definition shed light on the debate over the existence and nature of particular forms?[12] Aristotle certainly

---

[9] Michael Ferejohn emphasizes Aristotle's use of 'physical' as well as 'logical' material in these chapters in 'The Definition of Generated Composites'.

[10] See Ch. 2 Sects. 2.2–2.5.

[11] Aristotle talks not only of particular substances, like Socrates or this man, but of particular composites 'taken universally' (Z.10, 1035^b27–31, Z.11, 1037^a5–7). In speaking of man, he is concerned with particular composites seen in abstraction from what makes them particular. I take 'as universal' to modify 'a certain composite' in 1035^b30 to designate the composite 'as universal', which is composed from a universal form and a type of matter. Such a composite is an enmattered kind. I have been fortified in this reading of 1035^b27–31 by discussion with Myles Burnyeat.

[12] The case for particular forms is developed in recent books by Irwin, Frede and Patzig, and Witt. (T. H. Irwin, *Aristotle's First Principles* (Oxford, 1988), 250–9; M. Frede and G. Patzig, *Aristoteles: Metaphysic Z* (Munich, 1988); C. Witt, *Substance and Essence in Aristotle*

sometimes talks (even in the central books) in terms which suggest that
he accepts the existence of particular forms (as, for example, when he
speaks of this soul, the soul which is Socrates, in Z.11, 1037ᵃ6–10). However,
even if he does, it does not follow that particular forms can be the objects
of definition. For, even if there are both particular and universal forms, it
may be that only the latter are the objects of definition and of scientific
knowledge. When one approaches these issues with the *Analytics'* perspective in mind, the crucial issue is not whether Aristotle thinks that particular forms exist, but rather (i) what particularizes them, and (ii) whether,
and in what ways, such forms are prior to general forms.[13]

It is tempting to see the *Analytics* as providing the outline of an answer
to (ii). There, general forms alone can be used in explanation. As such they
must be prior in account and in knowledge (cf. Z.1, 1028ᵃ31–3), and, thus,
the primary beings. Particular forms (if any such were to be found in
the *Analytics*) would be derivative, and differentiated by reference to
the matter the general forms enform (the form of Man-in-this-matter, as
is perhaps suggested in *Metaphysics* Z.8, 1034ᵃ5–8). If the *Metaphysics*
follows this pattern, general forms will be explanatorily basic, and particular forms the result of such forms being instantiated in given quantities of
matter.[14] Indeed, if the answer to the 'What is F?' question is the same (in

(Ithaca, 1989).) Others who have taken this line include Albritton, Sellars, Heinaman, Lloyd,
Frede, and Whiting (R. Albritton, 'Substance and Form in Aristotle's *Metaphysics*', *Journal
of Philosophy* 54 (1957), 699–708; W. Sellars, 'Substance and Form in Aristotle', *Journal of
Philosophy* 54 (1957), 688–99; R. E. Heinamann, 'Aristotle's Tenth Aporia', *Archiv für
Geschichte der Philosophie* 61 (1979), 249–70; A. C. Lloyd, 'Necessity and Essence in the
Posterior Analytics', in Berti (ed.), *Aristotle on Science*; M. Frede, 'Substance in Aristotle's
Metaphysics', in A. Gotthelf (ed.), *Aristotle on Nature and Living Things* (Pittsburgh, 1985),
17–26; J. Whiting, 'Form and Individuation in Aristotle', *HPQ* 3 (1986), 359–77). The existence of general forms is explicitly defended in the *Analytics* (*Post. An.* A.24, 85ᵇ15–18). Aristotle's formulation of explanatory claims there invokes universals (*Post. An.* B.17, 99ᵃ21–4,
30–7), and apparently does not include singular terms referring to particulars (see G. Patzig,
Aristotle's Theory of the Syllogism, tr. J. Barnes (Dordrecht, 1969), 4–8). Particular forms,
however, may play their own distinctive role in explanation. In *GA* 5 they are used to explain
individual genetic differences (as J. M. Cooper argues, 'Metaphysics in Aristotle's Embryology; in D. Devereux and P. Pellegrin (eds.), *Biologie, logique et métaphysique chez Aristote*
(Paris, 1990), 79–84). Presumably, at least some perceptual forms are particulars (*De An.* B.5,
417ᵇ22–5).

[13] Some proponents of particular forms regard Aristotelian general forms as abstractions
(Frede and Patzig *Aristoteles: Metaphysic Z*), while others view them as real entities (Irwin,
Aristotle's First Principles 262–3). This issue is raised by Whiting ('Metasubstance: Critical
Notice of Frede-Patzig and Furth', *PR* 100 (1991), 638f.). Both groups can agree with the
defender of the priority of general forms on the following claims: (i) *Analytics*-style definitions are of general forms; (ii) there are particular forms; (iii) knowledge requires general
forms. The key issues on which these parties divide concern (i) the relative priority of general
and particular forms, and (ii) the ontological status of general forms.

[14] Forms (whether particular or general) are prior to composite substance (whether individual or taken universally) (cf. Z.3, 1029ᵃ5). If so, forms cannot be defined as the forms of
composites (or of the-matter-in-a-composite); for, this would be to treat the composite as
explanatorily prior to the form.

the *Metaphysics*) as the answer to the 'Why?' question, and the latter answer is tied (in the *Analytics* style) to explanation concerning universals, the relevant primary substances must be general forms.

It would be no small task to establish that this line of interpretation is correct. There are several steps that might be challenged. Some will deny that Aristotle (in the *Metaphysics*) holds that general forms are explanatorily prior (or prior in account) to particular ones. Maybe the latter are basic in the explanation of the *particularity* of particular composites. Others will argue that Aristotle (in the *Metaphysics*) did not accept the inference from the explanatory priority of general forms to their ontological priority.

The proper consideration of these responses lies outside our present project. However, it is a major advantage of the present approach that it brings into sharp focus two crucial questions. First, is the *explanandum* in the *Metaphysics* the particularity of particular substances or their unity?[15] For, if it is the latter, the *explanans* should be general (e.g. the essence it shares with other members of its kind: the essence of the kind). Second, if the *explanantia* are general, does it follow that they are prior in *being* to particular forms? If we could answer these two questions, we would have the basis for progress on the much-disputed issue of the role of general and particular forms. For, we would see more of Aristotle's motivation in this discussion.

However, while these questions are (I suspect) answerable, I shall not pursue them further here. Instead, I shall focus on Aristotle's discussion of the unity of particulars, and leave open the issue of whether he also attempts to explain their particularity.[16] My aim is only to show the *Analytics* model at work in *Metaphysics* Z, H, and Θ, and not to argue for (or against) the suggestion that particular forms are needed in this context. Indeed, this seems to follow Aristotle's own preoccupations. In Z.2–12 his concern seems to be to preserve (in the case of substances) his *Analytics* connection between definitions and universals and to secure his favoured hierarchy (*Post. An.* B.9). The issue of particular forms is not, it seems, a major interest in these chapters.

While the discussion of Z.4–12 appears to follow certain aspects of Aristotle's methods in the *Analytics*, there are several departures from that

---

[15] The question of unity may be asked about particulars as follows. Granted that this is a particular, what makes it a unity? (Answer: The Form F it possesses is combined in a given way with its matter.) This question does not involve the question: What makes this particular a particular? Indeed, in the former, its particularity is taken for granted. The question of unity can be taken either diachronically or synchronically. Aristotle (I shall assume) intends his answers to apply diachronically as well as synchronically.

[16] If he does aim to explain the particularity of particular substances, he will do so by invoking (in line with the explanatory approach) particular forms. So understood, particular forms are required if Aristotle is adopting the radical version of the explanatory approach which aims to explain the *particularity* of particulars.

model which might initially be surprising. For example, while definitions are said to be of one thing (Z.4, $1030^b9–10$, Z.12, 1037^b26), and regularly conceived in the genus-species mode ($1037^b20–2$, 1030^a12 ff.), Aristotle does not immediately employ the explanatory machinery he developed in the *Analytics* to answer the following question:

Why is two-footed, wingless, animal *a unity*? (Z.12, $1037^b13–15$: cf. *Post. An.* B.6, $92^a29–30$)

One might have expected him to seek a middle term which explains why two-footed belongs to animal, in the manner proposed in the *Analytics* B.8.[17] But instead he suggests in Z.12 that in the phrase 'two-footed animal', 'animal' refers to either nothing or nothing differentiated over and above the species ($1038^a5–8$), and that in certain cases the final *differentia* will be one thing alone (1038^a25 f.) which gives one unique essence (and, presumably, entails all the other *differentiae*). This suggestion does not invoke the *Analytics* model of seeking a unifying answer of the appropriate type to the 'Why?' question (which is only introduced in Z.17). Indeed, Aristotle's explanatory approach to definition is not deployed at all in Z.12.

Why is this so? In Z.4–12 Aristotle is attempting to answer the 'What is F?' question while using only some of the resources at his disposal. First, he deploys the general constraints on definition developed in the (explanation-free) parts of the *Analytics* (and the *Topics*) to claim that definition is of essence, is of one thing, and is connected in some way with genus and *differentiae*. Second, he argues, on the basis of his physical writings, that form is a plausible candidate for the role of essence in the case of substance. But these two moves do not take him very far. He has not as yet articulated a clear and determinate idea of form or essence which is to meet these conditions. How is the form of man itself to be conceived? Is it, for instance, merely the unanalysable *what it is to be a man*? Without the explanatory material introduced in Z.17, Aristotle does not have the resources required to specify the kind of form involved. Neither here nor in the *Analytics* can the definitional task be completed without the addition of material drawn from the theory of explanation.

Z.12 exemplifies a similar incompleteness. Aristotle suggests that one secures the unity of definition by finding one final *differentia* which entails all the others. But this proposal cannot apply (at least straightforwardly) to the case of man, considered as two-footed, *wingless*, animal (1037^b33). For, being two-footed does not imply being wingless (consider birds). It also does not work if man is considered as mortal, two-footed, wingless

---

[17] See Ch. 7 Sect. 7.4.

(see *Post. An.* B.6, 92ª29 ff.).[18] Further, if one devised one complex predicate (such as 'mortal-wingless-two-footed') which did entail all the rest, one would still need to show that this complex predicate was itself a proper unity. Either the Z.12 model fails to apply to many relevant cases or it presupposes the type of unity it is attempting to establish. Either way, it fails. Prior to Z.17 Aristotle has no way satisfactorily to resolve the issue of unity raised in Z.12. It is small wonder that he returns to it later in H.6 with the explanatory material in place (see Sect. 11.4).

Why does Aristotle proceed in this way? If he were following the *Analytics* model, one would expect him to motivate the introduction of explanation-based material in Z.17 by showing the incompleteness of attempts at definition without it. As in the *Analytics*, he should argue for the interdependency of the practices of definition and explanation by showing that the former by themselves are incomplete. The gaps in the account offered in Z.4–12 constitute one argument for that claim. Another (as I shall argue in the next Section) is provided by his suggestion in Z.13–16 that definitional concerns by themselves generate an impasse, which can only be broken by the introduction of explanatory material in Z.17. In this way, one can understand the pattern of argument throughout Z as (in large part) directed to establishing the interdependency of definition and explanation. In effect, Aristotle is arguing for the two structural features SF(2) and SF(3) introduced above.

11.3 Z.13–17, H.2: THE INTRODUCTION TO THE EXPLANATORY APPROACH

By the beginning of Z.17 Aristotle has reached an impasse. The general structure of his *aporia* is clear. He established in Z.13 that substance cannot be (in some sense) a universal, and in Z.15 that it cannot be a complex of universals (1040ª14–25). But definition, we already know, must be of something universal. Hence, particular composites, like Socrates (Z.15, 1039ᵇ20–1040ª7), cannot be definable substances. Nor can particular ideas (1039ᵇ8–14), nor particular eternal objects. So, it appears that there can be no such thing as definable substance.

Several of the detailed arguments in this aporetic section are interesting and recall discussions in the *Analytics*.[19] But the underlying pattern

---

[18] These issues are discussed by A. Falcon in 'Aristotle's Rules of Division in the *Topics*: The Relation between Genus and *Differentia* in Division', *Ancient Philosophy* 16/2 (1996), 377–88.

[19] See, in particular, Aristotle's arguments in Z.15 against the view that (e.g.) 'the sun' can be defined as 'what revolves around the Earth' or 'what is hidden at night' (1040ª29 ff.). I discuss these in App 1 n. 7.

of argument is particularly revealing. Aristotle begins with the claim that substance, unlike universals common to several kinds, is specific or unique to the kind in question (Z.13, 1038^{b}9–11).[20] This point by itself generates the central problem. Since no substance can be composed of universals or of other substances, every substance must be incomposite. But if this is so, none can be captured in a formula (1039^{a}14–19), since there can only be formulae of composites. So, there can be no definitions of substances.

This line of argument forms the basis for large parts of the discussion in Z.14 and 15. In Z.14 Aristotle states that if there were universal forms of a Platonic type, either particular species would be comprised of them or they would be different for each species (1039^{b}7–8). In the former case, they would not be unique. In the latter, they would be unique to the relevant species but unknowable (1040^{a}24 f.) and not describable in language (1040^{a}10 f.). One either uses universals common to many things to describe substance (in which case one fails to capture the uniqueness of an essence) or one can only specify the particular type of substance by a demonstrative (in which case it is not knowable in the appropriate scientific mode). If every type of substance is incomposite, none can be described in terms of a general formula (Z.13, 1039^{a}17–19).

Aristotle considers a possible reply to this dilemma, in Z.15:

universals may apply separately to many things, but taken all at once they apply to this substance. (1040^{a}14–16)

This remark immediately recalls one of the suggestions discussed in *Posterior Analytics* B.13.[21] In the *Metaphysics* it is rejected on two grounds. If the components of man (e.g. animal and two-footed) are separable universals, then everything that is predicated of man will also be predicated of them (*qua* components of man). So, man will not be the unique bearer of the relevant set of properties, since (e.g.) animal will bear the same set of properties (1040^{a}16–21).[22] Further, this proposal makes every

---

[20] This understanding of Z.13 follows the outline pioneered by Michael Woods in 'Problems in *Metaphysics* Z, Chapter 13', in J. M. E. Moravcsik (ed.), *Aristotle: Critical Essays* (New York, 1967), 215–38, and further developed in his 'Universals and Particular Forms in Aristotle's Metaphysics', OSAP, suppl. 1991, (Supplement), 41–56. A similar overall interpretation of Z.13 is developed by A. Code in 'No Universal is a Substance: An interpretation of Z.13, 1038^{b}8–15', *Paideia* (1978), 65–76, and in M. Burnyeat (ed.), *Notes on Book Zeta of Aristotle's Metaphysics* (London, 1979), ad loc. While I have followed the generalist reading of Z.13, problems similar to the ones I discuss will arise within a particularist interpretation of this chapter: 'What is unique to the particular in question?'; 'How is this knowable?'.

[21] This case is discussed in Ch. 9 Sect. 9.2.

[22] This argument does not look robust. If animal does share the properties of man (e.g. being two-footed, etc.), why not say that it only shares these properties derivatively *qua* participating in the composite man? If so, it would possess these properties in a different way from that in which man does. But perhaps Aristotle has a reply to this: If one understands

component prior to man, since they need not be destroyed if the composite is destroyed (1040^a21–2). But this gets the relevant priorities wrong. Not every component of the composite should be prior to man in this way. Some should be (e.g. possessing a soul of a given kind), but others should not. This proposal, by making all components prior, does not capture the kind of priority required of definition.[23] Merely to conjoin all the universals present in a composite is to give up the idea, central to the *Analytics* style of definition, of there being some prior basic feature at the centre of the account. At this point, the *Analytics'* constraints on definition are to the fore.

These chapters set the target for Aristotle's own investigations. What is sought (to define a composite substance) must be (in some way) a non-complex unity,[24] which is in the relevant sense prior and specific to the kind of substance in question. The challenge, raised in Z.13, is to show how a non-complex, prior feature of this type can be knowable at all. Aristotle notes (tantalizingly) that 'in some way there can be definition, and in another not' (1039^a21 f.). Presumably, he thinks that although substance is incomposite in some way, it can still be the object of definition. He now needs to show how such definitions would be knowable. Does he use the *Analytics* model to help him at this point?

There is considerable reference to the *Analytics* in Z.17, which marks the beginning of Aristotle's most systematic attempt to apply the explanatory style of definition to substance. Indeed, Aristotle indicates in 1041^a23–30 that his goal is to apply his explanatory model to the case of composite substances. In this passage he uses his favoured *Analytics* example of thunder (cf. *Post. An.* B.8, 93^b8–12, B.10, 94^a2–9) to illustrate his approach to composite substances.

He introduces his discussion by describing seeking the essence through asking the 'Why?' question:

The question is: Why does something belong to something else? And that it belongs has to be clear; otherwise, you are not asking anything. Take, for example, the question:

Why does it thunder?

[This is equivalent to:]

the role of animal in this way in the composite man, it is no longer *prior* to man (contrary to the hypothesis of 1040^a17–18). To meet this reply, the objector would need to separate various kinds of priority (explanatory, ontological, etc.), and this would far outrun his simple strategy of listing all the relevant universals in an unstructured way.

[23] Thus understood, this passage is fully consistent with Aristotle's position in *Post. An.* B.13. Definition merely by listing a set of shared universals fails to capture what is explanatorily prior. Listing shared universals either captures no priority or only the wrong kind of priority (in which all universals are equally prior).

[24] This entity could not be a property, since substances are prior to properties in Aristotle's hierarchy of being (Z.13, 1038^b23 ff., cf. Z.1, 1028^a30 ff.).

Why does noise occur in the clouds?

That way, the object of inquiry is something of something else. And similarly:

Why are these things (e.g. bricks and stones) a house?

So, it is clear that the cause is being sought. This is the essence, to speak generally. In some cases, it is the final cause—as perhaps in the case of houses or beds; in others, it is the efficient cause. For, this is the relevant cause. (1041^a23–30)[25]

In the case of thunder, something which comes into being, the efficient cause gives the relevant answer: fire being quenched (as we know from the *Analytics*). And on this basis we can construct a full definition:

Thunder is noise in the clouds caused by fire being quenched.

This full definition (as we learn in *Post. An.* B.10, 94^a1–7) follows the pattern of the explanatory syllogism:

Noise Φ nec fire being quenched.

Fire being quenched Φ nec those clouds/clouds in k.

Noise Φ nec those clouds/clouds in k.[26]

In the full definition of thunder, there are other elements beyond the efficient cause: e.g. noise in the clouds. These are parts of the definition in the *Analytics*, but they are not the answer to the 'Why?' question.

So, what is the analogue in the case of *house* (to take the first case to be discussed in detail in Z.17)? Aristotle proceeds extremely cautiously by asking the question:

---

[25] I construe '*logikos*' as referring to a manner of proceeding which is based on considerations of a general kind, not based on principles particular to a given science or subject matter (cf. *Post. An.* A.21, 82^b35 with Barnes's note.). By contrast, considerations are '*phusikos*' if they are specific to a given subject matter. (On this, see my discussion in *Aristotle's Philosophy of Action*, 128 n. 27.) In 1041^a31 ff. I agree with Ross (*Aristotle's Metaphysics*, II. 223) in construing 'the other cause' as naturally referring to the final cause, and, thus, take the whole sentence $^a31$–2 to elucidate the same distinctions as are marked out in the sentence $^a29$–30. Frede and Patzig, by contrast, (*Aristotle's Metaphysic Z*, II. 312–3) take 'the other cause' to refer to the formal cause alone, and contrast this with both efficient and teleological causes (as introduced by 'this sort of cause' in $^a31$). Thus, they see Aristotle as contrasting here the formal causes of (e.g.) mathematical objects with the efficient and final causes to be found in what comes into being and passes away. However, the preceding context does not mention mathematical (or other timeless) objects, but focuses rather on the transitory examples introduced in $^a29$. Further, in the subsequent lines, Aristotle's concern in using the phrase 'the being/existence' (at 1041^b5–6) is with similar cases of transitory objects. Thus, it is natural to understand this phrase in $^a32$ to apply to the same type of case. In general, in this passage, Aristotle appears to focus on a limited set of cases ('some . . . some . . .' in $^a29$), and not to aim at a general taxonomy of all cases of substances.

[26] The exact form of the C-place is unclear. I prefer 'clouds in k' to preserve their appropriate generality. By the inelegant symbol 'Φ nec' I intend 'belongs necessarily to'.

Why are these bricks or stones *a house*? (1041^{a}27, ^{b}6–7)

and answering:

because *what it is to be a house* belongs to them. (1041^{b}6–7)

But he does note that the general form of the relevant question is:

Why is the *matter* some definite thing? (1041^{b}7–8)

and that the general form of the answer refers to the essence of the thing, which is identified with the form (1041^{b}8).

At this point a further feature is added to the account of form: not only must it provide an answer to the 'What is it?' question, it must also serve to answer the relevant 'Why?' question by specifying the basic explanatory feature. The notion of form is to be constrained by two sets of demand: it should both supply an answer to the 'What is F?' question and at the same time provide the basis for the relevant type of (presumably teleological) explanation of why the substance is as it is.

But why is Aristotle so confident that these two questions are answered in the same way? Why is there *one* feature which satisfies both the definitional and the explanatory requirements? This question is inescapable if Aristotle seeks to follow independent and distinct definitional and explanatory routes to form.[27] For, what makes it true that these two routes both lead to the *same* destination? Why is there not one notion of form which answers the definitional question, and another which answers the explanatory one? But a similar question would also have arisen if Aristotle had progressively refined one notion of form. For, what would make it true that there is, in fact, just *one* notion of form which is held constant throughout these refinements?

The mutual dependency of definition and explanation provides an answer to these questions. According to this model (see SF(2) above), the definitional task cannot be completed without the addition of material drawn from the practice of explanation. Nor can the relevant type of explanation be specified without adverting to a feature which tells us what the substance is. The structure of *Metaphysics* Z appears to reflect precisely this interdependency. In the discussion up to Z.16 Aristotle had established that there can be no proper account of the definition of substances without recourse to the practice of explanation. Thus, in Z.17 the relevant explanatory material is introduced to spell out a proper definition of substances. But immediately it becomes apparent that the appropriate form of explanation is one which involves constraints drawn from the practice of definition. For, the feature sought as the

---

[27] See, e.g. Michael Ferejohn's paper mentioned above (n. 8).

explanatorily basic one must also answer the definitional question
(1041ᵃ26f.). Nor should this be a surprise, since it is a constraint on
Analytics-style 'structural' explanation that the *explanans* should tell us
what the kind in question is.[28]

In the *Analytics*, there is one feature (in the case of thunder and of
eclipse) which answers both definitional and explanatory questions.
Indeed, the two questions are so connected that neither can be answered
without the other. If this model is to be transferred to the case of substances (as seems to be the aim of Z.17), there must be one feature which
provides the basis for an answer to both definitional and explanatory questions. Since these questions are interlocked, if form is the answer to one,
it must be the answer to the other.

But is this type of explanatory approach to definition in Z.17 merely an
isolated fragment in the argument of the central books of the *Metaphysics*?
Are SF(2) and SF(3) confined to this chapter? It appears not. Large parts
of the next books constitute an attempt to implement this approach (or so
I shall argue).

The proposal introduced in Z.17 needs to be unpacked further. We need
to understand the reference of *house* in the question:

Why are these bricks *a house?*

Does it refer to the whole of the compound (matter and form) or to some
definite feature of these bricks (e.g. their being arranged in a given way)?
More generally, in Z.17 Aristotle's question is:

Why is the matter some definite thing? (1041ᵇ7–8)

We can only make progress with this question if we know how 'some
definite thing' is to be understood. Further, we need to understand
how the phrase *what it is to be a house* functions in the answer. For,
while we have reason to believe that this refers to a feature which is
the teleological cause, we do not know how to specify this in any detail. If
Z.17 gives a blueprint for further work, it does not tell us how to carry
through the project. These gaps are filled in H.2 and beyond in a manner
which carries further the explanatory approach to definition (or so I shall
argue).

In H.2 Aristotle begins by discussing the *differentiae* of matter: composition, time, position, etc. (1042ᵇ11 ff.). This is precisely the type of
move he should make if he is pursuing the explanatory approach. In the
Analytics he sought (in investigating substances) *differentiae* as *explananda*
which belong *per se* to the kind in question and mark it out from the
relevant genus.[29] If one construes matter as a genus (or analogous to one),
the relevant *differentiae* should mark out the matter involved in the sub-

---

[28] See Ch. 8 Sects. 8.3 and 8.4.   [29] See Ch. 9 Sects. 9.2 ff.

stance.[30] In the case of house, the relevant *differentia* of the matter (bricks and stones) is *arranged thus* (1043ª7 f.). Aristotle immediately notes that the final cause may be added as a *differentia* in some cases (1043ª8 f.), and that in this case it would be a covering for possessions and bodies (1043ª16–18, 32 f.). Indeed, Aristotle goes on to speak of 'being a possessions-protector' as the activity, form, and shape of the house. From these materials he can construct a full definition of house:

House = bricks and stones arranged thus as a covering for possessions and bodies.

Aristotle suggests that some *differentiae* may be causally more basic—the cause of each thing being what it is (1043ª2–4).[31] In the present example, the final cause will play this role: being a possessions-protector. So, one can now reframe the question raised in Z.17 as follows:

Why are bricks and stones (the matter) arranged thus (in given spatial arrangements, with a roof, etc.)?

The answer will invoke the basic form: In order for it to be a possessions-protector. For, it is its being this which explains why the bricks and stones are arranged as they are.[32] Further, it is because houses are essentially possessions-protectors that they contain *bricks and stones* which are arranged thus; for, this kind of matter possesses the right capacities to be a possessions-coverer, because it is water resistant, unmoved by wind, etc.

Definitions of this type could be related (by the methods of *Post. An.* B.10 94ª1 ff.) to a syllogism such as:

---

[30] Aristotle insists on the close connection between matter and genera in Z.12, 1038ª5 ff. On this, see, e.g., R. Rorty, 'Genus as Matter: A Reading of *Metaphysics* Z-H', in *Exegesis and Argument: Phronesis*, suppl. 1 (1973), 393–420.

[31] Aristotle writes that: 'it is amongst the *differentiae* that something must be sought which is the cause of each thing being what it is' (1043ª2–3). That this refers to one of the *differentiae* (or at least some limited set of these) is confirmed by Aristotle's subsequent introduction of the final cause (1043ª9), which is invoked in giving *the* activity of the house ('to be a covering for belongings and bodies', 1043ª16–17). Quasi-substances, like houses, are used as the nearest analogies for genuine substances (1043ª4–7).

[32] The connection between the matter (bricks, planks…) and the relevant feature (being arranged thus) should be a *per se* one, if the *Analytics*-style account is to be preserved in its entirety. That is, *being arranged thus* should belong to such bricks, planks, etc., and to nothing else. Either the relevant matter is defined as that to which *being arranged thus* belongs (perhaps in favourable conditions) or *being arranged thus* is defined as something which belongs to matter of this type. On this view, the relevant matter would form the grouping to which *being arranged thus* belongs. This group might be (e.g.) *house-material matter*. Bricks and planks would form species of matter of this type. Compare the case of deciduous trees and (e.g.) figs, discussed in Chapter 8 Section 8.3.

Being arranged thus Φ nec being a possessions-coverer.

Being a possessions-coverer Φ nec these bricks, etc.

Being arranged thus Φ nec these bricks, etc.[33]

In such a syllogism, *being arranged thus* would replace *being a house* as *noise* replaced *thunder* in one of the *Analytics* B.8 syllogisms (93^b9–12). In the *Analytics*, the question:

Why does *thunder* belong to these clouds?

is replaced by:

Why does *noise* belong to these clouds?

In the *Metaphysics*, the question:

Why does *being a house* belong to these bricks? (1041^b6)

can be similarly replaced by:

Why does *being arranged in a given way* belong to these bricks? (1043^a7–8)

In both cases, the answer is discussed by isolating a causally basic phenomenon, in the first case an efficient, in the second a teleological cause (as was predicted in 1041^a29–31; see also 1044^b1). In both, there is an immediate causal connection in the major premiss. It is because the bricks are used as a possessions-coverer that they are arranged thus. No further intermediate cause is being sought.

Analogous moves may be made in the case of man. The Z.17 question:

why is this body with this feature a man? (1041^b6–7)

could be reformulated in the H.2 style as:

Why is this body two-footed?

or

Why does being two-footed belong to this body?

However, Aristotle is proceeding at a very abstract level (1044^b16ff.), and does not make the form of the question determinate. He is clearer about the nature of the answer, *what it is to be a man*. This is unequivocally identified with *soul of a given kind* (1043^b2–4), which provides answers to the Z.17 question:

Why does being a man belong to this body with this feature (e.g. this shape)?

---

[33] In this syllogism, both the A- and B-terms are to be taken as species-form terms. Thus, in the major premiss, *being arranged thus* is taken as a consequential part of the form, derivative from *being a possessions-coverer*. Both of these are predicated of the relevant matter in the minor premiss and conclusion.

and its rephrased version:

Why does being two-footed belong to this body (with this feature)?

The answer would be that being a biped belongs to this body because its having two legs is required by what it is to be a man. On this understanding, the relevant type of soul serves as the teleological cause which explains why the body has given features.

If this account is correct, the unity of the composite substance, man, will depend on there being one basic feature (e.g. a soul of a given kind) which belongs immediately to the relevant matter. This feature should have the following properties:

(a) It should be linked immediately to the relevant matter in such a way as to explain why the matter is as it is.

(b) It should explain why the relevant matter is possessed of certain necessary, *per se*, properties (e.g. being a biped).

(c) It should constitute what it is to be the composite substance.

(d) Its unity should be basic and not further analysable. Thus, it should be a non-complex cause (of the appropriate type) specific to the kind in question.[34]

In the *Metaphysics*, since the relevant structure of explanation in the case of substances is teleological, the form must be the non-complex teleological cause which explains why the matter is possessed of certain features (such as being two-legged). Thus, the matter will be organized in the way required for the relevant type of movement (walking, running) characteristic of man. The relevant form will be that feature specific to the kind which explains why its other properties are as they are. It will be discovered by uncovering its basic role as in the explanation of the structure of composite substances.[35] Although simple causal features (such as souls) are not the subject matter of enquiry in the way composite substances are (cf. Z.17, $1041^{b}9$–11), they will be discovered by successfully tracing the 'Why?' question back to its ultimate teleological source, the non-complex cause of the thing being what it is (H.2, $1043^{a}3$ f.).[36]

---

[34] It should be noted that the unity of the soul, so understood, is compatible with its having parts, provided that the soul cannot be reductively analysed into its parts. That is, the soul may have parts provided that what it is to be a part is to be understood as (metaphysically) dependent on the unity of the soul.

[35] In the next Section I consider further the way in which the soul operates as a final cause (in commenting on H.6, $1045^{a}31$–3).

[36] In this case, the syllogism would run as follows:

Being two-footed belongs to being what it is to be a man.

Being what it is to be a man belongs to this body.

Being two-footed belongs to this body.

This line of thought is developed further in H.3 and H.4, where Aristotle states that while composite substances are definable, the primary elements from which they are composed are not (1043^{b}28–31). Primary elements are compared with the indivisible elements from which other numbers are composed (1043^{b}34 f., 1044^{a}1 f.). Thus, the primary substance (soul) in the case of living creatures must (at least) be a non-composite entity, which lacks the kind of internal structure possessed by composites (see 1043^{b}30 f.).

We are now in a position to understand Aristotle's reply to the *aporia* he set out in Z.13–16. This arose because it was difficult to see how if forms are non-composite they are knowable. Aristotle now has a solution: they are knowable because they are discovered to be the basic cause which explains why, in the case of man, being two-footed belongs *per se* to animal or matter of a given type. In a successful investigation of composite substances, one will find the specific differentiating cause which explains why the composite is (in other respects) as it is. The basic causal feature must be specific to the kind; for, otherwise it could not explain (in the appropriate way) why all and only members of a given kind have some necessary property. As in the *Analytics*, one will conclude one's search with the discovery of fundamental commensurate universals, unique to the kind in question. The differentiating cause will be universal in the sense that it is present in all and only members of the relevant kind. But it will not be a universal of the type which extends more widely than the kind (Z.13–15).

Soul of kind S can replace being what it is to be a man. As in the previous note, both the A- and B-terms (being two-footed, being what it is to be a man) would point to aspects of the form of man, which are predicated of the relevant matter (whether this be particular matter or matter of a given type). The B-term would indicate something sufficient to make this matter a human being (although it would not, of course, be sufficient to account for the existence/presence of this matter). In this way, Aristotle could answer (in a metaphysical mode) the question 'What is man?' (which is raised in 1041^{b}1, and is the immediate focus of the present discussion). This answer is, of course, not the one the biologist would give, since her concern (unlike the metaphysician's) is not with *what it is to be a man*, conceived of merely as that feature (whatever it may be) which explains why this body is a man/two-footed. Rather, she aims to spell out *what it is to be a man* in biological terms (See E.1, 1025^{b}8–10). The metaphysician, by contrast, could reasonably be satisfied with this style of account since his goal is to outline a style of account which can apply to *all* substances. (For a contrasting view, see Robert Bolton's paper 'Science and the Science of Substance in Aristotle's *Metaphysics* Z', *PPQ* 76 (1995), 454–7).

In *De An.* B.2 Aristotle envisages an alternative but similar syllogism. It appears to run as follows (413^{a}13 ff., cf. 414^{a}4 ff.):

Being alive belongs to soul.

Soul belongs to matter of a given type.

Being alive belongs to matter of a given type.

The matter in question is unified by its possession of the capacity for life. Thus, the connection in the conclusion is a universal *per se* one (See Ch. 8 Sect. 8.3). As in the case of planks and bricks, there may be differing species of this matter.

For, the latter will not yield the one basic (prior) simple entity required. Further, the relevant form or essence will be knowable on the basis of its role in the (appropriate type of) teleological explanation of the internal workings of a composite substance. The form in question must be capable of explaining why the other features of the substance are as they are. Thus, it could not be an invented simple such as man* (an invented indivisible form), since the latter could not make the other specific features intelligible in the required way (Z.17, 1041^{a}19–20). In Z.13 Aristotle asked how a form specific to one kind only could be knowable. Now we can see his answer.

It is significant that in H.4 Aristotle explicitly introduces one of his favoured *Analytics* examples (the eclipse of the moon (H.4, 1044^{b}9 ff.)), and compares it with the case of man (as, in Z.17, thunder is compared with man). In the case of the eclipse, the cause or form is only present in the definition if one invokes the efficient cause. As Aristotle notes:

What is eclipse? It is deprivation of light. But if 'by the Earth's coming in between' is added, one has the account which includes the cause. (1044^{b}13–15)

In this case, the efficient cause is a unique phenomenon necessary and sufficient to explain the eclipse of the moon. The analogy with the case of man is closely drawn. The form is the essence, which is identified with the teleological cause (1044^{b}1). Thus, even if non-composite, the essence can be discovered by uncovering the specific differentiating entity which is explanatorily basic; for, one can come to know it by detecting its distinctive causal role.[37]

In this Section, I have suggested that in Z.17 Aristotle introduces his *Analytics* explanatory theory in order to determine more precisely the type of form required for definition. This material is introduced because Aristotle's definitional project, begun in Z.4–12, cannot (in his view) be completed without the assistance of material drawn from the practice of explanation. For, the latter enables us to grasp the nature of the form, which is prior and an incomposite unity (in part) because it is a non-complex cause. Without recourse to the practice of explanation, we cannot overcome the *aporiai* of Z.13–16.

At the metaphysical level, the notion of form, thus understood, is held in place by two sets of conditions: it is the feature which answers the 'What is F?' question (Z.4–12) and at the same time supplies the basic cause in

---

[37] In H.4 Aristotle suggests that the matter of man may be the '*catamēnia*' (1044^{a}35), but also notes the importance of finding the matter which is unique to the thing in question (1044^{b}2–3). Elsewhere in these chapters the body appears to be the relevant matter (H.5, 1044^{b}29–31, H.3, 1043^{a}34–5, Z.17, 1041^{b}7). In H.4 Aristotle is giving examples of candidates for causes, rather than specifying them precisely. Indeed, throughout this discussion Aristotle seems more concerned to outline the general structure than to be precise about the detailed place-holders in his scheme.

the relevant teleological pattern (Z.17ff.). Further, this metaphysical conception provides the basis for an epistemic route to the discovery of the form. For, we can come to know it on the basis of its basic causal role. In these ways, Aristotle's discussion of form exemplifies the co-determination of essence and causation which we uncovered in the *Analytics*.[38]

11.4 THE EXPLANATORY APPROACH CONTINUED: PROBLEMS IN H.6

In the account suggested, the full account of man should read as follows:

Man: two-footed animal with soul of kind k.

to match:

House: bricks arranged thus for the sake of covering possessions.

In this account, *two-footed with soul of kind k* might be presented as the shape or activity, and *animal* as the matter.[39] Further, *soul of kind k* is the basic, simple, causal factor: the teleologically basic feature. *Man* is a unity because there is one such feature which explains why the relevant animal is two-footed.

In H.6 Aristotle takes up directly some of the issues raised in Z.12 and 17 and H.2–3:

What makes a composite one thing and not a heap? (1045^a8–12).

Why is man one thing, not many: two-legged, and animal? (1045^a19 f.).

Indeed, he ends the chapter by claiming to have found an answer to this question:

looking for the cause of one thing is the same as looking for the cause of it being one thing. (1045^b19 f.)

In the light of the account offered above, one would expect him to deploy his favoured explanatory model of definition (as captured in SF(3)) to

---

[38] Thus, it exhibits Structural Feature 3-SF(3)-mentioned in the Introduction to this Chapter.

[39] Aristotle is not always clear on how to categorize 'arranged thus' or 'two-footed': whether as matter or as activity/form. Sometimes they are taken as activity/shape compared with matter (cf. 1043^a5, 8). Sometimes they are omitted, and the shape/activity is specified using only the basic activity (possessions-covering/soul (1043^a16–18, $^a34$–5)). Sometimes they are described 'as matter' to the basic activity of the soul (cf. H.3, 1043^b10–13). This suggests that the notions of matter and form are relational: 'arranged thus'/'two-footed' is form with respect to body/bricks, but matter with respect to soul/possessions-covering. A certain degree of fluctuation in terminology should not disturb us at this point.

address these issues. I shall argue that this is indeed the case, although the content of the chapter is elusive and has been subject to a variety of different styles of interpretation.

Aristotle introduces his favoured case of man as a two-footed animal, and then writes:

if—as we say—one [presumably, animal] is matter and the other shape [presumably, being two-footed] and the one is potentiality, the other actuality, what is sought would no longer seem to be an insuperable problem (*aporia*). For, this is the same problem one would have if the definition of *cloak* were 'rounded bronze'. For, this name would be a sign for this definition, so that what is being sought is the cause of the bronze and the rounded being one. So the problem has gone away, because one is the *matter*, the other is the *shape*. What then is the cause of what is potentially F being actually F (in the case of things that come to be) besides what makes it so, the efficient cause? For, nothing other is the cause of what is potentially a sphere being actually a sphere; rather, this [viz. the cause] is what it is to be for each of them singly. (1045^a23-33)[40]

According to the explanation-involving model of definition, one would expect Aristotle to proceed as follows. If one considers the issue of unity using terms such as:

matter: shape

potentiality: actuality

there is no longer an insuperable problem, because one can see how to resolve it. The question is now in answerable form and we can discover what is sought: what makes it the case that (e.g.) potentiality and actuality are paired in such a way as to form a composite unity. The answer appears to be: because they have the same teleological goal which determines their essence. This goal, it appears, is intrinsic to the basic actuality (e.g. soul of a given kind), and at the same time determines the nature of the matter (body or animal), which is as it is for the sake of the goal.

Aristotle's claim marks a further step in the development of his

---

[40] On this reading, 'this' in 1045^a33 refers to *the cause* mentioned in $^a32$. Thus, both matter and form will share the same cause (e.g. the same goal), although not necessarily in precisely the same way. For, the goal might belong immediately to the form and only derivatively to the matter. If so, although they share the same goal, their essential natures may differ in some way. (On this point, I have been assisted by Lewis's note on my earlier formulation. See Lewis, 'Aristotle on the Unity of Substance', *PPQ* 76: 3/4 (1995), 260 n. 53, commenting on a less cautious claim in my paper.) On the dissolutionist view 'this' would refer not to the cause but to the fact of what is potentially a sphere being actually a sphere (viz. to there being a unified substance), which would give the essence of both actuality and potentiality as abstractions defined by their contribution to a unified substance.

teleological analysis of substances.[41] Had he simply followed the account sketched in Z.17 and H.2–3, he should have expanded talk of *shape* to include fundamental features of man (such as possession of the relevant soul). The shape, so understood, would determine the nature of the relevant matter, which is as it is for the sake of such a soul.[42] However, Aristotle makes the further move of introducing a goal intrinsic to the basic actuality (e.g. the soul) which makes that actuality what it is. There is, it appears, a goal which determines the nature of the actuality and of the required matter.[43] This goal is the explanatory basic feature at the centre of Aristotle's account. If the explanatory approach is to be developed in this way, Aristotle will need next to elucidate what this basic feature is.

There is, however, an opposed interpretation of this passage, which represents Aristotle as rejecting the explanation-involving account. It runs as follows.

If one invokes as basic notions:

matter: shape

potentiality: actuality

no further explanation of their unity is required, because no genuine problem remains. Nothing more could be said to explain the unity of a composite substance, precisely because these notions themselves are abstractions from that of a unified member of a kind.[44]

---

[41] This line of interpretation, sketched initially in my paper 'Matter and Form', has been developed further by Lewis in 'Aristotle on the Unity of Substance', *PPQ* 76 (1995), 222–65. While our approaches are similar, Lewis is more confident than I about the possibility of establishing the explanatory reading of Aristotle's project on the basis of H.6 alone.

[42] So understood, the proposition:

Soul of a given type belongs necessarily to body of type S.

would be explanatory bedrock, an immediate proposition (in the language of the *Analytics*).

[43] Aristotle did not need to make this further move to maintain the basic outline of the explanatory approach. That could have been defended while taking the actuality (and not its internal goal) as the relevant starting point. Aristotle may have introduced the relevant internal goal to illuminate the nature of the relevant actuality in a specifically teleological way. For discussion of similar cases, see my 'Aristotle: Ontology and Moral Reasoning', 135–40.

[44] Elements of the *dissolutionist* line of interpretation can be detected in claims such as:

potentiality and actuality are the same thing present together in that full activity which is nothing other than the manifestation of the one entity that both are' (L. A. Kosman, 'Substance, Being and *Energeia*', *OSAP* 2 (1984), 144)

or

Aristotle compares asking for an explanation of why *potentiality* and *actuality* are one with asking for an explanation of why anything is one. No answer is needed . . . because the

On this view, Aristotle, so far from attempting to perfect the explanatory approach in these chapters, is in fact abandoning it.

This alternative, dissolutionist, interpretation might be supported by a reading of the final lines of the chapter (1045^b17–23). These run as follows:

But—as has been said—the final matter and the shape are the same and one, the one potentially the other actually (*energeiai*: dative), so that it is similar to investigate:

What is the cause of one thing being F?

and

What is the cause of being one?

For, each individual thing is something, and what is potentially and what is actually are one in some sense. Therefore, there is no other cause (of it being one/being F) except that which brings it about that there is something which moves it from potentiality to actuality. Things that are without matter are, without qualification, essentially something one.

The dissolutionist interpreter may cede that the apparently explanatory question raised in 1045^b18–20 seems to be an important and sensible one: What is the cause of unity? However, she will conclude that these appearances are misleading, since in the final sentence Aristotle clearly says that there is no *other* cause of the unity of what is potentially F and what is actually F apart from the efficient cause. In her view, this means that if one excludes the efficient cause, there is no cause of unity at all. Rather, the unity of the composite substance is to be taken as basic and not in need of further explanation.

However, if the final sentence is interpreted in the way the dissolutionist interpreter suggests, it flatly contradicts the earlier passage (1045^a30 ff.) in which Aristotle makes the far more cautious claim that there is no cause of what is potentially F being actually F *except* the one essence of both. For, in the earlier passage, there may be a cause (other than the efficient one) of the relevant unity of the composite substance: (e.g.) the presence of a form, identified with the teleological goal, which determines the nature of the matter. The explanatory interpreter, by contrast, can avoid this inconsistency if he can show that the final sentences of H.6 mean only that (if one excludes the efficient cause) there is no cause of unity of substance

explanation of the thing is at the same time an explanation of its being one. (M. Burnyeat, *Notes on ETA and THETA* (Oxford Subfaculty of Philosophy, 1984), 44–5.)

However, neither Kosman nor the London Group opt wholeheartedly for the dissolutionist view. Other passages in these works suggest a somewhat different version of the nonexplanatory account, described below as the 'quick-fix' approach (see n. 59). Wilfred Sellars ('Aristotle's Metaphysics: An Interpretation', in *Philosophical Perspectives* (Springfield, 1967, 118)) appears to adopt the dissolutionist viewpoint without qualification.

distinct from the relevant actuality and potentiality (since these encapsulate all the causal features required to explain the unity of the composite substance). Can this explanation-involving interpretation of the final sentences of H.6 be sustained?

The argument in 1045^{b}18–22 is highly compressed, but (it appears) runs as follows:

(1) Each thing is one thing (*hen*) of a given kind (*ti*). (Premiss)

(2) The matter is the thing in potentiality, the form is the thing in actuality. (Premiss)

(3) It is similar to seek the cause of one thing being something and of it being one thing. (From (1) and (2))

(4) (3) follows from (1) and (2) since one thing *is something* because matter and form are joined as potentiality and actuality. But when matter and form are joined in this way there is *one* thing present.[45]

The key premiss is (2). In what way is the form *the thing in actuality*? According to the dissolutionist interpreter, this means that the form is the composite substance *seen as actuality*, while the matter is the composite substance *seen as potentiality*. On this interpretation, the notion of one composite substance is taken as basic. By contrast, the explanatory interpreter sees (2) as claiming that the form is *the thing in actuality*, because the thing (e.g. man) is to be identified (in strict use of H.2, 1043^{a}27 f.) with the *form* (as the man in actuality). On this view, the actuality is taken as basic and the matter is understood as potentially that actuality, where the latter is identified with the thing itself (i.e. the man).[46] Thus, the distinctive soul will be what makes man one thing and the thing it is. For, when matter and form stand to each other as potentiality and actuality, the actuality makes the composite what it is (e.g. man) and ensures that it is one thing. Thus, the actuality determines that the relevant matter is as it is.

Several considerations favour the explanatory interpretation of H.6. First, the questions raised in 1045^{b}18–20 appear to be genuine ones. Indeed, 'What is the cause of the unity of the composite?' is the very question which Aristotle had set himself in Z.17 and H.2–3. It would be surprising

---

[45] This case is immediately contrasted with that of objects which lack matter and are as such one without qualification (1045^{b}23). The latter group, which include (e.g.) forms, are mentioned here (as in 1045^{a}36–^{b}7) to distinguish them from things involving matter, which are (in the present context) Aristotle's main concern. Things without matter can be described as immediately one because they are free of the problems of unity which arise in discussion of enmattered things. For a somewhat contrasting view, see Verity Harte's 'Aristotle's *Metaphysics* H.6: A Dialectic with Platonism', *Phronesis* 41/3 (1996), 289–97.

[46] I am indebted to Michael Frede for advice on the interpretation of this sentence. For a somewhat contrasting view, see Theodore Scaltsas's discussion ('Substratum, Subject and Substance', *Ancient Philosophy* 5 (1985), 232–3).

if now, with no detailed preparation, the question was declared to be a pseudo one. Second, it does not seem that the theorists whose views are discussed in 1045ᵇ7–17 are asking a nonsensical or pseudo question. Rather they are raising a genuine difficulty (viz. that mooted in 1045ᵃ30–3) in a way which makes it 'aporetic', because (so formulated) it is difficult to resolve.[47] Once the question is correctly framed one can find a feature which explains the relevant unity: the common essence of the matter and form, which reveals the former as *potentially* F and the latter as *actually* F. For the form is the teleologically basic feature which explains why the matter is as it is.

In H.6, according to the explanatory interpreter, Aristotle introduces the notion of actuality as part of his explanation of the unity of a composite substance. So understood, matter and form will be shown to be unified because both are essentially directed to the same intrinsic goal. Indeed, talk of actuality and potentiality indicates (on this account) the ontology required to make these claims perspicuous.[48] If so, Aristotle's task in *Metaphysics* Θ will be to show how these notions can be used for this purpose, and to make clear the idea of the intrinsic goal of the relevant actuality.

If Aristotle tackles these issues in *Metaphysics* Θ, he will be following (and deepening) the explanatory approach. By contrast, if he is a dissolutionist, his strategy in *Metaphysics* Θ will be very different. For, then he will conclude at the end of H that:

There is no difficulty in seeing how:

potentiality: actuality

matter: form

are unified to form a unified composite substance. For, these notions are themselves abstractions from the more basic notion of a unified substance. Indeed, actuality is just that which together with potentiality yields a substance of this type.

If so, this is, effectively, the end of his enquiry, since he has shown that the issue of unity is a pseudo question. All he can do in *Metaphysics* Θ is confirm (once again) that there is no genuine issue of unity.

[47] That is, so formulated, the question produces perplexity. This might be because, so formulated, it leads to two conflicting answers, each of which has something to be said for it (*Top.* Z.6, 145ᵇ17 ff.). There is no requirement that *aporiai* can only be resolved by showing that there is no genuine question to answer. Indeed, usually, when there are *aporiai* there are genuine issues to resolve. See, e.g., the use of *aporiai* in the discussion of *acrasia* (*NE/EE* H.1, 1145ᵇ3 f., 21 f., 1146ᵇ6–8).

[48] This is not to say that the ontology is solely defined in terms of the relevant goal as 'whatever plays a given role A' in an appropriate structure. There is more to talk of actuality than is determined in this way.

Which of these routes does Aristotle follow in *Metaphysics* Θ? I shall argue, in the next Section, that he goes on there to develop the explanatory approach in ways required to fill the gaps left in H.6. If this is correct, Aristotle pursues the explanatory account from Z.17 to the end of Θ.

11.5 THE EXPLANATORY APPROACH CONCLUDED: Θ.6–10*

It might initially look as if Aristotle had abandoned his explanation-involving strategy in Θ.6–10. Indeed, in 1048^{b}7–9 some passages might suggest that he has finally opted for the alternative dissolutionist approach. Thus, he writes, in possibly the most disappointing sentence in the whole of the *Metaphysics*:

all things are not said to exist actually in the same way, but only by analogy . . . for the relation is either that of process to potentiality or substance [*ousia*] to some specific matter.

In H.6 Aristotle appeared to introduce talk of actuality and potentiality to clarify the relation between matter and form in a compound substance. But now it looks as if he is employing the latter to illuminate the former. The relevant potentiality (in a unified substance) is one which stands to its actuality as matter stands to its composite (e.g. the statue of Hermes (1048^{a}30–3, ^{b}2–5)). If so, the notion of the unity of a composite substance will be the basic one. If so, both matter and form will be conceived as abstractions from the notion of a unified composite. No account will be given of either except in terms of its role in a unified substance. If this is correct, Aristotle has abandoned the explanatory approach to the definition of substance.

Has Aristotle really discarded his explanatory strategy? If he is to maintain it, he must show how talk of *potentiality* and *actuality* can render perspicuous the unity of a composite substance. Also, he must elucidate the idea of an intrinsic goal of the actuality introduced in H.6. Is he doing either or both of these in Θ.6–10?

The analogy between the potentialities and actualities involved in processes and in substances holds the key to Aristotle's discussion. For our purposes, there are two crucial questions. What is the basis for the analogy? And, why is it merely an analogy? Aristotle's answers to these two questions are (I shall suggest) the ones required by the explanatory approach to definition.

Consider the case of processes. The relevant potentiality will be defined as one for a given type of process: (e.g.) the potentiality to be made into a house.[49] The resulting type of process will be the one it is because of its goal: the house being built. If processes differ in goals, they will be numerically distinct even if they always co-occur.[50] Since the process is defined by its goal (end point), the potentiality is essentially the potentiality to reach that end point. Here, the end point or goal defines the nature both of the process (to move towards that end point) and of the relevant potentiality. In a favoured Aristotelian example, house-building is defined as the process it is by its goal (viz. the house being built), and the potentiality thus exercised is defined as the potential to achieve this goal (viz. to build a house).

If substance is to be understood analogously, there should be a goal which reveals both its nature (conceived as actuality) and the relevant potentiality (its matter). Thus, both actuality and potentiality will be defined (directly or indirectly) in terms of the goal of the actuality (as suggested in H.6, 1045^{a}31–3). Indeed, it is because actualities and potentialities can be perspicuously represented in this way that they are introduced as the entities required in Aristotle's teleological account of substance.

Does Aristotle sustain the analogy between substances and processes in this way? Does the relevant actuality have an appropriate internal goal? There are reasons for returning an affirmative answer to both questions.

(1) In the case of processes, the goal is its end point. By contrast, in the case of substances (as in that of activities) the goal is immanent (1048^{b}21–3). Thus, the goal of being a house is realized when there is a house (1050^{a}26 f.). Once this goal has been achieved, a house can persist for a long period. By contrast, in the case of processes, once the goal has been realized, the relevant process is over. As Aristotle hastens to explain, the goals are of a different type in the two cases (1048^{a}18–36). This is why

---

[49] See *Phys.* Γ.1, 201^{a}16–18. I have defended this account elsewhere (*Aristotle's Philosophy of Action*, 19–27). For a contrasting account, see Mary Louise Gill's discussion (*Aristotle on Substance*, 186–94). My view rests on construing the relevant capacities for change as essentially *dynamic* capacities of substances. Others, by contrast, understand Aristotle to attempt to account for processes without taking such dynamic capacities as basic. Philosophical discussion of this issue requires study of the adequacy of definitions of change which do not rely on the presence of dynamic capacities (e.g. Can such accounts separate changes from a succession of distinct states, or from 'Cambridge', relational, alterations which are not genuine changes?). These issues raise exegetical problems concerning Aristotle's answers to Zeno's paradoxes of change. In my view, Aristotle employed dynamic properties of substances to answer Zeno's challenge, and this is why he accepted capacities for changes as basic. But a full defence of this suggestion is a major, and separate, undertaking.

[50] An example of this is, I believe, teaching and learning (*Phys.* Γ.3, 202^{b}5–22), which differ in goals (202^{a}21–4). See my discussion of this (*Aristotle's Philosophy of Action*, 11 ff.).

processes essentially *unfold* through time, while substances (like activities) *endure*. This difference between them is a result of a difference in the relevant types of goal.

(2) The internal goal in the case of the actuality of the soul is life (1050^a35 ff.). If the soul is conceived as the being which actually possesses the capacity for life, its goal is life. For, it is because its goal is life that the relevant actuality (being actually capable of life) is as it is. Indeed, the term 'actuality' can be predicated of the internal goal (e.g. life) or that which is intrinsically directed to that goal (e.g. the soul) ($1050^a21–3$).[51] Once we conceive of form as actuality (and matter as potentiality), we can see how both of them are what they are in virtue of being appropriately connected with this goal.[52] In this way Aristotle can sustain the analogy with processes. For, there too the relevant goal determines both the actuality and the potentiality.

While Aristotle defends the analogy between substance and process in this way, he also points out areas of disanalogy.

(3) The relevant potentialities and actualities are related in different ways in the two cases. (This is discussed in Θ.8.) Since the actuality in the case of substance does not occur in another thing or in itself as another thing ($1049^b5–8$), it cannot be related to its potentiality in the same way as an active potentiality is related to a passive one in the case of processes.[53] For, in the case of substances, the relevant interaction cannot involve efficient causation as may occur between distinct subjects of change.[54] For, the latter always operate in another object or in themselves considered as another object (e.g. a doctor healing himself (*Phys.* B.8, 199^b31, *Meta.* Δ.12, $1019^a17–18$). Thus, there must be an important difference between the type of explanation appropriate in these distinct cases.

(4) The other *relata* (capacity for change: matter) differ in ways which reflect the difference in types of goal in the two cases. In the case of persisting substances, the relevant capacity of the matter is *to be* a man and not *to become* a man. In many cases, the capacity to become an F will be lost when one is an F (e.g. a man). Once one is a fully-fledged man, one can no longer become what one already is (while still remaining that thing). This is precisely how the capacities essentially involved in *being* and

---

[51] I discuss these issues more fully in my paper 'Aristotle: Ontology and Moral Reasoning', 135–9.

[52] In *De An.* Aristotle appears to take this proposal further. Thus, while in *De An.* B.1 the soul is taken as the actual capacity for life in a body of a given type ($412^a19–21$, $412^b15–17$), in B.2 it is more precisely identified with that in virtue of which we are alive (in the immediate sense, viz. of having the relevant capacity for life (414^a13 ff.)). In B.1 the soul is taken as form *qua* actual capacity, but in B.2 as that in virtue of which that capacity is what it is. It is in the latter way that (e.g.) life can be understood as what makes the soul what it is. More detailed discussion of these *De Anima* passages must await another occasion.

[53] This seems clear at *Meta.* Θ.8, $1050^a21–3$, where Aristotle identifies the goal with the actuality.   [54] For a contrasting view, see Gill's, *Aristotle on Substance*, 213 ff.

becoming differ.[55] So, the type of potentiality which matter is will differ from the potentiality to become an F (which capacity belongs as such to a subject of change).[56] Matter will rather be essentially the potentiality to be an F.

Aristotle in Θ.6–8 uses these points to clarify the distinctive types of potentiality and actuality present in composite substances. Since his strategy depends on pointing to their distinctive roles in explanation, he is (it appears) carrying forward the explanatory approach to definition initiated in Z.17 and H. Thus, in 1048^b7–9 cited above, he should be seen as claiming that there is a unified substance when (and only when) there is a potentiality of type (2) tied to an actuality of type (1) in virtue of their sharing one teleological goal. If so, actuality and potentiality are the basic elements in Aristotle's ontology precisely because they are what is

---

[55] See *Phys.* 201^b10–12, 28–9, 202^a1. In these texts, the capacity to be a house appears to be the capacity to be, in certain conditions, arranged so as to protect belongings. This capacity is distinct from the capacity to become a house under the exercise of the builder's skill, as the conditions for its exercise are different. The one continues as long as the house survives, the other only as long as the builder builds. I have defended this interpretation elsewhere (*Aristotle's Philosophy of Action*, 19–21). For a contrasting view, see Michael Frede's discussion (in *Unity, Identity and Explanation*, 173 ff.). He suggests that something retains the ability to be an F precisely as long as it satisfies the conditions which made it initially appropriate material to be turned into an F. This may well be true in cases like houses (which Frede discusses), where the matter (i.e. bricks) remains relatively unchanged throughout the process of building and after the house is built. But it does not apply (in any obvious way) to cases where the matter alters through a developmental process, and is different at the end from at the beginning (e.g. the matter of a man); for, the matter of the developed man has lost the ability to *become* a man. This is one reason for regarding with some scepticism Frede's claim that the ability to be an F is the same as the ability to become an F, 'taken in a given way' (*Unity, Identity and Explanation*, 186). (This claim is separable from Frede's central contention that the notion of potentiality to be an F is different from the notion of power to change or be changed (*Unity, Identity and Explanation* 187).) However, it might be replied that, although the ability to become F is lost in some cases when one is actually F, it remains true that the ability to become F is one essential part of the ability to be F: viz. the ability to be F at some low level of actuality. Discussion of this point would take us far outside the present study. There is reason to doubt, however, that Aristotle commits himself to this view in these sections of the *Metaphysics*.

[56] This seems clear in Aristotle's discussion of processes (*Phys.* Γ.1, 201^a27–^b5), where bricks have the potential both *to become* and to be a house. In the *Metaphysics*, bricks are used as examples of the matter (Θ.7, 1049^a9–11, see H.2, 1043^a7–9) of the house. So, those things which are the *matter* of a house have at some point the potential *to become* a house. (For this view of the role of bricks in processes, see my *Aristotle's Philosophy of Action*, 19–20.) This does not require Aristotle to identify the potentiality to be an F with the potentiality to become an F, or to claim that it is *qua* the matter of an F that bricks have the potentiality to become an F (even though bricks could not possess the potential to be an F unless they also possessed the potentiality to become an F). Indeed, Aristotle appears to focus in the opening sections of Θ.7 (1048^b37–1049^a18) on the question of *when* something *first* has the potential to be an F, and does not attempt the more ambitious project of analysing this potential in terms of the potential to become an F (or vice versa). (Note the temporal notions: 'when' (48^b36), 'any time' (49^a1), 'already' (49^a2, 16).) The issues here are complex, and require deeper analysis. But that lies outside the scope of the present project.

needed to account (in an explanatory way) for the unity of a composite substance.

There is one further aspect of the explanatory approach to be considered. In Aristotle's account, the relevant actuality is a simple, indivisible, entity specific to the relevant kind which explains the presence of the other *differentiae* of its matter. But what kind of simple entity is involved in talk of (e.g.) immediates (1045^b2–4), simples (1041^b9–11), or incomposites (1043^b35)? If he is following the explanatory approach, the relevant actuality will be central to the relevant answer to the 'Why?' question. The relevant simple incomposite feature will be one which explains all the other relevant features of the composite. Indeed, the simplicity in question need amount to no more than the requirement that there be one basic cause or starting point (as in *Post. An.* B.9, 93^b21–2), which does not permit of further causal analysis. The simplicity at issue need be no more demanding than this.[57]

11.6 SUBSTANCE AND DEFINITION

I have sketched an account in which explanation is central to Aristotle's strategy for defining unified composite substances. If this sketch is correct, he is attempting to apply to this case the style of definition developed for *eclipse* and *thunder* in the *Analytics*. If so, his answer to the 'What is F?' question will be given by invoking the basic feature in a teleological explanation of why the other genuine features of F are as they are. In the case of man, the 'What is F?' and the relevant 'Why?' question will both be answered by reference to man's form: his soul. This plays a crucial explanatory role. It is because the soul is as it is that man is a two-legged animal with its distinctive shape. Matter of the relevant type is required if we are to fulfil our distinctive soul functions. Thus, Aristotle will introduce form and matter (and later actuality and potentiality) in the *Metaphysics* as the conceptual resources needed to provide the metaphysical basis for his *Analytics* style of explanation-involving definition. Further, with these resources, he can explain the unity of a composite substance on the basis of the explanatory interconnections he discerns between matter and form (understood as a simple unity).[58]

---

[57] On this issue, see Harte's 'Aristotle's *Metaphysics* H.6', 276–304.

[58] If Aristotle had attempted to explain the particularity of particular substances, he would have required particular forms in addition to the general ones discussed here. At that stage, a further question is pressing: Is he justified in using particular forms to explain particularity? If Aristotle is following either of these versions of the explanatory approach, he will not be concerned (in the first instance) to answer the epistemological question of how we identify or re-identify substances. Nor will he be concerned to address the modern metaphysi-

In this account, Aristotle's approach to definition depends (in *Metaphysics* Z, H, and Θ, as in the *Analytics*) on the view that the same answer should be given to the questions 'What is F?' and 'Why is F as it is?' Indeed, if the argument of Sections 11.3–11.5 is correct, definition by matter and form is a special case of the general account of definition developed in the *Analytics*. It differs only in introducing the concepts of matter and form (drawn from Aristotle's physical writings) to specify the terms required in an *Analytics* style of (teleology-involving) definition of composite substances. Aristotle does not, as LeBlond suggested, introduce at this point a further separate form of definition (over and above definition by causal basis and definition by genus and species).[59] Properly understood, these are all instances of one general, explanation-involving, form of definition which permeates *Analytics* and *Metaphysics* Z, H, and Θ alike.

If we see Aristotle as following this explanatory approach to definition, we gain further insight into the basic nature of form. So understood, it is the answer to the question 'What is this substance?' while at the same time being a fundamental feature in a teleological account of why the substance is as it is. Since it is a major claim that there is one thing that can play both these roles, Aristotle needed to develop an account of form which showed how it could play both these roles simultaneously.

This approach puts constraints on the notion of form. Forms, so understood, have to be capable of playing a certain role both in teleological explanation and in definition. For example, the form of man could not be the simple indefinable Man*, if the latter were not capable of playing the required role in the explanation of why man is two-footed that (e.g.) being rational does. Thus, even if it is true that he takes form to be (in some sense) a 'basic', 'primitive', or 'undefined' element,[60] its nature is tightly

cal question of how we can construct the diachronic unity of a substance from a collection of synchronic unities. While he is taking the unity of a composite as analysable, it is to be analysed in terms of simpler diachronic unities and not synchronic ones. The explanatory approach (as he defines it) is not to be assimilated to either of these modern projects.

[59] LeBlond made this suggestion in 'Definition in Aristotle', 63–79. See also Ch. 10 Sect. 10.1.

[60] These phrases are used by A. Code and J. Moravcsik ('Explaining Various Forms, of Living', in M. Nussbaum and A. O. Rorty (eds.), *Essays on Aristotle's De Anima* (Oxford, 1992), 129–44) in rejecting the functionalist interpretation of Aristotle (which I also reject). They proceed, however, as if the only alternative open to one who rejects the functionalist view is to represent Aristotle as treating 'forms' as undefined primitives, about which (to judge by their article) little, if anything, can be said. (Indeed, it is not clear how their forms differ from the Platonic unanalysable simples Aristotle rejects in Z.17, 1041[a]18 ff.) In effect, Code and Moravcsik fail to see the possibility of the distinctive mid-position which (in my view) Aristotle actually adopted. For, if I am right (see 'Aristotle on Hypothetical Necessity and Irreducibility', *PPQ* 68 (1988), 1–54), the relevant forms, actualities, etc. cannot be defined in abstraction from their role in teleological explanation (even though they cannot be defined simply as teleological causes). Code and Moravcsik miss the possibility of a viable Aristotelian mid-position between functionalism (of a suitably restrained form) and some form of dualism or vitalism.

constrained by the demand that it play a given role in explaining why the substance as a whole is as it is.

The constraints on definition (introduced in Z.4–12) are incapable by themselves of making fully determinate the relevant notion of form. As we saw above, they need to be supplemented by explanatory concerns in Z.17 and beyond. Taken together, they rule out the possibility of defining form merely as (e.g.) 'whatever occupies a given explanatory role'. For, what is sought is a feature which answers the 'What is F?' question by accounting for the presence of the ability to play a given explanatory role. Only then will the definition make the whole nature of the kind fully transparent. There can be no account of form (as was to be expected in the light of the interdependency thesis) which renders it incapable of playing both the required definitional and explanatory roles.[61]

The distinctive nature of this interpretation may become clearer if it is compared with two other accounts that have gained currency in recent years. One might be termed (as above) the dissolutionist approach, the second (perhaps somewhat pejoratively) the 'quick-fix' strategy.[62] Both reject the view that the theory of definition (in the case of substance) requires any support from the theory of explanation.

According to the dissolutionist, the starting point for metaphysical investigation is the unity of a persisting composite substance (whether Socrates or man) and not the form. In this account, matter (potentiality) and form (actuality) are (interconnected) abstractions derived from the basic notion of one unified substance. If so, there is no real question about the unity of the composite. It is taken for granted at the outset.[63]

A partial analogy may help to make the dissolutionist account clearer. In it, unified composite substances are analogous to sentences when taken (as for example by Frege) as the basic units in semantic theory. There, a predicate is that which together with a subject yields a sentence, while a subject is that which together with a predicate yields a sentence. It is a mistake to try to explain the unity of a sentence in terms of an independently specified type of interconnection between subject and predicate (for

---

[61] Aristotle's frequent comparison of form with shape is particularly appropriate in this regard (see, e.g., *Meta.* H.6, 1045^{a}28–9). For, the geometrical features of shape, such as we see in looking at shaped objects, serve to explain why objects with those shapes are apt to behave in certain ways. Thus, it is because objects are round that they roll. Their roundness does not merely consist in their ability to roll. What is being sought in the case of form is a feature which, like roundness, explains why objects with that form are disposed to act in certain ways. For some discussion of this issue, with reference to Aristotle's account of desire, see my *Aristotle's Philosophy of Action*, 238–40.

[62] Sometimes it is unclear whether a given author is advocating the 'quick-fix' or the dissolutionist viewpoint. See n. 44 and the passages cited there. I am indebted at this point to conversations with Pantazis Tselemanis.

[63] This parallels the dissolutionist reading of H.6 discussed above.

the relevant interconnection is itself dependent on the unity of the sentence).[64] It would be a similar mistake (according to this view) to attempt to explain the unity of a composite substance by means of an independently specified type of connection between matter and form. For the relevant *relata* are all abstractions from the basic notion of one composite (e.g. the sentence).[65]

If I am correct, Aristotle has serious objections to the dissolutionist project. First, the dissolutionist, in giving up the idea of form as the starting point for explanation, severs the connections between the answers to the 'What is F?' question and to the relevant 'Why?' question. If so, he is forced to surrender the constraints on definition which flow from the interconnections between definition and explanation (on which, if Sections 11.2–11.5 are accepted, the central argument of the *Metaphysics* turns). If so, he leaves the relevant notion of definition unconstrained. For, if form is not understood as what explains the relevant composite and its matter, what makes some features of the composite substance its form? Indeed, it seems as if (on this view) it is we who decide which of the range of possible *abstracta* is to be the form.[66]

Similar objections apply to the 'quick-fix' interpretation. In this account (unlike the dissolutionist's), *actuality* and *potentiality* are introduced independently of the notion of the unity of a composite substance, but without any further elucidation. It is claimed that, once they are introduced, one can see immediately that their interconnection will give rise to the appropriate type of unity.

This interpretation, however, fails to offer a perspicuous account of the type of unity in question. It merely introduces two unanalysed terms ('the correct *relata*'), and says that when they are *correctly related* there is the appropriate type of unity. But this suggestion appears empty until we know (at least) what either the 'correct *relata*' or 'the correct relation' is. Indeed, nothing prevents form (so understood) from being the simple unanalysable (Platonic) man*. Aristotle's notion of form must be more constrained than this.

---

[64] This analogy is, of course, only a partial one. Fregean subjects and predicates are not, unlike Aristotle's matter and form, in some way identical with one another. The latter pair are more closely related than the former.

[65] This amounts to a fuller statement of what is termed above (see n. 44) the dissolutionist viewpoint.

[66] The form of the composite is, in important respects, like a primary term in *Analytics* B.19. Both define the relevant matter which falls under them, and both explain why that matter is as it is. Primary terms define the *subject matter* in their genus, while forms define *the matter* which is part of the relevant composite. Further, the primary terms in a genus (like the point, unit, or dyad) are the basis for explaining why the derived elements in the genus are as they are. Similarly, the form explains why the matter (and composite) are as they are. I am indebted at this point to conversation with Michael Frede.

The 'quick-fixer' may reply that the 'correct *relata*' in the case of composite substances are analogues of potentiality and actuality in the case of processes. But what now is the basis of this analogy? Deprived of all connection with teleological explanation, the notions of form and actuality (so understood) appear unconstrained and obscure. For, they no longer figure as the central planks in an account of the unity of the composite anchored in an explanation of why the latter is as it is. Indeed, it is hard to see why anyone should believe that (so understood) they pick out features of reality.

11.7 CONCLUSIONS AND GAPS

In this Chapter, I have suggested that Aristotle's approach to the definition of composite substances in the central books of the *Metaphysics* follows the explanation-involving pattern set in the *Analytics*. This model can apply to substances and teleologically defined processes as well as to the efficient causal processes (like thunder and eclipse) discussed in the *Analytics*. (It would be a major task to seek to defend the sketch I have given on a line-by-line commentary basis. It would be a further major project to investigate whether this model also applies, in Aristotle's view, to numbers or qualities. Both tasks lie outside the scope of this work.)

Many questions about the *Metaphysics*, even ones closely related to our present theme, remain undiscussed. Little has been said about the role of matter in Aristotle's theory,[67] still less about the relation between the account of substance proposed in the central books and that offered in

---

[67] In *Meta.* Z.17, H, and Θ.6–9, Aristotle's positive remarks about matter are extremely cautious, and could (I suspect) be interpreted consistently with a variety of different positions. For one account, see my 'Aristotle on Hypothetical Necessity'. An alternative interpretation has been proposed (the so-called *disappearance view*) in which there is no matter present at all in the composite save as potentiality. In general, Aristotle is very careful in the central books of the *Metaphysics* not to commit himself to views beyond those strictly required for the success of his basic project. Thus, he restricts himself (I have argued) to showing how to understand substances within the explanatory style of definition developed in the *Analytics*. His reluctance to go further than is needed for his limited goal has generated two major exegetical debates. In the area of present discussion, there are two examples of lacunae of this type.

(a) Does he regard general or particular forms as prior (and in what ways)? (See Sect. 11.3.)

(b) Does he regard the capacity to become F as an element in the capacity to be F? (See n. 49.)

While some of these questions may be answered by Aristotle elsewhere, his discussion in the central books of the *Metaphysics* appears to leave them (probably designedly) open.

Metaphysics Λ.[68] These issues raise difficult and important questions about Aristotle's views on substance and definition, which cannot be considered here.

[68] For some remarks on this issue, see my paper on Λ.2 in '*Metaphysics* Λ.2: *Matter and Change*' in M. Frede and D. Charles (eds.), *Symposium Aristotelicum* (Oxford, 2000), forthcoming.

12

Biology, Classification, and Essence

12.1 INTRODUCTION

In the preceding Chapters, I have argued that Aristotle developed *one*, explanation-involving, account of definition. The interdependency between his account of the practices of definition and of explanation, uncovered in Chapters 8 and 9, rests on two claims:

(A) At the centre of each definition there is reference to one causally basic feature which explains the presence of other necessary features of the phenomenon.

(B) The definition is completed by the addition of reference to differentiating features, themselves parts of the nature of the phenomenon, whose presence is explained by the basic causal feature specified in (A).

These two claims provide the basis in the *Analytics* for an integrated approach to definition and classification. In the *Metaphysics* both play a role in Aristotle's account of definition and of essence. Are they also at work in his biological writings?

If Aristotle remains committed to (A) in his biological studies, he will look for definitions which refer to one causally basic feature of the required type.[1] If he adheres to (B), he will attempt to uncover a system of *differentiae* which captures parts of the nature of the relevant kinds in the way suggested above.[2] More precisely, he will look for *differentiae* which:

(a*) fit into a general and non-*ad hoc* procedure for deriving genuine kinds from other relevant kinds

and

(b*) are themselves explained by the basic underlying feature of the kind.[3]

Does Aristotle do either? In the *Analytics* Aristotle gives no example of a full definition of an animal kind. Nor does he point to any empirical science

---

[1] See Ch. 8 Sect. 8.2.
[2] For the outline of this strategy, see Ch. 10 Sect. 10.4.   [3] See Ch. 9 Sect. 9.4.

which can be ordered within a genus-*differentia* structure of the type he proposes. While he gives biological examples, he does not show how the science (as a whole) can correspond (even roughly) to the model of the *Analytics*. Still less does he establish that it does so. Are these gaps filled in the biological works? Or does Aristotle give up the *Analytics* account of definition and classification when confronted by the complexities of real science?

Aristotle's remarks in his initial discussion of biological classification in *De Partibus Animalium* A.2–3 render doubtful his continued adherence to claim (2). He had suggested in the *Metaphysics* that there should be *one differentia* which marked out the species (cf. Z.12, 1038^a25 f.), and implied the presence of all the rest.[4] But now he prefers an alternative in which correct division is by multiple *differentiae* (642^b21, 643^b9), applied to the genus simultaneously. It is not immediately apparent how simultaneous *differentiae* of this type are to fit into the *Analytics* model, with its step-by-step priority relations (as marked out in *Post. An.* B.13).[5]

Does Aristotle still adhere to (A)? In the *Metaphysics* (as was argued in the last Chapter) he developed a teleological account of the internal structure of composite substances, in which the essence is the single basic teleological cause of the substance being as it is. Do biological kinds correspond to this model? If they do not, his methods for establishing the unity of kinds (and substances *qua* members of kinds) will be in danger of collapse.

These two issues raise further questions about Stages 2 and 3 of the three-stage view, as presented above.[6] For, they bring into sharp focus two problems:

(1) What is required (at Stage 2) to establish the existence of a kind?

(2) Are there in the biological domain essences of the type required by Stage 3 of the *Analytics* model? Did Aristotle think there were?

Did Aristotle succeed in classifying biological kinds and uncovering their essences in the ways proposed in the *Analytics*? Did he develop that

---

[4] In the *Analytics* discussion of man (B.5, 92^a1 ff.), Aristotle mentions as possible *differentiae* mortal, two-footed, wingless, which appear to fall in different division trees. His problem is to say what unifies the different *differentiae* in distinct division trees. This could not be resolved by noting (as Aristotle does in *Meta.* Z.12) that in each separate division tree there is no need to represent intermediate stages (such as footed, in a tree which ends with two-footed). In this respect, *Meta.* Z.12 does not face the relevant issue of unity as squarely as *Post. An.* B.5 or *PA* A.2–3 do. This may be (as suggested in the previous Chapter) because *Meta.* Z.12 is only a first step in the *Metaphysics* towards resolving these issues, and the major advances are made in *Meta.* Z.17, H, and parts of Θ.

[5] See Ch. 9 Sect. 9.4. In the *Analytics* one had (in the case of three) the following *differentiae*: odd, prime and prime*. Even if the latter formed one *differentia*, they are posterior to the first *differentia*. Not all are simultaneous.   [6] See Chs. 2, 3, 7, and 8 above.

general framework further and make it more precise? Or, alternatively, did he surrender the whole project, and despair of maintaining in this area the paradigm of definition and classification to which he is committed in the *Analytics*?

I shall argue that some parts of the biological writings constitute a substantial vindication of ideas developed in the *Analytics* (and *Metaphysics*), but that others expose certain aspects of that model as deeply problematic. The route to classifying and establishing the existence of biological kinds can be seen as Aristotle's development of the account given in the *Analytics*. But his account of what is involved in establishing the unity of a kind involves a major modification of his *Analytics* model of definition. It is no exaggeration to say that the study of biological kinds precipitated a crisis in Aristotle's thinking about definition. Nor was it one which he could easily or painlessly resolve. Indeed, it is not immediately clear that he succeeded in resolving it all.

12.2 DIFFERENTIATION OF KINDS (1): *DE PARTIBUS ANIMALIUM*

In *De Partibus Animalium* A.4 Aristotle considers which method is to be used in describing the properties of genera and species. One method would require us to study each indivisible species separately ($644^{a}29$–$644^{b}1$). Aristotle rejects this on the basis that it is 'long-winded', forcing us to mention the common attributes of many species time and time again. He continues:

So, perhaps the right procedure is this: [a] so far as concerns the attributes of those groups (genera) which have been correctly marked off by common usage— *groups which possess one common nature apiece and contain in themselves species not far removed from one another* [my emphasis] (I mean birds, fishes, and any other group which though it lacks a name yet contains species generically similar)—to describe the common attributes of the group all together; and [b] with regard to those animals which are not covered by this, to describe the attributes of each by themselves; e.g. those of man, and of any other such species. ($644^{b}1$–7)

The passage contains the following thought. Certain genera have been correctly marked out by common usage: those that (i) possess *one common nature*, and (ii) contain species not far removed from one another. It appears that there will be one genus if and only if it contains (i) a distinctive *common nature* and (ii) species not far removed from one another.

This passage, however, is elusive. It does not say what is to count as one common nature of the appropriate type. Nor does it determine when species are not far removed from one another. Aristotle does state that:

it is practically by *resemblance* of the shape of their parts, or of their whole body, that the groups are marked off from one another—as groups of birds, fishes, cephalopods, testacea (644^{b}7–11)

and notes further that within these groups (*genera*) the parts differ only by 'the more or the less', by being (for example) larger or smaller, softer or harder (644^{b}13–16). But these remarks also are vague. It is not clear whether resemblance in shape of parts *constitutes* (in the central cases) sameness in nature, or whether it is rather that members of the same genus, marked out on different criteria, do in fact generally have similarly shaped parts.

Nor are Aristotle's remarks elsewhere on this topic in *De Partibus Animalium* free from obscurity. He writes in A.2 that the name 'bird' is given to one type of *likeness*, 'fish' to another (642^{b}14–16), and in A.3 that birds are marked out from fish by many *differentiae* (643^{b}12–14). But it is not clear whether he is concerned here with likeness in any feature whatsoever, or only in some favoured or more basic set of features (and, if so, which), or with likeness overall. Do all likenesses count equally, or only some? The passage remains unclear.

At the end of *De Partibus Animalium* A.5 Aristotle notes that the parts of the body 'are for the sake of some action' (645^{b}16–17) and exist for the sake of their natural function (^{b}19–20). Relevant actions include generation, growth, copulation, waking, sleep, locomotion (645^{b}33 ff.). Do these functions define similarity and difference in parts of animals independently of their shape? If so, does Aristotle propose (as a further thesis) that if animal parts serve the same function, they will resemble each other in shape? Or does he construe shape as definitionally basic, and hold as a further thesis that if animal parts resemble one another in shape, they tend to have the same function?[7][8]

In *De Partibus Animalium* A.5 Aristotle appears to take actions to be definitionally prior to the organs (or instruments) which perform the actions. For he writes:

---

[7] Aristotle notes that within such groups the parts of animals differ 'rather in terms of their bodily qualities' (644^{b}13), and not by analogy. But this leaves it unclear whether, within one group, the relevant parts are *fundamentally* similar in their bodily qualities (e.g. size, shape, etc.), or in terms of their possessing some other feature (e.g. having the same function).

[8] Similar remarks apply to *HA* A.1 (486^{a}22–5), where Aristotle again states 'of those whose genus is the same, that they differ by the more and the less'. These remarks are clarified (in this context) by Aristotle's actual method for distinguishing genera in *HA* A.3–6 (see below).

When actions are for different goals, the organs differ in the same way as the actions. Similarly, if one action is prior to another, the part to which it belongs will be prior. ($645^{b}28$–32)

If priority between actions determines priority between organs, this is (presumably) because actions are definitionally prior to organs. Indeed, to regard organs as instruments (as he does in $645^{b}15$–17) indicates that their goal or purpose is constitutive of their identity, and that any similarity in shape is secondary. Thus, what makes an axe what it is is the purpose for which it is designed. This will be so even if some are more like hammers in shape and size than other axes ($645^{b}18$ f.). All axes, no matter what their shape, will differ by the more and the less provided that they fulfil the same general function. Similarly, animal parts in different species will differ by the more and the less provided that they too fulfil the same general function. Thus, feathers in birds will differ only by the more and the less because they all play a similar role in the overall activities of birds (its complex action ($645^{b}17$), involving assisting flight, protecting the animal, etc.) in somewhat different ways.

This provides us with a route to understand Aristotle's remarks at the beginning of *De Partibus Animalium* A.4:

> While groups that differ only by excess (the more and the less) are placed in one group, those that are only similar by analogy are placed in different groups. I mean, bird differs from bird by the more and the less, as one bird's feathers are long, another's short, while birds and fish are similar only by analogy (for the bird, feathers, for the fish, scales). ($644^{a}16$–22)

So interpreted, birds will differ from each other by the more and the less because they act in the same way, even though their organs differ in shape. By contrast, birds will differ from fish because they have different characteristic actions, and their parts can be similar only by analogy. Thus, parts will be similar only by analogy even if they are identical or very similar as regards shape ($644^{a}24$ f.), provided that they play roles in different characteristic actions (e.g. the legs of birds and humans, or blood in different genera of animals).

If this is correct, in *De Partibus Animalium* A.4 Aristotle is not beginning with a non-theoretical idea of similarity in shape and deducing from it similarity in genus (as the first lines might suggest). For, birds (and birds' feathers) will differ from each other only by the more and the less because they are birds and feathers, items marked out in terms which depend on their possessing distinctive characteristic actions. Several features favour this view. First, it explains why Aristotle can allow that parts which are similar in shape are analogously related ($644^{a}24$ f.), when they belong to different species. Second, it explains why in some cases difference in shape indicates difference in organ, while in others the organ is the same and differs only in the more and the less ($643^{a}1$–3). In the former, but not the latter, the organs differ because they fulfil differing activities. Had Aristotle employed shape as the criterion for sameness/difference of an organ, he would have divided kinds in ways which do not respect these relevant, indeed essential, features (643^{a}27–9; cf.642^{b}12–20).

These passages suggest that Aristotle is relying on a theory of the nature of a genus, in which similarity in characteristic activity plays the central role. But the theory is not spelled out in these passages, since Aristotle does not say which actions play this role, or whether features other than characteristic activity can be equally central in genus determination. To this extent, the idea of a common nature is left indeterminate. Similarly, his remark that the first task of the biological writings is to describe the properties which belong *per se* to each group of animals (A.5, 645^{b}1–3) remains indeterminate because he has not precisely defined the groups involved. In the language of *Posterior Analytics* B.13, he needs to set out more precisely the appropriate differentiating characteristics which separate different groups of animals.

Aristotle refers, at the beginning of *De Partibus Animalium* B.1, to the *Historia Animalium* (646^{a}8–10). And it is there that he focuses most insistently on these issues and develops his own views most fully. He writes in *Historia Animalium* A.6, 491^{a}9 f.:

our goal is to establish first the differences that exist and the properties that belong to all.[9]

To detect the relevant differentiating characteristics is the way to discover what the genera and species are. Thus, in this passage, he is recalling the goal of *De Partibus Animalium* A.5: to describe the properties which belong *per se* to kinds, as marked out by their relevant *differentiae*. This follows the general prescription concerning the role of *historiai*: to discover what properties genuinely belong to which objects, so that one can more easily devise appropriate explanations (*Pr. An.* A.30, 46^{a}23–7). *Historiai* are, thus, essential first steps towards causal explanation, and ones which

---

[9] In 491^{a}5 ff. Aristotle is not merely trying to grasp any feature which distinguishes animals. If this had been his only goal, he would not have separated the *differentiae* of kinds from the properties that belong to them. (*'ta sumbebekota'* here, as in *PA* A.5, 645^{b}1, refer to genuine attributes.) That he does so shows that an essential element in the project in the *Historia Animalium* is to establish which kinds exist and which properties belong to them. To this extent, he must be engaged in the taxonomic task of laying out which kinds exist. In effect, Aristotle has a double aim: to determine which attributes belong to things and which (kinds of) things they belong to. His aim is not confined to the first of these. For a contrasting view, see D. M. Balme, 'Aristotle's Use of Division and Differentiae', in Gotthelf and Lennox (eds.), *Philosophical Issues in Aristotle's Biology*, 69–89. Balme sees Aristotle as having only one aim or intention in *Hist. Anim.*: '*The* intention is to investigate the means by which one may distinguish and define animals' ('Aristotle's Use of Division and Differentiae', 11). Thus, in his view, Aristotle's aim did not involve taxonomy (p. 9). This said, Balme is certainly correct to reject the view that in the *Historia Animalium* Aristotle's *one* aim was to provide a complete and exhaustive taxonomy of all animal kinds (pp. 83–4).

involve determining which genera and species, in reality, differ from each other (as in the immediately preceding passages of *Historia Animalium* A.6 and *De Partibus Animalium* A.4), and which properties genuinely belong to each kind or sub-kind.[10] So, we may raise, in considering *Historia Animalium*, two more specific questions:

(a) Does Aristotle succeed in clarifying the notion of a *common nature*, as introduced in *De Partibus Animalium*, in the way required to separate differing genera and species of animals? (Or, in the language of *Historia Animalium*, how far does he delimit the type of *differentiae* required for this task?)

(b) Does Aristotle succeed in marking out (in outline) the basis for species differentiation within a genus?

Positive answers to (a) and (b) would enable us to grasp what determines the basic system of differentiation at work in the biological writings. We should then be in a position to see how far Aristotle's biological classificatory scheme fulfils the two demands (a*) and (b*) of the *Analytics* paradigm. Does his use of the notion of common nature provide the basis for a non-*ad hoc* procedure for deriving genuine kinds, which points to features to be explained by the causal basis of the kind? Further, one may ask how far his use of the notion of common nature is of assistance in establishing the existence of a genus or species. Is it sufficient (or necessary) for knowledge of the existence of a genus or species that one knows it to possess a common nature of some type (possibly so far unspecified)? Is this what is required to know (in the terminology of the *Analytics*) that there is a cause or unifying principle which explains why (e.g.) fish exist in the way they do, even if one does not know precisely what the cause is?[11]

12.3 DIFFERENTIATION OF KINDS (2): *HISTORIA ANIMALIUM*

In *Historia Animalium* A.6 Aristotle lists seven main groups (great genera) of animals: birds, fishes, cetacea (all of these are blooded), hard-shelled

---

[10] *Historia Animalium* is the pre-syllogistic stage of scientific enquiry (*Pr. An.* A.30). It should be sharply distinguished from experience which is not at a sufficient level of generality to count as scientific (see Ch. 6, Sect. 6.2). Some have labelled this stage 'dialectical', although the methods seem far removed from Aristotle's explicit guidelines on dialectical method in *NE/EE* Z.2 or *Top.* Θ. There seems no reason to assume that everything that is not syllogistic is dialectical. In my view, *HA* and the *Rhetoric* contain examples of *historiae* which are neither syllogistic nor dialectical.

[11] In the terminology of Chapters 2 and 3, this is to achieve Stage 2 but not yet Stage 3.

animals, soft-shelled animals, 'softies' (types of cephalopod), and insects (490^b7–14), (these last four are bloodless). How did Aristotle arrive at this classification? Why did he exclude certain other candidates from the category of great genera (490^b15–491^a6)?

Aristotle's earlier discussion in *Historia Animalium* A.1–5 has laid the foundation for these claims. Birds have been marked out as feathered fliers (490^a6–7, 12–13), fish as gilled and (generally) finned, footless swimmers (489^b23–6). Most of them take in and emit water, and cannot live apart from it (487^a15–20). Cetacea are also swimmers, but lack gills and instead have a blowhole (489^b2–4). Also, they are viviparous (489^a34). Insects, so-called because of the insections in their bodies (487^a32 f.), do not take in air, although they live and get their food on land (487^a31 f.). By contrast with birds, flying insects have membranous wings (490^a9–11). The 'softies' (cephalopods) are swimmers, who have feet and fins, which they use for swimming (490^a2–4). The soft-shelled animals (crustacea) are all aquatic and capable of locomotion whether by swimming or walking (487^b15–18), while many types of hard-shelled animals (testacea) are aquatic but stationary (487^b14), take in neither water nor air, but obtain their food in the water (487^a25 f.).

Aristotle, it appears, has provided a justification for treating these genera as correctly marked out by common usage. He has done this by showing how these kinds exhibit genuine differences in the following respects:

(a) type of locomotion: walking, flying, swimming, stationary;

(b) method of breathing: some take in air or water, others do not;

(c) method of eating: where the animals find their food. (cf.487^a22–7).

In some cases modes of locomotion are the basic ingredients. Fliers are divided according to their method for doing so (feathers, membranous wings). In others, modes of breathing are basic (gills, blowholes, etc.). But each of these kinds is marked out using divisions within the life functions (locomotion, breathing, eating, etc.). It appears that it is these affections and actions that provide the basis for Aristotle's classification at this point (cf. *De Partibus Animalium* A.5, 645^b33 ff.). To have a common nature is (at least) to have a distinctive way of fulfilling some of these basic life functions.[12]

---

[12] It is striking that Aristotle does not include perceiving in his list of soul functions introduced in *PA* A.3 or *HA* A.1–6 to distinguish kinds of animals. However, since (e.g.) the perceiving of special sensibles, as described in *De Anima*, is essential for life and common to all, animals will not be differentiated in terms of their possession of the capacity to perceive. They may, of course, be differentiated in terms of *how* they perceive (since, as emerges later in *HA*, there are differences between their perceptual organs (A.10, 491^b34–492^a12, 23–6; 492^b13–21, etc.)). Differences in intelligence, however, are used as elsewhere to distinguish animals (*HA* A.1, 488^b15–18; cf. *Meta.* A.1, 980^a27 ff., *De An.* Γ.3, 428^a10–12).

The central role of *differentiae* of this type is illustrated by other aspects of *Historia Animalium* A.1–5. The discussion of parts follows the pattern of *De Partibus Animalium*: if the genus is the same, animals will differ by the more and the less (*HA*, A.1, 486ᵃ22 ff.). By contrast, if features belong to different genera, they will only be analogically similar (486ᵇ20–2). But, as before, the genera (such as bird and fish) appear to be taken as already determined. As in *De Partibus Animalium*, sameness and difference rest on sameness and differences in genus (and presumably, therefore, on difference in basic soul function).

Aristotle lists, in addition to *differentiae* with regard to part, differences in respect of life, activities, and dispositions (*HA*. A.1, 487ᵃ11–14). These cases also reveal some structure. Aristotle begins with water and land animals, but then breaks this classification down further in terms of patterns of feeding and breathing (487ᵃ14–ᵇ8). Differences in locomotion and reproduction, by contrast, are taken as basic, and not further analysed into more basic categories (487ᵇ8–32, 489ᵇ19 ff.). Similarly, in characterizing what is shared by all animals, Aristotle focuses on eating and digestion (488ᵇ29–489ᵃ8) and reproduction (489ᵃ8–16), but mentions touch only in passing (489ᵃ17–19). Thus, certain activities (such as feeding, moving, breathing, and reproducing) are taken as the central ones in characterizing differences between animals.

The central role of this favoured set of *differentiae* becomes clearer when Aristotle considers cases of groupings which fail to yield great genera. Wingless quadruped is briefly canvassed as a possibility in *Historia Animalium* A.6, 490ᵇ19 f., but not used elsewhere as a genus. By contrast, viviparous quadruped and oviparous quadruped are retained as relevant genera, although neither are great genera. Why is this? Aristotle notes that wingless quadrupeds divide into the viviparous and oviparous (490ᵇ20 f.). But while these are nameless groups, their namelessness cannot be the crucial factor. For, the immediate subdivisions within the retained genus of viviparous quadruped are similarly nameless (490ᵇ31 ff.). The relevant point here seems rather to be that the species within the suggested genus of wingless quadruped would be dissimilar in a certain crucial respect: method of reproduction (see *PA* A.4, 644ᵇ4–5). Further, Aristotle notes that viviparous animals all have hair, while oviparous ones have scales (490ᵇ21–3), pointing to a feature which is the analogue of hair in other animals (*GA* E.3, 782ᵃ16–19).

In this example, Aristotle is relying on two ideas. If one has a genus, the species which comprise it should perform basic life functions in a basically similar way (e.g. reproduction). Further difference in mode of reproduction is sufficient to show that there are different genera in the case of quadrupeds. Both show that Aristotle is concerned to secure his favoured genera on the basis of a unified common nature—in which shared ways of performing certain basic functions are of central importance (here, locomotion and reproduction).[13] In the case of a unified genus there is a distinctive way of moving, reproducing, feeding, and breathing. Difference with respect to one of these life functions undermines the unity of the genus.

If this is correct, a theory of what constitutes a *common nature* is at work in selecting the great genera in I.6, and deselecting others. Aristotle is not proceeding merely by counting up *differentiae* and seeing which animals share many of them. He is focusing rather on certain basic soul features which determine the great genera, and viewing subspecies as ones which perform these functions in roughly similar ways. This makes far clearer what a 'common nature' is: an organized collection of methods of moving, reproducing, feeding, and breathing.

A similar background theory is at work elsewhere in the *Historia*. Aristotle throughout employs a formula to associate animal kinds with given features:

As many as are X, some/all/none have P.[14]

In his discussion of the instrumental parts of blooded animals in *Historia Animalium* B.15–Γ.22, the following animal groups occupy the X-place:

viviparous quadrupeds (505^b32, 506^b25)

oviparous quadrupeds (505^b35, 506^b26)

viviparous quadrupeds with horns and which do not have teeth in both jaws (507^a34)

footless not internally viviparous (509^b5)

footed viviparous (510^a13 f., 517^b4 f.)

footless animals that are externally viviparous though internally oviparous (511^a3 f., 521^b25)

footed ovipara (517^b4 f.)

blooded animals that are internally and externally viviparous (520^b27, 521^b22)

---

[13] Why are serpents not a 'great genus'? Is it because this 'genus' too cuts across animals with different means of reproduction (oviparous/viviparous ($490^b24–7$)), where the species are too different from each other? Aristotle leaves this point in the air in A.6, but later treats serpents in certain respects like other oviparous land animals (B.17, $508^a9–12$), although he notes that serpents are divided as to their habitat (B.14, $505^b5–10$).

[14] This point is properly emphasized by J. Lennox in 'Divide and Explain: The *Posterior Analytics* in Practice', in Gotthelf and Lennox (eds.), *Philosophical Issues in Aristotle's Biology* and by Gotthelf in 'Historiae: Animalium et Plantarum', in W. W. Fortenbaugh (ed.), *Theophrastean Studies*, (New Brunswick, 1988).

In these cases, Aristotle uses features concerning locomotion and reproduction as the basis for his divisions between animals. Subsequently, when
he divides genera into species, he often does so by distinguishing the ways
in which the animals reproduce (internally, externally, viviparously, etc.).
He does, of course, draw further subdivisions (as at B.17, 507^{a}34) within
the groups marked out in this way. Thus, for example, he distinguishes
among viviparous quadrupeds those that have horns but lack teeth in both
jaws. But this latter demarcation is required because (in this context) he
is focusing on differences between types of stomach. Similarly, when he
distinguishes:

animals that have kidneys and bladders (B.16, 506^{b}32)

he does so in a context where these organs are the subject matter.[15] In
general, his basis for differentiation remains organized natures with distinctive means of reproduction and locomotion.[16] Thus, throughout these
sections, Aristotle's divisions rest (in the main) on differing ways of fulfilling the basic functions of reproducing, moving, breathing, and growth
(*PA*. A.5, 645^{b}33–5). Differences in these functions mark out distinct
genera, whether great or small.

Aristotle, in discussing the *common nature* of animals (in *HA*. A and B),
takes as basic, locomotion, breathing, and reproduction. Once great genera
have been marked out in these terms, he can distinguish differing sub-kinds
in a similarly structured way. After fish have been introduced as gilled,
finned swimmers (A.5, 489^{b}24–5), Aristotle uses the following *differentiae*
further to divide the genus:

(a) four-finned vs. two-finned vs. no-finned: B.13, 504^{b}27–35

(b) covered vs. non-covered gills: B.13, 505^{a}1 f.

(c) single vs. double gills: B.13, 505^{a}8 f.

(d) few vs. many gills: B.13, 505^{a}10–12

Thus, he can separate (on the basis of *differentiae* of this type) several
major species within the genus of fish (such as selachia (505^{a}1), muraena
(504^{b}34, cf. 489^{b}24–6), eels (504^{b}32, cf. 489^{b}24–6)), as well as other smaller
species (such as the mullet, parrotwrasse, perch, rainbowwrasse, carp,

---

[15] The only other case (in this section) which does not use life functions for division is
that of blooded animals (B.15, 506^{a}6, 13). But 'blooded' offers a shorthand way of referring
to the first three great genera (fish, birds, cetacea) mentioned in *HA* A.6, and to the other
cases of blooded animals later adduced (e.g. man; cf. B.15, 505^{b}29–32).

[16] A similar story is to be found in Aristotle's discussion of miscellaneous *differentiae* in
HA Δ.8–E.24. There, too, the X-places are filled by (e.g.) four-footed ovipara (536^{a}4 f.);
footed, blooded, and non-ovipara (538^{a}22 f.); man, footed, vivipara, blooded ovipara
(532^{b}33 f.); blooded oviparous quadrupeds (557^{b}32).

dogfish, swordfish, tapefish, and fishing frog, all discussed in *De Historia Animalium* B.13).

Fish have certain features in common (in Aristotle's account). They are blooded (505^{b}1 f.), and have a bladder (506^{b}5), although this may be differently placed in different fish (*HA* B.15). All have a gut of a given type (a feature they share with birds (508^{b}14)), although they differ from one another in the number they possess (508^{b}15–25). Aristotle notes that varieties of fish differ in these respects (at the level of species: e.g. angelfish, skate, pipefish, goby, burbet, etc.). But they are, nonetheless, all varieties of fish because they all carry out similar functions (e.g. nutrition of a given type) in similar ways, and possess the basic *differentiae* of fish (as gilled or finned swimmers).

Aristotle, by employing intuitions of this type about *common nature*, is able to vindicate the popular assumption that fish form one genus of animal, one whose species share similarity in function and in functionally related structural features. Against this background, he can proceed to mark out further major differences between fish: some, the scaly fish, are oviparous, while others are viviparous (B.13, 505^{b}2–4)—for instance, the selachia.[17] Indeed, he calls 'selachia' footless creatures which have gills and are viviparous (Γ.1, 511^{a}4–7).[18] They form a proper grouping with their own distinctive sexual *differentiae* (Δ.11, 538^{a}29) and bone structure, which reproduce in a distinctive manner (Δ.5, 540^{b}5 ff., Z.10, 564^{b}15 ff.). Here, too, Aristotle focuses on reproduction to distinguish lower-level types of fish, even though they all breathe and/or move in the way distinctive of fish. The genus has a common nature because all fish perform the same basic soul functions in similar ways.

Once this common nature has been established, Aristotle can distinguish between fish by contrasting their ways of performing other soul functions: generation (Γ), perceiving, hearing, sleeping (Δ), reproducing (E, Z), eating (Θ), migrating (Θ.12 ff.), hibernation (Θ.15), flourishing (Θ.19), illness (Θ.20), adaptation to their environment (I.37). Of these, procreation and eating are the most basic (in Aristotle's view):

One part of the life of animals consists in actions concerning procreation, another in actions concerning food. For, it is on these two activities that the interests and life of all are fixed. (*HA*. Θ.1, 589^{a}2–5)

---

[17] Why are fish one genus, even with this difference, while wingless quadrupeds are not? (A.6, 490^{b}20–1). Presumably, Aristotle thought that he had discovered enough of a common nature in the case of fish in terms of their locomotion, breathing, eating, etc. to sustain their claim to be a unified kind, but did not detect enough of a common nature on similar grounds amongst wingless quadrupeds. (But see Sects. 12.5 and 12.6).

[18] What happens to the fishing frog (505^{b}2)? He remains submerged in subsequent discussion.

Elsewhere he notes:

The habits of animals are all concerned with breeding and rearing of young, or with obtaining food . . . These habits are modified so as to suit cold and heat, and the variations of seasons. (Θ.12, 596^{b}20–4)

Aristotle, in discussing these activities, frequently begins his account by saying what all fish have in common: they all lack testicles (509^{b}3, 25), none have breasts or milk (521^{b}25 f.), all lack visible sense organs (533^{a}34 f.), all sleep (537^{a}1), and all feed on spawn (591^{a}7). He then proceeds to note that differing kinds of fish perform these functions differently.

Aristotle's discussion of the eating habits of fish in *Historia Animalium* Θ.1–12 provides an example of the relevant aspects of his method.[19] In Θ.2 he is mainly concerned to note differences in eating patterns between the different types of fish he has already marked out on separate grounds such as:

(a) types of gill: grey mullet, scarus, selachians, dentex[20]

(b) types of fin: conger, muraena, bass, gilthead, eels[21]

(c) types of gut or gall: amia, red mullet, goby[22]

(d) types of skin: tunny[23]

(e) types of breeding or spawning pattern: saupe, phycis, rock fish, sargue, channa, sea perch[24]

---

[19] In *HA* Θ.1–12 Aristotle is concerned to map differing ways of obtaining food on to his favoured genera (fish, birds, serpents and other scaly animals, viviparous, quadrupeds, and insects), and their subspecies. Thus, in the remainder of Θ.2 Aristotle operates with the following demarcations of aquatic animals:

590^{a}18: hard-shelled animals (testacea) that are incapable of motion

590^{b}1 ff.: mobile shellfish

590^{b}10 ff.: crustaceans

590^{b}32 ff.: soft-shelled animals

591^{a}1 ff.: octopus

591^{a}7 ff.: fish

He then notes their differing ways of finding food—as was to be expected given their differing natures—and marks further differences within the respective genera.
[20] Grey mullet (591^{a}18, cf. 504^{b}32), scarus (591^{a}14, cf. 489^{b}26 f.), selachians (591^{a}10, cf. 489^{b}24–6), dentex (591^{a}11, 505^{a}16).
[21] Conger (591^{a}10, cf. 489^{b}26), muraena (591^{a}11, cf. 489^{b}24–6), bass (591^{a}11, cf. 489^{b}26), gilthead (591^{b}9, cf. 489^{b}26), eel (591^{a}18, ^{b}30, cf. 505^{a}16).
[22] Amia (591^{a}11, cf. 506^{b}13), red mullet (591^{a}12, cf. 508^{b}17), goby (591^{b}14, cf. 508^{b}17).
[23] Tunny (591^{a}11, cf. 505^{a}27).
[24] Saupe (591^{a}15, cf. 543^{a}8), phycis (591^{b}13, cf. 567^{b}20), rock fish (591^{b}14, cf. 543^{a}5), sargue (591^{b}19, cf. 543^{a}7), channa (591^{a}11, cf. 538^{a}21), sea perch (591^{a}11, cf. 543^{b}1).

As before, distinct modes of breathing, moving, digesting, and reproducing play a central role. Aristotle shows how distinctive ways of finding food can be mapped on to types of fish already distinguished in terms of other soul functions. Thus, he confirms his earlier classification by showing how those distinctions are related to other differences in eating pattern. There are only three cases of fish species added in Θ.2: the dascyllus (591ª14), melanurus (591ª15), and the peraeas (ª24). All the rest have been already marked out in terms of other soul functions. Indeed, this is the general pattern in Aristotle's discussion of migration, hibernation, flourishing, and adaptation. In nearly all cases, the types of fish attributed different kinds of (e.g.) migratory pattern have been distinguished in terms of his basic *differentiae*. While he is prepared to add four further types of fish to his list at this point (e.g. black bream, 598ª10; weaver, 598ª11; braize, 598ª13; sea cuckoo, 598ª14), the remaining twenty-four have already been marked out on other grounds. Aristotle underwrites popular distinctions between species of fish by noting their relevant basic natures (modes of moving, breathing, digesting, and reproducing), while occasionally showing how further sub-groups differ in eating or migratory patterns. His theory of soul function directs his enquiry and helps him to vindicate popular claims of this type.

In the passages considered, Aristotle has used his theory of soul function to mark out fish as a genus and to draw further differences within this genus. Elsewhere in *Historia Animalium* he employs the same resources (in a somewhat different way) to separate different types of aquatic animal. Some live and feed in water, take in water and emit it (e.g. fish), while others live and feed in water but take in air not water and breed away from water (e.g. otter, beaver, crocodile) (A.1, 487ª18–20). Some, again, obtain their food in water, but take in neither water nor air (e.g. shellfish, sea anemones (487ª23–6)). Aristotle uses different modes of breathing and location of food to distinguish different types of water animal. As he remarks, these are connected since no water animal which takes in sea water gets its food from land (487ᵇ3–5). Thus, breathing and mode of nutrition play a decisive role in separating out animals which share the same habitat and in marking out different ways of being aquatic.

Aristotle, in his subsequent discussion of aquatic animals (*HA* Θ.2), is forced to further refinement by examining the activities of the dolphin (589ª31–ᵇ28, 590ª13–18). This case is problematic because the dolphin takes in and discharges water by its blowhole, while also inhaling air into its lungs (589ᵇ5 f.). Since it takes in and emits both water and air, it could be classified as both aquatic and terrestrial (589ᵇ7–14). Aristotle, faced with this problem, distinguishes further (*prosdioristeon* (589ᵇ13)) between aquatic animals as follows: some take in water (via their gills) for the same purpose as respiration—to cool their blood, while others, which take in water for the different purpose of obtaining food, do not use water to cool the blood but expel it via their blowhole (589^b15–18). These latter animals are *aquatic* in a different way from fish. Difference in breathing separates differing ways of being aquatic: one type of animal breathes by taking in water, the other by taking in air ($\Theta.2, 590^a14$).[25] Fish and dolphins, however, both take their food from the water, and so can be distinguished from animals which breathe like fish but obtain their food on dry land (the water newt (589^b25–8)). Here, too, Aristotle uses difference in basic soul functions (breathing, eating, and locomotion) to distinguish different ways of being aquatic. Once again, it seems that his investigations rest on a powerful background theory of what is to count as a *common nature*. When two animals without a common nature can both be characterized as *aquatic*, the latter term needs further clarification.[26]

Aristotle, it appears, in *Historia Animalium* is working with a set of assumptions about what it is to have a *common nature:* it is to possess the same organized set of soul functions involving (typically) locomotion, breathing, reproducing, and eating. To establish the existence of a great genus is to establish that there is an organized and distinctive set of soul functions of this type. Species are differentiated (in large part) by their differing ways of performing the same set of soul functions. Thus, to establish that a species exists is to establish that there is a nature which performs the set of soul functions characteristic of the genus in a distinctive manner.[27] In this case (as in that of the genus) one grasps that there is a common nature, even if one has not as yet grasped what that nature is: what the basis for the difference in soul function is.

If this is correct, Aristotle's project in the *Historia Animalium* is not that of determining the relevant genera and species merely by collecting a 'large group' of counter-predicable properties, and then using division to

---

[25] In 590^a14 f. Aristotle also adduces the mixture of the body (*krasis*) as a way of distinguishing different types of aquatic animal. This appears to depend on the surrounding medium by which the animal is cooled and the food it takes in (*GA* 767^a30 ff.). If so, it is determined by features relevant to breathing and food, and so is derivative from these more fundamental categories.

[26] Aristotle began his discussion of aquatic animals ($\Theta.2, 610^b1$–3) in a way which suggested that he was investigating a grouping which cuts across the great genera, and includes fish and cetacea together. But once his discussion gets under way he uses difference in soul function to underwrite the generic differences between fish and cetacea he had set out in *HA* A.6 (see above). Thus, while at the outset his approach might have appeared non-taxonomic, his procedure vindicates the division into great genera (on the basis of soul function) sketched above.

This whole discussion has important implications for Aristotle's view of dualizers. It suggests that dolphins 'dualize' only provisionally between being aquatic and being terrestrial. They do not dualize when the definitions of being aquatic are further tightened (589^b13 ff.). This point is investigated by Robert Parker in his review of G. E. R. Lloyd's *Science, Folklore and Ideology* entitled 'Sex, Women and Ambiguous Animals', in *Phronesis* 29 (1984), 184. See also Herbert Granger's: 'The *Scala Naturae* and the Continuity of Kinds', *Phronesis* 30 (1985), 181–222.

[27] This is further clarified at Stage 3 (see below).

establish the species. Nor does he merely seek those general *differentiae* which are distinguished by continuous variations of their sensible affections.[28] The significance he attaches to differences in basic soul functions shows that he is making major assumptions about what features are important in establishing genuine common natures. His enquiry is, in effect, the progressively more systematic elucidation of controlling concepts of this type, one which results empirically in differentiation into kinds and sub-kinds.[29] It involves both empirical data and a powerful background theory.[30]

---

[28] This is suggested by J. Lennox in his reply to an essay which forms an earlier version of part of this Chapter: 'Notes on David Charles on H. A.', in D. Devereux and P. Pellegrin (eds.), *Biologie, logique et métaphysique chez Aristote* (Paris, 1985), 173.

[29] I take it that an empiricist reading of the *Historia Animalium*, which saw it as concerned with establishing the existence of kinds and species, would represent Aristotle's method as follows:

Stage (A): Use counter-predication to establish genera as the locus of many such counter-predications.

Stage (B): Divide within such genera using further counter-predication and division to establish species (which differ only by the more and less).

On this account, Stages (A) and (B) will be innocent of background theoretical assumptions about what constitutes a common nature. Several considerations weigh against this view. First (as I have emphasized), Aristotle gives factors special prominence in selecting genera and species (as in the case of fish) which are closely related to his own views about their common nature. Second, within the genus of fish Aristotle notes that some are viviparous, others oviparous, some have an oesophagus (B.17), while all are blooded like other animals and have a gut like birds (508[b]14 f.). One needs to give some special significance to fish as gilled swimmers to sustain a common genus, given this type of diversity of sub-kinds. Finally, Aristotle does not treat some possible genera as genuine ones, presumably because their points of similarity are not significant enough: wingless quadrupeds (490[b]19 f.), the blooded (490[a]27), and (perhaps) those with lungs (shared by oviparous and viviparous alike (*PA* Γ.6, 669[a]26–8)). Of the latter, Aristotle remarks:

what is common to them is without a name, and it is not like the case of 'bird' which is the name given to a certain genus. This is why, as what is to be a bird is composed of something else, for these creatures lung possession is included in their essence (669[b]10–12)

The issue in this passage is whether 'what is common' to lunged creatures is itself a genus or kind. I doubt this for two reasons:

(a) This case is specifically contrasted with that of 'bird' which is said to be the *name of a genus*.

(b) The difference between these two cases explains why, while the essence of birds consists in something, the closest analogy is for these creatures to have being lunged included in their essence. This suggests that they lack an essence *qua* lunged creatures, and that being lunged figures in the essences of kinds which are marked out on other grounds (e.g. being birds, being vivipara, etc.).

For a contrasting view of this particular passage, see Balme, *Aristotle's De Partibus Animalium I and De Generatione Animalium I (With Passages from II. 1–3)* (Oxford, 1972), 120, and Lennox, 1990, 181 fn.3.

[30] While elements in the background theory may be a priori (e.g. the theory of definition and classification), the theory as a whole is not. Thus, it is an empirical matter to determine the relevant genera or species, what types of organized soul functions there are. Contrast

In these respects, Aristotle's pattern of differentiation follows the model set out in *Posterior Analytics* B.13. The *differentiae* will be features which are themselves parts of the nature of the kinds to be investigated. Further, the method is not an *ad hoc* one, since it is based on a few closely related basic concepts which are used to differentiate the relevant kinds (as is required by (a*) above). If there is an answer to the 'Why?' question which explains the presence of these differentiating features, all the essentials of the *Analytics* model will have been retained.

The biological works do not satisfy, however, all the desiderata proposed in the *Analytics*. The *Historia Animalium* does not provide a complete taxonomy of all animals, an exhaustive, hierarchic classification. For, the account (as has often been remarked) is incomplete in many respects. Aristotle's apparent aim in the *Historia* is to provide the basic outline for a system of classification rather than to carry it through in every detail. Further, the classificatory scheme (involving multiple simultaneous *differentiae*) does not (as was noted above) correspond precisely to the hierarchical scheme of *differentiae* (odd, prime, prime*) set out in the discussion of B.13.[31] However, that said, Aristotle aims to provide the resources (via his theory of common nature and soul function) for locating biological kinds within a classificatory scheme which retains several aspects of the *Analytics* model. This goal is to be achieved mainly by invoking the concepts of common nature and soul functions. This account has interesting consequences for our understanding of the three-stage view and of the general aims of the *Historia Animalium*. (See the next Section.)[32]

12.4 ESTABLISHING THE EXISTENCE OF KINDS: STAGES 2 AND 3

The discovery of a common nature is a central element in discovery of the existence of a kind (at Stage 2 in the three-stage view). To establish the

---

I. Düring's claim in 'Aristotle's Method in Biology' in S. Mansion (ed.), *Aristote et les problèmes de méthode* (Louvain, 1961), 218: 'even in his most advanced biological works his reasoning is based on a priori principles and book-knowledge more than on observation'. He notes that 'it does not seem reasonable to characterize his method as empirical' (p. 218).

[31] Ch. 9 Sect. 9.2.

[32] For a contrasting view, see David Balme's 'Aristotle's Use of Division and Differentiae', 80. He argues that 'the role of *Hist. Anim.* is to collect, screen and distinguish, and describe correctly the differentiae requiring explanation'. The basis for this claim is that Aristotle (a) did not systematically classify subgenera, and (b) involves within some subgenera a wide variety of animals. While both these points seem correct, they only show that Aristotle did not use his taxonomic resources to carry through the (immense) classificatory task of discerning all the groups of animals that there are. They do not indicate that he was

presence of a common nature at this stage in the investigation requires one to know that there is a unifying cause at work, even though one need not yet know what it is. Stage 2 takes us beyond Stage 1, where we lack knowledge of the existence of the kind. For, at Stage 2 we know that the kind exists and have some grasp on its internal structure.

How should Stages 2 and 3 be connected? There are two points of connection suggested by our earlier discussions:

(a) What is discovered at Stage 3 should provide the basis for the common nature discerned at Stage 2 (as the teleologically basic feature or (perhaps) shared type of material basis: (e.g.) degree of heat). If so, it is no accident that the genera and species marked out at Stage 2 match those which science explains, since the latter fills out and further explicates the guiding conception of a shared nature already implicit at Stage 2. If this notion had not been invoked at the second stage, and the genera and species had been marked out (e.g.) by counter-predication and division, it would have remained unexplained why Stages 2 and 3 are parts of one enterprise. If genera and species were determined by the method of counter-predication alone, there would be no reason why there should be any overlap between these kinds and those with the same Stage 3 essence. There would be no reason to believe that pre- and post-scientific classification would march in step as well as they seem to do (in Aristotle's account).

(b) In some cases, authority may rest with Stage 3 considerations in determining the nature of kinds. If there are not one but several distinct basic causes of apparently similar cases, the kinds involved will differ. Thus, Aristotle writes in discussing pride:

if we do not come to one but to two or more accounts, it is clear that what we are seeking is not a single thing but several. (*Post. An.* B.13, 97^{b}13 f.)

If there is not one thing common to all proud people, there are distinct types of pride. Thus, difference in internal cause (e.g. indifference to fortune, not brooking dishonour) forces difference in species of pride. However, this will only be so if at Stage 2 genera or species are marked out in such a way as to be revisable in the light of Stage 3 considerations. This could not be so if genera and species are marked out by the empiricist method of counter-predication and division alone. For, in that case there would be no reason to accept that Stage 3 considerations should possess the authority to correct pre-scientific classifications. The two enterprises might simply study distinct subject matters. By contrast, the

engaged in the wholly different task of merely collecting animal *differentiae*. Balme's view, although a healthy reaction against the earlier a priori interpretation offered by Düring of the *HA*, represents Aristotle as an 'out and out' empiricist, untrammelled in his biological investigations by any specific theoretical presuppositions.

assumption of a common nature at Stage 2 is precisely what gives authority to the results of Stage 3 enquiry, if—as in the case of pride—there turn out to be two or more distinct causes at work.

At Stage 2 one can establish that a kind exists by showing that it has a distinctive nature—even if one does not know in detail what this is. To establish that something of this type has a distinctive nature, it is sufficient to establish that it is an organized teleological structure. One may well be unaware at this point of what the basic teleological cause is.

In the biological examples, one could establish the existence of such a structure by showing that there is an animal with an organized set of distinctive basic soul functions involving locomotion, nutrition, breathing, or reproduction. In this way one could establish that a relevant *differentia* belonged to a wider genus in the way required to establish that one is confronted with an organized structure. Counter-predication by itself may provide evidence that there is an organized nature before one. But the presence of a common nature explains why, in some cases, there is counter-predication of the relevant type. Thus, one knows in the case of animal species and genera that such kinds exist when one knows that there is an appropriate type of organized nature.

Reflection on Aristotle's method in the biological works serves to illuminate some issues left unresolved and obscure in the *Analytics*. It is only in these writings that he spells out what is required to establish the existence of distinct genera and species. He is not merely following a pre-set *Analytics* model of scientific investigation. He is rather struggling to make that model at once more precise and more powerful, with the assistance of additional conceptual machinery based on the notions of common nature and soul function.[33]

It is clear, once Stage 2 is conceived in this way, why Aristotle should have laid out kinds and their features in the precise way he did in the *Historia Animalium* as a preliminary to causal explanation (*HA* A.6, 491^{a}9–11). He needed to set out the differences that exist between kinds and the properties that belong to each of them (491^{a}9 f.), and then to discover the fundamental causes of these kinds possessing these properties. The basic causes will be the essences of the kinds themselves (at their varying levels), which explain—at Stage 3—why the kinds have the properties they do. One cannot carry through this type of explanation without having the *explananda* in correct form. We need to grasp the properties which genuinely belong to things in a successful '*historia*' of this kind (*Pr. An.* A.30, 46^{a}24–6). We cannot do this if we do not mark out (prior to Stage

---

[33] This is comparable with Aristotle's introduction of new material such as matter, form, composites, in the *Metaphysics* to carry through his *Analytics*-based programme. The theory of soul function is developed in *De An.*, presumably as the prolegomenon to biological study (see *De An.* B.2, 413^{b}1–10, ^{b}16–414^{a}3).

3) the distinct genera which possess *per se* attributes or the attributes which belong to such genera (*PA* A.5, 645^{b}1–3). If we do not achieve this, we will not easily find the relevant explanatory syllogisms. Thus, it is an essential preliminary for explanation of this type that one grasp genuine kinds and their non-accidental properties. This is what grasping the relevant 'the that' consists in.[34]

So understood, Aristotle has two aims in this *historia*. To separate distinct genera and (where required) species and to determine which properties belong *per se* to them. His project is not merely to list *differentiae* and note their co-occurrence (as a preliminary to causal investigation). Nor is the *Historia Animalium* simply a collection of general features which can be used to distinguish different types of animal.[35] For, these suggestions ignore the use which Aristotle makes of *differentiae* in classifying distinct genera and species of animals. One should not conclude from the incompleteness of the taxonomy provided in the *Historia* that Aristotle had no interest in classifying the genera and species to which general features belong.

Aristotle could not have limited his goal to (e.g.) collecting *differentiae* if his explanations were to follow the model set out in *Posterior Analytics* B.16–18.[36] For, that can most easily 'get under way' if one has one genuine kind and one genuine property as *explananda*. If there are two distinct explanations of why what is apparently one grouping has what is apparently the same property, there must be either two genuine kinds or two distinct properties.[37] At the pre-explanatory stage (as in *Post. An.* B.13–15) one's aim is to grasp the relevant unitary kinds and their genuine features. One can sustain the belief that one has grasped a kind of the type needed in explanation (cf. *Post. An.* B.17, 99^{b}2–4) if one has grasped one common nature. Further, without the idea of one common nature, one could indefinitely divide kinds into further subspecies (e.g. salmon more than one foot long/less than one foot long) and offer explanations of why the distinct pseudo-kinds had their particular properties. The constraints imposed by the theory of *common nature* at Stage 2 prevent explanations of this form 'freewheeling' out of touch with genuine kinds.

---

[34] In recent years several writers have emphasized the role of *historiai* as preliminary to causal explanation (D. M. Balme, 'Aristotle's Use of Differentiae in Biology', in Mansion (ed.), *Aristote et les problèmes de méthode*; '*Genus* and *Eidos* in Aristotle', *Classical Quarterly*, NS, 12 (1962), 81–98; P. Pellegrin, *La Classification des animaux chez Aristote* (Paris, 1982), trans. A. Preus, *Aristotle's Classification of Animals* (Berkeley, 1986); 'Aristotle: A Zoology without Species', in A. Gotthelf (ed.), *Aristotle on Nature and Living Things* (Pittsburgh, 1985); Lennox, 'Divide and Explain'; Gotthelf, 'Historiae: Animalium et Planatarum'). This important line of reflection is fully consistent with seeing Aristotle as concerned also with establishing kinds (as Lennox notes, 1990, 173–4). Indeed, it seems impossible for Aristotle to do the first without doing the second.
[35] As Balme suggested, 'Aristotle's Use of Division and Differentiae', 88.
[36] See Ch. 8 Sects. 8.3 and 8.4.   [37] See Ch. 8 Sect. 8.4.

It should be no surprise, once Stages 2 and 3 are understood in the way suggested, that Aristotle's discussion of taxonomic issues in *Historia Animalium* is incomplete. It is only when the explanatory task is completed at Stage 3 that these issues can be finally resolved. It would not have been possible for Aristotle to have produced a complete taxonomy (even if— *per impossibile*—all the relevant *historiai* had been completed) without considering the basic explanatory questions addressed in *De Partibus* and *De Generatione Animalium*.

The overall model of classification in the *Historia Animalium* retains, as has been argued, many aspects from the *Analytics*. Further, the concession that kinds are demarcated by many *simultaneous differentiae* does not by itself undermine the basis of the *Analytics* approach to the nature of *differentiae* or to the unity of kinds. Man may fall under a variety of *differentiae*: (e.g.) two-footed, two-armed, straight-stander (*PA* A.3, 644^{a}7–11), and there still be one essence which explains all these other features (as the causally basic *differentia*). Further, these will all be *differentiae* of the appropriate type provided that they are explained by the relevant essence (answer to the 'Why?' question). In the case of fish and birds, the genera will be marked out by a variety of features which provide the basis for further (posterior) differentiation into species. The centre of the *Analytics* model is preserved provided that there is one basic teleological causal factor of the required type. In the next Section I shall investigate the extent to which this crucial assumption is vindicated in Aristotle's account of fish.

12.5 THE ESSENCE OF BIOLOGICAL KINDS (1): THE *ANALYTICS* MODEL AT WORK?

Fish are introduced (see Section 12.3) as gilled, finned and footless swimmers (*HA* A.5, 489^{b}23 ff.), within the wider grouping of blooded animals. Can one take one element in their natures as basic, and explain the other relevant features in terms of it? If Aristotle follows the *Analytics* pattern, as developed in the case of substance, the relevant feature should be the form, construed as the starting point in a teleological explanation of why the kind is as it is. So understood, the form can be used simultaneously to answer two questions: 'What is F?' and 'Why is F as it is?', in a manner exhibiting Aristotle's favoured interdependence of definition and explanation.[38]

On occasion Aristotle moves in precisely this direction. Thus, he writes:

[38] See Chs. 8, 9, 10.

since fishes have a swimming nature, as is stated in the account of their essence ... they have no separate limbs attached to their bodies. Since they are essentially blooded animals, they have fins because they are swimmers, but lack feet since they do not walk on land. (*PA* Δ.13, 695^{b}17–23)

Other aspects of the life of fish are explained in terms of their distinctive nature as swimmers, living in water and not on land.[39] This is why they have gills and not lungs to cool their internal heat (*PA* Δ.13, 696^{a}34 ff.; cf. *De Resp.* 10, 476^{a}12–15); for, gills allow them to admit water for these purposes. Similarly, they have fluid eyes in order to see long distances under water and to counteract the adverse effects of water on their visual capacities (*PA* B.13, 658^{a}4–7). Since their habitat contains fewer objects to strike against, they lack eyelids (658^{a}7–10). Further, because they live in water, they need to eat quickly with little mastication to prevent ingesting too much water with their food (*PA* B.17, 660^{b}11 ff., Γ.14, 675^{a}6 ff.), and so have small tongues and sharp teeth.

These remarks follow the pattern set out in some of Aristotle's (occasional) general comments about the internal and external parts of animals. He writes:

Just as each animal is equipped with those external parts which are necessary for its manner of life (*bios*) and its movements (*kineseis*), so it is with their internal parts. (*PA* Γ.4, 665^{b}2–5)

The distinctive parts of fish should be just the ones required for its distinctive manner of life and movement as a swimmer in water. Elsewhere Aristotle writes, in an apparently similar vein, that:

It is clear that the body as a whole must exist for the sake of some complex action. (*PA* A.5, 645^{b}16 f.)

If the relevant action is swimming in water, this should explain, as in the passages cited, why the external and internal parts are as they are. Further, Aristotle seeks to explain why fish as a genus perceive, eat, and breathe as they do in terms of their pattern of movement in water. Here, too, he follows the model set out as the ideal in *De Partibus Animalium* A.1, 640^{a}33–5.

The best way of putting the matter would be to say that because the essence of man is what it is, therefore a man has these parts; for, he could not exist as a man without them.

The essence is given by reference to the creature's soul, which constitutes its form (*PA* A.1, 641^{a}18–20). In the case of animals, the relevant parts of the soul will be determined by their capacities for movement, perception,

---

[39] It is assumed that they swim and move in ways different from dolphins, seals, etc. (as indeed they do!).

and digestion or nourishment (641^b5–8). In the case of fish, it seems that the essence is constituted by its ability to swim in water, and this explains why the other parts of its soul and its body are as they are. One teleologically basic feature appears to be determinative of the other distinctive necessary properties of fish.

Fish form a genus, with a distinctive set of properties, intermediate between properties common to all animals and those limited to given species of fish (*PA* A.5, 645^b22–4). Aristotle attempts to specify what is common to a wide range of animals, and then to note the relevant variations. In the latter cases, he notes (B.2, 648^a14–16):

> It should be supposed that the variations in parts either are to be referred to the functions of each of the relevant creatures or their essence or bring some advantage or disadvantage.[40]

Thus, in considering bones (*PA* B.9), he claims that they are similar in all viviparous animals, although bigger and harder in animals which, like the lion, are more violent in their lifestyle (655^a10–12). Birds have bones, but they are weaker than the bones of vivipara (655^a17–19), presumably to allow them to fly more successfully (cf. *PA* B.16, 659^b8–12, Δ.12, 694^a10–12). Here, Aristotle points to features which explain the relevant variations distinctive of the genus or species in question. This pattern of explanation is standard throughout *De Partibus Animalium* B, Γ, and Δ. Aristotle specifies general types of flesh, eyes, hair, tongues, teeth, mouths, horns, hearts, lungs, stomachs etc., notes which types of animals (e.g. all land creatures, blooded animals, vivipara, viviparous quadrupeds, etc.) possess them and then points out variations which he seeks on occasion to explain. Thus, selachia differ from other fish in having spines made of cartilage (655^a23 f.), partly in order that they can move in a more supple way, and partly because 'all the available earthy material has been used to construct their skin' (655^a25–8). While the variations may be specific to one kind of animal (e.g. the elephant (B.16, 658^b33 ff.)), or shared by a genus of animals (fish (B.13, 658^a4 f.)), Aristotle seeks to explain their presence by reference back to the distinctive nature of the animals involved.

Aristotle's method of analysis suggests that the basic features of distinct genera and species are those aspects of the movement and lifestyle which explain why kinds possess their other distinguishing relevant properties. The distinctive aspect of the fish is their ability to swim in given ways, and this is used to explain why they possess gills, fins, fluid eyes, small tongues, and sharp teeth. They fall within the wider grouping of blooded animals (*PA* Δ.13, 695^b20 ff.), but the wider grouping is not itself a genus (presumably) because the varieties of blooded animal are too diverse, lacking one uniform type of life and movement (*HA* A.6, 490^b16 ff.). Being blooded sets

---

[40] The last clause is discussed below.

limits on what type of further physical features fish possess ('if they have four fins, they cannot have legs' (*PA* Δ.13, 695ᵇ21 ff.)), but does not explain why they have fins rather than legs. The specific explanation of why fish have (e.g.) no separate limbs attached to their bodies (i.e. no legs) depends on their distinctive movement and lifestyle. Being blooded may be part of the nature of fish because it sets constraints on the bodies fish will have. But it need not be part of the essential nature of fish (as given in their definition) because it does not explain the presence of the specific qualities which fish possess.

In these ways, Aristotle follows the pattern of explanation set out in the *Analytics*, and further modified (in the case of substance) in the *Metaphysics*.

12.6 THE ESSENCE OF BIOLOGICAL KINDS (2): THE PARADIGM IN DANGER

Aristotle could not account for all features of the nature of fish in this way. They are all gluttonous because their equipment 'for reducing food is defective, as a result of which most of it passes through unused' (*PA* Γ.14, 675ᵃ19–22). Since they are gluttonous, it is well that their mouths are (in certain cases) underneath their tip so as to avoid overeating and to avoid death from this cause (*PA* Δ.13, 696ᵇ30–2). Aristotle does not, however, attempt to explain their gluttony in terms of their essence *qua* swimmers. These distinctive features are not explained by reference to this essential activity, but rather by invoking a disadvantageous feature of their composition. The *differentia* is one 'which brings some advantage or (in this case) disadvantage', but its presence is not explained on the basis of the essence and characteristic activities of the creature (*PA* B.2, 648ᵃ15 f.). Nor does Aristotle explain why fish have to have defective eating equipment (compare *PA* A.1, 640ᵃ36–7).

Similarly, when considering fish reproduction, Aristotle notes that they produce many eggs, because it is impossible for a large number to reach perfection, as many are destroyed (*GA* Γ.1, 751ᵃ27–30, Γ.4, 755ᵃ25–30). That they do so is a consequence of the nature of their habitat, and does not follow directly from the fact that they are swimmers. (After all, the water might have been as safe for them as for dolphins!) Similarly, in the eggs they produce the white is not distinct because they are small and 'abound in cold and earthy matter' (*GA* Γ.1, 751ᵇ18–20). But, again, Aristotle makes no attempt to link these features with fishes' essential nature as swimmers.

Aristotle, in discussing methods of reproduction, notes that some fish are viviparous (such as selachia *GA* B.1, 732^{b}22), while others are oviparous (732^{b}22–4). Similarly, he finds (among footed animals) that not all quadrupeds are viviparous (or oviparous (732^{b}16–19)). His conclusion is that we cannot correctly divide the relevant types of reproduction on the basis of differing means of locomotion (732^{b}24–6), since the cause of the former lies in differing degrees of internal heat and fluidity (732^{b}31 f.). Thus, selachia are more fluid in their internal composition than other fish which are hot and solid (733^{a}8–10), and this explains why the former are internally viviparous and the others are not. The relevant *differentiae* are related to the heat and fluidity of their bodies, and not to their differing patterns of swimming (cf. *GA* Γ.3, 754^{a}23 ff.). The differing means of reproduction 'criss-cross' over and within the animal genera marked out on grounds of locomotion (and other soul functions), and cannot be explained in terms of them.

Aristotle's problem is that his teleological and causal explanations do not have as a common starting point one basic feature (as they should according to the *Analytics* account). Some begin with claims about animals' bodily properties or the environments in which they live. But these are not referred back to the essential unifying feature of one type of swimming. Not all explanations begin with the essence of the fish.

Aristotle had prepared the way for some deviations from his favoured *Analytics* model in *De Partibus Animalium* A. Thus, in A.1, 640^{a}34–6, he had noted that if we cannot explain certain properties in terms of the essence alone, then:

the nearest must be done: viz. that there cannot be a man at all otherwise than with them, or that it is well that man should have them. (640^{a}35–^{b}1)

Further, he had remarked that actions and organs may be present because they are necessitated by the presence of others, without one set being prior to the other (*PA* A.5, 645^{b}33–4). However, these concessions do not fully capture the extent to which he has deviated from the *Analytics* paradigm. Fish (of certain types) are oviparous and lack adequate means of reducing food simply because this is how their bodily nature is composed. The relevant starting point for this explanation is a given fact about their bodily composition, not a set of related soul functions. Similarly, in discussing reproduction, variation between animals is explained in terms of their differing degrees of heat and fluidity, and not their distinctive types of locomotion, breathing, or digestion. Aristotle does not attempt to show that it is necessary (or good) that fish have these bodily properties in order to survive. Rather, he takes as basic the presence of such bodily features, and explains why fish—given that they possess these features—necessarily have others as well.

12.7 THE NATURE OF THE PROBLEM

Aristotle's problem is threefold:

(1) In the case of fish, considered as a genus, the *Analytics* model leads us to expect that their distinctive features will be explained by their essence as movers (of a given type) in water. However, no mode of reproduction follows from their lifestyle (so understood) or type of movement. Similarly, their distinctive style of eating results from their defective eating equipment, and is not a consequence of their distinctive form as water movers.

(2) Within this genus, there is considerable variation between species with regard to (e.g.) means of reproduction, number of gills, and type of gill covering. These variations do not seem to depend, in Aristotle's theory, on the distinctive lifestyles of the different species of fish, since they are not explained, for example in the case of selachia, by reference to their distinctive pattern of swimming.

(3) Differences in types of fish reproduction depend not on differing types of movement but on their differing degrees of heat and fluidity. So far from explaining the latter in terms of their distinctive mode of locomotion in water, Aristotle begins his explanations with (what appear to be) brute physical facts about the animals' degree of heat.

Throughout these discussions, Aristotle takes as his starting point a rich notion of a common nature. Distinctive species of animal, such as fish, have certain features which can be explained in terms of their basic soul function (e.g. swimming in given kinds of ways), but others (e.g. their digestive and reproductive capacities) which cannot be explained in this way. This departure from the *Analytics* model reopens a question which had apparently been resolved there: What is it that makes a given set of soul functions and bodily characteristics such as:

moving in way A, reproducing in way B, having a digestive system of type C, and having heat of type D

into a genuine unity? What distinguishes this group from (e.g.):

musical, grammarian?

In the *Analytics*, this question was answered by finding one feature which explained why (e.g.) fish moved in way A, reproduced in way B, breathed in way C.[41] Indeed, this was what secured the unity of the kind in question. The difficulty is to see how this solution can work for the common nature of fish, as this is understood in the biological writings.

---

[41] See Ch. 7 Sect. 7.5, Ch 8 Sect. 8.2.

These problems are not confined to the study of fish. Aristotle, in discussing why elephants possess long trunks (*PA* B.16, 658^{b}33 ff.), takes as basic their great size. While he notes elsewhere that this is a source of protection (*PA* Γ.2, 663^{a}5–7), he makes no attempt to show that it is best, or even good, that they have precisely the size they do. Rather, their specific size is taken as a basic datum in the relevant explanation.[42] Similarly, in large animals the presence of surplus earthy matter is taken for granted, while Aristotle comments that nature makes use of this surplus for further purposes of its own (*PA* Γ.2, 663^{b}31 ff.). 'Material nature' plays a role as a starting point in these explanations. (See, for the phrase 'material nature', *PA* Γ.1, 640^{b}28 f.)[43]

Did Aristotle, in his biological writings, fail to find a way of satisfying his own *Analytics* requirements for the unity of the relevant kinds? Fish turned out not to have the simple, unifying, essences which his theory predicted that they must have. They appear to lack the one teleological cause which explains their heat, faulty digestive system, and mode of movement. In place of one unified cause, we find a series of distinct and apparently unrelated causes serving as the starting points for different explanations.

This problem goes deep. If there is no one basic teleological cause of the required type, how can Aristotle mark out the kind's essence? In the *Analytics* we uncovered the essence by finding a basic cause of the relevant type. Essence and causation fitted together, precisely because there was one unifying cause of the appropriate type. Without it, Aristotle could not use his favoured mode of answer to the definitional 'What is F?' question.

Aristotle's problem is not confined to issues of definition. The absence of an appropriate answer to the 'Why?' question threatens to undermine his approach to classification. The presence of a unified essence was required (in the *Analytics*) to ground the claim of certain features to be *differentiae*.[44] His system of classification will be undermined if there is no one unifying cause of the appropriate type.

There is, it appears, a crisis in Aristotle's project. In biology, his favoured area of investigation, he failed to find the one, unitary, causal feature whose (postulated) existence provides the basis of his account of definition in the *Analytics* and the *Metaphysics*. Are we, at this point, witnesses to the collapse of a brilliant research programme?

Aristotle's difficulties stem from his commitment to three assumptions:

---

[42] This point is well illustrated in Allan Gotthelf's 'The Elephant's Nose: Further Reflections on the Axiomatic Structure of Biological Explanation in Aristotle', in W. Kullmann and S. Follinger (eds.), *Aristotelische Biologie* (Stuttgart, 1997), 85–95.

[43] This point is established by James Lennox in his 'Material and Formal Natures in Aristotle's *de Partibus Animalium*', in Kullmann and Follinger (eds.), *Aristotelische Biologie*, 163–81.   [44] See Ch. 9 Sects. 9.2 and 9.3.

(Assn A) The unity of a kind is determined fundamentally by the presence of a unifying feature, prior to all else, which is explanatorily basic (as indicated in Chapters 8–11).

(Assn B) The favoured mode of explanation for natural biological kinds is teleological (as indicated in Chapter 11), and the form is the teleologically basic explanatory feature.

(Assn C) The answers to the 'What is F?' and the 'Why is F as it is?' questions are the same (in the ways indicated in Chapters 8–10).

He cannot, having made (Assn C) countenance mysterious simple entities (e.g. an unanalysable soul of the fish) as the basis for his answer to definitional questions. Essences have to be features capable of fitting into a causal story of the appropriate type.[45]

Aristotle, on the basis of these three assumptions, must have believed that (in the case of fish) there would turn out to be a basic teleological feature which (i) explains the presence and character of the remainder of their other genuine properties, and (ii) defines what it is to be a fish. But real life failed to live up to his philosophical expectations. Aristotle could, of course, have regarded his investigations of fish as incomplete, and held on to the possibility of discovering the vital unifying feature. But at times (as in *GA* B.1, 732^{b}28 ff.) he appears confident that the explanations he invokes in terms of heat and bodily composition are genuine and that they cut across his favoured soul-function style of demarcation (in terms of locomotion or breathing, etc.). If so, at this point he seems to surrender the idea that there is, in this case, the type of unitary essence which his metaphysical and scientific picture requires.

Is this difficulty one which damages Aristotle's whole account of natural kinds and their essences? Or can it be isolated, or rendered innocuous, in some way? Perhaps in the biological works he followed a radically different approach from the one developed in the *Analytics* or the *Metaphysics*? The problem, however, cannot be evaded merely by saying that biology is one thing, metaphysics another. For, the present dislocation threatens to undermine the connection between Aristotle's model of science in the *Analytics* and his favoured example of an explanatory science: biology. Further, if his metaphysical picture requires a basis for the unity of kinds inconsistent with the findings of his biological science, surely he must reject (or limit) that picture itself?

In the next Sections I shall consider several responses to this difficulty, based on readings of parts of the biological works, and assess the modifications they require in Aristotle's account of essence (as we have understood it).

---

[45] Indeed, this is precisely why Aristotle rejected unanalysable Platonic forms in Z.17, 1041^{a}18 ff. (See Ch. 11 Sects. 11.3 and 11.6).

12.8 THE ESSENCE OF BIOLOGICAL KINDS (3):
THE CONSERVATIVE APPROACH*

The most conservative response would have been to show that Assumptions (A)–(C) are not threatened by the results of his biological investigations.

This response might have several ingredients. First, Aristotle might suggest that there is a unifying feature of the appropriate type in the case of fish, which has so far been ignored: the survival or flourishing of the creature itself. On this view, what would be essential for fish (as a genus) would be those features which both (i) are required for the relevant animals to survive as fish, and (ii) explain the presence of their derived genuine properties. There may be several explanatory basic features of this type (moving in a given way, reproducing in some way, eating in some way), but all will be elements in one basic essence because all are required for fish to survive *as fish*. In this way, all would be ingredients in one basic unifying teleological cause, even though they do not all follow from one separate form of activity (such as movement). Features which the creature necessarily possesses but which do not satisfy *both* (i) *and* (ii) (e.g. its inadequate digestive system) would be regarded as non-essential. What it is to be part of the essence of the fish is to be a constitutive part of the organized explanatorily basic bundle of capacities required for the fish to survive (*as such*).

In the account just sketched, a certain degree of heat may be necessary for the fishes' survival, but will not be part of their essence. The presence of a material base of this (general) type might be explained teleologically by the requirements of the form ('This is a way, but not necessarily the only way, for the fish to survive.') Indeed, the specific material basis uncovered might introduce a further degree of specificity beyond that supplied by its formal nature (see, for example, in the case of reproduction, Aristotle's discussion of selachia, *GA* B.1, 733^{a}8 ff.). Thus, one might explain the specific mode of reproduction in a given type of fish in terms of its precise degree of heat (even though that precise degree is only one of a possible range of temperatures good enough for the fish to survive or reproduce, and the fish's possession of this degree of heat was itself explained in different terms). In this account, it would be part of this fish's form that it reproduces *in some way*, but not that it reproduces in *the precise way it does*. For, the explanation of the latter would rest on (e.g.) a material explanation, whose starting point was not itself part of the form. In such an account, the form would not specify the precise way it reproduces, but only mention that it reproduces in some way.

Nor need the role of matter (on this conservative account) be confined to these two roles. It can also act to check the proper operation of the form, if the latter fails properly to control it. (See, for example, *GA* Δ.1,

766^{b}13 ff., 3, 767^{b}11–24.) In such cases, the presence of the matter would explain why not everything goes as it should. The matter would interact with the form in irregular and unpredictable ways in such a case. There are, thus, several ways in which matter could act as an explanatory starting point consistent with the form playing the role required of it in the conservative account.

This general approach would, no doubt, have been attractive to Aristotle. However, it is clear that it involves a major departure from the *Analytics* paradigm. For, what is at stake in the biological examples is the survival of the fish *as the fish*. There may well be modes of survival which might be enjoyed, if the internal natures of fish were somewhat adjusted, involving different, or additional, modes of breathing, reproducing, etc. But these would not all be modes of survival of *the fish*, since some of the changes would be too radical for their continuing *as fish*. That genus would have ceased to exist, and another have taken its place. Equally, man, if made more godlike, might enjoy a different form of flourishing. But this would not be *human* well-being, since the creatures involved would no longer have the relevant human capacities, and would have ceased to be the complex unity of nous and emotions which makes up human nature (*NE* K.8, 1178^{a}19–21). What, then, are the limits of well-being for *humans* or survival for *fish*?

There is a dilemma. *Either* survival for the fish requires (in the first instance) the survival of all of its present existing soul functions *or* it requires the survival of only some of them. The first alternative takes as basic and prior the continued existence of the genus (the fish) and not its form. Thus, its central notion (the survival of the genus as fish) is far removed from the independent unifying essence which serves as the starting point in the *Metaphysics* or *Analytics*. For, that was prior to all else (such as the composite), and not derivative from it. However, if the second alternative is preferred, one needs to determine which features are required for the fish to survive. What is needed is a further unifying concept which can determine what is required for survival as a fish. More generally, one would need the resources to mark out an ecology of natural groupings of soul functions, differentiated without any reference to the composite organisms they enform. But the expectation is disappointed. Aristotle fails to provide the basis for, or even the merest sketch of, this type of account. Indeed, at crucial places in his story, it is the *common nature* of the whole organism (and not features of its form alone) that provides the starting point of his account.

But did Aristotle, nonetheless, attempt the conservative route? There are reasons for thinking that he did not. Had he done so, he should have made great efforts to isolate the contribution of the form, emphasizing that while it is essential that fish reproduce *in some way*, it is not essential that they reproduce in the specific way they do. (Any mode would be good enough provided that it resulted in the relevant form being transferred.) However, there is no evidence of his drawing the crucial distinction between fish reproducing in some way and reproducing in the precise way they do. Further, had he followed the conservative strategy, he should have distinguished most carefully between the differing roles played by factors cited in teleological and in material explanation. But Aristotle does not do this. Thus, for example, in discussing the gills of fish, he first invokes degree of heat to explain the strength of their movement, and then uses the latter to explain why some fish have numerous rather than few gills (*PA* Δ.13, 696^{b}18–21). Similarly, in the case of the elephant, its mega-size and exceptional capacities are both invoked in (apparently) the same way in the explanation of why it has a trunk (B.16, 658^{b}34, see 659^{a}7 f.). Degrees of heat are taken as explanatory givens on the same level as soul functions, pattern of movement, or being a land animal.

Aristotle, it appears, did not take even the first steps along the conservative road. If he saw the difficulty, he did not tackle it by tinkering with the details of the *Analytics* account. If he had a solution, it must have been a more radical one.

12.9 THE ESSENCE OF BIOLOGICAL KINDS (4): THE RADICAL ALTERNATIVES*

Did Aristotle, confronted by these problems, envisage sweeping changes to his account of unity and definition? I shall consider three such solutions in order of increasing radicalism. (There are probably others.)

It may be suggested that Aristotle rejected, in his biological writings, the combination of assumptions (A) and (C) noted above. If so, he would have taken the form or essence as a unity (*one* form) independently of any explanatory role it might play. Thus, he would insist that there is a unique integrated form of the fish (made up, for example, of a combination of material and movement-based features) which constitutes its essence, quite apart from any consideration of its role in explanation.

This approach, in severing the *Analytics'* connection between essence and explanation, undermines Aristotle's grounds for taking certain features as essential and others as merely necessary. Further, once explanatory considerations are removed, Aristotle lacks an account of what makes something *one* integrated form. His route to satisfy his own Definitional Constraint is effectively undermined.[46] For these reasons, he would have found this approach unattractive. Fortunately, there is no reason to believe that he took it.

---

[46] See Ch. 8 Sect. 8.2.

An alternative suggestion runs as follows: perhaps Aristotle maintained assumptions (A) and (C) but rejected (B), and took the material base (and not formal features such as pertain to soul function) as essential and explanatorily prior.[47] However, this strategy, even if it could provide a satisfactory resolution to the issues of unity, runs strongly contrary to Aristotle's insistence in *De Partibus Animalium* A.1 and 5 that the soul is prior to matter in biological explanation (640^b25 ff., 641^a28 ff., 645^b30 ff.). Nor can it do justice to the central role given to teleological explanation in his biological writings (e.g. 640^a3 ff., 642^a14 ff.).

But perhaps Aristotle should have taken this route. Was his mistake to look for the explanatorily basic feature in the wrong place? Perhaps he should have replaced his teleologically based account with a material account, phrased (as today) in terms of genetic code, DNA structure, or capacity for interbreeding. Surely one of these would have enabled him to find the simple unifying feature demanded by the *Analytics* model? His mistake (as we can see with the benefit of hindsight) was not to have looked in the right place for the basic unifying feature his favoured model of definition required.

There are, however, reasons to doubt whether Aristotle's favoured model, even thus modified, can apply to biological taxa. Interbreeding occurs between distinct species, particularly among plants, fish, and amphibians. Hybridization is a common feature of the animal and plant kingdoms. Man naturally produces man (as Aristotle emphasized (*Phys.* B.3, 194^b29–32). But there is, it appears, as much intra-species genetic as morphological variation. Indeed, possession of genetic variety enables a species to survive in changing environmental circumstance. Thus, there may be considerable variation within species in 'genetic code', with differing gene combinations yielding the same phenotype.[48] There is as much similarity between the DNA of some dogs and that of wolves or cats, as between the DNA of two different types of dog.[49] There is reason to doubt that the genetic code will provide the simple unifying feature required for Aristotelian definition.

Did Aristotle opt for an even more radical alternative? Did he reject all of Assumptions (A), (B), and (C) and take as basic the idea of a common nature shared by all fish, consisting solely in the way they move, reproduce, breathe, and in their possession of certain morphological and material features. If so, the notion of a common nature will be the result of reflection based on examples of particular kinds of animals which are seen to form a natural grouping. But there will be no need to establish the existence of

---

[47] This alternative is explored by Robert Bolton in 'The Material Cause: Matter and Explanation in Aristotle's Natural Science', in Kullmann and Follinger (eds.), *Aristotelische Biologie*, 97–124.

[48] These issues are discussed by John Dupré in 'Biological Taxa', *PR* 90 (1981), 84–6. I am indebted to his discussion at this point.

[49] As Putnam observes in 'Aristotle after Wittgenstein', 132.

a unifying common cause to underwrite the unity of the kind. The authority for determining that there is a genuine kind will rest not with explanation or scientific method, but with common-sense observation and classification. The source of the relevant authority will be popularly held, well-entrenched views (*endoxa*) about kinds.

If Aristotle were to have adopted this most radical alternative, he could have said (in the *Analytics*) that:

biped   animal

is a clear case of a common nature, while:

musical   grammarian

is not, without defending the first claim by finding a basic feature which explains why being biped belongs to animal. That is, he could have taken at face value our intuitions about common natures without requiring that they be legitimized by scientific practice. If so, the locus of authority would lie with common beliefs rather than with scientific knowledge. Had he accepted this strategy in biology, he would have departed from, indeed rejected, his *Analytics* model of explanation and definition.

There is good reason to believe that Aristotle did not proceed in this way. In his discussion of 'the great genera' in *De Partibus Animalium* A.4 he reconciles himself to standard beliefs provided that they are correct. Since in *De Partibus Animalium* A Aristotle emphasizes the importance of scientific reasoning, causality, demonstration, and form (e.g. A.1, 640ᵃ1–6, 34 ff., 642ᵃ14 ff.), he appears to take as correct only those popular claims which are underwritten (in some way) by his scientific or metaphysical theory. Nor does he think that common opinion has achieved the proper method for analysing the relevant natural phenomena (A.1, 639ᵇ7–10). There are, in Aristotle's view, additional constraints introduced by the more rigorous and accurate study of nature itself, which can override popular opinion in certain areas.[50]

This dilemma has deepened. The authority for kind determination cannot rest solely with popular opinion. It can and should be corrected (according to Aristotle) by scientific method and informed discovery. But, in the case of biological kinds, those methods failed to uncover the unified essences which should (according to the *Analytics* model) determine the nature of the relevant kinds. Worse still, as indicated above, they give reason to believe that no such unifying essence is to be found. Although biological species are central cases of natural kinds, they appear to lack the non-complex feature which Aristotle took elsewhere as the source of unity of genuine kinds. Was he mistaken to attempt to assimilate biologi-

---

[50] This occurs, e.g., in the discussion of 'dualizers', where Aristotle clarifies the notion of 'sea animal' in the light of problematic cases.

cal species to his favoured model for natural kinds, the one which applies to the eclipse, to water, and to gold?

12.10 THE ESSENCE OF BIOLOGICAL KINDS (5): ARISTOTLE'S MIDDLE WAY?

Let us take stock of the last sections: the conservative holds that there must be one teleologically basic explanatory feature which underwrites the unity of the kind. The radical, by contrast, rejects the idea that authority for kind determination rests with teleological concerns of this type. In his view, either there is no theoretical basis for the unity of kinds or (if there is one) it lies in the material, not the teleological, cause. But neither conservative nor radical alternative appears to capture Aristotle's position. Did he find a position between these two extremes? Or did the problem defeat him?

If Aristotle found a 'middle way', it must be one which does justice to:

(i) the prominent role he accords to teleological explanation (Section 12.5)

(ii) the importance he attaches to material and efficient explanation (Section 12.6)

(iii) his need to maintain some measure of priority for the form over the composite kind (Section 12.8)

(iv) his insistence on underwriting popular ideas of common natures in an explanatory fashion (Section 12.9)

(v) the role he gives to *differentiae* marked out in terms of soul function (Sections 12.2 and 12.3).

Did Aristotle find, or envisage the possibility of, a route which satisfies these demands?

One might hope to render these claims consistent by taking the teleological factors as basic and relaxing the relevant unity condition. Thus, for example, one teleologically basic feature might explain many, but not all, of the kind's genuine features. The fish's distinctive mode of moving in a given habitat may explain a great deal of its common nature and generate enough *differentiae* to mark out the kind, even though it does not explain (e.g.) why fish reproduce precisely as they do.

If Aristotle were to relax Assumption (A)[51] in this way, the teleological

---

[51] See Sect. 12.7.

cause would constitute some aspect of the essence (in line with Assumption (C)), even though it is not the starting point for all explanations of necessary features of the kind. Other features (such as concern material composition or environment) would provide starting points for other important explanations, provided that they fitted together with the teleological cause in 'one common nature'. Thus, there would be a variety of connections between soul function and matter, some beginning with the former, others the latter, provided that they were all parts of one common nature.

Did Aristotle pursue this approach? If he did, how did he articulate the idea of 'fitting together' in one common nature? In his discussion of fish, he explains the presence of fins and absence of legs on the basis partly of their nature as swimmers, partly of their being blooded (*PA* Δ.13, 695^b17–23). Fish have fins because they are swimmers. Given that they are also blooded, they lack legs. Hence, the resulting features of fish are the outcome of a number of interlocking causal features. The fish, as a swimmer, needs to carry out certain activities. Given the matter it possesses, it can only perform these activities if it has certain bodily features and not others. While the relevant matter could have been used for several different purposes, in the fish it is used for certain specific purposes and not others. In this case, both material and formal natures are constrained by each other. Here, they 'fit together' in so far as their mutual interaction determines parts of the nature of the relevant kind.

Nor is this structure confined to fish and their fins. Aristotle remarks, in discussing the elephant, that its front feet are used exclusively to support its immense weight, while in other lighter four-footed animals front feet are used in place of hands to grasp objects (*PA* Γ.3, 659^a23–5). Given this use of its front feet, and its need to reach air quickly, the elephant must have a trunk of a given type: one which can be used for breathing and for grasping. Here, several individual features (weight, need to grasp, need to breathe under water) combine to determine one outcome. As was noted, certain aspects of the matter are taken as basic (e.g. weight (659^a7)). Nature, in effect, does the best it can with the material at its disposal (*IA* 704^b15–16). But the matter, so used, plays a role (together with the formal nature) in explaining certain distinctive features of the kind's nature.

This form of analysis is relevant to the other problematic cases raised above. The material nature can (together with the formal nature) explain why fish have eggs which are white and small, or why they eat in a gluttonous way. Both material and formal features interact to produce the distinctive outcome. Thus, fish need to reproduce, but the way in which they do so is the product of their distinctive matter. In this way, their formal nature combines with their degree of heat to produce the distinctive nature of their progeny. Similarly, fish need to eat, but the way they do so is the product of their distinctive physical constitution. Here, too, formal and material natures interact to produce the relevant outcome.

In this account, the unity of a kind will consist (partly) in the interaction of its explanatory features (whether formal or material) to determine some of its derived features. The notion of one *common nature* will not be grounded in the unifocal pattern, favoured in the *Analytics*, but instead in the interaction of several separate causal factors. The resulting unity might be termed an *interactive unity*, because it rests on the distinctive interconnection of several causal features, and not on the presence of one common cause or starting point.

Biological natures, so understood, will not conform to the *Analytics* ideal, but neither will they be the result solely of common sense reflection. When all goes well, Stage 2 claims to detect natural groupings will be vindicated by the discovery of interlocking connections of the type indicated. As in the *Analytics*, the relevant unity will be underwritten by some explanatory structure. On occasion we may discover that we have mistakenly lumped together as one two kinds, with distinctive formal or material natures. Thus, although Aristotle relaxes his *Analytics* account of unity, he is not driven to accept any of the radical solutions canvassed in the previous Section.

However, this said, Aristotle must, nonetheless, be prepared (on this account) to take as an explanatory starting point a given material nature, whose presence in an organism is not further explained. As a consequence, he must accept that there is no one starting point which is (i) explanatorily prior to all else in the way the *Analytics* model suggested, and (ii) the ground of the kind's unity. The nature and unity of biological kinds will no longer be made perspicuous through and on the basis of one explanatorily basic feature. Nor can Aristotle simply take such a feature as the basic essence of the kind.

How significant are these departures from the *Analytics* model? Aristotle, as we saw above, envisages biological investigation as starting from a differentiation of animal kinds into a variety of common natures (Section 12.5). The biologist will seek for the interacting formal and material natures which produce these kinds' distinctive features. The relevant material base (in successful cases) will play a role in underwriting the groupings with which we begin. In effect, the biologist is seeking to vindicate (or undermine) the types of common nature we mark out on the basis of our observation and practice as farmers, breeders, etc. He is not attempting here to explain *de novo* why a given type of matter is present in this type of animal.

These differences are major ones. Biological investigation is anchored in our practices and intuitions about what is to count as a common nature. The type of unity sought will be one which underwrites in some explanatory way (at least some of) our ordinary classifications. For this reason, biological taxa cannot be fully assimilated to the theoretical paradigm defined in the *Analytics*. Indeed, it should be no surprise, since our biological terms were not introduced in a way governed solely by that ideal.[52] In the biological case, progressive understanding of the idea of a common nature generates the type of interactive unities sketched above. It will not lead to kinds unified in the style of the *Analytics*, unless there happen to be such kinds which underwrite our everyday biological classifications into (e.g.) dogs and horses.[53]

Notwithstanding these differences, Aristotle's understanding of biological kinds still reflects certain features of his *Analytics* account. He can continue to distinguish between explanatorily basic and derived, necessary, features of the kind. Further, he can still treat some explanatorily basic features as essential, provided that they fit into a genus-wide sytem of explanatorily relevant features.[54] There may indeed be cases where (in the absence of one basic explanatory feature) it is not determinate whether (e.g.) mode of breathing or reproduction is essential or merely necessary. But, nonetheless, the explanatory structure of biological kinds approximates (in certain respects) to the *Analytics* paradigm. For, a set of relevant starting points, individually and jointly, still determines the kind's other necessary features.

12.11 CONCLUSION

In the previous Section, I sketched one way in which Aristotle's *Analytics* model could have been modified to accommodate his recalcitrant biological discoveries. Further, I noted some (far from conclusive) evidence of the presence of an approach of this type in Aristotle's biological writings. It would be worthwhile to investigate this issue further, but

[52] This leaves open (but does not entail) the possibility of the type of 'vagueness' in classification which Geoffrey Lloyd has argued is a characteristic of Aristotle's actual biological method. See, 'Fuzzy Natures', in his *Aristotelian Explorations* (Cambridge, 1996).

[53] Thus, even if artificially produced dogs (built by physicists) resembled natural dogs in their molecular structure, we would not regard them as dogs because we take mode of reproduction as an essential part of a dog's nature. Molecular biologists are better understood not as talking about dogs but about dogs*, a kind many of whose members are dogs. While evolutionary and molecular biology may 'involve different viewpoints', their debate should be seen not as one about 'what it is to be a dog', but about whether dog or (its homonym) dog* is the most useful biological category for us to adopt. The molecular biologist is, in effect, advocating a reform of our classificatory system, not claiming to tell us what that classificatory system 'really' is. On this issue, contrast Putnam's discussion in 'Aristotle after Wittgenstein'.

[54] There is, of course, the possibility of taking other features (e.g. material ones) as essential, provided that these generate their own genus-wide classification. I return to this issue in the next Chapter.

that major undertaking lies outside the scope of the present project.[55] However, for present purposes, there is a prior and more general question which needs to be addressed. If anything of the type suggested is (even approximately) correct, how (if at all) was Aristotle justified in surrendering, in his biological writings, some central parts of his *Analytics* account of the unity of kinds? What entitled him to offer respectively interactive and unifocal accounts of the unity of biological kinds and meteorological kinds?

Aristotle's silence on these issues is unnerving. Did he remain quietly (or perhaps grimly) optimistic that some future science would eventually succeed (where his had failed) in discovering *Analytics*-style unifying essences? Or was he transfixed by the problem, accepting that his theory had fragmented, with different types of definition for different types of kind? Did he think that he had an adequate theoretical justification for some departure from his *Analytics* paradigm? Or was it simply that (somewhat pragmatically) he followed the *Analytics* model when he could and settled for a modified approach when he could not?

In the final Chapter, I shall consider these issues further. While some aspects of Aristotle's theory of essence and natural kinds are unaffected by these difficulties, others remain on the danger list. The crisis has not yet passed.[56]

---

[55] I hope to pursue this issue further elsewhere.　　　[56] See Sect. 12.7.

13

Aristotle's Essentialism

13.1 LANGUAGE, THOUGHT, AND ESSENCE

There is one claim on which Aristotle and my modern essentialist (as introduced in 1.2) agree:

(A) The world falls into natural kinds with their own essential properties.

However, they differ in their understanding of (A) and in the grounds they offer for its truth.

For my modern essentialist, (A) is underwritten by our practice as ordinary (non-scientific) thinkers of individuating kinds of objects in terms of their explanatorily basic features. The source of claims about essential features lies in our pre-scientific conventions and intentions. His claim could be expressed as follows:

(B) It is because we (as pre-scientific thinkers) have such conventions that we treat certain features of kinds as essential.

My modern essentialist is a conventionalist. But his position is a species of a wider genus, whose defining claim may be presented as:

(C) It is because we (as pre-scientific thinkers) think as we do that we divide the world into natural kinds with their own non-accidental features.

(C) does not make it a matter of convention that we think as we do. Perhaps we could do no other. But common to (B) and (C) is the claim that the world (as we find it) is as it is (in some crucial respects) fundamentally because of the way we think.[1]

Aristotle, as I argued in Chapters 2–6, does not attribute to ordinary thinkers intentions or beliefs of the required depth to sustain either (B) or (C). In his view, ordinary thinkers can grasp terms for natural kinds without thinking of those kinds as possessing a fundamental and determining feature of the relevant type. In particular, the master craftsman can grasp a genuine kind term while lacking the idea of its possessing this type of hidden, basic, scientific structure (Chapter 6). While the idea of such a

---

[1] In particular, it is not the case that we think as we do because the world is as it is.

structure may emerge later in our practices, it is not (in Aristotle's view) a requirement for understanding a natural-kind term.

Aristotle's reasons for rejecting (B) and (C) carry a further consequence. If the ordinary thinker can grasp natural-kind terms without thinking of them as possessed of a determining scientific feature, the latter idea cannot be one which we need for our basic understanding of the world. In particular, it cannot be a principle of the type which simultaneously defines what it is to be a thinker and the world of which we think. Thus, Aristotle rejects what I termed in Chapter 1 the democratic version of Kantianism. For, according to that view, it makes no sense to ask whether principles such as these come from us or from the world. We cannot sustain the idea of separate contributions made respectively by us and the world.

In Aristotle's view (as I interpret him), the source for claims about natural kinds and their essences does not lie (in any of these ways) in our thoughts as ordinary thinkers. If such claims are to be vindicated, they will be sustained from resources in metaphysics rather than the theory of thought or language. In his account, the burden of proof is carried by the metaphysician and not by the intuitions of the ordinary thinker. The question is: How is this to be done?

13.2 CO-DETERMINATION AND INTERDEPENDENCY: ARISTOTLE'S BASIC POSITION

Aristotle, I have argued, is committed to the following three basic claims:

(D) Our practices of definition and of explanation are incomplete without the assistance of one another.

(E) Essences and *per se* causes are co-determined.

(F) The interdependency of our practices rests on the co-determination of essences and *per se* causes.

From these claims, two more follow:

(G) The type of intelligibility which we seek in definitions cannot be fully characterized without reference to the world and its causal structures.

and

(H) The world and its causal structures cannot be fully grasped by those who lack the type of definitional and explanatory practices we possess.

These five claims, as was noted in Chapter 10, separate Aristotle from conventionalist and Platonist alike. In accepting (G), he rejects the assumption that our own thinking contains within itself (independently of how the world is) the determinate intuitions about definition which the conventionalist requires. The very notions which are essential to definition (such as unity and priority) cannot be made determinate without dependence on the world and its causal structures. Further, in accepting (H), Aristotle rejects the view that the world's intelligible patterns are there to be grasped by anyone irrespective of their definitional and explanatory practices. The type of intelligibility we find in the world cannot be grasped by those who lack our definitional and explanatory practices.[2] In this way, Aristotle escapes the fatal oscillation between Platonism and conventionalism described in Chapter 1 (Sections 1.3 and 1.4).

These points can be placed in a wider philosophical perspective, which allows us to grasp more securely the questions at issue. Platonism (as I characterize it) is committed to three claims:

(i)   The world exists independently of us, complete with its own kinds and essences.

(ii) The world, its kinds, and its essences are visible to any proper thinker whatever their definitional or explanatory practices may be.

(iii) Our grasp on the relevant type of essences cannot depend essentially on our having certain definitional and explanatory practices.

For the Platonist, we grasp the relevant type of kinds and essences by seeing them in nature. What makes certain features essential is independent of our definitional practices, and a proper understanding of what it is to be essential should register this fact. Reality and essence are mind-independent in two distinct ways: (1) their existence is not dependent on the existence of any mind, and (2) their nature can be grasped by any mind whatsoever, no matter what its definitional or explanatory practices may be.

Aristotle (as is argued in Chapters 7–12) is not a Platonist (so understood). He rejects the second and third aspects of the Platonist account by denying that the type of intelligibility uncovered in constitutive explanation can be understood from a perspective innocent of the relevant definitional and explanatory concerns. The type of intelligibility we discover in nature cannot be grasped without reliance on practices of definition and explanation such as ours. But, nonetheless, the patterns we uncover in essentialist explanation are there to be discovered. In effect, Aristotle rejects the Platonist claims (ii) and (iii) above, while holding on to the basic realism embedded in claim (i).[3] In his view, there are essences whose

---

[2] See Ch. 10 Sect. 10.5.

[3] The two points of difference between Plato and Aristotle are related. The first registers Aristotle's resistance to the claim that definitions can be complete without the addition of material drawn from the theory of explanation. The second notes that if such material is

existence does not in any way depend on our explanatory/definitional practices, even though we cannot grasp them independently of those practices.[4]

If Aristotle rejects Platonism, he is not thereby driven to accept the standard conventionalist alternative. According to the latter, the type of intelligibility registered in essentialist claims is introduced by us and is grounded in our practices of explanation and definition. The conventionalist rejects each of the Platonist claims. He will maintain:

(i*)   It is not the case that the world's intelligible structure exists independently of us and our own system of definition and explanation.

and

(iii*) The intelligibility we detect in the world is a reflection of our own definitional and explanatory practices.

Simply put, if there are essences in nature, it is we who made certain features essential.

Aristotle denies the third conventionalist claim. As we noted in Chapter 10, the theory of definition (in the *Analytics*) cannot be completed without reference to how the world is, with its necessitating patterns of causation. The relevant form of intelligibility is not merely a projection from us on to an intrinsically unintelligible world. For, we cannot fully specify the type of intelligibility we seek without reference to the necessitating patterns that are to be found in the world. In Aristotle's view, the world's intelligible causal structure is something that exists independently of us and our system of explanation. Thus, while he rejects the Platonist claims (ii) and (iii), he does not do so at the cost of slipping into the standard conventionalist alternative. It is a strength of his position that he combines acceptance of the first, and most important, Platonist claim with a rejection (shared by the conventionalist) of the remaining two Platonist contentions. As elsewhere, he seeks to 'unpick' and retain the best elements from strongly opposed theories.

Aristotle's commitment to (F) and (G) also serves to distance his view from the form of Kantianism sketched in Chapter 1. According to my élitist Kantian, it makes no sense to ask what contribution comes from us and which from the world. Aristotle, by contrast, seeks to answer this question by saying that both we and the world make separable but incomplete contributions to the full account of good definition. Since it makes sense to

added the resulting definitions will not be visible from all points of view (since they will not be visible from a point of view innocent of our explanatory interests). For further discussion of Platonism, See Ch. 1 n. 37 and Ch. 10 n. 39.

[4] For further discussion of the apparent parochialism of this viewpoint, see Section 13.5 below.

distinguish these components, his view cannot be assimilated to that of the Kantian.[5]

These points can be made diagrammatically. Both conventionalism and Platonism are bipolar alternatives, made up of two distinct and complete ingredients:

(1) our thoughts □:□ the world

In conventionalism, we do the work in constructing a model of intelligibility which we then project on to the world. In Platonism, the world does all the work, offering to us its own type of intelligibility, complete and perfect in itself. We make no contribution but that of registering what there is. For that reason, the world's intelligible patterns can be grasped by any thinker whatsoever (provided that they have the resources to see what there is). There is no need of any particular definitional or explanatory practices to see what reality contains.

By contrast, Kantianism (as I have characterized it) is unipolar. There is no coherent question to ask about whether the relevant form of intelligibility flows from us or from the world. For, there is no way (in principle) of distinguishing between the world as we think of it and the thoughts we have about it. They are not merely governed by the same constraints, but are (strictly speaking) identical. In a diagram, this view might be expressed by one shape (and one of beguiling simplicity!):

(2) □: our thoughts of the world = the world we think about

Aristotle seems to accept neither bipolar nor unipolar model. He does not think that either we or the world individually construct the type of intelligibility we seek. For, although his account of definition begins with our practices it cannot be completed without reference to the causal structures we find in reality. Nor would the latter be fully intelligible to any who lack the relevant definitional and explanatory practices. It is not that there is no coherent question to be asked concerning the origin of the relevant type of intelligibility. Rather, it is the product of two separable but incomplete contributions made by us and the world (and its causal structures). There are two elements in a harmonious whole:

(3) our thoughts ⊏⃗⃖⊐ the world

Thus, Aristotle's viewpoint cannot be assimilated to any of the standard options set out in Chapter 1. He is neither a modern essentialist, nor a Platonist, nor a projectivist, nor a Kantian.

There are two further claims which are needed to complete Aristotle's account of essence and definition:

---

[5] Nor, given his acceptance of (F) and (G), can his view of definition and essence be a projectivist one. (See Ch. 10 Sect. 10.2.)

(I) Essential features form the natures of kinds, and as such are distinct from merely necessary properties which belong to those kinds because they flow from their essences.

The essential features are those which meet the definitional constraints: the basic essence is a unity, the causal source of those necessary features which differentiate it from other kinds (in the favoured definitional way). Features will be merely necessary if (i) their presence is derived from the relevant causal source but (ii) they do not differentiate the kind in the favoured definitional style.

To (I) should be added one further claim:

(J) There are some genuine biological natural kinds.

(A) and (D)–(J) constitute the central planks of Aristotle's essentialism. We have seen them at work offering distinctive answers to the two questions raised at the beginning of our investigation:

(1) What makes statements of the form: 'Man is essentially rational', true?

and

(2) How can we come to know that such statements are true?[6]

Claims about essences are not to be understood in any of the Platonist, conventionalist, or Kantian ways described above. Thus, Aristotle's attempt to answer the metaphysical question (1) cannot be assimilated to any of the three options discussed in Chapter 1.[7] Nor, in his view, do we come to discover such essences by following a method which is either wholly a priori or wholly a posteriori. Rather, the type of essence-involving explanation (as described in Chapters 8 ff.) involves both a priori (such as may concern the general notion of definition) and a posteriori elements (the latter drawn from an understanding of causation in this world). Neither element can be made fully determinate without the assistance of the other.[8] Here, too, Aristotle's viewpoint differs from the three options set out in Chapter 1.

Are Aristotle's views defensible? They seem to be coherent, but do they

[6] See Ch. 1 Sect. 1.1.

[7] For some philosophers (influenced by Wittgenstein) it is a mistake even to ask the question of what makes such statements true. For them, the task of the philosopher is to expose the confusions and fallacies involved in raising such questions in the first place.

[8] This point could be put slightly differently. One might suggest that one could grasp essences by a mixture of empirical observation and inference to the best explanation (as some suggest one can discover causal necessities in nature). However, the type of best explanation invoked in the Aristotelian picture involves not merely conditions such as simplicity and explanatory power, but also a priori ones derived from the theory of definition (e.g. that it involves an essence, that it makes the nature of the kind transparent).

withstand rational criticism? Are they properly motivated? Is there something they fail to capture?

13.3 THE DISTINCTIVE NATURE OF ARISTOTLE'S ESSENTIALISM. SOME OBJECTIONS

The subtlety of Aristotle's position emerges when one considers two lines of objection which have been urged against it. As will be clear, both fail to hit the intended target.[9]

Quine is justly famed for his criticisms of 'Aristotelian essentialism'. He characterizes the position he wishes to reject as follows:

this is the doctrine that some attributes of a thing (quite independently of the language in which the thing is referred to, if at all) may be essential to the thing, and others accidental.[10]

Quine takes commitment to 'Aristotelian essentialism' to be a bad thing. There is good reason to reject any view which makes this commitment. But why? What is so bad about Aristotelian essentialism? Do Quine's criticisms engage with Aristotle's actual views about the essences of kinds?

Quine sometimes complains that Aristotelian essentialism involves a form of 'favouritism' towards certain traits of the individual, an attitude Quine permits himself to describe as 'invidious'.[11] For, the Aristotelian is committed to taking some descriptions as 'somehow better revealing the "essence" of the object'. But why is this form of 'favouritism' a mistake? Aristotle has given a number of arguments in favour of treating some features as essential and others as accidental, based on his commitment to claims (D) and (E) above. Indeed, he attempts to show that 'favouritism' of this type is not merely justified, but is in fact required if we are to make sense of our talk of definition and of kinds.

If 'favouritism' need not be a vice, why is Aristotelian essentialism (by Quine's lights) 'invidious'? Quine speaks, somewhat gloomily, of the 'metaphysical jungle' of Aristotelian essentialism,[12] and indicates his wish to be rid of it. However, although Aristotle's views on essence may seem

---

[9] In Sections 13.5–13.8 my goal is to employ Aristotle's account of essence and explanation, as interpreted in previous Chapters, to respond to criticisms of his viewpoint. While I will not refer here to textual details, I shall rely on the exegetical work done in previous Chapters. In Sections 13.5 and 13.8 I shall depend on claims made in Chapters 7–12, while in Sections 13.6 and 13.7 I shall also draw on Chapter 6.

[10] 'Grades of Modal Involvement', in *Ways of Paradox*, (New York, 1956), 173–4.

[11] 'Reference and Modality', in *From a Logical Point of View* (Cambridge, Mass., 1964), 154. Quine focuses on the essences of individuals and not those of kinds (or of individuals *qua* members of kinds). But his arguments apply, *mutatis mutandis*, to kinds.

[12] 'Grades of Modal Involvement', 174.

complex, they are far from confused. So, why call for the logging companies? Why cut down this intriguing and beautiful piece of ancient woodland? Is Quine an 'ecological vandal'?

Quine offers two reasons. One takes as its starting point the rich and elusive ontology of possible worlds, deployed in modern discussions, to capture notions of essence. Here, we find talk of world-bound individuals, world-bound properties, and of individuals existing in different possible worlds. Quine, plausibly enough, finds these notions obscure and perplexing. However, none of them is required to underwrite Aristotle's actual talk of essence. He needs to advert only to the individuals, kinds, features, and properties (and their combinations) which make up this world. What Aristotle insists on is attention to the varying ways in which these features are attached to objects and kinds (as suggested by the copula-modifier view set out in Appendix 2). Thus, Aristotle can agree with Quine that all of reality is exhausted by the actual world with its objects and features, but not accept his further claim that all true/false statements are about what is actually-instantiated in this world. For, there will also be true claims about what is naturewise-instantiated (and what is possibly-instantiated) by the relevant objects. Aristotle's proposal, as it stands, allows us to talk of essence and possibility without becoming entrapped in the elusive possible-worlds machinery of modern discussions.

Quine has, I suspect, a further reason for wishing to be rid of Aristotelian essentialism, one indicated by his remark that (for Aristotle) essential features are so 'independently of the language in which they are referred to'. For Quine, there is simply no way to grasp ontological issues independently of the ways we use to describe reality. There can be no way of knowing which features are essential independently of our language, with its own system of definition, explanation, and classification. Indeed, from his perspective, we can make no sense of the idea that certain features are essential to an object (or kind) without using our own linguistic practices (of definition, classification, and explanation). However, Aristotelian essentialism, as Quine characterizes it, demands that we do just that. Hence, it must be rejected.

The crucial move is in the penultimate sentence. Why think that Aristotle requires us to make sense of the idea that certain features are essential without using our practices of definition and explanation? Quine, it appears, thinks that Aristotle must be committed to (what I have described as) Platonism, the view that we can 'see' (without any dependence on language at all) what is essential and what is not. But, if my interpretation is correct, Aristotle differs from the Platonist on precisely this point. For, while he will accept that:

(i) The world exists independently of us, complete with its own kinds and essences.

he will deny that:

(iii) Our grasp on the relevant type of essences cannot depend essentially on our having certain definitional and explanatory practices.

Indeed, in Aristotle's view, we need these definitional and explanatory practices to latch on to kinds and their essences.

Quine's objections may be effective against the Aristotle of legend, but they do no damage to Aristotle's actual position. For, Aristotle (as we have interpreted him) is not an Aristotelian essentialist such as Quine attacks. Why has Quine erred? It seems that he has assumed that the only alternatives are Platonism (the view he attributes to Aristotle) and some version of conventionalism in which talk of essence is a shadow cast by our linguistic practices, the result of our own grammar (or individuative practices) autonomously conceived. But, if I am correct, Aristotle held neither of these views. In his account, while we cannot grasp the essential features of kinds independently of our practices of definition and explanation, they are not mere reflections of our conventions and grammar. Indeed, his aim seems to be to reject Platonism while (at the same time) avoiding a purely conventionalist understanding of definition and essentiality.

One of Locke's objections to Aristotle's essentialism manifests a similar mistake. Locke once wrote:

To talk of specifick Differences in Nature, without reference to general *Ideas* and names is to talk unintelligibly. For I would ask anyone, What is sufficient to make an essential difference in Nature, between any two particular Beings, without any regard to some abstract Idea, which is looked upon as the Essence and Standard of a Species? (*An Essay Concerning Human Understanding* III. vi. 5)

Locke concludes from the fact that we cannot grasp which differences are specific ones without dependence on our system of classification and naming that there are no specific differences existing independently of us in nature. But why does his conclusion follow? Aristotle, it should be clear, would not accept it. For, while he will agree with Locke that:

(iii*) Our grasp of the relevant type of essences depends on our having certain definitional and explanatory practices.

he will not conclude that:

(i*) The world does not exist independently of us, complete with its own kinds and essences.

For, he does not make the assumption, crucial to Locke's argument, that:

(P) If a claim is graspable only from the point of view of our practices of definition and explanation, it must fail to be an objective claim about a reality existing independently of ourselves.

In Aristotle's account, it does not follow from the fact that certain features are visible only from within the perspective of our definitional and explanatory perspectives that they are not features of reality. This point is already clear in the analogy he draws between thought and colour perception.[13]

Both Locke and Quine (in their differing ways) fail to recognize the possibility of the distinctive mid-position, which Aristotle sought to occupy. Quine argues from a justified rejection of Platonism (as I have characterized it) to the inevitability of some form of conventionalism. Locke, by contrast, argues from the unobjectionable premiss (iii*) to the (implausible) rejection of realism about kinds and their essences. Thus, both Locke and Quine fail to address the position actually occupied by Aristotle. For, he was concerned to outline a position which combined a (plausible) realism about essences with the acknowledgement that we can only have knowledge of essences through a route dependent (in some measure) on our practices of definition. In this way, he combines the most attractive Platonist and conventionalist claims ((i) and (iii*)) in one unified theory.

13.4 FURTHER OBJECTIONS TO ARISTOTLE'S ESSENTIALISM

But is Aristotle's account stable? Does he really succeed in maintaining a form of realism while still accepting that we can only have knowledge of essences because we have our definitional and explanatory practices? Does his view collapse, under pressure, into either conventionalism or Platonism?

Many will think that this must be so. They will not believe that an account which begins from our interlocking definitional practices and explanatory practices could provide the basis for an acceptable form of realism. I shall consider four attempts to articulate this unease as a determinate objection to Aristotle's viewpoint.

Objection 1: We can easily avoid (it will be said) using the interconnecting practices of definition and explanation which Aristotle describes. Indeed, such practices constitute a self-contained game from which we could easily free ourselves. After all, since natures are not part of the data of perception, Aristotle's talk of nature, definition, and explanation must be a projection from us on to a world which itself lacks both natures and essences. Thus, we must be able to dispense with this talk and return to a conception of reality which is nature-free. Aristotle's starting point, in

---

[13] See Ch. 10 Sect. 10.5.

our practices of definition and explanation, must be too parochial to be required for a grasp on objective reality.

Aristotle does not share the objector's conception of the problem, or the empiricist starting point which motivates it. For him, as we have seen, perception is of cross-temporal moving objects.[14] Experience will add a preliminary mode of classifying objects in a demonstrative-based way as (e.g.) this illness, this man, this disease.[15] If all goes well, we will arrive at the understanding of the master craftsman who grasps what can and cannot be done with the objects he confronts, and aims to learn where limitations in what can be done stem from him and where from the nature of the kind itself, such that no extension of his skill could change it. The nature of the kind is what makes some things possible and others impossible for him. At this point, talk of natures intersects with our ordinary practices and interactions with the world. Far from being part of an isolated, cut-off, game, they are basic to the understanding we have as craftsmen of the world around us.

The master craftsman will raise questions such as: 'Why is it that if I do this, that happens?', 'What is it about the nature of the kind which explains why this happens after that?' These questions concern the nature of the kind itself, what can and what cannot (in principle) be changed and why. In asking these questions, the master craftsman aims to make the kind's necessary properties and his dealings with them intelligible to himself. For, he wishes to know what it is about this kind which makes certain things inevitable and others avoidable. While his grasp on the nature of the kind is incomplete, it represents a step in the direction of the type of understanding achieved in a successful definitional answer to the 'What is F?' question. Both aim to make the nature of the kind perspicuous to us. In this way, our definitional and explanatory practices arise naturally out of the master craftsman's understanding of his subject matter.

The master craftsman plays two roles in this account. It is through his understanding that we first have access to kinds, their natures, and their necessary features. These notions are embedded in his understanding of his dealings with the world (as encapsulated in such sayings as: 'That cannot be done, because . . .'; 'There is no point in trying that . . . it has to be done this way.'). They cannot be dispensed with unless we are also prepared to surrender the type of understanding which the master craftsman has of the world. For, his understanding essentially involves a modality-rich grasp on reality. The concepts of kind, nature, and necessity employed in the theoretical discussion of the metaphysician are rooted in the judgements of the master craftsman. It is through his involvement with kinds,

---

[14] See Ch. 5 Sect. 5.4.   [15] See Ch. 6 Sect. 6.2.

whether as carpenter or farmer, that we first gain access to the natures which the metaphysician studies.[16]

Secondly, the craftsman's understanding of natures is not exhausted by a series of claims of the form:

If I do this, that will necessarily happen.

For, he is able to respond creatively to new situations and demands ('How would you make something with this property?'; 'What can we do with this piece of wood?'). He has a sufficient grasp on the nature of the kind to be able to respond creatively in this way. Indeed, it is just this grasp which allows him to see (and explain to others) what can and cannot be done in dealing with (e.g.) the wood before him. Rather than taking as basic a series of unexplained necessities, he will see these as flowing from the nature of the kind. The metaphysician aims at a perspicuous understanding of this type. For, neither he nor the master craftsman can remain content with a series of brute unexplained modal facts. Nor can his understanding be exhausted by a series of modal claims about how the kind will react in a variety of situations. His grasp on the nature of the kind is manifested in his ability to generate such modal claims in a systematic way, an ability grounded in his grasp of its essence.[17] While the metaphysician achieves a deeper understanding of the nature of the kind, the perspicuous grasp he seeks is first exemplified by the type of practical knowledge possessed by the master craftsman.[18] For, both aim (in differing degrees) to make the nature of the kind intelligible. Indeed, the metaphysician's account is best seen as an extension of the type of understanding already achieved (in limited measure) by the master craftsman.[19]

Objection 2: According to Aristotle's view, we can only grasp the essences of kinds if we have interconnected practices of definition and

---

[16] See Ch. 6 Sect. 6.4. The master craftsman's practical engagement with kinds is causally necessary for his acquisition of thoughts about kinds and their properties. Further, such thoughts are legitimized by his craft involvement with kinds.

[17] Descartes' account of matter as extension, shape, and movement exemplifies the type of essentialist thinking at issue. His goal was to explain the remaining features of kinds in terms of these three basic ingredients, which required no further explanation. In this way, he aimed to make the relevant natures through and through perspicuous in the way which characterizes Aristotelian essentialist thought.

[18] At this point, we return to a question left open in Chapter 10 Section 10.5: What type of intelligibility does the metaphysician seek?

[19] This is why, as was noted in Chapter 6 authority lies (in the *Analytics* model) with Stage 3 over Stage 2 considerations. The master craftsman can reasonably defer to the metaphysician/scientist because the latter has achieved a deeper (but still perspicuous) understanding of the kind. This does not require the former to think in the very same terms (e.g. 'micro-physical structure') as the latter. It is enough if the master craftsman can see the metaphysician's account as a more revealing description of the same thing: the kind's nature.

explanation. But surely, it will be said, this perspective cannot legitimize realist claims about kinds and essences. Does not realism require that we be able, no matter what our definitional or explanatory practices may be, to 'see' the world's modal structure? Surely, if something is real, it cannot be accessible only to those who make particular assumptions about the nature of definition.

But why must a realist make this assumption? In Aristotle's account, the master craftsman (and not the low-level artisan) grasps genuine kinds as such. This is because he understands that their instances share an interconnected set of properties, which neither he nor anyone else can change. Without his engagement with the world we would lack the grasp we have on genuine kinds. No such understanding can be achieved by the person who stays at the level of experience. Further, without the master craftsman's practical engagement with kinds, we would not latch on (in the appropriate way) to the modal properties we need to grasp the fundamental nature of things. While we could lay out a map of what such structures might be, we would lack a proper understanding of their constituting the natures of kinds. They would represent an abstract topology and not an account of the physical world we inhabit.

At this point, we can invoke Aristotle's favoured analogy with colour perception. There are two points of comparison. First, without the master craftsman's understanding of kinds, we would be like those who are colour blind: unable to see what is there. As we need a properly functioning visual system to grasp colours, so we need the master craftsman's understanding to latch on to kinds. As the former does not undermine the realism of our colour judgements, so the latter need not undermine the status of our judgements about kinds. Second, without our experiential engagement with colours, we would not achieve an understanding of what colours are. We might have a grasp of (e.g.) properties of light reflectance, but we would not be able to understand what it is to be coloured. Similarly, without our craft engagement with kinds, we could map out an abstract topology containing interconnected scientific features. But the latter would not amount to a world containing genuine kinds. For kinds, as we understand them, are ones of the type involved in our craft engagement with the world.[20]

There is, in any event, good reason to interpret the judgements of the master craftsman realistically. For, he is up against a reality which limits what he (or anyone) can do, and which makes him act in some ways not others. Indeed, his understanding of that reality is what explains

---

[20] Thus, the master craftsman's practical engagement with objects is indispensible in our acquisition of thoughts about kinds. It is not merely one possible route, or even the one we happen to follow. Our definitional and explanatory practices are grounded, in the ways indicated, in the master craftsman's understanding of kinds.

why low-level artisans act as they do. There is a further reason to take his judgements as descriptions of an independent reality. For, if all goes well, they will be underwritten by the interlocking theory of essence and causation, which we have seen at work in a variety of contexts and situations. The latter makes the nature of the kind fully intelligible to us in the ways indicated above. In this way, the realism of Aristotle's account of essence and nature is supported from below by the master craftsman's grasp on kinds and from above by the interlocking theory of essence and causation. Both have important roles to play. The latter exhibits the metaphysical depth of the idea of nature. The former ties the theory to genuine kinds in the world, and prevents the theory being a purely abstract one, cut off from our practices, containing relations which we do not fully understand.[21]

Objection 3: Can we not envisage different classifications generating incompatible definitional claims? The master craftsman's conception of gold is dependent on the kind's having a nature, which he cannot change and which will limit and confine his possible activities. This nature can in turn be investigated by the metaphysician. But surely a tribesman could have a term 'ggold' which picked out all and only yellow metals found in a given place. Now, we might say, for the tribesman it is a necessary feature of ggold that it is yellow. But this will not be a necessary feature of our gold. Surely these are incompatible essentialist claims, both generated from different initial classifications of reality? If so, our talk of essence looks to be a reflection of our interests, not a way of capturing reality.

This objection permits of a simple answer. In the case described, the essential features do not belong to the same kind. For, the tribesman's kind is ggold, not gold. Thus, this is not a case of inconsistent claims about the same kind, but rather one in which there are consistent claims about different kinds. In a similar way, one can say that there are two separable kinds, dogs and ddogs, if the former are defined solely in terms of their evolutionary history, the latter their molecular composition.[22]

But this form of reply is, in some cases, over-concessive. For, it is not obvious that the tribesman, just now described, has grasped a natural-kind concept at all. His claims about ggold do not stem from any grasp on the internal nature of any kind, since his classification (for all he knows) may cut across several kinds. Nor do they arise from a craftsman's understanding of the interconnected set of dispositions. Even if he has latched on to a feature of the genus metal, he has not as yet acquired the thought of a natural kind or a natural-kind term.

---

[21] This is the ideal case. We shall consider below what happens when these two factors are not present in this optimal way.

[22] A somewhat similar objection is discussed in Chapter 12 n. 53.

Objection 4: But surely, it will be said, Aristotle must accept the follow-ing counterfactual claim:

[C] If our definitional practices had been different, the world would have contained different kinds and essences.

If so, he must think that we could have adopted equally good, but differ-ent, definitional practices, which would have led us to detect other kinds and other essential features. However, if so, his claims about essences will flow (in the final analysis) from us and our definitional practices and not from the world. Once again his position appears to collapse into a form of conventionalism.

In Aristotle's account, our definitional practices contain ideas of unity and priority which can only be made determinate by reference to the world and its causal patterns. Indeed, his basic claim is that our definitional prac-tices cannot be fully specified without dependence on the determinate causal patterns we find in reality. We do not, in his view, have a set of world-independent definitional practices which we can alter independently of how the world is. Rather, the world plays a role in determining which def-initional practices we have. So, how could our definitional practices have been different? Does the possibility of such differences lead inevitably to conventionalism about essences and kinds?

There seem to be three possible routes to support [C], which should be considered:

(i) Our definitional practices might have lacked the ideas of priority or unity.

(ii) Our definitional practices might have contained these ideas and been complete, in a wholly a priori fashion, without any reference to the world and its causal structures.

(iii) Our definitional practices might have latched on to different causal patterns in the world.

Do any of these possibilities in fact threaten the realism of Aristotle's account? It is far from clear that they do.

If our definitional practices had been different in the way suggested by (i), we would not have defined kinds with essences at all. Indeed, where would our idea of essence (or essence-revealing explanation) have come from?[23] We would have been as if colour blind, incapable of detecting

___

[23] One might think that if one insists that explanation of the relevant type must begin with the nature of the kind (or imposes on explanation perspicuity requirements which flow from essentialist thinking about natures) one's explanations will begin with starting points of the type required for definition. But this is only because one has built into one's account of explanation constraints motivated by the theory of definition.

what is there to be seen. If so, the possibility of (i) does not support [C] above.

What of (ii)? Surely our definitions could have been completed in a wholly a priori fashion, without reference to the world, in the manner favoured by Plato (independently of all connections with a posteriori causation)? If so, the world would have contained different kinds and different essences. While both Plato and Aristotle wished to be realists, does not this possibility undermine their claims? Surely here we are forced to collapse into conventionalism?

Aristotle's reply, if what has been said so far is correct, is a distinctive one. In his view, Plato's project (if successfully carried through) would amount to no more than an abstract description of a possible world, not to an account of genuine kinds (as we encounter them). It would be like a piece of abstract geometry, not a description of real space. For, it would not be grounded in the understanding of natures around us, first acquired through our craft engagement with the world, and deepened by our grasp on the world's causal patterns. Even if Plato's abstract model could be mapped on to the real world in some way, it could not by itself provide an understanding of the natures of genuine kinds. For those, we need grounding in causal patterns in reality.

And (iii)? In one case, if our definitional practices had been different in the way indicated, this would have been because the world itself contained different kinds and essences. In such an eventuality, [C] would be true, but its truth would not undermine the basic realism of Aristotle's account. For, the world would contain kinds and essences other than those it now does, because its causal structure would have been radically different from those we now encounter.

But could we not, consistent with the world as it now is, have devised quite different kinds? What is the special significance of (e.g.) our biological kinds, the ones we understand via the notion of common nature? Could we not equally well used kinds based on material causes, such as those legitimized by a new molecular biology? Surely we could dispense with teleologically based kinds of the type Aristotle envisages? I shall consider this objection further in discussing biological kinds below. It is in this area that some of the severest tests of the stability of Aristotle's position are to be found.

13.5 BIOLOGICAL KINDS

Aristotle holds that there are genuine biological natural kinds. This claim generates a number of objections. I shall consider three, the last of which reintroduces an issue from the previous Chapter.

Objection 1: Descartes and Locke

Descartes was an essentialist, but not an Aristotelian essentialist. He thought that the only essential properties were those of matter (such as shape, extension, and movability) and of mind (consciousness). Although he did not complete *Principles* V and VI (to be devoted to living things), his view seems clear. Either there are no Aristotelian biological natural kinds or (if there are) they are derived kinds, based in differences in kinds of matter (marked out using differences in shape, extension, and movability). Locke went one step further, claiming that:

There is no individual parcel of Matter, to which . . . Qualities are so annexed as to be essential to it, or inseparable from it. (*An Essay Concerning Human Understanding* III. vi. 6)

As soon as one considers objects merely as parcels of matter, rather than as pieces of gold or tigers:

the thought of anything essential to any of them instantly vanishes. (III. vi. 4)

There is no way (Locke claims) of deriving Aristotle's distinctions between natural kinds from the differing properties of matter. If so, there can be no real essences of the type Aristotle envisaged.

This line of criticism is not powerful. First, even in cases where one cannot derive higher-order demarcations from lower-order ones, there seems no reason to doubt the reality of the higher-order kinds. For, the higher-order demarcations are marked out by considerations (such as those which concern teleological explanation) which are not present at the lower level. It is a widely recognized feature of non-reductionist strategies that there need be no perfect capturing of the 'shape' of higher-order demarcations at the lower level.[24] Descartes and Locke appear to rest on the assumption that the only genuine kinds are either present at the lowest physical level or reducible to such kinds. But there is no reason either to believe this assumption oneself or to attribute it to Aristotle.[25] Indeed, there is reason to do neither.

What is more interesting are the assumptions which drive Descartes' argument. There are three:

(1) All genuine explanation must begin with principles that are *clear and distinct*.

(2) The principles of matter such as extension and movability are of this sort.

---

[24] See, for instance, the Introduction to D. Charles and K. Lennon (eds.), *Reduction, Explanation and Realism* (Oxford, 1992), 7–9.

[25] For consideration of Aristotle's use of the non-reductionist strategy, see my 'Aristotle on Hypothetical Necessity and Irreducibility', 20–44.

(3) The Aristotelian principles which govern movement, life, or animals are not of this sort.[26]

It would be a major undertaking to attempt to unpack and make clear Descartes' own conditions for perspicuous explanation. Was he tempted by the view that all proper explanations of the physical should be instances of the mathematical method, and as such graspable a priori, without dependence on empirical means?[27] But, whatever the precise details of Descartes' own position, there is a general line of response available to Aristotle: to challenge the assumption that our explanatory starting points must enjoy the type of perspicuity on which Descartes insists, a perspicuity far removed from the one that characterizes our dealings with the kinds around us. His starting points have the status of an abstracted pure geometry, not those of a science dealing with the world we understand. For Aristotle, as we have seen, the master craftsman, not the geometer, provides a model of the type of perspicuous understanding to which we, as metaphysicians, aspire. Aristotle's project begins with what is 'familiar to us' and ends with an account of what is 'familiar by nature'. As suggested above, the kind of intelligibility we aim for (in a completed science) will be recognizably of the general type as we, as master craftsmen, engaged at earlier stages of enquiry with the kinds that surround us. This is why the notion of 'what is familiar . . .' is the same in these two contexts. Thus, even if the idealized type of understanding which Descartes sought is possible, it is not part (in Aristotle's view) of a proper understanding of the world.[28]

[26] Thus, Descartes wrote: 'But what is a man? Shall I say a reasonable animal? Certainly not: for then I should have to enquire what an animal is, and what is reasonable; and thus from a sensible question I should descend insensibly fall into an infinitude of others more difficult' *Philosophical Writings*, ed. J. Cottingham, R. Stoothoff, and D. Murdoch (Cambridge, 1985), II, 16–17. The underlying claim seems to be that the starting points for one's enquiry should be immediately clear and self-evident. Thus, Descartes envisages a perfect description of the world, in which 'matter has a nature in which there is absolutely nothing that everyone cannot know as perfectly as possible' (*Philosophical Writings*, I, 90), and in which 'we can demonstrate a priori everything that can be produced' on this basis (I, 97).

[27] On this, see D. Garber, *'Descartes' Mathematical Physics'* (Chicago, 1993), ch. 3.

[28] Descartes saw large parts of the Aristotelian tradition as the systematization of the uncritical world view of the common man (see, for instance, *Philosophical Writings*, II, 293–8, 251–255), uncorrected by the findings of science. (On this, see J. P. Carriero 'The Second Meditation and the Essence of the Mind', in A. O. Rorty (ed.), *Essays on Descartes' Meditations* (Barkeley, 1986), 199–221.) It should be clear (on the basis of his method in the *Analytics*) that Aristotle was not committed to the project of merely systematizing the commonly held world view. (Consider, for instance, his rejection of the common-sense view of the void.) But equally Aristotle would reject the Cartesian demand that the starting points of science must satisfy some revolutionary new set of epistemic credentials (such as clarity and distinctness), wholly removed from those we normally impose in our everyday dealings with the world. On this latter issue, see Daniel Garber's *'Semel in Vita*: The Scientific Background', in Rorty (ed.), *Essays on Descartes' Meditations*, pp. 88–91.

Aristotle's reply comes into sharper focus when we consider his discussion of the role of *nous* in grasping first principles.[29] *Nous* grasps certain features as first elements in a science on the basis of an explanation-involving procedure of induction. Its epistemic authority is derived from, and vindicated by, the process of induction on which it rests. As such, *nous*'s grasp on first principles (as reported in *Post. An.* B.19) depends on seeing their role in sustaining a pattern of explanation and differentiation of the type set out in the preceding chapters of the *Analytics*. There is no need for the special type of familiarity (demanded in Descartes' rationalistic model) to account for our grasp of first principles.

Objection 2: Locke's Second Objection

Locke had other objections to kind essentialism apart from those already noted. One runs as follows:

> many of the Individuals that are ranked into one sort, called by one common Name, and so received as being of one *Species*, yet have Qualities depending on their real Constitutions which are as different from one another as from others, from which they are accounted to differ *specifically*. (III. vi. 8)

The kinds marked out by biology do not correspond precisely to the ones found at some lower level. Not merely are they not deducible from them, but their divisions do not map precisely on to those made at the level of fundamental science. Thus, Locke concludes, the kinds we mark out in biology are not genuine kinds. At best, they represent shadows cast by our own interests as classifiers and namers.

But Locke's argument is not strong. In Aristotle's view, kinds can be real enough, even if they are not mappable on to demarcations marked out in, and motivated by, fundamental physical science. As before, shapelessness at some underlying level is no bar to the reality of the biological kind in question. It is sometimes assumed that if the kinds demarcated in ordinary experience (such as dogs or cats[30]) cannot be reduced to 'fundamental' physical kinds, they must be dismissed as illusory, constructs of our language, mere *façons de parler*.[31] But Aristotle rejects this viewpoint. Biological kinds can be genuine even if they do not reduce to more basic ones. Failure of reduction is, in his view, no bar to reality. It is only some unquestioned reductionist dogma that can make it seem to be so.

---

[29] See Ch. 10 Sect. 10.3.

[30] Similar remarks apply to the kinds marked out in psychiatry, such as depression or various forms of obsessionality.

[31] See, e.g., the argument sketched by Stephen Schiffer in *Remnants of Meaning* (Cambridge, 1987), 70–1. He suggests that properties such as *being a dog* are 'pleonastic' (not genuine properties) since they are irreducible to genetic or evolutionary or phenotypical properties.

If this is correct, the arguments deployed against essentialism concerning biological kinds by Locke and Descartes are ineffective. Indeed, they fail to engage successfully with the position Aristotle actually adopted.[32]

Objection 3: Aristotle's Own Problem: Do Biological Kinds have One Essence?

Nevertheless, biological kinds do pose a problem for Aristotle. As we saw in the last Chapter, they fail to live up to his unity requirement for natural kinds, because they do not have one basic feature which explains the rest.[33] But Aristotle persisted in regarding these kinds as real. He did not conclude from this that such kinds are merely constructs, the products solely of our interests. Nor did he move towards introducing a fully scientific kind (perhaps marked out in some favoured material way), conforming to his unity requirement. Still less did he consider slicing fish up into a number of structured but slimmer entities (e.g. swimmers, breathers, reproducers), each with its own basic essence. Aristotle accepted fish as a real kind even though it failed to satisfy his ideal. The crucial question is: Is he justified in doing so? Can he resist being driven towards a properly scientific taxonomy, one which reflects his own *Analytics* ideals? How can he persist with interactive common natures of this type?

It might seem that this is not really a problem. The master craftsman will engage with kinds of this type (as farmer or breeder) and will have some understanding of their nature. Further, biological research will uncover some interconnected explanatory structure, even if this does not correspond precisely to that found in the ideal case. Thus, Aristotle has reason not to regard fish as our construct, even if the kind's unity is not grounded

---

[32] This is clear in one of Locke's other arguments against biological essentialism. He wrote:

There are animals so near of kind both to Birds and Beasts that they are in the Middle between both. (III. vi. 12)

Indeed, elsewhere he speaks of the 'continuum of things', and comments on the interbreeding of women and gimars (III. vi. 23) as producing borderline cases which do not fall precisely into one or other natural kind.

However, Aristotle himself gives a series of examples, far more realistic than the ones Locke provides, of cases which are borderline between animals and plants, in *Historia Animalium* 588[b]3–25. Indeed, there he speaks of 'the continuousness' of the change from animals into plants (588[b]11–13 (see 588[b]3–5)). It is no part of Aristotle's strategy to deny (a) that there are borderline cases between kinds, or (b) that there are anomalous cases of particular kinds. Indeed, as was noted in Chapter 12, there is nothing in Aristotle's strategy which precludes the possibility of genuine vagueness in nature.

[33] See final Section of Ch. 12.

in one essence of the appropriate unifying type. For the reality of the kind can be guaranteed without recourse to one essence.

But if things are that easy, why search for one essence in other cases? How can Aristotle rest content with the lack of a unifying cause in these cases, when in others he seeks for one? Surely, if ideally unified kinds were to be devised in biology, he would be forced to prefer these to the biological kinds he discusses (such as fish, elephants, and dolphins). Could he have held on to his favoured taxa in the face of other alternatives which conform more fully to his ideal? Conversely, if there are no biological kinds of the latter type, can he avoid regarding biology as a failed science?

The question is: can Aristotle reasonably rest content with the type of interactive common-nature kinds he uncovered in his biological studies? Can he justifiably stop at this point, without having found scientific kinds with *Analytics*-style unified essences? If the latter were to be found, could he resist regarding them as a 'better class' of kind?

Aristotle's idea of a biological common nature is grounded in our ordinary dealings with the world, the ones exemplified in our activities as farmers or fishermen, breeders or hunters. These are the kinds we are interested in understanding. Indeed, it is through our involvement with them that we acquire our thoughts about what it is to be a kind, as well as our grasp on specific kinds (such as animal, sheep, and dog.) Our craft involvement with these is our point of access to kinds whose natures we seek to discover. If these kinds play these two roles, Aristotle has reason enough to retain them even if they only approximate to his *Analytics* ideal. These are *our* kinds, the ones we want to understand. For, such understanding will deepen and extend the knowledge we have as master craftsmen of the kinds involved.

From this perspective, Aristotle's discussions of biological and non-biological kinds form a unified whole.[34] In the latter, but not the former, we find a unitary feature which makes the whole kind intelligible to us. This discovery recognizably extends the type of understanding which the craftsman has of his subject matter. In the former, by contrast, an extension of his understanding leads to the interactive kinds discussed in the last Chapter. We will only find unitary *Analytics*-style starting points in biology if we give up trying to make *our* kinds thoroughly intelligible to us. But, as we have seen, we have (in Aristotle's view) strong reasons not to take this step. For, we are interested in both cases in extending our craft-based understanding of the relevant kinds.

Is there a further Aristotelian reply? If the analogy with colour perception holds, we may not be capable of abstracting too far from our original starting point in craft involvement with our kinds. For, to do so would be

---

[34] To return to a problem raised at the end of Chapter 12.

to lose the type of intelligibility we seek. It is not that there is a truly objective world which exists somewhere inaccessible to us beyond our range. It is rather that, as in the case of colour, aspects of what is really objective can only be grasped by creatures with the type of experience we possess. So understood, the idealized scientific story (in which colours are replaced by wave lengths) cannot constitute a complete picture of the world. For, it cannot capture the nature of the kinds or colours with which we interact.[35]

This point can be pressed further. If we were to abandon *our* kinds in pursuit of the scientific ideal, the resulting account would be (at best) partial and (in the extreme case) one we could not fully understand.[36] Indeed, in the latter case, it might threaten our understanding of what it is to be a kind. While we may postulate entities which exemplify our theoretical ideal of unity, their necessary features need be nothing more than the product of our theorizing. In the limiting case, such idealized kinds will not possess natures of the type which limit (directly or indirectly) what we or other kinds (with which we can interact) can do.[37] If so, we would lose our understanding of what it is to be a kind endowed with genuine necessary properties. While we might develop, in complete abstraction, a beautiful 'logical' picture of the world, it would not be one which contained kinds whose natures were intelligible to us.

If this is correct, Aristotle can resist the drive towards a scientific account of kinds, with ideally unified *Analytics*-style essences. He can insist on the necessity of retaining certain of the kinds we understand as craftsmen, on pain of losing our basic understanding of what it is to be a kind. We cannot, in the world as we find it, rationally detach ourselves completely from our involvement with these kinds (the ones with which we and others causally interact). There are important limits on the distance we can travel from our starting point in pursuit of this scientific picture.[38] The world will not

---

[35] On the view just sketched, our understanding of *colour* cannot be given in a purely scientific account, couched solely in terms completely abstracted from our experience as perceivers of colour and of light. There are, no doubt, relevant truths about wave lengths, but they cannot account for what it is to be a colour. For accounts in which the *explanandum* is not the phenomenon we see will not be accounts of *colour*. There cannot be proper descriptions of colour, or of kinds, in which the *explananda* are completely abstracted from our experience or involvement with the world. This, no doubt, is why Aristotle was drawn to an account of colour in terms of the activity of light (see Ch. 5). For, this will be intelligibly connected to our experience of colour.

[36] For similar reasons, Aristotle will remain committed to natural substances (*De An.* B.1, 412ᵃ11–14, *Meta.* Λ.1, 1069ᵃ31 f.). For, to abandon these in pursuit of a scientific ideal would be to endanger the type of intelligibility at which he aims.

[37] They would be like mathematical entities rather than genuinely physical ones. Aristotle cannot, on this view, accept them as real kinds solely on the basis of their role in a coherent mathematical model of the world.

[38] Contrast the view sketched by David Wiggins in *Sameness and Substance*, 144. According to Wiggins, we are inclined to continue to employ terms such as 'dog' because of their

be fully intelligible if we abstract ourselves completely from the point of view, which is grounded in our craft engagement with objects and kinds. If so, Aristotle cannot dispense with his biological kinds even though they fail to live up to the standards he set in the *Analytics*.

This line of reply has the advantage of explaining Aristotle's use of colour and skill as analogues for the active intellect, in *De Anima* Γ.5. Both indicate the kind of intelligibility he seeks, one manifested initially in the understanding of the master craftsman and tied permanently (in some measure) to that perspective. However, while this line of thought seems attractive, it could only be sustained by a deeper study of Aristotle's grounds for resisting reduction.[39]

13.6 QUIETISM AND SILENCE

There is one further objection to be considered. Aristotle attempted to provide a metaphysical account of necessity in terms of essentiality and explanation. But was his work really necessary? Perhaps we have a perfectly good grasp of the relevant notions embedded in our understanding of linguistic expressions such as 'It is necessary that . . .', 'It is essential that . . .', or 'It is possible that . . .'? Is more required? Why do we need a metaphysical theory in which definition and explanation are interdependent?

This quietist strategy is to be distinguished from that of my modern essentialist. For, the latter seeks to ground our use of the relevant linguistic expressions in (e.g.) our acceptance of a set of conventions. The quietist does not wish to explain our practices either in this way or in the neo-Kantian fashion described above. Rather, he prefers to avoid all theoretical speculation, and rest content solely with our ordinary understanding of certain linguistic expressions.

Aristotle has several reasons for rejecting the quietist strategy. First, his distinction between 'It is necessary that P' and 'It is essential that P' has to be grounded in some way. If one removes the connections between

---

convenience in practice. In his view, such terms represent 'a stage . . . in some gradual process of the revelation of reality'. On the present account, the importance of such kinds is that it is through grasping them that we come to understand what it is to be a kind, endowed with modal features. For this reason, they are indispensable for thinkers with our abilities and sensibilities.

[39] For further discussion, see my *Aristotle's Philosophy of Action*, 213–34, and 'Aristotle on Hypothetical Necessity and Irreducibility'. The present conjecture is that Aristotle's grounds for resisting reduction are based (in part) on his requirement that the world be made fully intelligible to us (in the way in which his subject matter is intelligible to the master craftsman).

essence and explanation, what makes it true that (e.g.) the composite man is prior to body and mind, rather than the latter being prior to the former?[40] Indeed, it might turn out that the distinction between essence and necessity is a misguided one. It cannot be simply assumed that we possess determinate and justified notions of the necessary and the essential. This needs to be established.

Second, claims of the form 'It is necessary that man is rational' or 'All men are necessarily rational' can (in principle) be understood in more than one way. They might be interpreted (in Lockean fashion) as rooted *de jure* in our classificatory conventions. Alternatively, they might be taken (as Aristotle does) to reflect *de facto* metaphysical necessities. The latter, but not the former, are sometimes described as non-trivial necessities.[41] If we focus solely on sentences such as:

It is necessary that P

or

a is necessarily F,

these alternatives (and the questions they raise) are overlooked. Nor can we assume that non-trivial essentialism is in good order as it is. For, it is certainly conceivable that our practices might have developed so as to conform to some other (e.g. Lockean) ideal, which dispensed with non-trivial essentialist claims (so understood). If so, one needs to show that our apparent commitment to non-trivial essentialism is justified. But where we need justification, the quietist provides none.[42]

There is one further point: Aristotle provided an elegant and rich metaphysical theory of essence, necessity, and explanation to underwrite our

---

[40] On this issue, see Ch. 6. The problem is raised also by Kit Fine in 'Essence and Modality', *Philosophical Perspectives*, 8 (1994), 8.

[41] See Ch. 1 Sect. 1.3.

[42] This point can be made with regard to identity claims such as:

It is necessary that a = b.

Such claims can be defended by noting that 'a' and 'b' are to be used as rigid designators, and that:

'a = b' is true.

So understood, the claim that:

It is necessary that a = b

rests on our linguistic practices concerning designators, and the truth of the identity claim. But, alternatively, the truth of this claim might rest on the conjecture that:

'a = b' is necessarily true,

where this is understood to rest on the identity claim, and the further (metaphysical) thought that no object can be other than the one it is. It seems a worthwhile task to understand the differences between these approaches.

ordinary modal notions. Even if no such theory were strictly required (despite the remarks in the last paragraphs), it would still be desirable. For, it gives us a deeper understanding of the relevant notions than the quietist can provide. If quietism is to be defended, its advocates must show that Aristotelian metaphysically grounded theories are either impossible or undesirable. But these are major claims, themselves in need of sustained argument. They cannot be defended merely by declining to answer a set of naturally arising questions.

13.7 CONCLUSION

Aristotle developed a distinctive account of essence, nature, and necessity. It has four basic, separable, features. The first pair concern thought and meaning, the second metaphysics:

(1) It does not require the ordinary thinker, in grasping a natural-kind term, to have access to proto-scientific ideas of kinds, conceived as possessing an underlying physico-chemical structure.

(2) It does not require the ordinary thinker, in grasping a natural-kind term, to know of the existence of the relevant kind.

(3) In it, our practices of definition and explanation are interdependent. Further, this interdependency rests on the metaphysical thesis of the co-determination of essence and causation.

(4) In it, theoretical practices of definition and explanation are grounded in the activities and understanding of the master craftsman. Indeed, we cannot, on pain of losing the very intelligibility we seek, abstract ourselves completely from this original starting point.

(3), its central metaphysical claim, appears not to be vulnerable to the objections considered in this Chapter, and to have some advantages over its current major competitors, conventionalist, Platonist, Kantian, and quietist alike. That said, it is, in some respects, incomplete and in need of more detailed examination and development. Indeed, further work is required on both metaphysical claims.[43] Nonetheless, Aristotle's four claims are not mere relics from the prehistory of metaphysics. Rightly understood, they are still a living and thought provoking contribution to the subject.

---

[43] (4) is, I believe, central for a proper understanding of Aristotle's resistance to the reductionist (or eliminativist) scientific philosophies of his day.

Appendix 1
Aristotle on the Principle of Non-Contradiction

Several aspects of Aristotle's complex discussion of the principle of non-contradiction (PNC) in *Metaphysics* Γ.3–4 rest on his account of names and their signification. I shall focus on these and leave aside the many other issues raised in these chapters. My aim is to sketch the connections between part of this discussion and his account (as presented in Chapters 2–6) of similar topics elsewhere.

One of Aristotle's main arguments in Γ.4 begins as follows:

> If 'man' signifies one thing (as it does), let this be 'two-footed animal'. I mean by 'signifying one thing' this. If man is that (e.g. two-footed animal), then if anything is a man, that (e.g. being a two-footed animal) will be what it is to be a man. (*Meta.* Γ.4, 1006ᵃ31–4)

The line of argument appears to run as follows:

(1) 'Man' signifies one thing: e.g. 'two-footed animal'.[1] (Premiss)

(2) If anything is a man, being two-footed will be what it is to be a man. (From (1), combined with Aristotle's account of what it is to signify one thing)

The discussion of Chapters 2 and 4 provides a way to understand (1). 'Two-footed animal' may be a fully specified stage 1 account of what 'man' signifies (*Post. An.* B.8, 93ᵃ24). If so, the account will specify some non-accidental features of the kind. This is required if the name and the account are to have the same significance. Such accounts 'predicate one thing of one thing non-accidentally' (*Post. An.* B.10, 93ᵇ36–7). Thus, if 'man' signifies a genuine kind (i.e. a kind with instances) the full account may be represented as 'being two-footed belongs to animal'. Accounts of this type (unlike 'tied-together ones') require there to be a genuine kind in reality, which is non-accidentally a two-footed animal.

Aristotle characterizes what it is for a term to signify one thing in terms of there being one (and just one) stage 1 account of the type just specified which is correlated with the term:

'man' signifies the same as 'two-footed animal' and nothing else

This requires that the account of what 'man' signifies specifies some part of the distinctive nature of the kind. For, only then will 'man' and 'two-footed animal' signify the same thing (and nothing else). By contrast, 'pale' and 'artistic' cannot signify one thing (1006ᵇ15–18) since there is no genuine kind of pale objects with a distinctive nature signified by the term 'pale'.[2] There can be no account of these

---

[1] I take the latter phrase to specify a linguisitic expression, as signalled by the presence of '*to*' (1006ᵃ32).

[2] Aristotle is assuming, at this point, his favoured ontology of kinds as already in place. He is arguing that because there is a genuine kind (man), 'man' signifies one thing. He is not arguing that there is a genuine kind because 'man' signifies one thing.

terms which specifies a non-accidental feature of a genuine kind. (For similar reasons, 'goatstag' will fail to signify one thing in the appropriate way.)

In the argument, (1) together with these semantical assumptions supports (2). The relevant account of what the term 'man' signifies (viz. 'two-footed animal') (i) will have the same significance as 'man', and (ii) will specify a non-accidental feature of the kind. Indeed, it will only have the same significance as 'man' because it fulfils (ii). Identity of signification between these linguistic items rests on man (the kind signified) having the non-accidental feature mentioned in the relevant account. On this basis Aristotle can move from (1) to a claim about the real world in (2). For, his criterion for the identity of signification rests here on claims about the natures of kinds.[3]

It should be noted that, while the name and the relevant account have the same significance, it does not follow that 'man' signifies the fundamental essence of man, what it is to be a man. Aristotle is making the following points:

(3) 'Man' signifies one thing: the same thing as 'two-footed animal' signifies.

(4) 'A' and 'B' signify one and the same thing if and only if to be a two-footed animal is part of what it is to be a man.

But it does not follow from (3) and (4) that 'man' signifies part of what it is to be man. For, (4) is concerned only with the conditions under which 'man' and 'two-footed animal' signify one and the same thing, and says nothing about the precise signification of the term 'man'. Thus, (3) and (4) are fully consistent with 'man' signifying a kind which has a distinctive nature, and do not require the term to signify that distinctive nature itself. One can only derive the stronger claim if one adds the following premiss:

(5) To signify a kind which has a non-accidental feature is to signify that non-accidental feature.

But there is no evidence that Aristotle made this further (highly controversial) assumption in this passage.[4] It is enough for his purposes that the term does indeed signify one kind with its own distinctive nature.[5]

Our earlier discussion of accounts of what names signify brings into focus two further issues in the immediate context:

(i) One may grasp a stage 1 account of what some term signifies without knowing of the existence of the kind. It is, therefore, no surprise to find in (2) the

---

[3] In this interpretation, the subject matter appears to be the kind (man), and not particular men. This is the most natural interpretation as the name in question is 'man' throughout (e.g. 1006^{a}31, 1006^{b}14). While it is true that in 1006^{a}33 and ^{b}28 Aristotle writes 'if someone is a man', this phrase may merely reflect his attempt to ensure that the kind is a genuine one (i.e. has instances). Modern interpreters, who attempt to regiment this argument in first-order-predicate calculus, assume that the subject of his discourse must here be individual men. But their assumption (with its attendant scope problems) seems to be a construct more of their choice of logical grammar than of the text itself. That said, the ontology presupposed in these arguments merits further study.

[4] For a contrasting view, see T. H. Irwin's 'Aristotle's Account of Signification' in M. Schofield and M. Nussbaum (eds.), *Language and Logos* (Cambridge, 1982), 261–2.

[5] See, e.g. Ch. 4 Sect. 4.2.

phrase 'if anything is a man' in 1006ª33. For, it can be used to indicate the possibility (which Aristotle countenances elsewhere) of one's grasping this type of account without knowledge of the existence of the kind.

(ii) The account of what 'man' signifies will (typically) specify some non-accidental feature of man, but not the (basic) essence of the kind. 'Two-footed animal' plays precisely this role (see *Meta.* H.3, 1043ᵇ2–4), as this is a feature of man required by his essence (a given type of soul). It is again no surprise that in the immediate context the phrase 'what it is to be' can extend beyond the essence to other features. For, in 1006ᵇ13 ff. it and similar phrases are used to specify (the essenceless) what it is not to be a man. The term can naturally apply to features such as the one mentioned: being a two-footed animal.

To summarize: Aristotle's line of thought rests on several assumptions about signification:

(A) 'Man' signifies one thing.

(B) 'Man' signifying one thing requires that 'man' can be correlated with one type of account of what that term signifies: one which specifies a non-accidental feature of the kind.

(C) One can grasp an account of what 'man' signifies without knowing of the existence of the kind or of its basic essence.

(A) and (B) require that the name 'man' signifies something which has a nature of the relevant type. In this case, the kind signified will have as a non-accidental feature being two-footed. This follows, as we have noted, from Aristotle's account of what it is for the name and account to have the same significance (granted that 'man' signifies one thing). (C) reflects the semantic shallowness of stage I accounts.

In the dialectical context of *Meta.* Γ.4, (C) is important. In it, neither name nor account should specify the basic essence of the kind. For, Aristotle's argument should work not only against those few who reject the PNC but accept (e.g.) that:

(D) 'Man' signifies the essence of man.

It should be effective against those who hold that:

(E) 'Man' signifies a kind, which has an essence.

If the argument turned on (D), its value, considered as a defence of PNC, would be slight. For, sceptics about PNC could easily escape refutation by rejecting (D). Perhaps, they will say, 'man' signifies one thing, and that one thing is a kind which has an essence. But they may see no reason to accept that the name signifies the essence itself.

The shallowness of (E) should not surprise us. It is precisely what is required in contexts in which one should make as few (controversial) assumptions as possible. Indeed, it would be a mistake to invoke (D) at this point, with its 'scientific' assumptions about the basic essences of kinds. Since Aristotle is engaging with the sceptic at a 'logical' (*logikos*) level of discussion, he should use an account of what the term signifies which avoids semantically deep (and controversial) assumptions of this type. Indeed, the existence of such contexts provides him with a further motivation (over and above those noted in Chapters 2, 4, and 6) for ensuring that stage 1 accounts are semantically shallow.[6]

Assumptions (A) and (B) remain important as the argument develops. In *Meta.* 1006ᵇ28 ff. Aristotle writes:

If it is true to say of something that it is man, it must be a two-footed animal (for this is what 'man' signifies). If this is necessary, it is impossible that the same being should not be a two-footed animal . . . It is, therefore, impossible that it should be true to say that the same thing is a man and not a man.

This argument turns on the following claims:

(6) 'Man' signifies 'two-footed animal'. (Premiss)[7]

(7) If something is a man, man is necessarily a two-footed animal. (From (6))

(8) Man is not possibly not a two-footed animal. (From (7) and the definition of necessity)

(9) Man is not possibly not a man. (From (7) and (8))

(10) The same thing (viz. the kind) cannot be at the same time both man and not man. (From (9))[8]

The transition from (6) to (7) can be validated (with support from Assumptions (A) and (B)). An adequate account of what the name 'man' signifies will be one which specifies only features (e.g. being two-footed) which are non-accidental features of the kind (if the kind exists). If there is a genuine kind signified, it will be one which is non-accidentally two-footed (see (8)). While the kind will, no doubt, have its own basic essence, that need not be mentioned in the account of what the term signifies.

Aristotle's commitment to Assumptions (A) and (B) emerges elsewhere in his discussion. He anticipates that his dialectical opponent will deny that 'man' signifies one genuine kind by doubting that there are kinds or substances with essences of the appropriate type (1007ᵃ20–2, 34–5). He replies:

those who argue in this way do away with substance and essence. (ᵃ20–1)[9]

---

[6] For further discussion of Aristotle's method in this area, see A. Code, 'Aristotle's Investigation of a Basic Logical Principle', *Canadian Journal of Philosophy* 16 (1986), 341–57, and R. Bolton, 'Aristotle's Conception of Metaphysics as a Science', in *Unity, Identity and Explanation* 321–54.

[7] I take 1006ᵇ29–30 to be making a claim about the (linguistic) account of what 'man' signifies: 'man' signifies the same as 'biped animal' (following the pattern of 1006ᵃ32).

[8] As before, I take the subject to be a kind and not its instances. For a clear analysis of the problems which arise if one makes the latter assumption, see C. Kirwan *Aristotle's Metaphysics* Γ, Δ, E, (Oxford, 1971), 98.

[9] In this passage the focus of discussion is on the significance of the phrase: 'what it is to be a man' (1007ᵃ22, 23). Indeed, this is what is taken to signify one thing (1007ᵃ25). If so, in these lines (1007ᵃ23–6) *'ousia'* means *ousia tinos*: i.e. essence. But does *'ousia'* in 1007ᵃ20–1 mean this also (taking *'kai'* as epexegetic)? This seems unlikely since the next line appears to refer to substances (*autois*) as well as essences (1007ᵃ21–2). If so, Aristotle is arguing here that his opponents do away with substances because they do away with essences. This passage cannot be used to show that (e.g.) 'man' and 'the essence of man' signify the same, because it focuses on the significance not of 'man' but of 'what it is to be a man'.

Why are his opponents forced to this extreme? If they accept the proposed account of what it is to signify one thing (as encapsulated in (A) and (B)), terms like 'man' can only fail to signify one thing if they completely fail to signify a genuine kind. Aristotle expects that his opponents will remain faithful to this account of what it is to signify one thing, but will deny that terms like 'man' signify one thing by claiming that there are no such kinds in reality. Rather, in their view, 'man' will signify in the way 'pale' does. When their approach is generalized, all predications turn out to be of the latter type (accidental: see 1007ᵃ21–2). There will be no actual cases which fulfil the agreed conditions for signifying one thing.

Aristotle's reply is that if all predication is accidental, there will be no primary subjects (1007ᵃ33 ff.). If there are no substances, all sentences with prospective subject terms will dissolve into several parts said accidentally of each other (1007ᵃ35–ᵇ1). However, in his view, this is not possible. Accidents can be predicated of each other only if both belong to one substance (1007ᵇ3–5, 15–16). Therefore, if predication is possible, there must be substances (or kinds) to stand as the basic subjects of sentences in which 'one thing can be said of one thing non-accidentally'. But there can be such sentences only if the subject term signifies one thing, and this (in turn) will only be possible if there is a genuine kind which 'man' signifies.

Aristotle's attachment to his account of what it is to signify one thing (as encapsulated in (B)) is a permanent feature of this discussion. In his view, terms like 'man' will only cease to signify one thing if there are no genuine kinds. But the latter, he claims, is not possible. Significant speech requires that the language's basic subjects signify one thing (1006ᵃ21–23, ᵃ31–ᵇ12). However, such signification will not be possible if PNC is rejected. Hence, he concludes, conformity with PNC is required for any who engage in significant speech (at least for certain central elements in their language).¹⁰

In Aristotle's account, 'man' has the same significance as 'two-footed animal' because both signify the same kind and do so in a non-accidental way. If this were not so, the relevant account could specify an accidental feature of the kind. One further consequence should be noted: if 'man' signifies its kind in this way, the term could not retain its present significance and apply to anything else. For, if it did so, it would only specify this kind accidentally, and would not signify the same as the non-accidental description ('two-footed animal'). If so, there can be no case in which 'man' retains its present significance and signifies a different kind from the one it actually does.¹¹ 'Man' could not retain the significance it presently does were

---

¹⁰ But could one reject PNC for some non-central part of the language, where there is no essential predication of this type? Aristotle does not address this problem explicitly in *Meta.* Γ.4 and sometimes proceeds as if he is replying to a sceptic who rejects PNC universally. However, his remarks on accidental predication (1007ᵃ34 ff.) imply a strategy against a more limited scepticism. Aristotle suggests, in effect, that any case not involving essential predication can be reduced to a more basic one which does. Once this reduction has been effected, his argument can proceed as before.

¹¹ The significance of 'man' cannot be given by means of a description which happens to pick out the kind. See Aristotle's arguments in *Meta.* Z.15 against the view that (e.g.) 'the sun' can be defined as 'what revolves around the Earth' or 'is hidden at night' (1040ᵃ29 ff.). Aristotle argues that these accounts are mistaken since 'the sun' signifies a certain substance independently of whether it has these features (1040ᵃ33). His arguments are swift and compelling. First, 'the sun' would signify that substance even if it stood still or shone at night

it not correlated (non-accidentally) with the very kind with which it is now linked. But this is precisely what we should expect if (for Aristotle) the signification of this name is fixed by the identity of the kind with which it is correlated (by 'likening', as suggested in Chapter 4 Sections 4.1 and 4.2). For, that model makes it impossible for the signification of a name to remain constant if the name is 'likened' (in different contexts) to different kinds. In these respects, Aristotle's discussion of what it is for a name and account to signify one thing coheres well with the way in which (in his view) the signification of such names is determined (as interpreted in Chapter 4).

(1040^a31-2). Second, if something else revolved around the Earth or shone during the day, this would not be the sun (1040^a33 ff.). These two telegrammatic arguments count strongly against any attempt to capture the significance of the term 'the sun' in terms of contingent definite descriptions (in the Fregean mode). In Aristotle's view, the significance of 'the sun' must be fixed in such a way that the term attaches to the same substance in a wide range of counterfactual possibilities.

Appendix 2

Essence, Necessity, and the Copula

1 Issues of Logical Grammar

In *De Interpretatione* 16^{b}6ff. Aristotle isolates two aspects of the present-tense sentence:

Theaetetus thrives.

—the name and the *rhema* (verb). The latter expression has three roles:

(1) It signifies something (e.g. thriving).

(2) It co-signifies time.

(3) It is a sign (in affirmations) of being said of something else.

The verb (in addition to signifying the state of thriving) signifies when 'thriving' is predicated of Theaetetus, and asserts that 'thriving' is predicated of him. Of its three semantic roles, only the first is referential. The expression does not in addition refer to a time, or to a special binding agent. Rather, through (2) and (3), 'thriving' is asserted to be true now of Theaetetus.

These three semantic roles need not be played by one word alone. The verb can be replaced by a participle and the copula, as in the sentence:

Theaetetus is thriving.

Here, the copula performs the second and third roles:

(2) It indicates tense (e.g. now).

(3) It signifies a combination. (16^{b}24)

It does not, in Aristotle's view, signify 'being' by itself (16^{b}21). Its role is to express the combination of the items referred to: Theaetetus and health. The copula indicates that there is now a combination of health with Theaetetus.

In *De Interpretatione* 19^{b}19ff. Aristotle appears concerned to emphasize that 'is' is a third item in sentences along with terms such as 'man' and 'just'. It predicates in addition that 'just' is true of man, in the way in which all verbs signify, in addition, time. In the copula we have a word which lacks signification on its own, but which has this type of additional signification when combined with 'just'. It signifies the combination of 'man' and 'just', and is co-predicated along with the term 'just'. Thus, its role appears more closely linked with 'just' than with 'man'. For, it co-predicates with the latter and not the former.

Aristotle is developing a grammatical picture, in which the copula is aligned syntactically and semantically more closely with the predicate term (in this case, 'just') than with the subject.[1] This is certainly how he was taken by the ancient commentators Alexander and Ammonius. Thus, Alexander wrote (*In Analytica Priora*. 369.12–14): ' "to be" is not a term, but is added to the predicate terms in the analysis of the sentences into terms' (see *In. Apr.* 16.7–10). 'The predicate term is that to which "is" is added' (*In. Apr.* 406.32–4). Similarly, Ammonius writes ' "to be" is adjoined to the predicate term . . .' (*In Apr.* 23.27–8).[2]

In Aristotle's subject/predicate analysis of these sentences, the copula has a role (or series of roles) within the predicate. One such role is suggested in Aristotle's discussion of negation. In his view, the sentence 'A is just' has two opposites:

(1) A is-not just

and

(2) A is not-just.

(1) denies to A the positive state of justice, while (2) asserts of A the negative state of not-being-just. Corresponding to the latter is a further denial:

(3) 'A is-not not-just', which denies to A the negative state of being-not-just (cf. *De Int.* 19^{b}27 f.).

The negated copula (in (1) and (3)) has the distinctive role of denying to A a given state (whether positive or negative). In effect, it is a sign of the separation of that state from A. In these cases, Aristotle adds 'not' to the verb or copula (21^{b}19–23). If he were to employ a negation operator governing the whole sentence, it would be derivative from this central case.

Aristotle seeks to distinguish (1) and (2) in a variety of ways. Thus, for instance, in cases where no object is marked out by the grammatical subject, he takes (1) to be true, but (2) to be false. In his view, while imagined or fictional objects may be truly denied the positive state of being just, they cannot be truly asserted to possess a given negative state.[3] Such objects cannot possess either positive or negative states but they can be truly denied to possess such states.[4]

---

[1] There are occasions when Aristotle writes as if the copula is a third separate item in sentences of this type. For example, in *Pr. An.* 24^{b}16–18, Aristotle says that there are two terms in a proposition, which may leave a residue 'is' or 'is not' in cases where the copula is present. He writes

I call a term that into which a sentence resolves; that which is predicated and that of which it is predicated, when 'is' or 'is not' is either present or absent

But these claims are consistent with the account I offer above. For, neither deny that 'is' is to be taken as more closely aligned with the predicate than with the subject.

[2] See Jonathan Barnes's 'Grammar on Aristotle's Terms', in M. Frede and G. Striker (eds.), *Rationality in Greek Thought* (Oxford, 1996), 175–202.

[3] There are a number of complex issues about Aristotle's treatment of empty names. (See also Ch. 4 Sects. 2–4.) It may be that the name ((e.g.) 'Socrates') should be replaced in this sentence by a complex expression ((e.g.) 'the son of X and Y'.)

[4] There are other cases in which sentences like (1) and (2) differ in truth value. Take the sentence:

A is most of all (*malista*) B.

The negation corresponding to (1) is:

The copula is crucial for Aristotle's analysis of modal sentences such as:

Theaetetus is essentially a man

or

Theaetetus is necessarily two-footed

or

Theaetetus is possibly in Thebes.

Aristotle treats as parallel 'belonging', 'belonging from necessity', and 'being capable of belonging' (*Pr. An.* 29^{b}29 ff.). This strategy makes sense on the assumption that modal notions are treated as modifying 'belonging' in different ways. For, 'belonging' is that feature of a verb which indicates a mode of combination of (e.g.) man with Theaetetus. The modal notion is not treated as part of the predicate term 'man', since it does not form a new complex predicate term 'necessarily-a-man'. Rather, it modifies the way in which the feature, man, belongs to Theaetetus. Thus, Aristotle (as in his treatment of negation) is attaching 'essentially' or 'necessarily' to the copula, and not adding a new modal predicate (e.g. 'necessarily-two-footed') which is asserted (without modification) of the subject.[5]

Aristotle's remarks in *De Interpretatione* 21^{b}26 ff. appear to follow this pattern. He envisages the following order of sentence construction:

     white, man

[Addition 1] is, is not

[Addition 2] possible, not possible

Addition 1 is made to the terms 'white' and 'man', Addition 2 to 'is' or 'is not', now taken itself 'as a subject'. In Addition 1, 'is' acts as an indicator of the way in which man and white are connected (by combination rather than division). In Addition 2, 'is' is like a subject because, although it does not indicate an actual

A is-not most of all B.

while that corresponding to (2) is:

A is most of all not-B.

Similar differences are present in modal contexts:

Contrast: A is-not possibly B.

with

A is possibly not-B.

Similarly, one might contrast: A is-not determinately B.

with

A is determinately not-B.

For example, a child, not yet subject to proper training in virtue, may not possess the positive state of being just, but may equally not possess the negative state of being non-just (or unjust). Indeed, both (1) and (3) might be true in this case.

[5] Ammonius correctly describes modal notions as 'qualities of the belonging relation'.

subject, it is modified by 'possible' and 'not possible'. The latter indicates how the two genuine subjects (white and man) are combined, when white possibly-belongs to man.[6] The manner of the combination of the basic subjects is progressively specified at the two levels. At the first, it is said to be that of connection (rather than separation), at the second the form of connection is further clarified (as possibly-connected/not possibly-connected/essentially-connected, etc.).

Aristotle compares his use of modal notions with his use of 'true' and 'false'. In a simple affirmation, such as:

Theaetetus is a man

the predicate term 'man' is said to be true of Theaetetus. In modal sentences such as:

Theaetetus is necessarily a man

or

Theaetetus is possibly a man,

'man' is said to be necessarily-true or possibly-true of Theaetetus. For 'true of' mirrors at the metalinguistic level the role of belonging at the metaphysical level.

So understood, 'is' does not introduce a new entity which is then modified. For, Aristotle's crucial point is that 'is' functions *like* a subject without being a subject. Its initial role (as elsewhere) is to point to the way in which the terms (in affirmations) are combined. In the affirmative sentence:

a is F

the 'is' functions to indicate the feature F's belonging to a (by affirming 'F' of a). This claim is then modified to form:

F possibly-belongs to a

F necessarily-belongs to a.

If the first claim is taken as equivalent to:

F really-belongs to a

in the next two sentences 'really-belongs' is modified in different ways. In this way, 'necessary' and 'possible' are added to make affirmations of the subject (22^a7ff.). In affirmative modal cases, the modal addition (functioning in addition) indicates a predicate's being combined in a given way with the subject ($22^a11–14$).[7]

---

[6] The reference to 'the way in which two subjects . . . are combined' might suggest a reference to different possible worlds. But this is not necessary. (See the final paragraphs of Section 2 of this Appendix.)

[7] Ammonius (*De Int.* 230. 1–15) suggests that in this passage Aristotle regards the modal notions as modifying simple sentences. In his view, they say (in effect) that it is possible/ necessary that a given state of affairs exist, while 'it is true that' affirms that a given state exists. But Ammonius appears confused, since earlier he had taken the modal notions as adverbs like 'fast', 'well', and 'always'(214. 25). Indeed, he had introduced the notion of a mode by describing it as 'the manner in which what is predicated belongs to the subject'. Further, Ammonius' interpretation of this passage makes Aristotle's view of the logical grammar of modality (unnecessarily) different in *De Int.* 12 and in *Pr. An.* 29^b29ff.

If one takes 'possible' and 'necessary' as copula-modifiers in this context, one can explain Aristotle's complex discussion of the role of negation in modal contexts. The negation of:

A is-possibly wise

is

A is-not-possibly wise

and not:

A is possibly not-wise.

Why? Because at the level defined by Addition 2 one added 'possibly' to 'is' to form the

A is-possibly wise.

To negate this, one should go back to the previous level, and replace 'possibly' with 'not-possibly' to form:

A is-not-possibly wise. (See 22^{a}9 f.)

Here, the verbs 'to be'/'not to be' function like an underlying feature because it is these which are modified by 'possibly' or 'not-possibly' to form the relevant complex copula.

This view may be contrasted with another in which the negation of the modal claim:

(4) It is possible that a is F

is

(5) It is not possible that a is F.[8]

In this proposal, it is the first 'is' in (4) that is negated not the second. But this is not Aristotle's analysis. He looks for the verb which links 'F' and 'a', and negates that. The first 'is' in (4) is not the right type of 'is' for Aristotle to negate, because it does not express the required type of link between 'F' and 'a'. Rather, in his account, one should seek for the 'is' which links subject and predicate terms and then negate that.

2 Metaphysics and Logical Grammar

According to Aristotle:

Theaetetus is possibly a Theban

is to be understood as:

[8] This line of interpretation is favoured by Ammonius and John Ackrill, who describes Aristotle's formulations (in the style to be expected if one adopts the copula-modifier view) as 'dangerously elliptical' (*Aristotle's Categories and De Interpretatione* (Oxford, 1963), 149). My suggestion is that these formulations, so far from being 'dangerously elliptical', are metaphysically beneficial.

Being a Theban possibly-belongs to Theaetetus

and

Theaetetus is necessarily two-footed

is to be understood as:

Being two-footed necessarily-belongs to Theaetetus.[9]

In this case the relevant modal notion modifies the way in which the relevant property belongs to Theaetetus. Modal notions are taken as ways of modifying the belonging relation (e.g. *Pr. An.* 29^{b}36–30^{a}2).

The metaphysical significance of his approach can be illustrated by pointing to three rival views of the logical grammar of these sentences. In the first, one takes:

Theaetetus is actually an Athenian but possibly a Theban

to say (in possible-world idiom):

The actual-Theaetetus is an Athenian but the possible-Theaetetus is a Theban.

This account, in effect, introduces two world-bound individuals (Theaetetus-in-w1, Theaetetus-in-w2), and takes predicates such as 'being an Athenian' to be true or false of both of them. An alternative, which locates modal complexity in the predicate, interprets the relevant sentence as follows:

Theaetetus is actually-Athenian, but Theaetetus is possibly-Theban

or

∃w1 [Theaetetus is Athenian-in-w1] & ∃w2 [Theateteus is Theban-in-w2].

Here, there are two distinct world-bound predicates, 'Athenian-in-w1', 'Theban-in-w2', true of the same object. If these predicates are taken (as in Aristotle's account) to refer, there will be two new world-bound properties (in addition to, or in place of, the simple property of being Athenian). A third option understands:

Theaetetus is possibly a Theban

as involving a sentence-forming operator:

---

[9] In a similar fashion, he could analyse temporal contexts such as:

Theaetetus is now an Athenian

as

Being an Athenian presently-belongs to Theaetetus.

The future (in contrast to past and present) might be analysed in terms of possibility. Thus:

Theaetetus will be an Athenian.

might be analysed as:

Theaetetus is-possibly an Athenian.

There need be no reference to possible worlds or to an actual future in this analysis. These intriguing issues lie outside the scope of the present Appendix.

It is possible that Theaetetus is a Theban.

At the next level of analysis, this sentence is interpreted to mean:

In some possible world, Theaetetus is a Theban.

If Theaetetus is actually an Athenian, one might say:

In the actual world, Theaetetus is an Athenian, but in some possible world he is a Theban.

Here, we need to make sense of talk of possible worlds, and to consider whether Theaetetus is the same individual in the two worlds in question.[10]

Aristotle's copula-modifier view differs from the first two options in not introducing world-relativized objects or world-relativized properties. Nor is it a variant of the third option since it takes as basic the relation within the sentence between subject and predicate. It is not to be understood as involving reference to possible worlds. In Aristotle's account, the modal terms are syntactically adverbs, focusing on the modes/ways in which features are related to objects. In place of modal properties or world-bound individuals, one has a variety of ways in which non-modalized properties can belong to objects. His strategy allows him to keep the ontology simple (i.e. restricted to this world's objects or combinations of such objects and non-modal features which belong to objects in this world), and to treat modality (along with tense and negation) as ways in which these features belong to the relevant objects. His account of the logical structure of modal sentences reflects his relatively uncomplicated ontology.[11] For, he has no need of possible

---

[10] One might interpret this sentence without reference to possible worlds as follows:

In a story which corresponds to the way concrete reality is:

Theaetetus is Athenian,

while in a story which corresponds to the way reality might have been:

Theaetetus is Theban.

But, if one does this, one is committed to the existence of stories of this type (presumably told by someone) in order to understand the sentence.

[11] The beginnings of a more detailed proposal might run as follows.

(1) 'Socrates COP.F' is True iff F stands in relation R to Socrates.

(2) 'Socrates COP.negative F' is True iff F does not stand in relation R to Socrates.

(3) 'Socrates COP.possibly F' is True iff F possibly stands in relation R to Socrates.

(4) 'Socrates COP.necessarily F' is True iff F necessarily stands in relation R to Socrates.

One extension to the case of quantified expressions might run as follows:

(5) 'Every man COP.F' is True iff F stands in relation R to each individual of which 'man' is predicated (each member of the class of men).

(6) 'Every man COP.necessarily F' is True iff F necessarily stands in relation R to each individual of which 'man' is predicated.

(7) 'Every man COP. possibly F' is True iff F possibly stands in relation R to each individual of which 'man' is predicated.

(8) 'Some man COP.F' is True iff F stands in relation R to some individual of which 'man' is predicated.

objects, possible properties, or possible worlds to account for the truth of sentences involving possibility and necessity.[12]

Aristotle's logical grammar captures in a perspicuous way his metaphysical claims (as set out in Chapters 7–10). To recapitulate: essential features, in Aristotle's view, are simply the ones which belong definitionally to a kind. Thus, in the case of a given kind A:

(E) 'A is-essentially F' is True if and only if F is the feature which makes the kind A the one it is (in the ways discussed in Chapters 7–10).

A's necessary properties are ones whose presence follows (whether always or for the most part) from A's being F. Necessary properties will be ones whose presence is explained by A's being F. Thus:

(N) 'A is-necessarily P' is True if and only if A's being P follows either always or for the most part from A's being F.

A's possible properties (e.g. being Q) are those properties whose possession by A is consistent with A's necessary and esssential features. 'A is-not Q' does not follow from A's possessing its essential or necessary features.

(P) 'A is-possibly Q' is True if and only if it is consistent with A's essential and necessary features that A is Q.

Aristotle, it should be noted, usually takes A's possible properties also to be ones which are neither necessary nor essential.[13]

(9) 'Some man COP.necessarily F' is True iff F necessarily stands in relation R to some individual of which 'man' is predicated.

(10) 'Some man COP. possibly F' is True iff F possibly stands in relation R to some individual of which 'man' is predicated.

In (6), (7), (9), and (10), the scope in the metalanguage is the same as that in the object language. (There are important issues here which need further study.)

What is relation R? In one version, it might be 'really belongs to'. In another, somewhat parallel, one might take R to be the relation of 'true of', and F to stand for the predicate 'F'. If so, one might proceed as follows:

'a is F' is True iff 'F' is said truly of a.

'a is not F' is True iff 'F' is said not-truly of a.

'a is necessarily F' is True iff 'F' is said necessarily-truly of a.

'a is possibly F' is True iff 'F' is said possibly-truly of a.

'All a's are F' is True iff 'F' is said truly of each a.

'All a's are necessarily F' is True iff 'F' is said necessarily-truly of each a.

In this version, one might use Tarski's mechanisms of satisfaction further to analyse the relation 'true of'.

Detailed analysis of these issues would take us far afield. For further discussion of related topics, see Paolo Crivelli's 'Notes on Aristotle's Conception of Truth', in M. S. Funghi (ed.), *Studies in Honour of F. Adorno* (Florence, 1996), 153–4.

[12] See the discussion of Quine's objections to talk of necessity in Ch. 13 Sect. 13.4.

[13] Standardly, Aristotle takes:

It is not that Aristotle attempts to read his metaphysics directly from his favoured logical grammar.[14] It is rather that it is an advantage of the latter that it expresses in a perspicuous way the metaphysical realities (as he sees them).[15] The latter requires neither possible worlds, nor possible-world-bound objects or properties. All that is needed is that certain causally basic features make those kinds the ones they are (in the way captured by his co-determination thesis).

possibly p

to be equivalent to 'p is neither impossible nor necessary'. But on occasion he allows for a second (aberrant) sense of:

possibly p

which is equivalent to:

not necessarily not p.

In the latter case, he permits the inference:

necessarily P possibly P

to stand. (*Pr. An.* A. 13–22)

[14] For a minimalist view of this kind, see Mark Johnstone's 'Is there a Problem about Persistence', *PASS* 61 (1987), 107–55.

[15] Others have argued that one can vindicate Aristotle's modal logic by using his copula-modifier account of modal statements. For a recent attempt to do this, see Richard Patterson's *Aristotle's Modal Logic* (Cambridge, 1995). For studies of similar attempts in medieval philosophy, see Simo Knuuttila's *Modalities in Medieval Philosophy* (London, 1993) and Henrik Lagerlund's, *Modal Syllogistics in the Middle Ages* (Uppsala, 1999). In this Appendix I am concerned only with the connections between Aristotle's logical grammar and his metaphysics.

Bibliography

ACKRILL, J. *Aristotle's Categories and De Interpretatione* (Oxford, 1963).
——'Aristotle's Theory of Definition: Some Questions on *Post. An.* 2. 8–10', in
  E. Berti (1981), 339–58.
ALBRITTON, R. 'Substance and Form in Aristotle's *Metaphysics*', *Journal of
  Philosophy* 54, (1957), 699–708.
ALEXANDER, in *In Analytica Priora*, ed. M. Wallies (Berlin, 1883).
——in *In Aristotelis Metaphysica Commentaria*, ed. M. Hayduck (Berlin, 1891).
AMMONIUS, in *Analytica Priora* I, ed. M. Wallies (Berlin, 1899).
AVGELIS, N. and PEONIDIS, F. (eds.). *Aristotle on Logic, Language and Science*
  (Thessaloniki, 1998).
BALME, D. M. 'Aristotle's Use of Differentiae in Zoology', in S. Mansion (1961),
  reprinted in Barnes, Schofield and Sorabji (eds.) 1, 183–93.
——'*Genos* and *Eidos* in Aristotle', *Classical Quarterly*, NS, 12 (1962), 81–98.
——*Aristotle's De Partibus Animalium I and De Generatione Animalium I (With
  Passages From II. 1–3)* (Oxford, 1972).
——'Aristotle's Use of Division and Differentiae', in A. Gotthelf and J. G. Lennox
  (eds.) (1987), 69–89.
BAMBROUGH, R. *New Essays on Plato and Aristotle* (London, 1965).
BARNES, J. *Aristotle's Posterior Analytics* (Oxford, 1975), 2nd edn. (Oxford,
  1994).
——'Grammar on Aristotle's Terms', in M. Frede and G. Striker (eds.) (1996),
  175–202.
——SCHOFIELD, M. and SORABJI, R. (eds.). *Articles on Aristotle* 1: *Science*
  (London, 1978), 3: *Metaphysics* (London, 1979).
BERTI, E. (ed.), *Aristotle on Science* (Padua, 1981).
BODEN, M. (ed.), *The Philosophy of Artificial Intelligence* (Oxford, 1990).
BOGHOSSIAN, P. 'What the Externalist Can Know A Priori', PAS 97 (1997),
  161–75.
BOLTON, R. 'Essentialism and Semantic Theory in Aristotle: *Posterior Analytics*
  II. 7–10', *Philosophical Review* 85 (1976), 515–44.
——'Aristotle on the Signification of Names', *Language and Reality in Greek
  Philosophy: Proceedings of the Greek Philosophical Society* 1984/5 (Athens,
  1985), 153–62.
——'Definition and Scientific Method in Aristotle's *Posterior Analytics* and the
  Generation of Animals', in A. Gotthelf and J. Lennox (eds.) (1987), 120–66.
——'Aristotle's Method in Natural Science', in L. Judson (ed.) (1991), 1–29.
——'Division, définition et essence dans la science aristotelicienne', *Revue
  Philosophique* 2 (1993), 197–222.
——'Aristotle's Conception of Metaphysics as a Science', in T. Scaltsas, D. Charles,
  and M. L. Gill (eds.) (1994), 321–54.
——'Science and the Science of Substance in Aristotle's *Metaphysics* Z', *Pacific
  Philosophical Quarterly* 76 (1995), 454–7.

BOLTON, R. 'The Material Cause: Matter and Explanation in Aristotle's Natural Science', in Kullman and Follinger (1997), 97–124.

BONITZ, H. *Index Aristotelicus* (Berlin, 1970).

BOWEN, A. C. (ed.), *Science and Philosophy in Classical Greece* (Pittsburgh, 1989).

BRENTANO, F. *Psychology from an Empirical Standpoint*, trans. C. Rancurello, D. B. Terrel, and L. McAlister (London, 1973).

—— *The Psychology of Aristotle*, trans. R. George (Berkeley, 1977).

BREWER, B. *Perception and Reason* (Oxford, 1999).

BROACKES, J. 'Aristotle, Objectivity and Perception', *Oxford Studies in Ancient Philosophy* 17 (1999), 51–113.

BROADIE, S. *Nature, Change and Agency* (Oxford, 1982).

—— 'Aristotle's Perceptual Realism', in J. Ellis (1993), 137–59.

BRODY, B. 'Why Settle for Anything Less than Good Old-Fashioned Aristotelian Essentialism?', *Nous* 7, (1993), 351–65.

BURGE, T. 'Individualism and the Mental', *Midwest Studies* 4 (1979), 73–121.

—— 'Cartesian Error and Perception', in P. Pettit and J. McDowell (1986), 117–36.

—— 'Intellectual Norms and Foundations of Mind', *Journal of Philosophy* 83 (1986), 697–720.

BURNYEAT, M. (ed.), *Notes on Book Zeta of Aristotle's Metaphysics* (Oxford, 1979).

—— 'Aristotle on Understanding Knowledge', in E. Berti (1981), 97–139.

—— *Notes on ETA and THETA* (Oxford Subfaculty of Philosophy, 1984).

—— 'Aristotle voit du rouge et entend un "do": combien se passe-t-il de choses? Remarques sur *De Anima*, 2, 7–8', in G. R. Dherbey (1996), 149–67.

BUTLER, T. 'On David Charles' Account of Aristotle's Semantics for Simple Names', *Phronesis* 42 (1997), 21–34.

CARRIERO, J. P. The Second Meditation and the Essence of the Mind', in A. O. Rorty (ed.) (1986), 199–221.

CASTON, V. 'Why Aristotle Needs Imagination', *Phronesis* 41/1 (1996), 20–55.

—— 'Aristotle and the Problem of Intentionality', *Philosophy and Phenomenological Research* 58/2 (1998), 249–98.

CHARLES, D. *Aristotle's Philosophy of Action* (London, 1984).

—— 'Natural Kinds and Natural History', in D. Devereux and P. Pellegrin (eds.) (1985), 145–67.

—— 'Aristotle: Ontology and Moral Reasoning', *Oxford Studies in Ancient Philosophy* 4 (1986), 119–44.

—— 'Aristotle on Hypothetical Necessity and Irreducibility', PPQ 69 (1988), 1–54.

—— 'Teleological Causation in the *Physics*', in L. Judson (ed.) (Oxford, 1991), 101–28.

—— 'Supervenience, Composition and Physicalism', in D. Charles and K. Lennon (eds.) (1992), 265–96.

—— 'Aristotle on Names and Their Signification', in S. Everson (ed.) (1994), 37–73.

—— 'Matter and Form: Unity, Persistence and Identity', in T. Scaltsas, D. Charles, and M. L. Gill (eds.) (1994), 75–105.

—— 'Aristotle and Modern Moral Realism', in R. Heinaman (ed.) (1995), 135–72.

——'*Metaphysics* Λ. 2: Matter and Change', in M. Frede and D. Charles (eds.) (2000), forthcoming.

——and LENNON, K. (eds.), *Reduction, Explanation and Realism* (Oxford, 1992).

CHIBA, K. *Aristotle on Explanation: Demonstrative Science and Scientific Inquiry* (Hokkaido, 1992).

CLARK, P. and HALE, B. (eds.), *Reading Putnam* (Oxford, 1994).

CODE, A. 'No Universal is a Substance: An interpretation of Z.13, 1038^{b}8–15', *Paideia*, 2nd Special Issue, (1978), 65–76.

——'Aristotle's Investigation of a Basic Logical Principle: Which Science Investigates The Principle of Non-Contradiction?', *Canadian Journal of Philosophy* 16 (1986), 341–58.

——and MORAVCSIK, J. 'Explaining Various Forms of Living', in M. Nussbaum and A. O. Rorty (eds.) (1992), 129–46.

COOPER, J. M. 'Metaphysics in Aristotle's Embryology', in D. Devereux and P. Pellegrin (eds.) (1990), 55–84.

——'Aristotle on Emotion', in D. J. Furley and A. Nehemas (eds.) (1994), 193–210.

CORCORAN, J. *Ancient Logic and Modern Interpretations* (Dordrecht, 1974).

CRIVELLI, P. 'Notes on Aristotle's Conception of Truth', in M. S. Funghi (ed.) (1996), 147–59.

CUSSINS, A. 'The Connectionist Construction of Concepts', in M. Boden (ed.) (1990), 368–440.

DESCARTES, R. *Philosophical Writings*, ed. J. Cottingham, R. Stoothoff, and D. Murdoch, 2 vols (Cambridge, 1985).

DETEL, W. *Aristoteles Analytica Posteriora* (Berlin, 1993).

——'Why All Animals Have a Stomach: Demonstration and Axiomatization in Aristotle's *Parts of Animals*', in W. Küllman and S. Follinger (eds.) (1997), 63–82.

DEMOSS, D. and DEVEREUX, D. 'Essence, Existence, and Nominal Definition in Aristotle's *Posterior Analytics* II.8–10', *Phronesis* 33 (1988), 133–54.

DEVEREUX, D. and PELLEGRIN, P. (eds.), *Biologie, Logique et Métaphysique chez Aristote* (Paris, 1990).

DHERBEY, G. R. (ed.), *Corps et Ame* (Paris, 1996).

DUMMETT, M. *Frege* (London, 1973).

DUPRE, J. 'Biological Taxa', *Philosophical Review* 90 (1981), 66–91.

DÜRING, I. 'Aristotle's Method in Biology', in S. Mansion (1961), 213–21.

EBERT, T. 'Aristotle on What is Done in Perceiving', *Zeitschrift für Philosophische Forschung* 37 (1983), 181–98.

ELLIS, J. (ed.), *Ancient Minds: The Southern Journal of Philosophy* 31, suppl. (1993).

EUSTRATIUS, *In Analyticorum Posteriorum Librum Secundum Commentarium*, ed. M. Hayduck (Berlin, 1907).

EVANS, G. 'The Causal Theory of Names', *PASS* 47 (1973), 187–208.

——*Varieties of Reference* (Oxford, 1982).

EVERSON, S. (ed.), *Companions to Ancient Thought 3: Language* (Cambridge, 1994).

——*Aristotle on Perception* (Oxford, 1997).

FALCON, A. 'Aristotle's Rules of Division in the Topics: The Relation between *Genus* and *Differentia* in Division', *Ancient Philosophy* 16/2 (1996), 377–88.

FEREJOHN, M. 'Definition and the Two Stages of Aristotelian Demonstration', *Review of Metaphysics* 36 (1982), 375–95.

—— *The Origins of Aristotelian Science* (New Haven, 1991).

—— 'The Definition of Generated Composites in Aristotle's *Metaphysics*', in T. Scaltas, D. Charles, and M. L. Gill (eds.) (1994), 291–318.

FIELD, H. 'Mental Representation', *Erkenntnis* 13 (1978), 9–61.

FINE, K. 'Essence and Modality', *Philosophical Perspectives* 8 (1994), 1–15.

FORBES, G. *The Metaphysics of Modality* (Oxford, 1985).

FORTENBAUGH, W. W. *Theophrastean Studies* (New Brunswick, 1988).

FREDE, M. 'Substance in Aristotle's *Metaphysics*', in A. Gotthelf (ed.) (1985), 17–26.

—— *Essays in Ancient Philosophy* (Minnesota, 1987).

—— 'The Definition of Sensible Substance in *Metaphysics* Z', in D. T. Devereux and P. Pellegrin (eds.), *Biologie, logique et métaphysique chez Aristote* (Paris, 1990), 113–29.

—— 'Aristotle's Notion of Potentiality in Metaphysics θ', in T. Scaltsas, D. Charles, and M. L. Gill (1994), 173–93.

—— (ed.), *Aristotle and Moral Realism* (London, 1995).

—— 'La Theorie aristotelicienne de l'intellect agent', in G. R. Dherbey (1996), 377–90.

—— and CHARLES, D. (eds.), *Metaphysics Lambda: Symposium Aristotelicum* (Oxford, 2000).

—— and PATZIG, G. *Aristoteles Metaphysik Z* (Munich, 1988).

—— and STRIKER, G. (eds.), *Rationality in Greek Thought* (Oxford, 1996).

FUNGHI, M. S. (ed.), *Studies in Honour of F. Adorno* (Florence, 1996).

FURLEY, D. J. and NEHAMAS, A. (eds.), *Ethical-Political Theory in Aristotle's Rhetoric* (Princeton, 1994).

GARBER, D. '*Semel in Vita*: The Scientific Background', in A. O. Rorty (ed.), *Essays on Descartes' Meditations* (Berkeley, 1986), 81–116.

GILL, M. L. *Aristotle on Substance: The Paradox of Unity* (Princeton, 1989).

GOLDIN, O. *Explaining the Eclipse: Aristotle's Posterior Analytics* 2. 1–10. (Michigan, 1996).

GOMEZ-LOBO, A. 'On the So-called Question of Existence in Aristotle, *An. Post.* 2. 1–2', *Review of Metaphysics* 34 (1980), 71–91'.

—— 'Definitins in Aristotle's *Posterior Analytics*', in D. O'Meara (ed.) (1981), 25–46.

GOTTHELF, A. (ed.), *Aristotle on Nature and Living Things* (Pittsburgh, 1985).

—— and LENNOX, J. G. (eds.), *Philosophical Issues in Aristotle's Biology* (Cambridge, 1987).

—— 'Historiae 1: planatarum et animalium', in W. W. Fortenbaugh (ed.) (1988), 100–35.

—— 'The Elephant's Nose: Further Reflections on the Axiomatic Structure of Biological Explanation in Aristotle', in W. Kullman and S. Follinger (eds.) (1997), 85–95.

GRANGER, H. 'The *Scala Naturae* and the Continuity of Kinds', *Phronesis* 30 (1985), 181–222.

HAMLYN, D. W. *Aristotle's De Anima II and III* (Oxford, 1968).

HARTE, V. 'Aristotle's *Metaphysics* H.6: A Dialectic with Platonism', *Phronesis* 41/3 (1996), 276–304.

HEINAMAN, R. E. 'Aristotle's Tenth Aporia', *Archiv für Geschichte der Philosophie* 61 (1979), 249–70.

HICKS, R. D. *Aristotle: de Anima* (Cambridge, 1907).

HUFFMAN, C. A. *Philolaus of Croton* (Cambridge, 1993).

HUGHES, G. 'Universals as Potential Substances', in M. Burnyeat (ed.) (1979), 107–26.

HUSSEY, E. *Aristotle's Physics III–IV* (Oxford, 1983).

IAMBLICHUS *De Communi Mathematica Scientia*, ed. N. Festo (Leipzig, 1891).

——*In Nicomachi Arithmeticam Introductionem*, ed. H. Pistelli (Leipzig, 1894).

——*Introductio Arithmetica*, ed. R. Hoche (Leipzig, 1866).

IRWIN, T. 'Aristotle's Account of Signification', in M. Schofield and M. Nussbaum (eds.), *Language and Logos* (Cambridge, 1982), 241–66.

——'Aristotle's Concept of Signification', in M. Schofield and M. Nussbaum (eds.) (1982), 240–66.

——*Aristotle's First Principles* (Oxford, 1988).

JACOBS, W. 'Aristotle and Nonreferring Subjects', *Phronesis* 24 (1979), 282–300.

JUDSON, L. (ed.), *Aristotle's Physics* (Oxford, 1991).

——'Chance and "Always or for the Most Part" in L. Judson (ed.) (1991), 73–99.

——'What Can Happen When You Eat Pungent Food', in N. Avgelis and F. Peonidis (eds.) (1998), 185–203.

KAHN, C. 'The Role of *nous* in the Cognition of First Principles in *Posterior Analytics* 2. 19', in E. Berti (1981), 385–414.

KARASMANIS, V. 'The Hypotheses of Mathematics in Plato's *Republic* and his Contribution to the Axiomatization of Geometry', in P. Nicopoulos (ed.) (1990), 121–35.

KIRWAN. C, (ed.), *Aristotle, Metaphysics Γ, Δ, E* (Oxford, 1971).

KNORR, W. R. 'Construction as Existence Proof in Ancient Geometry', *Ancient Philosophy* 3 (1983), 125–47.

KNUUTTILA, S. *Modalities in Medieval Philosophy* (London, 1993).

KOSMAN, L. A. 'Understanding, Explanation and Insight in the *Posterior Analytics*', in E. N. Lee, A. P. D. Mourelatos, and R. M. Rorty (eds.) (1973), 374–92.

——'Substance, Being and *Energeia*', *Oxford Studies in Ancient Philosophy* 2 (1984), 121–49.

KRETZMANN, N. 'Aristotle on Spoken Sounds and Significance by Convention', in J. Corcoran (ed.) (1974), 3–21.

KRIPKE, S. *Naming and Necessity* (Oxford, 1980).

KULLMAN, W. and FOLLINGER, S. (eds.), *Aristotelische Biologie* (Stuttgart, 1997).

KUNG, J. 'Aristotle on Essence and Explanation', *Philosophical Studies*, vol. 31 (1997), 361–83.

LAGERLUND, H. *Modal Syllogistics in the Middle Ages* (Uppsala, 1999).

LANDOR. B. 'Definitions and Hypotheses in *Posterior Analytics* 72^{a}19–25 and 76^{b}35–77^{a}4', *Phronesis* 26 (1981), 308–18.

LEAR, J. 'Aristotle's Philosophy of Mathematics', *Philosophical Review* 91 (1982), 161–93.

LEAR, J. *Aristotle: The Desire to Understand* (Cambridge, 1988).

LE BLOND, J. M. 'Definition in Aristotle', in J. Barnes, M. Schofield, and R. Sorabji (eds.) 3 (1979), 63–79.

LEE, E. N., MOURELATOS, A. P. D., and RORTY, R. M. (eds.), *Exegesis and Argument, Phronesis,* Suppl. 1 (1973).

LENNOX, J. G. 'Notes on David Charles on H. A.', in D. Devereux and P. Pellegrin (eds.) *(*1990), 169–84.

—— 'Divide and Explain: The *Posterior Analytics* in Practice', in A. Gotthelf and J. G. Lennox (eds.) (1987), 339–59.

—— 'Between Data and Demonstration: The *Analytics* and the *Historia Animalium*', in A. C. Bowen (1989), 261–94.

—— 'Aristotelian Problems', *Ancient Philosophy* 14 (1994), 53–77.

—— 'Material and Formal Natures in Aristotle's *de Partibus Animalium*', in Kullman and Follinger (eds.) (1997), 163–81.

LESHER, J. H. 'The Meaning of *Nous* in the Posterior Analytics', *Phronesis* 18 (1973), 44–68.

LETOUBLON, F. 'Les dieux et les hommes: le langage et sa reference dans l'antiquité grecque archaique', in *Language and Reality in Greek Philosophy: Proceedings of the Greek Philosophical Society* 1984/5 (Athens, 1985), 12–99.

LEWIS, D. 'Counterpart Theory and Quantified Modal Logic', *Journal of Philosophy* 65 (1968), 113–26.

LEWIS, F. 'Accidental Sameness in Aristotle', *Philosophical Studies* 42 (1982), 1–36.

—— 'Aristotle on the Unity of Substance', *Pacific Philosophical Quarterly* 76: 3/4 (1995), 222–65.

LLOYD, A. C. 'Necessity and Essence in the *Posterior Analytics*', in E. Berti (1981), I. 46.

LLOYD, G. E. R. 'Who Is Attacked in *On Ancient Medicine?*', *Phronesis* 8 (1963), 108.

—— *Aristotelian Explorations* (Cambridge, 1996).

LOCKE, J. *An Essay Concerning Human Understanding,* ed. P. J. Nidditch (Oxford, 1975).

MACKIE, J. *Ethics: Inventing Right and Wrong* (New York, 1977).

MACKIE, P. Review of *Necessity, Essence and Individualism: A Defense of Conventionalism*, A. Sidelle *Mind* 99 (1990), 635.

MANSION, S. *Aristote et les problèmes de méthode* (Louvain, 1961).

MARCUS, R. B. *Modalities* (Oxford, 1993).

MATTHEWS, G. 'Accidental Unities', in M. Schofield and M. Nussbaum (eds.) (1982), 223–40.

McDOWELL, J. 'On the Sense and Reference of Proper Names', *Mind*, 86 (1977), 159–85.

—— 'Singular Thought and the Extent of Inner Space', in P. Pettit and J. McDowell (eds.) (1986), 137–68.

—— 'Putnam on Mind and Meaning', *Philosophical Topics* 20 (1992), 35–48.

McGINN, C. 'The Structure of Content', in A. Woodfield (ed.) (1982), 207–58.

McKIRAHAN, R. *Principles and Proofs* (Princeton, 1992).

MIGNUCCI, M. 'Puzzles About Identity: Aristotle and his Greek Commentators', in H. J. Wiesner (ed.) (1985), 57–97.

MILLIKAN, R. *Language, Thought and Other Biological Categories* (Cambridge, Mass., 1984).

MODRAK, D. *Aristotle: The Power of Perception* (Chicago, 1987).

MORAVCSIK, J. M. E. (ed.), *Aristotle: Critical Essays* (New York, 1967).

MORROW, G. (ed.), *Commentary on the First Book of Euclid's Elements* (Princeton, 1970), 9. 19.

MUELLER, I. 'Aristotle on Geometrical Objects', *Archiv für Geschichte der Philosophie* 52 (1970), 156–67.

——*Philosophy of Mathematics and Deductive Structure in Euclid's Elements* (Cambridge, Mass., 1981).

NICOPOULOS, P. (ed.), *Greek Studies in the Philosophy and History of Science* (Dordrecht, 1990).

NUSSBAUM, M. C. *Aristotle's de Motu Animalium* (Princeton, 1978).

——'Saving Aristotle's Appearances', in M. Schofield and M. Nussbaum (eds.) (1982), 267–94.

——and RORTY, A. O. (eds.) *Essays on Aristotle's De Anima* (Oxford, 1992).

O'MEARA, D. (ed.), *Studies in Aristutle* (Washington, 1981).

OWEN, G. E. L. '*Tithenai ta phainomena*', in S. Mansion (ed.) (1961), 83–103.

——'Aristotle on the Snares of Ontology', in R. Bambrough (ed.) (1965).

PACIUS, J. *In Porphrii Isagogen et Aristotelis Organon Commentarius Analyticus* (Frankfurt, 1597).

PARKER, R. 'Sex, Women and Ambiguous Animals', *Phronesis* 29 (1984), 174–87.

PATTERSON, R. *Aristotle's Modal Logic* (Cambridge, 1995).

PATZIG, G. *Aristotle's Theory of the Syllogism*, trs. J. Barnes (Dordrecht, 1969).

PEARS, D. 'Ifs and Cans', *Questions in the Philosophy of Mind* (London, 1975), 142–92.

PELLEGRIN, P. *La Classification des animaux chez Aristote* (Paris, 1982), trans. A. Preus, *Aristotle's Classification of Animals* (Berkeley, 1986).

——'Aristotle: A Zoology without Species', in A. Gotthelf (ed.) (1985), 95–115.

PELLETIER, F. J. and KING-FARLOW, J. (eds.), *New Essays on Aristotle* (Calgary, 1984).

PETERSON, S. L. *The Master Paradox* (Princeton Ph.D. thesis, 1969).

——'Substitution in Aristotelian Technical Contexts', *Philosophical Studies* 47 (1985), 249–57.

PETTIT, P. and J. MCDOWELL (eds.). *Subject, Thought and Context* (Oxford, 1986).

PHILOPONUS in *Analytica Posteriora*, ed. M. Wallies (Berlin, 1909).

PUTNAM, H. *Philosophical Papers*, 3 vols. (Cambridge, 1975).

——'Meaning and Reference', in S. P. Schwarz (ed.) (1977), 119–32.

——*Reason, Truth and History* (Cambridge, 1981).

——'Aristotle after Wittgenstein', in R. W. Sharples (ed.) (1993), 117–137.

——'Comments and Replies', in P. Clarke and B. Hale (1994).

QUINE, W. V. 'Grades of Modal Involvement', in *Ways of Paradox* (New York, 1956), 156–174.

——'Reference and Modality', in *From a Logical Point of View* (Cambridge, Mass., 1964), 139–159.

RORTY, A. O. (ed.), *Essays on Descartes' Meditations* (Berkeley, 1986).

396 *Bibliography*

RORTY, R. 'Genus as Matter: A Reading of *Metaphysics* Z-H', in E. N. Lee, A. P. D. Mourelatos, and R. M. Rorty (eds.) (1973), 393–420.

ROSS, W. D. *Aristotle's Metaphysics*, 2 vols. (Oxford, 1924).

—— *Aristotle's Prior and Posterior Analytics* (Oxford, 1949).

SALMON, N. *Reference and Essence* (Oxford, 1982).

—— *Frege's Puzzle* (Boston, 1982).

SAMBURSKY, S. 'Philoponus' Interpretation of Aristotle's Theory of Light', *Osiris* 13 (1958), 114–26.

SCALTSAS, T. 'Substratum, Subject and Substance', *Ancient Philosophy* 5 (1985), 215–40.

—— CHARLES, D. and GILL, M. L. (eds.), *Unity, Identity and Explanation in Aristotle's Metaphysics* (Oxford, 1994).

SCHIFFER, S. *Remnants of Meaning* (Cambridge, 1987).

SCHOFIELD, M. and NUSSBAUM, M. (eds.), *Language and Logos* (Cambridge, 1982).

SCHWARTZ, S. (ed.), *Naming, Necessity and Natural Kinds* (Cornell, 1977).

SELLARS, W. 'Substance and Form in Aristotle', *Journal of Philosophy* 54 (1957), 688–99.

—— 'Aristotle's Metaphysics: An Interpretation' in *Philosophical Perspectives* (Springfield, 1967), 73–124.

SHARPLES, R. W. (ed.), *Modern Thinkers and Ancient Thinking* (London, 1993).

SIDELLE, A. *Necessity, Essence and Individualism: a Defense of Conventionalism* (Ithaca, 1989).

SLOMKOWSKI, P. *Aristotle's Topics* (Leiden, 1977).

SMILEY, T. 'Syllogism and Quantification', *Journal of Symbolic Logic* 27 (1962), 58–72.

SMITH, R. 'Immediate Propositions and Aristotle's Proof Theory', *Ancient Philosophy* 6 (1986), 47–55.

SORABJI, R. *Necessity, Cause and Blame* (London and Ithaca, 1980).

SPELLMAN, L. 'Referential Opacity in Aristotle', *History of Philosophy Quarterly* 7 (1990), 17–33.

THEMISTIUS, *Analyticorum Posteriorum Paraphrasis*, ed. M. Wallies (Berlin, 1900).

THEON SMYRNAEUS, *Expositio Rerum Mathematicarum*, ed. E. Hiller (Leipzig, 1878).

TSELEMANIS, P. 'Theory of Meaning and Signification in Aristotle', *Language and Reality in Greek Philosophy: Proceedings of the Greek Philosophical Society 1984/5* (Athens, 1985), 194–203.

UPTON, T. 'Naming and Non-Being in Aristotle', *Proceedings of the Catholic Philosophical Association* 59 (1985), 275–88.

—— 'Aristotelian Hypothesis and the Unhypothesized First Principle', *Review of Metaphysics* 39 (1986), 283–301.

WATERLOW, S. *Nature, Chance and Agency* (Oxford, 1982).

WEDIN, M. 'Aristotle on the Existential Import of Singular Sentences', *Phronesis* 23 (1978), 179–96.

—— 'Singular Statements and Essentialism in Aristotle', in F. J. Pelletier and J. King-Farlow (eds.) (1984), 67–88.

—— *Mind and Imagination in Aristotle* (New Haven, 1988).

WHITING, J. 'Form and Individuation in Aristotle', *History of Philosophy Quarterly*, 3 (1986), 359–77.

—— 'Metasubstance: Critical Notice of Frede-Patzig and Furth', *Philosophical Review* 100 (1991), 607–39.

WIESNER, H. J. (ed.), *Aristoteles Werk und Wirkung* (Berlin, 1985).

WIGGINS, D. *Sameness and Substance* (Oxford, 1981).

—— 'Putnam's Doctrine of Natural Kind Words', in Clark and Hale (ed.) (1994), 201–15.

WITT, C. *Substance and Essence in Aristotle* (Ithaca, 1989).

WOODFIELD, A. (eds.), *Thought and Object* (Oxford, 1982).

WOODS, M. 'Problems in *Metaphysics* Z. Chapter 13', in J. M. E. Moravcsik (ed.) (1967), 215–38.

—— 'Particular Forms Revisited', *Phronesis* 36 1 (1991), 75–87.

—— 'Universals and Particular Forms in Aristotle's Metaphysics', *Oxford Studies in Ancient Philosophy* (1991, Supplement), 41–56.

ZABARELLA, J. *Opera Logica* (Frankfurt, 1608).

Index Locorum

General Index

Index Nominum